SEEK AND HIDE

SEEK
AND
HIDE

The Tangled History of
the Right to Privacy

AMY GAJDA

VIKING

VIKING
An imprint of Penguin Random House LLC
penguinrandomhouse.com

LIBRARY OF CONGRESS CATALOGING-IN-PUBLICATION DATA
Names: Gajda, Amy, author.
Title: Seek and hide : the tangled history of the right to privacy / Amy Gajda.
Description: [New York] : Viking, [2022]
Identifiers: LCCN 2021048491 | ISBN 9781984880741 (hardcover) | ISBN 9781984880758 (ebook)
Subjects: LCSH: Privacy, Right of—United States.
Classification: LCC KF1262 .G35 2022 | DDC 342.7308/58—dc23/eng/20220131
LC record available at https://lccn.loc.gov/2021048491

Printed in the United States of America
1   3   5   7   9   10   8   6   4   2

Book design by Daniel Lagin

For my sister Sally,

bold and beautiful,

pathbreaking and lifesaving,

a sweetheart,

now a star

CONTENTS

Introduction   ix

A Quick Primer on Law, Procedure, and Precedent   xv

PART I
THE RISE OF PRIVACY

1. Brandeis's Secret   3

2. Hamilton, Jefferson, and the Greatest Evil   12

3. Love and Pictures   29

4. The Warrens Make the Paper   38

5. Who Was Kate Nash?   52

6. "The Right to Privacy"   67

7. The Right to Know   80

Coda Part I: The Death of Sam Warren   92

PART II
THE RISE OF THE MEDIA

8. A Different Kind of Fire   101

9. The Law Won   114

10. Holmes and Brandeis and the (Regulated)
    Marketplace of Ideas   131

11. Be Decent   144

12. Pandora's Box, the Source of Every Evil   157

13. Bodies and Breathing Space   169

14. Real Chutzpah, Real Housewives   191

Coda Part II: It Does Not Follow   201

PART III
WATCH OUT!

15. Miss Vermont, Judge Mikva, and the Wrestler   213

16. Girls Gone Wild (Privacy in Public)   225

17. Kate Nash Redux (Privacy in Data)   231

18. The Right to Be Forgotten (Privacy in the Past)   242

19. A President and His Tax Returns (Privacy in Politics) 251

Epilogue: Dignity and Liberty   263

Acknowledgments   277

Notes   279

Bibliography   341

Index   359

INTRODUCTION

I t would seem that a pair of tights and a snap camera started it all.

That's because the scandalous leg gear and the troubling new technology got a mention in the fourth paragraph of an 1890 law review article by the attorneys Louis Brandeis and Sam Warren, one that many say marked the start of the legal right to privacy in the United States. The law partners wrote that a theatrical performance that same year had sparked "a somewhat notorious case."

The story goes that Marion Manola, singer-actress and star of Broadway's *Castles in the Air*, wore gray silk tights as a provocative part of her art. Tights back then set tongues wagging: they had a sensual cling at a time when women wore thick dresses that plunged to the ground and sashayed around there so that no one much knew what shoes looked like either. Tights on a stage actress allowed men to see the curve of her hips to her toes.

Such distraction was not universal, however, and Manola's silken legs failed to move the day's theater critics. *Castles in the Air* is "a perfect abyss of weariness" was *The Evening World*'s assessment. *The New York Times* called it "an apparent failure." But Manola's trim and attractive figure kept audiences coming nevertheless. The theater manager, recognizing even meatier marketing potential, wished to capture an image of Manola in her ensemble. "She is my chief soprano" was his public explanation.

Newspaper headlines from Friday, June 13, 1890, made clear that Manola absolutely, positively refused. New York: SHE WON'T BE TAKEN IN TIGHTS. Chicago: WILL NOT BE PHOTOGRAPHED IN TIGHTS. In Boston, the *Globe* put it patronizingly: MISS MANOLA IN DISTRESS: WILL RESIGN RATHER THAN BE PHOTOGRAPHED IN HER TIGHTS. Live performance was one thing, but still photography seemed an invasion entirely different.

Then came trouble, just as any careful reader would have expected. Quite literally the next evening, as Manola ran toward the open arms of a costar in the second act, a flash of light and a puff of smoke erupted from the Broadway Theatre's balcony. The manager had placed a snap camera in an upper box! A photographer had captured Manola and the "not too slender, not too plump, graceful, and shapely contents of the darker gray tights"!

News coverage of the outrage appeared at about the speed of the snap flash. "The million and a half people in New York are not bothering them-selves about the silver bill, the federal election law, or the other issues which interest the country at large," *The Atlanta Constitution* reported. "The New Yorkers have nothing in view but Miss Manola's tights, and just at present they are discussing nothing else."

Women rallied to Manola's cause, crediting her for standing firm against a clear male desire to exploit a woman's choice; the "entire sympathy of all of her sex and of the best part of the community" stood with the actress. Some men, on the other hand, struggled to understand why this particular photo was such a big deal. They'd seen Manola's silky legs before, not only on Broadway, but on cabinet cards published when she'd starred in the risqué *Boccaccio*. Her tunic back then sported a tantalizing fringe that covered her pelvic region just so, with tight light tights doing the rest of the work.

We'll never know what Manola's legs looked like during her *Castles in the Air* performance, however. A judge immediately sided with the actress, her sex, and the community's best and ordered that the manager never, ever develop the photo, let alone publish it. And the story might have ended there.

But the idea of that personal invasion fit perfectly into a narrative build-ing in the mind of the attorney Sam Warren back in Boston. Warren saw a different sort of marketing potential in Manola's legs; the viral tale could help support his call for what he called a newfangled right to privacy. This was solid proof that cameras could (and people would) capture embarrass-ing images from real life far beyond the woodblock portraits that already tormented the rich and powerful so. Heck, the so-called snap or detective camera was even marketed in such a privacy-invading way: ads promised that it could record the countenance and pose of an unsuspecting victim who would be unaware until it was too late. Mrs. Grover Cleveland, a friend of Warren's, had it particularly bad: she was HAUNTED BY AMATEURS, headlines read, the dozens of hopeful photographers who waited for a glimpse of the First Lady. Some of their cameras were shaped like purses. Others looked so much like handguns that police could have shot to kill a paparazzo and nobody would have questioned it even for a second. The autograph-seeking fans who similarly frenzied around the French actress Sarah Bernhardt to invade her "privacy" during her U.S. tour in the 1880s? They now had a weapon much mightier than the pen.

Today, the 1890 plea "The Right to Privacy," written by Warren and his law partner the future Supreme Court justice Brandeis, is used to support legal protection not only for the haunted and the hunted, but also to justify protection for everything from sexual intimacies and private scandals to police eavesdropping and computer data. Judges routinely laud the reasoning and quote the language of "The Right to Privacy" in publication cases—as well as in cases involving presidential privilege, civil rights, drug testing, freedom of information, and many others. The 1890 article, those judges say, is seminal and brilliant and famous and historic and a landmark and the foundation for nearly every single privacy-related right that we have in modern times.

But here's the thing: the right to privacy as a legal concept has *always* existed in some sense in U.S. law, ever since the very first long-form newspaper reported titillating scandal in 1690 and was immediately shut down. Warren and Brandeis helped things along to be sure, but privacy, the notion that certain private information is sacred and ought to be protected not just from government but from everyone, causes of action called truthful libel or even ridicule, already had a fairly firm foundation by 1890, and it grew from there. It's just that nobody's heard much about it, for reasons that probably have more to do with our focus on press freedom than anything else.

And privacy has always meant basically the same thing: that people generally have the right to keep certain things quiet, to define themselves for themselves against the interests of others. It means that they—we—have the right to be secluded, to stop others from peering in on us as we go about the more intimate parts of our lives, to become who we were meant to be in that seclusion, to remake ourselves, to put up a shell, to curate features of our identity against interested neighbors and against prying media, and to sue those who peer and those who publish what they've seen. As courts began to suggest in the nineteenth century and continue to suggest today, privacy means the right to be let alone.

That free-for-all marketplace of ideas that we hear so much about? The concept of truth as the highest value? The public's unfettered right to know? The chilling warning that once things are out in public, we can't take them back? Such privileges have never really existed in the United States in the way that most people think of them. Our right to privacy—the right to decide our public face and who we are in our most intimate moments even when we've shared those moments with others—is not a right born of today's new and invasive technologies but has long persisted as a counterbalance to truth and press and speech freedoms and the right to know.

That's why the story of Marion Manola is a perfectly modern one as well. Today, there are many who capture others through cell phones or hacking or data trackers or hidden cameras in public bathrooms or even fancy door-bells that start recording audio and video the instant someone walks by in the dark. What might become of that information, that truth in the hands of others, is the essence of the right to privacy.

But as this book also shows, too much privacy can be a bad thing. Privacy can protect those who wish to bare their live bodies to a selective few, but it can also shield those with dead bodies to hide. That sort of privacy protection and resulting restrictions on the truth and the right to know can lead to despots and dictators and can erode democracy. It can and did help facilitate the silence about evil injustices that existed before #MeToo and Black Lives Matter, because strong privacy interests can end up protecting those sorts of wrongdoers too.

The history of the right to privacy bears all this out. Those who have pushed for privacy as a legal concept over time—Alexander Hamilton and Thomas Jefferson, Samuel Warren and Louis Brandeis, Grover Cleveland and Donald Trump among them—have had parts of their lives that they'd rather the public not know, those sorts of things that might have had a dampening effect on their careers and livelihoods and their families' peace. Many like them have tried to use privacy as a sort of invisibility cloak to end public inquiry, and it's been a pretty good strategy at times: a claimed privacy right in information can shut things down, depending upon the strength of privacy law at the time or how ethical the publisher or speaker feels like being.

That tension between the right to privacy and the right to know the truth and make use of it is what this book is about. The line between the two is an elusive one, and one that the U.S. Supreme Court itself has repeatedly and forcefully refused to draw. "We do not hold that truthful publication is automatically constitutionally protected," the justices wrote at the dawn of the internet, "or that there is no zone of personal privacy within which the State may protect the individual." By the time of smartphones, the justices had poetically protected the "privacies of life" found within them, using the same phrase that Louis Brandeis had used decades before when he served on the Court, language that the Supreme Court had originally written in 1886, four years before "The Right to Privacy" was published.

But there's much that happened before and after all that. The history of the right to privacy includes the brashness of media from the very beginning: that newspaper report from 1690 that the king of France "used to lie with [his] Son's Wife" and the resulting government shutdown of its presses for distastefulness; the lecherous Founding Fathers' struggles with how to tamp media interest in their private lives; shockingly graphic early tabloids; the journalist Nellie Bly's deeply invasive fakery; magazines with "nothing of any possible value" that published photos of dead bodies; all the way up to and beyond *Gawker*'s choice to upload a decidedly not safe for work celebrity sex tape against the celebrity's wishes, giving a billionaire the entry to help shut it all down.

It's the story of the rise of technology that leads to new media and those who wish to stifle that media for cultural, political, ethical, and deeply personal reasons. But it's also the story of that very human right to be let alone and what interests should define an individual and ultimately triumph, even when others claim a right or an interest in her and what she's doing with her body.

Marion Manola, who struggled with morphine addiction, died young. She told others that she'd learned her lesson from her *Boccaccio* portrait and didn't want her daughter to see her mother's body as some sort of advertisement in Manhattan shopwindows ever again.

Samuel Warren, who had his own emotional struggles, also died young. There, it's pretty clear that a loss of the privacy he fought so hard to defend led to his death. Louis Brandeis, meanwhile, lived on in influence from a seat on the nation's highest court, but his confirmation nearly didn't happen because of what had happened with Sam.

These stories of pain from prying, of a privilege from the press, and the way the law has responded to them, all help shape the continuum of the right to privacy in the United States. That continuum is less of a line at times than a curlicue that occasionally circles back on itself, a tangle that favors privacy or publication when society appears to need it or when someone important fancies as much.

We may think that we've never needed the right to privacy as much as we do today. But that's what nearly every generation before us has thought too. Their stories—their mistakes and their victories—can help us decide where we might draw today's right-to-privacy line in these privacy-worried times of data brokers, internet snoops, and free-for-all publishing.

Through it all, it's pretty clear that privacy will ultimately win out. And as good as that may sound right about now, it's not always the best thing.

A QUICK PRIMER ON LAW, PROCEDURE, AND PRECEDENT

This introductory material is meant largely for readers new to the process of law in the United States. It's what most students learn during their first few weeks of law school, the foundation for their legal education and eventually their law practice.

First, there are four main types of law in the United States: constitutions, statutes, regulations, and the common law or court-created law.

The Constitution of the United States needs little introduction here. It's (mostly) all-powerful, and when the Supreme Court suggests that a particular federal constitutional provision means X, all lower courts within the federal and state court systems must also find that it means X. This concept is known as stare decisis, which, in effect, keeps rogue judges in line by forcing them to apply the law that a high court says is applicable as that higher court has defined it. Even though the facts may be somewhat different in a new case and even though that case may be heard in a court at a level several notches below the Supreme Court, lawyers and their clients know that X is how the constitutional provision will be interpreted because the U.S. Supreme Court has decided as much and stare decisis binds all lower courts to that decision.

In this book, the First Amendment's promise of freedom of the press, speech, and expression is the part of the Constitution that is most at issue. But because the U.S. Supreme Court has never decided precisely when the right to privacy trumps the freedom to publish a truth, even though it has suggested repeatedly that it does, lower courts are freer to decide what the

First Amendment means in an invasion-of-privacy context. That's why you'll find that some courts come to somewhat different conclusions about how to balance privacy and press freedoms, not only throughout history, but also very recently. The Supreme Court's lack of guidance on this precise point is an important reason why.

States also have their own constitutions. These can be important in privacy cases because some, like California's, have a provision explicitly protecting an individual's privacy. The federal Constitution does not have that sort of language in it—the word "privacy" does not appear—but the Supreme Court has found that protection for privacy is implied by a variety of constitutional rights even so, and that's why lower courts have necessarily decided as much too. The right to privacy in abortion choice is one example. A state constitutional provision can be found unconstitutional under the federal Constitution, but there's little interplay other than those scenarios. A state constitution, for example, can promise *more* protection than the federal Constitution, which is why I say that the U.S. Constitution is *mostly* all-powerful, but it cannot constrict rights guaranteed by the federal Constitution.

Enacted law—statutes or legislation passed by Congress and state legislatures—is another type of law. Statutes are powerful because, similar to stare decisis, courts within that particular jurisdiction are bound by them because they reflect what the people say the law is through their legislators. Judges therefore must faithfully use a statute to decide a particular case when it is applicable unless they decide that the statute is unconstitutional or has some other type of flaw. A statute might prohibit certain behavior; relevant to this book, back in the early days of the United States, Congress passed the Alien and Sedition Acts, statutes that made it illegal to say negative things about the government or the people in it. In this book too there's mention of federal tax law and a current statute on the books that protects the privacy in federal income taxes. Those are examples of enacted law.

Statutes passed by a state legislature apply in that state only. Criminal law is a good example of typical state-based legislation, and because every state can have its own say about what makes a particular crime, first-degree murder is defined differently in different states, everything from a premeditative mindset (just like on TV shows) to who the victim is (in some states, first-degree murder is only the killing of a particular person, like a police officer or an EMT). More relevant to this book, New York has a long-standing privacy statute defining the right to privacy in a unique way. That statute applies only in the state of New York, meaning that state courts there (or federal courts there hearing a state-law claim) *must* use that statute to decide privacy cases, but courts outside New York are not bound by it at all. Privacy is not statutory in most states, however; it has developed in most states through the courts, through the so-called common law.

Relatedly, regulations are laws created by government agencies. They play a very small role here. One good example is a Federal Communications Commission regulation that punishes a broadcaster when certain swearwords or particular nudity makes it out over the airwaves; that provision, in effect, punishes the publication of accuracy, of truth, in order to protect social propriety, an interest that courts have supported. (The FCC doesn't control either the internet or cable, which is why you can hear and see so much more there, even though traditional over-air broadcasters remain bound.)

And finally, there's the common law or court-decided law, which is the most significant source of legal protection for privacy in most states. Because of stare decisis, once a high court in a particular state decides a case involving particular facts in a particular way, all other courts in that state must decide any new case with similar facts in precisely that same way. Change occurs only when the previous decision is thought to be unconstitutional or no longer relevant because of society's progression. A good privacy-based example is the outing of gay or lesbian individuals. Formerly, some courts had decided that that sort of information, if revealed about someone who did not want it revealed, would be "highly offensive" and therefore an invasion of privacy. But as society has grown to be more inclusive, more modern courts have decided that to reveal someone's sexual orientation is not highly offensive at all and therefore *not* an invasion of privacy. This does not consider the impact on the individual's safety, however, and a few modern courts have started to consider this in some cases, and they can because the common law permits courts to adjust the scope of legal protection in step with shifting social concerns.

The common law usually doesn't include such a dramatic shift, however. In privacy cases, for example, when a court needs to decide if a particular act of intruding into another's seclusion is highly offensive or not, it will look to see what higher courts in that jurisdiction have decided regarding similar behavior in previous cases. When the high court in a given state decides that a particular act of intrusion is indeed highly offensive, all lower courts within that state, because of stare decisis, must follow in lockstep regarding that particular behavior, even if the lower court judge disagrees with the higher court's assessment. The judge's hands are as much bound as if the decision were a statute. Lawyers also call this application of law from a higher court in that state or jurisdiction binding precedent.

This application of prior court decisions—what we call the common law—relying on and creating a foundation of legal principles based on case outcomes on which other courts may build, makes the United States fairly unique. Only a small number of countries in the world, tracing their legal heritage to England, are common-law countries; most follow a civil-law system, in which a civil code or statutes create all law.

The common law is how most law, including much of the law of privacy, has developed throughout the United States. Because each state is its own jurisdiction, however, unbound by decisions outside its borders other than the Supreme Court (and even then only in a very small number of relevant cases), different states have done things differently as privacy law has developed. In privacy, for example, the vast majority of states have accepted the four main privacy torts, those that arose through the common law. We call those misappropriation (the use of another's identity, usually in advertising), intrusion into seclusion (the peering in on another when that person is in a secluded space), publication of private facts (the revelation of another's secrets), and false light (like defamation, but the false information need only be highly offensive and not reputation harming). But not all states have done so.

In those states that have accepted those privacy torts, judges (or, more rarely, legislatures) created a right to sue for privacy invasions out of necessity; a scenario had suddenly occurred involving intrusive new technology, for example, or a particularly intrusive publication, and because it was new, there was no law on which to rely, so *something* needed to be done. As a real-life example from the 1950s, the owner of Sad Sam's Tavern in Waukesha, Wisconsin, liked to enter the tavern bathroom, take photos of women going to the bathroom there, and show them to his patrons. Because that sort of thing had never been explicitly addressed in the law before, the Wisconsin Supreme Court needed to decide if such behavior was an invasion of privacy.

If you've ever read a court decision, you'll note that nearly every sentence is followed by a citation to another court decision; stare decisis and the way the common law works and develops are why, because it's important to build on existing law when deciding *any* case. But if there is no binding precedential court decision on point and no relevant statute in the state and if the state constitution doesn't address the scenario, a court would need to rely on something else in order to find an invasion of privacy for the very first time or instead suggest that the legislature change state law by enacting a new statute or regulation. Wisconsin's high court in the case involving Sad Sam's bathroom photographer chose the latter option. It decided that privacy was an issue best left to the legislature to define, and so the Wisconsin legislature nearly immediately responded by passing a law making such bathroom photo taking illegal.

That wasn't the Wisconsin court's only choice, however. In the absence of a binding court decision or controlling statute in its own state, a court can rely on persuasive precedent, which usually means a decision from a court outside the state. Out-of-state decisions are not binding but may offer a rationale or policy perspective that persuades a court in a different state to adopt the judgment as its own. That Wisconsin court could have looked to neighboring states, for example, to see how they defined a privacy invasion and could have relied on those court cases to craft its own legal rule for Wisconsin.

That's why even out-of-state and lower court decisions about privacy are important and are described here; privacy is still thought to be a relatively new legal wrong, and the internet has created even more troubling brand-new scenarios—so courts deciding privacy cases often look to other states' decisions, especially when facts are unique.

And that brings us to dicta. "Dicta" means language in a court opinion that is not strictly necessary to resolve the case being decided but suggests how the court might rule in a different hypothetical case. A court might say, for example, as did a federal appellate court in Illinois, that the case in front of it was not a privacy invasion, because the information published was rather innocuous, but then add that if the disclosure had involved nudity or sexual information or medical information, it would have violated privacy. That latter part, the court's response to a hypothetical set of facts, would be dicta. Dicta can be persuasive even though it is not binding because such language tells lawyers and judges how that court and perhaps others would likely decide a case involving facts like those.

It works the same way at the U.S. Supreme Court. Even though the justices have yet to decide a case in which the right to privacy has bested freedom of the press or freedom of expression, they've suggested in dicta in a number of cases that it does.

Then things come full circle. If a state legislature or if Congress doesn't like the way courts are headed in a particular area, they can pass legislation to change things, and as long as that legislation doesn't violate constitutional provisions or is otherwise illegal, courts must abide by the legislation even though they don't agree, as explained above. In other words, statutes can trump the common law but never the Constitution.

The necessity of finding and relying on authority of some sort on which to base a judicial decision is why two legal publications have shaped so significantly the development of the right to privacy in the United States. The first is "The Right to Privacy," the scholarly law review article written by Samuel Warren and Louis Brandeis published in the brand-new legal magazine called the *Harvard Law Review* in 1890. (As you'll see, it too relied on certain persuasive precedent in arguing that a right to privacy was important and should exist in the United States. Its authors had to do that in a common-law sense; lawyers too must rely on some legal precedent to build their arguments, or other lawyers and judges will be unpersuaded and unimpressed.) If a court deciding a privacy case in 1891 wished to find an invasion of privacy in a given case (say, the use of a man's name and signature on lozenge tin labels without his permission) and there was no preexisting case law in that state on which to rely, then the court could always point to a law review article as one of the reasons it had decided the case as it did. (And this really happened in 1891 in a lawsuit involving lozenge tins; the court cited

"The Right to Privacy" weeks after its publication as a reason it embraced the right to privacy on those facts.) Courts at all levels and in all states and the federal system routinely cite "The Right to Privacy" even today; many consider it the most important law review article ever written because it was so influential as courts developed the right to privacy in the United States and arguably worldwide.

The second and perhaps even more significant publication that helped shape privacy law in the United States is the Restatement, a series of volumes published by the American Law Institute on a variety of fields of law, almost like an encyclopedia. Each Restatement is drafted through a collaborative process by well-regarded judges, lawyers, and law professors who seek to synthesize and restate prevailing legal principles, bringing order and clarity to the sometimes confusing jumble of underlying court decisions. If a court cannot find binding precedent in its own jurisdiction, reliance on the Restatement could well be considered the next best thing because it often restates the law from other jurisdictions and, therefore, as most states see it.

The Restatement that covers privacy rights in tort law (the law that generally gives people the right to sue others for money for wrongful injury as opposed to putting the offender in jail) has proved to be especially powerful. Because the "right to privacy" as a phrase was so new in court decisions when Restatement authors first drafted a privacy provision in the 1930s, judges back then looked to it for guidance. That became routine when the second Restatement of Torts was published in 1977 and framed the four privacy torts. Today, many courts, including the U.S. Supreme Court, very often rely on or at least cite the Restatement in their privacy-related decisions. In this way it too has been highly influential in the development of privacy law throughout the United States. Now that nearly fifty years have passed and technology and publication have changed dramatically, the American Law Institute is working on a new Restatement of privacy law.

You'll also find here mention of a few criminal cases involving privacy and freedom-of-information cases involving privacy and other types of cases that directly involve *government* behavior and don't directly pit publishing or other typical expressive freedoms against privacy. But these cases, especially those decided by the U.S. Supreme Court, including the famous *Roe v.*

Wade, are important because they help define which dimensions of life we consider private and when privacy rights outweigh freedom of the press and speech and the right to investigate and publish truth.

The idea of the common law is that law builds on itself and grows (or shrinks) in step with society's evolving needs. And that's what makes privacy so interesting today. Society needs it, the law is there on which to build, and the only question left is, which way do we as a society want to go, especially when the right to privacy is so often pitted against that other critical right, the freedom of expression?

PART I

THE RISE OF PRIVACY

Chapter One

BRANDEIS'S SECRET

t was 1884 and Louis Brandeis was just another budding Boston lawyer getting ready for oral argument before the members of the Massachusetts Supreme Judicial Court. The justices were all men, all lined up at a bench behind a do-not-approach railing, with marble busts of the learned looking down from niches above. Brandeis's friend Oliver Wendell Holmes had joined the Massachusetts high court just the year before.

Brandeis was about to argue his very first right-to-privacy case. It's one that in later years he didn't like to talk about, and in any event it's been overshadowed in history by things that occurred six years later. Brandeis would lose the battle that day, but that was not at all surprising; he was representing a publisher at a time of grave concerns about privacy, after all.

In the mid-1880s, at the height of the Gilded Age, the exterior of polite society gleamed, but things festered underneath. Sensational newspapers had exploded onto the scene, eager to expose the nation's underbelly, book publishers were trying to keep up with readers' growing taste for scandal, and the rich and powerful complained bitterly that these newfangled publishers had become far too interested in private matters.

Had there been a poll that day in 1884, in fact, most everyone in the United States would have said that they were against Louis Brandeis. His client, A. Williams & Company, had published a book titled *Cape Cod Folks* that reveled in the humiliating secrets of Cedarville, a cloistered hamlet on Cape Cod. It was written by a young woman, boarding-school bred, who'd slummed it as a schoolteacher for a couple of seasons. She'd lived among the townsfolk, had become their friend and confidante, and had secretly taken fastidious notes in preparation for an exposé of their small-town lives. The author of *Cape Cod Folks* was initially anonymous, but everyone in Cedarville knew straightaway that it was Sally Pratt McLean.

Cape Cod Folks became a best seller; reviewers, who thought it a novel, gushed over what they called the remarkably realistic prose. The author had a "keen eye for the ridiculous," they said, and the "quaint and homely" queer characters offered genuine amusement as they went about their lives in "a poor little apology for a village," "one of the most desolate and forlorn places on the cape." McLean "d[id] not spare their poverty, their ignorance, their awkwardness, their pettiness; all these [were] told with a sharp pen, with genuine disgust, or with hearty laughter."

One key story line featured a decrepit character named Grandpa Fisher, hopelessly confused, weak, and defenseless, dyeing his scraggly gray hair black so that he might look like a man of thirty, only to end up, in the author's assessment, neither old nor young, human nor inhuman. There was an etching at the front part of the book that showed as much.

Then there was Zetta, one of the older students. She confessed that she'd been wooed by a sailor into doing the "worst." "Oh, I wish I was dead!" she told her teacher. "It's the sin and the shame."

And who wouldn't be captivated by Lorenzo Nightingale, Grandpa Fisher's neighbor, an unsophisticated youth just a smidge from manhood who'd made a heartfelt boyish pass at the teacher? "I should like to kiss you just once to-night and mean it," he told her, and then did it more than once. If he set off to work real tight, and maybe came back lucky in a few years, might he have the teacher's hand in marriage? Or would she continue to trifle with him even then, simply because he was raised poor and ignorant?

It took awhile, but readers outside Cedarville soon caught on that those quaint and homely, queer and amusing, awkward and poor characters appeared both on the pages of *Cape Cod Folks* and on one single page in the U.S. census. As one critic put it, the trouble with the book was that it was "too true."

In response to growing alarm about the truth of it all, the publisher promised to change the real-life names in future editions. It also sent out a sorry-not-sorry apology saying that it "deeply regret[ed] that the feelings of anyone should be injured by the innocent fun contained in the book."

Adelaide Fisher, the thirty-one-year-old daughter-in-law of Grandpa Fisher, was one of those injured. She'd brought Sally Pratt McLean to town and had given her room and board; Adelaide's husband was away at sea, she had her hands full with two little kids, and she longed for some adult company.

For a while, Adelaide didn't trust Sally. But then she did.

Adelaide was particularly devastated by her portrayal in the book: McLean had described her as a frail little woman, not pretty, with a tired, tense look about the mouth and a way about her that made her seem sorely discontent. It was easy for Adelaide to get out of temper, and she often slapped the children. She missed her husband terribly, and she worried about his fidelity, especially when letters from the sea stopped coming. Adelaide had turned to religion for comfort, and when she led the town prayer meetings in song, her voice was strangely sweet and rapturous in its pathos and pathetic quaver. "Shall we meet beyond the river," she sang, where "sorrow ne'er shall press the soul?"

Precisely eleven months to the day of the book's announcement in *Publishers' Weekly* came word that Adelaide had died. The official cause of death was consumption, but everybody knew what had killed Adelaide Fisher: "the unpleasant notoriety forced upon her by that book," as her doctor put it, the embarrassment of it all. She'd left behind her mariner husband, an eight-year-old daughter, and a seven-year-old son.

Before she died, Adelaide had joined in a lawsuit for libel and ridicule against the publishers of *Cape Cod Folks*. Grandpa Fisher had joined it too, and together with three other plaintiffs they argued that the book had crushed their dignity; they'd taken Sally Pratt McLean into their homes out of kindness and friendship, and she'd proved to be a "viper." Eventually, four of the five plaintiffs agreed to cash settlements with Brandeis's client, A. Williams & Company, and thereafter dropped out of the lawsuit.

The sole holdout was Lorenzo Nightingale, the teacher's would-be suitor. He took his case to a jury, the publisher argued in response that it had every right to publish the truth about his mostly unrequited love, and jurors awarded Lorenzo $1,095, quite a lot in 1884, about $30,000 today.

The day after the verdict, the *Boston Daily Advertiser* criticized *Cape Cod Folks* as "an attack . . . on the proprieties of private life." Many in this age of increased reading and writing, the *Advertiser* suggested, believed that no verdict could be too excessive for simple country folk who deserved life, liberty, and the pursuit of happiness and had instead been humiliated by those who would steal into intimate moments and reveal them. The *Nightingale* case pressed the question of how far publishers may legally violate the decencies and proprieties recognized in the ordinary relations of life. It wouldn't be long and shouldn't be long, critics said, before readers would demand the same sort of restraint from the greatest offenders, the day's newspapers that seemed increasingly hell-bent on reporting the same sort of embarrassment and scandal.

Louis Brandeis, whose reputation was on the rise throughout the Northeast, was brought in by the publisher on the *Nightingale* appeal. He found himself in a bit of a hole there, given all the pushback in the court of public opinion. A clever lawyer needed both to protect his client and to recognize in some way Nightingale's profound embarrassment at the revelation of otherwise private passions.

The trouble was—and Brandeis surely knew this—that his friend Oliver Wendell Holmes, despite being the son of a famous poet, was no fan of the day's increasingly unrestrained publishing. Holmes had become a judge the same year that Joseph Pulitzer had purchased *The World* in New York City, promising a change in methods, purposes, and principle in the newspaper, and a Pulitzer sort of sensationalism was already creeping into the Boston papers. A defiant Holmes, in a very early case that questioned a newspaper's right to publish truth, had therefore held *The Boston Herald* liable for publishing a 100 percent accurate story about a certain attorney who was facing disbarment. To give the public knowledge of such a personal thing, Holmes had written in *Cowley v. Pulsifer*, was inappropriate, because it threw no light upon the "administration of justice."

You might think that all newspapers would have rallied against the Holmes decision as some sort of unconstitutional restriction on their news judgment, but they didn't. There were indeed rumblings of such a defense mostly in state courts back then, and some judges had written things like "a free press [is] one of the strongest bulwarks of liberty, and the people of this country have ever guarded it with jealous care," but it would take decades before the First Amendment itself would prove so protective in an official sense. Besides, some newspapers at the time proudly distinguished themselves from their more scandalous cousins; the *Boston Daily Advertiser*, for example, headlined its story about the *Cowley* decision A LEGAL LIMIT TO "ENTERPRISE" and found that limit perfectly agreeable. In light of *Cowley*, the *Daily Advertiser*'s editorial read, "It [would] not be unreasonable to hope that before long the honest citizen m[ight] find some way to make his privacy respected."

Holmes kept that newspaper clipping in his papers until he died. He'd also asked that the permanent privacy of his personal letters be secured by burning or some other destructive method. "I don't know whether you feel so," he wrote to a friend named Harold Laski many years later, "but I like to think that no more of me will be made public than what I have made so."

But that's a privacy story for the twentieth century.

The Holmes bench book for 1884–85, his personal record of court cases and their outcomes, suggests that Holmes himself was to write the opinion in the *Cape Cod Folks* case but then, for some unknown reason, Justice Walbridge Field agreed to take over. This was surely an additionally ominous sign for Louis Brandeis. That's because, like Justice Holmes, Justice Field had sided with the plaintiff and against a newspaper in a case involving a truthful article. There, journalists had accurately reported that a local minister had been forced out of his church for brutalizing his daughters through "horsewhippings for trivial offences, systematic starving, feeding of rotten meat, and positive dishonesty and faithlessness in his family relations." Editors testified that they'd shared the news in the interest of society and the public good.

Justice Field wasn't at all impressed with that judgment call: the truth of the words published is not an absolute defense, he wrote, because what counted was whether the newspaper had acted with a malicious intent in revealing the truth, the heart of the plaintiff's claim. The public's right to know, after all, had its limits, and because the jury had found such limits perfectly satisfactory in this particular case, its verdict would stand: the newspaper owed the horsewhipping, philandering minister $1,000. Case closed.

By the time Brandeis stood in front of the Massachusetts Supreme Judicial Court in 1884, in fact, more than 250 court opinions from across the

United States had mentioned the word "privacy" in some way. Courts had focused on the privacy of the home (the "right of quiet occupancy and privacy was absolute and exclusive"), and on the "privacy of domestic life" or, even better, the "sacred privacy of domestic life." Others had noted the privacy inherent in sexual relations ("illicit intercourse of parties is generally consummated in the strictest privacy and secrecy, and is known only to the parties themselves") and the privacy in telegrams (the "destruction of the happiness of whole households" would otherwise be "brought to light and hawked through the country by scandal-mongers"). It all suggested the need for strong privacy protections especially within the family: "Of what occurs in the privacy of the family circle," outsiders "can know but little or nothing" because "lifting the veil from the domestic sanctuary [would] expose to public view the secrets and scandals of private life," a violation of the common law (or court-decided law). A California judge had written quite specifically that the conversation of intimate friends may not be shared either and that any invasion of domestic circles would encourage an evil "system of espionage abhorrent to American ideas." Sure, that case involved a police informant who'd spilled the beans, but the language was powerfully protective more generally.

Meanwhile, in Michigan, Justice Thomas Cooley of that state's supreme court had come up with a catchy phrase in his influential treatise on tort law that neatly described such privacy sensibilities: the right to be let alone. He'd also joined in an opinion several years earlier that said flat out that the general public "has no concern whatever with the lawful doings and affairs of private persons." Cooley's "right to be let alone," in fact, had caught on much more quickly than a related phrase on the other side of the coin minted that same decade: the "right to know" the truth of things.

This body of law and opinion seemed to give the *Cape Cod Folks* plaintiffs a sound legal path to victory and the defendant an impending defeat at the Massachusetts Supreme Judicial Court, but nothing was spot-on precedential, so Brandeis argued in a sort of Hail Mary pass that his client's behavior was wrong but not actionable. Yes, there'd been emotional harm done to Lorenzo Nightingale, the young man who'd bared his heart to a teacher who'd then told the rest of the world about it, Brandeis argued. But that sort of wrong wasn't yet on the law books—libel meant harm to reputation, he argued, and ridicule "laughs *down*," not with or up—and this was therefore only a breach of the canons of propriety and good manners. The civil law didn't address eavesdropping or looking into one's windows either, Brandeis noted, so it certainly didn't recognize this publication-related "invasion of the plaintiff's domestic privacy."

As proof of the law's failure to support privacy, Brandeis mostly cited cases from England that really weren't all that helpful to him; this brief didn't sing like those that he'd later become famous for, those that incorporated compelling facts, public policy matters, and nonlegal argument. He surely must have been thinking that Lorenzo Nightingale was a much more sympathetic plaintiff than a brutalizing excommunicated minister or an attorney facing disbarment.

Even the facts weren't on Brandeis's side in a case that he himself had called a privacy invasion.

Oral argument at the time was usually followed by a published decision within a few weeks. So when the rest of October, November, December, January, February, and March all passed with no word from the court, Brandeis surely knew that he was in trouble. An opinion in the publisher's favor would have been easy to write, because all that the justices would have needed to say was that the law didn't recognize a privacy claim, just as Brandeis had argued in his brief and at oral argument. No legal support for something called a right of privacy? Short opinion quickly written.

But if the court had decided that folks like Nightingale had a right to privacy by name? That sort of intricate opinion that built upon layers of existing law would have taken a little longer. Importantly, such an opinion would have also stopped the *Cape Cod Folks* gravy train; Brandeis's client had already published more than seventeen revised editions as the lawsuit dragged on, and revenue from those had to have been a consideration.

Meanwhile, on a more personal level, it probably didn't help matters when Brandeis's cousin, a famous medical doctor, suddenly went missing, and newspapers around the nation began to report intriguing details about the man and his immediate family. Had the prosperous Dr. Richard Brandeis suddenly gone insane? Was he wandering around demented, leaving his wife prostrated from grief and anxiety? Or did his disappearance involve something more sinister? Nobody, surely not even a publisher's lawyer, could celebrate that sort of spotlight on family tragedy.

Louis Brandeis therefore did what any thinking defense lawyer would have done and he settled Lorenzo Nightingale's claim. That meant the case ended right there, before any decision on the appeal by the court. Nobody knows for sure what the publishers paid Nightingale because nobody can find the case file at any Massachusetts courthouse; they say that back then, after settlement, everything was destroyed because the case could no longer be revived and there seemed no reason to keep anything. Only the handwritten trial court notation, Justice Holmes's bench book marked "settled by parties before decision," the court docket, old newspaper accounts, and Brandeis's appellate brief bound with others as a memento for his daughters prove that it ever happened.

That means we don't know for sure what legal precedent the plaintiffs used to support their claims for libel and ridicule against Brandeis's client in the *Cape Cod Folks* case. But there's a hint in news coverage of the case, and an interesting twist. The magazine *The Literary World*, surely helped along by the plaintiff's lawyers, suggested that the patriot Alexander Hamilton, now dead some eighty years, would have seen it Lorenzo Nightingale's way: Hamilton, the editorial read, had embraced and supported the ideal of a free press to some extent for sure, but had also condemned mischievous, painful writing that ridiculed others.

That is pretty much correct. And Hamilton is not the only Founder who seemingly would have supported Nightingale and the other plaintiffs in the *Cape Cod Folks* case. At the time the United States was getting under way, a good number of pleas for privacy—through cases involving seditious libel and otherwise—had led to some powerful, albeit questionable, decisions against publishers. Some called the cause of action behind it all *truthful* libel, the notion that truth could be as harmful to reputation as falsity if not more. That sort of anti-press punishment for truth sprang in part from England's notorious Star Chamber, a real-life court that had ordered in the fifteenth, sixteenth, and seventeenth centuries that rogue publishers' ears be cut off, that their noses be slit, or that they be branded or imprisoned for life for publishing truth, usually truth that revealed government wrongdoing.

Brandeis wouldn't include Star Chamber cases in his later arguments for privacy because that would have been bad company: Nobody wanted the evils of the Star Chamber lurking behind a new legal principle. But he surely recognized the relationship because he would credit key progeny in his *Cape Cod Folks* brief, sparked in large part by a troubling long-ago decision involving George Washington, John Adams, Thomas Jefferson, and Alexander Hamilton.

Back in the early nineteenth century, decades before Brandeis would defend the *Cape Cod Folks* publisher in Boston, there was a case in New York called *People v. Croswell*. The Founders played major roles. And just like in the *Cape Cod Folks* case, it pitted privacy against a publisher, and privacy ultimately won out.

Chapter Two

HAMILTON, JEFFERSON, AND THE GREATEST EVIL

Alexander Hamilton and Thomas Jefferson weren't the first to invade privacy by publishing naughty truths in the newspapers. But it was close. And by bickering over such revelations, they helped along the right to privacy in the new United States.

Cutting pieces like that were the norm back then. Most newspapers were ramped-up, coarser versions of modern-day partisan media; they published mostly what was politically useful, and fake news made for as much good copy as excited coverage of duels, which helped keep male-combat-for-honor fashionable, and the sort of fiction that was said to work on women's romantic inclinations and make them act improperly. New York's population stood at about thirty-three thousand, and growing citification had smoothed the rusticity of the shepherd, but it was clear to the elite that such evil communications worked against civility by corrupting morals and disgracing national manners.

That sensibility eventually found its way to the nation's courts. "One of the greatest blessings ever bestowed by Providence on His creatures"—the liberty of the press, one judge in Pennsylvania wrote in the early days of the United States—"was capable of producing . . . the greatest mischief," the "greatest evil."

Hamilton was one of the milder media mischief makers, at least to start. Maybe, just maybe, he wrote in 1792 under the nom de plume Catullus in the *Gazette of the United States*, Jefferson's real character and tantalizing secret life would be revealed soon. In the meantime, he'd drop a hint: Jefferson's

Quaker-like simplicity—his quiet, modest, retiring nature—concealed a voluptuary, a man who reveled in sensual pleasures, a debauchee.

"For god's sake, my dear Sir," Jefferson wrote to James Madison in response, "take up your pen, select the most striking heresies, and cut him to pieces in the face of the public." Jefferson had to put a stop to Hamilton's taunting prose because he knew what was coming: whispers in Charlottesville at the time were that Jefferson was having a sexual relationship with one of his slaves, Sally Hemings. Hamilton as Catullus suggested that that news would be breaking in the papers soon enough.

That didn't happen. But four years later, in 1796, when President George Washington announced he'd be stepping down and there were rumblings that Jefferson would make a fine replacement, Hamilton returned to the pages of the *Gazette*. This time, he wrote as Phocion and began a multipart editorial campaign to examine the pretensions of Thomas Jefferson and his secret life.

Example one: Why had Jefferson written a letter to a fellow philosopher expressing his belief that all peoples might be equal? This apparent shift in Jefferson's stance on emancipation had come shortly after his return from France, where he had "imbibed" the subject of racial integration. (Paris, it is said, was where Jefferson had first come to know the fourteen-year-old Hemings, the half sister of Jefferson's deceased wife.) How could a mixing of the races have been any sort of worry for Jefferson anyway, Hamilton asked, when he must have seen all around him the sufficient marks of an enslaved person mixing with his (or her) master? Besides, who wanted a sensualistic aristocratic epicurean philosopher president anyway?

Alexander Hamilton/Catullus/Phocion soon learned firsthand that people in glass houses shouldn't throw stones. Hamilton had his own secrets, and Thomas Jefferson's comrade in arms (for the moment, at least) was the despised newspaper editor James Callender, a man who gleefully spilled the beans about the Federalist powerful. The Anti-Federalist Jefferson found Callender's writing politically useful, of course, so he paid Callender to put together certain pieces and served as an anonymous source for Callender's reporting.

Callender would happily reveal in turn in the innocuous-sounding pamphlet *The History of the United States for 1796* that Hamilton was not who *he* appeared to be: that this great master of morality in public had had an illicit correspondence with another man's wife. The dirt was 100 percent true; Hamilton, married and the father of a toddler, had been locked in a torrid affair with a woman named Maria Reynolds. The day that the states ratified the First Amendment was the day that Hamilton received a letter informing him that Maria's husband had learned of their illicit love . . . and might want some cash to keep things quiet.

Quiet was not kept. Callender's explosive piece included a series of letters between Hamilton and the entrepreneurial Mr. Reynolds that proved it all true. "Included are fifty dollars," one letter in Hamilton's hand read. "They could not be sent sooner." (This sort of revelation was tit for tat in Callender's mind because Hamilton had once spoken publicly of some of George Washington's personal letters, including those marked private that had asked for writing help. Hamilton ought to have concealed the imperfections of his friend, Callender had argued, a sensibility in line with law that had, since 1710, made it a crime to open another's letter. Postmaster General Ben Franklin had later protected letters even more stridently by ensuring that mail carriers not leave them around for others to see.)

Back in Charlottesville, Thomas Jefferson must have been pleased with such revelatory hubbub. He made a quick notation in his June 1797 financial ledger: "Pd. Callender for Hist. of US."

Hamilton's response to it all was a ninety-five-page booklet complaining about his own loss of privacy. He found "mortifying disappointment" in Callender's "Scandal-Club" publication that had devoured "even the peace of [Hamilton's] unoffending and amiable wife." Was nothing sacred? Sure, Hamilton admitted that he had in fact had an amorous connection with Mrs. Reynolds, but this sort of intimacy wasn't appropriate for public consumption. If "any little foible or folly can be traced out in one, whom they desire to persecute," Hamilton warned, referring to the publishers of the day, "it becomes at once in their hands a two-edged sword, by which to wound the public character and stab the private felicity of the person."

That sort of thing—a stab to the private felicity of a person that wounded his public character—suggested a legal cause of action, something that would support a lawsuit at the time. Hamilton, a lawyer, likely knew that they called it truthful libel in some places and plain old regular libel in others and that it meant that anything harmful to a person's reputation, even if true, could be punished. Libel, including truthful libel, had been helped along post–Star Chamber by an important British law book published in the 1760s, Blackstone's *Commentaries on the Laws of England*, one that had been highly influential in the United States too. It said that a publisher certainly could put whatever he wanted to in his newspaper and that freedom of the press was essential to a free state, but if that publisher published something "improper, mischievous, or illegal, he must take the consequence of his own temerity." This included the publication of embarrassing truth, something like a tidbit about a husband who'd been unfaithful and had suffered his wife's wrath in response; such a revelation, Blackstone believed, was punishable because it exposed the husband publicly and made him look ridiculous. The worry was that when private, personal, truthful things got reported, the emotional damage and desire for physical revenge would be even more profound to the outed individual than had falsity been published.

Sensibilities were similar stateside. "This is an age," one publisher in Philadelphia wrote in 1789, "when the prying eye of curiosity penetrates the privacy of every distinguished person," with table talk and trivial pursuits both exposed with "the pomp of importance, by some officious hand, engaged to furnish anecdotes for the world." At a time when newspapers carried ads promising strict privacy in the teaching of dancing, the treatment of seminal weakness in either sex, and the curing of venereal complaints, the trend, the writer said, appeared to be to veil such puerilities.

They didn't call it a right to privacy. "The greater the truth, the greater the libel," they used to say.

———

You don't hear much about truthful libel today. The story of the fight against *seditious* libel—criticism of the government or criticism of official conduct by government officials in order to undermine them (hence seditious)—is widely celebrated in history books, in part because of the romantic tale of the New York newspaperman John Peter Zenger, who in 1734 criticized a colonial governor and then persuaded a jury to find him not guilty for doing so. We've erected historical markers for John Peter Zenger, we've named a ship after him, and if you ask anyone who's studied journalism, his name is synonymous with freedom of the press. Trouble is that a jury nullification in a single case did very little to change the law generally, and the government kept right on arresting journalists for saying bad things about it, even in New York, all the way through to the Cleveland administration and beyond, at times cloaking a government official's private life through what was, in effect, a seditious libel charge.

Truthful libel, in contrast, the idea that truthful reputation-harming details about an individual could be punished, had no such poster child. It too punished the publication of truthful information about the government and its officials, but everyday people could also sue using it when they felt that newspapers had invaded their domestic privacy.

There was one important difference. During the time of Hamilton and Jefferson and Callender, seditious libel had become an on-the-books federal crime. The Alien and Sedition Acts, passed in 1798 during the Adams administration, were meant to impede the work of Anti-Federalist newspaper types like Callender, who was both an alien, having come to the United States from Scotland, and seditious. Criticize the government? Go directly to jail; Congress had decided as much.

Libel, as well as truthful libel, on the other hand, was also a common-law concept, the type of law that had developed through the courts, one that would be every bit as precedential as laws passed by legislatures, just usually not as instantly sweeping. Truthful libel wasn't all that controversial either. Even the beloved John Peter Zenger had approvingly published supportive musings: that there were some truths not fit to be told, including private and personal faults and failings, which if published can only cause mischief and do no good.

The First Amendment's promises of freedom of speech and freedom of the press, meanwhile, didn't fit much into the landscape back then; such principles didn't have the same reverence or power as they do today. Not only was everybody still figuring out what those promises meant, but the Bill of Rights applied only to the federal government anyway, not yet to the states, and certainly not to individuals or private enterprise. Through it all, words on paper that seemed pretty darned absolutist like "no law" should abridge "the freedom of speech, or of the press" turned out to be not so protective of speech or the press after all.

This privacy-related puzzlement about the First Amendment began even before it was ratified. My question is this, the Massachusetts Supreme Judicial Court justice William Cushing wrote to John Adams in 1789, is it wrong to deem and adjudge any publications of the press punishable if they reveal instances of "male conduct" by politicians that are immoral and repugnant but are also absolutely true?

Cushing, who later became one of the first five justices on the U.S. Supreme Court, then answered his own early #MeToo question: doubtless publishers may and ought to be restrainable from injuring the characters of such men. Adams responded favorably to Cushing's assessment too: yes, a scandalous truth published for no good reason would mean that the plaintiff would prevail. Then, as president, Adams put his words into action by signing the Alien and Sedition Acts, which threatened that if anyone "shall write, print, utter, or publish, or shall cause or procure to be written, printed, uttered or published . . . any false, scandalous and malicious writings or writings against the government" or the president or members of Congress "or to excite against them . . . the hatred of the good people of the United States," the writer, printer, utterer, or publisher could be fined $5,000 and thrown in prison for five years. Adams would also complain bitterly about notorious, indecent abuses of the press throughout his life.

And despite their artful rhetoric about the importance of a free press, it's pretty clear that most of the Founding Fathers fell right into line with Adams. Even though we may remember more their pro-press language— because those are the phrases that publishers most often remind us of—the powerful men of eighteenth-century America preferred privacy as a cause.

Ben Franklin, for example, agreed that "every Person has little Secrets and Privacies that are not proper to be expos'd even to the nearest Friend," and said that when he published his pamphlets and newspapers, he "refus'd to print such thing as might do real Injury to any Person," including personal reflections and all libeling and personal abuse. He noted the difference between "private letters between friends" and those "written by public officers to persons in public station, on public affairs," and suggested that the former should be kept out of others' hands. He also suggested that he would cheerfully consent to exchange his liberty of abusing others in the press for the

privilege of not being abused himself by those who could tear "private character to flitters."

Alexander Hamilton, who would come to play an even more important
role in the right to privacy, found laws for "restraining and punishing incendiary and seditious practices" important to preserve confidence in the government and believed that writings leveled against any government official
should be actionable as libels.

James Madison, the author of the First Amendment, wrote in 1800 that
he and other key players were "not unaware of the difficulty of all general
questions which may turn on the *proper boundary* between the liberty and
licentiousness of the press."

George Washington assured a foreign friend that the United States had
"infamous Papers—calculated for disturbing if not absolutely intended to
disturb, the peace of the community"—and said that certain newspapers
were "outrages on common decency."

But, perhaps not surprising, it was Thomas Jefferson, third president
of the United States—a man who wrote ciphered letters to friends to keep
things secret, who asked that certain of his letters be destroyed by burning,
and who had significant secrets to keep—who was the clearest in his condemnation of the press and its publication of truthful but hurtful items. He
found "the pain of a little censure" in newspapers "more acute than the pleasure of much praise" and therefore said his greatest wish was "to avoid attracting notice," "to keep out of view in every thing of a private nature." He
was frustrated with "the publication of what ha[d] not been intended for the
public eye," especially his own private sentiments. "And do you not think I
had a right to decide this for myself?" he would ask his correspondents.

In 1786, Jefferson wrote the now-famous line that the country's "liberty
depends on the freedom of the press, and that cannot be limited without
being lost." But by 1803, as president, Jefferson shared a confidence with
Pennsylvania's governor that he had "long thought that a few prosecutions
of the most eminent offenders" of journalism excess "would have a wholesome effect in restoring the integrity of the presses" and that such prosecutions would "place the whole band more on their guard." "The restraints
provided by the laws of the states are sufficient for this if applied," he suggested, surely meaning the law of libel and, therefore, truthful libel.

And it was Jefferson who wrote in another letter to Madison that the federal Constitution left that sort of protection up to the states, including "how far the licentiousness of speech & of the press may be abridged without lessening their useful freedom, and how far those abuses which cannot be separated from their use should be tolerated rather than the use be destroyed."

It's no wonder that newspaper editors got into trouble back then for publishing what others considered private truths. The framers recognized—and at times indulged in—the power of exposure to punish and destroy enemies. But they also embraced a concept of press freedom that recognized limits, including one built upon what they considered the gratuitous, unjustified exposure of private information.

Some newspapermen, of course, didn't quite see it that way.

Somewhere along the way Thomas Jefferson and his buddy James Callender had a falling-out.

There's a backstory here too. In 1800, again with financial help from Jefferson, Callender had published a pamphlet titled *The Prospect Before Us*. There, he called the Adams administration a "tempest of malignant passions" that had "extinguish[ed] the only gleam of happiness that glimmer[ed] through the dark and despicable farce of life." Adams himself was a "hoary headed incendiary." And, Callender said, it had all started with the dreadful George Washington, the man who "could not have committed a more net and pure violation of his oath to preserve the constitution" by entering into a treaty with England against the wishes of Congress.

Callender was in trouble. Not only was George Washington a saint, but the Adams administration's Alien and Sedition Acts were, in effect, making it a crime to write scandalous and malicious things against the government, and truth was a defense by statute, not necessarily by rote, which is what Callender found firsthand when he was arrested. Jurors took all of two hours to find him guilty and sentence him to nine months in jail. There was a difference between liberty of the press and its licentiousness, the judge had explained.

Callender's life behind bars in the Richmond jail was horrendous. He wrote a remarkable series of letters to Jefferson explaining, among other things, that he was in very bad health owing to the stink and the shrieking insane. But through it all, he'd managed to publish parts of a new edition of *The Prospect Before Us*. "This letter will inclose a few pages of the second part of The Prospect," he wrote to Jefferson in August 1800 from jail. "But next week, I Shall send some Sheets that You have not seen before."

A few months later, Jefferson was elected president, and because the Alien and Sedition Acts had automatically expired, Callender was released from custody. Given all that he'd done for Jefferson and the party, all that material that he'd published criticizing Hamilton's private doings and Adams's more public ones, Callender expected some sort of political payback, maybe even a postmaster job.

But Jefferson told Callender no. In response, Callender warned Jefferson that he knew secrets about him that he'd happily spill. Jefferson appeared confident when he wrote to James Monroe that Callender was wrong, that Callender knew nothing that Jefferson himself was not willing to declare to the world.

But that must have been an overstatement.

"It is well known," Callender wrote thereafter in a newspaper called *The Recorder,* "that the man, whom it delighteth the people to honour, keeps, and for many years past has kept, as his concubine, one of his own slaves." This revelation about Jefferson was profoundly newsworthy, Callender wrote, and not something that should be excused as everyday boys-will-be-boys behavior. "Her name is Sally," and Jefferson had chosen her to bear his "several children," including a son who looked exactly like him. Earlier Federalist newspapers had been correct, Callender wrote, Jefferson had in fact selected "African stock whereupon he was to engraft his own descendants."

There was more. Callender revealed that Jefferson had paid him $100 to publish those nasty things about George Washington and John Adams. *The Prospect Before Us*? That pamphlet had had Jefferson's hands all over it too, just like *The History of the United States for 1796.*

Callender's piece wasn't the end of it. A couple of months later, somebody calling himself Junius Philaenus published a sixty-four-page pamphlet titled *A Letter to Thomas Jefferson*, clearly written for a larger audience. In it, Philaenus urged women not to be bewitched by the new president's charms because Jefferson was already taken: "A certain black strumpet, yelep'd

Sally, enjoys [his] love and [his] embraces." Jefferson, who'd used the partisan newspapers to further his ambitions—Jefferson had, Philaenus suggested, "bribed [Callender] to become a villain and then dictated for his pen" falsehoods against the venerable—had all the time been hiding a "private" secret, that he lived "in the habits of open and shameless prostitution with one of his own slaves." He was but a coward philosopher.

That tirade sounded an awful lot like Phocion from years before. Could Junius Philaenus be Alexander Hamilton?

The person who published the responsive pamphlet *Letters to Alexander Hamilton, King of the Feds* just a few weeks later sure thought so. It was subtitled "A Reply to a Scandalous Pamphlet Lately Published Under the Sanction, as It Is Presumed, of Mr. Hamilton." Junius Philaenus's work, this second pamphlet read, bears such evident symbols of Hamilton's patronage that it was impossible not to see the mark of the beast on its forehead. Hamilton had disavowed being the patron of the licentiousness of the press and yet had clearly "made more use of that Instrumentality to carry on intrigues against the peace and happiness of the people than any other man in America."

In the wake of both tantalizing tidbits—the information about Jefferson's relationship with Sally Hemings *and* Jefferson's support for the seditious *Prospect*—Jefferson got off pretty easy. The pamphlets did not circulate widely, and newspapers of all sorts hesitated to republish the first; it would surely be a libel even if true. The second seemed easier to defend, but even that wasn't certain. Some trusted Jefferson and his claim that his payments to Callender were but charity money, paid to a sad, sad man who'd become a raving alcoholic.

But the intrigue continued and would soon directly influence the course of privacy law in the United States.

The Wasp was a four-page Federalist newspaper designed to sting. Its masthead featured a nasty-looking eponym, and its very first edition in 1802 promised that it would strive to displease, vex, and torment its partisan (read: Jeffersonian) enemies. "If there, perchance, should come a Bee," the first paragraph of the first column read in reference to a newspaper that supported Jefferson, "a Wasp will come as soon as he." An editor named Harry Croswell had founded the new publication, and he welcomed James Callender's report confirming what the Federalists already knew, that President Jefferson wasn't what he appeared to be.

"Mr. Jefferson paid one hundred dollars to Callender for libelling George Washington and John Adams," Croswell wrote. But even he steered away from the whole Sally Hemings thing.

Soon after, state authorities in New York indicted Croswell for a libel on Jefferson. *The Wasp*'s editor, the indictment read, was a malicious and seditious man with a depraved mind and a wicked and diabolical disposition who had scandalized and vilified President Thomas Jefferson in order to bring Jefferson into great hatred, contempt, and disgrace. By republishing what Callender had written about the president, Croswell had most grossly slandered the private character of Jefferson, who, the government added, was well known to be virtuous.

By this point, seditious libel had lapsed and was no longer a federal statute, but that disappearance had no effect on state law. Croswell had defamed the president of the United States—he had grossly slandered the private character of Jefferson by republishing Callender's claims—and that sort of libelous behavior remained against the law in New York.

Croswell responded quickly. His arrest, he said, was a direct attack upon the freedom of the press and showed a palpable hostility to the freedom of discussion. He hoped that Jefferson would be on his side. After all, truth had been an on-the-books defense to statutory seditious libel, and Jefferson had wrapped himself in the flag several months earlier by writing that public men should submit to slander as a part of a national duty to press freedom. Surely Jefferson would live his rhetoric and absolve Croswell.

But Jefferson remained absolutely, positively silent.

So Croswell and his attorneys began to formulate a defense proving the truth of it all through the man who'd reported the information about Jefferson in the first place. The way they'd planned it, not only would James Callender testify that, yes, Jefferson had paid him to say those things about Adams and Washington, but he'd bring with him to court two letters from Jefferson that proved Jefferson's role in *The Prospect Before Us*.

Your Honor, we call James Callender to prove the truth of the matter!

The star witness unfortunately failed to appear, at least in court; Callender turned up dead that same week. He'd drowned in Richmond's James River in water that was about three feet deep and was buried the same day. An official inquest that came days later called the drowning accidental, the result of drunkenness. The Jeffersonian newspapers called it a suicide, brought on by the shame of Callender's type of journalism. John Adams thought that the miscreant might have been killed: plunged in by an enemy. Indeed, the Federalist newspapers pointed out that Callender had been in the process of bringing to light Jefferson's real character. "The grave cannot always arrest the pursuit of vengeance," they warned.

But here the grave did arrest one pursuit. There's little disagreement that Jefferson did pay Callender; personal letters and Jefferson's notations prove as much. But it took until the year 2000 for the Thomas Jefferson Foundation to officially recognize that Callender and Hamilton had been right all along with regard to the Sally Hemings story, that Jefferson had indeed been in a sexual relationship with his slave. And, as late as the 1960s, Callender's revelatory pieces on Jefferson were described by one biographer as merely scandalous tittle-tattle about Jefferson's private life.

It's pretty clear that even had Callender lived, a defense of truth wouldn't have done much good in Croswell's case. After all, privacy sensibilities that protected the individual through "the greater the truth, the greater the libel" remained a part of the common law of New York, and so truth often helped prove a newspaper's licentious wrong.

Federalist newspapers at the time were outraged at the suggestion that published truthful revelations about Jefferson's back-channel maneuvers would be too painful for him to bear and should therefore be officially repressed. "Mr. Jefferson's tools have resorted to the common law," the *Washington Federalist* wrote, that "not only prohibits the truth from being given in evidence, but has established it as a principle, that the greater the truth, the greater the libel." What Croswell had published, they argued, was important information involving a politician's manipulative relationship with a notorious publisher. Had the victory for newspapers after the end of the statutory Alien and Sedition Acts actually been a profound defeat in that the common law now kicked in and it didn't recognize truth as a defense? Moreover, they asked, where was Jefferson, the patriot who'd wept with anxiety at the suppression of truth three years earlier after the passage of those laws?

The Bee of course was on Jefferson's side. "The liberty of the press is a precious invaluable right," its editorial read, but "its licentiousness is a scourge to any well ordered government." Printers hiding behind some sort of sacred mask of liberty, it wrote, should not be allowed to publish anything and everything they wanted about those individuals who held public office.

That meant that in 1803 Harry Croswell was brought before a New York jury on charges of libeling Thomas Jefferson through his republication of Callender's quite accurate allegations. The prosecutor reminded jurors of *The Wasp*'s editorial line: that the liberty of the press was a most invaluable privilege but that its stinging licentiousness was a growing and intolerable evil. Without the ability to call witnesses or otherwise prove the truth of the matter, the defense had little to say in response, and the jury took an evening to find Harry Croswell guilty.

And this is where the former secretary of the Treasury, partisan multinamed editorialist, and philanderer Alexander Hamilton reappears. Now a New York lawyer in private practice—someway, somehow, surely because the case was ultimately all about Thomas Jefferson's bad behavior—he agreed to participate in *The Wasp* editor Harry Croswell's appeal.

Maybe Hamilton wasn't the best choice for a case that would impact the future of press freedom to report the truth. He still had a bit of a chip on his shoulder about the media, being a victim of Callender himself.

Nevertheless, they say that Hamilton gave it his best. He spoke for six hours before the New York high court on behalf of Croswell's right to publish accurate, albeit painful, facts about Thomas Jefferson. Hamilton was "like a torrent," they said, "bold, strong and overpowering," pouring "his resistless course to the amazement of democracy." On that day, "truth, proud, powerful and fearless, asserted its majesty." Hamilton's oration was so good that newspapers predicted it would "never be forgotten by the advocates of federalism and rational liberty." Hamilton had taken a "bold stand in favour of the press" and thereby offered an "essential service to his country" and "to freedom."

The trouble was that Hamilton didn't argue that the press should be totally free to report the truth, no matter the cost to privacy. Not surprisingly, he argued in line with long-standing Blackstonian libel principles that an unrestricted press would be a bad thing, a "pest of society," a "terrible liberty" that would "encourage vice, compel the virtuous to retire, destroy confidence, and confound the innocent with the guilty." "The Liberty of the Press," he argued instead, "consist[ed] . . . in publishing the truth, *from good motives and justifiable ends*, though it reflect on government, on magistrates, or individuals." Punishment for a truthful story might come, for example, if a publication revealed "a man's personal defects or deformity." That sort of truth would be far too painful for anyone to bear, and would instantly harm reputation even if true, and so publishers who published such things would of course be liable.

Then this addendum, certainly sparked by the revelation of his interlude with Mrs. Reynolds: if the publisher "uses the weapon of truth wantonly; if for the purpose of disturbing the peace of families; if for relating that which does not appertain to official conduct," then that publisher should be punished.

You might think of it as a call for a right to privacy, by sensibility if not by name, in the face of scandalous yet absolutely truthful reporting. Hamilton was all for drawing a protective line, so long as he got to draw it.

And the Croswell case clearly crossed that line, Hamilton explained in a right-to-know sort of way: this was important news; this was coverage that revealed what Jefferson had done to harm the honor of the country and its national legacy of inestimable value. Freedom of discussion and freedom of the press, Croswell's trial attorneys had already told the appellate court, were essential to the liberties of the United States because they enabled the people to select their rulers with discretion and to judge correctly their merits. Croswell's reporting had opened some eyes, and that was the whole point of press freedom: to report certain truths (what we today might call inconvenient truths) about those in leadership, just not too much.

The government argued in response that the truth of what Jefferson had done was irrelevant here. The press had the right to free discussion of public measures, yes, but such right should not descend to expose private vices. To reveal defects and foibles to the public eye, even with regard to a president, "corrupts the morals of the community, tends to drive useful men from office, and to render the press a vehicle to scatter firebrands, arrows and death."

And in the end, maybe because ultimately those two arguments had a certain synergy that protected privacy, with or without a line to cross, the government effectively won, and Hamilton lost. The New York justices split on whether Croswell should be able to prove the truth of what he'd published, and so, by procedure, Croswell lost his bid for a new trial. A jury never did hear that Thomas Jefferson had paid Callender to say nasty things about George Washington and John Adams, even though it was completely true.

Alexander Hamilton died just five months after he argued the Croswell case. He was shot over privacy interests in a duel with Aaron Burr after a newspaper published Hamilton's suggestion that Burr had something amiss with his "private character" and therefore should not be trusted with the reins of government. Hamilton died at the home of William Bayard, a close friend, a curious coincidence because the Bayards would come to play nearly as important a role in the right to privacy as would Hamilton.

In response to the violence involving the nation's best, the Commonwealth of Virginia passed a law it called "An Act to Suppress Duelling." "All words" that would be considered insults and that would lead to violence, the statute read, "shall hereafter be actionable." There was no mention whatsoever of any defense stemming from the truth of those words. "Indeed," a Virginia court interpreting the statute wrote, truth may be all the more harmful should it involve information about "an obvious bodily or mental imperfection, or with a well known stain upon the reputation of a near relative, or with a notorious disgrace which he has himself incurred."

And with that, the nation's best were protected doubly.

The *People v. Croswell* case itself isn't all that well known in legal circles. It's far from powerful precedent anyway because it's a state court case that mostly consists of arguments by counsel that resulted in a split decision at a time when the First Amendment mostly just sounded good.

But its restrictive ideals and language lived on. Recall that in 1803, the same year that Croswell was convicted of libeling the then president, Jefferson, Jefferson had suggested to Pennsylvania's governor that it might ultimately help society and journalism itself if more publishers faced libel charges. Jefferson had included in that letter an article by a Pennsylvania journalist, Joseph Dennie, that he thought appropriate, a "good . . . instance" for a potential arrest, a writer "to make an example of." While nobody's sure what precise clipping Jefferson sent along, it could well have been one that mentioned Jefferson's relationship with "Black Sall" because the timing would have been right.

And, just like that, Dennie, the author of that particular Black Sall article and similar anti-Jefferson reporting, was indicted for what was effectively truthful libel in Pennsylvania. Dennie, the government said, had reviled, depreciated, and scandalized the characters of the Revolutionary patriots. By the time of that trial, the *Croswell* case had already been decided, so the judge instructed the jury by quoting Alexander Hamilton that "'if one uses the weapon of truth' wantonly, for disturbing the peace of families," it's a libel, because the "matter published is not proper for public information." And this: "The liberty of the press consists in publishing the truth, from good motives and for justifiable ends." But this time the jury went the way of the John Peter Zenger jurors and found the publisher not guilty.

Not all juries saw it that way, however, and throughout the nineteenth century truthful libel refused to die or be killed. "If every man who does not enjoy an unblemished reputation . . . were fair game, in a country where the liberty of the press is so much perverted and abused," a New York judge wrote shortly after the *Croswell* decision, "few, indeed, would escape." He criticized specifically the public papers "who sport with the feelings of others, under the professions of zeal for the public good."

Decades later, Hamilton's argument in the *Croswell* case—that there was, in effect, a limit to what truth could be published about an individual in order to protect his privacy, to respect his feelings and his family's feelings—found its way into the Massachusetts high court decision by Oliver Wendell Holmes that restricted the publication of a truthful article about an attorney facing disbarment, for example. There, Holmes wrote that there was a distinction between filing something in court and "subsequently printing it in the newspapers, or otherwise publishing it to strangers who have no interest in the matter."

As precedent, Holmes cited a case that had quoted Hamilton in *Croswell* directly and that then wrote this: "No state of society would be more deplorable than that which would admit an indiscriminate right in every citizen to arraign the conduct of every other, before the public, in newspapers, handbills or other modes of publication, not only for crimes, but for faults, foibles, deformities of mind or person, even admitting all such allegations to be true." That case, *Commonwealth v. Blanding*, involved a newspaper reporter who'd reported that a customer had died of alcohol poisoning at a local tavern; the reporter was convicted despite its truth because, the court decided, that sort of thing didn't belong in a newspaper. "Private vices," the court wrote, should be left "to the corrections of conscience."

And in certain press-privacy line-drawing cases involving much more decidedly private things, that remains the law in the United States today: despite the protective language of the First Amendment, and the modern sense of the public's right to know certain information, once talk turns to truthful but humiliating secrets about a person, at times even a public figure or public official, there must be a solid reason for the speaker to reveal such information or the speaker can be liable.

The fact that this restriction sprang in part from uncomfortable truths involving Thomas Jefferson that the public would have surely wanted to know? That's made little difference. And by now you've probably recognized that protection for the powerful is a familiar theme in the history of the right to privacy.

Chapter Three

LOVE AND PICTURES

Henry Denis was a lawyer in New Orleans who put his bursting heart on paper and sent his would-be ladylove a letter expressing interest in a courtship. It was 1810, just a few years after Alexander Hamilton had eloquently argued against the wanton weapon of truth, and to express one's innermost feelings in such a concealed, sealed way seemed a safe enough bet.

The ladylove, however, was bemused. Henry Denis wasn't her type, and who was he to think as much anyway? So, in an early version of social media shaming, she forwarded Denis's letter to a local newspaper called *Friend of the Laws* for publication. That would give everyone in town the opportunity to read just how presumptuous Henry Denis had been in his quest for love.

Denis, being learned in law, recognized that a judge might have something to say about the newspaper's planned reveal; he asked for an injunction ordering that his letter not be published. Judge François Xavier Martin of the Orleans Territory's Superior Court instantly agreed.

That didn't end it. *Friend of the Laws* wasn't about to be bound by a judge, oddly enough, so it published an ad explaining that readers who wished to gratify their curiosity could get a glimpse of the Denis love letter at the newspaper office, the local courthouse, or the print shop.

They came; they read.

Judge Martin was angry, so angry that in 1811 he wrote one of the very first court opinions protecting what had been mostly statutory privacy in intimate letters while slamming the newspaper for its attempt at a workaround. Henry Denis's words had been written for his crush alone, in confidence and in mystery, Judge Martin wrote, and the newspaper's purpose in sharing them with all of New Orleans was to reveal Denis's sacred secrets and to wound his feelings. That wasn't right. It didn't matter that the woman had received the letter without asking for it or that Denis had sent it to her freely and without restriction; publishing what was inside the envelope was the sole prerogative of the sender and not the recipient.

"How many serious things, proper to be communicated in the privacy of one's correspondence, are unfit for the public eye," Judge Martin asked, knowing that nearly all who read his opinion would agree that nothing of that sort was fit to be shared. A wife who wrote about family disquietude. A father who confronted his daughter about her errors of conduct. A brother who revealed family secrets, expecting privacy in the shame. And, of course, a man who bared his heart to his would-be ladylove. The newspaper's behavior was not only a villainous outrage on good manners and decorum but also a civil violation of the law—a tort—and a criminal wrong. Judge Martin fined the newspaper editor $50 and sent him to jail for ten days.

The judge added two things, just to be clear: the truth of it all didn't matter a whit, and freedom of the press was no defense whatsoever.

Judge Martin, writing in the Orleans Territory in the early nineteenth century, was among the first to build on privacy-related legal interests furthered along by *Croswell*. And, soon after, judicial concern not only about embarrassing truth's *reputational* harm but also about its potential for *emotional* harm became more common in the pages of court decisions. A publication meant to inflict that sort of psychic damage simply didn't seem written with a good motive and for a justifiable end because people's feelings were more important than a few public laughs at their expense.

So directly in line with such sensibilities came early privacy-relevant language throughout the first half of the nineteenth century like this: the law draws around individuals providently for their peace because humans are sympathetic creatures who deserve protection against publications calculated to exclude them from society. That, from the U.S. Supreme Court, meant among other things that to publish that a man had the itch and smelled of brimstone was a wrong even if true because the information made the man appear ridiculous. The happiness of individuals was just as important as societal quiet and good order, and all people no matter their positions in life needed the same level of security and peace. Courts began to salve "the wounded feelings of an honorable man," recognizing that the "very truth" of the words "g[a]ve venom to the sting of insult" and his feelings would be "doubly outraged" if his whole life were investigated to prove it all true. "It imports nothing," another court wrote, "that a man's personal defects, his family misfortunes, his mental peculiarities, &c should be insultingly proclaimed to him." Unless the embarrassing information was truly important news, a mighty narrow and utterly subjective category, the publisher would be liable, and it didn't matter much if the person were a public official or a private citizen.

Take, as a striking example, a newspaper article that accurately reported that some tenderhearted maidens in New Hampshire had attended a party. That was scandalous enough in the mid-nineteenth century, but then came this bombshell: "kisses were bestowed on ripe lips and cheeks" there, cheeks previously "innocent of such sweet tokens." Of course this sort of reporting was punishable. The truth was scandalous and odious and disgraceful and had ridiculed those maidens just as much as saying that they'd smelled sulfurous, the court explained.

It's no wonder that the law back then was described as a privacy-sensitive cherub who held a flaming sword at the gateway to the garden of life, repelling anyone who might dare disturb the sanctuary of domesticity.

Perhaps the cherub's sword was lit by altruism. More likely, it flamed in warning because judges too had rather suddenly become points of interest in the press and well recognized what embarrassing and scandalous information might be published about them next. That's the way journalists saw it at least: that the ones who complained most about press licentiousness were the ones most conscious of their own wickedness, the ones who feared exposure. The Englishman Charles Dickens, for one, had complained in the 1840s that the American press had its evil eye in every house and that no private excellence was safe from its attacks, but he would soon attempt to institutionalize his wife so that he could continue his secret affair with a young actress.

Back in the time of *Croswell*, newspapers were mostly *un*interested in digging deeper into the bench and the men who sat on it. Consider this single-sentence story from 1800 that gave readers precisely what they needed to know about the placeholders at the nation's highest court: "Alfred Moore, of North Carolina, is appointed one of the Associate Judges of the Supreme Court of the United States, to supply the place of James Iredell, deceased." Or this coverage from an early Supreme Court correspondent who gushed that he was highly pleased with the appearance of the "Judges of the Supreme Court of the United States in their ROBES OF JUSTICE, the elegance, gravity and neatness of which were the subject of remark and approbation with every spectator."

But as the nineteenth century got well under way, there arrived the cheaper daily press, independent publications that, to elite readers at least, allowed the "shock of disgust" to fly "with electric rapidity" across the country, giving "all classes and conditions of people, the wise and the unwise, the illiterate and the learned," the news of the day. This was a real problem. At a time when etiquette books advised that proper people not accustom themselves to scandal, penny papers had started up with the promise that they would canvass freely the character and pretensions of public men and spun themselves as the great levelers, elevators, and democratizers. "The Cheap Press," one fan wrote at the time, "its importance cannot be estimated!"

Judges suffered from all that leveling. One wasn't very smart. Another needed to comb his matted wad of hair. A third wouldn't be at work for a while because he'd "concealed from even his personal friends the fact that for many years he ha[d] suffered from hemorrhoidal tumors." Elegant robes, journalists had increasingly decided, shouldn't be an impenetrable shield for such pointed criticism or intriguing life circumstance.

Judges warned in response about the growing boldness of a press that, without correction, "would form a rampart from behind which the blackest scurrility and the most odious criminations might be hurled on private character with impunity." And they'd often summon Hamilton: that everyone, including judges, had a right to keep secret vices, foibles, and infirmities from the public. Embarrassing truthful revelations, they would say, caused pain to the tender and holy relations of life.

Which gets us back to New Orleans and Judge François Xavier Martin. Word on the street was that he was "a person notorious for his libidinous amours," lecherous and bawdy. He too, they said, was well acquainted with the pangs of secret love. So it should not be at all surprising that after a different New Orleans newspaper published a story about a bacchanalian rout and orgies involving a different judge who "in debauch kept the tavern in a roar all night," the privacy-sensitive Judge Martin sent the writer to jail even though it was all true.

And just as Judge Martin schooled in the Henry Denis case, press freedom back then still didn't count for much. If the First Amendment gave publishers the right to violate secrets, courts would say, it would be a troubling and strange construction, an "extraordinary pretension" never intended by Congress. Other judges would often wax poetic about the "liberty of the press" but quickly make clear that journalism was "subject to legal control," adding that "there can be no right in printers, any more than in other persons, to do wrong." Court decisions that "discourag[ed] that licentious abuse of the liberty of the press" were a necessary tool, judges explained, to combat "a great and growing evil [that] ought to be diminished." "To claim that a man may write and publish what he pleases, however scandalous," one instructive decision from the mid-nineteenth century read, "is upon the same principle that the highwayman desires the privilege to plunder and rob." Protection for the privacy in personal letters became paramount. "No one," a court in the 1840s wrote, "can justify the purloining of private letters, and publishing them for the purpose of wounding the feelings of individuals, or of gratifying a perverted public taste."

The same sort of privacy-centric sensibility became a part of state constitutions too. "There are in private life many things that had better remain untold," one Michigan legislator had argued during discussions about that state's constitutional convention, and "public good did not require the propagation of private scandals" or that "the privacies of domestic and of social life should be unbarred to the vulgar public gaze." Michigan ended up protecting freedom of speech and freedom of the press but, in Hamilton style, protected only truth "published with good motives and for justifiable ends" and held publishers "responsible for the abuse" of privilege.

It all began to irritate journalists. What about the First Amendment? Under what legal principle does an American judge dare tell a printer that certain truths are off limits because the privacy of the individual was more important? Forlorn lovers had suddenly found consolation for the frowns of their mistresses in the law of all places, despite the truth of it all. Didn't judges recognize that journalism itself had the sole power to decide what was news?

But that didn't persuade the judges of the first half of the nineteenth century. To them, in cases of private correspondence and other secrets, the liberty of the press didn't include the power to publish whatever the press wanted. Instead, it was "the right of every private citizen to have the privacy of his life respected," and the "irrelevant gossip of envious or unfriendly neighbors against men who stand well with the public" was as offensive to journalism as it was to the men themselves.

Then came the pictures.

Illustrations in newspapers had been around for a while, of course. A drawing of a wasp had adorned *The Wasp* way back in the days of Croswell, and innocuous monthly magazines had included drawings of flora and fauna as soon as technology and budgets allowed. This meant that readers back then were quite familiar with the occasional woodcut in ads like one from 1840 for a circus that featured two sleek racing horses and one clunky, misshapen, junior-high-school-art-class bareback rider that appeared female-ish. Such images and the white space around them broke up the lines upon lines and columns upon columns of news words that all butted up against one another in teeny tiny typeface before some layout genius invented headlines.

That's why the fairly sudden use of drawings to illustrate news stories in the mid-nineteenth century caused such alarm. First, the illustrations had the irrepressible allure of a siren's song; the nonlinear anomalies and white space around them immediately drew the eye. Second, they made news stories come alive in a way that words alone could not; you might think of them as the day's video of accident scenes. Third, it seemed that nobody on staff could accurately etch a human body if his life depended on it.

Consider "The Emperor Napoleon in His Coffin as He Appeared at St. Helena After Having Been Disinterred in the Presence of His Generals," a disconcerting image that took up half of New York's *New World*'s front page in 1841. Napoleon's corpse was in excellent condition and had been miraculously preserved, others had claimed, but the poor guy sure looked mighty bad in the sketch.

At least he'd been dead for twenty years and wasn't around to see it. The Reverend Dr. Hardy was very much alive in the 1840s when he made the front page of *Vox Populi*, a newspaper from Lowell, Massachusetts. In the name of counseling, the Reverend Hardy had bounced a young woman up and down on his lap to great community scandal, and somebody at the paper had dutifully tried to sketch the scene. Hardy appeared every bit the part of a lecherous cartoon vampire, his forehead taking up about two-thirds of his heavily eyebrowed face and his banged dark hair akin to a poorly placed wig from the Dollar Store. "Look, we say, upon this illustration of the way they do the thing where brother Hardy comes from," the newspaper ordered, as if it needed to, because everybody in town had already looked.

Thirty miles away in Boston, the *Weekly Mail* had illustrated its sadly spelled TRIAL OF ALBRRT J. TIRRELL FOR THE MURDER OF MRS. M. A. BICKFORD with a clown-like drawing of the perp, who appeared to be wearing heavy eye makeup and bad lipstick, a more angelic drawing of the victim, who wore a tantalizingly low-cut dress, and a sketch of the two-story "house where the murder was committed." That all took up the upper quarter of the front page. Other newspapers might have used six hundred or so words to describe Tirrell—because "much curiosity always exists in the human heart to know how a man looks who has done any deeds"—but the *Weekly Mail* knew that a picture was worth more than all that.

Within a few years, national publications including *Ballou's Pictorial* and *Frank Leslie's Illustrated Newspaper* had started up, focused heavily on illustrations to tell news stories. The Civil War introduced drawings of battlefield carnage and other startling scenes in publications like *Harper's Weekly*, some with dead bodies added for additional gore. The *National Police Gazette* began to push the envelope too with gruesome scenes of death apart from war, including the moment the bullet struck President Lincoln. Mark Twain turned an especially critical eye on that newspaper and called it indecent; it was proof, he said, that there was too much liberty of the press and too little wholesome restraint. (Newsmongers who sold the *National Police Gazette* would eventually be convicted for distributing indecent pictorial newspapers calculated to debauch public morals because, courts explained, there was a distinction between stating a fact as news, however horrid it may be, and putting truth into pictures. Such publications by their very coverage, those courts would say, hampered the enjoyment of private life.)

Then, also around the time of the Civil War, came *The Illustrated Police News*. It was a foldable sixteen-page tabloid published in Boston that featured full-page sensational woodcuts on the cover like, say, a police raid at a brothel where officers had uncovered an incriminating sock of one of their own. Inside, readers would find multiple illustrations and comparatively very little writing: one issue featured the drawings of the hanging of two orphan boys, a self-murder by gun, a child trampled to death by a horse, a double-murder scene with two surviving toddlers crawling around their parents' bodies, and death by snow house. There were twenty or so woodcuts in each edition of *The Illustrated Police News*, the vast majority of which featured gruesome death, horrific injury, or hellacious sex crime.

Some considered Boston and environs the absolute hotbed for this sort of shockingly invasive literary trash. The region had also given the world both *Vox Populi*'s ministerial knee bounce and the *Weekly Mail*'s winsomely sensual murder victim, after all. And it had all started there in 1690 with *Publick Occurrences*'s revelation of a king's affair with his son's wife and the resulting shutdown of its presses. Boston-area publishers had a veritable lineage of scandalmongering.

So in the early 1870s, a student editor in Cambridge, Massachusetts, at a new college newspaper, started a recurring column that critiqued news publications. He blamed a large part of journalism's growing public relations problem—the widening rift between rich people like him and the evermore envelope-pushing press—on the increasing use of illustrations. In a column he called "Our Exchanges," he applauded one newspaper's woodcut of a boathouse, but worried that it was but the camel's nose, a sign that this publication too would "follow the example of most illustrated papers, and become sensational."

Samuel D. Warren was one of the editors at what was then called *The Magenta*, soon to be renamed *The Harvard Crimson*. Perhaps the most surprising part of his growing disdain for journalism and its sensationalistic privacy invasions was not that the future coauthor of "The Right to Privacy" was a journalist himself but that it was his family who'd helped news publishing along in a major way: the Samuel D. Warren Company produced the paper that helped grow newspapers in the United States.

Chapter Four

THE WARRENS MAKE THE PAPER

S am Warren, the man whose words would one day inspire a nation to embrace the right to privacy by name, couldn't remember ever being anything but very, very rich. The Warrens had started out as rag brokers back in the day when paper was made from that sort of thing, but quickly found their way into the wood pulp paper mills that more easily fed a growing newspaper readership. They sold paper to publishers like Houghton Mifflin, Scribner & Co., and *The Atlantic* too, and there would be lots of reading material at home, all because the Warrens had made the paper that held the words. The Samuel D. Warren Company would eventually become a $1.6 billion business, a part of Scott Paper.

Sam was born in 1852, just four months after *The New York Times* first published, and his childhood was one of private tutors, boarding schools, and a six-story town-house mansion on tony Mount Vernon Street with so many bedrooms that no one found much need to count them. Ultimately, two mansions would be joined as one to give the parents, five kids, and seven servants loads of elbow room. The family had had its tragedies to be sure—two-year-old Josiah had died in 1853 from scarlet fever, and three-year-old Henry had fallen from a carriage and would face a lifetime of pain and disfigurement—but the Warrens' disposable income put them near the top of the richest people in Boston. They were among the first to get an "electric machine" that Sam's brother Fiske would drive along public highways, frightening both skittish humans and horses, and that sort of shocking wealth made life mighty comfortable.

All the money in the world couldn't change one thing, however. Ned, the second youngest of the Warren children, was bullied because he was gay. Not by the Warrens themselves. In letters throughout Ned's life most of his family seemed supportive, and the siblings would eventually speak of Ned's male partner much as we would a man's husband today. He, in turn, praised Ned's siblings and Sam in particular as "a fine, strong, and tender man."

But in the early years Ned's classmates were relentless. They'd noticed that Ned's handwriting was a little too round and that he enjoyed art and dressing up. After Ned wore his sister's fancy boots to school one day, the other boys started calling him Tassels because that's what the song said that girls with curls wore. Then the boys started beating on Ned.

Decades later, Ned would play a role in a story that would prove fatal to Sam. He'd also nearly bring down Louis Brandeis.

You might say that Sam Warren, his siblings, and the penny press all grew up together in the second half of the nineteenth century. By 1860, when Sam was eight, there were three thousand newspapers in the United States, up from just two hundred at the start of the century, led by increases in reader literacy and education and drops in newspaper prices. By the time Sam was sixteen, Charles Dana had purchased the New York *Sun* and had begun winning readers over with pointed coverage of murder, scandal, and society gossip. *The Sun* was said to make vice attractive to its readers even in the morning, which meant that high-society Victorians had more to worry about than salacious woodcuts. They also had an ever-growing problem with newspapers' words.

Consider DEATH FOR MURDER, the uncomfortable story in the *New-York Daily Times* about an execution that offered readers a second-by-second account of the last moments of a condemned man at the gallows: "As he went up, a long, tremulous, agonizing cry—partly a wail, partly a moan, was heard from his now distorted lips," then "two or three undulating spasms, a heave of the bosom once or twice, a contraction and lifting of the arms below the elbows where they were secured, and there hung a corpse!"

Or coverage of the Sickles tragedy. Sure, most of whispering Washington had already known about the private scandal that had sparked it: the strikingly handsome Philip Key, son of Francis Scott Key, had been showing up at Congressman Dan Sickles's residence in an unremitting fashion especially when the congressman was away. (Who could blame Mrs. Sickles for her wandering eye? Her husband had sparked his own scandal when he'd taken the notorious prostitute Fanny White to Europe thinking that nobody back home would find out.) After an anonymous letter tipped the congressman off to his wife's indiscretions, Sickles shot Key dead in Lafayette Square just outside the White House, "snapp[ing] his pistol at the head of his victim while the body was quivering in the agonies of death."

"A scandal in high life" was the way some newspapers put it.

And that pretty much captures Victorian high society's—and Sam's—growing problem with newspapers. Back in the days of Callender and Croswell and well into the mid-nineteenth century, the discord in the newspaper business had mostly centered on people in politics, a backbiting that often stemmed from party discord, but as the penny presses took firmer hold and tempted their readers with scandalous sensationalism that invaded the privacy of interpersonal relationships, society's polarizing schism, the trouble with newspapers, became socioeconomic: the elites wanted their privacy, and readers of the penny papers wanted to know why.

So, yes, there was trouble in 1872 when the free-thought and free-love duo of female publishers at *Woodhull & Claflin's Weekly* daringly reported a story headlined THE BEECHER-TILTON SCANDAL-CASE: Brooklyn's beloved preacher, the Reverend Henry Ward Beecher, had had an affair with his friend's wife. Worries about potential liability had caused the regular press to shy away from the story, and Beecher himself had threatened from the pulpit in the months before that "to betray the secrets of a household" was "an odious immorality" perpetrated by "moral outlaws" who spread "shameless news," invading "the privacy of domestic life," but sisters Victoria Woodhull and Tennie Claflin explained that, law and religion be damned, the public should know that someone who'd preached against indiscriminate trysts had frequently partaken of them. Like many publications of the day, the women would often only hint at the names of people involved in shame: that "Mr. ——," once poor now rich, "was 'the man' of a woman who kept a 'respectable' house of prostitution." But in the case of the Reverend Beecher, the *Weekly* went full invasive and used his name flat out.

There was more. Woodhull and Claflin also exposed the shenanigans at New York's French Ball in the same edition: magnificent hussies were in attendance there, some of whom weren't more than fourteen, schoolgirls clad in short dresses and leg-hugging tights, and the "best men" who attended, including one identified by name, plied the children with wine and then debauched them. "Such is the real character of men high in social and financial life" is what Woodhull and Claflin told their readers.

Within a few hours, police arrested the "wickedest women in New York," Woodhull and Claflin, for libel and for sending obscene literature through the mails even though it all appeared to be true. It would take a couple of years and some time in jail, but a jury eventually vindicated the two, refusing to hold them liable for reporting real-life intrigue. Meanwhile, the Beecher-Tilton scandal case, already rich with privacy issues, had turned into the much more public *Tilton v. Beecher* lawsuit for out-of-wedlock sexual intercourse, meaning civil adultery, and some newspapers devoted entire sections to the tantalizing claims brought by Mr. Tilton. One featured a drawing of the Reverend Beecher with Mrs. Tilton atop his knee, both looking a lot more lifelike than the vampirish reverend from just a couple of decades before.

That body of law that had protected privacy interests in the first half of the nineteenth century? It had waned a bit. Increasingly, judicial opinions had started to become "animated with a generous anxiety to maintain freedom of discussion" and a stronger interest in the First Amendment more generally. Newspapers were only too happy to run with that.

So it's no wonder that by the 1870s well-placed Victorians called newspapers bundles of scandal that offered disgusting publicity about the vile details of what was carried on in the sanctity of the home and other privacies of life. Publishers had burst into the sacred realm of a man's family relations—Parties! Weddings! Only the vacuous working class cared!—but they had also dashed open the ghastly chamber of domestic wrongs. Such papers had no respect for personal privacy, Victorians would say, the right of every person and the unfailing mark of societal refinement. "Flee from a woman who loves scandal, as you would flee from the evil one" was the going advice. But newspapers instead set about wooing her.

E. L. Godkin—a magazine editor who had founded *The Nation*, a man with a "towering influence on all thought concerning public affairs" through-out the Victorian era—had been trying for a while to rally the publishing troops to rise to higher standards. What business is it of ours, he'd written in 1870, if a minister left his wife and kids for someone else? Surely that was a strictly private affair, a personal tidbit with which the discriminating pub-lic should have no concern.

Not many, but a few newspapers were starting to see it his way. By the early 1870s, journalists in Missouri had formed the very first press associa-tion, motivated to change journalism from its catch-as-catch-can printer roots into a profession with stricter ethics standards. And in 1875, the Black American press met for the very first time with the same motivations, to "shape a policy of their own."

But an overall shift in a self-policed ethical direction would take de-cades. In the meantime, Sam Warren, at Harvard, showed that he had already taken that strong ethics turn.

In 1873, Harvard College was open only to males and mostly only to the af-fluent. Students shopped at Cambridge grocery stores with shelves full of crackers, pickles, beer, and "everything appropriate to a student's side-board." Tailors enticed them with "perfect fitting pantaloons," gossamer hats, and "cravats, gloves, collars, and all the little Fancy Articles usually required to complete the toilet." And of course there were extravagant and exclusive secret societies that were quite obviously nobody else's business.

So imagine the consternation when a Harvard freshman dared share private matters about the membership of certain secret societies with main-stream Boston newspapers. Who would do such a thing! Editorial board members at Harvard's new newspaper, *The Magenta*, Sam Warren surely among them, decided that it was their duty, they used that word, to write a biting editorial that would teach the little tattletale the proper closemouthed way to behave on and off campus.

The Magenta, soon renamed *The Harvard Crimson*, had started as a friendly competitor to a sports-heavy campus newspaper, and its motto from the get-go—"I won't philosophize, I will be read"—was meant as a sort of lure to undergraduates who fashioned themselves literary. The paper would be published fortnightly during the college year at fifteen cents a pop with a subscription rate of $1.50. But a serious lack of interest scuttled the whole subscription thing.

Lord Byron's words portended *The Magenta*'s lofty goals. In its first issue, student editors explained that they would keep things intentionally clear and soft; their newspaper would not be one of those sensational tabloids containing childish rumor and crude gossip, they explained, the privacy-invading prose that had become increasingly common in cities across the United States (by then there were four thousand newspapers). "We shall be content with the humbler task of satisfying the curiosity of our readers about what is going on in Cambridge," they wrote, though they recognized the difficult nature of such a task given their contributors' innate inclinations. College journalism had a borrowed vice, you see, and even Harvard students had gutter-born thoughts that would cause them to write recklessly and crudely. *The Magenta* tried to hold firm to a higher path.

By November 1873, however, the fancy gloves were off. How dare that loose-lipped freshman reveal to Boston newspapers secret society secrets! The list of new club members didn't concern the general public in the least, was obviously an offense to those concerned, and was precisely the sort of private thing that should never, ever be published in a newspaper. The student tattler who'd reported it all to the Boston dailies? "We are perhaps too merciful in withholding his name," the editors of *The Magenta* wrote, while hinting strongly at precisely who that freshman was.

Turns out that they were wrong about a lot of things. "In an editorial of our last number we made certain statements damaging to the reputation of a member of the Freshman Class," the very next edition of *The Magenta* read, but no apology followed, and instead the editors sought to explain themselves. First, they'd had it on good authority that the unnamed-yet-named individual was the culprit. Second, who wouldn't have been outraged and acted fast to condemn the bad actor and the privacy invasion that he'd wrought? In the end—and they did suggest that this would be their final word on the subject—*Magenta* editors blamed the whole thing on the Boston papers and suggested it was *they* who needed to learn from the experience.

"Henceforth," the editors instructed the working journalists across the river, "secrets of importance only to those whom they concern may remain secrets."

Soon, a broader biting critique of journalism began to appear regularly in the pages of *The Magenta*, courtesy of Sam Warren. In his recurring media criticism column, Sam could be savage and sometimes extremely complimentary. He found the Bowdoin newspaper shockingly flimsy. He credited *The New York Times*, a paper that, like him, had been around for twenty-two years, with a "marked improvement in general tone and character." And he had high praise for *The Atlantic*'s variety and style, which was not surprising, given the Warren family connection. You have to wonder what he thought of the Bangor newspaper report that his parents had been thrown from a wagon near the paper mills and had suffered nasty bruises. Or the one that shared with readers that his grandparents had happily celebrated their golden wedding anniversary at a small gathering at the Mount Vernon Street mansion. When he'd write "The Right to Privacy," he'd specifically complain about those sorts of more gossipy items.

Just a few months before his graduation, Sam's grandparents gave him a scrapbook titled *News Cuttings: A Ready Reference Receptacle for Scraps of Print, from Our Chief Sources of Knowledge, the Newspapers*, but Sam chose to save instead mostly mementos from Harvard's exclusive clubs. The scrapbook was jam-packed. Not only had he been elected editor in chief of *The Magenta*—the position "for which I have been much interested," he'd explain in his yearbook autobiography—but he belonged to the Institute of 1770 (the literary speakers' club that he also covered), the Hasty Pudding Club (even then known for its satirical performances; Sam was secretary), the Glee Club, the Porcellian Club (perhaps the most elite social club of them all at Harvard; Ned longed to join but was never invited), the O.K. Society (another elite social club), Delta Kappa Epsilon (a traditional fraternity), and the Cercle Français (no wonder so many editorials in *The Magenta* noted the beauty of the French language and encouraged students to learn it). Surely it couldn't have been this particular Samuel Warren who, *The Boston Globe* reported, had been found suffering from liquor seizures on a Boston wharf in the summer of 1874.

Perhaps most poignant were the lyrics for Harvard's class of 1875 song.

They appear twice in *News Cuttings* because Samuel Warren wrote them. The future for the class of 1875 didn't look too bright:

The Future now, in accents stern,
Calls us from careless hours,
And bids us in real life to learn,
That earth is not all flowers.

But when dark shadows cross our way,
And hope is lost to sight,
From college days will gleam a ray,
To pierce the blackest night.

Within a few months, Sam surely would have written that from law school days would gleam that ray because it was there that he would meet the man who would become his dear friend, his confidant, his law partner, and his family's lawyer: Louis Brandeis.

Dane Hall wasn't a particularly attractive building on Harvard's campus. The home of Harvard Law School looked pretty much like a big old brick house without the charm, a squat two-story albatross situated among soaring Victorian peaks that had somehow lost its colonnade years before in an unfortunate cross-campus move. When Dane Hall burned in the early twentieth century, there were few tears for the loss.

But in the autumn of 1875, Samuel Warren and Louis Brandeis walked with little reservation into Dane Hall, the law school back then, to become first-year law students.

Harvard Law School was a two-year program at the time, which made Sam and Louis part of the class of 1877, along with about sixty other young men. Back then, there were precisely seven faculty members including the president of Harvard, Charles Eliot, who had a law degree, and John Arnold, the law librarian, who didn't.

The degree from Harvard Law School, the LLB, the equivalent of a bachelor's degree in law, would be Brandeis's first and Warren's second. It's not clear precisely when the two met, but Sam eventually helped Louis read from assigned textbooks when Louis's eyes tired, and they'd become fast friends by graduation, a strong relationship that would continue until Sam died in 1910.

Students back then got in to Harvard Law by proving that they understood a foreign language and volume 4 of Blackstone's *Commentaries*, the British law book written in the 1760s that had influenced Alexander Hamilton and other Founders, the one that included the legal mandate that while a free press was essential, a publisher who'd published something "improper, mischievous, or illegal [would necessarily] take the consequence of his own temerity." Brandeis had also prepared by reading Kent's *Commentaries on American Law*, likely the 1873 version, the one edited by Oliver Wendell Holmes, a Boston lawyer at the time and a Warren family friend. If a libel exposed "personal defects, or misfortunes, or vices," the *Commentaries* read in part, the truth of that libel would aggravate its evil tendency, and besides nobody should care about such things because they were injurious to the peace and happiness of families and brought only private misery, public scandal, and disgrace.

As 1Ls, Sam and Louis took the same sorts of classes that law students take today: Torts, Property, Contracts, Criminal Law, and Civil Procedure. On the very first page of Brandeis's notes on torts, so presumably on the very first day of class in his very first year, he wrote this:

The absolute rights of man are:

1. Rights of personal security
2.   "   "   safety
3.   "   "   liberty
4.   "   "   reputation
5.   "   "   property

Any injury to those rights, Brandeis wrote, would be compensable in tort. A broad reading of that sort of law would later help to make him famous.

In the second year of law study, only two courses were mandatory, Evidence and Jurisdiction. And that was it for formal preparation in the law, though Harvard would begin requiring three years of study the very next year. It all cost students around $750, which included everything from tuition to rent to food and utilities. Warren had the money, so it was no big deal—as a wealthy student, he was focused more on asking professors about things like trusts and property ownership, information that would prove devastatingly important to him in later years—but Brandeis had to take out a family loan.

After graduation, with Brandeis first in the class and Warren second, Sam was invited to join Oliver Wendell Holmes's Boston firm. Louis had initially moved to St. Louis to practice, which is where his sister Fannie lived, but was soon back in Boston too, drawn by letter after letter from Sam suggesting that the two of them go into practice together. The idea made good business sense, Louis told his family, because Sam was fine in mind and character and had the type of bulldog perseverance and connections that would help bring clients along.

On August 16, 1879, came the official announcement in the *Boston Post* that Samuel D. Warren Jr. and Louis D. Brandeis had opened a new law firm. "The former is well known to Boston," the squib read, "and the latter gentleman who comes from Louisville, Ky., took exceptionally brilliant rank at the Harvard Law School Commencement a couple of years ago." That same week, newspapers around the nation exploded with word that the former governor of Rhode Island had shot a U.S. senator from New York in the streets of Narragansett, a seaside enclave for the privileged, because the senator had been sleeping with the governor's wife. The press was wrong for printing such a story, many said, because it invaded the governor's privacy and his domestic circle and was therefore nobody else's business.

Back in Boston, Sam's connections brought work but hit-or-miss payment, so Louis supplemented his income by working as a law clerk to Justice Horace Gray of the Massachusetts Supreme Judicial Court. That decision involving the minister who'd horsewhipped his daughters that held that the truth of it didn't matter and that the newspaper would still be liable because of family privacy sensibilities? Louis Brandeis was Gray's clerk when that case was argued. Two years later, Brandeis would argue the *Cape Cod Folks* case there.

It wasn't all work. On weekends, Sam and Louis would head up to the

Warren family's summer place to boat and swim. Or they'd have dinner at the Warrens' double mansion on Beacon Hill, amusing themselves in "the most unBostonian manner" afterward. Before long, given all the vacant rooms in the back mansion, Louis moved in with the family, and the Warren home became Louis's home as well.

Throughout this time and for years beyond, the two would hang with Oliver Wendell Holmes, drinking and talking of the highest good, Brandeis would say. There were alcohol-enriched larks to the zoo, shared tickets to cultural events, visits to the Holmes family beach house, and frequent meetings at a local tavern. Holmes read through Brandeis's work prepublication, and Holmes's dinner parties became ground zero for any discussion of Holmes's own legal publications, including his musings on torts. It was right about then that Holmes gave his famous lectures on the common law with Brandeis in attendance and very likely Warren too: that tort law helps protect against various forms of harm, balancing as best it can "the reasonable freedom of others with the protection of the individual from injury," and that the "life of the law has not been logic: it has been experience" based on the "felt necessities of the time."

In short, both Warren and Brandeis had become an important part of Holmes's young inner circle, and by the time Holmes got appointed to the Massachusetts high court, leaving behind a teaching post at Harvard that Brandeis had helped secure, Brandeis felt comfortable enough to drop him a congratulatory note: "As one of the bar I rejoice. As part of the law school I mourn. As your friend I congratulate you." Later, after President Theodore Roosevelt nominated Holmes to the U.S. Supreme Court, Holmes thanked Brandeis for giving him courage at the most crucial of times.

There was one more thing. Warren and Brandeis helped along the fledgling *Harvard Law Review*, the publication founded in 1887 that would eventually make them both hugely famous in law circles. Today, the *Harvard Law Review* is a scholarly periodical of great influence; judges, law professors, and lawyers read its articles written by distinguished academics to better understand the state of the law and the law's likely future. But back then, the *Review* was in its infancy, a "magazine" of about fifty pages that cost thirty-five cents, one of only a small number of legal-scholarship-focused publications in the country. Louis Brandeis had been one of seven Harvard alumni and faculty to help start the *Harvard Law Review*, promising "very valuable assistance" to student editors. Such a publication, they all hoped, would "show something of the progressive and scientific spirit" that characterized "the study of law," but they considered their publication "experimental."

And, indeed, soon after its appearance, the *Harvard Law Review* appeared to be faltering. "They couldn't make the thing go," Brandeis would later say. So he helped to drum up potential authors and suggested that what the *Review* needed was publicity. Sam kicked in the money so that a copy would go to every member of the Harvard Law School Association, an entity composed of Harvard Law graduates that was also started by Brandeis. Today, both the *Harvard Law Review* and the Harvard Law School Association are robust fixtures nationally and internationally.

Their law firm became successful too, successful enough that Brandeis felt he could turn away clients like Mark Twain, who'd come to the firm inquiring about some sort of libel action lost to time (Brandeis was skeptical of both the claim and the man). Sure, Brandeis had had something he called nervous indigestion for the first few years of practice, and in the early days both he and Warren worried about whether the next client would show, but business quickly boomed.

Brandeis would say that he'd achieved that level of success, his seamless entry into elite Boston society in the days when an outsider usually had trouble gaining admittance, because of Sam's connections. But Brandeis credited himself too and his knowledge of art and music and his very own embrace of Boston's puritan ideals. It was an Old Testament kind of town, Brandeis would say, and he liked that. Sam said that he found in Boston a dignity that no other city could match.

It was right around this time, in the early days of their law firm, that Joseph Pulitzer purchased *The World* in New York City and the penny press assault on privacy moved into high gear.

And then Sam fell in love. We know this not from any notes he wrote or any diary entries or anything personal like love letters because those were all destroyed or are kept safely tucked away by family. We know it from newspaper coverage.

The press wasn't much interested in the Warrens to start. They were among the richest families in Boston, yes, but the newspapers of the 1870s and early 1880s mostly gave only occasional mention of their philanthropic work or their attendance by list at innocuous social events. Occasionally, there'd be a story about the paper mills in Maine, and there had been that mention of the wagon accident and the family anniversary in the 1870s, but coverage of the Warrens as an important Boston family was all pretty sparse.

Contrast that with *An Album of Portraits of Celebrities*, a booklet put out by a New York publisher in the early 1880s. Inside were etchings of thirty-two men considered the most famous in the United States, two per page: an actor (some guy named Lester Wallack), an inventor (Thomas Edison), a couple of newspaper editors (those at *Harper's Weekly* and the New York *Sun*), and sixteen politicians. One of them was a U.S. senator from Delaware named Thomas Bayard, a man who'd run for president twice before and who would soon be named secretary of state under Grover Cleveland. It was at his relative's home that Alexander Hamilton had died decades before.

Sam was about to become the celebrity politician Thomas Bayard's new son-in-law.

The news about it came in late 1882. The engagement of Mabel Bayard, "a daughter of Senator Bayard, to Samuel D. Warren, of Boston, is announced," the "News Observations" column in the Raleigh newspaper read. Ditto in *The Washington Post* and *The Cincinnati Enquirer. The New York Times* previewed the wedding in "The Gossip of Washington," and *The Boston Globe* added the announcement to its "Table Gossip" column, explaining that it had learned of the engagement from the New York *World*. By the end of the year, Sam Warren was so familiar to Washington that the *Post* would announce when he'd come to town and where he was staying. Both the *Times* and the *Post* along with many, many other newspapers covered the wedding itself, calling it the marriage of the season, a "long expected event, for which there had been hopes and fears, heart flutterings and silent longings": ten ushers, eight bridesmaids, the bride's satin dress, the many in attendance, the gifts, and more. "There was a bridegroom, too," *The Washington Post's* story read, "but bridegrooms are seldom much noticed on occasions of this kind," although others highlighted that Sam was indeed a Boston millionaire. About a hundred wedding attendees, many of them family members, signed a Tiffany & Co. scroll as witnesses, the fashion at the time among the rich. Newspapers said that hundreds had been invited.

Through it all, a legal argument had started to take root in the mind of Sam Warren. As Brandeis later recalled, "it was . . . a specific suggestion of [Warren's], as well as [Warren's] deepseated abhorrence of the invasions of social privacy," that led the two of them to write the law review article "The Right to Privacy." Brandeis himself had been cajoled into the collaboration, he said. "This, like so many of my public activities," Brandeis wrote, "I did not volunteer to do." After all, he'd changed his middle name to Dembitz in honor of his uncle, a longtime journalist at *The Nation*, the magazine edited by E. L. Godkin. Brandeis said he was inspired by Lewis Dembitz's "longing to discover truths."

That didn't sound much like someone focused blindly on the right to privacy. But Sam had that blind focus. And he had friends in high places who had it too.

Chapter Five

WHO WAS KATE NASH?

Buried safely in the Brooke Russell Astor Reading Room for Rare Books and Manuscripts at the New York Public Library, guarded by lions, is a series of what appears to be unpublished love letters written by Grover Cleveland.

Cleveland, bachelor president, married a young woman named Frances Folsom while he was in his first term in office and had a devoted wife, young children, and everything else to make him happy when he died. He seemed the perfect family man by many biographical accounts.

But there at the library in an archival folder is a letter that would have been written during Cleveland's marriage and sent to someone named Kate Nash: "I must stop with the assertions that I love you dearly and had rather receive a little of the comforts which you could give me than any other thing. I am not without hope that I may still be yours."

And this letter: "I will not give you up entirely nor banish you from my heart. I will not forget all your trials in days gone by, nor your unselfish love, nor your constant prayers. I have been cruel to you and I know that I have often been heedless and unappreciative, but I cannot bid you farewell now. . . . I will not be driven away from you and you shall not say I must not see you any more."

Adding to the mystery is an unsigned introductory note in the folder that says this: "The following letters, written by Grover Cleveland to Kate Nash, the woman he loved before his marriage . . . constitute a very remarkable series of documents in the life of a President of the United States. Their tenor is such that, although it is preferable that they should not be published till many years have elapsed, they cast no discredit on the character of the great Democratic President. The fact of his relation with Kate Nash has long been known, and his opponents tried to make capital out of it at the time that Cleveland was running for the Presidency."

But Kate Nash is not mentioned in any of the standard Cleveland biographies, and information about the two of them doesn't appear by name in any of the main historical newspaper databases.

The dates in most of the letters have been "clumsily changed," the introductory note continues, inked in a seemingly different hand by an unknown someone, perhaps postdating them with "the idea of blackmail." Whatever the backstory, somebody took the time to type out each of these handwritten letters and place the typewritten copies into the archival file so that future readers wouldn't need to struggle with Cleveland's cursive.

Blackmail maybe. But there's a letter there surely written when Cleveland was famous because he mentions that little girls have been sending him birthday presents even though it had once been a day that he and Kate had celebrated alone. Either way, whether he was governor of New York or president of the United States, Frances Folsom was in his life at the time he wrote that and had been for a while. That letter ends abruptly on page 1: "I do not forget you and never shall." It picks up on what appears to be page 3: "So I hope you will assure this love and tell me all about yourself and how you are situated and what I can do for you always holding you tight in memory."

Who was Kate Nash? And if her relationship had been a thing when Grover Cleveland was rising to the presidency, why don't we know anything about her?

The intrigue in Cleveland's life began early. Back before he became so famous that he appeared with Senator Bayard in the 1882 *Album of Portraits of Celebrities* as governor-elect of New York, he was a lawyer in Buffalo in practice with a man named Oscar Folsom. Folsom's daughter had turned eleven just three days before he died in a buggy accident. Grover Cleveland had known the girl since she was a baby—he'd bought her her baby carriage, she'd called him Uncle Cleve, and from her babyhood he'd had the warmest of feelings for her—so of course it made sense that, given the tragedy, he would act as a sort of surrogate father. She had a mother, but Cleveland became her guardian and she became his ward.

The little girl, Frances Folsom, grew up and, many said, became of striking appearance in every way. When she turned eighteen, still a mere schoolgirl, Grover Cleveland started dating her. People could hardly believe the mismatch. Cleveland was nearing fifty, wasn't a pretty man and was portly to boot. Turns out, though, Frances had fallen in love with him, and a leaked letter proved as much: Cleveland had been her foster father, she'd written to a friend, but at some point familial love had turned to something different. White House chambermaids spilled the beans on the other side too, letting reporters know that the president kept a picture of Frances on his dresser where he would always see her and that they'd been awfully spoony when she'd last visited the White House.

Cleveland called such reporting "an outrage upon all the privacies and decencies of life" and demanded the two get the same "right of privacy" that newsmen themselves expected. What would they report on next? What sort of nightshirt he wore? He promised that he'd now shut the media out of the White House completely. Then he burned his personal letters.

They married in 1886 when Frances was twenty-one and Cleveland was a few months shy of fifty.

But the smarminess of that love story isn't the real reason Republicans would soon suggest that Frances Folsom hadn't married well. Before the wedding in the White House, and even back when Frances was a child, there'd been rumblings that Cleveland was a drunk who'd frequented prostitutes and had secret children. Once he became the Democratic nominee for president, it had all exploded in stories "sensational and disgusting enough to form a serial in the Police Gazette," stories with headlines like A TERRIBLE TALE and CLEVELAND'S PRIVATE LIFE. Yes, Cleveland had had a child out of wedlock, but, no, that wasn't all. He'd secreted that child away to an orphanage, tricking the mother, Maria Halpin, into relinquishing custody. He'd then had the boy christened Oscar Folsom, the name of his former law partner, as some sort of paternity deflection to save face.

Either way, Frances Folsom was implicated in the story that hit the papers smack-dab on her twentieth birthday: the child was either her soon-to-be stepchild or her half brother.

Reporting would soon shift toward the latter as the presidential election neared. Maria Halpin, this version of the story went, was no angel but a woman who got around, and Cleveland was no debauchee but a hero who'd accepted responsibility to hide his law partner's shame. The Reverend Henry Ward Beecher, who'd been miraculously cleared by a jury for breaking up the Tilton marriage despite those knee-bouncing newspaper drawings, was only too happy to endorse Cleveland for president, telling journalists that no respectable paper "had the right to put in matter that addressed itself to the faculties that lay below the ears." In any event, E. L. Godkin over at *The Nation* asked, would voters rather elect an unchaste man or an influence peddler as president?

The unchaste guy won.

The media gave the couple decent privacy during their honeymoon, thanks in part to police who circled the Allegheny mountain cottage where the two stayed, but some reporters were said to have hidden in the bushes hoping for a glimpse of anything worth reporting. In any event, the honeymoon soon ended in every way: An insider at the White House leaked that President Cleveland had ordered that only positive clippings about the wedding be sent his way. Another told a reporter that Mrs. Cleveland preferred the company of older men, especially a certain senator and a certain congressman. Mrs. Cleveland's maid told someone who told someone else who told a reporter that the First Lady darned her own stockings and polished her own shoes. They said that there was only one bill that President Cleveland didn't dare veto and that was his wife's millinery bill. Meanwhile, the commander in chief was up to three hundred pounds.

America had a "morbid craving" for information on the Clevelands, it was said, and the media was mighty happy to oblige; the more insider tidbits that lifted the veil of privacy, the better. And while we're on the subject, why wasn't Mrs. Cleveland appearing as often in public? This air of mystery about the First Lady's absence was an open secret among the Clevelands' close friends, *The Boston Herald* reported, a gentle way of saying that too many questions should not be asked about the "life of the *family* at the White House." Ahem.

Just a few days after that report—a suggestion that Mrs. Cleveland was pregnant, even though their first child wouldn't be born for several years—President Cleveland spoke at Harvard's 250th anniversary celebration. He focused briefly on the glories of Harvard to start but then laid into the press with what some said were tears of wrath and indignation rolling down his cheeks. His talk then turned to what he considered his rights of privacy, though he didn't call it that. He was due the same level of decency that should be accorded every citizen, he argued. He was tired of the gossip in newspapers that concerned his personal affairs. These were "silly, mean and cowardly lies" found every day in newspaper columns, tidbits that "violate[d] every instinct of American manliness and in ghoulish glee desecrate[d] every sacred relation of private life." Cue "The Star-Spangled Banner," quite literally.

Samuel Warren was surely in the audience that day for that now-famous Cleveland speech. Not only was Sam's father-in-law, Secretary of State Bayard, one of the speakers, but it was at Sam's alma mater, and everybody who was anybody in Boston was there.

And every one of them was on Cleveland's side. "All who were listening to him," E. L. Godkin wrote of the speech, "seemed to share the emotion with which he alluded to the way in which he and his family had been pursued by the newspaper 'ghouls.' They felt for him and with him as the victim of newspaper enterprise." Cleveland's talk was not an unwarranted attack on the newspapers of the day, Godkin wrote, it was "a great public service."

But the president's message resonated with Sam in an especially profound way because his family had suffered a different sort of ghoulish coverage just a few months earlier. That January, Sam's sister-in-law twenty-eight-year-old Katie Bayard had died of heart disease exacerbated by what the media called "social exactions," meaning that she stood in the doorway of the Bayard home on a chilly night welcoming guests because, as was usual, her sickly mother wasn't up to it. When Katie didn't join the family the next morning, her sister found her in bed, with "a peculiar expression," and screamed to everyone, "Katie is dead!" She was indeed dead at that moment, or so doctors later relayed to newsmen. The family thereafter gathered around the "still warm but unconscious form" and had attempted to revive the young woman but couldn't. A period of heartrending distress followed, with Mrs. Bayard first passing out, then lying prostrate on a sofa.

"There seems no doubt that Miss Bayard was killed by overwork," the newspapers theorized, a "victim" of Washington's entertaining scene furthered along by her mysteriously malingering mother.

They buried Katie a few days later. Newspapers reported that Sam was supposed to have accompanied her remains to Wilmington but for some unexplained reason didn't. Meanwhile, Mrs. Bayard, they said, was "seriously indisposed." The family had asked for privacy, but media reported from the church as well as the cemetery.

Within days, Mrs. Bayard, fifty-one, was dead too, of something newspapers called "congestion of the brain" "caused by grief at the loss of her daughter." She'd rarely been seen outside her house, they said, had been mostly sedentary for years, a "hopeless invalid" who had mainly relied on Katie to get things done. What would such a woman do now that Katie was gone? Survival looked unlikely, newspapers had predicted, and that turned out to be true.

They reported great detail from that death scene too: Mrs. Bayard had suffered mostly delirium before she died with only occasional and slight returns to sanity. Once she was gone, no family was with her body as it was moved from the house to a waiting car, "in order that they might be spared the annoyance of being gazed at by the morbidly curious throng." In Delaware, the daughters were too overcome to attend the transfer of their mother's remains to the church. The same sort of funeral and burial coverage given Katie Bayard followed in newspapers across the nation.

And lest it appear that Victorian mourners appreciated such journalistic attention, they didn't. E. L. Godkin had already written that such reporting—"especially in cases of bereavement or misfortune," tragedies in human life that give so much pain, "often as exquisite pain as mortals know"—should be punished through what he might have called truthful libel, just as the law allowed in France. Publishers in the States should focus more on ethics principles, he wrote, expanding on his absconding minister example, because "nothing is better worthy of legal protection than private life" or "the right of every man to keep his affairs to himself, and to decide for himself to what extent they shall be the subject of public observation and discussion."

Invasive death coverage was bad enough, but Sam and his family had also started to suffer the sort of invasive general gossip that so annoyed Grover Cleveland. Sam's engagement and wedding had been followed by blurbs about where the family would be vacationing and who would be vacationing with them. Readers were there, in effect, when the Warrens visited overseas and spent time at their seaside home at Mattapoisett and when Mrs. Warren entertained the Dilettanti Club and gave a luncheon. Reporters covered the Warrens' costly art purchases and revealed that the Warrens were building a wharf at their summer property, and then a stable, and then a boat. Newspapers across the nation inexplicably picked up an article about the secretive India Wharf Rats social club in Boston that had outed Sam as a member; the Rats enjoyed themselves in ways that would not be allowed in tonier clubs, the papers reported, and had caused their fellow aristocrats horror "over the escapades of [the otherwise] dignified members, whose names [were] supposed to be synonymous with sobriety and propriety."

All this time, Grover and Frances Cleveland and Sam and Mabel Warren were growing closer. At first, the Warrens had attended White House events or dinners in honor of the First Couple surely orchestrated by Secretary Bayard. But then Mrs. Cleveland began to visit Mrs. Warren at the Warren summer place at Mattapoisett, and the couples started to enjoy more intimate dinners together at Sam and Mabel's homes. Breakfasts too. Eventually, society columns noted that the Warrens and the Clevelands had become close friends and that Sam had started to serve as a sort of intermediary between the Clevelands and Sam's fellow Bostonians.

At the same time, in contrast, Sam's friend and law partner, Louis Brandeis, was of very little society-page interest to the press beyond broader coverage of the Dedham Polo Club at Karlstein, Sam's country estate in Dedham, where Brandeis was also a member. Louis's single mention in *The Boston Globe*'s "Table Gossip" column came when the Union Club named him as a new member, and on that very day the column noted that Mabel Warren was in Delaware for her sister's funeral.

Instead, Brandeis was mostly in the paper for professional reasons: the *Cape Cod Folks* litigation, for example, or word that he'd been admitted to the U.S. Supreme Court Bar so that he might argue his first case there, one about railroad land taxes. His sister Fannie had died tragically on an extended visit to their parents' home in Louisville in 1889, but coverage of that was all handled quite tactfully by local papers: she "had been ill [for] some time and her death was not unexpected." Fannie had suffered from depression and had stopped eating in the weeks before her death. The day before she died, Louis wrote to his father advising the family to let nature take its course with Fannie, that they shouldn't force her to eat.

That sort of tragedy would have been of keen interest to folks at *The World*; Pulitzer's paper routinely published stories headlined MRS. ANNIE FISHER, AFFECTED BY FITS OF MELANCHOLIA, TAKES HER LIFE BY DRINKING CARBOLIC ACID or DEPRESSED SINCE THE DEATH OF HER HUSBAND, MRS. WEIL TAKES POISON AND EXPIRES. And it's not as if *The World* discounted news out of Louisville: ROASTED TO DEATH: THREE MEN DIED IN SIGHT OF THEIR HELPLESS FRIENDS was datelined there. When authorities decided after a multiyear search that the missing Dr. Brandeis, Louis's cousin who'd gone missing in New York City, was legally dead, *The World* described his mysterious disappearance this way: "On that bleak December day, he walked out to Broadway and disappeared in the throng of Christmas shoppers—walked, as it were, into a vortex and carried down to bottomless depths, out of the sight of man, away from all who knew and loved him." But it also pointedly noted that the family had originally waited four days to notify police about his disappearance.

Pulitzer was pushing bolder and more sensational coverage designed to draw the average reader in, and his articles went well beyond tragedies. Tell readers about the richest of the rich, the aristocratic class of four hundred in the United States, Pulitzer had instructed *World* editors and reporters. "Tell them how they spend their money; what they say; how they live; what their ambitions are," tell such stories with pictures and tell them interestingly with words, because readers craved such sensation. If the journalists did that sort of reporting, Pulitzer promised, a huge increase in readership would follow.

He was right, of course. And directly in line with all that, *The World*'s first real foray into the illustrations that Sam Warren so hated was a series of caricatures it called "Wall Street 'Nobility'"—the very rich Vanderbilt and Villard, Gould and Jewett—published one Sunday in early 1884. That page, its artist would later suggest, "proved the starting point of the great boom in daily newspaper illustration" because circulation "took an immediate jump and continued its upward course on succeeding Sundays, when the city fathers, the local politicians, the militia and other bodies were limned in black and white."

But when women were sketched, looking blotchy in all the wrong places, the artist said, an assistant district attorney for New York warned Pulitzer that he could be indicted for criminal libel. "The protest was grounded less on the basis of the distortion of fair features," the artist explained, "than on the argument that the privacy and sanctity of American homes had been ruthlessly invaded and forced into the garish glare of vulgar publicity" through illustration.

Perhaps what's most ironic about this is that it was Sam's family's paper company that had made these sorts of illustrations possible too. "Lovers of well-printed wood-engravings" owed the Samuel D. Warren Company "a special debt of gratitude," *The American Bookseller* had suggested in the 1880s, because the company was first to produce the sort of paper that made such drawings in financially conscious publications like daily newspapers economically feasible.

Meanwhile, just outside Washington, Nellie Bly, reporter for Pulitzer's *World*, was taking her boss's instructions to tell stories about the powerful to heart, and First Lady Frances Folsom Cleveland didn't suspect a thing as she lay in a hammock one September day at Oak View, the First Couple's twenty-seven-acre getaway manse. The Clevelands had Victorianized the old stone farmhouse just a couple of years before, adding a full-on front porch, pointy roofs, and a turret. They were a couple under siege, after all, just as Cleveland had suggested at Harvard a couple of years before, and in response they'd closed part of the White House grounds to prying visitors. Outsiders weren't welcome at Oak View either, obviously.

No matter. Bly was doing a story on the wives of the 1888 presidential candidates, and an interview with the incumbent First Lady would be an important part of it. She'd said that she planned to get a quotation or two, maybe, but also to gather information about Mrs. Cleveland's appearance and, perhaps, "her history." That meant that a gotcha approach would work best.

Mrs. Cleveland must have seen the stranger coming up the way because, within seconds, she jumped from her hammock and ran headlong into the house, leaving only the blur of a blue silk sash behind. But Bly found a headline nevertheless by stealing her way inside Oak View: there was a shrine of sorts to President Cleveland just inside the library, with candles surrounding his terra-cotta bust; the main hall was carpeted, and other rooms had wooden floors and throw rugs; rich light-colored furniture was everywhere; thin baby-blue brocade draperies surrounded French windows; and there were four hats on the hat stand. By the time the crack security team sent Bly on her way, she'd inexplicably decided that this all indicated Mrs. Cleveland was being kept from human contact by the president and his team. The poor girl couldn't even lounge on the piazza and gossip with friends in peace, Bly wrote, apparently without a twinge of introspection.

By that point, nearly everybody in the United States knew who Nellie Bly was. Born Eliza Jane Cochran, she'd taken the name Nellie Bly at the start of her newspaper career in Pittsburgh. After a move to New York, she'd instantly made a name for herself by feigning mental illness that put her in a madhouse on Blackwell's Island. The resulting story led to powerful change; the government promised greater assistance for patients there and had cleaned things up. But that sort of investigatory work into public enemies took time and there were newspaper columns to fill, so Bly necessarily expanded her reportage: "Should women propose?" she asked in one story, got her fortune told by a witch in another, and had herself "dragged from a hotel and locked up all night in a station house" for a third. She snuck into an opium den, had her horoscope read, spent a day in a diet kitchen, and jumped into pool instruction to explain what it was like for those afraid of the water. Ads for her mostly quirky, sometimes important stories in the *Sunday World* appeared all week as a lead-up to the romp.

And then Bly turned to even more pointed stories about how the 1 percent lived and, given that nobody knew what she looked like back then—her first photo in *The World* would come only after she'd circumnavigated the world—she went incognito.

"Frolics at the French Ball: Nellie Bly Tells of the Fun and Breeziness

After Midnight" was a result. At the ball, wine flowed as it had a decade before in the Woodhull and Claflin days, as did the women in tights and short dresses who threw bounties of kisses well after midnight. A famous actress (could it have been Marion Manola?) was drunk on the dance floor as if wine had been free and plenty all night. Men followed women where men shouldn't go, just to be sure that no one else would snag their catches. And that pretty girl in the short red gown too inebriated to walk into the wine room without assistance? She'd been confined the year before in the Blackwell's Island madhouse; Bly recognized her from there, and, no, it wasn't clear which location was preferable.

"Nellie Bly at the Summer Resorts: Her Observations of Men, Women, and Things at Newport and Narragansett Pier" came later. The glum and miserable rich spent their dreadfully stupid evenings gossiping about everybody in sight. Those who should have been happy there—a millionaire, a couple whose names made the society columns, a woman high atop society—all had looks of positive unhappiness about them. One rich young man had a lisp, a nasal tone, a face like a mudsucker, and yet five women clung to him; these daughters of fortune, far from striking beauties, were after one thing, and that was to continue to live the high life that they'd become accustomed to. Meanwhile, their male potential suitors were so stuck on themselves that they didn't notice just how clingy their own bathing suits were.

By that time, daily readership of *The World* had reached nearly 350,000.

Bly's sort of undercover reporting—a window on reality opened to readers, at times for no worthy reason—inspired other journalists. A *World* reporter threw himself overboard from a New York ferry just to see what his unsuspecting fellow passengers and the crew would do. GIRLS WHO BATHE, a later exposé of the same seaside resorts that Bly had attended, focused on an engaged maiden and her new boyfriend, a married flirt who still loved her husband, and two "girl lovers" who hung out together, all completely unaware that a reporter was among them taking notes. A *World* reporter hid in plain sight at a public telephone office and reported some of the "great many amusing incidents" overheard there, including heartfelt calls from homesick children and philandering fathers "unable" to make it back home. Another hid in a sofa to report on conversations at a police station. And somebody at *The World* stole his or her way into the life of the novelist Frances Hodgson

Burnett of *The Secret Garden* fame: she was eccentric and odd, she preferred the company of young men, and her marriage was a failure, which was not surprising given that "women are not proverbial for their love of sex."

The exposé-for-the-sake-of-itself with its many privacy invasions became such a thing that successful people literally began to wonder whether the stranger next to them was a regular person or a reporter for *The World*, even as they rushed to buy the new issue. Other newspapers of the day, including *The New York Times*, began to ask how dare these journalists turn people's lives inside out to the public gaze and reveal the privacies of life simply to gratify public curiosity. Surely the law could and would step in to help Mrs. Burnett—they suggested that quite literally, calling it the "Right to Privacy"—but also the many others who deserved protection from intrusive behavior that led to emotional harm.

Nellie Bly apparently came around to that point of view at least to some extent. Just a few months before she left *The World* to marry a millionaire, she wrote a poem that seemingly offers a window into her emotional struggles and, perhaps, how they related to her work:

Were you ever caught by the tide of blueness and swept to the land of misery?

Sometimes you know the boat that carries you. It may be lack of work, loss of money, a false love, a death, and still again you may not know what it is.

You only know that a pall falls upon you through which life looks too miserable to endure . . .

You wonder why you are so unhappy; you fail to account for your wretchedness.

The author of *American Nervousness: Its Causes and Consequences*, a treatise published in the 1880s, had already put his finger on it: "The periodical press [has] increased a hundred-fold the distresses of humanity."

And now the story returns to Kate Nash, woman of mystery and apparent pen pal of Grover Cleveland.

It's clear that the dates on the letters in the rare book room of the New York Public Library aren't quite right or, better put, appear to be edited. The letter in which Cleveland asks for Kate's comforts? The date on it, December 18, 1894, appears to be written in a different hand and in a different pen. Same with the date on the one in which Cleveland says that he won't banish Kate from his heart. Perhaps the dates were changed by someone to make them align with Cleveland's marriage, to make them all the more scandalous, as the introductory note in the archives suggests.

That theory seems bolstered by another letter in the collection, one apparently written to Kate from a man named Wilson Bissell. Bissell had been Grover Cleveland's law partner, campaign manager, and general fixer, and it was Bissell to whom Cleveland, as president-elect, confided that he needed to sneak into Buffalo in order to attend to some "financial arrangements" too sensitive for even Bissell to handle. But maybe that trip involved a different-from-Frances "former ward" of Cleveland's who lived in Buffalo, a "young woman," it was said, "who had lost her money through no fault of her own."

The Bissell letter is dated 1888, though that date also appears altered. In it, Bissell says that he's worried that a person he calls C has opened and read a letter from Kate and that Bissell fears some sort of imminent romantic crisis. C is likely Cleveland, just as the introductory note in the archives suggests. "I feel sure that he will misinterpret it," Bissell writes in what reads as a bit of a panic. "So far as this does or can affect me I do not care one whit but I am anxious as to what effect it will have upon you and him." The letter sounds very much as if Bissell were Kate's paramour, a secret previously unknown to C, who was also romantically involved with her.

In any case, there were many secrets to be kept.

It's not clear who Kate Nash was, given the common name, but there are some intriguing options. First, there was a Kate Nash who lived in Washington, D.C., at the time Cleveland was elected, a recent graduate from Wesleyan College in Ohio, the daughter of a military man, and just about the same age as Frances Folsom. She held a New Year's reception one year in conjunction with one at the White House and had a relative named Nellie, significant because Cleveland refers to a Nellie in one of his letters.

Then there's a Kate Nash who lived in Cazenovia, New York, close to where Cleveland grew up, who would have been about thirty when Cleveland took office. This Kate Nash never married, had a sister named Ellen, and worked as a post office clerk in the small town, which could be relevant because Wilson Bissell eventually became postmaster general during Cleveland's second term. There's an intriguing note in the Library of Congress's Index to the Grover Cleveland Papers too: that "several Cleveland scrapbooks and a box of letters and telegrams which had been stored at Cazenovia" were shipped to Cleveland's official biographer, but mysteriously might have never made their way back to the Library of Congress for cataloging. This Kate Nash's family, contacted through an ancestry database, knew of no connection with Grover Cleveland, however.

A third Kate Nash—also a Miss Nash—is listed in the 1892 federal census for Rochester, a city mentioned in Bissell's letter. Based on census records, she would have been about twenty when Cleveland became president.

Finally, there's a Catharine Nash born in Buffalo around 1863, so would have been in her twenties when Cleveland was gaining political ground. When she was seventeen, she appears to have worked as a dressmaker and, later, as a store clerk. She might have had five children, only two of whom survived, and census records suggest that she might have been divorced at some point. Nellie was her younger half sister. But her family knew of no connections with Grover Cleveland either.

The point of the Kate Nash story is threefold. First, some authors contemporaneous with Cleveland equated him with Thomas Jefferson because they both attacked the press for intruding on what they called their private lives. Cleveland's romantic life—one that people in Buffalo had talked about for years and one that would soon come back again to bite him in a way that implicated Sam Warren's family—suggests that there was fire behind that smoke. As Cleveland himself put it in a letter to a friend when he was governor of New York and headed out on a hunting trip, "I understand arrangements have been made for me to kill a deer (this game is spelled differently from that I am accustomed to)."

Second, when we laud "The Right to Privacy" as a groundbreaking work that moved us forward on a path to privacy and protection from others, we laud language influenced at the very least indirectly by a man—men, really— with much to hide. Back in 1874 when Cleveland was asked his thoughts on the Tilton-Beecher adultery case as part of a newspaper inquiry into what lawyers thought of the scandal, he responded that Mr. Tilton, the wronged husband, had failed to make an adequate case against the Reverend Beecher, suggesting that Beecher was innocent "beyond question." A child would be born to Maria Halpin—perhaps Cleveland's son—within a month.

And finally, if you're creeped out about the amount of information that's available on public databases about all of the Kate Nashes from the 1880s, and about the fact that a stranger can peruse all of it, including family trees, and thereafter make contact with Nash relatives, consider what they know about each of us today, who has access to all that data, and what will become of it in the future.

Chapter Six

"THE RIGHT TO PRIVACY"

Remember how newspaper columns in the mid-1880s suggested that First Lady Frances Folsom Cleveland liked the company of other older men?

One of those men was the ruggedly handsome editor of the Louisville *Courier-Journal*, Henry Watterson. By the time President Cleveland's reelection campaign was in full swing in the late 1880s, supported by the Warrens and Louis Brandeis and other Democrats, rumor was that Watterson had invited Mrs. Cleveland to the theater one night. When she'd returned to the White House, President Cleveland had "upbraided her, called her wicked names, and finally slapped her face" in jealousy.

Watterson was said to have been a witness and the one who'd first told the story, but he later denied it. Others said that it had started with John Ingalls, a Republican U.S. senator from Kansas, but he denied it too: he'd openly criticized the president in the past, he explained, but he would never question Cleveland's behavior "as a private individual or in his private capacity." Then a minister told a reporter that he'd rather shake hands with a cloven animal than the president, and that pretty much sealed the rumor's believability. In any event, perhaps the cruelty shown Kate Nash was more than emotional, because whispers of domestic abuse in the White House had started popping up just after the Clevelands' honeymoon and maybe it was all true.

There was more. At the Democratic National Convention in 1888, a mysterious someone had slipped intriguing pieces of paper under the doors of the electors. Every citizen in Buffalo, the papers said, knew of the "beastly and revolting Bacchanalian orgies" that Cleveland had participated in there that had continued throughout his governorship and into the presidency. It was a debauchery that "would have made Caligula envious": an apparently indescribable sort of revoltingly horrible heinousness that once kept the Hog Incarnate wallowing with mad abandon inside a Saratoga resort for two days. This so reviled the First Lady that she'd left the White House for a hotel, then for New York, and then for Europe, vowing never to return, and she'd only come back for politics' sake. It all proved that the president was indeed the Beast of Buffalo.

Some called this an attack on Cleveland's private life too.

Cleveland denied it all, of course, but that was his method of dealing with matters that he'd rather the press and the public not know. "I tell you this in strict confidence," he once wrote to Thomas Bayard, Sam's father-in-law, "the policy here has been to deny and discredit [the] story." Newspapers had gotten wind that Cleveland was fighting cancer, information that was absolutely true.

Back at the 1888 Democratic National Convention, experts said that the allegations of debauchery appeared to have come from the inside, from the Democrats themselves, part of a plan to stop Cleveland's nomination because insiders knew that it all would come out sooner or later in the scandalous, licentious press and, when it did, the Republicans would win the presidency. The mystery papers also named Secretary of State Bayard repeatedly: that previous political attacks against him—that he'd made a laughingstock of U.S. diplomacy, that his difficulties and embarrassments as secretary had left the president angry, and that he was becoming increasingly irritable because he was going deaf—had also come from within.

Word came down pretty quickly that the scoundrels who had placed the papers would face libel charges if they could be found. They never were. But what they said would happen happened: Cleveland won the Democratic nomination, but he didn't win his home state and he lost the presidency. They'd also predicted that he'd never be welcomed back in Buffalo, and Cleveland never did live there again and didn't even show for his mother-in-law's wedding to a hometown man. Buffalo had become the place that Cleveland said he hated above all others.

You have no idea, he would say, "how I fairly yearn to be let alone."

Scribner's Magazine for July 1890 looks like a larger-sized paperback book with a golden construction paper cover; glossy paper wasn't yet the norm for magazines, but the Samuel D. Warren Company was working on that. There aren't all that many illustrations in *Scribner's* because illustrations hadn't yet taken firm hold in all publications, but those that are there offer a window into the Victorian's world. People dressed fully at work and at play, including corsets and sweepingly long dresses for women and free-standing starched collars and jackets for men. There were pianos for entertainment and fountain pens for writing and Edison miniature incandescent electric lights to illuminate the dark. People rode in horse buggies and on bicycles built for two, handlebar mustaches optional but quite obviously encouraged.

Technology? Something that called itself the World Typewriter was suddenly available, "the only one that can be conveniently carried by the traveler and can be used anywhere." Portable cameras too, as Broadway's Marion Manola well knew. One ad asked, "What's the News?" and then answered that detective cameras with fine picture-producing qualities were now available for purchase. By then, such contraptions were pocket-sized and allowed instantaneous photographs "of any persons or thing you meet anywhere."

A hint of that sort of use was on page 5 of that issue of *Scribner's*. An editor at the *New-York Tribune* had just published a book titled *Tin-Types Taken in the Streets of New York*, a series of stories from the metropolis accompanied by "racy" sketches. Turns out that the ad was an overpromise; there were only drawings inside *Tin-Types*, but a tripod camera loomed on the book's spine to suggest the advent of street photography, an art that Jacob Riis was already practicing around the tenements of New York. Sketches drawn from Riis photographs had appeared a few months earlier in *Scribner's*, some featuring sorry-looking tenement lodgers, passed-out bar patrons, and street tramps, each of which was marked "drawn from photograph."

Also by that time the *New York Illustrated News* tabloid was incorporating the same sort of drawn-from-photograph illustrating of its far more scandalous pages. One cover in 1890 featured a full-page etching of a busty woman whose blouse had fallen down just so. CAUGHT BY A CAMERA FIEND, the headline read, A SOCIETY YOUNG LADY OF RED BANK, NEW JERSEY, WHILE SUNNING HERSELF AFTER HER MORNING BATH, IS PHOTOGRAPHED IN HER GAY AND LIMITED ATTIRE BY A SNAP SHOT FROM A STRANGER'S CAMERA. The camera fiend's behavior and the drawing that resulted were surely inspired by the *Illustrated News*'s continuing interior masthead call for "portraits, sketches, and news of an interesting character" that, it promised, would be "liberally paid for if used."

It's no wonder that one of Brandeis's favorite magazines, *Puck*, featured on its cover in 1890 a cartoon of a young woman dressed in a pink robe soiled with the ink of scandal thrown by "Jack the Inkslinger," a reporter dressed in black with stolen papers reading "sensational journalism" and "private matters" and "family secrets" bulging from his pockets. Its caption read "Public morality must suffer at the hands of our newspaper scandalmongers."

This surely all chilled Sam Warren. He especially had time for such reading because, by 1890, he was no longer practicing law at the Warren & Brandeis firm. He'd left to run the family paper company with his brother Fiske after their father's death two years before; Louis had helped draw up those plans and the resulting trust. The paper trade, of course, remained robust, and it's relevant that Sam spent at least part of the summer before "The Right to Privacy" with the Clevelands, who'd rented a beach house just five miles up the road from the Warrens' once Benjamin Harrison took over the presidency.

Louis, meanwhile, had gotten some hands-on experience at newspaper publishing of all things, so had started to understand journalism from the inside. He and other "high-brows" in Boston, he'd explain, had attempted to change the *Boston Post* into "a worthy Bostonia sheet" in the late 1880s but had lost money at the venture instead. (At one point a few years later, he'd consider becoming the editor of the *Post* but ultimately decided against it.) He'd also fallen in love and was now writing a series of adoring notes to his intended, Alice Goldmark, whom he'd marry a few months later. He wouldn't be able to send along any photographs, he explained to her, given that he'd been on "bad terms" with his photographic portraits ever since he was a law student and had taken care to destroy them all.

In any event, both surely saw the July 1890 *Scribner's* because it was an article titled "The Rights of the Citizen: To His Own Reputation" by E. L. Godkin that, like Marion Manola's tights, got a mention in the fourth paragraph of the Warren and Brandeis article: that an "able writer" had recently argued that the law needed to remedy "the evil of the invasion of privacy by the newspapers."

Godkin had written yet again that intrusions on privacy, the sort of newspaper gossip marketed like a commodity to the masses, threatened the very happiness and dignity of individuals. A person had the right to decide for himself how much "personal thought and feeling," how much information about tastes and habits, private doings and family affairs the public should get. Great pain comes when others learn of the human folly, misfortune, indiscretion, and weakness once known only by family, Godkin suggested.

The law could help, he argued, and truthful libel's mantra—the greater the truth, the greater the libel—seemed perfectly logical given the emotional harm at stake. But he admitted that that refrain didn't appear as palatable in modern times.

Perhaps another refrain, one shorter and to the point, would be more persuasive.

Volume 4, issue 5 of the *Harvard Law Review*, published when the *Review* was still young, appears unremarkable. Its fifty or so pages and its layout are just like the issues that had come before: a couple of scholarly articles by the Harvard affiliated followed by short notes about new cases and other blurbs about things of interest to lawyers (including, earlier, news that legal research was becoming a bit easier thanks to a new American digest containing descriptions of many state and federal cases). Its cover was made from the same sort of construction paper as *Scribner's Magazine*, and it was about that same size.

There, on the first page of that unremarkable volume, begins "The Right to Privacy," the seven-thousand-word *Harvard Law Review* article that many say is the most important ever written because it became the foundation for most privacy law that exists today. Its twenty-eight pages and fewer than fifty paragraphs beat out an article on interstate commerce, a squib about a case that held that a family itself could sue for criminal libel, and a note about a recent Iowa court decision that awarded a meteorite to the owner of the land on which it had embedded itself and not to its finder.

That the two attorneys would choose the *Harvard Law Review* in which to publish made good sense. By that time, Warren and Brandeis had joined the Brandeis-promised stable of on-call attorney-writers upon whom students could rely, and "The Right to Privacy" was their third article (the two earlier ones focused on water law; more were promised but never written). Moreover, by that time, the *Review* was "rapidly outgrowing the experimental stage of its life," and had started to show real potential as a publication of influence.

The opening paragraph of "The Right to Privacy" suggests in line with Godkin that the time for an official right to privacy had arrived. Sure, Warren and Brandeis wrote, the principle that "the individual shall have full protection in person" was "as old as the common law." But sometimes, additional protection was needed, sometimes "political, social, and economic changes [required] the recognition of new rights." The law "in its eternal youth," they argued, could grow to recognize those rights, "to meet the new demands of society." One of those rights would be and should be the right to privacy, called that by name.

Together, they made five main supportive points, arguably in this order:

1. Newspapers are bad. The day's newspaper enterprise was overstepping in every direction proper bounds, trading in information stolen by infiltration into domestic circles. Stories that mentioned sexual relations were a particular problem, Warren and Brandeis wrote, and were clearly published for one reason: to satisfy prurient tastes. Gossip had become a trade, they said, columns were filled with it, it was unseemly, it was potent for evil, and it both belittled and perverted. (That all may sound like an overreach, but what was spun as a scholarly study of newspapers that same year called the press "a horrible octopus . . . ever ready to publish scandalous . . . matter.")

2. Certain technology is a threat. Cameras. Instantaneous photos, especially those taken surreptitiously. Modern devices for recording or reproducing scenes or sounds. Modern devices able to penetrate the confidences

of a relationship without any participation by one of the injured parties. Methods that allowed for the reproduction of women's faces and forms "colored to suit a gross and depraved imagination." (That last part was surely sparked not only by the Marion Manola story and maybe what the *New York Illustrated News* was up to, but also by Grover Cleveland's disgust at what had by then become a sort of free-for-all use of Mrs. Cleveland's image and name in advertising.)

3. People inherently need privacy, in an emotional and a legal sense. Privacy is absolutely necessary to human happiness. Man needed to be able to retreat from the world to a place of solitude, to be let alone. The law could and should enable that by suppressing descriptions of private life, habits, acts, and relations of an individual as long as that individual was a private person. If the person was a well-known politician, there was greater leeway, but the publication of such information could be punished if the news had no legitimate connection with their fitness for office.

4. The elites understood what was best for society and were therefore the best to make this sort of thing happen in the best way. The ignorant and thoughtless (surely meaning those in the Pulitzer-reading lower classes) had come to believe that newspaper gossip was important news, and when such fluff filled their brains, it dwarfed their thoughts and aspirations. Thinking people needed to step in to take action to protect the naive who could afford but a penny, and in doing so, the thinking would protect society itself.

5. Existing law could be tweaked to create this right. But, for heaven's sake, not libel, they argued with a certain level of cheekiness given the ubiquity of Blackstone, Brandeis's experience with *Cape Cod Folks* (still routinely condemned in 1890 for revealing Cedarville's secrets), and the mention of truthful libel's relationship with privacy in Godkin's essay. Libel, Warren and Brandeis wrote, was about protecting material things and not the human spirit or feelings. Instead, this new right to privacy would necessarily need to spring from intellectual property rights or artistic rights because those involved the quality of being possessed and protected the inviolate personality, not just the materiality of the person, though it's not precisely clear what they meant by that. Breach of

confidence would work too, which was a contracts notion. We also might look to the law of France and to the law of England.

Who wrote what in "The Right to Privacy" isn't clear, but that look to France was probably Warren's idea; there are four paragraph-long quotations in French in the article with no translation whatsoever, which sounds like something that would have come from the pen of a member of the Cercle Français, although Brandeis knew some French too. And by writing in a foreign language that not all understood—"En prohibant l'envahissement de la vie privée, sans qu'il soit nécessaire d'établir l'intention criminelle, la loi a entendue interdire toute discussion de la part de la défense sur la vérité des faits," is a key example—the two managed to slip in language that paralleled precisely the-greater-the-truth-the-greater-the-libel concept. In untranslated French, it became pleasingly palatable.

That nod to England could well have been Brandeis. "The Right to Privacy" mimics his *Cape Cod Folks* brief in a sense because it uses several quotations from British cases and statements from British lords for support.

But as Alexander Hamilton could have told them, Warren and Brandeis did not need to reach over the Atlantic for help: proper and justifiable truth remained a legal concept and judges had continued to decide as much. "The right of privacy," one Missouri judge had explained in the 1870s, protects "family secrets" and other "private affairs," the publication of which would destroy individual peace and happiness. "It would be a barbarous doctrine," another in Louisiana wrote a few years later, "which would grant to the evil-exposed the liberty of ransacking the lives of others to drag forth and expose follies" and any constitutional promises of freedom did not protect such a publisher.

In any event, the point of the article wasn't to find every single privacy-supportive judicial opinion even if such a thing were possible back then. It was to get lawyers and judges to sit up and take notice of the problem, to work to change public opinion, and, thereafter, to change the law. A few days after "The Right to Privacy" appeared in print, Louis predicted that that would happen with the right to privacy. "Most of the world is in more or less a hypnotic state," he wrote to his fiancée, Alice, "and it is comparatively easy to make people believe anything, particularly the right."

And indeed the two authors at times used beautiful language in the pages of "The Right to Privacy" to help make people believe, some of which is still routinely quoted by courts and scholars and change makers today because it fits modern-day privacy concerns just as well:

- "The intensity and complexity of life, attendant upon advancing civilization, have rendered necessary some retreat from the world, and man, under the refining influence of culture, has become more sensitive to publicity, so that solitude and privacy have become more essential to the individual."
- "Instantaneous photographs and newspaper enterprise have invaded the sacred precincts of private and domestic life."
- "The press is overstepping in every direction the obvious bounds of propriety and of decency."
- "Numerous mechanical devices threaten to make good the prediction that 'what is whispered in the closet shall be proclaimed from the house-tops.'"

Recall that Warren and Brandeis put one main limitation on their right to privacy, a nod to the right to know, a concept that was slowly finding firmer foundation in law by phrase in 1890 too. A privacy claim couldn't spring from information that was of public interest. If a politician had a speech impediment or couldn't spell, Warren and Brandeis suggested, that could well be information that was of public concern and therefore would be an inadequate basis for a privacy claim. But those sorts of things—matters that could affect a politician's ability to do his job effectively—were about it, because, they argued, even public men had the right to keep certain things private and away from popular curiosity. Journalists clearly shouldn't be able to investigate the lives of prominent public men to ferret out past scandal, they wrote for example, because those sorts of details of private lives should not be laid bare for inspection. (That must have been a nod to Grover Cleveland.)

Finally, in a footnote, the two authors included proposed statutory language drafted by one of the Warren & Brandeis associate attorneys that would have, in effect, reinstated criminal libel in Massachusetts: "Whoever publishes in any newspaper, journal, magazine, or other periodical publication any statement concerning the private life or affairs of another, after being requested in writing by such other person not to publish such statement or any statement concerning him, shall be punished by imprisonment in the State prison not exceeding five years, or by imprisonment in the jail not exceeding two years, or by fine not exceeding one thousand dollars."

And that was "the right to privacy" as Warren and Brandeis imagined it: people had the right to enjoy life, a right to happiness, and a big part of that enjoyment was the right to be let alone, the right to keep newspaper reporters with their worrisome new technologies out of private life, including the private lives of public men.

"Our hope," Brandeis told Alice that same month, "is to make people see that invasions of privacy are not necessarily borne," to make readers "ashamed of the pleasure they take in subjecting themselves to such invasions."

Theirs, he said, was an effort "to start a back-fire" for privacy, just "as the woodsmen or the prairie-men do."

"The Right to Privacy" indeed eventually "attracted a good deal of attention," Brandeis would later write in his unpublished autobiographical notes. Not only was its topic decidedly current and much of its language lovely, but the two authors did their best to create public opinion through "the semblance of lively public interest." Brandeis, some said, had the real talent here, a certain "formula" "of stirring up public discussion and demand" that he would "put into play" at appropriate times, and for many years he kept among his files at the law firm one devoted to privacy. It was there that he would place assorted letters and newspaper clippings, leaving a paper trail of what might be considered marketing outreach to help start those back-fires for privacy.

Warren and Brandeis's first step was to write to certain highbrow newspaper and magazine editors, some of them friends, so that they might publish news about the article to extend privacy's reach beyond the *Harvard Law Review*. The *Boston Post*, of course, was first; it lauded "The Right to Privacy" in an unsigned editorial on December 19, 1890, four days after the law review article's official publication, and then again a few weeks later. This was an unusual response to an academic article, and it's possible that Brandeis or Warren wrote both of those pieces. "I have been making public opinion by wholesale," Brandeis had suggested to his brother in the months before. "The press is full of our editorials" and "the law reviews of our articles."

Sam meanwhile sent along page proofs of "The Right to Privacy" to *The Century Magazine*, suggesting that its reporters write an article on the topic. "The subject seems to me one of the most important that can be suggested, and I am not hopeless of a remedy for existing evils," he wrote. Then came pieces in the Warren family–affiliated *Atlantic Monthly* (calling "The Right to Privacy" "a learned and interesting article"); the Brandeis family–affiliated *Nation* through Uncle Dembitz (a "strong" argument for the right to privacy); *To-Day* (a "remarkable" work that focused on a subject of "interest" and "importance"); and *The New England Magazine* ("very timely and very interesting," "erudite," "valuable and significant"). There was a *Life* article too, and while that one pretty much suggested that Warren and Brandeis seemed a little too thin-skinned, its author agreed that something needed to be done to stop "shocking wrongs" in publishing. "The Right to Privacy" even got a mention in the pages of Pulitzer's *World* in an article decidedly against interest headlined PRIVACY IS A SACRED PRIVILEGE.

Eventually, Warren and Brandeis managed to drive up so much interest among friends and colleagues in the publishing world that some newspapers began to suggest that the right to privacy was "coming to be one of the most important rights of the citizen" long before the law itself would officially and uniformly say such a thing.

The next step was to repeatedly encourage the student editors of the *Harvard Law Review*, where Brandeis remained an active trustee, to remind readers of the importance of the article. "The Right to Privacy" appeared in volume 4 of the *Harvard Law Review*. Volume 5, published in 1891, told readers about a court decision that had lauded the article as "an able summary," one that "well deserves and will repay the perusal of every lawyer." By volume 7, published in 1893, the *Review* was calling "The Right to Privacy" an "able article," the "only scientific discussion of the subject," and a smart extension of the plea for the "right to be let alone." When a judge halted the publication of two actors' photos as part of a who-is-better-liked readers' poll, *Harvard Law*

Review student editors found it "pleasant" to note that the court had used "The Right to Privacy" in its reasoning. In 1905, Brandeis was still sending notes about potential privacy coverage to student editors, one suggesting that a recent case proved that the right to privacy remained a lively subject. "Certainly," the student editor assured him in response, "we shall use this one for all it is worth." And indeed the *Harvard Law Review* noted the case five times in the following four volumes.

Next came the most obvious way to influence law. Warren and Brandeis sent a copy of "The Right to Privacy" to judges and others of influence, including the seven hundred or so members of the Harvard Law School Association, the organization for alumni that Louis had started. In the copy sent to Justice Holmes, still then on the Massachusetts high court, Sam enclosed a note explaining that a panel of New York judges had recently cited "The Right to Privacy" in an opinion relating to privacy. "Whatever one may think of this decision, the principle at issue seems to be of importance, at least from a social point of view," Warren wrote. "It is satisfactory to know," Brandeis would jot in similar notes to colleagues, "that the right of privacy is gradually becoming established." By 1897, the right to privacy found its way into a Boston-based law dictionary: "Privacy," the entry read. "The right of privacy has been defined as the right of an individual to withhold himself and his property from public scrutiny, if he so chooses," crediting in part Samuel D. Warren and Louis Brandeis.

What seemingly went largely unnoticed by anyone concerned, however, was that in 1891, in an opinion written by Justice Horace Gray, the man for whom Brandeis had clerked at the Massachusetts high court, the U.S. Supreme Court had mentioned the right to privacy in a concrete way for the first time in a tort context. The case involved a woman injured on a train who had refused the defendant railroad company's request that she "submit to a surgical examination" to prove her injuries. She had the right to be let alone, the right to keep her nude body to herself, Justice Gray and the other justices decided, though they never cited "The Right to Privacy." That privacy right involved the inviolability, the dignity, of the person, the Court wrote, and was indeed both sacred to and guarded by the common law.

Despite that sort of increasing judicial interest, Sam always thought that the best way to make the right to privacy a fixture would be privacy legislation passed by Congress or by state legislatures. Without it, Sam worried, the courts would be unreliable in their embrace of the privacy ideal, given the often haphazard, state-by-state jurisdictional patchwork that judges might sew through the common law. And indeed by 1910, the lawyers' magazine *Case and Comment* put it this way: "A study of the cases in which this doctrine of privacy has been considered shows a surprising lack of progress toward the development of any fundamental principles or clear outlines of the alleged right."

But Sam and Louis needn't have worried. Privacy protection just as they had envisioned it was indeed growing and would eventually come more fully into effect with the help of hundreds and hundreds of judges across the nation. Statutes would come later too. It's just that Sam wouldn't live to see it happen.

He would live to see rumblings in law of that different sort of right that got a quick nod in "The Right to Privacy," however: the right to know. And here, Sam's friend Grover Cleveland in his second term as president becomes an even more powerfully tangible protector of privacy and an enemy of published truth.

Chapter Seven

THE RIGHT TO KNOW

W. Calvin Chase, the editor of *The Washington Bee* during Grover Cleveland's two terms as president, earns only a quick mention in Frank Luther Mott's authoritative nine-hundred-page epic titled *American Journalism,* published in 1962. Mott called *The Washington Bee* one of the "most important" of the "Negro papers" in the 1880s and described Chase as its "fearless editor."

Given John Peter Zenger's eight full pages, that underestimates things.

In short, nearly a century after Thomas Jefferson kept Harry Croswell in jail for reporting uncomfortable truths that were said to have invaded privacy, Cleveland did exactly the same thing to Chase, helped along by weaponizing the same sort of privacy-relevant law that Jefferson had relied on decades before.

W. Calvin Chase was a Black man, which is important in terms of both what happened to him and maybe why history doesn't much remember. And what Mott could have added to *American Journalism* was this: that Chase had a reputation as a fraud-attacking bulldog, that he was a journalist who lived the public's right to know, "never fail[ing] to expose, in the most condemnatory manner, any fraud, unjust attack or evil, that caught his vigilant eye." His masthead featured a hive swarming with angry bees and a promise that there would be "Stings for Our Enemies" and "Honey for Our Friends." "We will tackle all skunks" is how Chase put it the same year that Warren and Brandeis published "The Right to Privacy." He had, others said, a "strong penchant to attack prominent people."

It's through that sort of mindset and that sort of publishing that Chase became "an influential source of his era's black social and political thought" as "he dominated black journalism in the nation's capital when it was the center of Afro-American political and intellectual life." Black and white newspapers alike lauded *The Washington Bee*, "the organ of the colored people in Washington," as interesting, stalwart, newsy, and creditable. For the most part, they also appreciated the self-assured Chase himself.

Such credit did not extend to the White House, however. By the 1890s, Chase's relationship with Grover Cleveland might well have been described as awfully prickly.

The prickliness had started once the *Bee* endorsed James Blaine in the 1884 election, and Chase had later worried in an opinion piece that Cleveland's inauguration might lead to violence against Black citizens. When Chase thereafter led a contingent of Black leaders to the White House to invite President Cleveland to that year's Emancipation Parade, Cleveland held up a copy of *The Washington Bee*, suggested that Chase had put Cleveland's life in danger, and asked all to condemn the newspaper. "I hope the colored citizens of the District will not allow themselves to be influenced by the editors of such sheets as this," Cleveland had said. Then he fired Chase from his steadier day job working as a clerk in the War Department, suggesting "incompetency."

That meant a president who guarded secrets and who'd helped inspire a new movement for privacy now had a full-time bulldog journalist on his hands, a man all the more eager and able to tell the people about government misdeeds and the people behind them. "It is an unwritten law of this land," *The Times* of Philadelphia wrote the year that President Cleveland fired Chase, "that the people have a right to know what their servants in public capacities are doing." Unwritten in law for the most part, maybe, but by that time tens of thousands of newspapers had used the right-to-know phrase in news articles and editorials, lighting their very own back-fires for the sort of revelation of information that pushed, sometimes righteously and sometimes not, against Victorian notions of privacy.

W. Calvin Chase seemed the man to get the job done.

Today, the right to know is a crucial part of finding and reporting truth, the foundation for modern freedom-of-information laws, statutes passed by legislatures that give individuals the right to receive local, state, and federal government documents, from the most important to the very mundane, simply for the asking. It's how journalists learn about and publish information that officials may not want revealed, like expenditures in the agencies and extraterrestrials in the skies. But information in the state's hands can at times contain scandalous secrets as well, certain materials that individuals don't want others to know. And that's where the right to privacy comes in.

It's a clash that's mentioned in a sense in *Marbury v. Madison*, the 1803 case that gave the judiciary the last word on the meaning of the Constitution and established the power of judicial review. The same year that a jury found Harry Croswell guilty of libel, the Supreme Court told the attorney general of the United States that he need not answer certain questions about the judicial commissions at issue in the *Marbury v. Madison* dispute, that "if he thought that anything was communicated to him *in confidence* he was not bound to disclose it." But whether the papers had ever been in his office at all was a different type of nonconfidential impersonal information, it was "a fact which all the world have a right to know."

Some seventy years later, just a few years before Warren and Brandeis started law school, the Illinois Supreme Court picked up that phrase and that sentiment: the people have "the right to know," the decision's introductory material reads, "why the liberty of any citizen is restrained, and for what he is confined." The people's right to learn about the arrestee extended to the criminal charges against him, the reason for those charges, and his status and condition, because the people had both a responsibility to look after an arrested individual and an interest in observing the criminal process against him as it unfolded, those judges wrote.

Soon, other courts in other places decided that the people had the right to know by phrase about other types of governmental behavior: the validity of election outcomes and the validity of government titles held by government workers; contracts agreed to by the government and whether companies were living up to them; contents of reports created by the government; certain information about public offices and officers; and what was going on in legislatures and in the courts.

The right to know therefore became increasingly linked with government: the people's interest in learning about the state's activities, the people's right to understand what was going on inside their institutions, if not necessarily, given the sensibilities of "The Right to Privacy," the right to know everything about the private character of their elected representatives.

It all seemed easy enough, but soon any right to learn about government wasn't solely about the often boring details of bureaucracy because, rather suddenly, divorce was becoming increasingly common. Sure, people should know about courts as institutions, but what if a divorcing couple wanted to keep embarrassing testimony from reaching outside ears? Newspapers had revealed titillating rumors about knee-bouncing extramarital affairs for decades, but such opaque reporting could suddenly liven with truly intimate secrets and tearful courtroom testimony and maybe even photographs of in-court meltdowns.

What about the right to know about those sorts of things?

One of the very first court decisions to answer that question started with a one-sentence squib published by a California newspaper just a couple of years after "The Right to Privacy" appeared. Barbara Price had started divorce proceedings against her husband, Elijah Price, and in 1892 the *San Jose Daily Mercury* decided that its fifty thousand readers might like to know about the family dispute.

The Prices weren't famous. They were two seventy-something Californians with a fruit farm near San Jose and some property in San Francisco who apparently didn't love each other much anymore. But for some reason—most likely because a courthouse insider had tipped off the newspaper that there was dirt to be had—a reporter for the *Daily Mercury* glommed on to their divorce story.

It didn't help matters when William Lorigan, the county judge hearing the case, ordered that the courtroom be emptied, that courtroom doors be bolted and barred, that no insider breathe a word of what would be revealed inside, and that no reports be published should anyone on the outside hear what had happened. Mrs. Price's lawyer had asked for such restrictions; he knew that the testimony would be of such a character as to bring "hot blushes to the cheeks." And the judge agreed that precise details of such a low and filthy divorce, including injuries "some poor, unfortunate girl may have suffered," should be kept from those on the outside.

Cheek-reddening testimony in divorce cases wasn't all that unusual back then. In the 1890s, even as divorce became an increasingly viable option for dissatisfied spouses, the state was mostly interested in keeping families together, so couples would be granted a divorce only if one of them proved fault on the other side: this required the irrefutable details and indignities of adultery or abandonment or unnatural sexual practices or extreme cruelty through physical or emotional abuse. There was a certain synergy with the Pulitzer-type papers in such cases because the shame of divorce made for (these are actual words used in divorce coverage in the 1890s) "sensational" stories containing "spicy details" and "choice morsels" for the "waiting ears" of an eager readership.

Readers of the *San Jose Daily Mercury*, for instance, a paper that seemed to report the details of divorces the way modern-day news organizations report crimes. Just a few days before the Prices came before the judge, the *Daily Mercury* had published word that a different wife's philandering had been proved in part by the sound neighbors had heard of *two* pairs of shoes dropping to the floor at bedtime when the husband was out of town. The courtroom doors had been tightly closed during that testimony too, and such exclusion was 100 percent allowable because California law gave judges the right not only to keep spectators in divorce and similarly revealing cases out but to order "any issue of fact . . . therein to be private." The law's purpose was twofold: to protect those testifying about certain matters from public shame, and to shield those in the audience who might otherwise be shocked at the indiscretions.

When a judge orders a reporter out of a courtroom and tells that reporter not to publish what he might later learn happened inside, it becomes a challenge of sorts to find out what was so god-awful embarrassing about the case that the press should be restrained. In the Price divorce, the secret was that Mr. Price had found pleasure in the arms of "younger and livelier female companions," including prostitutes, and that Mrs. Price, a beleaguered mother of thirteen, had found herself inflicted with a loathsome disease. We know all this because the reporter from the *Daily Mercury* paid no attention whatsoever to Judge Lorigan's order and reported precisely what had happened in the Price courtroom in stories his newspaper headlined A WIFE'S WOES and THE PRICE CASE: AN AGED COUPLE FIGHTING FOR SEPARATION IN COURT.

As the publisher of *Friend of the Laws* had learned decades earlier in New Orleans, when a reporter does something that a judge has ordered him not to, it becomes a bit of a challenge to the judge, and within a few hours Judge Lorigan ordered the *Daily Mercury*'s editor in chief arrested for criminal contempt of court. "Liberty of the press and freedom of speech are not absolute rights," the judge explained, citing in part words from Justice Thomas Cooley.

You might not think of the Price case as one that perfectly pits individual privacy against the public's right to know—that anyone had the *right to know* that Mrs. Price had a loathsome disease inflicted upon her by her philandering husband—but that's the way newspapers would spin the conflict, and somewhere along the line the information about Mrs. Price's venereal troubles got wrapped up in the Constitution. Editorial upon editorial in California newspapers, eighty or more of which were republished by the *Daily Mercury*, likened Judge Lorigan's courtroom to the infamous Star Chamber and the judge himself to one in a place like Russia that didn't have the First Amendment. "If newspaper men are to be debarred from publishing facts for goodness sake," one California newspaper editorial asked, "what are they to publish?" Publicity, not secrecy, in divorce cases should be required by law because newspaper coverage helped show that some spouses colluded in order to divorce and divorce itself was bad for society.

As the contempt case against the editor of the *San Jose Daily Mercury* made its way up to the California Supreme Court, the newspaper suggested that no thinking person could see the judge's decision any other way than as a trampling of constitutional principles and a violation of the right to know. ALL CONCUR, ALL AGAINST IT, and OF ONE MIND were headlines attached to stories that told readers that free speech was on trial, that the press had an "unbounded liberty" to publish what it pleased, and that the Constitution meant what it said when it warned "against the abridgment of the liberty of the press." No judge, editors wrote, could punish a newspaper that published "any news which its enterprise and industry had enabled it to procure" because such punishment would be unconstitutional.

It made for highly persuasive copy, and eager readers learned a lot about the rights of a free press—except, as you've surely recognized by now, given all the law that by that point had protected privacy in families, letters, conversations, body examinations, and sex, the free-press principle wasn't quite that crystal clear.

In the *Price v. Price* divorce case, Mrs. Price ultimately won. In keeping with strong interests in a different sort of privacy, however, Judge Lorigan rejected the "disgusting results" of the detective work that the family had done that had proved that Mr. Price had visited houses of ill repute, so the related cruelty allegations against him did not stand. Instead, the judge found that Mr. Price had deserted Mrs. Price by living elsewhere, and therefore she got the divorce, some of the California property, and $25 monthly alimony.

In the contempt case springing from the *Price v. Price* newspaper coverage, the press won. Just as the newspapers had predicted, Judge Lorigan had no right, the justices of the California Supreme Court decided, to kick the *Daily Mercury* reporter out of the courtroom and to prevent him from reporting news from the trial.

But that's because the court focused on the language of the statute that allowed judges to remove people from courtrooms certain to bear witness to lurid testimony. The whole point of that statute "was to secure decorum in the conduct of trials involving the relation of the sexes, and to protect witnesses of refined sensibilities from the ordeal which they might otherwise have to pass through in giving testimony of a delicate or filthy nature in the presence of a crowd of vulgar or curious spectators," the court reasoned. The statute didn't specifically say that reporters could be kept from reporting juicy details. But the court added that it didn't need to because "every one who has the welfare of society at heart will doubtless agree" that "the policy of a law which would prevent the publication of such matters" was a fine one.

"Freedom of the Press Cannot Be Curtailed" was the two-column subheadline to the *Daily Mercury*'s front-page story about the decision. Newspapers throughout California similarly headlined their stories A RIGHT TO KNOW and ALWAYS A WINNER and THE PEOPLE WON.

But that focus on journalism's right to publish what it had decided the people had the right to know was all wrong because the California Supreme Court did not say that there was a freestanding right to know or that the press would always win in such cases or that the Mrs. Prices of the world had no right to sue newspapers for revealing their sexually transmitted infections. Instead, the justices expressed more or less the opposite conclusion, citing Justice Cooley's treatise in part: "liberty of the press must not be confounded with mere license," and "liberty of the press stops where a further exercise would invade the rights of others."

What's perhaps most interesting about all this is that if you read the oral argument transcript from the California Supreme Court in the contempt case, the attorney for the *San Jose Daily Mercury* himself had argued for precisely that sort of limitation on his client's reporting, just as had Alexander Hamilton in *Croswell* and, in some sense, Louis Brandeis in the *Cape Cod Folks* case. "The liberty of speech and of the press is [the reporter's] by natural right, consecrated and made inviolable by the Constitution of the State" is what the attorney for the *Daily Mercury* told the California Supreme Court. "The only limitation placed upon that liberty is the condition that it shall not be exercised to the injury of others."

But headlines like THE LIBERTY OF THE PRESS CAN NEVER BE SUCCESSFULLY ASSAILED IN CALIFORNIA created the public perception—back-fires perhaps as intentional as those lit by "The Right to Privacy"—that the press was free to report any truth whatsoever under the Constitution. And helped along by similar headlines and editorials in more modern times, some people still think that's the law.

Spin it however the papers might try, just a few days later a judge back in Boston, concerned about "too much publicity," ordered journalists not to report anything from the courtroom regarding testimony in a breach-of-promise-to-marry case; it was one that involved a woman who'd said yes both to an engagement and to a man's premarital advances, so the testimony was sure to be scandalous. Privacy, not freedom of the press or the right of the people to know, would win out that time.

And in Washington, D.C., privacy would soon win again in a way that threatened not only the First Amendment but democracy itself.

By the second Cleveland administration—Cleveland had won the presidency back from Benjamin Harrison two years after publication of "The Right to Privacy"—the stalwart *Washington Bee* editor W. Calvin Chase's main investigative focus was not on Grover Cleveland himself (at least to start) but on a man known as C. H. J. Taylor. Taylor was the Cleveland-appointed recorder of deeds for Washington, D.C., and like Chase, a Black man. Taylor's job was to maintain all property records in the nation's capital.

A property records office might sound a little boring, but Chase's sources and his experience told him to keep digging because something seemed amiss. Others in powerful places had also started an investigation, and in 1894 the Civil Service Commission found Taylor guilty of soliciting campaign funds from his employees in violation of government rules. As even more tantalizing rumors about Taylor's behavior swirled—they said that he'd "been in hot water ever since he went to Washington"—the commission urged President Cleveland to remove Taylor from office immediately.

Nothing happened. For weeks. Taylor was "one of President Cleveland's discoveries," *The Evening World* explained, and the president was surely hoping that as time passed, everyone would forget that a government investigation had proved that one of his appointees had done wrong, sort of like what had happened with regard to his own personal indiscretions.

Chase waited five months, and then his *Washington Bee* exploded. Taylor not only had violated every law known to man but was "morally unfit to hold the place which he has disgraced since he has been recorder of deeds," Chase wrote. To top it all off, Grover Cleveland had had all the nasty details about what was happening in Taylor's office in hand for months: Taylor's escapades had included "insults to females, whom he ha[d] asked to visit his office after office hours for purposes contrary to the laws of common decency," a sexual proposition to a woman who'd lost her husband just three days before, and much more.

Today, most would agree that the public has a right to know about sexual harassment taking place within a government office or, as Hollywood and other allegations show, any office, really: that society needs to know the names of those who hold positions of authority and use those positions to proposition others and that journalists need to report on such incidents in order to stop them in an individual and a collective sense.

In 2018, journalism like that led in part to the #MeToo movement and won the Pulitzer Prize.

But more than a hundred years before, in 1895, the government considered Chase's reporting in his *Washington Bee* not only an invasion of Taylor's privacy but also a violation of libel laws.

The courtroom was mostly packed throughout Chase's several-day trial. Those in attendance heard troubling details about Recorder of Deeds Taylor and the office environment from witnesses Chase had called to prove the truth of what he'd written: that Taylor had in fact made an indecent proposal to a woman in the office, that he had in fact visited a house of ill repute, that he had in fact told an employee that she must have no other man but him. Several women testified that after they'd rejected Taylor's advances, he'd fired them. Others suggested that there had been an illegal abortion and a woman's death along the way. This was all relevant to the right to know, Chase argued, that one of the duties of the press was to inform the public about the character of its public officers, all for the public good and in the public interest.

The prosecution argued in response that Chase had published articles that wrongly exposed Taylor's "private character."

Here's how the judge instructed the jury: that the truth of the sexual harassment in the office wasn't enough to absolve Chase from liability for his reporting, that "even if the defendant should prove the truth of every charge against Taylor, he would then have to show to the entire satisfaction of the jury that he had published the charges with good motives and justifiable ends." As a part of that determination, the jury would need to consider whether Chase should have instead gone directly to Grover Cleveland to tell the president what he knew about Taylor's behavior instead of publishing it for all to read in the newspaper. "If the only object of the defendant was the removal of an unworthy person from office," the judge explained to jurors, that wouldn't be a properly motivated and justifiable revelation because it was the president alone who possessed the power of removal.

Not surprising, given that sort of instruction, it took the jury an "unusually prompt" fifteen minutes to convict editor W. Calvin Chase of libel. To add insult to injury, the judge refused to grant Chase bail, and so guards immediately took him to jail. Chase was later sentenced to three months behind bars despite his attorney's plea that, given Chase's leadership and standing, "to send him to prison, even for a day, would disgrace him to such an extent as to retard the race for twenty years at least." But those newspapers that covered the verdict didn't mention race much or the verdict's importance in the Black community.

On the other coast, the California newspapers that had loudly proclaimed press freedom in banner headlines a couple of years before in the Price case were quiet. One in San Francisco reported the story of W. Calvin Chase's detention at the bottom of page 3, middle column, in a squib as short as the original announcement of the Price divorce proceedings: "W. Calvin Chase . . . was to-day sentenced to ninety days in jail." The *San Jose Daily Mercury* didn't report the story at all, ever.

W. Calvin Chase, meanwhile, edited his newspaper from prison just as James Callender had several decades before and suggested that the president might offer him mercy. "This American government was founded upon a great principle," Chase wrote in his "Our Incarceration" column, "and one of the greatest and fundamental principles of its constitution is that the liberty of the press shall not be abridged." The Washington press joined in what was called an earnest effort to induce a pardon and Chase wrote that he hoped he'd soon be free.

President Cleveland let Chase stew behind bars for a few weeks and then resoundingly rejected his request for executive clemency, using words that harked back to those he'd used in his speech at Harvard years before: "this convict maliciously published an outrageous libel in a newspaper," a "dirty weapon" that had been used as part of a detestable crime to satisfy revenge. "It has become so common, and is so seldom punished," Cleveland fumed, "that I cannot reconcile Executive clemency in the case here presented with the duty I owe to decent journalism, the peace of society, and the protection of those constantly subjected to libelous attack."

So the story ends this way: W. Calvin Chase spent three months in jail in 1895 (he'd threatened to sue Cleveland for his incarceration but never did); Recorder of Deeds Taylor kept his position throughout the Cleveland administration because everybody seemingly had indeed forgotten about the original Civil Service Commission report of his wrongdoing, and nobody reported much anymore on Cleveland's own scandalous past or otherwise because they knew what could happen if they dared do so.

It's doubtful that this was the right to privacy as Sam Warren or Louis Brandeis imagined it. But maybe it became as much as time went on, given what was about to happen in Boston newspapers.

Coda Part I

THE DEATH OF SAM WARREN

Perhaps it's all a figment of a researcher's educated imagination, a modern-day reader's assessment based on her knowledge of the coming tragedy, but Sam Warren's handwriting becomes increasingly impossible to decipher in the two decades after he and Louis Brandeis published "The Right to Privacy." It's a visual to his unraveling made all the more poignant by the language itself.

When Justice Oliver Wendell Holmes sent Sam copies of some of his speeches, for example, surely a generic professional gesture sent to many other lawyers the same year that Holmes would join the U.S. Supreme Court, Sam wrote back that the enclosures had given him a life pleasure that was growing increasingly rare. "I am deeply indebted to you," he told Holmes. "Perhaps you will lunch with me sometime soon." In a letter to Louis a couple of years later, Sam wrote that he needed emotional support and especially appreciated the more personal notes that Louis sent along. "As the years go by, I need it more," Sam wrote, "there are few in life who are close as you." Their friendship, Sam said, helped to ease his mind: "I wish I saw you oftener."

In short, just as Louis Brandeis's star was rising—he'd become a famous lawyer and millionaire with three servants himself by this time and could seemingly pop in on Justice Holmes for tea and dinner whenever he pleased—Sam's star was crashing straight back to earth. It was as if Sam were weighted down so heavily, Brandeis told his wife, Alice, that "he had temporarily exchanged places with Atlas."

This worldly weight wasn't about any loss of riches or about any downturn in the papermaking business. That was all still mostly fine, and the gossip columns still referred to Sam as "the well-known paper manufacturer" and millionaire, and by then he had nine servants to Louis's three. Sam's trouble instead was within the Warren family and ultimately what outsiders knew about it all.

Much of that strife sprang from the reorganization of the family business and the resulting family trust, work that Louis had done the year before he and Sam had written "The Right to Privacy." "I cannot think of the family and its doings," Sam had written to Louis back then, "without including you as a most influential part." Louis had been "a very present help in time of trouble and a sure advisor at all times" for Sam and the Warrens over the course of many years.

But then he wasn't.

The Warren family trust, drafted at least in part by Louis, had placed Sam in charge of the Samuel D. Warren Company and had given Sam a larger share of the profits of what had by then become a $4.5 million company. And it was Sam as trustee who'd reported back to non-trustee family members about how the company was doing financially, which, according to Sam, was not always well. If you'd asked Sam's brother Ned, he would have said that Sam had become mind-blowingly rich while Ned had become increasingly poor. "Whenever difficulties of this kind arise," Ned wrote in a family letter, "my mind turns . . . to those who, judging by the expenses they undertake, are quite capable of helping me out." When the family agreed to lend Ned tens of thousands of dollars to help with his indebtedness, it was Sam who advised Ned to cut down on his expenses and to live more frugally. The family—again through Sam—also asked for proof from Ned's doctor that Ned's malingering had some sort of medical foundation.

Ned, by that time, had moved to England and had started a male-only commune of sorts where Oscar Wilde's friends would eventually find refuge and where Ned would lecture on Uranian love. He'd started to collect Greek and Roman antiquities that would later make their way into the museums of the world, and he would become known for his keen ability to spot treasures. He saw beauty in Auguste Rodin's *Kiss*, for example, and commissioned an anatomically correct version—"L'organe génital de l'homme doit être complété"—from the sculptor.

But he'd also started to collect bizarre sexual curiosities, pornographic antiquities at times shocking even to a modern eye that he'd later gift to the Boston Museum of Fine Arts, where Sam was a trustee and about to become board president. The MFA refused to show them: many included huge, distorted penises or images of men having sex with boys. Today, there's a famous work at the British Museum that's called the Warren Cup. It shows a man holding a boy in a shockingly sexual way, and it's named for Ned, who bought it from an antiquities dealer. Ned's gifts might have sent shock waves through proper Boston society, but Ned seemingly intended the affront. "The collection," he'd later explain, "was my plea against that in Boston which contradicted my (pagan) love"; the gift to the MFA was meant as "truly a paederastic evangel."

Through it all, Sam would say, he liked to keep family matters within the family because, to him, family dignity was what mattered most. This made the trouble with Ned especially worrisome. "Ned hates me as the author of all his ills," Sam wrote to his sister after Ned expressed an interest in learning more about how the Warren trust had been put together and how it operated. "I would like to step out that another take my place who can hold the family together." But that wouldn't happen.

It was right about then that Ned first hired a lawyer. What about the money and the business and the salaries at the Samuel D. Warren Company? What about the treatment of workers, both at the business in Boston and at the mills in Maine? Why shouldn't Ned be named a trustee so that he'd have a bigger voice in what was being done with all the money? Eventually, Ned's lawyer would uncover methods, the lawyer said, that had given Ned far less income—up to $1 million less—from the business and the trust. In response, Ned threatened to sell off his share of the company, leading to the potential collapse of it all.

The biggest blow came in December 1909. Just before Christmas, Ned filed a lawsuit demanding that a court step in to make things right. The worst of it was that Boston newspapers took notice of the squabble. "The litigants are members of the well known Boston Warren family," the *Boston Post* noted, "in the forefront of Boston society." WARREN BROTHERS SUED, the headline in *The Boston Daily Globe* read, and its story reported that Ned had asked the judge that Sam be removed as trustee, repeating Ned's lawyer's claim that Sam had padded his personal income by leasing property back to himself through the trust. Ned had therefore asked for new leaders of the family business, the story read, those "who will take steps to recover from S. D. Warren any money he may not be adjudged entitled to." The suggestion was that Sam had diverted nearly $1.5 million.

Brandeis didn't escape scrutiny either. One story noted that he had been the one to draw up the trust papers; another explained that the family had been assured that giving Sam considerable power was "well calculated to effectuate their wishes and protect their interests," which had turned out not to be true. Three days before Christmas, the *Post* included drawings from the courtroom of Sam and Ned captioned "Members of the Warren family, whose dispute over a huge estate will be settled by a master." Sam looked especially old.

That was much tamer newspaper coverage than what might have been because, despite increasing rumblings about a privacy privilege, newspapers even in proper Boston had grown increasingly nasty in their criticism of the lives of the elite over matters trivial and some less so. One earlier story had focused on Mabel Warren, Sam's wife, and had scolded her for not doing her usual amount of entertaining. Another suggested that Sam's older son seemed in conquest of a particular Boston debutante. While that young woman's proportions were Junoesque, her younger sister was "a trifle too large" and had broken two saddles in one week while riding horses. Sam's son's budding relationship was "an affair to be watched," even though he and his Junoesque girlfriend had scarcely spoken at a society event and seemed to be quarreling.

That was all bad enough given Sam's fragile emotional state and his hatred of family intrusions, but the final blow could well have been Louis's decision to assign the Warren trust matter to another attorney at the law firm. Louis had been called to assist a major publisher in a case involving allegations of government wrongdoing; his work promised to bring in $25,000 plus expenses to the firm along with good publicity. Given what Louis felt was his partner's comparable level of expertise with the Warren file, he asked the partner to represent Sam's interests. He'd also admittedly found the whole Warren affair to be "dragging painfully" and likely wanted out.

"I don't suppose you know how near, how very near I have come to losing my grip entirely during the past year," Sam had once written to Louis in the early days of their partnership, "but I believe I shall retain it, and your apparent confidence in me, helps me much."

So on a weekend in late February 1910, just a few days after *The Boston Globe*'s "Table Gossip" had reported that his namesake son and now daughter-in-law had returned to Boston after a European honeymoon, Sam took the train to Karlstein, the Dedham retreat he'd named for the rock where Charlemagne had rested during troubled times. He spent some time walking the property, they say, chopped some wood, and then shot himself. He'd turned fifty-eight the month before.

"There is no doubt," one newspaper put it, that the legal proceedings "which threatened to disclose family skeletons, worried Mr. Warren."

The media would never report the tragic truth of Sam's death. Instead, the story that made the papers across the nation was that Samuel Warren had died of apoplexy, a cerebral hemorrhage. "Mr. Warren had gone from his Marlboro street residence to Dedham on Friday," the *Boston Post* had reported, "in the hope of gaining rest from the strain brought on by the suit over the control of the property left by his father," and had died of apoplexy caused by exhaustion. That's what the doctor would write on the death certificate, and that's what the family spokesman would tell the many journalists who'd assembled in Dedham, giving Sam the cloak of privacy for the moment at least in death.

Louis Brandeis was that spokesman: "Mr. Brandeis stood as a guard between newspaper reporters and any members of the family," the *Boston American* reported; he'd rushed to Dedham from Washington immediately after learning of the tragedy and was the one "in charge of things at the Warren house." APOPLEXY, SAYS BRANDEIS, one newspaper headline read.

Only a couple of the articles about Sam's death suggested that something seemed fishy. Warren "had been noticeably depressed," one of those articles noted, and another suggested that his death was shrouded in a great deal of mystery. If Sam had been sick, that second newspaper had asked rhetorically, how come he'd had the strength to walk from the train station to Karlstein and then chop wood?

But nobody published the answer to that question, and Sam's body was brought back to his Back Bay mansion for the funeral. Louis Brandeis was an usher; Justice Holmes apparently did not attend. *The Boston Globe* accidentally identified Sam as "Mr. Russell" in its story about it all.

In later years, Brandeis would refer to Sam's suicide as "the Warren tragedy," and he'd keep a photograph of Sam tacked to the wall of his study until the end. "Boston failed to appreciate one of the noblest of her sons," the then justice Brandeis would write to Sam's children, six years before his own death. Sam, Louis told them, had integrity, a rare generosity, and great tenderness. He sent along some letters that Sam had written in the early days of their partnership that he said showed as much, some of which suggested that Sam didn't much like law practice and that Sam understood that the key to the firm's success was Louis's own advancement.

Precisely one month after Sam died, Louis received word from *Hampton's Magazine* that it would be profiling him for the June edition and wanted a good photograph. Louis's secretary sent one along, apologizing for its being "somewhat broken" but explaining that it was the only one available. The short biography told readers that Brandeis was a "lawyer and publicist," an "unofficial Attorney-General for the Public Interest" whose "way of doing something for the public has been to arouse the public to do something for itself." The photograph looked fine.

A few months later, a disgruntled man who'd been fired from his city job shot the mayor of New York, William Gaynor, in front of reporters and photographers who'd gathered to see the mayor off on an overseas trip. Mayor Gaynor ultimately blamed Hearst newspapers for the gunman's attack—if Pulitzer's "World has ever done a thing to make the masses gape, Hearst has gone it one better," critics used to say—suggesting that the assassination attempt had been inspired by Hearst's sensationalistic criticism of Gaynor's policy decisions. The mayor also blasted the photographers who'd taken pictures of the attempted assassination. "I could not bear to have them looking at me in the plight I was in," Gaynor said. "I hope [those] pictures were not published." But they were. It all caused *The Century Magazine* to ask, "How many more of the people's representatives in high places must be sacrificed to false ideas of the liberty of the press!"

Meanwhile, the *Harvard Law Review* had published an article titled "Freedom of Public Discussion" that explored "the nature and extent of the freedom which the law permits in the discussion of matters of public inter-est." But nobody much talked about that piece, and it mostly withered into obscurity.

With the end of 1910 came word that a settlement had been reached in the Warren family trust dispute. "The terms of the settlement are private," *The Boston Globe* reported, explaining that the only related document on file at the courthouse was one showing that the parties had agreed to a dismissal. Surely it was Brandeis who'd moved to seal it all.

That meant Sam Warren had gotten his wish for family privacy in that moment too, even in a matter that had captured the public's attention and interest. Nobody would find out until much later that Ned had indeed re-ceived a sizable sum from the company and that that's why he'd agreed to drop the case. It would all become important when Woodrow Wilson nomi-nated Louis Brandeis to the U.S. Supreme Court.

All the while, the back-fires of the right to privacy continued to burn. And then a famous no-holds-barred journalist poured gas on the flame, and, surprisingly, the growing blaze for privacy as a legal right ultimately led courts to begin to trust and therefore to back journalism more often.

PART II

THE RISE OF THE MEDIA

Chapter Eight

A DIFFERENT KIND OF FIRE

The famous journalist Upton Sinclair was dead asleep early one Sunday morning in March 1907 when an explosion rocked Helicon Hall, the colony he'd created for fellow writers and intellectuals in Englewood, New Jersey. Sinclair had published *The Jungle* the year before—work that had exposed the disgusting world of Chicago's meatpacking industry, led to stronger government food safety standards, and made him a household name—and he told reporters that an enemy's bomb was surely the cause of the blast.

That explosion and resulting fire would help along the right to privacy in the United States. You might think of it this way: Sam Warren and Louis Brandeis attacked sensational journalism from the outside as lawyers through the law, but Upton Sinclair would attack it from the inside, from a journalism ethics point of view as a journalist, powerfully blasting onto the media criticism scene in a way that would have shocked the far more refined E. L. Godkin.

Along with Nellie Bly and Ida Tarbell, Sinclair is credited with being one of the nation's first investigative reporters, a hardworking, ready-to-ferret-out-wrong journalist christened with the memorable nickname "muckraker" by Teddy Roosevelt. But the story is more complicated than that. Roosevelt hadn't lauded muckraking journalism in his 1906 speech, quite the opposite. He'd complained in line with language in "The Right to Privacy" that "gross and reckless assaults on character" in the press had created "a morbid and vicious public sentiment" and that "hysterical sensationalism" was the "poorest weapon wherewith to fight for lasting righteousness." Roosevelt called out those "evil," "vile and debasing" publications that formed an "epidemic of indiscriminate assault upon character." The muckrakers were of that type, he said, those "whose vision [was] fixed on carnal," and they continually raked for muck, for "the filth of the floor."

But investigative journalists latched on to the term as a badge of honor.

Sinclair's undercover work on *The Jungle* didn't instantly endear him to his fellow journalists either, however, and for good reason. He'd made a bad misstep back in 1902 starting out as a writer when he'd tricked nearly every single newspaper in the United States into believing that the author of a book *he'd* actually written was a young poet who'd killed himself immediately after sending a final manuscript to publishers. Sinclair's secretary had earlier laid the groundwork for *The Journal of Arthur Stirling* by sending a fake obituary to *The New York Times*, and the *Times* had unwittingly published it: "STIRLING.—By suicide in the Hudson River, poet and man of genius, in the twenty-second year of his age, only son of Richard T. and Grace Stirling, deceased, of Chicago. Chicago papers please copy."

"The reporters took it up," Sinclair boasted, even though he'd forgotten to include a first name, "and published many biographical details about the unfortunate young man" who did not exist, mostly because a fellow who called himself S. had offered them a short biography of the ill-fated poet in the journal's preface: Stirling had lived in poverty as a lonely wandering spirit, his previous work had been repeatedly rejected by publishers, he'd drowned himself in the Hudson with a heavy dumbbell and a strong rope, and only then did his dream of publication finally come true. "The reality of this," the bought-in *Boston Journal* wrote of *The Journal of Arthur Stirling*, "is one of its undeniable qualities."

Sinclair thought it all a harmless hoax, joke work that capitalized on his desire "to raise a sensation," but the reporters and editors who'd been tricked were aghast. "This matter of a faked biography is going too far" is what the Massachusetts *Springfield Republican* wrote, "to sell a book for what it is not is overpassing the limits of jest." That sentiment became universal in newsrooms, and as word of the hoax spread, there "came denunciation on the part of the many editors who had been deceived." Upton Sinclair, they said, was both a mediocre writer and a megalomaniac.

After Sinclair investigated and wrote about meat processing for *Collier's* and in *The Jungle*, he bolstered his journalistic credibility among readers, most of whom had likely forgotten about the whole Arthur Stirling brouhaha. But other journalists didn't and wouldn't forget, and given Sinclair's questionable track record many in his profession doubted that the revolting information about how sausage was made was true. "Upton Sinclair, not being a journalist," was the way the journalist George Seldes began a sentence that slammed Sinclair for "numerous errors in judgment and criticism."

There was another reason some in the post-Victorian era looked at Sinclair with strong skepticism. The avowed socialist was building a "home colony" on property in Englewood, just across the Hudson River from the Bronx. Sinclair had a small income, a small family, and a small farm, he'd said, but needed to "be free to turn his attention to intellectual pursuits." By sharing things like childcare and dishwashing, cooking and farming—"there have been months when I have done all the house-work, the cooking and washing of dishes, and taken care of the baby and a sick wife besides," he'd complained—others could join him in thinking big thoughts and doing big things. White people only, please.

Sinclair regretted the need to share this personal information, his "private affairs," with others, but he felt it would help to get the colony going. The plan seemingly worked well. Within a few weeks, the local post office reported that the number of letters sent to Sinclair equaled those sent to Grover Cleveland, who had by that time retired in Princeton.

It was about then that some libraries started banning *The Jungle* as unfit for their shelves for its general repulsiveness. And that Upton Sinclair reported that he'd started receiving death threats.

Sinclair's Helicon Hall, the name he'd given the colony, was up and running by late 1906, the year *The Jungle* came out in book form. Outsiders were intrigued because rumors were that the colony was a "free-love nest" and that Sinclair had started it both as a socialistic experiment and to keep several mistresses close. To investigate the rumors, "predatory journalists" and sketch artists—Sinclair called them the "gutter press"—had entered the property "in various disguises and under various pretexts in order to peer into [members'] private lives" simply to draft "burlesque copy" for newspapers. "They wrote us up on that basis," Sinclair said, on the rumors, "not in plain words, for that would have been libel—but by innuendo easily under-stood."

"All that we wish," he told *The New York Times*, "is to be let alone."

The explosion at Helicon Hall in 1907 killed one and injured several oth-ers. Sinclair thought it was arson, but it turned out to be a gas leak. Officials later reprimanded Sinclair for not having appropriate fire escapes in what they said was, in effect, a hotel. Meanwhile, additional rumors were swirling, so investigators grilled Sinclair with "suggestive questions" not only about the "hidden secrets" of communal life but also about the community buzz that maybe somebody on the inside was responsible for the blast.

It wasn't a purely theoretical line of questioning. Members had said that they'd removed Sinclair from his leadership role shortly before the fire be-cause they were worried about imminent financial ruin, a colony "hopelessly in debt." There was more: the day before the blast, Helicon Hall had been slapped with a $1,000 lawsuit by a workman who'd not been paid. The fire would have helped in a financial sense, it seemed: Helicon Hall had a $26,000 mortgage and a $40,000 insurance policy. It was all circumstantial, Sinclair complained, and yet the innuendo had quickly found its way onto "the front pages of the yellow newspapers of the country."

Soon, insurance proceeds paid everyone off and coverage of the fire dropped from the headlines. But that didn't make things easier for Upton Sinclair. Given his newfound celebrity through *The Jungle*, the investigator became the target of investigation as Hearst-branded and other sensational newspapers turned to the types of stories that had similarly riled Sam Warren and friends: what Upton usually had for breakfast (one cup of cold water—no ice—and six uncooked prunes) and whether he'd gone under-cover at the Vanderbilt mansion the Breakers disguised as a servant (he said that he hadn't). Meanwhile, whispers from knowing secretaries and ticket agents were that Meta Sinclair, Upton's wife, had had a post-fire nervous breakdown. "I have this to say," Upton Sinclair told reporters after rumors that marital difficulties might also be at issue, "there never has been nor will be anything but perfect devotion between us." That, he said, was "all that the public ha[d] a right to know in the matter."

The biggest bombshell would drop four years later: Meta, dissatisfied with Upton's self-absorption, had taken up with a "tramp poet" from Kansas,

Harry Kemp, and she admitted that Kemp wasn't the first in her sinful search for the perfect mate. Upton Sinclair responded that he wanted a divorce. And then the couple and the poet met with reporters to talk through it all. Upton didn't believe in marriage anyway, it appeared, and the new couple said that they wouldn't ever marry. It was as if the collusion that had so worried marriage-supporting newspapers in the 1890s were taking place right in front of reporters' eyes.

And thus came additional investigation into this duo of quirky relationships—Meta and Upton; Meta and Upton and Harry—with resulting headlines like these:

- **SINCLAIR FREAKY, PAPA-IN-LAW SAYS: MR. FULLER BELIEVES AUTHOR WILL BE GREAT MAN IF HE WILL EAT MORE MEAT** (Meta's father: "One night . . . [Sinclair] chewed a prune for 20 minutes"); and
- **SINCLAIR FIGHT ON** (tramp poet Kemp: "I realize now that I was the goat and was caught, and here I am"); and
- **SINCLAIR TOLD ME TO TAKE HIS WIFE** (tramp poet Kemp: "He encouraged me in my attentions to Mrs. Sinclair"); and
- **KEMP DRIFTED INTO LOVE** (Upton "preached free love," and "Meta was unhappy" with this particular type of genius).

There were hundreds and hundreds of stories as the divorce wound its way to and through court: no, there hadn't been any agreement between the two to seek a divorce; no, Meta Sinclair had not spent significant time in Mississippi with Mary Craig Kimbrough, the woman who would soon become Upton Sinclair's second wife; and yes, all that Meta Sinclair wanted was to "settle her affairs with Mr. Sinclair as quickly and quietly as possible."

Upton tried unsuccessfully to have the divorce case sealed—he'd hoped that a lot of what he said would not get out—and Meta begged for reporters to drop the story. "It is really none of anyone else's business, you know," she told them. "To put it quite plainly, I am sick of the publicity and notoriety that has come to me" and "must decline to add further to my embarrassment."

In the end, once the divorce was finalized, Upton Sinclair left the United States for the Netherlands, telling reporters that he was sick of the "gossip and inquisitiveness over his matrimonial troubles" in his birth country. The "journalistic jackals," he said, had screamed with glee as they'd rendered the carcass of his dead love relationship, publishing the "shameful details" of his "domestic misfortune"—"all the intimate details of where [he] slept and where [his] wife slept and what [he] saw [her] doing"—despite "the privacy guaranteed [him] by law."

That frustration with the press that started with Helicon Hall and continued straight through to Holland would lead to a different sort of manifesto from Upton Sinclair. Titled *The Brass Check: A Study of American Journalism*, it too revealed how sausage was made, and it too would help create profound and lasting change in an industry. Sinclair didn't know the law the way Warren and Brandeis did, but he knew journalism, and he had the power to start back-fires for privacy too.

Upton Sinclair would surely never admit it, but *The Brass Check*, his mostly self-interested plea for ethics, his attempt to jolt journalism into recognizing personal privacy, reflected in part his experience in writing for magazines. Driven by editors like E. L. Godkin, highbrow periodical publishers continued to place ethical and, at times, practical restrictions on embarrassing but interesting truthful information even at a time when newspapers were decidedly sensational.

At *McClure's*, for example, the muckraker Ida Tarbell, by that time a similarly famous author after her stunning investigative piece on the disturbing practices of Standard Oil, was working to tamp down an article written by Edith Wherry. Wherry had come to *McClure's* with "The Shame of S. S. McClure, Illustrated by Letters and Original Documents," an exposé featuring the publisher's trysts, involving at least one in office, and wanted it published in the pages of *McClure's* own magazine. The revelations of McClure's extramarital intimacies never happened, thanks in part to Tarbell's interference (McClure was not only her boss but a friend) and, likely, a philanderer-financed catch-and-kill.

At about that time Tarbell had also been trying to woo the retired president Cleveland into writing an autobiographical series for *McClure's*. The plan was that Cleveland would write his life recollections and that she'd serve as his editorial adviser. The former president kept putting her off. "The project requires me to exploit myself and my doings before the public," Cleveland wrote. "I do not see how I can do this." But Cleveland did trust Tarbell enough to suggest that she come to visit the Clevelands during the summer, for "the Tarbell-Cleveland fantasy" of putting something on paper. "I have frequently thought no one could help me so much as you," he told her.

That could well have been true because by this time Tarbell had also become fairly close friends with Frances Cleveland and they'd had at least one adventure in New York City together including the opera, dinner, and a sleepover at Tarbell's apartment. Mrs. Cleveland had also invited Tarbell for dinner—for a "cosy time" together with the couple in Princeton—more than once. Who knows what Ida Tarbell knew about the Clevelands and kept under her hat for reasons of friendship or perhaps of ethics. "Somehow I have an idea that you know me well," Grover Cleveland had written to her, and indeed she could have. In any event, Cleveland's reminiscences—surely juicy ones if he'd included everything—never got published by *McClure's*.

Many years later, long after Cleveland had died, Tarbell put together her own reminiscences of certain journalistic interactions she'd had with Cleveland, but before she did, she had an important ethics-related question for Mrs. Cleveland. "Have I your permission," Tarbell asked in 1938 about letters the thirty-years-dead Cleveland had written in 1907, "to use the paragraphs marked in the letters?" Of course, Mrs. Cleveland replied, "I always think of you as one of my real friends," and "your letter makes me feel I have been right in doing so."

Journalists through the decades have been criticized for becoming far too chummy with politicians and for stretching ethics to protect friends, for keeping under their hats for privacy reasons things that many other people thought ought to have been reported. Where to draw the appropriate line between private life and news is a challenge made all the more difficult when the bond between politician and press is a personal one.

President Teddy Roosevelt understood and used this dilemma to his fullest advantage. He'd procured an early agreement with the mostly adoring journalists who covered him: he'd give them unprecedented accessibility and would "keep them posted" on key information as long as they promised never to "violate a confidence or publish news that the President thought

ought not to be published." Those quotations are from a former Washington correspondent for the New York *Sun* who'd revealed as much in his autobiography, adding that Roosevelt considered it a perfectly reasonable gentleman's agreement. The Washington press corps, it seems, came obediently along, hesitating to publish what President Roosevelt felt was inappropriate news. And when Joseph Pulitzer's *World* strayed by suggesting that something seemed fishy with regard to the Panama Canal purchase, Roosevelt had Pulitzer indicted for criminal libel. He later sued a journalist for suggesting he was an alcoholic, and won.

President Woodrow Wilson—the president who would nominate Louis Brandeis to the Supreme Court—was not quite as agile as Teddy Roosevelt in keeping the press quiet, but it was close, and the secrecy involving Wilson was more than health related (a stroke disabled him during his second term, but coverage of that was incomplete). By 1916, the ethics-sensitive Tarbell had left *McClure's* along with several other of its famous muckrakers, the magazine had turned just a touch more scandalous, and Wilson was up for reelection. And so came a thinly veiled work of nonfiction fiction, an account based on a scandalous rumor about President Wilson too delicate to be reported pretty much anywhere but overseas: that Wilson had had an affair while married, that he had promised the woman that their relationship would become official once his sick wife died, and that he was worried about the potential for a resulting breach-of-promise lawsuit with all its nasty publicity because he'd ultimately married someone else. The other woman in *McClure's* "That Parkinson Affair" was paid off with $30,000 and eventually went away.

The woman's name in real life was probably Mary Allen Hulbert.

Historians will never know how accurate the *McClure's* fictionalized story about President Wilson, his first wife, Ellen, his second wife, Edith, and his girlfriend Mary was because not only was the information repressed back then but someone destroyed the real-life letters Wilson had written to Mary, a love at least in spirit while he was president and married to another.

President Wilson too "resented invasions of family privacy."

Upton Sinclair returned to the United States from Holland after more than a year, bursting with inspiration from his tangles with media and how very differently he'd been treated by overseas journalists who respected his talent and held no grudge. And thus he wrote *The Brass Check*, a journalistic attack on those in the United States who had attacked his privacy, those who fed eager readers and growing coffers by invading others' lives. "There is more than one kind of parasite feeding on human weakness," he wrote in 1919 after describing a procedure in which men exchanged money for brass tokens that they later used at bordellos, "there is more than one kind of prostitution which may be symbolized" by a brass check, and that is journalism.

The day's journalism, he argued, was much too fixed on the sort of muck that had troubled Roosevelt: sensational coverage was "a characteristically American procedure," a way that newspapers in the United States made both the famous and the not-so-famous into "public scarecrow[s]" by publishing "scandals about [their] private life." Even if reporters weren't explicit in the language that resulted from their "pernicious intrusion into private affairs," Sinclair wrote, all one had to do was read between the lines to figure out who and what personal information was behind the story.

He knew, he said, because he'd lived it. Predatory journalism had made a monkey out of him and had driven others to ruin and suicide. Many of the stories that revealed personal failings were sparked by tipsters inside telegram offices and other places who'd report what they read and heard to gossip reporters, and such relationships were all part of the economics of reporting.

Upton Sinclair went on for more than four hundred pages about the privacy invasions and other wrongs that people like him had suffered at the hands of journalism. He urged reporters to unite to create their own standards, their own "ethical code," one that featured at its core a sense of duty to the public. The chapter "Cutting the Tiger's Claws" suggested that the *law* needed to strengthen to protect people's privacy and to take journalism down a notch too.

The response to *The Brass Check* among journalists was about what you'd expect. Sinclair had earlier complained that he couldn't catch a break from newspapers still stinging from his *Journal of Arthur Stirling* days and that reporters wouldn't put his name on lists of great writers even though many others had. New York's "leading newspaper," Sinclair said, refused to publish his articles and even his name, and the Associated Press refused to cover him unless he was involved in something "considered disgraceful."

The Brass Check made him into even more of a pariah. Only a few newspapers published reviews, and those that did did so mostly mockingly. *The New York Times* was among those that refused to run an ad for the book, but it did cover at length a talk about it by Dr. James Melvin Lee, director of the journalism department at NYU and author of *History of American Journalism* (neither Sinclair nor Tarbell nor W. Calvin Chase made *History*). Lee first suggested that Upton Sinclair should not be believed because of the Arthur Stirling hoax. Then he discounted several of Sinclair's claims and eventually "delivered a general eulogy on the accuracy and fairness" of certain press.

In response, Sinclair published a pamphlet he titled *The Crimes of the "Times"* that suggested Lee had received his training in journalism ethics from a barbershop weekly. And back and forth and back and forth—Sinclair biting at Lee and *The New York Times*; *The New York Times* and Lee biting at Sinclair. It got so bad and the factions were so strong that the director of the Columbia University School of Journalism told his students that year not to be like Upton Sinclair.

But despite all that dissension, all that hatred even, something in *The Brass Check* eventually resonated with a journalism industry already finding its professional footing. Upton Sinclair would eventually put it this way: "I know that we still have many bad and prejudiced newspapers, but many are better than they were. I think that *The Brass Check* helped to bring about the improvement." Even *The New York Times* and George Seldes would both come around. Through Sinclair's work in *The Brass Check*, the journalist Seldes admitted in an editorial in the *Times*, Upton Sinclair ultimately "influenced a generation of reporters" by teaching them through personal experience what was wrong with the profession of journalism.

The drive for ethical tenets was given a different sort of rousing push in 1920 when the well-respected Walter Lippmann, founder of *The New Republic*, published a small book he titled *Liberty and the News*. "The present crisis of western democracy," Lippmann had warned, "is a crisis in journalism." Among other things, publishers of the yellow press held a troubling and significant power over everyone, by "snooping at keyholes and invading the privacy of helpless men and women."

Things were so bad, Lippmann wrote, that surely the next generation would "bring the publishing business under greater social control." Would it be possible to establish a "Court of Honor," he asked, that would use "higher law" to help correct privacy-invasive wrongs, to help enforce "a grace like fairness" in newspaper publishing in a way that protected people and their private lives?

He said that he doubted that such a thing could happen, even though, given an increasing shift in the courts toward a right to privacy by name, it already had.

And in an overlapping series of events that ran from the first decade of the twentieth century to the 1940s involving a box company executive with an ulterior motive, a journalism-despising Supreme Court justice, an early revenge porn publisher with absolutist views, and a president with a secret baby, courts and journalism both would come to more fully embrace the sort of privacy that Walter Lippmann—and Sam Warren and Louis Brandeis—had dreamed of.

What's perhaps most ironic about Upton Sinclair's ethics awakening, at least with regard to the right to privacy, is that it didn't come early enough to protect a member of the Warren family, Sam's brother Fiske. If you've visited the Boston Museum of Fine Arts, perhaps you've seen there an oversized portrait of a lovely woman and her daughter in varying shades of pink by John Singer Sargent. Sargent painted *Mrs. Fiske Warren (Gretchen Osgood) and Her Daughter Rachel* in 1903. After acquisition, the museum delightedly noted its "long-standing relationship with the Warren family: Fiske Warren's brothers, Samuel D. Warren and Edward Perry [Ned] Warren, were important collectors and patrons of the MFA."

In 1914, Upton Sinclair published what he said at the time was a novel about the very rich he titled *Sylvia's Marriage*. He described it as "the story of a Southern girl who marries a wealthy Bostonian and Harvard man and bears a child blinded by gonorrhea." Some credited *Sylvia's Marriage* as a "very human and convincing story" of married life, a shocking work that explored sexual matters in an accurate, truthful manner, one of the very first to explore such a delicate subject.

Gonorrhea or any similarly sexually transmitted infection was not something people talked about much back then, as a glance at the pages of *The Cincinnati Enquirer* from 1914 helps show. "Men!" an ad for Dr. Howell's practice read. "Business men, salaried men and wage earners of all classes and conditions are coming to me for treatment. Why not you?" Dr. Howell specialized in illnesses like blood diseases, prostatic diseases, piles, and other rectal diseases. But some of his expertise was too delicate for mention. "If your trouble is of a private or special nature," another section of the ad read, "you can have perfect privacy by coming to my offices. They are located in a large business block with two public entrances, elevators and stairways. This means for you real privacy not obtainable elsewhere."

There was real shame back then.

Sinclair would later reveal that he'd fashioned the husband Douglas van Tuiver in *Sylvia's Marriage*—the appallingly snooty Harvard man who'd frequented a prostitute and who'd brought gonorrhea home to his wife and child—after Fiske, the youngest Warren sibling. Who knows how accurate it all was, especially given Sinclair's eagerness to mislead in the Arthur Stirling fiasco, but there's a strong parallel in the book with Warren family privacy concerns at least: after being found out, the character in the novel is "terrified of the gossip" about his personal life and what the newspapers might know and might well report, fears that seem perfectly reasonable given that the prostitute in the book had a habit of reading society columns with friends and translating for them the subtle allusions and veiled scandals that she knew could be found there.

It was just the sort of worrisome scenario that had inspired and was condemned by "The Right to Privacy."

Walter Lippmann, who'd gone to Harvard, had read Sinclair's scathing portrayal of the Harvard-educated superrich and had told Upton Sinclair that such a man did not exist, but Sinclair knew better. "I would have been embarrassed" at Lippmann's criticism, Sinclair would later write, "had I not known certain facts that, unfortunately, I was not at liberty to mention." Sinclair's former secretary had been hired by Fiske Warren, you see, and Upton and his new wife had become friendly with Fiske and his wife, Gretchen, so they apparently knew certain things. Whether the information was accurate or not, readers of Sinclair's autobiography were left with what Sinclair himself would have called innuendo easily understood.

Poor Fiske Warren surely had no idea that it was he who'd somehow become the fictional scoundrel in *Sylvia's Marriage*. We know this because, despite wartime paper shortages, an eager-to-help Fiske—by this time, Upton Sinclair's "old friend"—had agreed to supply Samuel D. Warren Company paper so that Sinclair could self-publish *The Brass Check*, the book that thereafter would help lead journalism to a strong, uniform, national code of ethics that protected privacy.

Chapter Nine

THE LAW WON

What if, you might now be wondering, an author publishes a work that suggests that an identifiable real-life person has a sexually transmitted infection such as gonorrhea? And what if that real-life person wishes to sue the author? What would the law have to say about that?

The answer would depend on how that real-life person—named or unnamed, purported fiction or not—would answer a key question posed in an initial consultation with a lawyer: Is the information about the sexually transmitted infection false or is it true?

And that's an entry into how the law more commonly began to recognize "the right to privacy" as both a right and a phrase in a rather surprising way, how the back-fires for privacy by name grew more officially in the nation's courts just as ethics in journalism was becoming more official too.

First, a quick backgrounder inspired by Douglas van Tuiver's troubles in Upton Sinclair's *Sylvia's Marriage*. Today, if an author publishes such a work, and if the identifiable real-life person (a pseudonym makes no difference) answers that the information about gonorrhea is *false*, the real-life person could sue for defamation. Even today, at the law's most basic, putting aside multiple modern nuances including our more open approach to such matters and the actual malice standard that protects a publisher under certain conditions, if someone says that someone else has an STI and they don't, it can support a solid defamation case.

That's been the law for a long time with regard to that sort of disclosure in particular; recall that man noted by the Supreme Court who was said to have had "the itch" and therefore a successful libel claim. So of course when a ne'er-do-well in Georgia told another man in front of others in the mid-nineteenth century that he was "a clappy d[amne]d son of a bitch" who'd "been rotten with the clap this two or three years," the plaintiff won his libel case too. "The disease imputed to the plaintiff by the defendant, no one could fail to understand," the court wrote, and such a condition "would most certainly exclude him from all good society."

Recognition of the lasting harm in that sort of misinformation (or lie) and the individual's rightful reinstatement within society are what defamation is all about. Usually the plaintiff needs to offer some proof of reputational harm, but not in this case. In the 1930s, the first Restatement of the Law of Torts—the powerfully influential encyclopedia-like law book written by well-respected legal experts that restates the common law in a cohesive way as guidance for judges so that they can "render their judgments in a consistent and reasonably predictable manner" throughout the United States—maintained that allegations of "a presently existing venereal or other loathsome and communicable disease" were so harmful to reputation that damages would be presumed with no proof necessary. Statements about another's gonorrhea were that clearly, horribly, and sure-to-harm-the-reputation bad.

Invasion of privacy involves published information that has the potential in some cases to exclude people from society too, but it's different from defamation in modern times because it necessarily involves the revelation of *truthful* information. It's what Warren and Brandeis argued for. And of course, long before the Warren and Brandeis article, early courts had found that truthful allegations of a "loathsome disease" were also in themselves exclusionary: so scandalous, so offensive that truth was no defense because the speaker's "social and relative duties" had been violated simply by the mere mention of the affliction. These sorts of illnesses were exactly the sorts of unmentionable "private vices," "the offences, faults or foibles of men," that early courts had punished. Women had valid claims too. As Oliver Wendell Holmes put it in his edition of Kent's *Commentaries on American Law*, "To say that a married woman has the pox is actionable *per se*."

Today, the law calls that sort of invasion of privacy "publication of private facts" or "publicity given to private life," and it's found its way into common law in the United States through what Walter Lippmann might well have called Courts of Honor. It was helped along by a leading light of academia, William Prosser, who published his own influential law review article on privacy in 1960 and then worked on the second Restatement to help solidify the tort's acceptance. Publication of private facts is one of the things that Hulk Hogan sued for when the *Gawker* website published a sex tape featuring him.

But that's getting ahead of the story a bit.

Publication of private facts may be the type of privacy tort that Warren and Brandeis pined most for in their *Harvard Law Review* article, but it wasn't the first that courts and legislatures began to embrace. Remember that mostly throwaway line in "The Right to Privacy" that condemned reproductions of women's faces and forms "colored to suit a gross and depraved imagination"? The one that seemed designed to help Marion Manola and Frances Folsom Cleveland fight off those who wished to exploit their names, faces, and worse? In roundabout fashion, that's the sort of tort-based privacy law that "The Right to Privacy" first inspired.

Later, in the 1930s, the first Restatement of Torts would define privacy in a way that put publication of private facts first. "A person who unreasonably and seriously interferes with another's interest in not having his affairs known to others" is liable for invasion of privacy, it read, but a person who exhibits another's likeness to the public is liable for invasion of privacy too.

That second part involving use of likenesses is today the privacy tort called misappropriation, and it gives everyone the right to sue for the misuse of their name or photograph, generally in advertising. Mrs. Manola and Mrs. Cleveland inspired it, but a teenager named Abbie helped it become the law.

Rochester Folding Box Company started manufacturing cardboard containers in Rochester, New York, at the turn of the twentieth century. It quickly became successful based in large part on the hundreds of thousands of small cigarette boxes that it shipped to Japan with lettering in English designed to make local tobacco seem more exotic. The company's lithography and printing division worked directly with clients to come up with marketing schemes like that one. And it was that division that got Rochester Folding Box into headline-making trouble.

At just about the time that Upton Sinclair was writing *The Journal of Arthur Stirling*, so a little more than ten years after "The Right to Privacy" appeared in the *Harvard Law Review*, the Franklin Mills Flour Company hired Rochester Folding Box to create a poster that it hoped would lure grocery shoppers into buying its brand of flour. They decided on a lithograph featuring a picture of a young woman and the tagline "Flour of the Family."

The wordplay wasn't all that clever, really, because the flower/flour phrasing had been done before. One ad for Minkota Milling Company, for example, showed a smiling, sturdy older woman, hand on hip, in a jaunty derby hat, long-sleeved blouse, and floor-length skirt, with a giant bag of flour atop her shoulder. "The flour of the family" that also read.

But the ad designed for Franklin Mills Flour had a different vibe. This time the woman seemed fragile and young; this time she wasn't looking at the camera at all but seemed focused on something far off in the distance; and this time she wasn't wearing the day's proper body-covering clothing but a light-colored blouse with an elastic ruffle pulled down off her shoulders just far enough to reveal her collarbone and perhaps a bit more. "Flour of the Family" this ad read too, and it tucked off into a corner very small photos of a box, a barrel, and a bag of Franklin Mills flour.

The product wouldn't have attracted the eye the way the young woman did.

Her name was Abbie Roberson, she was seventeen, and that portrait was meant for her boyfriend's eyes alone. (Abbie would later suggest that that so-called boyfriend, an unnamed lawyer, had had a hand in the transfer to Rochester Folding Box. "Little did I realize what they were going to do with it," she would say.) She'd found out about the poster in the same way that Marion Manola had a couple of decades before: she'd walked by a store and had seen herself in the window. What she didn't know until later was that Rochester Folding Box had published twenty-five thousand such posters and had sent them across the country, mostly to grocery stores, but they'd found their way into warehouses and saloons too.

Abbie was "made sick," she said, at the misuse of her portrait. Doctors had already diagnosed her with a failing heart, so her angry family was all the more inspired to sue Rochester Folding Box and its flour-making client. The family's lawyer argued specifically that Abbie's privacy had been invaded.

Elbridge Adams was a thirtysomething lawyer and one of the founders of Rochester Folding Box, a company that by that time was on its way to becoming the third-largest box manufacturer in the United States. That meant that when Abbie Roberson filed her lawsuit for invasion of privacy, Adams had both the law degree and the finances to go full throttle on defense. But he didn't, really. Borrowing a page from the Louis Brandeis *Cape Cod Folks* playbook, Adams argued simply that, *Harvard Law Review* article on privacy or not, no law prevented his company from doing what it had done. No law and no court decisions on point meant that, sorry, judges were powerless to protect Abbie. (This wasn't entirely accurate; in 1891, in the first case to mention the six-month-old Warren and Brandeis article, a court in New York had upheld Sir Morell Mackenzie's claim against the Soden Mineral Springs Company for using his signature and name on every box of its lozenges without his permission. The plaintiff, the court reported, had argued that "the acts complained of are an unwarrantable invasion of the reasonable right of privacy," "citing, *Article in Harvard Law Review*, December, 1890, *on the Right of Privacy*.")

The teenager in the Flour of the Family ad was just as successful at the trial court level as Sir Mackenzie. "Every woman has a right to keep her face concealed from the observation of the public," the judge wrote, her image protected as a natural extension of the "sacred" "privacy of the home," a necessity for "domestic and individual happiness."

Journalists, eager to highlight the differences between the reporting that they did in newsrooms and the selling of advertising that took place in another part of the newspaper building entirely, praised the decision. "The unauthorized circulation of the portraits of pretty girls or well-known men for advertising purposes," an industry publication read, "has grown to be an evil that ought to be suppressed."

Abbie won at the intermediate-level appellate court too; those judges cited Judge Cooley's right to be let alone. To argue for privacy in pictures featured in advertisements may be a new strategy, the court wrote, but "the principle upon which that right depends is not novel" and has "well-established principles" that support it.

Detective camera buffs were starting to get worried. "This decision is interesting to all who photograph," a magazine for photographers advised in an understatement, "and should be noted."

But, in the end, Elbridge Adams and his folding box company won; he made the same the-right-of-privacy-is-not-a-legal-actionable-right argument at New York's highest court, the court of appeals, and in 1902 the judges there finally bought it. Sure, Chief Judge Alton Parker wrote for the 4–3 majority, the right to privacy had been "presented with attractiveness" in the *Harvard Law Review* in 1890, but it was ultimately an idea "bordering upon the absurd." Who was to say what would be a violation and what wouldn't be, for one? The best example was smack-dab right there in front of them. "Others would have appreciated the compliment" in having been found lovely enough to have their faces featured in advertising, Judge Parker and his colleagues told Abbie, so where was the harm?

That meant that privacy as a legal conception was instantly dead in the state of New York and pretty quickly the decision rippled out beyond advertising. One New York court ruled, for example, that a man who'd been arrested for swindling the Earl of Rosslyn during a card game had no ground to stand on when he asked that police remove his photo from their so-called rogues' gallery, their collection of mug shots. "He (Owen) seeks to prevent publication of the picture as an invasion of his rights of privacy," the judge hearing the case said, "but the Court of Appeals has repudiated the doctrine that the rights of privacy has any existence in law."

The swindler would be pleased to know that the internet age has made certain courts far more accepting of his argument.

Judge Parker would soon become more agreeable to the whole idea of privacy too. After he ran for president of the United States in 1904 in an ill-advised bid to take down Teddy Roosevelt, he suddenly understood the need for such a right: persistent "camera fiends" had started to follow him everywhere, and his wife had to leave home "to escape the sleepless surveillance of surreptitious snapshotters." Newspapers noted Parker's about-face. "Curses and chickens are not the only things that come home to roost," one in Rochester wrote. It thereafter published this ditty about a fictional girl named Maud:

> *Judge Parker, passing down the way,*
> *Was hailed by Maud one later day.*
> *Said she to him: "I do not like*
> *My picture up along the pike;*
> *By this I'm losing my good name*
> *And being put to every shame."*
> *But when she asked, in trembling tone,*
> *If she hadn't the right to be let alone,*
> *The Judge remarked he'd never heard*
> *A proposition so absurd.*

Privacy-related legislation in New York happened nearly immediately, inspired by Abbie's plight. The New York legislature passed a law it titled "An Act to Prevent the Unauthorized Use of the Name or Picture of Any Person for the Purposes of Trade." Thereafter, any person whose name, portrait, or picture was used in advertising without permission could sue the advertiser, and such a use was a crime to boot.

You might think that privacy advocates would rejoice in that history, but early recognition of that sort of right to privacy by statute in New York pretty much ended there, and since that day New York's main privacy law hasn't changed all that much. The type of privacy that Warren and Brandeis lobbied for—the publication of a private fact as a privacy violation—is nearly universal in the United States and elsewhere but effectively does not exist in New York, where privacy rights are traditionally joined mostly with commercial use.

And this is why, in 2015, residents in New York City who believed that they were safely ensconced in their glass-windowed low-rise apartment building lost their case against a photographer who'd captured images of them and their children close-up in night and day for more than a year using a telephoto lens from a building across the street. Here too the photographer's unwitting subjects were surprised to see their images in public, this time for sale in an art gallery promoted as a series titled *The Neighbors*. The intermediate appellate court hearing the case applied New York's privacy statute and found little protection for the plaintiffs because the photographer had intruded for art's sake, but it lobbied the legislature for change. "Needless to say, as illustrated by the troubling facts here, in these times of heightened threats to privacy posed by new and ever more invasive technologies," the court wrote, "we call upon the legislature to revisit this important issue, as we are constrained to apply the law as it exists." New York's high court refused an appeal.

New York, therefore, was an outlier from the time of the *Roberson* case. "The right of privacy, or the right of the individual to be let alone, is a personal right," a Georgia court for one wrote early on in its rejection of the *Roberson* decision, crediting "The Right to Privacy" in part. "The principle is fundamental and essential in organized society that every one ... shall respect the rights and properties of others" even when they have rights of their own. Other states soon joined that chorus.

The common law, therefore, was beginning to coalesce in many places around two sensibilities: that a right to privacy existed in the first place, built upon ideas and values that had always been a part of the jurisprudence of the United States, *and* that such a right would surely abridge some level of another's freedom but that that was okay given privacy's importance. Alexander Hamilton's argument in *Croswell*—that the publication of truth was protected as long as there was good reason to publish it—had helped to lay the groundwork, and from there the Warren and Brandeis argument that protection for the inviolate personality should be called the "right to privacy" was gaining ground. Cases that protected privacy in letters and in nudity and in medical conditions and otherwise offered some sense of off-limits topics. It was all about the right to be let alone, as Michigan judge Thomas Cooley had first suggested, and Abbie's case became a rallying cry for why.

Meanwhile, in academia, Roscoe Pound, a famous professor and dean at Harvard Law School, and friend to Brandeis, argued for privacy in 1915, at just about the time that Upton Sinclair was writing *The Brass Check*, and his focus too was mainly on journalism's oversteps. There was a need in the law to recognize privacy more strongly, Pound wrote, given "the invasion of privacy by reporters in competition for a 'story,' [and] the activities of photographers." He urged that more courts accept invasion of privacy as a cause of action by name because it was reasonable that a person's "private personal affairs shall not be laid bare to the world and be discussed by strangers," as had happened, he said, in the *Cape Cod Folks* case, and he praised that early plaintiffs' victory.

All that such a court need do was limit the right when there were important competing interests involved, he wrote, as if that sort of thing would be simple.

At some point along the way, Elbridge Adams, a distant relative of the Adams presidential dynasty, had the same sort of privacy turnaround as had Judge Parker: the founder of Rochester Folding Box, the one who'd argued that he had the right to use Abbie Roberson's boudoir shot to advertise flour, suddenly began arguing in support of a right to privacy.

Maybe the shift was inspired by the sensationally intrusive coverage of his would-be father-in-law's death from a heart attack the night before Adams's wedding: it was after a hearty dinner at the hotel when the man "began to stagger, and sank upon the bed, as if completely exhausted," and then he expired. Or maybe he knew at the time that his marriage was in trouble and didn't want the precise details of his extramarital sexual behaviors getting out. He would eventually argue that he had a constitutional right not to answer philandering-related questions during the divorce hearing, in fact, and by that time had persuaded a judge to seal and lock away all papers from the couple's child custody dispute.

But his sudden embrace of privacy was most likely one of simple business. Everyone in the world by Adams's own assessment was angry about the *Roberson* decision against the teenager Abbie, and the whole matter was easy enough to trace back to one particular company with clients as far off as Japan who could simply take their need for boxes elsewhere. Adams therefore began to argue in magazines and in law reviews that the law needed to change to "meet a condition of modern society which [was] becoming intolerable." The intolerable condition wasn't advertising, mind you, but "journalistic, and even so-called literary, invasions of privacy." Courts should simply extend the law of libel in order to tamp down what was a growing disregard for others, he wrote. He supported jail for journalists too—"a fair attempt to remedy the evil" of those who would publish "all the prurient details of a family scandal or a divorce suit."

You might say that his methods of persuasion here were even better than his company's marketing schemes because he'd suddenly made people refocus on the likes of Joseph Pulitzer and William Randolph Hearst and forget about the wrong that Rochester Folding Box had done to Abbie Roberson. Moreover, through an ingenious use of passive voice, he routinely failed to identify himself as the attorney for the company. Even Brandeis might have been fooled; he sent along an Elbridge Adams law review article titled "The Right of Privacy, and Its Relation to the Law of Libel" to students at the *Harvard Law Review*, and others, suggesting that the Adams article linking truthful libel with privacy showed that the right to privacy remained "a vital force," was finding judicial recognition, and was "a very live one with many people."

In any event, within months of the final *Roberson* decision favoring his business, Elbridge Adams had become so strong a privacy advocate that he was invited to speak on the topic at the American Social Science Association annual meeting in Boston. Louis Brandeis was there too giving a paper titled "The Incorporation of Trades-Unions." It would be a few years before he'd join the nation's highest court.

With Brandeis likely in the audience, Adams praised "The Right to Privacy" as "one of the most brilliant excursions in the field of theoretical jurisprudence which the recent literature of the law discloses." He didn't much mention the *Roberson* decision, but instead argued in line with the Warren and Brandeis article that the day's journalism had resulted "in a lowering of social standards and of morality," that it belittled and perverted the understanding, vulgarized the tastes, and dwarfed the thoughts and aspirations of the people.

Then, at the very end of his talk, Adams quoted Justice Henry Billings Brown of the U.S. Supreme Court: Justice Brown, Adams told the crowd, had given a talk at a meeting of lawyers in 1900 in which he'd said that despite all the scandalmongering that everyone was so concerned about, it would be "impossible" to remedy the evil in newspapers.

Adams probably didn't know, but Justice Brown had been thinking about the right to privacy in the context of the press for quite a while, mostly for personal reasons. We'd expect this today because of his notorious role in the 1896 case *Plessy v. Ferguson* in which he'd written for the Court that separate railway cars for the races would be entirely constitutional, but there'd been surprisingly little criticism of *Plessy* at the time.

And what Justice Brown had said at that lawyers' meeting was a little more tempered than what Elbridge Adams had remembered; it was "exceedingly doubtful," Justice Brown suggested, "if any *legislation* be practicable which shall tend to restrict the excessive license indulged in by newspapers."

So, reading between the lines, maybe the common law could find a way. Maybe it already had.

Coincidence or not, the right to privacy had started to seep with greater force into U.S. Supreme Court jurisprudence at just about the time that Justice Brown took his seat on the high bench in 1890. Recall that the justices had written this in 1891 in that torts case involving an injury to a woman on a railroad train: "No right is held more sacred, or is more carefully guarded, by the common law, than the right of every individual to the possession and control of his own person" and thereafter cited Justice Cooley: "The right to one's person may be said to be a right of complete immunity; to be let alone."

In a parallel effort to protect their own privacy, to be let alone with or without supporting laws, Brown and his fellow justices had taken fairly tight rein on journalists assigned to cover them: note taking inside the courtroom was not allowed, sketching of the justices inside the courtroom was forbidden, and any writing papers whatsoever would be confiscated.

Those efforts didn't help much in a direct sense. First, there'd been a series of shocking leaks to the media about the Court and its decisions in those years; newspapers in several key cases had reported days in advance of the official hand down precisely what the outcome would be. All it took, reporters explained, was a little liquor to loosen justices' lips. Newspapers also published stories about the justices' salaries; their gambling problems; and their apparent senility. They'd stalked an unknowing Justice Harlan on a streetcar and reported on the conversation he'd had there. "I only want to live long enough to see the United States of South Africa established," Harlan had told his companion.

Intrigued media had a sharp focus on Justice Horace Gray, Louis Brandeis's former boss too. The longtime bachelor had risen to the U.S. Supreme Court just a couple of years after Brandeis had worked as his clerk and, at age sixty-one, had finally gotten engaged to a fellow justice's daughter. That announcement became "the sensation of the season," newspapers reported, in part because Gray had a "decided fondness" not only for sweets but for pretty girls and had earlier said that choosing just one to marry would be difficult. That house that he'd purchased with windows strategically placed so that neither light nor people could peer in? Turns out that it wasn't meant for Annie Van Vechten (a woman gossip columns said was Gray's girlfriend but who was more likely a girlfriend of Grover Cleveland's sister Rose). It was for Justice Gray's fiancée—or maybe his sister.

That tells you that the family members of the justices did not escape journalists' interest either as the turn of the century neared: a justice's wife's apparent alcoholism (her love of "libations to Bacchus") had once again caused her to promenade unsteadily around a supper room, then fall into the arms of an army officer; a justice's granddaughter's affair with her married "Adonis lover" had become the talk of Washington; a justice's daughter's sickness had required the curing waters of a Pennsylvania resort; a different justice's daughter had had a sad lesson in love, given her new husband's liquor habit and his flagrant excesses.

But even with all that published intrigue, Justice Brown's relationship with the media of the day was a uniquely prickly one. First, he'd had the misfortune of becoming a federal judge in Detroit in the years that sensational papers were really starting to crank. That meant that in 1885, five years before he'd join the Supreme Court, reporters in Michigan were particularly excited to learn that he'd shot a burglar who'd come into his house in the middle of the night. The story made national news and some pretty sensational headlines. As the burglar loomed with gun and lantern in hand asking for jewelry and cash, the judge had reached into his bedside commode, pulled out a revolver, and shot several times. The fact that the burglar had fired back and made a getaway made the story all the juicier.

When police captured a suspect, journalists of course wanted an interview with his famous judicial victim and wouldn't take no for an answer. "A reporter for *The Free Press* visited Judge Brown's residence at 10:45 last night," *The Free Press* itself reported with stunning bravado, "and for ten minutes vigorously sounded the door bell without obtaining a response."

That single burglary event and its excited news coverage were surely what started Justice Brown on the road to despising the press. It didn't help that during his impending confirmation to the Supreme Court, journalists had erroneously reported that he'd killed the man. Then, after Judge Brown officially became Justice Brown, things got more personal. Journalists began to report that his eyesight was fading, that he and his wife apparently could not have children, and that she, once vibrant, had mysteriously become an invalid. They'd also accurately reported on a talk that the justice had given at Yale, his alma mater, in which he'd made a terrible joke involving his wife: "I feel like the man who was told at his wife's funeral that he would have to ride to the graveyard with his mother-in-law." The man would do it if he had to, Justice Brown said, "but it would destroy all the pleasure of the occasion."

So precisely six years to the day of his visit to Yale and a significant amount of news coverage later, Justice Brown gave a different sort of speech, this time to the annual meeting of the New York State Bar Association apparently with Elbridge Adams in attendance. This time, he ripped into the day's journalism, and this time he demanded privacy. Modern critics might think of Justice Clarence Thomas as going too far in his condemnation of the press—"The media often seeks 'to titillate rather than to educate and inform'" is what Justice Thomas wrote in a dissenting opinion in 2019 that also criticized "the litigation and relitigation of criminal trials" in news stories—but Justice Thomas's complaints are mild compared with what Justice Brown had to say.

Brown told the crowd of lawyers in a talk curiously titled "The Liberty of the Press" that invasion of privacy by turn-of-the-century newspapers had become a real problem in the United States. Rumor had it that newspapers had sent reporters to Washington solely "to blacken the character of particular men," that they'd spied on houses and had listened from stairwells to unearth domestic scandals, that they'd stolen messages from wires to report private information—all proving a "sad degeneracy" that had made U.S.

newspapers disturbingly different from those in much more refined England and France.

Sensational American dailies had been especially cruel in their "assaults upon private character," Justice Brown said, because, after all, "there are probably but few men who have not, at some period of their lives, yielded to temptation" and who wished to keep those illicit life events to themselves, but unscrupulous papers instead ferreted them out for exploitation. (Turns out there was fire behind that smoke. After Justice Brown died, his friend and biographer curiously used titillating excerpts from Brown's personal diaries in the biography, including word that Justice Brown had fallen "violently in love" with another while married. His biographer also shared that Justice Brown was very fond of young ladies and that he "never failed to notice a pretty woman whom he met.")

And, finally, Justice Brown noted in his talk that scandal-ridden, sensational newspapers—those most prone to invade the sanctity of private character and use photographs and other illustrations to invade "one's right to privacy"—were usually the ones screaming the loudest for First Amendment press freedom and the right to publish whatever they wanted.

Justice Brown wasn't the only justice who felt that way; if you look for it, you'll find subtle appearances of the Brown sort of promotion of privacy and condemnation of the press reflected in a number of Supreme Court opinions from around the turn of that century. Justice Brown himself wrote in an utterly unrelated case involving sailors' work contracts that the First Amendment was not as meaningful as some thought: "The freedom of speech and of the press (article 1) does not permit the publication of libels, blasphemous or indecent articles, or other publications injurious to public morals or private reputation." The justices as a group had already recognized in dicta in 1885 the privacy in sexual relations, noting "the intimacies of the marriage relation," and in 1886 had embraced what they called "the privacies of life" including the "sanctity of a man's home" that deserved protection in the name of constitutional liberty and security.

Lower courts soon joined in. That sort of published rhetoric from the justices in speeches and court opinions, in addition to increasingly glowing accolades for "The Right to Privacy," gave other judges nascent confidence to slap media down for invading privacy:

- Yes, a photographer who had published a photo of dead, unclothed conjoined twins would be liable for invading the parents' right to privacy. "The most tender affections of the human heart cluster about the body of one's dead child," Kentucky's high court wrote.
- Yes, the *National Police Gazette* would be liable for its story exposing a woman's apparent tryst at a New Jersey hotel. The topic was not a matter of news, was not an item of general interest to the public, but was instead an example of "the license which the press assumes to itself in the ruthless hunt for sensational news, and in the unsparing invasion of private affairs with which the public has no concern."
- Yes, a journalist would be liable for sneaking into a jury room and hiding behind curtains in order to listen to deliberations, take notes, and then publish precisely what he'd heard.
- Yes, those who published others' personal letters of "extreme affection" would also be liable. The very nature of that correspondence "may be such as to set the seal of secrecy upon its contents."
- And, yes, public officials would have similar protection for their private lives, because "a person who enters upon a public office, or becomes a candidate for one, no more surrenders to the public his private character than he does his private property."

In 1902, Justice Oliver Wendell Holmes joined the U.S. Supreme Court and continued his interest in the jurisprudence of privacy there. Early on, he joined Justice Brown in an opinion holding that a libel action against a newspaper in the Philippines would stand, even though the precise words that the newspaper had used had come directly from court testimony and were therefore accurate. Here, however, the courtroom quotations had been transformed into headlines in a sensational way, the justices reasoned, and there in the Philippines truth was protected only if it had been published for good reason and justifiable ends. Sensationalism was neither good nor justifiable.

And the Court's interest did not wane after Justice Brown retired in 1906. Justice Holmes and his colleagues that year upheld a contempt citation against two Colorado newspapers for publishing certain articles and cartoons that suggested the Colorado Supreme Court was a political body. The newspapers had argued informally that "if there is one department of the government more than another that should receive the scrutiny of the public press it is the judiciary" and more formally that it should be protected constitutionally because what it had published was the truth.

But the newspapers were wrong on both counts, the Court said. Freedom of the press, Justice Holmes wrote for the majority in holding the newspaper liable, extended mainly to that information that was necessary for the public welfare, and punishment for overstepping would extend to the *true* as well as the false. As support, he cited in part the many-decades-old *Commonwealth v. Blanding*, the case in which a judge punished a newspaper for accurately reporting that a man had died of alcohol poisoning in a particular bar—the one that had quoted Hamilton in *Croswell* directly and then stated, "No state of society would be more deplorable than that which would admit an indiscriminate right in every citizen to arraign the conduct of every other, before the public . . . for faults, foibles, deformities of mind or person, even admitting all such allegations to be true."

In 1915, the year in which both Roscoe Pound and Upton Sinclair were becoming dismayed with the exploitative excesses of media, Justice Holmes agreed with the rest of the Supreme Court that it was perfectly constitutional to subject "Mutual Weekly" newsreels to Ohio's board of film censors. Newsreels were a "means of making or announcing publicly something that otherwise might have remained private or unknown," and therefore they were "mere representations of events, of ideas and sentiments" and had real power for evil.

Those Supreme Court cases might not have directly involved the right to privacy by phrase, but they helped along the sensibility that restrictions on the publication of truth could indeed exist in a world that also respected the press at some level. It's probably no coincidence that World War I was raging by this time and that the federal government had urged citizens collectively in posters and elsewhere, "Do not become a tool of the [enemy] by passing on the malicious, disheartening rumors which he so eagerly sows. Remember he asks no better service than to have you spread . . . gross scandals . . . drunkenness and vice . . . to bring anxiety and grief to American parents."

Louis Brandeis would join the Court in 1916, and two years later the justices held that Toledo's newspaper could be held liable for editorials and cartoons that lobbied for a particular outcome in a pending court case involving Toledo's streetcar system. "Freedom of the press" was a right like every other and therefore "subject to the restraints which separate right from wrongdoing."

It's true that Justice Holmes and Justice Brandeis dissented in that case, but the five paragraphs that they wrote in opposition were mostly based on the language of a particular statute at issue. After all, they valued the privacies of life just as much as their colleagues did.

Chapter Ten

HOLMES AND BRANDEIS
AND THE (REGULATED)
MARKETPLACE OF IDEAS

There's a certain mystique around the Supreme Court duo of Justice Oliver Wendell Holmes and Justice Louis Dembitz Brandeis. Holmes and Brandeis are First Amendment legends, having built the foundation for the powerful constitutional protection that freedom of expression enjoys in the United States today.

There's a First Amendment concept known as the marketplace of ideas, and we have Holmes and Brandeis to thank for that robustly speech-protective rhetoric in a 1919 case called *Abrams v. United States*. And the two kept at it all the way through to 1931 in a case called *Near v. Minnesota* that credited the power of the press and condemned prior restraints.

But there's something that's often missed in poetic language from Holmes and Brandeis that celebrates First Amendment interests: both justices continued to care deeply about privacy. And that language is there too if you look for it, even in the most supportive of First Amendment cases.

First, consider how strongly both felt about privacy in their personal lives.

Holmes, fifteen years older than Brandeis and a son of fame, had urged his pen pals—and there were many—to keep his letters private and began marking them as such. There was good reason. He would send notes to his friends on Supreme Court letterhead (despite his colleagues' strong disapproval), including those to "good looking" Clara Sherwood Rollins, a novelist thirty-three years his junior. He had "many longings" to see her and "so love[d]" her letters that would she please send him another "intimate" one with no coquettishness? (Some friends in memoirs called Justice Holmes downright "lusty," which sounds about right.)

He would also tell those pen pals that he well understood the importance of secrecy in their own letters, given "the feeling of family privacy" within many, and he promised that he would not reveal to anyone "anything that had the least touch of privacy." In line with that, he'd worked to stop the publication of one of his famous poet father's letters. "I am much obliged to you for your consideration in consulting me," he wrote to *The Century Magazine* when editors planned publication. "I should regret very much to see that [letter] published. Manifestly, it was not written for the public eye."

Fanny Holmes felt exactly the same way about keeping certain things secret. "She hates to have people talk or know of her private affairs," Holmes wrote to a friend about his wife. And Holmes blamed part of his family's loss of privacy directly on the press. Newspapers seemed motivated solely to reveal that men in the public eye "were all rascals," he'd said after about a decade on the Court, and he hinted that greater control might be warranted to stamp out the "free field" of "reporters uncontrolled" in the day's journalism. He hoped that journalists would one day shift toward the publication of "real information" regarding "important matters" and began to worry that certain people he would chance to meet at the Court—one a woman he described as "a casual unknown dame" who'd appeared at his office—were undercover reporters. It's no wonder that Holmes biographers continually note his "deep sense of privacy."

And the interplay between personal and professional was surely clear to Holmes. One month after the Supreme Court decided a case approving government seizure of private letters (Holmes and Brandeis in dissent: "plaintiff's private papers were stolen," and such behavior shocks "the common man's sense of decency and fair play"), Holmes sent that letter to his friend Harold Laski asking that Laski destroy their correspondence. "By the by I never have asked you to burn my letters," Holmes wrote, "but I should like to feel that their permanent privacy was secured in that or some other way" because, Holmes said, he liked to think that only that which he wanted made public about himself would be made public. (Holmes would have been mortified to learn that not only did Laski keep the letters, but that particular one and hundreds of others have been published in a two-volume set of books titled *Holmes-Laski Letters*, spanning from 1916 to 1935. Oddly enough, the part of the letter about Holmes's interest in privacy in his letters has been replaced with an ellipsis in the book.)

Brandeis felt the same about privacy, of course, given his history as co-author of the most famous law review article on the subject, though was a bit more confident in certain of the day's journalism; he'd by then developed a strong friendship with Norman Hapgood, an editor at *Collier's* and *Harper's Weekly* who believed that ethical journalists should not publish certain truths including "private facts" and who criticized journalists for their unwritten rule that news coverage of journalism itself should promote only the positive, lest journalism foul its own nest. Sure, Brandeis would eventually write that article that he'd promised for years titled "What Publicity Can Do" where he'd suggest that sunlight was the best disinfectant, but in it he argued only that investment bankers should be forced to reveal key financial information to potential investors; there's nothing at all in the piece regarding private revelations about public men or women.

Behind the scenes, Brandeis continued his work for personal privacy. He taught family members to keep private affairs private and not to discuss them publicly, and he'd tell his daughters to be sure that they not reveal particular letters. He also destroyed most of the correspondence kept by his longtime secretary. Certain family troubles, including his wife's depression, could have been a key reason that he wanted to keep family information from others. And of course his biographers have routinely noted his desire for privacy, as did friends. "Privacy was one of the things that mattered to him"; he guarded vigilantly the citadel of his privacy.

It's no wonder those interests found their way into Holmes-Brandeis jurisprudence too.

There's a famous case that appears at first read to be completely unrelated to privacy called *Lochner v. New York*, a 1905 Supreme Court decision in which Justice Holmes wrote a famous dissent while Brandeis was still a practicing lawyer. *Lochner* involved the appropriateness of government regulation of business and a baker named Joseph Lochner who'd asked his employees to work more than ten hours per day, which was a violation of New York law.

Most of the justices at the Court sided with Lochner, finding New York's regulation on workweek hours unconstitutional. If the baker and his bakeshop employees agreed that more hours were needed each week, they explained, it was for the bake staff to negotiate through contract; to decide otherwise would restrict the individual liberty promised by the Constitution.

But Holmes in dissent felt that some government regulation was appropriate. "It is settled by various decisions of this court," he wrote, "that state constitutions and state laws may regulate life in many ways." Liberty to Holmes didn't mean unfettered power to act however one might like. Instead, under the Constitution, the government should protect "fundamental principles as they have been understood by the traditions of our people and our law." He didn't mean originalism as much as current understanding of constitutional principles and how legal rights had developed through social norms over time, "the right of a majority to embody their opinions in law." He criticized the Court's ruling as one "decided upon an economic theory which a large part of the country does not entertain."

Brandeis joined the Supreme Court several years later, after a painful confirmation process that involved significant inquiry into his role in the Warren matter. At the hearings, Ned Warren's attorneys had argued that Brandeis had designed a plan to funnel millions to Sam Warren while Ned received a mere pittance, even though Brandeis had surely recognized that such a deal wasn't fair. Boston lawyers joined in the condemnation, and the Warren case, it was said, "probably claimed as much of the attention of the [judicial nomination] subcommittee as any other single matter." It all made banner headlines across the nation too, leading Brandeis to suggest that he would "have preferred to be let alone" until retirement. There was the suggestion—and anti-Semitism surely played a role here too—that Brandeis's nomination was about to fail.

But then Sam's sister, Cornelia Warren, wrote Brandeis a note condemning the attacks, suggesting that she hoped for his confirmation so that the country would have the benefit of Brandeis's "unselfish devotion to the public good." In response, Brandeis asked that the Warren family consider a note to the Senate Judiciary Committee saying as much, one that "should . . . make clear beyond peradventure the facts . . . that during all of the period not only you, but [all] understood and approved of everything that was done," including Ned's "long approval" of the trust. Brandeis said that he was especially concerned that the attacks on him during the hearing had also attacked Sam's memory when Sam "was indeed the soul of honor."

Maybe such a letter eventually found its way to the committee but maybe not, because it took several months after that for Brandeis to finally be confirmed.

Nearly immediately after that confirmation, as the 1920s neared, the justices decided several matters using language that danced around the right to privacy in the abstract, in cases famous and not, with Holmes and Brandeis uniting on most of the outcomes. Holmes and Brandeis and the rest of the Court wrote that the First Amendment promise of speech freedoms "would not protect a man in falsely shouting fire in a theatre," for example, because the "character of every act depends upon the circumstances in which it is done." They explained that "the First Amendment . . . cannot have been, and obviously was not, intended to give immunity for every possible use of language." And they slammed newspapers' power to do "injury to reputation" and suggested that it was highly important that the ancient doctrine "'Whatever a man publishes he publishes at his peril' should be strictly enforced."

That all led to the 1919 *Abrams* marketplace-of-ideas decision, a wartime case involving the publication of a handout titled "Revolutionists Unite for Action"—"Workers of the World! Awake! Rise! Put down your enemy and mine!"—and a law passed the year before that made it a crime to publish such materials. The Supreme Court majority decided that the First Amendment did not protect the publishers given that their words were meant "to excite, at the supreme crisis of the war, disaffection," specifically a strike of workers at ammunition factories.

But Justice Holmes dissented, and Justice Brandeis joined him. Their theory of the Constitution, they wrote, was that "free trade in ideas" was the best way to reach the desired ultimate societal good, "that the best test of truth is in the power of the thought to get itself accepted in the competition of the market." That marketplace-of-ideas language is found in writings by John Milton and John Stuart Mill, whom Holmes had recently reread, and it was the first time that Supreme Court justices had suggested that First Amendment principles encouraged more speech, more publication, in order to give people the most information so that they might ferret out truth from sampling many voices. (Holmes also read H. G. Wells, and just the year before Wells had included similar phrasing in a novel: "When Joan left Highmorton she came into the marketplace of ideas. She began to read the newspaper.")

Such language sounds broad and reads almost like a First Amendment–based celebration of the right to speak at will and to publish willy-nilly whatever one would like without regard to consequences, but that's not what Holmes and Brandeis meant. First, they limited their language of protection to *opinion* statements in the context of what was a clear and present danger *to the government*—"Of course I am speaking only of expressions of opinion and exhortations, which were all that were uttered here," Holmes wrote—and he suggested that each of the earlier cases that pushed back on such a marketplace in the context of war speech had been decided rightly.

Second, as stuck as Holmes was on the importance of privacy in his personal life, he couldn't have possibly intended that humiliating truths be allowed to rent a stall in his marketplace. Private information—say, another's intimate family letter or nude image or highly personal medical diagnosis—is all the more hurtful the more it is shared, and it needs no additional public discussion and assessment to determine its veracity.

And remember *Lochner*? Holmes was the one to suggest the importance of government regulation despite broadly worded promises of liberty written in the Constitution, particularly when that regulation was based on fundamental principles springing from the traditions of people and of law, perhaps even the *Commonwealth v. Blanding* protection for "faults, foibles, deformities of mind or person," and other protections for medical information and sexual information and nudity that by that point had long been a part of societal and legal norms.

Brandeis too. Three months after the *Abrams* decision, he complained to Felix Frankfurter, then a law professor at Harvard who would later become a Supreme Court justice himself, that the "general American trouble is that we make public what should be private [and] treat as private what is strictly a public matter," such as "the degree and nature" of then president Woodrow

Wilson's health. A few months later, he wrote that some words were indeed "within the permissible *curtailment* of free speech" and that the decision of where to draw the appropriate line would always be one of degree, just like "many other rules for human conduct." Free speech needed protection from both tyrannical majorities, he explained, and "abuse by irresponsible, fanatical minorities." In *Whitney v. California* too, a famous case from the 1920s upholding punishment for speech that threatened violent insurrection in which he famously warned that "men feared witches and burnt women" when they lacked access to full information, Justice Brandeis wrote quite clearly that in his view First Amendment rights are "fundamental" but "not in their nature absolute." And Justice Brandeis joined Justice Holmes's unanimous opinion for the Court that decade that found that "men's affairs" should not be made public simply because they work for companies involved in interstate commerce, that to "direct fishing expeditions into private papers" would "sweep all our traditions into the fire."

What that all means is that the Holmes and Brandeis marketplace of ideas was surely one subject to regulation, especially it seems with regard to privacy. Theirs was not a willy-nilly marketplace at all, free for anyone to publish anything at any time without consequence; it had scales of decency, you might say, that weighed other values and sometimes tipped in that other direction.

Justice Frankfurter, friend to them both, would eventually put it this way: it was very easy to pluck certain memorable phrases from opinions written by Holmes and Brandeis that suggested a sort of near First Amendment absolutism, but it would be wrong to do so. Justice Holmes had specifically fought against such a tendency, Frankfurter said, believing that when certain ideas "become encysted in phrases," those phrases "thereafter for a long time cease to provoke further analysis." "Freedom of the press," Frankfurter wrote, after suggesting that both Holmes and Brandeis were far from First Amendment absolutists, "is not a freedom from responsibility for its exercise."

And then, as even more substantive proof of privacy concerns in the worlds of Holmes and Brandeis, came *Olmstead v. United States*, a 1928 case involving a police investigation into unauthorized liquor sales during Prohibition. Police had rather routinely tapped telephone lines so that they could overhear conversations between bootleggers who used secret caches and secluded ranches, and buyers whose interest in intoxication was put at two hundred cases a day.

Olmstead is why Brandeis is doubly famous for the right to privacy.

Brandeis had played a behind-the-scenes role in the Supreme Court's decision to hear the case in the first place. First, he'd tried to persuade Scripps-Howard newspapers to report on the covert government behavior in part so that his fellow justices might come to recognize the problem of police wiretapping into private homes through phone lines. One editor had finally taken the bait, Brandeis relayed to his friend Felix Frankfurter, and a series titled "He Snoops to Conquer" resulted, one that outed "espionage in private and public affairs." Second, he asked Frankfurter to request copies of the series so that editors would recognize the public's interest in the topic. That would lead to additional coverage, he hoped, leaving his fellow justices all the more inspired to grant certiorari and hear the case.

Brandeis got his cert grant but not his preferred outcome because, in the end, a majority of the Supreme Court decided that the government wiretap was constitutional. "The [Fourth] Amendment does not forbid what was done here," the majority wrote. "There was no searching. There was no seizure. The evidence was secured by the use of the sense of hearing [without] entry of the houses or offices of the defendants." Holmes and Brandeis both disagreed in the name of privacy, of course, and it's Brandeis's dissenting opinion that's become famous and the modern approach to police wiretaps.

Brandeis's dissent tracked "The Right to Privacy" in many ways, but he never cited it, perhaps, some say, for reasons of modesty. He wrote that in modern times "subtler and more far-reaching" devices had been created to invade privacy, making it possible for others to reveal what was "whispered in the closet." He was especially worried about newer technology, he wrote, including the "evil incident to invasion of the privacy of the telephone" that made it possible to listen in on even the most confidential of conversations. He foresaw cloud-based storage and hacking to some extent: he predicted that the day would come when people "without removing papers from secret drawers, [would be able to] reproduce them in court" and thereafter reveal to a jury "the most intimate occurrences of the home." (He'd been just as worried about "radium and photography" and the developing power of television to peer back into a house to learn its secrets, and maybe even "advances in the psychic and related sciences" that could allow others to "explor[e] a man's unexpressed beliefs, thoughts, and emotions," but his in-the-present clerk urged him to scratch all that as very obviously impossible.)

And, finally, Brandeis credited the Founders for their strong sensibilities with regard to privacy. "They sought to protect Americans in their beliefs, their thoughts, their emotions and their sensations," he wrote. "The makers of our Constitution undertook to secure conditions favorable to the pursuit of happiness," recognizing the "significance of man's spiritual nature, of his feelings and of his intellect." These and the "privacies of life," he wrote, quoting that Supreme Court case from 1886, were of far greater importance than an unwarranted governmental quest for information that had some possibility to lead to a criminal conviction.

Holmes wrote a separate dissent, in part because Brandeis had droned on a bit, a complaint he had generally. "I fear that your early stated zeal for privacy carries you too far" is what he'd told Brandeis, and in *Olmstead* he explained that Brandeis had "given this case so exhaustive an examination" that he needed to add but a few sentences. One of them included the now-famous phrase that he thought "it a less evil that some criminals should escape than that the Government should play an ignoble part."

In any event, for some years to come, privacy interests in some ways swept the Court, much of it in nuanced dicta. "It has always been recognized in this country, and it is well to remember," one majority opinion from 1929 reads, connecting things up specifically with "the right of privacy," "that few if any of the rights of the people guarded by fundamental law are of greater importance to their happiness and safety than the right to be exempt from all unauthorized, arbitrary or unreasonable inquiries and disclosures in respect of their personal and private affairs."

And a few years later, Brandeis would write this for a unanimous Court: "The State has, of course, power to afford protection to interests of personality, such as 'the right of privacy.'"

Treatises on newspaper law were taking notice. They'd gone from not mentioning privacy as a legal right at all to including entire chapters devoted to it, even though, as one suggested, the right to privacy hadn't yet been clearly defined.

Then, in the middle of it all, landed a case that the journalist Fred Friendly would later say had saved freedom of the press.

The reality of that Supreme Court decision is not so clear.

The famous Supreme Court case of *Near v. Minnesota* began in a column filled with remorse and urgency in the very first edition of *The Saturday Press*, a twelve-page tabloid-sized newspaper—more of a newsletter, really—published in Minneapolis in September 1927. Its editors, the journalists Jay Near and Howard Guilford, apologized in their introductory remarks for being linked in the past with "a local scandal sheet" and suggested that they'd learned their lesson from their indiscretions. "We heartily regret ever in years gone past, having penned a line about the amorous misadventures of our fellow men," they wrote, "and we apologize to the public at large for each and every line."

You might wonder about their sincerity when, in the same column, they asked for dirt on those who'd been blackmailed by their peer publications in such a way, suggesting that hundreds in Minneapolis who'd dallied outside marriage had been threatened into paying a ransom of sorts to kill newspaper stories of personal scandal. Near and Guilford wanted to investigate that journalistic practice, they said, to talk with those "whose homes would be wrecked and the purpose for which they paid money defeated, were their better halves to discover their misfortune." They'd planned to write a news story about it all and promised to keep whatever information they received from informants confidential.

An interior masthead suggested that *The Saturday Press* would be "a weekly 'who's who and why,'" however, so dalliers must have been nervous about what was to come.

They needn't have worried for two reasons. First, despite its initial fixation on this particular type of personal scandal, *The Saturday Press* seemed mostly bent on investigating and revealing systemic wrongdoing in the city, including what Near and Guilford suggested was government-aided commercialized gambling and gangster rule. There were occasional disturbing blasts of anti-Semitism and racism in their stories to be sure, but the real focus of *The Saturday Press* throughout its initial nine-issue run was the revelation of government corruption in Minneapolis and the officials who seemingly helped things along.

Second, the police chief instantly ordered *The Saturday Press* removed from newsstands and threatened to arrest anyone who sold the paper. Guilford and Near, he said, had violated Minnesota's nuisance law, one that banned "malicious, scandalous and defamatory" newspapers, the types the law said were just as much an annoyance to the public as "houses of prostitution," "itinerant carnivals," overgrown "noxious weeds," and barking dogs.

It was action reminiscent of what had happened to Callender, Croswell, and Chase. But this time the newspaper editors would take their case to the U.S. Supreme Court, and this time they'd win.

It would be quite literally a painful road to victory in many ways: Guilford was shot a few days into the dispute, which was little surprise because he and Near had been warned that they'd be killed if they published what they knew.

The Minnesota Supreme Court sure didn't ease the pain when it ruled against *The Saturday Press* before trial. The newspaper was, the court wrote, the sort of publication that contained "a selection of scandalous and defamatory articles," information that had been "treated in such a way as to excite attention and interest so as to command circulation." The revelation of men's sins, "the evils of scandal," were detrimental to public morals and welfare, and the newspaper had "no constitutional right to publish a fact merely because it [was] true."

It all made the publication illegal if a jury agreed, and so the court ordered that Near and Guilford stand trial. They did, a jury found them guilty, and eventually the Minnesota Supreme Court again refused to give the two a break, advising that Near and Guilford simply publish a less scandalous newspaper, one "in harmony with the public welfare" that would keep them out of trouble with the government.

But then, in 1931, the U.S. Supreme Court decided to hear the case, for the journalist Fred Friendly *the* pivotal moment in the history of journalism and First Amendment jurisprudence. And in the same year that the Great Depression raged and someone identified as "Anonymous" published *Washington Merry-Go-Round*, a *Primary Colors*–like look at key players in the nation's capital and their political antics, the U.S. Supreme Court reversed the Minnesota court's ruling. The justices held that such a restriction on *The Saturday Press* preventing its publication was an unconstitutional prior restraint, an act on the part of the government in violation of the First Amendment liberty of the press to quash a publication simply because it found its promised focus worrisome. If officials could do what those in Minneapolis had done, constitutional protections including press freedom would be reduced to mere words on a page. The Minnesota statute, the Court said, was "the essence of censorship."

SUPREME COURT OPINION UPHOLDS THE CONSTITUTIONAL FREEDOM OF THE PRESS, *The Kansas City Star* reported in its headline; The *Miami Herald* read FREEDOM OF PRESS UPHELD IN DECISION. Hundreds of other newspapers joined in: COURT APPROVES PRESS FREEDOM; U.S. SUPREME COURT UPHOLDS THE FREEDOM OF THE PRESS; SUPREME COURT GUARANTEES FREEDOM OF THE PRESS.

But the justices—Holmes, Brandeis, and the rest of the majority—hadn't been that broad at all. Sure, the language that struck down the Minnesota statute was powerfully protective of the press, but it was not at all absolutist. The justices had written, for example, that the press could indeed be restrained before publication in certain cases. "No one would question but that a government might prevent . . . the publication of the sailing dates of transports or the number and location of troops," they wrote with regard to government interests. And they suggested that prior restraints might also be appropriate in cases involving certain private interests as well. The footnote there referenced a Roscoe Pound article in which he specifically argued that injunctions would be appropriate in invasion-of-privacy cases in order to prevent emotionally harmful exposure in the first place.

There was more. The justices repeatedly explained that their opinion in *Near* had nothing at all to do with subsequent punishment for publication. "Liberty of speech and of the press is also not an absolute right, and the state may punish its abuse," they wrote, repeating the line from Blackstone that if someone publishes information that is "improper, mischievous, or illegal," he must take the consequence of his own temerity. They threw in for good measure a reference to Justice Holmes's favorite case, *Commonwealth v. Blanding*. "The preliminary freedom extends as well to the false as to the true," they wrote, "the subsequent punishment may extend as well to the true as to the false."

This all reflected a strong distinction made by Justice Brandeis during oral argument in the *Near* case between information of public concern that should be made *public* because the public had the right to know it, such as information about certain government activities, and information that should be kept *private*, such as deeply personal information about individuals (and their marriages). "You are dealing here not with a sort of a scandal too often appearing in the press," Brandeis told the attorney for the government in *Near*, "and which ought not to appear to the interest of anyone." The revelations in the Near and Guilford newspaper, in contrast, concerned government corruption, "a matter of prime interest to every American citizen," information that they had the right to know.

Even in *Near*, therefore, the decision that was said to have saved freedom of the press, there exists a strong sensibility that freedom of speech, press, and expression does not mean freedom to publish all information whatsoever simply because it is true. As additional support, remember that line from Brandeis, written for a unanimous Supreme Court that said the government has the power to protect interests of personality such as the right of privacy? That was written by the Court in the years *following* the Supreme Court decision in *Near*, setting up cases that would come especially in the latter part of the twentieth century that more directly pitted the right to publish against the right to privacy.

But something else was happening at the time of *Near* that made those subtleties in language supporting the right to privacy less important. By 1931, Walter Lippmann, the journalist who'd worried about the "crisis" of journalistic invasions of privacy, had become editor of *The World*. And, as his editorship suggested, "reliable and comprehensive" newspapers had painted the more sensational "yellow journalism" "in a corner."

In other words, just as the right to privacy was becoming more of a norm in law, it was also becoming an accepted norm in journalism, exactly what Upton Sinclair had urged in *The Brass Check*. It would turn out to be a confluence that would ultimately make guarding privacy through the law increasingly less necessary. For a while.

Chapter Eleven

BE DECENT

Upton Sinclair wasn't the only media type hell-bent on instilling in journalism a respect for privacy back in the days of *Lochner* and *Olmstead* and *Near.* You might say that a missed stroke at a 1922 Washington, D.C., golf tournament helped to move things along in a big way too.

President Warren G. Harding, the golfer at issue, was all lined up to sink a putt at the Washington Country Club as part of a press-sponsored tournament, and the atmosphere was tense. If things went well, he could pull ahead of the members of the D.C. press corps and claim tournament victory. But even though the ball was at the lip of the cup, an easy tap, "a battery of motion picture machines, several of which sounded like airplanes," suddenly went off as Harding swung, and the ball arced away. The frustrated president seemed ready to break his putter in two but then remembered that he was on camera, walked calmly to the scoreboard to see where he stood, and ended up taking fourth. HARDING, FUSSED BY CROWD, LOSES PRESS GOLF HONOR BY A STROKE one headline read.

Harding's ethics advice to the nation's press started in earnest just after that missed putt. Within days, he'd gathered newspapermen to complain about the problems he'd seen in papers; the journalism of the day was too often focused on sensational stories that could do real emotional harm to an individual, he told them. Why not highlight instead the more stalwart citizens who righteously served government and country? Why focus on the negative?

This admonition had far more gravitas than Grover Cleveland's grousing. That's because, on his way into politics, Harding had owned and worked at the Marion, Ohio, newspaper for years, and his ethics-driven Harding's Creed, the privacy-respecting rules for his newsroom, had become legendary in journalism circles: be decent; boost, don't knock; there's good in everybody; never needlessly hurt the feelings of anybody; don't reveal misdeeds of a relative in a way that will bring embarrassment to an innocent family; never let a suggestive story get into type. Harding's Democratic opponent for the presidency, James M. Cox, had been a newspaperman too, but only one candidate, various Republican-leaning newspapers suggested by repeatedly republishing Harding's Creed, had a plan to make journalism more respectable.

The press listened with eager, sympathetic ears. "If he had been discussing his own private household," *The Baltimore Sun* wrote after Harding's "heart-to-heart" with reporters, "he probably would not have exhibited more sensitiveness." "The President speaks in such matters as a newspaper man," *The Christian Science Monitor* added, "and when his hearers chance to be those of that profession, he makes an impression."

The New York Times held out. "President Harding has some fairly fixed ideas upon what should and should not be published," it wrote, and "these ideas do not coincide with the stand of some newspapers that suppression leads to abuses and unwarranted control of public opinion."

Perhaps the *Times* knew just how hot the brewing Teapot Dome scandal would become; Harding's secretary of the interior, Albert Fall, would eventually go to jail for accepting bribes involving federal land leases. Harding's meeting with reporters had come not long after *The Wall Street Journal* had reported that something seemed amiss.

Or perhaps the *Times* knew that the married President Harding had had longtime affairs with at least two women, one of which had continued throughout his presidency and had produced a child. Harding kept love letters from those relationships safely tucked away and told his personal secretary to burn them when he died. Not all found their way into the fire.

In any event, Harding was on a tear after that golf tournament, lobbying for cheerful benevolence in the press as personal and professional scandal swirled around him.

One year after *Wall Street Journal* journalists scooped the Teapot Dome scandal, and just as the right to privacy by phrase was becoming more accepted in the nation's courts, the members of the American Society of Newspaper Editors, ASNE, met as a group in Washington to help draft national standards of behavior for journalists. And, of course, they invited the former journalist President Harding to join them.

By that point, the early 1920s, professional meetings involving journalists were fairly routine, even though this was the first for ASNE. Recall that Black journalists first met as a group in the 1870s to "shape a policy of their own." By 1882, those journalists called themselves the Colored Press Association, their annual meetings included topics like "Journalism and Journalism Ethics" by 1887, and W. Calvin Chase of *The Washington Bee* had become a leader of the organization by the 1890s—just before a judge sent him off to jail and President Cleveland kept him there for reporting truth about a political appointee.

As the Chase saga suggests, it's true that Black journalists had trouble at times drawing political speakers to their podium, so their meetings were different in that sense. Virginia's governor, Charles O'Ferrall, for one, refused their invitation to speak after the member Ida B. Wells had persuaded her colleagues to vote as a unified voice against lynchings of Black men in the South. The brutes were not the lynchers themselves, Governor O'Ferrall had irritatedly explained in a letter to Chase, but those Black men who'd committed "a certain crime" worse than death and were of course "summarily dealt with" in response. "I would not think of accepting an invitation to address any convention or assembly that indorses . . . the course of Ida Wells in her slander of the people and civil authorities of the South," the governor had written.

But this was the 1920s, and ASNE members were mostly white (the nonmember Lester Walton, a Black reporter for the New York *World*, had sent a telegram petitioning members to capitalize the *N* in "Negro" and to leave the word out of headlines completely, but his request was referred to committee). Plus, ASNE's invitation to President Harding was special. The editors had told him that they wanted to "pay their respects" to a fellow editor whom they'd named a special member and to get his input on their ethics plan.

Harding happily accepted. He had more lobbying to do.

Harding's audience wasn't what he would have found in the late nineteenth century in another way. Most of the journalists gathered in Washington for the ASNE convention weren't scrappy catch-as-catch-can printers like in the old days, and some had even graduated from formal journalism programs.

Those programs had had a lackluster start. In 1875, Cornell University taught journalism in an effort to better what its president had called the deplorable and very serious deficiencies in the profession, but the program lagged. Washington and Lee University would deny in 1875 that there had ever been "any prescribed course of study" in journalism in its halls, but that wasn't exactly true, because Robert E. Lee had tried but failed to start one in "practical printing and journalism" just after the Civil War as part of his rehabilitation of the South.

By the time "The Right to Privacy" was published in 1890, such training had gained a bit more of a foothold. University of Missouri students were starting to take classes in journalism, and students in the University of Pennsylvania's Courses in Journalism program started learning "Newspaper Practice" and the "Law of Libel and Business Management." *Reporting for the Newspapers*, a small book with chapters titled "What Is News" and "A News Story Analyzed," appeared in 1901. By 1914, instructors at Columbia's journalism school—one endowed by Joseph Pulitzer, curiously enough, who also endowed the Pulitzer Prize awards there—used newsreel films to teach students how to write with "real news values." And by the year of Harding's missed putt, Fisk University had included in its journalism curriculum a course called "Ethics of Journalism," lectures that "discuss[ed] the proper responsibility to the public on the part of newspaper writers."

A formal national ethics standard seemed the next logical step; journalists were said to be "agitating for a set of rules of conduct" that would create the same sort of "ethical standardization" that doctors and lawyers had.

There were several local and regional ethics codes to cobble from at the time in addition to Harding's Creed, mostly all turn-of-the-century or later creations, and very nearly all of them similarly touched on privacy. The 1915 University of Missouri Journalist's Creed, for one: "no one should write as a journalist what he would not say as a gentleman," and news should contain clean and "helpful truth." The Oregon code read that "mercy and kindliness" were important, that news should not be sensational, and that "if the public or social interest seems to be best conserved by suppression," reporters should suppress. Journalists in Kansas had passed a resolution that rejected spy-like behavior and criticized the publication of gossip and scandal "however true." *The Emporia Gazette* had refused to publish the details of divorces by the early 1920s, because "the harrowing details that mark the wreck of any home are not news" and "are often salacious, sometimes debasing, and always abnormal." *The Detroit News*, in turn, told its reporters to be generous especially if a woman slipped into naughtiness because she may be in crisis: "printing the story may drive her to despair; kindly treatment may leave her with hope"; and "no story is worth ruining a woman's life—or man's either." An Ohio ethics code seemed a nod to *Cape Cod Folks*, advising newspapers never to "subject innocent persons to disgrace, ridicule, or contempt by unwarranted publicity." Even the Hearst papers had an ethics code, but their "omit things that will offend nice people" was tempered with the suggestion that "most sensational news can be told if it is written properly."

Back in Washington as the journalists and their codes came together at the American Society of Newspaper Editors convention, the featured speaker, President Harding, received the same level of unqualified respect that the *Sun* and the *Monitor* had given him earlier. He was "the most distinguished journalist in the world, the Editor-in-Chief of the United States of America," those who introduced him said to great applause, even though every single person in that room had surely heard the talk about both Fall and the extramarital fallen. Harding had titled his talk "Journalism," and his biggest point was this: there was never a time when a code of ethics—a "strict" one—was more important to the press of America.

Sure, he was appalled at the lack of accuracy in newspapers, he said, and reports of his broken-in-anger golf clubs were totally wrong, but newspapers also needed to be more decent. Comforting truth was better than scandal, he advised, which meant that "everything of a vicious character except that which [was] necessary as a public warning" should be kept out of papers. News of arrests was a special problem along with "the excessive publication of sensational vice." He'd learned as much from his experience at *The Marion Star*, he told his fellow editors, after a man had begged him in the interests of family to keep his misdeeds out of the paper, when Harding did as the man requested, and when the man reformed. It was time, Harding said, for editors to do as he'd done, to repay their debt to America for journalism's freedoms by drafting an ethics code that would omit those sorts of stories that tended to destroy the faith in society. There were "often times when the news ought to be suppressed," he said.

What he didn't say, of course, was that an emphasis on ethics and suppression—an interest in privacy, really—could help him personally.

The very first national code of ethics for journalists in the United States was voted into existence that day. ASNE's "Canons of Journalism" had seven separate sections: "Responsibility"; "Freedom of the Press"; "Independence"; "Sincerity, Truthfulness, Accuracy"; "Impartiality"; "Fair Play"; and "Decency." The final two sections had the most relevance to privacy. "A newspaper should not invade private rights or feelings without sure warrant of public right as distinguished from public curiosity," one line in "Fair Play" read. The "Decency" section suggested that "details of crime and vice" should be omitted for the general good. Drafters said that they'd used that precise language to be responsive to complaints from politicians and others in high places that reporters had assumed "a right to violate with pen and camera, the constitutional privacy" of individuals, especially those involved in scandals or disasters, and they'd specifically called privacy a "right" in discussing those provisions.

The provisions worked. Many in the profession considered the new ASNE ethics code "the Bible of the American journalist." But, as with the other Bible, a passage could have alternate meanings depending upon reader interpretation, and the privacy provisions were balanced with lines like "Freedom of the press is to be guarded as a vital right of mankind" and "it is the unquestionable right to discuss whatever is not explicitly forbidden by law." And so, in 1934, the ethics-sensitive Upton Sinclair was the first to report that the newspaper baron William Randolph Hearst was having an affair with an unnamed film actress—his "movie mistress"—who turned out to be the Hollywood star Marion Davies.

President Harding praised the new ASNE code, especially the privacy-protecting part. He died about three months later. Four years after that, one of Harding's mistresses published *The President's Daughter*, a "proper and true account of the relations of the author with Warren G. Harding," including the fact that she'd fallen in love with Harding when she was thirteen and he was in his forties. Their first kiss would come when she was eighteen and he was in his early fifties, after Harding, then a U.S. senator, had invited her up to a New York hotel's "bridal chamber" so that their discussion of a possible job and her admiration of him "might continue . . . without interruptions or annoyances." Later, he'd register her at hotels as his niece. Police had tried to stop publication of *The President's Daughter* at the direction of a group known as the Society for the Suppression of Vice; they confiscated the book's plates and printed pages for its "obscene, lewd and indecent" passages "descriptive of improper activities" involving President Harding. But the book was published anyway, the passages weren't obscene or lewd or indecent, and that's when readers learned that at just around the time Harding missed that putt on the golf course in Washington, D.C., and had that heart-to-heart with journalists, he had told his mistress that he wanted to make their brand-new baby "a real Harding." If only he could.

In 1929, two years after *The President's Daughter* came out, a jury convicted Secretary Fall of bribery. And in more modern times, the Library of Congress released in 2014 some of the letters that President Harding had hoped would be kept secret. "Won't you please destroy?" President Harding had asked one of his girlfriends. "You are not always careful with letters, and if you destroy, you won't need to be careful."

In the 1930s, a little more than a decade after ASNE passed its first code and just around the time of *Near*, journalism scholars began to study how closely newspapers followed their relatively new ethics provisions. Some sensational tabloids remained sensational, though they'd lessened considerably in number just as Walter Lippmann had predicted, and those that remained weren't the same. Even the notorious *Police Gazette* by that time promised readers "Boxing News, Views and Broadway Gossip" and mostly delivered that pabulum. What the scholars called "conservative" newspapers practiced journalism far more ethically, and their numbers had grown and were growing. *The New York Times*—a newspaper that had marketed itself for decades as "the model of decent and dignified journalism"—was near the very top of the ethics-abiding group, just a bit behind *The Christian Science Monitor*, and many others followed on that ethics-abiding list. Concerns about privacy and its conflict with "printing all the news" were another differentiating factor between "conservative" and "semi-conservative" and "sensational newspapers," the scholars reported; the many that fell into one of the conservative camps had become increasingly concerned with "the right to privacy" and an individual's personal reputation.

And this decided turn toward ethics is why Frank Mott in his book *American Journalism* called the 1920s "the beginning of the end of the worst phase of 'gutter journalism'" and found that by the 1930s the end of World War I, the ravages of the Great Depression, and the rumblings of a new war had all affected news sensibilities. Walter Winchell's lighthearted and sometimes mistake-filled celebrity gossip column was not the norm; by that point, many newspapers featured instead steady, responsible Pulitzer Prize–winning reporters and columnists who stood for and stood up for growing newspaper responsibility.

So complete was journalism's shift toward professionalism and so great was its growing respectability that in 1937 Walt Disney published a Big Little Book for children titled *Mickey Mouse Runs His Own Newspaper*. Mickey's policy at *The Daily War-Drum* was "to print the truth," to reveal "the gangsters and crooked politicians" in town. You know the rest: Mickey reported on corruption, the bad guys went to jail, and Mickey received a mayoral commendation. That photograph taken surreptitiously by a *Daily War-Drum* reporter who had "a camera an' a nosey disposition"? Mickey refused to publish it. The very next year, Superman first disguised himself as the *Daily Planet*'s reporter Clark Kent, and Brenda Starr would get her start at *The Flash* on the comics page two years later.

And so it went. Journalism became less licentious and more Edward R. Murrow, and its professionalism slowly began to turn the nascent right to privacy in Supreme Court dicta and common-law court decisions into something far more conceptual and less of a battle zone. Nationally, cases in state and federal courts that used the phrase "the right to privacy" or its iterations barely grew in number, from approximately 65 in the 1920s to 100 in the 1930s to 180 in the 1940s. If nobody invaded privacy, nobody needed to sue for it.

But don't be fooled. Privacy in a legal sense was never at any risk of dying.

The best example of this from around that time was surely the sex-crazed, celebrity-obsessed journalist Frank Harris, best known for his work for *Pearson's Magazine*. It's true that celebrity journalism had been a thing long before Winchell's infamous column—following the 1882 *Album of Portraits of Celebrities* booklet, *The Motion Picture Story Magazine* was up and running in 1911 and paparazzi shortly thereafter were "armed with the new flashlight contrivance and ready to catch the elusive celebrity"—but nobody had ever written truth like Frank Harris had. His goal, he said, was to teach young people "how to use their machine gun[s] of sex" and, in doing so, pit press and expression and speech freedoms directly against the right to privacy.

That meant readers of Harris's autobiographical series *My Life and Loves*, published in multiple volumes throughout the 1920s, learned that the author Guy de Maupassant had once visited six prostitutes in one hour; Guy had stamina and syphilis. The illustrator Aubrey Beardsley first had sex with his own sister. And the poet Walt Whitman had "half a dozen illegitimate children and perverse tastes to boot."

But the most graphic of revelations in Harris's reportorial account involved his own real-life, noncelebrity conquests (student Kate, adult Laura, teenager Grace, many more, all identified) and their detailed bodily responses to his physical wooings. Some of the vignettes involve girls, and some involve what we'd surely consider sexual assault, including one that he describes as his most amatory experience. Friends do not escape his revelations; one real-life teacher had shared a deeply personal sexual problem with Harris and agreed to a bizarre remedy, all of which Harris described in gruesome and highly embarrassing detail. ("I went at once in search of whipcord, and tied up his unruly member for him night after night" offers some sense of the story.)

Frank Harris argued that he had the right to reveal all that, that, as a journalist, he'd always fought for the Holy Spirit of Truth and, here, he would once more. "I am resolved to dare speak whatsoever I dare do," the preface to volume 2 of *My Life and Loves* reads. He'd already fashioned himself a First Amendment soldier, criticizing the Supreme Court in a *Pearson's* essay for putting Eugene Debs in jail "in direct contradiction of the Constitution."

But he found few comrades this time. Upton Sinclair called the Harris autobiography vile, inexcusable, and poisonous. Others worried that *My Life and Loves* would taint all journalism and become "a serious blow to the cause of freedom."

The broad taint never materialized, but the government did ban *My Life and Loves* pretty much instantly. England did the same. Such punishment was easy enough, given that Harris had mainly published his work in Paris and the government could stop the books in customs on the rock-solid grounds of obscenity: while privacy required a wronged plaintiff motivated to sue, courts as early as 1811 agreeably prohibited the entry of "pernicious animals, or *an obscene book*, or infectious goods, or anything else that the Legislature shall deem noxious or inconvenient." Today, obscenity remains one of the categories that the Supreme Court routinely suggests has very little First Amendment protection, given its "slight social value as a step to truth" and how that smidge of value is "clearly outweighed by the social interest in order and morality." In modern times, the Supreme Court has suggested the same thing about privacy violations too.

Old copies of *My Life and Loves*, therefore, quite literally warned, "MUST NOT BE IMPORTED INTO ENGLAND OR U.S.A."

The ban on *My Life and Loves*—the law's rejection of Harris's Holy Spirit of Truth—continued well beyond the time of *Near*. Twenty years after its initial appearance, judges in the 1940s sent bookshop owners in the United States to jail for selling the Harris work, and in 1959 reports were that smuggled-in copies were going for up to $150 on the black market.

An edited-for-certain-content version of Harris's autobiography finally appeared in an official sense in the United States in 1963. That same year, a magazine called *Eros* published "expurgated" excerpts—"I had hardly any sex-thrill with either sister" truncates things nicely—and a federal judge decided that they helped to support a criminal obscenity conviction against *Eros* because, given the prose, the judge had "little difficulty" finding all "the requisite elements." There was no "saving grace" here either, no claims of the work's contribution to great literature that had saved books like *Lady Chatterley's Lover*.

The U.S. Supreme Court affirmed the *Eros* obscenity conviction in 1966, two years *after* deciding the landmark *New York Times v. Sullivan*. *Sullivan* strongly protects publications on First Amendment grounds, creating the actual malice standard that makes it difficult for a famous person to win a defamation case, and there the Court wrote that the whole point of the First Amendment was "to secure 'the widest possible dissemination of information from diverse and antagonistic sources'" and warned that freedom of expression should not be handicapped. But not even *Sullivan* could save *Eros* from *My Life and Loves*.

Given all this, is it any wonder that it takes some digging and a significant amount of cash to land original physical copies of *My Life and Loves* today? One single autographed volume was going for more than $1,000 recently, probably because some sellers spin the series as "a landmark in erotic literature" what with its "blunt, colorful depictions of [Harris's] sexual exploits." But that's whitewashed reality because these are graphic, deeply personal stories about people in their most intimate moments, people who had no idea that they'd be revealed in such a way. As the poet Robert Browning told Harris when Harris asked about Browning's sex life, there are "things that the public has no right to know."

But Frank Harris was an outlier whose focus on truth at all human emotional costs would soon be quieted in the groundswell of overall goodness that journalism was well on its way to becoming. In response to a stronger embrace of ethics principles, courts began to put into words that they deferred to journalists' news judgment and their assessment of the public's right to know. One decided that filming an Arctic expedition was okay even though the explorers didn't want the journalists there. The "heroic adventure" was one of great public interest, the court wrote, and "news concerning it or its progress, [was] a matter to which the public [was] entitled." "Certainly, this Court should proceed with caution before it attempts to sit as a censor and to interfere with the traditional right of the Press to print all printable news," another court wrote.

In the next century, however, the Frank Harris story, as told by Frank Harris, would become a much more common one as media transformed itself in the age of the internet.

In more recent times, ethics has swept mainstream newsrooms, and modern journalists understand that they can lose their jobs if they fail to abide by certain ethics standards. This means that, today, Frank Harris would be fired at the first *rat-a-tat* of his machine gun of sex, freedom of expression or not. Those privacy-based ethics provisions are solid and universal:

- National Public Radio: "With all subjects of our coverage, we are mindful of their privacy as we fulfill our journalistic obligations."
- *The New York Times:* "We do not inquire pointlessly into someone's personal life."
- Radio Television Digital News Association: "The right to broadcast, publish or otherwise share information does not mean it is always right to do so."

Today, an organization called the Society of Professional Journalists oversees the national code of ethics for journalists, and that code too contains privacy-related provisions. The "Minimize Harm" section, for example, suggests that "ethical journalism treats sources, subjects, colleagues and members of the public as human beings deserving of respect." It reads in part,

—Balance the public's need for information against potential harm or discomfort. Pursuit of the news is not a license for arrogance or undue intrusiveness.

—Show compassion for those who may be affected by news coverage.

—Recognize that legal access to information differs from an ethical justification to publish or broadcast.

—Realize that private people have a greater right to control information about themselves than public figures and others who seek power, influence, or attention. Weigh the consequences of publishing or broadcasting personal information.

—Avoid pandering to lurid curiosity, even if others do.

—Balance a suspect's right to a fair trial with the public's right to know.

—Consider the long-term implications of the extended reach and permanence of publication. Provide updated and more complete information as appropriate.

There are counterbalances in this latest code too, those that tell journalists to "seek truth and report it" and to be "courageous in gathering, reporting and interpreting information." That means that, just like in Upton Sinclair's time, it's often a question of interpretation and, given a particular set of facts, some newsrooms will tend toward privacy while others will publish. In many situations, there is no 100 percent right answer.

At the turn of the twenty-first century—during the Wild West of a new thing called the Internet that we blessed with a capital *I*, when suddenly anyone with a keyboard and a connection could make publishing happen—there was a grassroots movement to draft a similar code of ethics for those who had started what came to be known as weblogs or blogs. The movement failed. Bloggers, many of whom were delighted to be blasting through the gates of propriety, said they were worried that any such code would tie their hands, that it would curtail their First Amendment freedom to express themselves.

The First Amendment part of their concerns made little sense, given that, as the history of the right to privacy shows, the law has often punished egregious revelations without regard to who did the publishing; bloggers or Facebook posters or online commenters don't have special freedoms to invade privacy or harm reputations simply because they're not journalists and don't know any better.

But they were right to worry about a standardized code in one sense because, by the first decade of the twenty-first century, some judges had become frustrated with modern media, and in response had started to use the Society of Professional Journalists' code as a weapon against journalism itself. If journalists violated an ethics provision, these judges decided, that helped to establish the journalists' liability. Privacy rights would triumph, supported even by the defendant.

In response, the Society of Professional Journalists placed a brand-new warning at the very end of its ethics code explaining that the code "is not intended as a set of 'rules' but as a resource for ethical decision-making." "It is not—nor can it be under the First Amendment—legally enforceable," the SPJ added hopefully.

But this is all getting a bit ahead of our story, because before there were renegade bloggers who happily invaded the privacy of the innocent and naive, there was a writer for *The New Yorker* and his target, William Sidis, child genius. Perhaps you've heard of him.

Chapter Twelve

PANDORA'S BOX,
THE SOURCE OF EVERY EVIL

Here's what a judge wrote in 1804 in the *Croswell* case, the one in which Alexander Hamilton argued for qualified press freedom: when we say freedom of the press, we can't possibly mean it in an absolute sense, because total press freedom "would be emphatically Pandora's box, the source of every evil."

That sounds hyperbolic, but not in the case of William Sidis, child genius.

Sidis's story started, in effect, in 1910, when he was eleven years old and already an undergraduate at Harvard. In his second term, he was asked to give a lecture he titled "Four-Dimensional Bodies," an overview of the fourth dimension and related mathematics. Distinguished professors, it is said, sat, listened, and "gazed in wonder."

Journalists gushed. *The New York Times* ran a seven-column story featuring a drawing of young Sidis; the lead paragraph compared him with Jesus at the Temple. Some papers suggested he was the Greek mathematician Euclid reincarnated. *The Baltimore Sun* headlined its story WILLIAM J. SIDIS, 11 YEARS OLD, *THE* MOST WONDERFUL BOY *IN THE* WORLD.

"It's very strange," Sidis told the *Sun* reporter that day in what was described as the clear high voice of an eleven-year-old, "but you know I was born on April Fool's Day."

As you might have guessed, the little guy nearly immediately cracked under the pressure. Within hours, Sidis took to bed, saddled with "the grip" and "overstudy," and newspapers reported that he was "breaking down." In its story headlined THE PRODIGY'S COLLAPSE, *The Washington Post* offered an incongruous prescription: withdrawal of news interest. The mystery illness had likely come about, the *Post* suggested, because William's parents had failed to protect him "from the wearisome exclamations and admirations of injudicious observers."

Coverage continued even so. When Sidis graduated from Harvard College in 1914, Warren Harding's *Marion Star* chose BOY WIZARD IS NOW A GRADUATE as the headline for its laudatory one-paragraph story, and that was precisely the tone in most newspapers. But then Sidis, you might say, slipped at a time when most newspapers had yet to develop a *Star*-like ethics code. He told a reporter that he would never marry and that he'd taken a personal vow of celibacy, a promise to himself that he'd commemorated with a medal. He was seventeen. Some newspapers called him a freak.

After that, reporters stopped gushing.

Sidis, whose dream was to become a lawyer, entered Harvard Law School that next fall. And it's possible that he heard those words from *Croswell* equating press freedom with evil there because Roscoe Pound, who taught at Harvard and knew Sidis, used *Croswell* as precedent when he wrote about the right to privacy. Pound is the one who argued in his *Near*-cited law review article that injunctions were appropriate in privacy cases.

Maybe Sidis would have made an outstanding lawyer, but we'll never know because he dropped out in his third year, just before graduation, even though his grades were fine.

That sealed the deal. Sidis officially became a national oddity, a "curious tragedy," "a remarkable instance of the rise and fall of an infant prodigy," who'd taken a job as a clerk in New York City clad in "an inexpensive, ill fitting suit," adding machine at his side, for $23 a week. In 1924 alone, more than two hundred newspapers across the nation carried word of his wretched failure in life with headlines like SAD CASE OF WILLIAM J. SIDIS: ALL HEAD AND NO HEART.

"Today," the New York *Daily News* reported, he "asks merely that he be let alone."

But not even that was what made Sidis most famous.

As William Sidis was making his way in Manhattan, the right to be let alone was continuing its rather slow but steady pace toward acceptance by name in the nation's courts. Sure, many newspapers had embraced ethics, but not always, and courts were still willing to find invasions of privacy in certain situations.

Some judges protected health matters in particular. One decided that a newspaper could be liable for publishing a news story and photograph featuring a deceased child born with his heart outside his body. Like those of the earlier conjoined twins, the plaintiff-parents had argued that the publication violated their right of privacy, that the circumstances of their child's birth and death were not for public consumption, and the court agreed. Another sided with a plaintiff against a newspaper that had published her abdominal X-ray; she had a viable claim for a right to privacy even though the image accurately and alarmingly showed that a doctor had indeed left a clamp inside her. And a third court held a newspaper liable for publishing a photograph of a woman lying outside, overcome by gas fumes. Privacy, that court wrote, sprang from an individual's basic right to liberty, and privacy was essential to human happiness.

Criminal matters received strong protection from some judges too. One found a newspaper liable for publishing photographs of a criminal defendant against the judge's orders. "The liberty of the press does not include the privilege of taking advantage of the incarceration of a person accused of crime to photograph his face and figure against his will," the court wrote, embracing in some sense the card swindler's claim from years before. Another ruled that a former prostitute had a right to privacy in her past life, condemning the crime reenactment program that had featured her story. "Right-thinking members of society," the court wrote, should permit people "to continue in the path of rectitude" rather than throw them "back into a life of shame or crime."

And all this is why, despite relatively sparse mention of a "right to privacy" by phrase in court decisions, the well-respected American Law Institute in the late 1930s came to embrace it anyway. Restatement authors—those respected judges, law professors, and lawyers tasked with restating the common law—drafted and enacted "Interference with Privacy." This Restatement provision is the one that recognized the existence of a valid legal claim against a person who "unreasonably and seriously interferes with another's interest in not having his affairs known to others"; such interference would include times when "intimate details" of one's life were exposed to the public or when "photographs of a person in an embarrassing pose are surreptitiously taken and published."

And lest those judges lacking precedent but deciding privacy cases be led astray by constitutional language promising press freedoms, the ALI offered three solid examples of ways in which media would be held liable for invading privacy:

1. by following a person around for a week and thereafter publishing an article detailing that person's behavior;
2. by publishing a film of an abdominal operation surreptitiously recorded from an operating room's skylight; and
3. by secretly capturing a photograph of a "hideously deformed" person and thereafter publishing it and "stating truthfully that [his] condition resulted from inexpert treatment at birth" in an article on the need for better medical care in rural communities.

The famous would be treated somewhat differently, Restatement authors wrote, because they "must necessarily pay the price of even unwelcome publicity," but those public people would be protected too when the publisher exceeded the bounds of what the authors called "fair comment" on their current or past behavior.

It was a momentous development in the legal community. The right to privacy had become official in some sense, a part of what might be considered the nation's most influential law book, a definition that could (and ultimately did) sweep through courts throughout the United States, thereby creating a national standard. But those on the outside heard little about it, from newspapers or otherwise. As worries about Hitler's power spread, President Franklin Delano Roosevelt focused instead on how constitutional freedoms had promoted national strength; the United States had become powerful "without a scratch on freedom of speech, freedom of the press or the rest of the Bill of Rights," he'd said. (Just a few years before, however, he'd unsuccessfully pushed for a code of conduct for newspapers as part of the Depression-era National Recovery Act and had envisioned bestowing on compliant newspapers an image of a blue eagle as a sort of presidential seal of approval.)

Given the Restatement's endorsement, the right to privacy continued on even so. The 180 or so cases in state and federal courts throughout the United States that mentioned the right shortly thereafter in the 1940s included one that found in line with earlier courts that a newspaper could well be liable for publishing a picture of a man as part of criminal coverage (privacy "is still in its infancy," the court wrote, but the plaintiff had a valid argument that "the use of his photograph, as published in connection with a magazine story of a crime, and not as news, violated his right of privacy" and caused him ridicule). Another held a newspaper liable for publishing a story about a "starving glutton" who had a rare medical condition. The author Marjorie Kinnan Rawlings of *The Yearling* fame had included a truthful but "vivid and intimate character sketch" of a neighbor in her book *Cross Creek*—"My profane friend Zelma, the census taker, said, 'The b——s killed the egrets for their plumage until the egrets gave out. They killed alligators for their hides until the alligators gave out. If the frogs ever give out, the sons of b——s will starve to death'"—and Rawlings found herself potentially liable too. That detailed description of her oblivious and trusting friend's use of profanity made a solid case for invasion of privacy.

The courts that decided as much would often cite Warren and Brandeis, Cooley and Pound, and then suggest that the information wasn't the sort of thing that a discriminating reader would want to read anyway. Many came to agree, in company with Alexander Hamilton decades before, that these sorts of privacy cases were simply matters of deciding what was of appropriate public concern, "whether the occasion or incident [was] one of proper public interest." It's just that a small number of judges were bolder news editors than others; they felt freer to tamp down the public's right to know when, as in the Restatement examples, the facts seemed particularly private. Privacy meant "the unwarranted appropriation of one's personality," one legal publication read in 1942, "the publicizing of one's private affairs with which the public has no concern," and was "predicated upon the constitutional guaranties of life, liberty, and the pursuit of happiness."

It's getting ahead of things just a bit, but the notion that press freedom would be tempered by privacy thereafter percolated beyond the nation's borders and reached countries around the globe, due in some part to American Law Institute sensibilities. As World War II raged, the ALI suggested a new project that it called the "International Bill of Rights." The "Personal Rights" section stated that "freedom of opinion and of speech" was "the right of everyone," and the use of the phrase "freedom of *opinion*"—and not freedom to *publish*—underscored the importance of the right to privacy. The draft contained an even more direct privacy provision: that "everyone shall have the right to be free from interference with his private life and activities" and that governments around the world had a duty to ensure that people were protected in such a way.

The American Law Institute never enacted its own International Bill of Rights, but the draft provided the foundation for the Universal Declaration of Human Rights, one of the best-known, most cited, and most followed human rights documents in the world, adopted by the United Nations in 1948. The declaration's original author explained that he'd read numerous documents on human rights before drafting, that the "best of the texts" from which he worked "was the one prepared by the American Law Institute" and that he therefore "borrowed freely from it."

Article 12 of the Universal Declaration of Human Rights reads, "No one shall be subjected to arbitrary interference with his privacy, family, home or correspondence, nor to attacks upon his honour and reputation. Everyone has the right to the protection of the law against such interference or attacks." Article 19 reads, "Everyone has the right to freedom of opinion and expression; this right includes freedom to hold opinions without interference and to seek, receive and impart information and ideas through any media and regardless of frontiers."

Those articles in the Universal Declaration of Human Rights in turn influenced the European Convention on Human Rights, adopted in 1953 and the most important human rights document in Europe, including its article 8, which protects privacy ("Everyone has the right to respect for his private and family life, his home and his correspondence"), and its article 10, which protects expression ("Everyone has the right to freedom of expression").

And because privacy rights and press rights are, in effect, given equal weight in those documents, protection of people—the right to privacy— many times prevails. In 2016, for example, the highest court in the United Kingdom told its newspapers that they could not publish a story that had been widely distributed on the internet about a man identified only as "PJS," who was married to a major celebrity and yet had had an affair with two others. Such a publication seemed a clearly unjustified invasion of privacy, the court decided, "however absorbing it might be to members of the public interested in stories about others' private sexual encounters." There, article 10 was little counterbalance against the importance of the unnamed celebrity's right to privacy.

Ironically, therefore, as Europe and the world shifted toward greater protection for privacy, helped along by what was ultimately the sort of privacy initially suggested by the American Law Institute, the United States continued the weight of its legal protections more toward the press and the freedom to publish. The United States–based *National Enquirer*, for example, was only too happy to name Elton John's husband, David Furnish, as the mysterious PJS.

But before all that, just a few years before the International Bill of Rights would begin to find support in other countries, the former child genius William Sidis was nearing forty and living in an apartment in South Boston with, as it turns out, very little privacy. And, in many circles at least, that's what he was about to become most famous for.

There's a certain incongruity in the July 10, 1937, issue of *The New Yorker* if you know to look for it. The cover features a cartoon of a young woman sunbathing nude on the roof of a skyscraper. She's curled in a near-fetal position, looking up with sudden alarm, clutching her arms to cover her chest with a towel.

Spreading across the rooftop is the shadow of an airplane passing overhead. Someone is watching.

But the concern for privacy ends with the cover. Just inside the magazine, the "Talk of the Town" column contains a rant against the Newspaper Guild, what was then a newly formed union for journalists with its own ethics code. (Newspapermen, the guild believed, should be guided "by a decent respect for the rights of individuals.") Making journalism isn't like making steel, someone at *The New Yorker* had written, because steel is the sort of thing that requires hard, cold uniformity while journalism's vibrancy required a multitude of voices from people free to follow their own drummers.

"Unless newspapermen in the aggregate are disorganized in their personal life," "The Talk of the Town" reads, "they are valueless to society" and devitalized. Instead, journalistic temperaments needed to be free to be individualistic, not totalitarian, not idealistic in a norms sense, and no group norm should be imposed to curb the news judgment of the individual journalist. Bluntly put, an organized press with strict standards threatened a newspaperman's freedom. And while we're at it, "What *is* a newspaperman, anyway?"

The humorist and cartoonist James Thurber could well have had a hand in that particular column. Thurber was assigned "The Talk of the Town" when he first joined *The New Yorker*, he's credited with giving it a voice, and he continued his contributions to the column into late 1937. He also wrote at least one additional piece humorously discrediting ethics for reporters and suggesting that journalistic standards led to less interesting writing.

And for the former child genius William Sidis at least, someone *was* watching, namely a woman connected with *The New Yorker* and Thurber. By then she'd attended the class on American Indians that Sidis led weekly in his boardinghouse room and, without identifying herself as a journalist, took notes about what Sidis said there, what he did there, and how things looked there.

The woman then returned to the magazine and supplied the information to Thurber, who in August 1937 published a piece titled "Where Are They Now? April Fool!" It was an exposé of William Sidis, the freak, now fully grown and ever more pathetic. The point, Thurber would later say, was to show parents how not to raise their children. This time, *The New Yorker* cover featured a cartoon of an older woman using a finger to test the waters at the beach.

Thurber wrote under the pseudonym Jared L. Manley, and he walked the reader through Sidis's sad life just a couple of years before he'd famously publish "The Secret Life of Walter Mitty," a short story about a man who dreamed of being something he was not and ended up facing a firing squad.

The portrait of Sidis was scathing. Even as a child, Thurber wrote, Sidis "had something of the intense manner of a neurotic adult" and had in fact "had a general breakdown" at age eleven after the 1910 Harvard lecture. Once he recovered, Sidis had thereafter had what Thurber called "a general maladjustment to his abnormal life." Phobias developed. Sidis said that he wished to live in seclusion; he claimed that he simply hated crowds but instead obviously hated people. He'd flowered into adulthood in "bizarre fashion," working at Wall Street firms as an accounting clerk and publishing a book on streetcar transfers through a vanity press. Some of his jobs had caused him such stress that he would weep at work and then quit. His small room—a "hall bedroom" in a boardinghouse in "Boston's shabby south end"—featured discolored pinkish flowers and two photos, one of him as a child and one of a lost, perhaps unrequited love. He couldn't bear responsibility or intricate thought. "All I want to do is run an adding machine," he'd said during class in "intense but halting speech," "but they won't let me alone."

And this is the way Thurber's piece ends: "'It's strange,' said William James Sidis, with a grin, 'but, you know, I was born on April Fools' Day.'"

Whether William Sidis, nearly forty, had in fact said nearly the identical thing to the class interloper that he'd said thirty years before to a *Baltimore Sun* reporter seems unlikely, and perhaps it was cribbed. In any event, Sidis sued for invasion of privacy based on Thurber's essay and a snide mention in a follow-up "Where Are They Now?": that readers "may recall a recent account of [Sidis's] accomplishments" in a prior issue.

The real accomplishment was *The New Yorker*'s because Sidis's case is now a part of media law lore, the first time, experts say, that American law "began, in an American way, to favor the interest of the press at the cost of almost any claim to privacy."

It started at the trial level, where the judge dismissed Sidis's invasion-of-privacy claim, explaining that most successful privacy cases involved extraordinary circumstances beyond this sort of revelation, such as the photograph of a dead child or the publication of a prostitute's life history. "I think I am safe in saying that the right of free speech and freedom of the press is still preserved throughout this country," the judge wrote, "and that under our laws one may speak and publish what he desires provided no offense against public morals or private reputation is committed."

On appeal, the three-judge panel for the Second Circuit, a highly influential federal court in New York, agreed. This time the court wrote that Sidis was once a public figure of whom great things were expected and that therefore his failure at life was "a matter of public concern." It would "be unwise," the court noted in what was essentially a nod to Thurber's news judgment, for the law to bar that sort of expression in newspapers, books, and magazines.

The Supreme Court voted not to hear Sidis's appeal. Coincidence or not, Louis Brandeis had retired from the Court the year before. And in between, the justices had written this: "A free press stands as one of the great interpreters between the government and the people. To allow it to be fettered is to fetter ourselves."

Newspapers enthusiastically covered the pro-press court decisions in the *Sidis* case and crowed at its description of the breadth of press powers. Some ridiculed Sidis and, along the way, schooled him about the business of journalism. "Life again made a mockery yesterday of the bizarre efforts of William James Sidis," someone at *The Boston Globe* wrote. Didn't Sidis realize that his "shyness toward the press" had itself become "newsworthy" and that his protestations simply made his life all the more worth retelling? In fact, as a result of the lawsuit, "newspapers all over North America and elsewhere [would now] publish stories about Sidis that never would have been published" had he not attempted such a "spectacular appeal" against the press and its news judgment. In honor of what it called Sidis's "failure," the *Globe* mockingly named him "America's Clerk-of-the-Week."

What *The Boston Globe* and other papers didn't report, however, was that William Sidis had renewed his claim against *The New Yorker*, for a tort that sounded a lot like what today we'd call intentional infliction of emotional distress and, maybe, a touch of truthful libel. He argued that *The New Yorker* had published its story "without justifiable motives or good ends," leaving him "suffer[ing] greatly in his peace of mind and sense of dignity." In 1944, he won that case, in effect, by settling with the magazine for an undisclosed amount.

"I feel that it was at last some sort of victory in my long fight against the principle of personal publicity," Sidis wrote shortly thereafter in a letter to a friend. He said that he was quite concerned for other young people who'd attracted the attention of the media early in their lives, in particular the day's antiwar protesters, that they might otherwise remain unwitting public figures throughout adulthood and be "pillor[ied]" by the press in the decades to come.

Three months later, William Sidis's landlady found him seriously ill in his room at the boardinghouse; she took him to the hospital, and he died a few days later of a brain hemorrhage. He was forty-six. Newspaper headlines announcing his death identified him as the "mental genius who gave up thinking," an "obscure," "broke," and "destitute" loner who "fled from his own mind into obscurity."

They described *The New Yorker* article as one that had focused on Sidis's "career."

Friends of William Sidis thereafter wrote letters to those newspapers, arguing that journalists had gotten things wrong yet again, that Sidis was not a pauper, not antisocial, not a recluse, but a likable man with a fine personality who'd paid his way in life, had numerous friends, and cared deeply about history. He was out of the ordinary, they said, not bizarre.

"William Sidis had one great cause" is how one letter to the editor in *The Boston Globe* put it, "the right of an individual in this country to follow his chosen way of life." Whenever he saw someone suffering from a loss of "'life, liberty, and the pursuit of happiness,' he fought in any way he could," that friend explained, including for the right to privacy. It was the newspapers that had characterized him as abnormal and erratic, the newspapers that had dogged him since he was a small child with adverse publicity.

Back at *The New Yorker*, James Thurber, who wasn't a lawyer, liked to say that the takeaway of the Sidis case had been "once a public figure," even in childhood, "always a public figure," and that his article would be "forever celebrated" because of the legal precedent it had created in "all so-called" right-to-privacy cases. He was right about the celebration part, at least in certain circles.

But similar to Elbridge Adams's shift after the Rochester Folding Box victory, the attorney who'd filed the brief for *The New Yorker* at the Supreme Court in the *Sidis* case, Morris Ernst, the man who also defended James Joyce's *Ulysses* against obscenity charges, thereafter wrote a book he titled *Privacy: The Right to Be Let Alone*. There, he lamented press intrusions and called privacy a "vital legal right."

He also took his press clients to task for reporting only on journalism's victories, never its losses in the courts or otherwise, and for "declin[ing] to report events which in turn might encourage the reading public to exercise some of their rights against invasions by the press." He called it a conspiracy of silence.

Louis Brandeis had died several years before but might have had some hand in Ernst's seeming shift: the two had become so close that Ernst would say that he loved Brandeis and that whenever he touched a lamp that Brandeis had gifted him from the Supreme Court, he felt that maybe the spirit of Brandeis was transmitted into him by brass and twinkling light.

Today, there's a yellow yield-type signal next to the Second Circuit appellate decision in *Sidis* as it appears in both of the major legal research databases. That yellow means caution, that the case may no longer be as powerful a precedent as it once was, that more modern courts have shifted away from its ultimate outcome and have said as much. That's a pretty accurate assessment of today's law of privacy.

But first would come decades of post-*Sidis* deference—a favoring of the press at the cost of almost any right-to-privacy claim—in cases involving magazines that published death photographs, newspapers that published rape-victim-naming stories, and gossip columns that published squibs that outed heroes.

The evils of Pandora's box, that judge in *Croswell* might say, had been loosed.

Chapter Thirteen

BODIES AND BREATHING SPACE

Weegee, the news photographer born Ascher Fellig, was often first to arrive at New York City murder scenes in the 1930s and 1940s. His photos showed it all: dead men on sidewalks and dead women on boardwalks, many with blood still draining from bullet holes in their bodies. Those sorts of pictures weren't routine in most newspapers—the New York *Daily News* cover shot featuring a leather-masked murderess dead in the electric chair was unusual—but in an odd reversal from *McClure's* days magazines were another story. Black-and-white last moments captured by Weegee and his imitators were snatched up by the era's infamous true-crime periodicals.

Headquarters Detective: True Cases from the Police Blotter was one of them, a magazine that routinely featured on its staged cover a scantily clad and often bound young woman looking in horror at what was surely a giant bowie knife coming at her just off camera. Startling real-life crime scene photographs came sprinkled inside: the bodies of two men dumped on a roadside, the bludgeoned body of a woman lying dead on a bed with blood seeping into the mattress, and another woman's body, nude, her face mutilated from the "six times the slayer sank his knife," all in the June 1940 edition alone. Today, mainstream publications would never publish such bold scenes of random death; it's a violation of journalism ethics in most newsrooms to publish photos of any dead body without good reason, and maybe only the horrors of war or terrorism or starvation would suffice. But

Headquarters Detective was one that pushed the envelope of propriety with its focus on death, period.

It also pushed the envelope of law. The New York state code in the 1940s made it a crime to publish or sell magazines "principally made up of criminal news or stories of deeds of bloodshed, or lust," part of a legislative effort to stop the glorification of violence that state lawmakers believed sucked young people into a life of crime. But in 1948, after the justices at the U.S. Supreme Court opened the pages of *Headquarters Detective* and caught a glimpse at what was inside, they wrote this memorable line: "Though we can see nothing of any possible value to society in these magazines, they are as much entitled to the protection of free speech as the best of literature."

That 6–3 decision in *Winters v. New York*, with Justice Brandeis's friend Felix Frankfurter in dissent, helped along the idea that all truthful information would be forever protected under the Constitution and that truth was what mattered most. *Winters* had come a year after a private group of male academics with degrees in law, history, and political science calling themselves the Hutchins Commission on Freedom of the Press (no journalists need apply) had handed down its finding that journalism was still a privileged industry, a mighty public power, in need of law in part as guidance. "If [journalists] are irresponsible," commissioners had warned, "not even the First Amendment will protect their freedom from governmental control," and "the amendment will be amended." *Winters* seemed a sharp rebuke to the Hutchins Commission.

In any event, in the decades after *Winters*, memorable and powerfully press-protective language continued at the Supreme Court. The justices wrote that speech that embarrasses doesn't lose protection and that speech that offends can't be suppressed in the marketplace of ideas. The First Amendment requires adequate breathing space, they wrote, and press responsibility can't be legislated and isn't mandated by the Constitution.

The cases include the most famous of all time that promote press and speech and expression freedoms: the legendary defamation case from 1964, *New York Times v. Sullivan*, with language powerfully protective of the press ("safeguards for freedom of speech and of the press . . . are required" by the First Amendment, and "debate on public issues should be uninhibited, robust, and wide-open"); *Time v. Hill* from 1967 ("exposure of the self to others in varying degrees is a concomitant of life in a civilized community," and "the risk of this exposure is an essential incident of life in a society which places a primary value on freedom of speech and of press"); and the Pentagon Papers case from 1971, a three-paragraph decision after which many of the justices wrote separate opinions ("The people shall not be deprived or abridged of their right to speak, to write, or to publish their sentiments; and the freedom of the press, as one of the great bulwarks of liberty, shall be inviolable": Justice Hugo Black, citing James Madison).

There were multiple others. It was a time when courageous reporting from civil rights struggles, from Vietnam, and from Watergate told the truths of everyday hatred, of war, and of presidential misdeeds, and in response a whopping 72 percent of Americans said they believed in and trusted the media. Supreme Court opinions with their powerfully memorable rhetoric seem reflective of that.

This meant that when privacy and press were pitted at the Supreme Court, the press won, even in increasingly difficult cases. To many on the outside, privacy interests surely seemed the right call, but instead the Supreme Court solidified the primacy of press freedom and, in a way, celebrated truth and the people's right to know.

In 1975, the Court decided that a grieving father whose seventeen-year-old daughter had died after an apparent gang rape had no claim against a television station that had broadcast his daughter's name in violation of a state statute that made it a crime to identify a rape victim. Media has a "great responsibility," the justices wrote in *Cox Broadcasting v. Cohn*, "to report fully and accurately the proceedings of government," including trials, and "interests in privacy fade when the information," such as this victim's name, "appears on the public record." Moreover, this sort of news story had social value as a step toward truth, and to punish media for such reporting would "invite timidity and self-censorship" and lead to suppression.

In 1977, the Court protected media for reporting the name of an eleven-year-old boy who'd been arrested, for taking his picture, and for videotaping him as he left court, all in violation of a lower court order. "Members of the press were in fact present at the hearing with the full knowledge of the presiding judge," the Supreme Court explained in *Oklahoma Publishing Co. v. District Court*, and therefore acquired the information lawfully, so to punish their reporting of truth, even though it involved a child who would otherwise be protected, would abridge First Amendment press freedoms.

A couple of years later, in 1979, the Court held in *Smith v. Daily Mail Publishing Co.* that media could not be punished for publishing the name and photograph of a fourteen-year-old boy who'd shot a classmate despite a state statute that made it a crime to publish such information without court permission. Journalists had learned the boy's name at the scene and therefore to hold them liable for such accurate reporting would be unconstitutional. "If the information is lawfully obtained," the Court wrote, "the state may not punish its publication except when necessary to further an interest more substantial than is present here."

Then, ten years later, in 1989, the Court decided in *Florida Star v. B.J.F.* that a newspaper would not be liable for publishing the name of a living rape victim in violation of both a state statute and the newspaper's own policy. An intern had found the information in a police report and had written a blurb for the police blotter naming the victim and explaining with surprising detail that an unknown man had run up behind her, placed a knife to her neck, then "undressed the lady and had sexual intercourse with her" before fleeing. Thereafter, the named victim received harassing phone calls that included new threats of rape and was forced to move from her home. Nevertheless, the Court wrote that it would be unconstitutional to hold the press liable for its accurate reporting: first, the media had acquired the victim's name legally; second, the government itself had supplied the information; and third, the state statute that suppressed such information targeted only media and could have been more evenhanded.

There was a celebration of truth throughout this period on the access side too, an ever-growing sense that the public did indeed have a right to know certain information. In the wake of Watergate, Congress threw open the files of federal government agencies by amending the 1966 federal Freedom of Information Act so that the press and the people could evermore "pierce [the] veil of administrative secrecy and open agency action to light of public scrutiny." Sure, FOIA has nine exceptions, including personal privacy, and Congress had passed the Privacy Act of 1974 in order to beef up protection for information the government held on individuals, but FOIA's right-to-know language mandated that each agency "shall" make most government records available to the public as a sort of "full agency disclosure." Many similar state statutes suggest flat out that any document created by a government employee—including emails and texts in particular cases—is presumed open to the public the instant it's created.

Shortly after FOIA's expansion, recognizing the change that was afoot, the American Law Institute reformulated the Restatement's privacy section. That privacy would continue to be the institute's concern despite all the openness in Congress and at the Supreme Court and despite polls that showed only about 33 percent of the public was worried about personal privacy wasn't surprising, really, because in response to all that openness some had started to fret that certain information the government had on them—they called it data—might be shared and published. In addition, the Restatement needed change because the initially scant lower court decisions suggested that privacy had shifted to become four distinct torts or civil wrongs: misappropriation (as in the *Roberson* case, the use without permission of another's image or name or identity in advertising or otherwise); intrusion into seclusion (as in the earlier Restatement example involving a surgery surreptitiously shot through a skylight, the peering in on someone who is in a secluded space); false light (similar to a traditional defamation case, but the falsity at issue only need be highly offensive); and publicity given to private life (the publication of private information that is highly offensive and not newsworthy, the tort at the heart of the Warren and Brandeis *Harvard Law Review* article).

But here, for the first time, Restatement authors predicted that in light of Supreme Court protection for accurate reporting and its language celebrating the power of the First Amendment and the people's right to know even in shocking cases involving rape victims and juvenile arrestees, truth could well become the ultimate defense against a privacy claim after all.

And, this time, Restatement authors used as an example not the hideously deformed plaintiff who'd had a valid claim against a newspaper for publishing his photo but the *Sidis* decision:

> A is an infant prodigy, who at the age of twelve lectures to leading mathematicians on the fourth dimension. On arriving at adolescence he develops an abnormal dislike for publicity, abandons his mathematical

pursuits, obtains employment as an obscure clerk and leads a very secluded life. Twenty years later B Magazine seeks him out and publishes
an article on his life history, disclosing his present whereabouts, employment and manner of life, and such matters as his collection of
street car transfers and his interest in the lore of an Indian tribe. This
is not an invasion of A's privacy.

By 1989, the time of the *Florida Star* decision, Ken Starr, then a judge on
the federal appeals court for Washington, D.C., suggested with worry that
there'd been a seismic cultural and sociological shift in the United States:
support for the Warren-and-Brandeis right to be let alone, he said, had been
replaced with the helped-along-by-Watergate right to know. The underlying
issue—what he called "the assault on privacy"—was one that was "fundamental to human decency" and dignity, he said, and how much we should
learn about others' intimate lives, including public officials and public figures, how deeply journalists and others should dig, and how much they
should reveal. He would release his report on President Bill Clinton's affair
with a White House intern within the decade in language nearly as revealing
as that in *My Life and Loves*—"on one occasion, the President inserted a
cigar" is one portion of one example—exposing not only a president but also
a once-unknown twenty-two-year-old.

In the meantime, journalism celebrated the growing legal shift toward
truth, the right to know as a trump to privacy, and the supremacy of First
Amendment freedoms. One book about Supreme Court decisions written for
journalism students explained that absolutist views on press rights from
concurring and dissenting justices at the Court would appear more often in
its pages without apology because its journalist-author felt most sympathetic to that viewpoint. Another suggested that the press had but two limitations: libel and obscenity. "Legally," a third read, "the right of privacy is
not a major impediment to reporters and editors who seek to tell us about
what is going on in the world." Many highlighted the *Sidis* case. By 1970,
Newsweek magazine suggested that privacy was dead on a cover that featured prying cameras, microphones, and computers; inside it wrote that
Americans had surrendered "both the sense and the reality of their own
right to privacy." That same year, an excited *Look* magazine told its readers

that sexual privacy was dying too: that protection for sexual behavior had arisen in Victorian times and there was no longer a need for it. A few years later, *Time* magazine suggested that in First Amendment cases, it was "clear that the news media [had] prevailed, at least in the court of law," and by 1997 *Time* reporters confirmed that Americans' "right to be let alone had disappeared" in a cover headlined THE DEATH OF PRIVACY.

In 2001, the Supreme Court seemingly solidified the shift against privacy and toward the right to know when it decided *Bartnicki v. Vopper* in favor of media. There, a radio station had aired the audiotape of a surreptitiously recorded cell phone call between two teachers' union negotiators in which one had suggested the use of violence. Even though federal law made it a crime to record a cell phone conversation, and even though it seemed clear that the radio station knew as much when it aired the tape (one that had been recorded by an unknown person and thereafter sent to the station), the Court ruled 6–3 that it would be unconstitutional to hold the station liable. What union officials had had to say about potential negotiation tactics was a "public issue," the justices wrote, making the information published real news, not simple "domestic gossip or other information of purely private concern." In fact, this was precisely the sort of case that Warren and Brandeis had in mind when they argued in "The Right to Privacy" that privacy doesn't prohibit publication of matters of public interest, the Court said, and here at least, in the clash between "individual privacy" and the "full and free dissemination of information concerning public issues," the latter won out.

But what that balancing test suggested was that privacy might still be a viable claim at the Supreme Court; it's just that, at that point at least, with the internet in its infancy, in the main cases heard by the Court, the balance had shifted on unique facts in favor of truth and the public's right to know. "Our Bill of Rights assures the press freedom to report and comment" is the way that Justice Arthur Goldberg had put it just a few weeks after the Court decided *New York Times v. Sullivan*, "yet, at the same time it guarantees to all a certain modicum of privacy," a privacy that the press had the responsibility not to invade.

And, indeed, despite the seeming primacy of press rights in Supreme Court cases during the 1950s through today, sometimes by name, sometimes outside government-related behavior, sometimes well outside dicta, and sometimes in words that can only be described as strident, the Supreme Court also recognized the importance of privacy. The language that promoted press and speech freedoms may be more familiar because it's often what we read and hear, but for seventy years, even in decisions that the media seemed to have won wholesale, privacy-promoting language is there too.

Consider that in the 1950s in *Beauharnais v. Illinois*, what might be considered an early hate speech case, the Court upheld the criminal conviction of a man who had published certain racist material. "There are limits to the exercise of these liberties (of speech and of the press)," the Court wrote, suggesting that "personal abuse" played no essential part in the exposition of ideas and differentiating between emotionally painful public ridicule and the idle gossip of a country town. In *Sweezy v. New Hampshire*, a case in which the justices decided that a professor had the First Amendment academic freedom not to respond to government questions about socialist activities, including groups considered subversive by the House Un-American Activities Committee, they criticized the government and ultimately McCarthyism for "making his private life a matter of public record" and equated that part of life with constitutional liberty. In *Watkins v. United States*, the Court wrote that congressional investigative powers could not "be inflated into a general power to expose where the predominant result [could] only be an invasion of the private rights of individuals," including "an individual's right to privacy," that "ruthless exposure of private lives in order to gather data" puts "constitutional freedoms in jeopardy," and the very next year held in *NAACP v. Alabama* that the "inviolability of privacy in group association" meant that the NAACP need not reveal its membership to government.

In the 1960s, in *Mapp v. Ohio*, a criminal case involving police who rifled through a woman's personal "lewd and lascivious" books and pictures, the Supreme Court again linked the "privacies of life" with "personal liberty." The "right to privacy," the Court wrote, was "no less important than any other right carefully and particularly reserved to the people." In *New York Times v. Sullivan*, the Court poetically noted that a "pall of fear and timidity imposed upon those who would give voice to public criticism is an atmosphere in which the First Amendment freedoms cannot survive," but it also suggested that for libel and other types of "repression of expression" there was "no talismanic immunity from constitutional limitations." An inquiry into "good motives and justifiable ends" in libel cases officially ended in *Garrison v. Louisiana* after the Court found it unconstitutional, but the justices specifically noted that the case did not concern the "abhorrence" involved when "a man's forgotten misconduct, or the misconduct of a relation, in which the public has no interest, should be wantonly raked up, and published to the world on the ground of its being true." *Griswold v. Connecticut*, the case in which the Court decided that state restrictions on birth control were unconstitutional, came in the 1960s too, and the Court wrote that the right to privacy sprang from the Constitution's First Amendment—that "the First Amendment has a penumbra where privacy is protected from governmental intrusion"—and noted that privacy was older than the Bill of Rights. They wrote in a self-incrimination case the next year that they had "respect for the inviolability of the human personality and the right of each individual to a private enclave where he may lead a private life." In the Sam Sheppard case, one involving excessive media publicity of a murder trial in which Sheppard claimed that a bushy-haired stranger had killed his wife, the Court took media to task for its sensationalism; the trial court judge should have warned reporters, the Supreme Court wrote, about the "impropriety of publishing material not introduced in the proceedings," and it especially criticized journalists for the way they "heavily emphasized" Sheppard's "illicit affair," pejoratively calling it "gossip." In *Time v. Hill*, a false-light case in which the Court held that *Life* magazine would not be liable for certain inaccuracies in news photographs of actors re-creating a crime scene, justices noted that by that point thirty-four states had recognized privacy in some way; they also contrasted the imagery at issue in the case with revelations that threaten community standards of decency. Then, as proof of something beyond the pale, the justices cited the original Restatement's example of the "hideously deformed" person who had a viable privacy claim against a newspaper that had published his picture to quite accurately illustrate an article on the results of poor rural medical care.

The 1970s was the decade of the "Fuck the Draft" jacket (yes, the Supreme Court held, its wearer could walk courthouse halls), and it brought the most significant shift toward protection for speech and press and truth and a public right to know, but privacy interests found their ways into those cases too. In *Rosenbloom v. Metromedia*, a defamation case, the Court looked to

Warren and Brandeis's "Right to Privacy" when it suggested that only certain information would be of appropriate "public or general interest": information about science and the arts, a college football cheating scandal, the integration of a university, police arrests for obscenity, and all people involved in those events would be newsworthy. But, the Court wrote, "we are not to be understood as implying that no area of a person's activities falls outside the area of public or general interest."

The decade also brought the Pentagon Papers case, in which the Court held in a three-paragraph opinion that an injunction against the newspaper publication of a secret government report titled "History of U.S. Decision-Making Process on Viet Nam Policy" would be unconstitutional (Justice Black: "It is unfortunate that some of my Brethren are apparently willing to hold that the publication of news may sometimes be enjoined" in other sorts of cases). In *Branzburg v. Hayes*, the Court ultimately held that the Constitution does not support a reporter's privilege that would allow journalists to keep sources secret (Justice White for the majority: it's true that "without some protection for seeking out the news, freedom of the press could be eviscerated," but "the press is not free to publish with impunity everything and anything it desires to publish"). In *Doe v. McMillan*, the Supreme Court found Congress had immunity for publishing a report about failing schools that contained truthful information about particular Washington, D.C., schoolchildren, including their names, absences, poor reading levels, failing test papers, disciplinary problems, sexual activities, and criminal violations. But the justices suggested that others would not be immune for such a publication and that constitutional, common-law, and statutory right-to-privacy claims seemed satisfied, given the potential danger to children's "reputations, good names, and future careers." Even the First Amendment–sensitive justices William O. Douglas, William Brennan, and Thurgood Marshall agreed that the complaint was viable; they wrote that they were particularly worried that "the age of technology has produced data banks" into which Social Security numbers, arrest information, juvenile delinquency behaviors, and other misdeeds and indiscretions are entered, all of which may be devastating to the person in adulthood.

That same year, the Court decided *Roe v. Wade*, holding that the Constitution protected a woman's right to choose to have an abortion and suggesting that the right to privacy had been given a constitutional dimension all the way back in 1891 in that decision written by Justice Gray involving personal injury to a railroad passenger and her "right to be let alone," to refuse the inspection of her body by a doctor hired by the defense. The justices wrote that they recognized that "a right of personal privacy, or a guarantee of certain areas or zones of privacy, does exist under the Constitution." It sprang from the First Amendment, the Court wrote (citing a case that had found a right to keep certain obscene materials for private reading); the Fourth Amendment (citing Brandeis in the *Olmstead* case); and the Fifth Amendment (citing the "right to be let alone" railroad decision, one involving the potential for self-incrimination). It appeared in the Fourteenth Amendment's "concept of personal liberty" and, more collectively, "in the penumbras of the Bill of Rights," to create a "guarantee of personal privacy," they wrote.

The very next year, just days before Richard Nixon resigned the presidency, the Court decided in *United States v. Nixon* that he must release subpoenaed White House tape recordings to a lower court as part of its "search for the truth" with regard to Watergate, but the justices also noted that privacy in communications was important for all. A few years later, the justices decided in the related *Nixon v. Administrator of General Services* that the public interest inherent in Nixon's White House tapes outweighed his privacy in them and that therefore government archivists would have access to them, just as a federal statute mandated, to preserve their historical value. But they also suggested that public officials, including presidents, "are not wholly without constitutionally protected privacy rights in matters of personal life unrelated to any acts done by them in their public capacity," specifically naming "matters concerned with family or personal finances," materials shielded from public view in presidential libraries, and materials containing a "legitimate expectation of privacy." It thereafter decided in *Nixon v. Warner Communications* that broadcast media and audio companies had at that time no right to recordings of the White House tapes, that with regard to the precise voice audio the public's right to know did not trump Nixon's privacy interests, including his potential embarrassment from snippets that might be edited to titillate. The Court also curiously threw in mention that "painful and sometimes disgusting details of a divorce case," those that would "promote public scandal," should not be released by courts either. (Archivists eventually released all portions of the tapes not protected on personal privacy grounds to the public in 2013.)

The nation's bicentennial year, 1976, was the year in which even stronger privacy concerns appeared in several decisions at the Supreme Court. In *Time v. Firestone*, the Court proved James Thurber wrong when it held that a woman who had married into the Firestone family and who, at the time of her marriage, had become a public figure could again become a private person in a legal sense and therefore need not prove the actual malice necessary in a defamation case. Information about divorce proceedings, the justices wrote, would do little to advance uninhibited debate on public issues. It's true that in *Paul v. Davis*, the Supreme Court refused a man's constitutional privacy claim brought against police who'd published his mug shot on a list of active shoplifters, but in *Air Force v. Rose* the justices decided that Air Force Academy cadets' ethics and honor case files should be redacted before release because of the privacy interests involved even though the information had previously been made public.

That same year, the Court held in *Nebraska Press Association v. Stuart* that a judge could not block media from publishing confessions from defendants in criminal cases, but also warned that the First Amendment carried with it a fiduciary duty to publish responsibly, a concept that the Court said was routinely acknowledged by editors and publishers "but not always observed." In a case the next year involving the news broadcast of a fifteen-second human cannonball act, the Court found that media could be liable. "Wherever the line in particular situations is to be drawn between media reports that are protected and those that are not," the Court wrote, it was quite certain that the First Amendment did not protect the media "when they broadcast a performer's entire act without his consent." That same year, the Court wrote in *Whalen v. Roe* that there was a "threat to privacy implicit in the accumulation of vast amounts of personal information," some of which would be embarrassing if disclosed, and that the duty to keep such information private and an "individual interest in avoiding disclosure of personal matters" "arguably has its roots in the Constitution." In 1978, they decided that news media had no automatic First Amendment right to interview inmates and otherwise investigate a suicide at a county jail to ferret out the truth, suggesting that inmates were "not like animals in a zoo to be filmed and photographed at will by the public or by media reporters, however 'educational' the process may be for others"; they'd thereafter decide that media would have access to ordinary criminal trials, but still later hold that the privacy interests of victims or potential jurors could keep media out. In *Landmark Communications v. Virginia*, the Court decided that news media would not be punished for reporting on confidential judicial review proceedings, though it rejected the media's request for an absolutist approach that would have protected all reports of truthful information. (That was the same year the Court decided that the Federal Communications Commission could punish radio stations that had played a George Carlin "Filthy Words" monologue; the First Amendment did not protect such publication of words that described sexual and excretory activities.) And, in 1979, in *Herbert v. Lando*, the Court held that defamation plaintiffs had the right to investigate the newsroom decisions that had led to certain articles, but it wrote that it worried too about media's "undue self-censorship and the suppression of truthful material."

In the 1980s, a time of seeming transition from more powerful First Amendment–driven decisions to those respecting certain privacies (and a time when suddenly 68 percent of Americans expressed concern for their personal privacy, sparked perhaps in significant part by data privacy concerns), the Court held that Henry Kissinger had privacy in his official business and personal telephone conversations while he served in the White House. A few years after that, in *Seattle Times v. Rhinehart*, the justices upheld a lower court's order that had protected on privacy grounds the names of members and donors to a religious group called the Aquarian Foundation started by a mystic who called himself Brother XII, despite press interest in the organization. The next year, they found "no public issue" in an individual's credit report, that such a report was not a matter of public concern. In 1988, justices ruled that a high school principal didn't offend the First Amendment when he prevented the school newspaper from publishing two articles; the justices reasoned in *Hazelwood v. Kuhlmeier* that the content of the articles (one on teen pregnancy and another on divorce) raised "the need to protect the privacy of individuals whose most intimate concerns [were] to be revealed in the newspaper." That same year, the justices decided in *Hustler Magazine v. Falwell* that *Hustler* magazine would be protected by the First Amendment for publishing a parody ad that suggested Jerry Falwell had had sex with his mother in an outhouse, but the Court warned that "this does not mean that any speech about a public figure is immune from sanction in the form of damages." Also in 1988, the justices wrote in a case involving picketing outside a home that "a special benefit of the privacy all citizens enjoy within their own walls . . . is an ability to avoid intrusions" and that a state can protect those interests. It's true that the Court ruled in *California v. Greenwood* that police could search trash bags left outside for pickup without a warrant, suggesting that anyone putting out trash should anticipate the "snoops" that might come around, but the very next year it held that there was privacy in so-called rap sheets, compilations of individuals' criminal histories. "To begin with," the Court wrote, "both the common law and the literal understandings of privacy encompass the individual's control of information concerning his or her person," and such privacy interests extended even to crimes disclosed to the public in the past as part of the public record, and this was true even when the individuals at issue had committed crimes of significant interest to the community.

And even though it's getting ahead of things just a bit, in more modern times, from the 1990s on, the Court decided a series of cases that seemingly shifted even more toward privacy. It held that journalists who'd promised confidentiality to a source and later accurately published the source's name could be sued for breach of contract despite the First Amendment; the Constitution's promise of press freedom "does not grant the press . . . limitless protection" from laws that restrain the right to publish truthful information, the Court wrote, suggesting that the *Florida Star* case didn't apply to *this* publication of truth because the press had acquired the source's name unlawfully through a promise it didn't keep. The Court also decided that police can be liable for inviting the media on so-called ride alongs in which journalists accompany police on arrests. In that case, *Wilson v. Layne*, it wrote that privacy protected the home and the people inside it from police-facilitated media coverage of their arrests, rejecting media's arguments that such coverage ensured accurate reporting on police issues. In *Lawrence v. Texas*, the justices protected intimate sexual conduct on privacy grounds: there is "an emerging awareness that liberty gives substantial protection to adult persons in deciding how to conduct their private lives in matters pertaining to sex" and people "are entitled to respect for their private lives." The justices also protected Vince Foster autopsy photos in *National Archives and Records Administration v. Favish*, suggesting that, at least with regard to the Freedom of Information Act, family members have privacy interests in death images of their loved ones, that those left behind should be allowed "to secure their own refuge from a sensation-seeking culture for their own peace of mind and tranquility," protected especially from the pain and the privacy violation that would occur when such images would appear randomly on the internet. "We have little difficulty," the Court wrote in *Favish*, "in finding in our case law and traditions the right of family members ... to limit attempts to exploit pictures of the deceased family member's remains for public purposes" and cited a Restatement example: parents had a successful privacy claim when a photograph of a dead child was published against their wishes.

In *Snyder v. Phelps*, the funeral picketing case, the Court decided that Westboro Baptist Church members had a First Amendment right to hold up signs that said "God Hates Fags" and other hateful things because such speech was ultimately focused on matters of public concern including homosexuality in the military. But the Court suggested that a similar attack "over a private matter," including something like an individual's credit report or her sexually explicit video, could well lead to a different outcome. It also suggested in a footnote that a targeted attack published on the internet against a grieving family like the Snyders might be treated differently. That same year the Court acknowledged in *NASA v. Nelson* that it had earlier "referred broadly to a constitutional privacy 'interest in avoiding disclosure of personal matters'" and "assum[ed]" "that the Constitution protects a privacy right of the sort." And in a criminal case decided in 2018, *Carpenter v. United States*, the justices rejected warrantless tracking through cell phone towers, explaining that they were worried that even though ultimately people were traveling in the open, the "privacies of life" including familial and sexual associations would otherwise be discovered, building upon language written in *Riley v. California* in 2014 about the privacies found on cell phones, mundane matters for the most part, but also occasionally much more "intimate" information, including photographs of "private life," information about health concerns, addictions, and other such "private information" similarly linked with "the privacies of life."

Though we think of many of these cases as ones that largely support freedom of the press and free expression, throughout all of them runs a consistent thread: language referring to and protecting a privacy right that refuses to be sacrificed to other freedoms.

And here's the thing: even in those rather shocking Supreme Court cases in which the privacy of rape victims and juvenile offenders took a backseat to freedom to publish truth, the justices wrote lines that aren't as famous, like this: "There *is* a zone of privacy surrounding every individual, a zone within which the State may protect him from intrusion by the press, with all its attendant publicity." In the case against the *Florida Star* newspaper brought by the rape victim identified only as B.J.F., the Court wrote this: "we do not hold that truthful publication is automatically constitutionally protected, or that there is no zone of personal privacy within which the State may protect the individual from intrusion by the press, or even that a State may never punish publication of the name of a victim of a sexual offense," because there is "sensitivity and significance" in privacy interests that are just as profound as those inherent in press interests.

Finally, in *Bartnicki*, the case involving the publication of a cell phone conversation, recall that three justices dissented, meaning that they would have found the radio station liable for its broadcast. Of the six who voted with the majority, two justices wrote separately to suggest that not only was there no blanket right to publish truth, but some truths in particular were "truly private" and therefore off limits entirely, including a "videotape recording of sexual relations" between two celebrities and the portrayals of "intimate private characteristics" of an individual, and maybe even information about the divorce of a wealthy person.

Adding those two justices to the three who dissented means that in 2001, had the information at issue in *Bartnicki* been considered both private and not newsworthy—involving sex or other intimate information, as the concurrence explained—the Supreme Court would have sided at least 5–4 with privacy and against the right to know. It also suggests that, that year at least, Hulk Hogan would have been victorious at the Supreme Court had his case against the *Gawker* website for publishing his sex tape been heard by the justices.

But the most important part about all this privacy-related jurisprudence and language from the 1950s until the dawn of the internet and beyond is that hardly anybody really paid all that much attention to it. The focus was almost entirely on how media seemed increasingly free, how First Amendment interests had triumphed in *Sidis* and in other cases, and how the Supreme Court had protected even those who'd outed rape victims. As a result, the public learned little about its right to privacy. It's nowhere near the perfect experiment, but it's nonetheless interesting that a search for "freedom of the press" on a popular newspaper database yielded 951,000 hits in 2021, while both the combined "right *to* privacy" and "right *of* privacy" appeared in newspapers just about half as often.

James Reston, the *New York Times* executive editor who'd voted to publish the Pentagon Papers, used to say that the twentieth century was the era of the journalist. And it surely was; literary and immersion and long-form journalism grew, and reporters seemed solidly protected by First Amendment free-press promises. In the journalism of this period, some have said, the facts danced. But, almost stealthily, in 1969, there arrived a key case that shut a journalist and his important story down.

Here, in the era of the journalist, the facts danced and privacy won.

It's hard to decide which scene from the 1967 documentary *Titicut Follies* is most difficult to watch because that's the point: the cinema verité film reveals the horrifying plight of many locked inside Bridgewater State Hospital, the stone-block bastille forty minutes south of Boston that contained those we used to call the criminally insane.

The worst could well be the skeletal man being force-fed, a rubber tube inching its way up his nose while his doctor's cigarette, nearly half of it ash, dangles perilously above. It could be the one featuring the dead body of an inmate—is it the man who'd been force-fed or just a nameless other?—packed into a drawer for later mostly solitary burial, cotton balls delicately placed into the eye sockets. Maybe it's the man plunged into a bathtub, joyful when filthy bathwater seeps into his mouth, or the one who reveals that he sexually abused children to a psychiatrist more intrigued with his masturbatory behavior. But the worst is probably the scene featuring Jim, a former schoolteacher, naked inside an empty prison cell, stamping round and round louder and louder, growling through his teeth as guards repeatedly ask why he can't keep his own cell clean.

The title *Titicut Follies* isn't meant to titillate. "Titicut" is what locals called the land around the prison, and "Follies" refers to the variety show that drugged-up prisoners and pumped-up guards put on for the public each year. Vaudeville turned out to be a real moneymaker: the first show earned $1,500 to help pay for televisions and stereos—"material needs"—that the inmates wanted but the state wouldn't pay for. It became an annual tradition.

Who knows why the state of Massachusetts allowed the lawyer turned filmmaker Frederick Wiseman inside prison walls for eight weeks to film the variety show and so much more. Maybe it's true that state officials knew just how bad things were and hoped to "stir up community interest to improve the institution" at election time. Or maybe, as antics by some in the film suggest, the guards wanted to be movie stars. In any event, Wiseman spent nearly two months and $35,000 capturing everyday prison scenes like psychiatric appointments, prison transfer hearings, pill dole outs, and naked, near-naked, and sloppily clothed prisoners shuffling about or singing nonsense in the yard or picking their noses, many aware of the camera but too drugged or incompetent to care. Wiseman didn't film the inmate Albert DeSalvo, the Boston Strangler, because guards had asked him not to, but he did tens of others and got signed releases from about a hundred of the competent.

Wiseman premiered his documentary *Titicut Follies* at the New York Film Festival in 1967, and it instantly became the hottest ticket. Who wouldn't want a glimpse inside a prison for the criminally insane? Who were these men? What did they look like, and how did they act? How was Massachusetts treating them? It might sound creepy stalker, but the many modern television series that focus on life in the slammer prove that people want answers to those sorts of questions. Here, the answers were particularly difficult: some men seemed too sane to be there, most looked and acted drugged out of their minds, and it was clear that Massachusetts through its doctors and its guards wasn't doing its job to care for them. This seemed the people's business. As Wiseman put it, "public institutions in a democracy are meant to be transparent, open to public inspection," and change "can only happen when the public is informed."

Frederick Wiseman's investigation into Bridgewater never got much of a chance to have its Bly–Blackwell's Island moment in the disinfecting light of the sun, however. The day of its premiere, the Massachusetts attorney general, Elliot Richardson, filed a lawsuit arguing that the film showed inmates in "extremely intimate and confidential situations." Richardson hired the Morris Ernst law firm in part to make his argument in favor of inmate privacy, and despite *Near v. Minnesota*'s strong language against prior restraints where important news is concerned (and that very first right-to-know case that suggested the people should learn much about those in the care of government), he won a temporary restraining order that prevented any future showings of the film.

The Boston Globe recognized the interests on both sides and punted. "The right of the inmates to privacy should certainly be protected," it wrote. "But so, if possible, should the right of the public to see the film." Massachusetts legislators who funded state institutions sided overwhelmingly with inmate privacy. "Where the hell are the liberals and advocates of civil rights?" one asked. "Where the hell are they now?" The answer was that counsel for the Massachusetts office of the American Civil Liberties Union had represented Frederick Wiseman at first but pretty quickly dropped out and thereafter punted too, explaining that the ACLU couldn't take a stand because "civil liberties on both sides [were] in conflict with each other." (It's the same way in more modern times with revenge porn; the ACLU at times stridently and successfully argued against statutes that would punish those who publish nude photographs of others on revenge porn websites, suggesting that the First Amendment rights of the poster supplanted the right to privacy of the outed usually female victim, while the organization suggests on its website that it fights more generally for privacy in "the control individuals have over their personal information.")

In the *Titicut Follies* case, a Massachusetts judge eventually heard a month's worth of testimony—arguments against the ban and in favor of the right to know from the filmmakers, and arguments for the ban and in favor of the right to privacy from state officials—and he thereafter banned the film permanently. It was a "nightmare of ghoulish obscenities," the judge said, in which inmates were pictured without their permission. "No amount of rhetoric, no shibboleths of 'free speech' and the 'right of the public to know' [could] masquerade this pictorial performance": it was work that trafficked in embarrassment, loneliness, and human misery. Then the judge ordered that Wiseman turn over all copies of the film and all of its outtakes so that they might be destroyed.

In 1969, the Massachusetts Supreme Judicial Court—where Louis Brandeis had clerked, where Oliver Wendell Holmes had first judged, and where *Commonwealth v. Blanding* had originated—mostly endorsed that ban. Because not a single one of the inmates was newsworthy, the court wrote, citing in part Warren and Brandeis's "Right to Privacy," and because the documentary was "a collective, indecent intrusion into the most private aspects" of the inmates' lives, the ban would stand with three asterisks. First, the film could be shown to "legislators, judges, lawyers, sociologists, social workers, doctors, psychiatrists," students in those fields, and related organizations, because they were the people who could do the most good with the disturbing revelations in the film. Second, Wiseman could keep his outtakes but couldn't ever publish them. Third, Wiseman had to amend his film to include "a brief explanation that changes and improvements [had] taken place in the institution since 1966." That message still appears at the end of the documentary after scant credits have rolled:

Screen One: The Supreme Judicial Court of Massachusetts has ordered that "a brief explanation shall be included in the film that changes and improvements have taken place at Massachusetts Correctional Institution Bridgewater since 1966."

Screen Two: Changes and improvements have taken place at Massachusetts Correctional Institution Bridgewater since 1966.

That same summer, Mary Jo Kopechne died in a car accident in Chappaquiddick, Massachusetts. And some people argued that maybe even Ted Kennedy and certainly the people around him that night had the same right to privacy that the Massachusetts Supreme Judicial Court had given the inmates a few weeks before.

Now, you might think that the justices at the U.S. Supreme Court would have an interest in a state court decision that banned a documentary revealing malfeasance at a state institution. But the justices voted not to hear the *Titicut Follies* appeal despite the Harvard law professor Alan Dershowitz's right-to-know and marketplace-of-ideas pleas on behalf of Frederick Wiseman: "No amount of 'free debate,' written or oral, can be an effective substitute for a documentary film which shows to members of the general public the very conditions about which they should be concerned." Justices William Brennan, John Marshall Harlan II, and William O. Douglas wanted the Court to take up the case, recognizing that it perfectly presented the clash between the right to privacy and the right of the people to know. It was, they wrote, a First Amendment issue not easily struck. But they couldn't persuade their fellow justices to grant certiorari.

In the meantime, *Titicut Follies* remained banned across the United States. Two decades passed. In 1987, Wiseman and his lawyers argued that given the passage of time and given that many inmates had either died or been released, the ban should be lifted. The judge, balancing press rights with privacy rights, agreed, but only if Wiseman blurred out the faces of those who'd never signed a release. Dershowitz called that ruling preposterous and a shame on the Commonwealth, suggesting that *Titicut Follies* was "not a film about faceless people." So Wiseman refused, and the ban continued.

Finally, in 1991, nearly a quarter century after that Massachusetts judge first condemned the film, the judge decided that press freedoms and the right to know finally outbalanced the right to privacy and that *Titicut Follies* could be seen by the general public, unblurred and unedited. Not only had even more time passed, but one of the featured inmates who'd originally objected to the film was writing a book and had changed his mind about its stigmatizing aspects. In any case, its message had remained powerful. The prison's superintendent that year credited *Titicut Follies* with contributing to mental health reform in Massachusetts; the mere suggestion of its horrors had motivated a taxpaying public to pressure legislators to make permanent change. But the superintendent also noted his continuing concern for the inmates' privacy.

Ultimately, Wiseman would say that he shared at least some of that concern. "I don't flatly reject the privacy issue," he told a reporter just before the film's second premiere, "but the right of privacy is not an absolute right legally."

Wiseman, a lawyer, would know. By 1991, bolstered by those memorable Supreme Court decisions and quotations supporting First Amendment press and expression freedoms and discounting the language that protected privacy, courts across the United States had mainly ruled against privacy rights of individuals whose private information had been revealed. Scholars in turn even more confidently published law review articles that suggested that the Warren and Brandeis privacy tort was dead and that the Constitution was a "nearly insurmountable" barrier in privacy cases.

The media lawyer Floyd Abrams was delighted. "The American press has never been more free, never been more uninhibited, and—most important— never been better protected by the law," he wrote. The whole *Titicut Follies* fiasco seemed an anomaly and ultimately turned out to be a win; privacy in a legal sense was indeed dead.

In September of that year, *Titicut Follies* opened in theaters across the United States. Ads for the film promised that it was a "stark and graphic portrayal of the conditions that existed at the State Prison for the Criminally Insane in Bridgewater." They called it "A MAJOR FILM EVENT," the at-last public showing of "Frederick Wiseman's brilliant and controversial documentary banned from public viewing for 24 years," a look at "society's treatment of the least of its citizens" on the big screen.

Some ads featured a single prominent image placed with enough white space around it to catch a reader's eye: it was a photograph of that dead inmate in his coffin.

You might say that in response to all that freedom, media had grown a little cocky.

Chapter Fourteen

REAL CHUTZPAH,
REAL HOUSEWIVES

B y the time the court lifted the ban on *Titicut Follies* in the early 1990s, it wasn't only documentaries that had dipped into cinema verité; television had started to get real too, a trend kick-started in 1973 when PBS broadcast the true tale of the Louds in its series *An American Family*, "shar[ing] their most private moments with a public audience." Camera-enhanced *Cops*—the show that followed police officers as they infiltrated drug dens, set up DUI stings, and wrote tickets for U-turns—had burst onto television screens. *Totally Hidden Video, America's Funniest Home Videos,* and a re-warmed *Candid Camera* all battled it out for most cringe-worthy snippets from real life. And *Unsolved Mysteries* focused armchair detectives on head-scratching crimes like an "Ohio woman's disappearance" and "the deaths of three bikers in Tennessee." Such programming had mushroomed into a new genre some had started to call reality television.

It was into all this reality that a car containing forty-seven-year-old Ruth Shulman, her husband, and her two teenage children tumbled as they plunged straight off I-10 and into a drainage ditch near Riverside, California, in 1990. Things didn't look good for Ruth; first responders found her entangled in the wreckage, her knee sticking out from the upside-down car. Ruth said she thought she was dreaming and kept asking how the others were. They were mostly okay, but she needed oxygen and she couldn't move her feet.

"I just want to die," she eventually told the nurse who'd arrived by rescue helicopter and had crawled under the car to help.

We know all this because that flight nurse wore a tiny microphone designed to pick up conversations in the open air. A television series titled *On Scene: Emergency Response*—a "look at real-life emergencies and the people who save lives"—had trained its cameraman with his nurse-worn microphone to be every bit as attentive to the accident scene as was the flight nurse, to capture through video and audio "the action" of "sensational, sometimes fatal car wrecks," and to shoot from arrival at the scene until the hospital doors closed behind the victim.

Ruth Shulman had had no idea that she'd been videotaped that day in what she called her gruesome, traumatic, and intensely private moments. She and her family found out only when their own *On Scene: Emergency Response* episode aired—touted in television listings as "auto accident" or "delirious head-injury patient resists treatment." The accident had left Ruth a paraplegic, and she was still in the hospital when she watched the Jaws of Life remove her crumpled body from the wreckage and when she heard her own wishes for death at the scene and inside the rescue helicopter.

"I was not at my best in what I was thinking and what I was saying and what was being shown," Ruth would later say, "and it's not for the public to see this trauma that I was going through."

But the public did in fact want to watch; *On Scene: Emergency Response* ranked 34th of more than 150 syndicated television programs in the early 1990s. The producers claimed that the program was an educational and often graphic reminder of the dangers of driving and other behaviors, but admitted that viewers' motivations were less high-minded. "All media that uses a camera is voyeuristic," those producers had explained, and they'd promised that "as long as there is tragedy and people want to watch it, we'll produce it."

So Ruth Shulman sued, arguing that *On Scene: Emergency Response* had invaded her privacy by publishing her private facts: what she'd said, what she'd looked like, and what her medical report was that day. She admitted that the accident itself might have been of some public interest but that close-up shots and crisp audio of her suffering at the scene and inside the rescue helicopter were not. "There is no social value to hearing a human being's emotional reaction to having her spinal cord severed" is how her lawyer put it.

Media lawyers argued in turn that Ruth was looking in the wrong place for monetary compensation, that the *accident* caused her injuries, not the media, and that the First Amendment promised press freedom even in the most uncomfortable of situations and was entitled to zealous protection.

A quick aside about releases in such scenarios, contracts similar to those gathered by *Titicut Follies* producers. Ruth was in no shape to have signed a release even if one had been offered to her. But had she been okay, and had she signed it, any release would have likely wiped away her right to sue. Today, those recorded as part of a reality program broadly acknowledge that "any injury [they] suffered may have been filmed and can be exploited" by the producers and that "material may [be revealed] about [them] of a personal, private, intimate, surprising, defamatory, embarrassing, disparaging, unfavorable, or unattractive nature." All this, those releases say, might well expose them to "public ridicule, humiliation or condemnation," and that, even so, they waive all tort claims, including the possibility to sue for "violation[s] of the right to privacy" "in any form." Many lawyers at the time of *Shulman* also believed that such releases weren't necessary when things happened in public, that media was free to capture and publish images and sound taken outside, no matter how disturbing.

In the *Shulman* case, those lawyers were partially right.

The California Supreme Court began its decision in *Shulman* with quotations from Warren and Brandeis's "Right to Privacy": the two authors' worry back in 1890 that newfangled "instantaneous photographs" had overstepped "in every direction the obvious bounds of propriety and of decency"; their prediction that other devices threatened to broadcast closeted whispers; their assessment that, rather suddenly, private information had been "spread broadcast" in the daily newspapers. In modern times, the California Supreme Court justices wrote, it had all gotten much worse, because now an onslaught of media of different types had sprung up, ready to satisfy the public's love of gossip, its "curiosity about the private lives of others," and its interest in the stories of neighbors' misfortunes and frailties.

But Ruth Shulman lost her publication-of-private-facts claim in 1998 despite that rhetoric because the court decided that First Amendment interests and the public interest in her calamity trumped her trauma. "The sense of an ever-increasing pressure on personal privacy notwithstanding," the court wrote, "it has long been apparent that the desire for privacy must at many points give way before our right to know . . . about the events and individuals of our time." This included Ruth Shulman and her accident. And then came the sort of deference encouraged by *Sidis*. "In general, it is not for a court or jury to say how a particular story is best covered," the justices explained, because "courts do not, and constitutionally could not, sit as superior editors of the press."

The lawyers for *On Scene: Emergency Response* had expected such an outcome; they'd argued in court and elsewhere that First Amendment principles and protection in such cases was "well-settled." Newspapers covering the case similarly suggested that the *Shulman* court had simply "upheld many of the long-established principles protecting the media in covering news events."

But others saw a greater nuance in the story of Ruth Shulman. "The law is literally unfolding and developing before our eyes," the media lawyer Lee Levine had told the *Los Angeles Times* a few months before the *Shulman* decision came down. There were "no legal rules yet," he said, at least not definitive ones regarding privacy and how much might be published about a person. He sensed there would be more to the story.

That sensibility would turn out to be spot-on. Because there was another part to the California Supreme Court decision in *Shulman* that went a different way.

It's no wonder that the *Shulman* court decided what it did with regard to publication of private facts in the 1990s. By then, not only had the *Titicut Follies* ban been lifted, but media had beaten back a long series of invasion-of-privacy claims in deferential decisions that, like *Shulman*, hailed the First Amendment, lauded truthful information, and emphasized the importance of the public's right to know over the right to privacy.

Those decisions oftentimes were far from lofty, however. Probably the most famous involved a magazine's right to publish photographs featuring a man with his pants unwittingly unzipped, a decision from the 1970s, and, in the 1980s, a newspaper's right to publish a photograph of a woman escaping an abduction wearing only a dish towel.

Throughout that period, media had also won privacy-based cases after outing those who'd had an involuntary sterilization, a psychiatric history, a secret adoption, an incestuous birth, and a woman who'd been the victim of a rape plus her real first name and a photo of her house. A news photographer had trespassed onto a psychiatric hospital's grounds in order to take a photo of an infamous patient alleged to have been involved in a child's death and had ended up including another patient in the published shot; the court called it all privileged conduct. News stories about named college basketball players' lousy grades and resulting serious academic troubles were protected too because the public had an interest in college sports.

One appellate court decided that Oliver Sipple, the disabled marine who'd saved President Gerald Ford from an assassination attempt by knocking away the would-be assassin's gun, had no right to privacy in his sexual orientation even though he hadn't shared the information with most others and even though his family had deserted him when a gossip column had outed him as gay: the news tidbit, the court wrote, contributed to better public understanding because it helped "dispel the false public opinion that gays were timid, weak and unheroic." Sipple had argued in broken, anguished speech that his sexual orientation was a part of his private life "and ha[d] no bearing on [his] response to the act of a person seeking to take the life of another." A person's value was in "how he or she responds to the world in which he lives, not on how, or with whom a private life is shared," he'd said. No matter. The right of the people to know that men who are gay can be brave too was more important.

That right of the people to be informed would also eventually help along media in a case involving a victim whose rape had been videotaped by her attacker. She'd turned the videotape over to police as evidence, police had shared it with a television news reporter, and the reporter's news story had used forty seconds of the victim's "naked feet and calves" and "portions of [her attacker's] naked body," his "upper torso, his arms and hands" "moving above and around" the victim's body during the assault. "By airing the videotape," the federal appellate court wrote in rejecting the victim's privacy claim, "the media defendants heightened the report's impact and credibility by demonstrating that the allegations rested on a firm evidentiary foundation and that the reporter had access to reliable information."

All the while, judges routinely explained that they dared not overturn journalism's news decisions. "Courts do not have license to sit as censors" is what the court that had found the sterilization newsworthy wrote; they shouldn't second-guess what experienced journalists had decided was news. The one that had okayed the photo of the dish-towel-wearing abduction victim agreed that courts shouldn't interfere with "a newspaper's privilege to publish news in the public interest." And the court in the videotaped rape case explained that it refused to "engage in after-the-fact judicial 'blue-penciling' which might have a chilling effect on freedom of the press to determine what is a matter of legitimate public concern."

In the wake of all that media-supportive law, law and journalism students throughout the latter part of the twentieth century continued to learn much about protections given publishers, and working journalists were advised by journalism organizations that "when a person becomes involved in a news event, voluntarily or involuntarily, he forfeits the right to privacy." Outsiders who questioned the media's right to publish certain private things got hit with the First Amendment—that "efforts to protect [society] from politically or socially incorrect expression" shared "the unfortunate common objective of protecting our freedom by proposing to take some of it away"—and a shaming comparison with those who suggested that public schools stop teaching evolution.

Confident journalists thereafter argued that they had the First Amendment right to sell T-shirts and coffee mugs featuring photographs of car accident victims because such images were newsworthy; they argued that the reporter's privilege protected them from being forced to reveal the names of anonymous commenters on news stories, likening internet trolls to Watergate's Deep Throat; and they argued that they had the right to access certain information from state university undergraduate applications—parents' names, parents' addresses, and the applicants' recommenders—because college applications to state schools were public documents and federal student-privacy law wouldn't apply to mere applicants.

By the early twenty-first century, some media had started collecting from police the mug shots of everyday people who'd been arrested for crimes large and small, thereafter publishing them with little regard for their news value or the fact that charges might later be dropped. Mocking sorts of games like

"See the Mug Shot, Guess the Crime" appeared, even in rather highbrow publications: Had the pictured and named woman with overdone makeup been arrested for "crimes against humanity; being too sexy; assaulting her boyfriend with hugs; [or] stealing eye shadow"? Was the young man in the dark shirt busted for "stealing sex toys while dressed as a ninja; breaking and entering; ejaculating on a stuffed horse at Walmart; [or] having sex in a church"? Choose wisely for maximum points; only one answer is correct.

The *New York Post* tabloid meanwhile put a remarkable full-page photo of fifty-eight-year-old Ki Suk Han on its cover; Han had been pushed onto subway tracks by an emotionally disturbed man and was helplessly clinging to the side while facing an oncoming subway train. DOOMED, the *Post* cover read in bold type just below Han; to his right the subhead read "Pushed on the subway track, this man is about to die." And about a second later, Han was indeed crushed to death by that subway train, leaving his survivors forever "haunted" by that image of Han's final moment of life.

Meanwhile, the post–*Titicut Follies* age of reality television had grown to include shows like *Lockup*, *The Real World*, *Big Brother*, and *The Real Housewives* of various cities, some scripted reality and some not. Offerings on videotape like *Faces of Death* that included exactly what you'd imagine appeared, as did television shows that revolved around audio from real-life 911 calls (accessed through freedom-of-information laws) and video from real-life visits to the emergency room (accessed through agreement with some hospitals), and who was to say what the public wanted to know and what it had the right to know and what it should know. One thing was clear, *Time* magazine announced at the dawn of the twenty-first century, voyeurism had now become TV's hottest genre and proved the nation's "passion for peeping."

Bob Woodward and Carl Bernstein of Watergate fame had started to worry. The United States now seemingly had "a scandal press corps," and "the weird, the stupid, the coarse, the sensational" were all becoming "our cultural norm—even our cultural ideal." The Pulitzer Prize–winning journalist Anthony Lewis argued that the law needed to shift: "the First Amendment's guarantees of freedom of speech and of the press are fundamentals of our freedom," he wrote, but "if they succeed in totally overriding the interest of privacy, it would be a terrible victory."

Fast-forward to *Punk'd* and *Scare Tactics* and maybe even *Borat: Cultural Learnings of America for Make Benefit Glorious Nation of Kazakhstan* (court: "it is beyond doubt that Borat fits squarely within the newsworthiness exception" to privacy for the way it "challenges its viewers to confront" the average American's response to a fake Kazakhstani journalist), and it's no surprise that in the midst of it all, in the midst of these visuals of people getting pranked and scared and outed on video and elsewhere, and in spite of decades of deference that had protected publications that published dishtowel-wearing women and unzipped men, some judges had started their own Warren and Brandeis–like rethinking of how the law looked at this kind of privacy right.

Maybe the numbers tell the story best. Within just a few years, journalism had become part of the media, trust in it had fallen from a post-Watergate high of 72 percent to 32 percent, and privacy interests had risen to 79 percent. Mentions of the right to privacy in court decisions that had numbered only around 400 in the 1950s grew to 1,150 in the 1960s, and then to more than 4,000 in the 1970s, to 6,100 in the 1980s, to 7,500 in the 1990s, all the way up to 25,600 in the first two decades of the twenty-first century.

News would lose in nearly every sense. And, surprisingly, *On Scene: Emergency Response* would be one of the first official victims.

It's true that the most important takeaway from Ruth Shulman's 1998 privacy case against the reality program *On Scene: Emergency Response* was that the First Amendment interests in reporting the truth that the public had a right to know beat out any right to privacy she had in her image and words. The "video documentary," the court explained as a wrap-up to that part of its opinion favoring the media and disfavoring her privacy, had used a degree of truthful detail that was "not only relevant, but essential to the narrative" of news about the accident.

But then the justices shifted gears. Publication of private facts was not the only privacy right that had been accepted by the courts by then: there was also the tort of intrusion into seclusion. And so, in that same opinion that celebrated the public's right to know over an individual's privacy, Ruth Shulman won in a different way. The publication of her image and words was protected, the court decided, but not the intrusive means of making the video itself.

That small microphone on the rescue helicopter nurse placed by the cameraman? That was precisely the sort of technology that made it possible to broadcast the closeted whispers that Warren and Brandeis had worried about, the device that allowed television viewers to be transported from their sofas into Shulman's crumpled car and then onto her life-flight helicopter. "We are aware of no law or custom permitting the press to ride in ambulances or enter hospital rooms during treatment without the patient's consent," the court wrote, and a "patient's conversation with a provider of medical care in the course of treatment" carried significant expectations of privacy. It all seemed to support a valid claim for intrusion, the Restatement provision that made it wrong to peer in on another electronically or otherwise when they are in a secluded place.

That meant the *On Scene: Emergency Response* broadcast was necessarily protected because the media had the right to air newsworthy details from an accident scene, but the intrusive methods behind that broadcast, specifically the taping of accident victims at their most vulnerable through what was, in effect, a hidden microphone, were not. It wasn't a complete victory for Ruth Shulman, and maybe had it all happened on the highway within earshot of others, she wouldn't have had a right to privacy even in an intrusion sense. But that different sort of scenario would be left for a different court on a different day, and Ruth could claim a partial victory. Her lawyer considered it more than that; he called the outcome "a major defeat for media corporations who have cloaked themselves with the First Amendment in order to trample over privacy rights."

Media lawyers for the most part pooh-poohed the suggestion that that part of the *Shulman* decision would have any sort of broad impact on journalism given the protections of the First Amendment. "For the legitimate news media," one said, "I don't think this changes the rules of the road in any sense."

And, indeed, just four months after the *Shulman* verdict, things in the reality television genre had seemingly gotten back to normal: a production crew moved into an Idaho town to film a TV show they called *The World's Nastiest Neighbors*, a hidden-camera look at how real-life people would respond to fake boors (so-called brain-damaged people who danced in the streets, used bullhorns to announce public gatherings, and mud wrestled on their front lawn). Here too technology enabled the production. "A camera crew taped the neighbors' reactions," secretly using larger hidden cameras inside the boors' house and smaller ones, including one disguised as a pair of sunglasses. The worried real-life neighbors eventually called the police on the boors and police discovered the ruse, but the program found a home on television even so. Hidden-camera programs "may be offensive to some," a network executive explained to *The New York Times*, "but tend to do well in the ratings."

It was into this mix of growing boldness among publishers, nascent rumblings from certain courts that media had at times overstepped the bounds of privacy, and growing concern among the public about personal privacy that Congress introduced Section 230 of the Communications Decency Act.

That turned out to be a big mistake.

Coda Part II

IT DOES NOT FOLLOW

More than a century ago, some predicted the world of the internet. It wasn't pretty.

"I should tremble," one journalist wrote in 1875, just as Louis Brandeis and Sam Warren were entering law school, "to see a paper issued by a really strong man who was also vile in his tastes and unscrupulous in the material he employed to cater to the wants of the public." The seer suggested that Americans always seemed hopeful, always believed "that every change [would] bring about better results" and that, as far as publications were concerned, a "higher and better type" would always develop from what had gone before.

"But this does not follow," he warned.

He would know. He'd by that point published a hoax pamphlet extolling interracial relationships in an early version of political misinformation meant to chill readers.

Zoom ahead to the mid-1990s. The internet was pretty much brand-new, and (surprise!) pornography already seemed to be proliferating there, documented for all by the image of a shocked child on *Time* magazine's 1995 CYBERPORN cover. Members of Congress wanted to make sure the little guy wouldn't come across any such thing again—Representative Christopher Cox of California, father of two, warned that "there is in this vast world of computer information . . . some things in the bookstore, if you will, that our children ought not to see"—so they began to enact laws that would "deter online porn merchants from pandering to children" and "ban indecent and obscene communications over the global computer network Internet and on computer services."

There was some First Amendment outcry about the indecency ban, as you might imagine, and that part of the law eventually fizzled. But Congress also had concerns about who might be responsible should a website try its best but fail to remove something objectionable. Rumors were that a court had recently held the web service company Prodigy liable for a defamatory comment left on one of its web-based bulletin boards. Prodigy mostly facilitated family-friendly internet access! How could it check every single one of its sixty thousand daily posts, assess them, and remove every single potentially objectionable one? Not only would that become an *I Love Lucy*–like conveyor belt of words that just kept coming faster and faster, but liability concerns would force any innovating internet company straight out of business. The internet might die in its infancy.

So to protect Prodigy and the internet itself two House members, Cox, a Republican, and Ron Wyden, a Democrat, drafted an amendment in response: "No provider or user of interactive computer services shall be treated as the publisher or speaker of any information provided by an information content provider." That meant that while websites would remain liable for information their employees posted (because that sort of publication would have originated with the company itself), if they invited the public to post on bulletin boards and otherwise interact, they would not be responsible for that user-generated material. The idea, Congressmen Cox and Wyden said, was to encourage internet companies to be vigilant, to remove anything nasty from their domains without worry that they'd become publishers by doing so, to self-regulate without the liability fears of a publisher. No liability meant that even if something bad somehow stayed up despite those best efforts, internet companies and websites couldn't be sued for it.

"We want to make sure that everyone in America has an open invitation and feels welcome to participate in the Internet," Congressman Cox told his fellow legislators when he introduced the measure. Others in Congress agreed, suggesting that it was a "thoughtful" way "to protect our children from being exposed to obscene and indecent material on the internet," to "help keep smut off the net" by encouraging web-based companies to clean their own houses.

Section 230 of the Communications Decency Act passed through Congress quickly, and President Clinton signed the bill into law on February 8, 1996, crediting it with serving "both the private sector and the public interest."

That may sound naive. Today, Section 230 is at the heart of discussion about the internet's wrongs, the reason many on both sides of the aisle are pushing for internet regulation, greater website responsibility, and an amendment to Section 230 if not its abolishment.

But if you time warped back to the birth of Section 230, you'd find it an oddly unplugged time. Only about 20 percent of households had computers, and less than 10 percent of Americans had ever accessed the internet, news stories said, necessitating such helpful descriptors as it's "like a gigantic electronic filing cabinet" and it "lets people access information stored in computers around the world by using browser software that lets computers retrieve pictures, video, sounds and text from remote sites." Even Congressman Cox had suggested in floor debate on Section 230 that it was only "recently" that he and his fellow lawmakers had become acquainted with it all.

Back then, as excited news reports that routinely announced brand-new websites explained, Yahoo ("http://www.yahoo.com/") helped surfers find "cool stuff" on the web like Big Entertainment of Boca Raton ("http://scifi.com/pulp/teknation/tnation.html") and the Hartford Fire Department ("http://www.tiac.net/users/ellfire"). Electronic mail, called that, had just begun, with two companies promising the possibility of *free* email services by 1996's end: Freemark Communications and Juno. And on the very day that President Clinton signed Section 230 into law, newspapers marveled that "sites with sounds" had increasingly started to appear.

It all proved that the internet was not just a fad, as was the worry, but an admittedly "fringe medium" that was "gradually catching the attention of businesses and consumers." Some suggested that the internet could well be the most important invention since Velcro.

Without a doubt, Section 230 helped to grow the internet; it helped facilitate everything from reader comments on nytimes.com to restaurant reviews on yelp.com to musings on reddit.com and posts on questionable websites far beyond. Section 230 not only protects all such websites, it's likely that not one of them would be the same had Section 230 not existed.

Under it, no matter how horrid, how defamatory, how privacy invading the comment, the review, the critique, the photograph, or the video, *The New York Times*, Yelp, Reddit, and those less ethics-bound websites are not liable as long as it's posted by someone outside the organization.

Add to that a public with an expansive understanding of First Amendment freedoms and little regard for or understanding of the right to privacy—confident legal advice on one participatory website read precisely this way: "The first amendment garuntees your right to free speech and you CANNOT get in trouble or be held accountable for any type of dafamation as long as it is is the truth"—and the internet seemed the true marketplace of ideas, a filing cabinet full of truthful information with some falsity thrown in that would be just as protected as the best of literature.

"One reason the Web is so great is you can do whatever the hell you want," a cyber expert said back then. "There really aren't any rules."

And so, just as the racist seer had warned in 1875, the vile and the unscrupulous took notice of not only the internet but Section 230. And as much as pixels might have seemed a hopeful change, the shift away from Samuel D. Warren Company paper did not make things higher or better, at least when it came to privacy.

Some web surfers looking for cool stuff on the internet a few years after the passage of Section 230 would have come across a website that called itself The Dirty, innuendo absolutely intended.

There, among hundreds of similar posts, they'd see two photos of a young woman, maybe in her teens or early twenties. She was lying on the floor of what appeared to be a small bedroom in a named city, staring blankly at the camera, arms above her head, apparently utterly out of it, perhaps unable to move. There was vomit all over the carpeting.

NO ONE INVITED HER, the headline above her photos read. This explanation followed: "This bit*ch threw up all over our room, and pissed herself.... Then she woke up in the morning and had the nerve to ask for new clothes to wear and to take a shower. ARE YOU KIDDING ME!"

Nik Richie, founder of The Dirty, added this in response: "I can't believe she threw up that much and is still fat. Mathematically it doesn't make sense."

There were seventy-two comments on the original post from 2011, and a decade later they were still there, as was the original post, all searchable, all available online even though the young woman who might have had too much to drink was likely by then in her thirties. Two commenters named her; others called her a pig and a cow. The most troubling suggested that the original poster should have raped her.

It's both ironic and utterly predictable that Congress's attempt at a more welcoming internet for all, the law that its sponsors said was meant to re-move perverse incentives for cyberspace's anything-goes culture and one that would serve the public interest, led to websites like The Dirty. Nik Richie, for one, credits Congress in his very first frequently asked question: "Can I sue the dirty for publishing false information?" Answer: "In a word—NO." "Under a federal law known as the Communications Decency Act or 'CDA,' website operators like TheDirty are generally not liable for 'publishing' con-tent from third party users."

It's the same for invasion of privacy. Today, under Section 230, the un-fortunate young woman on the floor of that bedroom in 2011 would not win a claim against The Dirty no matter the accuracy or inaccuracy of the post. Her only recourse would be against the poster, and, if traceable, that poster likely had far less income than The Dirty, where, back then, a single banner ad cost $10,000 a month.

We know that The Dirty isn't liable despite making all that money off others' misfortunes because somebody posted there loads of nasty stuff about a woman named Sarah Jones, a professional cheerleader and high school teacher: that she'd slept with every Cincinnati Bengals football player, that she'd had sex with one of them in her classroom, and more. She asked Nik Richie to take it all down, Richie refused, and Jones sued. (This was be-fore she'd fall from grace for bedding a student, but that was surely one of the reasons Richie chose to fight this particular claim.)

"You dug your own grave here Sarah" is what Richie posted in an open letter on his website. "With all the media attention this is only going to get worse for you."

He was right. Journalism and media backed Richie and The Dirty. The Reporters Committee for Freedom of the Press, CNN, and *Gawker*, among others, argued in their joint amicus brief that Section 230 had become the new overarchingly protective law for publishers online, that it was "grounded in core First Amendment standards," and that it stood for "expansion of free speech on the internet." The ACLU joined in an amicus brief too, arguing that a decision against The Dirty "threaten[ed] the broad diversity of protected speech" online. Facebook, Google, Microsoft, and other internet giants argued the same in their own brief: that Section 230 "remains critical to the development and robustness of the Internet" and its growth as "a medium for free expression."

The arguments worked; Sarah Jones lost. "Congress enacted [Section 230] to preserve a free internet," a federal appellate court wrote, "and that enactment resolves this case." Sure, Richie had chosen what posts to put up and had routinely added his own comments to others' posts, but Section 230 was clear; there would be no liability if the offensive words were written not by Richie himself but by a pseudonymous other, and the suggestive name The Dirty didn't matter a bit either.

And so, the same year that the *Jones* case was decided, web surfers could also find nineteen-year-old Brittney on The Dirty, a young woman who was, the poster said, a "home wrecking whore" who had "rode more dicks then [*sic*] most 30 year old women" and who also had chlamydia. The website published her nude photos with strategically placed stars and a thought bubble. You could see her face.

Section 230 rulings, like the one in *Jones v. Dirty World*, emboldened other websites that trafficked in emotional and reputational harm of named or identifiable individuals: dirtyphonebook.com (she's "a cute little bi-sexual Taiwan hooker that lives in Vegas now"), Juicy Campus (she's "been around with everyone in my frat and other guys"), Blipdar (she's "a desperate slut," a "decent fuck [and] cumrag"), College ACB (she's "a huge whore who will say anything to get a guys dick in her mouth"), and even peopleofwalmart.com (he, pictured leaning over the customer service desk, appeared to have defecated on himself). Today, websites like cheatersandbastards.com publish posts like one that suggested that a pictured and named woman, a "filthy whore" and a "disgusting cow," had "fornicate[d] with her nephew." "Warning," the website suggests: "This site contains truth . . . [and] freedom of speech." It promised that it would remove nude images, posts about children, and copyrighted images, but that "all other requests [would] be ignored and discarded." Because, under Section 230, it can.

Section 230 has also facilitated revenge porn websites like myex.com, one that literally suggested that the angry "get revenge" by sending in nude photos of the exes who'd wronged them. The angry did, and the devastatingly raunchy pictures—usually of women, usually named and searchable by city ("find someone you know," the website advised)—were headlined in 2015 with phrases like SHOW YOU MY EX BITCH and CHEATING HOE, multiple clickable nudes-meant-for-one off to the side. Some put its earnings at $20,000 a month. Today myex.com has disappeared, but similar websites remain, including one on which people post requests for nude photos of "College Bitches," named women who are students at named colleges. Sometimes their requests appear to be answered with downloadable files. "Anyone have K—— D——?," one poster recently asked, identifying by name a female student at a named college. The answer appeared to be no, but a different poster offered up a different named woman's photographs. "Anything of K—— B——?" that reply instead suggested and included a smiling photograph of a young woman and a file attachment.

Section 230 protected people accused of trafficking in humans too; a federal appeals court granted the website backpage.com immunity from sex advertisements featuring minor sex-trafficking victims because of the statute. "This is a hard case—hard not in the sense that the legal issues defy resolution," the court wrote, "but hard in the sense that the law requires that we, like the court below, deny relief to plaintiffs whose circumstances evoke outrage." Since then, Congress has amended Section 230 to carve out that sort of immunity for trafficking, but the heart of Section 230 remains.

A great tragedy is that people have killed themselves after such online revelations. The Rutgers freshman Tyler Clementi for one, who in 2010 jumped from the George Washington Bridge after his roommate posted a secretly recorded video of Clementi's intimate moments. A few years later, doctors writing in the *Journal of the American Medical Association* linked "the social-media age" with rising suicide rates, depression, and anxiety among young people, a media-critical assessment remarkably similar to that published in

American Nervousness more than a century before and one that aligns with what Facebook's own damning internal assessment showed.

Those who posted "No One Invited Her" surely recognized a link; they said that they would feel "kinda bad" if the young woman lying on the floor "looks at this post and offs herself." The creator of Is Anyone Up?, the very first revenge porn website, saw the same potential. "Let's be real for a second," he told *The Village Voice* in 2012. "If somebody killed themselves over that? Do you know how much money I'd make? At the end of the day, I do not want anybody to hurt themselves. But if they do? Thank you for the money."

And it's not too much of a stretch to say that Section 230 also helped along more modern types of seer-like political disinformation: social media sites, for example, have little reason to look into who has posted certain false material designed to manipulate voters during a crucial election or those considering vaccines during a dangerous pandemic if they aren't liable for it.

Ultimately, of course, the Reporters Committee for Freedom of the Press, CNN, the ACLU, Facebook, and Google were all correct about how most courts have come to describe Section 230. The statute is the cyber First Amendment, a law that "encourages the unfettered and unregulated development of free speech on the Internet," one court wrote in 2003, one designed by its own language to "promote the continued development of the Internet" in line with U.S. policy, and to "preserve [its] vibrant and competitive free market." That's the language of Section 230 that many focus on.

But sort of like with the original First Amendment, there's a nuance to Section 230 that isn't often highlighted. At its very start, the statute reads directly in line with what its sponsors said its purpose was, one that suggested that indeed they had a higher and better vision for the internet: to "offer a forum for a true diversity of *political* discourse, unique opportunities for *cultural* development, and myriad avenues for *intellectual* activity." Section 230's focus was on the expansion of the sort of "*educational* and *informational* resources" that "benefit[ed] . . . *all* Americans." Congress even suggested for good measure that "harassment by means of computer" wouldn't be protected by the CDA.

In any event, after the decision in *Jones*, Nik Richie called himself "an American Hero who saved the internet." But by that time, because of websites like his that caused emotional harm, other courts had started to double down more than had the *Shulman* court, to write that they were tired of what was happening with media online and elsewhere and to conclude that privacy needed to be respected more stridently. Nik Richie and his supporters might have won the battle, but a war was in the offing and modern judges seemed to be lining up on one side in particular.

The freewheeling internet continued to do whatever the hell it wanted just the same.

PART III

WATCH OUT!

Chapter Fifteen

MISS VERMONT, JUDGE MIKVA, AND THE WRESTLER

To hear Tucker Max's side of the story, he met a former Miss Vermont at a Boca Raton gym, and within hours they were at it in the back of a Ford Explorer. It wouldn't be the only time the two would come together in what he described as a weeks-long celebration of breasts and loins, eager bodies and soreness, and a multistate journey of sex in gazebos, kitchens, and public bathrooms. Much of it, or so Tucker Max opined, revealed "an inexperienced girl reacting to her first real sexual encounters." He used her real name.

"I didn't know what sex was before you," Miss Vermont was said to have said just before their breakup. "You infiltrate me and my body craves you."

Tucker Max put all that and more on his website in 2003 in a post he titled "The Miss Vermont Story," one that even he described as a kiss-and-tell "outside the bounds of all social norms." No matter; this was modernity, part of a new trend "of people putting their lives on the Internet in what's called Web logs," sort of like an old-fashioned diary entry, experts necessarily explained, but one published "online for the world to read." It had a Dirty-esque feel, but this was Tucker Max himself telling the tale, so there would be no Section 230 immunity.

Tucker Max believed instead that the First Amendment would protect him, that he had the "freedom of speech guaranteed by the Constitution" to say what he said in his "autobiographical account of their relationship."

Tucker Max's worldwide narrative didn't have the excruciating detail of *My Life and Loves* or the visuals in *Titicut Follies*, sure, but it was graphic enough, uninhibited enough some might say, to shock. There was another difference: the point, its author said, wasn't a warped sort of sex ed or nudity for its own sake but to call Miss Vermont out on her pageant platform in favor of sexual abstinence. "I normally don't like writing about the specific details of relationships or hook-ups for many reasons," Tucker Max assured the readers who'd also perused his "Midget Story" ("the time I had sex with a midget") and "Tucker Tries Buttsex; Hilarity Does Not Ensue" ("Jaime: 'But . . . I've never done it.' Tucker: 'I've never done it either; it can be our thing'"), but he was tired of "putting up with the giant hypocrisy."

He never once used the phrase "the public's right to know," and maybe his news decisions shouldn't be given deference even though books at the time were titled things like *We're All Journalists Now*, but he did throw out adjectives like "truthful" and "autobiographical," and because he'd gone to law school, he likely knew that an argument that a story was true and of public interest was a strong counterbalance to any invasion-of-privacy claim. This was, after all, a state's top beauty queen (!) who was telling young girls(!) one thing about abstinence while doing another (!). In any event, he ended "The Miss Vermont Story" not with any high-mindedness but with another slam: "Thank god for her sake she's attractive, otherwise she'd starve to death."

Miss Vermont sued, arguing that Tucker Max had shared private stories about their alleged sexual affairs on the internet. Tucker Max argued that Miss Vermont was a hypocrite, someone who held herself out as the personal embodiment of temperance, responsibility, and abstinence, while behaving less than virtuously, and deserved public accountability.

A Florida judge sided with Miss Vermont and ordered that Tucker Max take "The Miss Vermont Story" down.

Given the chronology of The Dirty, you might imagine what happened next: Journalists who somehow saw their own freedoms implicated immediately pushed back. "Don't chip away at 1st Amendment," one impassioned newspaper editorial read; another was headlined JUDGE'S RULING HARMS OUR FREEDOM TO PRINT VIEWS. Some readily equated Tucker Max with their colleagues in *Near v. Minnesota* who'd been prevented from reporting on government corruption ("the same principle generally applies," one wrote, "there is no doubt whatsoever that the judge's order . . . is completely at odds with the First Amendment"). They schooled that "even the disreputable have

right to free speech," that the judge's ruling was but "cyberphobia," "a rationale to take away freedoms that are so integral to this nation's history and
greatness." Some blamed Miss Vermont for her temerity just as they had
William Sidis decades before: Why would someone who wanted to be let
alone publicize herself by filing such a lawsuit? Miss Vermont may value her
privacy, one column read, "but we hold the First Amendment more dearly."
"It's not good manners" to kiss and tell as Tucker Max had done, another
suggested, "but it's in the Bill of Rights."

Eventually, a withered Miss Vermont dropped her lawsuit, and Tucker
Max instantly put his story of their sexual relationship back up, thanking
those who'd supported him for championing his—our—constitutional freedoms. "I am proud that I was able, in a small way, to serve my country by
defending, and ultimately defeating, an egregious attack on the 1st Amendment," he wrote. "If you read the briefs and have even the slightest understanding of American law, you knew she was fucked before she started.
Literally and figuratively."

By that point, the ACLU had joined the First Amendment groundswell
against Miss Vermont, filing an amicus brief on behalf of Tucker Max that
suggested the internet was the closest thing to a "true free marketplace of
ideas," a bastion of "breathtaking utility," "openness," and boundless communication.

Despite the bravado from many corners, it's not at all clear that Tucker Max
would have won had Miss Vermont's lawsuit against him continued. It's
doubtful, in fact.

Several years before his post, at just about the time of *Shulman* and the
passage of Section 230, a well-respected judge named Abner Mikva retired
from the D.C. Circuit Court of Appeals, the highly influential federal appellate court in Washington where he'd sat ever since President Jimmy Carter
had appointed him. As he did, he warned in what he called a "scary message"
for media that change was in the air.

"Watch out!" he wrote. "There's a backlash coming in First Amendment
doctrine."

This ominous warning came from deep inside the judiciary. There was a growing feeling among Mikva's colleagues across the United States, he said, that deferential First Amendment Supreme Court decisions in the 1960s, 1970s, and 1980s had gone too far to protect media, that judges in years past had defended "harmful" reporting too strongly, and that they no longer believed that the First Amendment should be or was meant to be so protective. He blamed "the state of journalism," including a decline in standards, for provoking the backlash. Judge Mikva didn't highlight the nuance of language in Supreme Court cases, but he didn't need to; he and his colleagues knew it was there and knew that they were on solid ground.

Judge Mikva was right. Within a few years, as television became more real, as the internet really took hold, and as journalism morphed into media, there came a series of privacy cases in which courts refused *Shulman*-type deference to the public's right to know and instead embraced privacy in situations far less intrusive than the sex story from Tucker Max's keyboard. Those who'd become accustomed to what some scholars now called the more "romantic" view of First Amendment rights, those who believed in absolutism or close, soon recognized that there were limits.

Sports Illustrated was one. A court in California reprimanded the magazine for publishing a typical Little League team photograph—adults in the back, kids all around them—that illustrated a story about coaches who abuse their players. A small number of the pictured boys had been victims of one of those men, their coach, and so they sued the magazine for invading their privacy by outing them in that way. Not only should the magazine have blurred the kids' faces, the court wrote, but state law protected such children from exposure and "public policy favors such protection." The magazine had argued that the typical team photo helped show that such tragedy could happen to any team and to any players.

The *Chicago Tribune* too. An Illinois court upheld a privacy claim against the newspaper for publishing the loving words that a mother had said to the body of her dead son in a hospital room, words overheard by reporters and included in a story about a rise in gang violence that also featured a photo of the victim's body on a gurney. "A jury could find that a reasonable member of the public has no concern with the statements a grieving mother makes to her dead son," the court wrote, "or with what he looked like lying dead in the hospital, even though he died as the result of a gang shooting." There, the newspaper had argued that the mother's quotations—"I love you, Calvin. . . . I have been telling you for the longest time about this street thing"—had helped to personalize an otherwise data-driven story.

And then a federal trial court in Washington, D.C., ruled against the *Washington Examiner*'s innocuous gossipy tidbit that a television news producer had "hooked up" with high-profile men, including a popular basketball coach. It was "unlikely that an unmarried, professional woman in her 30s would want her private life about whom she had dated and had sexual relations revealed in the gossip column of a widely distributed newspaper," the court wrote. The woman's "personal, romantic life [was] not a matter of public concern."

Maybe, these judges seemed to be saying, this utile, open, and boundless marketplace of ideas all the more invigorated by new media needed some regulation too.

And then, at this time of turnabout at the dawn of the twenty-first century, they started to protect public officials.

Those who watched the 1990s-born television magazine-style show *Dateline* became familiar with a segment that producers called "To Catch a Predator." It featured the stories of mostly men drawn to suburban houses by tweens who'd taken to social media to complain of boredom.

Turns out that the tweens who posted were actually adult internet vigilantes and the narrative was very nearly always the same: the man sent along some nasty description of what he wanted to do with the tween, he showed up at the house for sex, the kid in the house quickly disappeared, the show's host, Chris Hansen, popped in to confront the man about his nefarious plans, the man attempted to run away, and police arrested him outside on the lawn. Hidden cameras recorded it all, inside and outside, giving shocked parents around the nation a window into stunningly common and otherwise hidden predatory internet behavior.

"To Catch a Predator" was so popular that it eventually became its own show.

Then came the story of fifty-something Bill Conradt, the chief felony prosecutor and district attorney for a county just outside Dallas. We'll never know Conradt's side of why or how it all went down, but for whatever reason he responded to an I-am-bored-my-parents-are-away post by a boy who said he was thirteen. Conradt told the tween that he was nineteen, that he liked young boys for sex, and that he wanted to feel up this particular young boy and thereafter do much more with him. Conradt also sent along penis photos. The two communicated in that way for days.

To Catch a Predator's anchor, Chris Hansen, never had the chance to confront District Attorney Conradt with that lurid transcript, however, because Conradt didn't show up at the suburban house. The decoy actor texted and called and pleaded, and when Conradt never arrived, frustrated police decided to arrest him anyway, given that communicating in such a way with a child (or someone one thinks is a child) is a crime. They got a search warrant and an arrest warrant, and, journalists and cameras in tow, they went to Conradt's house to take him into custody. Conradt must have known what was about to go down because, just as soon as police entered, he shot himself dead.

"When these people came after him for a news show, it ended his life," Conradt's sister said after his suicide. In 2007, she sued NBC in his name.

Now, you might think that if media could identify the victims of rape without liability and show video of the crime, if media could publish pictures of patients at mental hospitals, if the public had the right to know what a car accident victim looked like and precisely what she said while pinned, NBC might have the right to investigate and report on this sort of behavior by a public official whose job it was to prosecute such crimes.

But you'd be wrong; this time privacy would win, and *Dateline* would get no deference because a federal judge ruled that Conradt's sister should indeed get the chance to tell a jury about the emotional harm he'd suffered at the hands of NBC when it showed up to cover his arrest. That jury, the judge wrote in 2008, "could find that NBC persuaded the police officers to engage in tactics principally for dramatic effect and to make a more sensational television show," all the while knowing that such coverage would "publicly humiliate a public servant who had always been an upstanding member of the community."

Most chilling for the journalists must have been the judge's use of the Society of Professional Journalists' Code of Ethics against them, suggesting that a jury could find the journalists' behavior unlawful because Chris Hansen and company had failed to "recognize that gathering and reporting information may cause harm or discomfort," had failed to "show good taste," and had failed to "avoid pandering to lurid curiosity." It's why the SPJ quickly placed that hopeful language at the end of its code suggesting that code provisions were not legally enforceable under the First Amendment.

The case settled within weeks.

By 2019, the well-respected judge who'd decided that journalism's ethics code could help determine its own liability, Denny Chin, originally appointed by President Clinton, had been elevated by President Barack Obama to the highly influential federal appellate court for the Second Circuit, one that covers New York, Connecticut, and, coincidentally, Vermont. It was that same court that had decided the *Sidis* case decades before. And Judge Chin proved Judge Mikva right yet again when he was one of three judges who that year ruled that the former vice presidential candidate Sarah Palin had a valid defamation claim against *The New York Times* for an editorial that incorrectly linked a Palin political action committee publication with violence against politicians. Judge Chin and his colleagues had not only told the lower court that a jury should decide the case but explicitly laid out the evidence that, to them, would help prove the actual malice necessary.

It was that same year that Justice Clarence Thomas argued in a concurring Supreme Court opinion that *New York Times v. Sullivan* should be overturned. *Sullivan*'s protection for publishers was, Justice Thomas wrote, a "policy-driven" decision "masquerading as constitutional law."

Journalists were shocked; whatever had happened to deference? But Judge Chin, for one, was unmoved. "I do think," he wrote in a law review article that same year, "that media and journalism have evolved to the point where perhaps the same kind of respect and deference that journalists once enjoyed is no longer warranted." He pointed to the devolution of publication on the internet, "the difficulty of erasing information that's out there," and ever-increasing data collection as reasons for society's greater sensitivity to privacy concerns.

Put another way, deference was done, and Judge Chin was clearly not alone in thinking so. The year after the *Conradt* case, a federal appeals court in Atlanta decided that *Hustler* magazine could be liable for posthumously publishing a series of nude photographs of Nancy Benoit, a professional wrestler who'd been murdered by her husband. The right to privacy, here in death through misappropriation, sprang from the Constitution, that court explained, and even though Benoit had died in a newsworthy way, her photographs served "no 'legitimate purpose of disseminating news . . . and needlessly expose[d] aspects of the plaintiff's private life to the public.'" *Hustler* "would have us rule that someone's notorious death constitutes a carte blanche for the publication of any and all images of that person during his or her life," the court wrote, "regardless of whether those images were intentionally kept private and regardless of whether those images are of any relation to the incident currently of public concern." *Hustler* didn't have that right.

That's the decision that some media defense lawyers say helped pave the way for what became one of the most prominent examples of the pushback against media in favor of privacy: the professional wrestler Hulk Hogan's claim against the tabloid website that called itself *Gawker*.

This is the way *Gawker*'s story and therefore the privacy dispute between Hulk Hogan and the *Gawker* website began:

> Because the internet has made it easier for all of us to be shameless voyeurs and deviants, we love to watch famous people have sex. We watch this footage because it's something we're not supposed to see.

Gawker headlined its news story EVEN FOR A MINUTE, WATCHING HULK HOGAN HAVE SEX IN A CANOPY BED IS NOT SAFE FOR WORK BUT WATCH IT ANYWAY and published it in 2012 with an accompanying video secretly taken with a bedroom ceiling camera that showed the famous professional wrestler and reality television star fully nude, penis visible, having sex of different sorts with an accommodating friend's wife in the accommodating friend's bed. Audio of sex sounds and subtitles of sex talk included.

Hulk Hogan asked *Gawker* to take the video down, and when *Gawker* refused, he sued for invasion of privacy.

Gawker was no stranger to that sort of threat. It had built its reputation on flouting journalism's ethics codes to publish things that mainstream media would not, including a feature it called "Gawker Stalker" that reported the whereabouts of celebrities in real time. But its coverage was way broader than that. The same year it published the Hulk Hogan sex tape, it brought worldwide attention to a North Carolina teen in an article it headlined FEMALE HIGH SCHOOL STUDENT ACCUSED OF FLASHING VAGINA IN YEAR-BOOK PHOTO. School officials had accused the eighteen-year-old of "exposing her hooha," Gawker wrote, by "lifting her graduation gown" in a photo published in the school's yearbook—Gawker called it a "crotchbook"—and Gawker included in its story a photograph of the high school student in cap and gown, with black bars covering her face and pelvic area. In a lawsuit that got comparatively little coverage, the teenager sued for the emotional harm she'd suffered at Gawker's hands, and Gawker argued in response that it had the First Amendment right to publish what it had.

The court sided with the teen. This wasn't a news story about a genuine public controversy, the court wrote, but one that pandered to the lurid and voyeuristic. Gawker's argument that it was protected by New York Times v. Sullivan principles fell flat.

Gawker was just as righteous and resolute in the case involving Hulk Hogan. "The Constitution does unambiguously accord us the right to publish true things about public figures," Gawker editors wrote in support of their news judgment to publish the Hogan sex tape, and they suggested that any judicial order against them would be "contemptuous of centuries of First Amendment jurisprudence."

Many commentators agreed that the law was on Gawker's side. And then, at trial in 2016, a Gawker editor testified that he believed he had the right to publish nearly all sex tapes. Was there a limit? Hogan's attorneys asked. If one featured a child, he answered. A child under the age of four.

The Florida jury thereafter went the way of the crotchbook court and awarded Hogan $140 million and drove Gawker into bankruptcy. Shockwave-inspired headlines from stunned newspapers read FIRST AMENDMENT TRASHED and EVEN THE LOATHSOME HAVE RIGHTS, and some said that the judge in the Gawker case had "encroach[ed] on editorial judgment" and had therefore chilled the press. "America has incomparable free-speech protections," one writer reminded readers, and "in this new era, we need to keep it that way." It's true that the Hulk Hogan case was bankrolled by the billionaire Peter Thiel, a man who'd been outed by *Gawker* as gay years before, but as was clear by that point in cases involving everything from hookups to *Hustler*, this outcome was straight in line. The right to privacy had already wakened and was rallying back with full-nelson force.

Thereafter, the Hulk Hogan jury verdict itself proved persuasive, even though the case ultimately settled for $31 million without an appeal, without any precedent-setting appellate court decision supporting Hulk Hogan's privacy. Post-*Gawker*, *The Washington Post* reported, plaintiffs everywhere had come down with what it called "Hulk Hogan Syndrome" and were suddenly "winning big."

But even plaintiffs backed by billionaires don't win big in privacy cases unless the law and judicial temperaments support them. And now it was headline-makingly clear that both did, that the "First Amendment could no longer be invoked as a secure shield" against perceived privacy invasions, even by the press. Some judges were clear about the internet-inspired cause. "As the ability to do harm has grown," the Ohio Supreme Court wrote when it accepted a privacy tort for the first time after years of rejecting it as being too similar to defamation without defamation's protections, "so must the law's ability to protect the innocent."

The floodgates thereafter opened. One court in 2016 found ESPN potentially liable for posting a star National Football League player's medical chart showing that he'd had a finger amputated. The amputation itself was of public concern, the court wrote, because the loss of a finger could affect an athlete's ability to play, but a jury could find that posting the medical chart was of purely private concern, given the privacy in medical information throughout history and later embodied in HIPAA. Another court right about then found that *Chicago Sun-Times* reporters who'd used data from the Illinois driver's license database to report on police officers' physical characteristics could be liable for invading privacy. "Where members of the press unlawfully obtain sensitive information that, in context, is of marginal public value," the court wrote, including the hair color, eye color, and weight of those officers who'd participated in a lineup that, given those identifiers, seemed to favor a politically well-connected arrestee, "the First Amendment does not guarantee them the right to publish that information." A third court decided in 2018 that an author who'd written a book about campus

Title IX complaints had potential liability for publishing "intensely private" text messages sent by a student to a professor because they weren't essential to the story and therefore weren't of public concern. And a fourth court that same year found police liable for allowing cameras from the reality show *The First 48* to record images of an arrestee without his consent. The filming and broadcast constituted a seizure of the man's image and were violations of his right to privacy; showing him walking down a police hallway and being interrogated by police served no legitimate purpose and violated his constitutional rights.

And in line with that language from the Ohio justices, other courts seemed to focus their condemnation on internet-based communication in particular. One ruled that a website could be liable for publishing video from a fatal accident scene, including the victim in his last moments of life, even though the video hadn't been obtained by the intrusive means condemned in *Shulman*. "Not all speech is of equal first amendment importance," that court wrote, "and where matters of purely private significance are at issue," the constitutional concerns are not as rigorous. The boxer Floyd Mayweather could be liable for publishing on social media his former girlfriend's sonogram photograph and accompanying medical report, suggesting that an abortion had led to their breakup. Such information "falls outside the protection accorded a newsworthy report," the court wrote, because "those images served no legitimate public purpose." And despite early ACLU arguments, state high courts began to rule that those people who posted revenge porn images could be punished for invading privacy. "This is a unique crime fueled by technology," the Illinois Supreme Court wrote, a problem of staggering depth, and privacy as it had developed through history supported the idea that "nonconsensual dissemination of private sexual images" was a "strong candidate for categorical exclusion from full First Amendment protections."

From one perspective, not a single one of those outcomes, not even the Hulk Hogan case itself, is all that surprising given the course of the right to privacy in the United States, and they're all why Tucker Max probably would have lost the privacy claim brought by Miss Vermont had her case continued. Privacy in sex and nudity and medical information and messages and family tragedies has a rich history in the common law and statutory law in the United States, so every one of those cases had a strong foundation on which to build. Some of the judges eager to do so looked all the way back to 1890 and cited Warren and Brandeis's "Right to Privacy" and could have cited cases from well before that.

So maybe it shouldn't be a shocker either that today—when police cameras routinely peer down city streets, when we raise our hands so that our bodies can be scanned at airports, when neighbors' drones fly through the air capturing movements outside and inside, and when omnipresent data trackers record what we like to read online and share that information with others—the impulse to expand legal protection for privacy has reached far beyond what even Warren and Brandeis suggested.

Can someone have privacy in a completely public place? Yep. What about privacy in data, including in the information found in open-file public records? Sure. Could the "right to be forgotten" exist in the United States, allowing the suppression of information already made public? It already does.

And while all that might seem like overdue relief in this age of invisible invasion, where now well more than 80 percent of people are concerned about a loss of privacy, there is a legitimate question about its costs. Maybe in our zeal for privacy, as Justice Holmes might say, we've gone too far in the direction of Sam Warren to cabin other important and competing rights.

Maybe the most important question today is this: Whatever happened to the right to know?

Chapter Sixteen

GIRLS GONE WILD
(PRIVACY IN PUBLIC)

There are tens of millions of doorbells with magical powers throughout the United States. They can see rather clearly in the light of day and pretty decently in the darkness of night at about a 160-degree angle or about half a city block from wherever they are placed, and they begin to record audio and video whenever someone walks by.

These doorbell-recorded videos—neighbors chatting in the morning with dogs in tow; a drunk young woman's mid-afternoon fall to the ground; a food delivery in darkness; a mother reprimanding her small daughter for not being an appropriate member of the family as the two hurry along the sidewalk at 1:00 a.m., all recent examples from a home in a residential part of New Orleans—are instantly uploaded to the doorbell owner's phone, but people watching and listening and recording are possible at any time by simply pressing a button on the app that turns the doorbell on. These recordings can thereafter be sent along to anyone: police, a neighborhood watch website, followers on social media.

What's most relevant here with regard to privacy is that many of the people walking and talking in day and night clearly (given what they do and say) have no idea that the doorbell is automatically watching and listening when they pass. In 2021, *The Washington Post* described the awkward scenario this way: "Millions of unsuspecting people—including camera owners' neighbors, peaceful protestors and anyone else walking down a residential block—are recorded without their knowledge or consent." Small red lights appear when some doorbells are tripped on, but they really aren't all that noticeable, even in the dark. It's not all that far from Dave Eggers's world in *The Circle*, where cameras look like weeds and sticks and capture the unknowing, and it makes Marion Manola's concerns about snap cameras during theater performances seem remarkably quaint.

Quaint, because some pretty graphic private things happen in the dark. "If you've ever peed outside this New Orleans bar," one newspaper revealed to the great dismay of tipplers who had in fact peed and kissed and done other questionable things right there, "you may have been caught on camera," a camera that also had its own Instagram account.

You might be thinking that there's no privacy in public anyway, that the law would have little to say about such things when people are out in the open. And that's partially true. Traditionally, someone walking and talking outside had no valid privacy claim. The most recent Restatement, for example, says this: "A is drunk on the public street. B takes his photograph in that condition. B has not invaded A's privacy."

But think about the line in "The Right to Privacy" about whispers in closets being broadcast from housetops and then consider that (1) these doorbells are pretty darned stealthy and (2) darkness might offer someone walking and talking outside at least the semblance of security and seclusion—the sense that if one can see no one, no one is watching or listening. The Restatement also says this: a privacy invasion can take place by looking in "upstairs windows with binoculars" or through the use of some other technological aid like a telescope. "Even in a public place," it adds, there may be some things about a person that remain private, "such as his underwear or lack of it."

That's why Ruth Shulman had a valid claim for the privacy tort known as intrusion into seclusion, and the fact that she was *outside* along a public roadway when the production team showed up to record her words didn't matter. "Fundamental respect for human dignity" was at issue in any event, the court wrote. Ruth Shulman's attorney had a more concrete takeaway. "It has now been affirmed that the right to privacy exists in public places," is how he put it.

He's increasingly correct; modern courts increasingly suggest that "the privacy that we enjoy, even in public," as one federal appeals court wrote in 2020, "is too important to be taken for granted." That sort of sensibility protected the fully clothed young girls who'd been photographed and videotaped at public events by a self-professed pedophile, for example, who'd thereafter uploaded the images to his "girl-love" website. "Even if photographs are accurate and taken in public places," the court wrote in upholding a permanent injunction against the man's behavior over his argument that such a prior restraint would be unconstitutional, "there can be a cause of action for invasion of privacy." Children and their parents, the court reasoned, should be able to go out in public to parks and stores and bowling alleys and ice rinks and not worry that an evil stranger's camera might capture them there.

That sort of privacy in public had been helped along by the girls and women who appeared in the early twenty-first-century video series *Girls Gone Wild*, one that featured, as a court described it, "a variety of young women exposing their [breasts and] buttocks and genitals in public places." Courts routinely decided that those who bared and thereafter sued *Girls Gone Wild* producers had valid claims to privacy. A rowdy Mardi Gras party attended by multiple strangers could be a private place, one court ruled, shielding an attendee's behavior. Another decided that the waters on a public lake could be private too, protecting a woman who'd removed her bathing suit top on a boat within eyeshot of a *Girls Gone Wild* photographer.

But there's another more sinister side to this type of privacy; those sensibilities in part are also why, until very recently, authorities confiscated cameras and arrested those who attempted to record police activity in public places. As late as 2021, a federal appeals court refused to find officers liable for detaining a citizen-photographer who'd recorded their use of force in public; it wasn't clear at the time that recording public police activity was constitutionally protected, the court explained.

Those sorts of legal decisions raise multiple additional right-to-know questions. Does a right to record police in public mean that we also have the right of access to police bodycam footage too? Or should, as one court recently suggested, serious consideration be given "the objections of individuals whose privacy interests are implicated" in such "sensitive determinations" regarding the release of bodycam video? If sensitive determinations are important, what if surviving family members of tragedy do not want any video released? Maybe it's no surprise that modern courts have found that the sharing of gruesome images taken outside at an accident scene can create liability for the sharer because such photos involve "sheer morbidity and gossip," without "any official law enforcement purpose or genuine public interest." But who gets to say what's genuine public interest and what's not? Especially when it all happens in a public place.

Given all these potential privacy interests in public spaces and the nuances that can lead to unclear outcomes, consider this scenario: A man invites another man to lunch; they're involved in litigation on different sides, but the dispute involves business matters and they remain friends. The restaurant is cozy, with tables at typical distances from one another, and the two sit at one of them. They thereafter spend five hours discussing the lawsuit as others dine nearby and as waitstaff hovers.

The lunch ends, the lunch mates say goodbye, and shortly thereafter a video of the conversation appears on YouTube. Turns out that the one who'd invited the other had used some sort of secretive recording device—a court suggested that the camera appeared to be in his shirt pocket—and the lunchtime conversation was now available for the world to watch and listen to.

A federal appellate court decided in 2016 that the man who'd been unwittingly recorded had a valid claim for invasion of privacy against his old friend. Sure, the conversation had taken place in a public restaurant with others around, the court wrote, but the guy with the camera had "hoodwinked" the other into believing that the conversation was just between the two of them. Any suggestion that there is no privacy in a conversation that occurs in a public place, the court added, "is wide of the mark."

A little more than a decade before, at just about the peak of *Girls Gone Wild*, the columnist William Safire had told his many readers that "as the law now stands, there is no privacy in public places"; that meant, he said, that "a whisper to your spouse on your front porch is the public's business." He'd written that column shortly after the terrorist attacks of September 11, 2001, at a time when Safire believed that the public's passion for privacy had troublingly disappeared, when interests in the "right to be let alone" had been replaced with "the right to stay alive." And it's true that at that moment, a time when terrorism was at the forefront of most minds, 44 percent of people in the United States suggested that they believed that surveillance of public places intruded only "somewhat" or not at all on personal privacy.

But two decades later, we have watchers of all stripes with omnipresent smartphones, listening doorbells, and flying camera drones. Now we have sixteen-hour voice-activated recorder pens that fit into shirt pockets and promise clear audio recording from up to forty-five feet away and the ability to upload it all with a click. "Put the pen in your pocket or just leave it out in plain sight," a spy gadget website suggested. "It doesn't matter, because nobody will give it a second look since it's so natural to have pens laying around." There are rock-shaped hidden cameras too for outside use, commercially available facial recognition technology for use inside that might soon "interpret facial expressions, detect sweat . . . or identify an elevated heart rate," and there's talk of "smart contact lenses" that, experts say, are sure to present "legal and etiquette issues . . . including norms around when and where devices can record voice and video."

And cameras aren't the only worry for those in public view; inadvertent technological self-incrimination is. Today, commercially available geolocation tracking data can be correlated to a particular cell phone, as a priest learned in 2021 when a Catholic news organization reported that its "analysis of app data signals" had been "correlated to [the priest's] mobile device" and showed that he had "visited gay bars and private residences while using a location-based hookup app." That description of current technology led one *New York Times* commenter to call it "a structural failure [of law] that allows real-time data on Americans' movements to exist in the first place and to be used without our knowledge or true consent." Even when, it seems, those Americans, at least at some point, are outside and visible to others.

That means that today Safire's worry about a lack of privacy outside is but a blip in a time of terrorism, and that's made all the more clear by a recent decision from a Texas court that decided flat out that a resident's front porch could indeed be a "private space." There, those familiar with magical doorbells will want to know, the darkness on the porch and therefore its seclusion had an awful lot to do with the outcome. Intriguingly, that sort of privacy is also the way of the world. In Europe, for example, a homeowner's camera that surveils public spaces, including a footpath to the home, can violate another's right to privacy. And so, of course, Prince William and Kate Middleton won their privacy lawsuit after paparazzi in France took photographs of them on their villa's balcony from about half a mile away; Middleton was nude, but very much outside. Surely any U.S. court that followed the Restatement would have protected them too, given its readiness to link vision-magnifying binoculars and telescopes with intrusion.

Most important, the concept of privacy in public spaces in the United States seems bound to expand along with the technology that threatens it. Twenty years ago, the U.S. Supreme Court even put a First Amendment–sensitive constitutional spin on it all, suggesting that "fear or suspicion that one's speech is being monitored by a stranger, even without the reality of such activity, can have a seriously inhibiting effect upon the willingness to voice critical and constructive ideas."

Those justices had expressed the same appreciation for privacy in public on a personal level. Justice Elena Kagan suggested that she walked a line in public, keeping certain thoughts to herself, and, given modern technology, predicted that privacy would become "a growth industry for the [U.S. Supreme] Court." United States marshals would confiscate recording devices at Justice Antonin Scalia's public speeches, and he suggested in that context that he had the "First Amendment right not to speak on radio and television" when he did not wish to do so. And Justice Sonia Sotomayor wrote of the "profoundly disconcerting" and "overwhelming" "psychological hazards" of life in the public eye and celebrated the "veil of privacy" she had at the Court. She had intentionally not invited media to one public event of eight hundred people, she said, to ensure that her conversation with an actress onstage might be more intimate, that they might "talk like girlfriends" with the legacy media's cameras away.

She later called privacy "the spear of an individual's individual freedom." And she said it as part of the Arthur Miller Freedom to Write Lecture sponsored by PEN America, a group whose mission it is to defend threats to free expression.

Turns out those modern jurists are just as worried about an even more insidious form of invasion, one involving data privacy.

Chapter Seventeen

KATE NASH REDUX

(PRIVACY IN DATA)

I f someone wanted to learn about the life of a person in modern times the way I wanted to learn about Grover Cleveland's girlfriend Kate Nash, they'd have a treasure trove of information far beyond the piecemeal census reports, birth and death records, and occasional newspaper clippings that Kate inadvertently left behind, most of them just a few keystrokes away.

And some investigations are not so benign.

In the summer of 2020, a federal judge in New Jersey, Esther Salas, watched her child die at the hands of a racist, misogynistic lawyer inexplicably angry about a delay in a case in Judge Salas's courtroom. It was easy enough for him to figure out where the Salas family lived, where the family went to church, and much more. He brought a gun with him.

"There are companies," Judge Salas said in an emotional plea for privacy after her son's murder, "that will sell your personal details" and leverage them "for nefarious purposes." The gunman had a "complete dossier" on her, she said, compiled in part by "a free flow of information from the internet." She asked for privacy even in her home address.

If you've ever had that sort of thing compiled in an official sense, you'll know that the word "dossier" sounds about right. And if the wrong person finds the right person with access to the right databases, they can buy their very own data-driven dossier about anyone. That's how a British tabloid was said to have learned the "home addresses, cellphone numbers, Social Security numbers and more" of the actress Meghan Markle, Prince Harry's future wife, and her family: a private investigator in the United States compiled data and sold it to an editor who thereafter contacted extended relatives to report on Markle family strife.

To get a sense of the types of information that might have been revealed in both instances, let me share information about my own dossier, my background check. Despite my relatively placid life—no criminal history, no bankruptcies, no foreclosures, no evictions, nothing that would stand out should someone really want to have a look at what I'm about—the private detective I hired to see what he could find came up with more than two hundred pages of data.

There's the mundane, information that has mostly always been of public knowledge, like my current home address. Traditionally, that sort of information wasn't protected because it's public record and generally many people know it.

But then my dossier swerves into unnerving territory. It includes nearly every single address I've ever lived at since childhood, many of the homes with purchase price and square footage, some with interior photographs and floor plans. For places we own, there's mortgage information; for those we've sold, there are the names of the current owners and, at times, the interest rates on their mortgages and how much they owed at sale.

There's my birth date. There's my Social Security number. There are my voter registration records going back ten years. There are seemingly all of the phone numbers I've ever had in my life. There's my driving record and a photo of my driver's license. There's another photo of me scraped from the internet. There's our current car (with license plate number) and the cars we got rid of more than a decade ago, along with their new owners, their new addresses, and their most recent plate numbers.

My last name is often misspelled so there's a list of my aliases of sorts. There's also a list of my relatives, including my immediate family and their birth dates by month and year, but also nieces, nephews, and very extended family (my sister-in-law's brother, as one example, whom I might have seen once at a wedding) with the first five digits of their Social Security numbers, their current email addresses, their current and past phone numbers, and their current and past addresses. It's the same for the people on my lists of "likely" and "possible" associates, many of them neighbors who would otherwise be unknown to me.

And most troubling for them—especially the more attenuated family members and neighbors—the report also includes information about their own bankruptcies, liens, judgments, criminal history, and such. Even my so-called possible associates are outed that way.

I also have key information about the other Amy Gajdas out there (my report says that there are three of us in the United States) and their immediate relatives, including, for one, her last known internet protocol address, a series of numbers linked to her individual computer or household that can be used to track her online even if she's using a pseudonym.

Finally, there's my social media report, which is admittedly paltry given that privacy interests rightly or wrongly caused me to shun social media from its very start. But here's what the company that investigated my presence on Facebook and elsewhere promises those interested in learning about a target's posts: "In a single search, you can discover more about a subject's digital identity through information not readily accessible via other forms of public records data—helping you gather information and assess risk more effectively."

This all doesn't cost much. My most recent background check, including all of the above, priced out at $150. And similar data about me and the vast majority of others in the United States, including birth date, relatives, current and past addresses, purported annual salary and net worth, purported employment, purported ethnicity and religion, is available on the internet for the price of a promise that the reviewer "WILL NOT use this information to stalk anyone" and "WILL NOT publicize their info or spread gossip." Some of that information is wrong, but a lot of it is right.

What's even more troubling is that there are investigatory companies that promise that they can access far more than all that data if the price is right. Medical records are said to cost $450; prescription information $400; school transcripts $450. Credit card activity costs $150 per month; bank account activity the same. The most expensive searches are $600 and up, and those include international bank records, insurance information, and employment history with salary. Everything from gate access codes to hotel bills to frequent-flier account data is said to be available for a price.

And if that brings chills, consider this ever more modern twist: Amazon knows that I own a bulldog. I've never told Amazon that I own a bulldog.

Amazon just *knows*. And if Amazon knows that, think of what else is out there, connected up with any one of us, someway, somehow.

I became aware of Amazon's interest in our bulldog after I accessed the data that Amazon has collected on me over my many years of being a customer. (This is thanks to the California Consumer Privacy Act, also known as CCPA, a 2020 law that gives California consumers the right to request "the categories and specific pieces of personal information" that a business has collected on them. In what is surely recognition that such a law will come to be commonplace, some companies make that data available to anyone who asks for it. Besides, these sorts of data requests are old hat for many companies; Europeans have had this right since 2018 through the General Data Protection Regulation.)

When one requests available data from Amazon, the company sends approximately eighty folders, each with its own subfolders, many marked with insider titles like "Retail.CustomerAttributes.zip" and "Digital.PrimeVideo .Viewinghistory.zip" and "PaymentOptions.1.AmazonPayBrowserBehaviorData .zip." And there, like nesting dolls inside my data file, appeared "HomeSer-vices.HomeInnovationTechnology.Pets.1.zip." In that folder came a subfolder marked "pets" and within that an Excel spreadsheet also marked "pets." There were five words inside that file: "bulldog," "Your Pet," "Dog," "ACTIVE." All true.

How Amazon knows this remains a mystery. I contacted the company but was never successfully connected with anyone who knew. Maybe Amazon learned about my dog from my internet browser's cookies (looking back, I think I might have had to identify the breed on a pet website at some point when I ordered medication or registered her microchip; a website privacy officer friend knows it was through cookies that she received free samples of baby formula for her "upcoming due date," even though she'd never told the company she was pregnant) or maybe the information about my bulldog came from a data collection company that learned it that way or another.

One of those data collection companies is Experian, "a global leader in consumer and business credit reporting and marketing services," as it describes itself. Experian maintains files on more than 200 million individuals in the United States and many more around the world, and it too offers those who request it a copy of their personal data through the CCPA. My data file there—sent only once I confirmed what the company already instantly knew: our current bank, the name of my employer from nearly thirty years ago, and the fact that we once owned a minivan—was similarly intriguing. Experian considers me a "Highly Likely" "Lux Womens Retail Shopper," a "Somewhat Likely" "Mid Low Furniture Shopper," and an "Unlikely" "Memorial Day Shopper," all of which it appears to have learned in part from what it says is my "geolocation data," perhaps the same sort of data that recently sank that priest. Most of my nearly forty shopping preferences and holiday-related categories are pretty accurate—yes to certain outlets, no to big-box stores, yes to summer break travel—but Experian also has me pegged as a "Manager" with "Some College" who is somewhat likely to visit theme parks, all of which isn't accurate but which may be for another Amy Gajda, I suppose.

Experian gathers its information about us, it says, from its "sources": "Automotive Companies, Business to Business Companies, Consumer Packaged Goods Companies, Consumer Survey Companies, Consumers, Authorized Data Compilers, Electronics Companies, Parenting Product Companies," and thirteen others. It shares the information it collects, it says, with "third parties," such as "Public Institutions, Health Product Companies, Media and Publishing Companies," and seventeen others, including "Regulatory Authorities or Law Enforcement" and "Insurance Companies."

And Experian may well know more about me than what it revealed. "We also maintain data about consumers that is considered Personal Information," Experian explained in my data report, "but is subject to protection under other federal and state laws," laws that include "the Fair Credit Reporting Act [and] the Driver's Privacy Protection Act" but also "the Health Insurance Portability and Accountability Act" that protects medical records. Experian also masked (even for me) what it calls "sensitive information," and that included, intriguingly here, my home address.

Imagine if even more data that's out there someplace were available to certain askers, if it were possible to add to any data report on an individual information from things like wearable fitness trackers, car black boxes, grocery store frequent shopper cards, news consumption (certain journalism websites do track and share), and DNA test results. (One of the websites that I've used under a fake name suggests that I'm related to nearly four thousand other users, and while its promise that it will not share "any person's data (genetic or non-genetic) [with] an insurance company or employer" gives me some comfort, as do new state laws restricting police access, I have wondered how many of my very distant cousins might be in those lines of work.) That would be a very full picture of an individual, right down to the building blocks.

It's also data that not only advertisers, employers, and insurers would like to get their hands on but also potential blackmailers and seemingly even killers, and, traditionally at least, the more information that we share about ourselves with others, online or off-, the less privacy we can claim in the information.

It's no wonder that so many have joined Judge Salas in her quest for data privacy, that today 93 percent of Americans say they would switch to a company that prioritizes data privacy, and that 65 percent want control over precisely what sorts of data companies collect (the remaining 35 percent must have misunderstood the question). An interest in data privacy is a "very strong, deep-seated feeling," the polling company explained, and anyone who thinks that such interests will go away "is in denial."

But data privacy is not solely a modern concern; judges and key others have long recognized the privacy-eroding danger in the compilation of information data points. In the 1950s, about a decade after the creation of the first real computer, recall that the U.S. Supreme Court wrote that it was concerned about "ruthless exposure of private lives in order to gather data" and suggested such behavior put "constitutional freedoms in jeopardy." In the early 1960s, computer scientists began to recognize that their "acquisition of vast new stores of information" could produce "an almost embarrassingly intimate picture" of an individual. Books titled *The Privacy Invaders* ("Even as you read this the most intimate details of your life are being recorded, bought and sold") and *The Naked Society* ("Here's how snoop devices are being employed by Big Government, Big Business, and Big Education in their sneak attack on YOU") appeared in response. By 1966, Congress was holding hearings to investigate the relationship between "the computer and invasion of privacy."

It was in the 1970s, just after the Harvard law professor Arthur Miller's *Assault on Privacy: Computers, Data Banks, and Dossiers* came out, and after *Newsweek* published its "Is Privacy Dead?" cover featuring a looming computer, that the Supreme Court suggested that public school data compiled about particular students should be protected and some justices worried specifically that technology had produced data banks into which key information would be placed to peg a person as a delinquent forever. The very next year, Congress credited the legacy of Warren and Brandeis's "Right to Privacy" and its protection for "the 'sacred precincts of private and domestic life'" and passed the Privacy Act "largely out of concern over 'the impact of computer data banks on individual privacy,'" limiting what the government could collect and release about individuals. A Supreme Court decision that recognized "the threat to privacy implicit in the accumulation of vast amounts of personal information in computerized data banks" followed. The 1980s is when the justices protected the compilation of arrest records too, noting "the implications of computerized data banks for personal privacy."

Right about then, *New Media* magazine predicted that databases created by individuals' interactions with computers would soon prove to be "digital gold," a data-driven treasure trove for companies that might want information on particular users or just generally, and *MacWorld* magazine warned that computers doing that sort of collecting could well make privacy for individuals a thing of the past. That meant that by the time Congress began to consider ways to *limit* liability for websites and internet service providers in the mid-1990s through Section 230, 68 percent of Americans had already expressed growing concern about privacy intrusions relating to computers and collection of their data. And *that* meant that when a Sun Microsystems executive told them in 1999, "You already have zero privacy—get over it," they didn't.

Today, the number of Americans concerned about data privacy has grown to 98 percent by some measures. Now we have doxing, short for dropping documents, "the practice," as one court explained, "of disclosing a person's identifying information (e.g., their home address) on the Internet to retaliate against and harass the 'outed' person." Now the congressional hearings are titled *Facebook, Social Media Privacy, and the Use and Abuse of Data*. And now the American Law Institute has launched a new law reform project called "Principles of the Law: Data Privacy."

This anxiety about data has extended to modern court decisions too, especially in recent years, meaning that big data has led to big privacy concerns and big outcomes favoring privacy. One court hearing a privacy case arising from Cambridge Analytica's use of Facebook data to target political ads in the run-up to the 2016 presidential election suggested that personal photographs and videos, watched videos, religious affiliation, political views, and relationship information could all remain private information even if shared with friends on social media. "When you share sensitive information with a limited audience (especially when you've made clear that you intend your audience to be limited)," the court wrote, "you retain privacy rights and can sue someone for violating them." Another court suggested that social media companies might well be restricted from scanning faces in photographs for identification purposes because such a use could violate privacy. That court noted that both common law and "literal understandings of privacy" included "control of information" about a person, even a person's facial appearance. Birth dates have been protected by some courts as have cell phone numbers and Social Security numbers and internet browsing histories.

One federal court recently decided that a lawsuit could go forward based on claims that the publisher-defendant had released the plaintiff's "personal reading information," including his periodical subscription information, to "data mining companies" that had thereafter aggregated it with "intimate and highly-detailed demographic and personal information" including his name, age, gender, income, employer, and "home address." Federal judges in 2021 similarly allowed lawsuits claiming data privacy rights in "detailed cradle-to-grave dossiers" and in voice-activated, speech-intercepting personal assistants to continue. And all the way back in 2004, a federal appellate court found privacy in an individual's *redacted* abortion records. "Even if there were no possibility that a patient's identity might be learned from a redacted" medical report, that court wrote, there would be a privacy invasion upon release.

Some of those court decisions spring from interests in biometric privacy, privacy in things like "a retina or iris scan, fingerprint, voiceprint, or scan of hand or face geometry." That's a list from the 2008 Illinois Biometric Information Privacy Act, the first statute to protect such information. Lawmakers back then had worried that compromised data bits such as Social Security numbers could be changed, but that biometrics "are biologically unique to the individual" and therefore, once compromised, forever compromised. Given the strength of that Illinois law, users recently won a $650 million settlement against Facebook for its "Tag Suggestions" program, one that looked for and identified people's faces in photographs. The federal trial court judge overseeing the case called it "a landmark result," "a major win for consumers in the hotly contested area of digital privacy."

That's Illinois, but a number of other states, including Delaware, New York, Texas, and Washington, have enacted biometric privacy statutes of some sort or are working on legislation that is likely to create some level of privacy in that and other types of data. In California, lawmakers have defined biometric information similarly as "imagery of the iris, retina, fingerprint, face, hand, palm, vein patterns, and voice recordings" but also as "an individual's physiological, biological, or behavioral characteristics," "keystroke patterns or rhythms, gait patterns or rhythms, and sleep, health, or exercise data." There has been some attempt by Congress at a national biometrics privacy law too.

And it's laws like those that may temper certain artificial intelligence efforts that impact privacy. Scraping of individuals' photos online and the later extraction of certain biometric identifiers in order to identify them "violates privacy and chills speech," one recent lawsuit argued. The AI company at issue in that case was said to have a database of more than three billion photographs of people taken and identified from social media and other websites, information it was said to have shared with police interested in learning the identities of certain people. In his representation of that AI company, the noted media defense lawyer Floyd Abrams, the one who'd celebrated a free and uninhibited press in the 1990s, argued in an intriguing parallelism that the company's conduct is fully protected by the First Amendment. Meanwhile, a different company offers all users the ability to scan the internet for a particular face for free, a tool that by 2021 had "become wildly popular among strangers looking to 'essentially stalk' women around the Web." Those women and others, those "who put those pictures on the Internet—with their children, their parents, the people who might be vulnerable in their life," a technology researcher told *The Washington Post*, "were not doing it so they could feed a database that companies could monetize."

Which brings us in a roundabout way to deepfakes. It's likely that those same sorts of arguments on both sides—privacy versus freedom of expression—will arise in cases involving the videos that appear to be someone they are not, named for the "deep learning" artificial intelligence required to generate the realistic videos of today, an unauthorized use of faces and identities so much the concern of the Clevelands and Abbie Roberson way back when.

And maybe, just maybe, all this talk about biometric identifiers, internet scans for photographs, and deepfakes makes celebrity pleas for privacy in their unauthorized photographs a bit more understandable. "When someone takes a photo of you that isn't flattering in bad lighting or doesn't capture your body the way it is . . . you should have every right to ask for it to not be shared" is what the reality television star Khloé Kardashian argued when an unauthorized bikini photo found its way to Instagram without her permission. "My body, my image and how I choose to look and what I want to share is my choice."

That's life, but in a sense even in death there's worry. As Experian's data-sharing language suggests, some insurance companies now use big data to decide "whether and what kind of [life insurance] policies to provide customers," to "draw on thousands of data points to provide a more personalized analysis" about prospective policyholders than "outdated actuarial tables." Put another way, that an applicant is said to be either a "quick-service-restaurant frequent visitor" or a "frequent gym goer" tells them something.

So, yes, Judge Salas got her heartbreakingly poignant wish for privacy, even in the data point about where she lives. New Jersey passed a law within four months of her son's murder making it illegal to disclose on the internet or otherwise the home addresses and telephone numbers of "active, formerly active, and retired judicial officers, prosecutors, and law enforcement officers" and certain of their family members. In a Section 230 conflict of sorts, the law also forces publishers to take down the information within seventy-two hours after a request for removal.

All that law decided by courts and all those statutes passed by legislatures also convincingly suggest that others who want privacy in certain data points will eventually get it, perhaps even some level of privacy in *their* home addresses too. Indeed, in 2021, the U.S. Supreme Court noted the "privacy concerns" in such commonly available data and worried in a tax law case that "anyone with access to a computer [can] compile a wealth of information about anyone else, including such sensitive details as a person's home address." Such data compilations, the justices reasoned, created "heightened risk" for donors to charities of all sorts, a risk that included "threats and harassment" from "intimidating and obscene emails" and "protests, stalking, and physical violence." Those worries were so significant, the justices decided, that charitable donors' names and addresses could be kept secret even from the government.

Similar worries have led Google Maps to blur pictures of an individual's home if requested. Facebook has a similar procedure, one that impacts journalism: if a news article "shows your home or apartment, says what city you're in and you don't like it, you can complain to Facebook," a recent report explained, and thereafter "Facebook will then ensure that nobody can share the article." All this is beginning to sound very much like Europe, where "data protection is sacrosanct" and where "even the most trivial details," such as address, job, and age, "are not allowed to be disclosed to third parties" without consent.

Which circles back to those lengthy dossiers available online or at a price that contain current home addresses and so much more. For those who've ever been arrested, related data, including mug shots, will appear in those more than two hundred pages. That would include adult criminal history, perhaps even from a decade or more before, even when the person has changed his or her ways.

And that implicates the next privacy right now gaining new life, the surprisingly American right to be forgotten.

Chapter Eighteen

THE RIGHT TO BE FORGOTTEN
(PRIVACY IN THE PAST)

The news made headlines in Detroit in 2013: federal authorities had arrested four suburban police officers after a major multiagency, months-long investigation.

The allegations against the officers were horrendous. "Beating and then taking a bribe from a man facing trial" is how the *Detroit Free Press* began its news story about the wrongdoing. "Scheming to protect and deliver what they thought was cocaine. Even agreeing in principle to kill someone for $20,000." It sounded like something straight out of Hollywood, the reporter wrote, a movie script about dirty cops.

But even though six photographs of people appeared on the same page as that story in the *Free Press*, not a single one of them featured a police officer in federal custody. That's because federal marshals had given journalists the officers' names but refused to give them the officers' mug shots. Those arrestees, the marshals said, had a right to privacy in the photos, and the fact that the alleged felons were in law enforcement only added to their humiliating potential, and therefore to the officers' interest in privacy.

That was an intriguing argument, made all the more so because the federal appellate court for Michigan had decided two decades earlier that an individual's privacy interest in his mug shot was exactly zero, that it didn't exist at all, given the quintessentially public context of law enforcement and the public's right to know about such matters. Even if any privacy interest in such photos should exist, the court had written in 1996, the right to know—

the "significant public interest in the disclosure of the mug shots of the individuals awaiting trial"—plainly trumped.

And so the *Detroit Free Press* and tens of other supportive media organizations argued in federal court that the U.S. Marshals Service in Detroit was flouting the law by refusing to hand over the photographs of the officers in their custody. Not only should the public have access to mug shots more generally, the argument went, that very court had previously decided as much.

But something major had happened in the twenty years since that appellate decision; by 2016, the internet no longer needed definition. Now most people in the United States could read and share news stories and websites that featured arrestee photos forever and ever, it seemed. That meant, the appellate court judges now decided, it was time to reconsider that earlier holding that mug shots had zero privacy.

As you've probably guessed, the judges flipped.

It was mostly about the right to be forgotten, the court suggested without using that precise term, a present-day worry about what someday would surely be those arrestees' interests in privacy in the past. Back in 1996, the time of the zero-privacy-in-mug-shots decision, "booking photos appeared on television or in the newspaper and then, for all practical purposes, disappeared," the court wrote. But now things stayed up online, remaining available long after people who'd been arrested had served their time and changed their ways. "Today, an idle internet search reveals the same booking photo that once would have required a trip to the local library's microfiche collection" and would have otherwise been "forgotten," the judges wrote. These older mug shots—a moment in time that remained stagnant forever and ever—hampered "professional and personal prospects" and "could haunt the depicted individual for decades."

So, no, the public wouldn't be seeing any of those mug shots of the police officers arrested for taking bribes and for conspiring to distribute cocaine in the suburbs of Detroit. And they wouldn't be seeing the mug shot of the former owner of the San Francisco 49ers National Football League team taken in a different case either. "A mug shot preserves, in its unique and visually powerful way, the subject individual's brush with the law for posterity," the court hearing that latter case wrote, and a concept like posterity meant that rivals could release it years later "to perpetuate [the arrestee's] criminal association."

Additional courts soon fell in line with that sort of reasoning, especially involving past crimes. One initially ordered that certain information about a man's criminal history be removed from a website created by the defendant; the information had been published not to inform the public, the court had written, but to harass the man, and moreover "the details about his past are likely not newsworthy twenty-five years after the fact." Another upheld arrested individuals' privacy interests in decades-old incarceration information, including mug shots and crime details that had been published as part of a searchable government database.

This concern about an individual's otherwise forgotten past might sound somewhat familiar. In 2014, the European Court of Justice ordered an admittedly accurate but decade-old newspaper article about a man's debt proceedings de-indexed so that it would be much more difficult to find during an internet search. Such information was currently harmful to his attempt to turn his life around more fully, the court wrote, and was "inadequate," "no longer relevant," and "excessive" in relation to "the light of the time that has elapsed." The decision had created a right to be forgotten, some said, and journalistic assessments of that law's relevance in the United States came back pretty quickly: "an individual's right to privacy is often on par with freedom of expression" in Europe, one newspaper in New York wrote, but "the opposite is true in the United States"; nope, another in Philadelphia suggested, Americans flat out do not have a right to be forgotten, and any European right will surely not cross the Atlantic. The idea of an individual's right to curate the past and to suppress once-public information was simply incompatible with freedom of the press and the public's right to know.

But those breezy assessments weren't precisely correct. After all, the law in the United States wipes away certain bankruptcies from credit reports after seven years, and the Supreme Court has relatedly decided that individual credit reports are not matters of public concern. Sure, that's not precisely the same as what the European court decided, but it's close.

What's all the more interesting is that recent U.S. court decisions respecting privacy in the past have extended well beyond past crimes and money troubles. One found a valid claim for invasion of privacy after a man who'd been "unambiguously male" since 2008 was outed for having had a female designation at birth, aligning itself with an earlier court that had found similar privacy interests in an individual's years-old gender-affirming surgery. Another court sounded a lot like Judge Holmes in the 1880s when it wrote that older information that revealed a government prosecutor's "incompetence and insubordination" from twenty years before would not be revealed because the public's right to know had "greatly diminished" over time, making the information far less important than the man's "strong interest in avoiding decades-old disclosures." And remember the case involving *Hustler* magazine that found privacy interests in a murder victim's nude pictures? That court wrote that *timeliness boundaries* limited the amount of information that could be published without liability because older information simply didn't have the same level of importance as did current information to any right to know.

It's not only judges who feel that way about privacy in the past. By 2020, nearly 90 percent of people in the United States supported at least some aspect of a right to be forgotten and told pollsters that they especially valued privacy in certain information (like embarrassing photos and deeply personal medical records, they said) *and* the importance of making that sort of information inaccessible, even after an initial publication. In California, the push for such protection was so strong that the law there now gives minors the right to erase the past, the ability to remove old "content or information posted" by them on any website or social media platform.

That's all in line with the surprisingly rich history of a right to be forgotten in the United States: the internet may be new enough to be bringing these issues to the fore, but notions about privacy in the past are quite old. Even before official publication of "The Right to Privacy" in 1890, courts had written that it would be "barbarous" to allow the "evil-disposed" the freedom to ransack others' lives by "drag[ging] forth and expos[ing] follies, faults or crimes *long since forgotten*" and "expiated by years of remorse and sincere reform"; others worried that without appropriate protections very old scandalous newspaper articles might be reproduced at any time "to wreck honorable old age." And we might think of "sharenting" as brand-new in an internet age when parents go online to share health and other information about their offspring sure to rile and perhaps even harm their children once grown, but publishers as early as 1895 suggested that a girl might sue her mother for agreeing that the child's nude photo be published in a medical journal. If the girl was later shamed by the photo, the suggestion went, "she would have been justified in later suing her mother for indecent exposure of her person when she was a speechless and helpless infant."

So in 1931, when that California court ruled that a former prostitute had privacy in her life history—that the publication of "unsavory incidents" in her past was a violation of her constitutional right to happiness; that society's object was "to lift up and sustain the unfortunate rather than tear [them] down"—it wasn't all that odd, really. Even Pulitzer's notorious *World* had refused to touch that sort of news in its glory days: a young man had come to editors in the late 1880s with similar dirt on a different, now-virtuous young woman. The story "was declined on the ground that the woman was doing nothing to forfeit her right to privacy," *World* editors explained, and "was fully entitled to be let alone."

So strong and so routine was this sensibility that by the late 1970s the American Law Institute's experts wrote in their latest Restatement on privacy that lapse of time could indeed make a once-public bit of information private again. They used as their example the main character in Victor Hugo's *Les Misérables* and his criminal past: "Jean Valjean, an ex-convict who was convicted and served a sentence for robbery, has changed his name, concealed his identity, and for twenty years . . . led an obscure, respectable and useful life in another city far removed," the modern Restatement reads. "B Newspaper, with the help of Police Inspector Javert, ferrets out Jean Valjean's past history and publishes it, revealing his present identity to the community." Jean Valjean had a potentially valid claim for invasion of privacy under those circumstances, Restatement authors explained, because there had been "a disclosure of the present name and identity of a reformed criminal," causing "his new life [to be] utterly ruined by revelation of a past that he has put behind him."

By that time, a federal appellate court had decided that if an interviewee changes his mind about being interviewed, the interview, in effect, resets, the past is wiped away, and the reporter doesn't have the right to publish the information learned. And a court in Pennsylvania had decided even more clearly that "offensive facts that occurred 25 years ago" could become private again with the passage of time and that a focus on past facts was "quite different from socially valuable news reporting."

And so the Restatement authors also wrote this in the latest Restatement: that privacy exists in "sexual relations," "unpleasant or disgraceful or humiliating illnesses," and "most intimate personal letters," sure, but there's also privacy in "some of [a man's] past history that he would rather forget." Given the court decision involving the former prostitute, they surely meant to include women too.

Modern courts continue to cite that last part—privacy in an individual's past—with no seeming worry about its First Amendment freedom-of-expression-related implications whatsoever. And that's probably why, by 2015, media defense attorneys suggested that "developing legal trends" favoring the right to be forgotten "pose[d] serious threats" to publishers in the United States.

They were likely also concerned about supportive language in U.S. Supreme Court decisions. The same year that the justices decided *New York Times v. Sullivan*, for example, recall that they suggested there might well be privacy in "a man's forgotten misconduct" and that truth alone wouldn't necessarily be good enough reason for revelation. The decision from 1973 that protected student data did so in part because of the "grave damage" to the students' "future careers," those times that would surely come "in later years" when the former students had "outgrown youthful indiscretions." And 1976, the year in which the justices decided that the passage of time could make a once-famous woman into a private figure again, was also the year in which the Court decided that there would be privacy in disciplinary information previously released about Air Force Academy cadets because so many even on the inside would have forgotten the particulars.

But it was in 1989 that the justices most strongly embraced right-to-be-forgotten sensibilities. It's true that the Freedom of Information Act decision in *U.S. Department of Justice v. Reporters Committee for Freedom of the Press* focused mostly on not the publication but the *release* of data—that the government's creation of rap sheets from public arrest information should be kept from reporters—but the justices also wrote more broadly that an individual's "privacy right at common law" in personal information depended in significant part on "the extent to which the passage of time rendered it private." As one example, the Court wrote, "the ordinary citizen" has privacy interests "in the aspects of his or her criminal history that may have been *wholly forgotten.*" There, the justices also quoted Warren and Brandeis's "Right to Privacy" for support, that the average citizen who gives expression to sentiments and emotions at one point in time still has the "power to fix the limits of the publicity which shall be given them."

That sort of fixing is happening in newsrooms today. More than 120 years after Warren and Brandeis wrote that individuals had the power to limit truthful information about the past, mainstream journalists are now more commonly responding to requests to take down older news stories that embarrass. A newspaper in Cedar Rapids, Iowa, explained its new policy this way:

> In the era of the Internet, a simple mistake, poor decision or minor crime can show up in search results and impact lives for a long time.
>
> The Gazette has been receiving an increasing number of requests from people who say they're being impacted long after charges were dropped or their court case has been completed. Whether it's a job search, housing or kids Googling a parent's name, it's difficult to fully put the incident behind them.
>
> There are many reasons we write stories about public safety and arrests. While details of many of the stories are gleaned from publicly available records, the passage of time changes how newsworthy the story is.
>
> Using [certain criteria, including the nature of the incident and possible expungement], The Gazette will consider requests for removal of non-felony and non-violent criminal offenses. Other cases will be handled on an individual basis.

And as that sort of guidance suggests, mug shots are becoming more of a relic in some newsrooms too: not only have certain states prohibited their release especially in instances involving lower-level crimes, but news organizations are increasingly refusing to use them on ethics grounds, recognizing, just as the federal court sitting in Detroit did, that the photos "live forever" on the internet.

The *Chicago Tribune* is one. It once published daily a "Mugs in the News" feature, one hundred booking photos of individuals arrested the day before for crimes both notorious and mundane. In 2021, the *Tribune* announced that it not only would no longer publish most booking photos but also would begin the arduous task of removing most of them from old articles in its archives. The newspaper suggested it had a new commitment to "compassionate coverage" of those entering the criminal justice system given how often mug shots reinforce racial stereotypes, punish the underprivileged, and imply guilt long before a trial that could well find them not guilty.

Intriguingly, the shift extends beyond newsrooms and beyond criminal histories. In a practice that *The New York Times* has suggested is not well known, Google too will now, more broadly, "remove harmful content from individuals' search results." A reporter there attempted such a request—one based on a pseudonymous experimental post written by him, that he was "an unqualified loser"—and within a week of his submitting the request for removal, "it was gone."

You might be wondering what these examples from media have to do with the law. Societal norms play a role in the right to privacy; courts will often look at what society itself has decided is privacy-worthy, protectable information. How better for courts to analyze whether published information is "highly offensive" than to look at how modern society generally treats such information. "The protection afforded to the plaintiff's interest in his privacy must be relative to the customs of the time and place" is what the Restatement says, which makes a recent *Washington Post* headline—"THE RIGHT TO BE FORGOTTEN": SHOULD TEEN'S SOCIAL MEDIA POSTS DISAPPEAR AS THEY AGE?—more than just a headline, especially when the answer seemed to be yes.

This probably all sounds good, but this particular type of past-protective privacy extended to its fullest has clear power to impact the public's right to know about its government leaders. After all, as Grover Cleveland and Warren Harding could have told you, those at the very top of politics have past lives that they've worked hard to hide from public view.

Consider here, then, an article from Oregon's *Willamette Week* titled "The 30-Year Secret." There, the reporter Nigel Jaquiss revealed that three decades earlier Portland's mayor, Neil Goldschmidt, a man who'd also served as Oregon's governor, had had sex with a fourteen-year-old girl, a relationship that had lasted three years. Goldschmidt had hired her as a babysitter for his kids and instead "would often take her down to her parents' basement, to hotels and other private spots and have sex with her." The girl turned young woman thereafter fell on hard times; Goldschmidt eventually agreed to pay her $250,000 to stay quiet, and annual payments depended on her staying mum. Rumors swirled nevertheless, Jaquiss heard them, he investigated, and he broke the story of Neil Goldschmidt's predatory behavior. It all won Jaquiss the Pulitzer Prize.

It's true that Goldschmidt never brought an invasion-of-privacy lawsuit against *Willamette Week*, and had he, he surely would have lost. But there was the suggestion that one might be in the offing. In a meeting with journalists before publication, Goldschmidt's attorney warned that the mayor's relationship with the fourteen-year-old babysitter was "a private matter" because, in part, the relationship had "occurred almost 30 years" before.

That sort of legal argument might sound ludicrous, especially for a public official, but recall that Jean Valjean of both *Les Misérables* and Restatement fame had become a mayor by the time his past life of crime was revealed, and he'd committed his indiscretions only two decades before, not three.

Given current trends, therefore, a politician's plea for privacy in the past might just work someday in the right sort of case. And consider, if so, the implications for the public's right to know and for democracy itself if the *president* of all people has an overarching right to privacy in public, in data, and in the past.

It could happen because it already has.

Chapter Nineteen

A PRESIDENT AND HIS TAX RETURNS
(PRIVACY IN POLITICS)

In November 2020, three professional photographers grabbed their cameras and long-range lenses and lined up along a Potomac River footpath in Maryland just outside Washington, D.C. Each photographer's camera sat atop a tripod: the longest of their lenses was about the length of a man's arm, it was meant to capture faraway things, and shots would be blurry otherwise.

The photographers weren't there to capture birds. They were there to capture a lame-duck president.

About a mile away in Virginia, on the other side of the Potomac, the incumbent president, Donald Trump, wearing a white Make America Great Again cap and a dark blue zippered jacket, stepped out of a golf cart, lined up his shot, and swung his club. It was a move far more momentous than the one President Warren Harding had taken and missed on a different Washington-area golf course decades before: Pennsylvania had just been called for Joe Biden, and that meant Biden would become the next president of the United States. At one point, President Trump looked across the river toward those long-range lenses and schlumped. But this time the presidential fuss couldn't be blamed on airplane-like camera sounds.

Just a few weeks before, as the COVID-19 pandemic and the election season both raged, a military helicopter had flown President Trump the few miles from the White House to Walter Reed Medical Center for some sort of treatment. He'd tested positive for the coronavirus that had already killed more than 200,000 people in the United States alone, many of them, like President Trump, older and with preexisting medical conditions.

This was huge news; the leader of the free world was sick enough to be hospitalized, and it wasn't too much of a stretch to think that maybe he might not get well.

But the president's doctors refused to tell Americans much at all about how their leader was doing, or about the course of the president's illness or the president's precise treatment or his vital signs or the first time he'd tested positive for COVID-19 or the last time he'd tested negative. In fact, doctors were "relentlessly positive," painting a "rosy picture of his condition," *The New York Times* reported.

Maybe that's understandable in context. Not only had President Trump claimed a right to privacy in his health information and called journalists interested in it sick and dangerous, but military doctors at Walter Reed had signed nondisclosure agreements. An NDA was unusual for a politician and especially a president; HIPAA covers interactions between doctor and patient, as would ethics provisions, and military confidentiality would surely also play a role. But Trump had made the doctors sign NDAs in 2019 anyway, the year he'd been rushed from the White House to Walter Reed for a different "undisclosed health issue." HIPAA doesn't offer individuals the right to sue for a violation, but it's quite easy to sue for damages and win if someone violates an NDA contract. Trump's doctors surely understood that.

It was only later, once Trump left office, that we found out just how bad things were when he had COVID-19. The president had had "extremely depressed oxygen levels," a *New York Times* investigation revealed, "and a lung problem associated with pneumonia." Doctors at the hospital had thought it likely he would need to be put on a respirator. He could have died.

Such secrecy in the face of public interest was not unusual under President Trump. Four years earlier, before a different contentious presidential election, candidate Trump had refused to reveal his past tax information to voters, even though every other presidential candidate post-Nixon had done so for transparency's sake. Trump suggested then and throughout his tenure in the White House that it was all about some kind of Internal Revenue Service audit; he was under investigation, he said, and he wouldn't dare release old tax information until some far-off time when all that bureaucratic nastiness was over. But in court filings and on Capitol Hill, his lawyers said it was really all about his privacy. There was a we're-all-in-this-together spin to the argument too; Trump's secretary of the Treasury, Steven Mnuchin, assured reporters that the government "will protect the president as [it] would protect any taxpayer" with regard to their right to privacy in tax returns. The Biden administration has similarly warned that unauthorized disclosures of such confidential tax information is illegal.

Before we dive too deeply into any real discussion of the propriety of presidential privacy in public places or in medical data or in past tax records or otherwise, it's important to note that the official tort law of privacy gives the president pretty much none. The father of modern privacy, William Prosser, wrote specifically in 1960 that "perhaps there is very little in the way of information about the President of the United States, or any candidate for that high office, that is not a matter of legitimate public concern." And the most recent Restatement, the one from 1977, suggests that the president of the United States must put up with the revelation of information that would otherwise be private because it goes with the territory.

In short, Ruth Shulman might have had some level of privacy at her accident scene because a tiny piece of technology had allowed everyone to listen in on an otherwise unknown woman's pain. A famous NFL player might have had privacy in his medical records because all he did was play football and therefore the doctors' specifics on his finger amputation weren't anybody else's business. And a man with a decade-old financial misstep might have deserved some level of privacy in Europe because that record had prevented him from finding gainful employment.

It's one thing if you're a random victim in a highway accident; it's another if you're president of the United States, or so one might imagine.

But Donald Trump mostly kept his privacy, if only by dragging his feet, and our attention. He never did release those tax returns, and by the time he lost to Joe Biden, nobody in the general public had laid eyes on the forms, aside from a few reporters who'd told readers that Trump had serious financial worries but hadn't published the documentary proof. Sure, *New York Times* journalists eventually scooped Trump's COVID-19 condition too, but that happened only *after* he left office; what Americans saw in real time was that Trump suddenly got better, took a helicopter back to the White House, and triumphantly ascended its outer stairs with a hint of a breathing problem and a camera awareness befitting a former reality television star. And while other photographers on a different payroll did indeed snap photos of President Trump schlumping on a golf course the day he officially lost his bid for reelection, somebody protected Trump's golf moves on a different day by driving a giant white box truck in front of news photographers wherever they went.

Who knows how many other times privacy prevailed in the past, in data, and in public in the course of President Trump's political story? After all, that pussy-grabbing boast on tape remained a secret until he was nearly president, so we'll never know if an earlier release and appropriate response from the network that cast him as a termination-happy billionaire would have changed the course of U.S. history.

It's true that privacy for political leaders exists elsewhere in the world by tradition and by law and that publishers there need to be careful about revealing too much, even about the highest of officials. Just ask *Closer* magazine, which published a 2014 story about François Hollande, the president of France, and his affair with the French actress Julie Gayet that included photos of the two of them taken separately outside Gayet's apartment on the street. The news story, which was true, and the innocuous photographs, which were accurate and authentic, had invaded their privacy, a court decided, and it ordered that *Closer* pay the equivalent of $20,000 in damages to Gayet for her post-publication emotional harm. Recall that in Europe the European Convention on Human Rights protects quite literally *everyone's* privacy in private life, in family life, and in home life. It's true that freedom of expression is protected there too, but very clearly privacy, even privacy that involves a public official, can win that duel. So strong is that sort of sensibility in Germany that when Chancellor Angela Merkel started shaking during appearances and assured the public that all was well, *Süddeutsche Zeitung*, a major German newspaper, wrote that health was a private matter, even for a chancellor. Deutsche Welle, Germany's equivalent of Voice of America, published an editorial suggesting that all media stay in line because Merkel too was "entitled to a privilege all other Germans claim for themselves: the right to privacy."

But that level of privacy would be pretty outrageous, it seems, in the United States, a nation in which modern tradition and law, especially the press-empowering First Amendment, say that the people have the right to know by phrase especially about their government, its people, and their doings and where the Restatement labels nearly everything a president does of public concern. "The public *needs* to know" how a president "is carrying the burden of responsibility and making use of the immense power of his office," the cultural anthropologist Margaret Mead wrote even before Watergate pulled the rug out. The people need to know about a president's "unacknowledged political or social alliances" and "whether his actions, public and private, are consistent with his words" so that voters aren't "duped or misled" about the most powerful man in the country or someone who wants to become that.

The trouble with the right to privacy, therefore, is that it's seductive. Privacy in public, privacy in data, and privacy in the past all sound pretty darned great until they're used by law or tradition to protect not only the helpless but also the most powerful, thereby shrinking public knowledge about the nation and its key players. President Trump, a man who very clearly craved and basked in the media spotlight from his reality television days forward, nonetheless wanted to keep media out of what he considered his private life, and for the most part he succeeded. And if *he* had privacy, surely that suggests all public officials and public figures beneath him would.

Donald Trump was not alone in his private presidency, moreover. When President Barack Obama first entered the White House, he promised a new era of sunshine and announced a presumption that government information would be released simply for the asking. He then closed his administration up so tight that journalists suggested it was the most impenetrable ever. A requirement that the White House approve certain FOIA releases, for example, agency officials said, "had been used to prevent the release of information embarrassing" to his administration, and it all seemed positively "Nixonian."

The best pre-Trump example, however, must be President Bill Clinton. Back when he was governor of Arkansas and the front-runner for the presidency, he made an impassioned plea for privacy in his family life, suggesting that the press had engaged "in a game of gotcha" by reporting allegations that he had been unfaithful. Hillary Clinton sat beside him and said flat out she thought it was "real dangerous in this country if we don't have some zone of privacy for everybody." And then when Clinton won the presidency and did what he did in the Oval Office with an intern because he surely thought that privacy on some level would protect him, he pleaded with the eager narrativist Ken Starr to stop the prosecution's "pursuit of personal destruction." "Even presidents have private lives," President Clinton said.

And, just like governors, they do and did, at times simply because we've let them, proved in the past by Grover Cleveland's secret girlfriend and Warren Harding's secret baby. It's certainly no coincidence that those men in particular helped privacy along: one through a strong friendship with a privacy-focused lawyer who'd literally set out to protect the powerful and the other through an orchestrated friendship with fellow newspaper editors who'd mostly come to believe as he did that respectful decency for all was the answer to journalism's bad post-sensationalism rap.

That their legacies, that privacy-sensitive ethics provisions and privacy-sensitive law can combine in powerful ways to protect even a president, is especially clear in the tale of John F. Kennedy, who like Harding was once a journalist. The big news when Kennedy was running for president was that he was a Catholic, and when he spoke about his religion at the American Society of Newspaper Editors convention in Washington in 1960—it was up to the press "to concentrate on the issues, the *real* issues," he scolded, instead of arousing "needless fears and suspicions"—not a single swooning journalist had a follow-up question. "Well, Senator," the ASNE president said that day, "I do not know whether you silenced your critics, but you silenced the questioners."

Maybe it's a coincidence, but later during that meeting those in attendance heard a talk titled "The Flow of the News to Marilyn Monroe." There, *The New York Times*'s managing editor, Turner Catledge, introduced a speaker-reporter named Lester Markel this way: When Lester takes up a story, he examines his subject and embraces it "very passionately." "He views it from every angle, every curve; he takes hold of it with firm and impressive touch, and he never lets go until his subject is thoroughly exhausted." The talk's title suggested that Marilyn Monroe, the curvy and exhausted subject, was the average newspaper reader, Markel thereafter explained to much laughter, and that she did "discuss some things intelligently" (more laughter). Journalists knew back then about Kennedy's womanizing and maybe even about any relationship he had with Monroe—she was good friends with

Markel and had suggested that she could tell him anything, so he, for one, surely knew of any involvement—but the rule was "if private behavior didn't interfere with public business, then it stayed private."

It's not clear when or if those journalists ever found out about Kennedy's own successes with a White House intern—a nineteen-year-old woman whom Kennedy had "seduced" in the White House marital bedroom—and, if so, whether they considered that relationship private too, but the implications for #MeToo behavior more generally are staggering here. As James Reston of *The New York Times* explained, reporters even then were "far too close to the men in power and, therefore, far too inclined to let . . . sympathy or affection for [the powerful] get in the way" of their reporting. Some continue to call journalists' decisions to look the other way in such situations even at the White House a "gentlemen's agreement" because it was a gentleman's game. Helen Thomas was an anomaly there, covering Kennedy for United Press International, but she wouldn't become UPI's chief White House correspondent until 1970. It took five years after that before she'd be invited to join the Gridiron Club, a long-standing organization of Washington bureau chiefs with bylaws that officially kept women out, even for social events.

That Secret Service–like level of good-old-boy respectful quiet from journalism in extramarital situations and the like led in turn to a growing confidence from those who held the presidency. By 1961, the Kennedy White House told journalists that "at times" they would "not be informed of the President's whereabouts." After some pushback from the press corps, Press Secretary Pierre Salinger assured journalists that President Kennedy recognized that "he has little, if any, claim to privacy" or any freedom from the public's interest in even "the most personal details of his life" and thereafter suggested that if the press ever felt that President Kennedy had hidden himself, "a complaint should be lodged."

There was none.

The very next year, ASNE members, in effect, solidified respectful privacy in politicians' lives when they very nearly uniformly agreed that the story of the presidential hopeful Nelson Rockefeller's divorce should stay out of major newspapers even though Rockefeller himself had announced the split. Such information was "gossip," those at ASNE's annual conference told the *Look* magazine reporter who'd criticized them for missing what he called "the biggest political story of [the] year." The divorce concerned Rockefeller's "private life," the editors explained, and "had nothing whatever to do with [Rockefeller's] public conduct."

And then, after the Kennedy assassination, there came even greater self-reflection on the part of those ethics-embracing editors. Television had not only gone live from Dallas to give viewers on-the-spot reports as things happened but constantly replayed scenes of presidential tragedy and transition, public detail, and family scenes, ensuring that all American living rooms would be witness to the action. This proved that journalism needed to corral itself even further, editors said, to practice even greater "professional self-discipline," lest it lose "the hallowed privilege of press freedom to arbitrary and fettering controls" from law.

Perhaps by design, thereafter, at that very same conference in 1964 is when Justice Arthur Goldberg of the U.S. Supreme Court told ASNE members that despite the weeks-old and powerfully press-protective *New York Times v. Sullivan* it might be time to "revise and refurbish" journalism's codes of ethics. "Our Bill of Rights assures the press freedom to report and comment; yet, at the same time it guarantees to all a certain modicum of privacy," he'd said in that talk he titled "Freedom and Responsibility of the Press." The rights were not incompatible, he'd explained, and freedom of the press could coexist happily in the legal world right along with privacy rights.

In any event, certain judges thereafter suggested that the law of privacy needed to change to protect President Kennedy even in death; that Jackie Kennedy and the Kennedy children would have the right to keep paparazzi from invading their privacy even when they were outside; and that President Kennedy's autopsy records would be protected on privacy grounds because, even though he was dead, "medical records . . . are usually considered private." Those words from Margaret Mead arguing for a decrease in presidential privacy for the good of the nation? They were written during a dustup over a book about Kennedy's death that Jackie Kennedy found too privacy invading, including details about the Kennedys' last night together, how she tended to her husband's wounds after the shooting, and letters that she and her daughter, Caroline, had placed in his coffin.

Recall that privacy in a president's "personal communications" has been protected too, even when that president was Richard Nixon, because snippets from recorded White House tapes might prove embarrassing. Courts have also shielded the former president George W. Bush's National Archives document requests because "the American public stands to gain little from knowing what the former officials are researching" and "the invasion of privacy on the former officials and their designees is great." President Obama's FBI background check, including his birth certificate, would be kept out of public hands too if that's the way Obama wanted it: one who runs for the presidency doesn't sacrifice all privacy, one federal court explained.

And don't be too quick to pooh-pooh the former president Trump's claim to privacy in income tax returns either. It's true that all the way back in 1925, Justices Holmes and Brandeis joined the rest of the Supreme Court when they ruled that a newspaper shouldn't be punished for publishing income tax records. But the justices didn't say that newspapers had a blanket right to do so, only that the law as it stood back then made income tax records open for public inspection, which in turn made the problem "one of statutory construction." That meant it was up to Congress to decide whether secrecy or publicity should prevail.

Half a century later, somebody at the Internal Revenue Service illegally disclosed President Nixon's tax return, and thereafter there was "an upsurge of opposition to public disclosure of tax information." Today, "The Right to Privacy" is one of ten provisions in the IRS's Taxpayer Bill of Rights, and "The Right to Confidentiality" is another. "In general," that document reads, "the IRS may not disclose your tax information to third parties unless you give us permission." The federal law from which that stems reads that "no officer or employee of the United States" or former officer or employee "shall disclose any return or return information obtained by him in any manner."

Today, the Restatement agrees that income tax returns are not public and therefore that it would be an invasion of privacy to publish them. Sure, it doesn't say anything about *presidential* tax returns, past or present, but the language protecting privacy in tax information is there, in our most modern and influential Restatement of the Law, and in 1989 that same language was quoted by the U.S. Supreme Court, that an income tax return "is not public and there is an invasion of privacy when it is made so."

This is surely why *The New York Times* anticipated public blowback after its news story that revealed key information about the then president

Trump's tax returns. "Some will raise questions about publishing the president's personal tax information," *New York Times* editor Dean Baquet wrote. "But the Supreme Court has repeatedly ruled that the First Amendment allows the press to publish newsworthy information that was legally obtained by reporters even when those in power fight to keep it hidden." And that's absolutely true, but then there's also that language about the revelation of tax returns in that 1989 case.

Privacy, therefore, may not be brimming with protections for presidents and other politicians just yet because the powerfully persuasive Restatement says what it says about the predominance of the public's right to know and, as Baquet notes, the First Amendment does protect newsworthy information. But taken to the extreme, this murky mash of law and ethics continues to have real potential to quash important information about those in power. After all, today privacy is growing because judges have decided that it should be growing and they have the power to go for more. Those courts at times have used "The Right to Privacy" as precedent, meaning that the article too has remained a constant and at times convenient weapon even in these high-profile, high-power situations. The historian Arthur Schlesinger, a friend to John F. Kennedy, once interpreted "The Right to Privacy" as an essay that "rigorously confined the policy of exposure to secrets bearing on public concerns" and drew a line that divided proper from improper curiosity. "If a politician takes a bribe it is the public's business," Schlesinger wrote, invoking Louis Brandeis specifically, "if he has an affair, it ought to be his own."

That's an overreach—while Warren and Brandeis wrote that privacy protected "the wholesale investigations into the past of prominent public men," they never drew a precise line—but Schlesinger's words show that the back-fires of privacy continued to burn in the most influential of places and from the most influential of persons long after 1890 to help protect the powerful. Even Richard Nixon name-dropped Brandeis in his ill-timed 1974 "American Right of Privacy" presidential radio address, one in which he suggested he would "provide a personal [right-to-privacy] shield for every American" that would "safeguard personal information against improper alteration or disclosure." Within days, authorities indicted Nixon aides in the Watergate scandal, and six months later Nixon himself would resign and argue for privacy in it all, in effect.

Sure, *ethics* principles in many modern newsrooms protect the powerful too. They continue to suggest that a politician's private life should be his own unless he's involved with a lobbyist, for example, or has been hypocritical in some way, such as voting against gay rights while involved in such a relationship. But privacy-centric *law* is surely its own powerful influence. Today, why should news organizations publish what might bring an expensive privacy-based lawsuit when they're already in such difficult financial straits, when they may feel too short staffed to investigate a scandalous truth fully, and when the law that seemingly would have once put a quick end to any privacy claim now seems to embolden one?

It's not such a ridiculous question. Rumors had swirled for years that the U.S. senator Larry Craig had a habit of propositioning strangers for sex in public bathrooms, but it took until his arrest for such behavior for mainstream media to report on it all. As some evidence of law's power to create that type of chill in newsrooms, consider the infamous politician Roy Moore's recent lawsuit for intentional infliction of emotional distress against Sacha Baron Cohen of *Borat* fame. Cohen had pretended to be an antiterrorism expert in a *Borat*-like sting involving an unaware Moore and had boasted about a new body-scanning, pedophile-finding wand. The wand beeped as it neared an incredulous Moore, who, during a U.S. Senate race the year before, had faced allegations that he had once had relationships with teenagers. Cohen's attorneys had argued that Moore's lawsuit should be dismissed, that the First Amendment very obviously protected the production, and that producers needed the "breathing space" to satirize "an indisputably controversial public figure," but a federal judge initially refused to dismiss the case.

All of this suggests that today the former president Trump's or any president's, or senator's, or mayor's, or candidate's broader claims to privacy in public, in data, and in the past can't be dismissed out of hand, given the forces aligning to defend those walls around them.

And that's all the more alarming for the right to know because not all that long ago a high public official from a different branch of government, Justice Stephen Breyer of the U.S. Supreme Court, suggested, in effect, that he'd also been thinking about privacy in those ways and that all three made good legal sense. Privacy "protect[ed] the personal integrity of individuals," Justice Breyer explained, and such protection was made all the more difficult by new technology, including computers, cell phones, and surveillance cameras. "These devices challenge one of the traditional guardians of privacy," he said, "the fallibility of human memory":

> When you walk down the street and your neighbors see what you are doing, they will forget. Or when I say something silly I think one good thing is that everybody is going to forget about it pretty soon. But not with tape recorders. Not with computers. Not with surveillance cameras. Not with machines that remember everything.
>
> The result is that the law of privacy is a little out of date in certain respects and it has to be changed. Everybody thinks it has to be changed, but not everyone agrees how.

That question of change—in effect, how to decide when privacy of the individual trumps the rest of the world's right to know—is mighty dangerous territory too.

Epilogue

DIGNITY AND LIBERTY

Queen Elizabeth knighted the British musician Cliff Richard in 1995. It was the first time that a rock star had ever been honored in such a way, and that made good sense: Richard's fourteen number one singles and his seven chart-topping albums had made him a legend. Many say that Sir Cliff, his knighted name, paved the way for the Beatles and for the rise of rock and roll itself.

So in 2014, it was especially huge news when police searched Sir Cliff's home as part of a criminal investigation. An allegation had been made against him "about an incident in the 1980s," police said, "involving an adolescent boy under the age of 16": that that boy and his friend "had been sexually assaulted by Sir Cliff in a dressing room after a Billy Graham event" at a soccer stadium. The authorities took the accusation seriously enough that they got a search warrant for Richard's house in Berkshire. They also notified the BBC that an investigation involving the icon was under way, the sort of leak that's not that unusual in the United States at least.

Sir Cliff was in Spain when he watched the BBC's helicopter hover outside his home to give viewers a you-are-there view of the police activity. It was a common enough sort of coverage—the BBC had a helicopter on retainer, and Sir Cliff's place was situated in a wooded area, necessitating aerial video—but Sir Cliff didn't see it that way. "It was an extraordinary thing for the BBC to do," he later said. "It kind of put the BBC stamp on this, almost telling people, 'We think this is true.'"

The investigation never amounted to anything, and police never arrested Sir Cliff for any crime. So, in response, he sued the BBC for invasion of his privacy. He argued that his dignity had been forever damaged by the BBC's quite accurate news story that a police investigation was under way involving him.

In 2018, the High Court of Justice in London sided with Cliff Richard. "Sir Cliff had privacy rights in respect of the police investigation and . . . the BBC infringed those rights without a legal justification," the judge wrote, rejecting the BBC's arguments based on freedom of the press and freedom of expression. Instead, the judge criticized the BBC for its sensationalism, for its breathless coverage of the search. He also imposed aggravated damages because the BBC had had the audacity to nominate its story about the police activity for Britain's Scoop of the Year Award. "Indeed," the court wrote, Sir Cliff Richard's "public status emphasises the need for privacy in a case such as this." Not only did the report "not contribute materially to the genuine public interest in the existence of police investigations," but "public figures [were] not fair game" for "gossip-mongers" like the BBC.

In the end, Sir Cliff Richard won more than £2.2 million in damages and attorneys' fees, the equivalent of approximately $3 million, for what the court said was damage to "his dignity, status and reputation," even though the story about the investigation itself was true. And Sir Cliff thereafter moved to the United States, saying he preferred "the anonymity in America" and suggesting, in effect, he would have greater privacy there.

Richard may indeed have greater anonymity in the United States because he's less likely to be identified walking down the street or perusing shelves in the grocery store, but privacy law in the United States as it currently stands offers him little support. In fact, we're often told that while Britain and other countries value the *dignity* that Sir Cliff Richard argued for in his privacy-based case, the law of the United States, in sharp contrast, values *liberty* and freedom and the First Amendment–fueled right of journalists to report the news, especially news about public figures like Cliff Richard.

Liberty of the press and liberty of expression were part of the privacy equation from the very beginning, proved by those discussions in 1789 between William Cushing and John Adams about any right to publish truthful but embarrassing facts about politicians. Today, it's clear that protection for such coverage stems directly from the First Amendment and from the people's right to know, and there's no better evidence than *Florida Star*, the 1989 Supreme Court case that rejected a crime *victim*'s claim to privacy. There's little need here to reiterate the importance of it all: the powerfully press-protective *New York Times v. Sullivan* says that the First Amendment requires "safeguards for freedom of speech and of the press" so that "debate on public issues should be uninhibited, robust, and wide-open." Without it, with a president like Cleveland or Harding or Trump in charge, we'd never learn important truths about government activities or about politics or about political leaders. And that would put an end to democracy as we know it.

Even the skeptical Sam Warren and Louis Brandeis recognized as much in "The Right to Privacy" and drew a line that protected press freedoms in privacy cases. "It is only the more *flagrant* breaches of *decency* and *propriety* that could in practice be reached," they wrote, "and it is not perhaps desirable even to attempt to repress everything which the nicest taste and keenest sense of the respect due to private life would condemn." "The right to privacy does not prohibit any publication of matter which is of public or general interest," they wrote. They didn't say a thing about cabining stories about police activity, for example.

But what the history of the right to privacy teaches is that despite what breezy headlines have suggested about freedom of the press as the forever-winning cudgel, the United States does not value that liberty exclusively. And, at times, again from the very beginning, an individual's *dignity*, often by word, has been an important consideration in privacy-relevant decisions. Dignity is why the New Orleans judge François Xavier Martin ultimately protected Henry Denis's love letter from publication in a newspaper in 1811. Dignity is what the plaintiffs argued they'd lost in the *Cape Cod Folks* case in the 1880s, and in the 1890s, it's what E. L. Godkin suggested privacy intrusions especially threatened and, later, why the U.S. Supreme Court suggested privacy protected the woman who'd refused a doctor's examination after a train accident.

Dignity is also what a Michigan judge linked in the 1950s with the right to be let alone (privacy was "a matter of human dignity"), and dignity interests are why the former first lady Jackie Kennedy was able to keep paparazzi away from her family ("a different rule," the court wrote, "could have a most pernicious effect upon the dignity of man"). It's literally by word the reason why the California Supreme Court protected Ruth Shulman at the accident scene: that "fundamental respect for human dignity requires the patients' anxious journey be taken only with those whose care is solely for them and out of sight of the prying eyes (or cameras) of others." And even though Judge Denny Chin never used the word itself, he was surely thinking about dignity when he wrote in the case involving *To Catch a Predator* that NBC had "publicly humiliate[d] a public servant who had always been an upstanding member of the community." That's also the case that most closely suggests that maybe, just maybe, Sir Cliff Richard's dignity-centric argument about privacy in an ongoing police investigation might one day be viable in the United States too.

Warren and Brandeis themselves found dignity by name an appropriate counterbalance to press freedoms. They wrote that at some point the "dignity . . . of the individual must yield to the demands of the public welfare or of private justice," suggesting that dignity could and should hold its own against a right to know. Warren often said how much he valued dignity itself, the dignity of the family. Sure, his motivations are suspect, but that doesn't make his sensibility wrong. Clearly, it's not too far a stretch to say that a focus on dignity makes good sense in an era of revenge porn, when the dignity interests of the individual are undeniable. Or that a dignity focus seems appropriate when, in a time of pandemic, victims of domestic violence were summoned to appear publicly on Zoom to describe their plights before a judge and a judging internet, especially when such hearings were recorded and stood the chance to go viral. One shaken woman's hearing had more than one million views on YouTube before it was taken down.

The *dignity* of individuals in privacy cases, moreover, is often linked in a constitutional sense with their own *liberty*. In other words, it's not only the First Amendment promise of *liberty of press and speech* that's a part of the Constitution but also "the Blessings of liberty" that the Constitution bestows on individuals and the Fourteenth Amendment's promises to them of life and liberty. In the 1880s, the first time Supreme Court justices used the phrase "the privacies of life," they called the liberty of the individual in that context a "sacred right." Later, in the days of McCarthyism, the justices linked privacy with constitutional liberty, and in more modern times they've suggested that people "are entitled to respect for their private lives" and that constitutional liberty's substantial protection for the individual was behind it all.

The Supreme Court justice Stephen Breyer—the justice who suggested the law needed to change to recognize the viability of privacy in public, in data, and in the past—said straight out during his confirmation hearings that the Constitution is "a document guaranteeing people rights that will enable them to lead lives of dignity" and that privacy through constitutional liberty is a big part of that.

Warren and Brandeis mentioned that sort of liberty in "The Right to Privacy" too, that liberty protects a "man's spiritual nature, . . . his feelings and his intellect," the "uninterrupted enjoyment of his life." Today, that's the sort of privacy from which data protections often stem. "We are beginning to learn about how much may be lost in a culture of transparency," an expert wrote about data privacy twenty years ago, "the capacity for creativity and eccentricity, for the development of self and soul." "The man who is compelled to live every minute of his life among others and whose every need, thought, desire, fancy or gratification is subject to public scrutiny," another wrote years before that, "has been deprived of his individuality and human dignity."

Words like "feelings" and "enjoyment," "creativity" and "eccentricity," "need" and "gratification" may sound familiarly constitutional too. The "pursuit of Happiness," like liberty, is an unalienable right, the Declaration of Independence reads, a self-evident truth. That so many courts have linked happiness with constitutional promises—that justices have written that the right to keep "private affairs, books, and papers from the inspection and scrutiny of others" is "essential to peace and happiness"—is why scholars suggest that Justice Brandeis was focused on "a core constitutional right," the "pursuit of happiness," in his *Olmstead* dissenting opinion when he argued for privacy, the right to be let alone.

Today, those long-standing sensibilities fit seamlessly with the 99 percent of people in the United States who say that they believe that the right to privacy is essential to or, at the very least, important to their own sense of *freedom*, their own liberty, and those people include Justice Sotomayor, who told that audience of freedom-of-expression proponents that privacy was the weapon that best protected liberty interests.

What this all ultimately tells us, then, is that there's been no linear, inexorable progress of the law of privacy—or of free expression—that wraps things up neatly here at the end, no ultimate vindication of one interest over the other. Instead, the best that can be mustered from curlicued lessons of history here is that protection for the right to privacy must inevitably balance an individual's dignity, liberty, and right to be let alone with the liberty of free expression. Alexander Hamilton suggested that such a balance was needed when he argued in *Croswell* that the press would be protected if its motives for publishing truth were good and the ends justifiable. Warren and Brandeis wrote in "The Right to Privacy" that any rule of privacy would require "an elasticity which shall take account of the varying circumstances of each case." And in modern times, Judge Chin invoked hundreds of his fellow jurists and the Restatement itself when he said that "there has to be some balancing involved" in a privacy case, a balancing that considers both "the impact of disclosure on the privacy rights of the individual versus the public's interest in knowing."

Without such a balance, history shows that the right to privacy would protect what some have called the "best men," leaders inclined to use the law as muscle to prevent further inquiry into their lives. Shakespeare's "best men" were "moulded out of faults" and made "much more the better for being a little bad," and it was in Shakespeare's time that England's Star Chamber punished journalists in horrific ways for publishing those truths. In the United States, privacy interests protected Thomas Jefferson, who worked behind the scenes to ensure that journalists who went too far in reporting truth learned their lessons; Grover Cleveland, who cloaked himself and others with privacy and kept journalists in jail; and Warren Harding, who bedded a teenager who'd come to him about a job. It protected plain old regular men too, those who, like the abusive former minister in the 1880s, argued that "raising the curtain upon domestic privacy" was a greater evil than exposing the truth about domestic violence. And it also helped to protect even more dark secrets about police and producers that movements like Black Lives Matter and #MeToo worked to reveal.

But as these pages have made clear, it's possible that the privacy balance can swing too far in the other direction, in favor of truth and freedom of expression no matter the human cost. This became most striking at the dawn of the internet, when grow-the-web economic interests bestowed on pixels a special sort of First Amendment–inspired protection that Samuel D. Warren Company paper never got. And, all the while, revenge porn publishers got rich off others' pain.

How did *Let Us Now Praise Famous Men* (a book about the poor that "recognize[s] the stature of a portion of unimagined existence" and "human divinity") become People of Walmart (a website about the poor that "roll[s] back dignity" by mocking misshapen shoppers who can't afford a more elite grocery experience)? "The deck seems stacked against those with traditional (and expensive) journalistic standards—and in favor of those who can disseminate the most sensational information as efficiently as possible" was Justice Neil Gorsuch's assessment in 2021.

So if we could wave a wand just as magical as today's smart doorbells, maybe its first and best use here would be to amend Section 230 to carve out from protection those publishers who create websites designed to cause emotional harm through embarrassing revelations and other sorts of mocking, those websites created with clear maliciousness. Such a move would mean they would face the same sort of privacy-based liability that publishers on paper face and would not be absolved automatically from their varying levels of heinousness. We've been told repeatedly by companies with a lot to lose that Section 230 protects free expression and underpins democratic values, but when you see the very real individual harm it enables, the quashing of the dignity and liberty and privacy of individuals—many of them women—it's clear that it goes too far to protect expression. Besides, it wouldn't be all that drastic a change anyway, because that sort of liability for others' posts exists already; *all* websites are currently liable for a random poster's intellectual property violations. Section 230, despite its effort to grow the internet at much human cost, has always protected copyright and trademark from digital exploitation.

And maybe once those sorts of cases and others like them hit the courts and those courts necessarily balance an individual's dignity, liberty, and privacy interests with free press and free speech rights, they'd do well to be guided by journalism's own ethics provisions, just as Judge Chin suggested.

I once thought such nuanced language dangerous in judicial hands, concerned about the impact on journalism itself and the ways that fed-up judges might curtail real news just as Warren Harding dreamed; surely shielding a public servant on those grounds is as chilling as the SPJ has argued. But now the small risk of overzealousness in those limited cases seems justified given the crushing harms in others. Why *not* suggest that even vigilance can become unduly intrusive at times? Why *can't* we recognize the importance of public enlightenment and, at the same time, "balance the public's need for information against [an individual's] potential harm"? Why *shouldn't* journalism itself and the decency it's built up for a century now help lead us to decide what is appropriately published and what goes too far? Real journalists perform those balancing acts daily by trade anyway, and it protects journalism to differentiate itself from other publishers. History shows this. We are not all journalists.

Put another way, society may not be able to force an ethics buy-in among all who publish—those who rioted and broke into the Capitol in 2021 in a bizarre effort to support Donald Trump, livestreaming it all the way, have argued that they were but journalists seeking truth, as one example—but the law has that power.

That sort of ethics-founded balance in privacy cases isn't really all that far off from what the U.S. Supreme Court itself has suggested is appropriate anyway, the ways it has defined, in a tempered way, what the public should be concerned about in a constitutional sense and when privacy might instead prevail. In *Snyder v. Phelps*, the justices wrote that a matter of public concern "is a subject of *legitimate* news interest; that is, a subject of general interest and of *value* and *concern* to the public." Before that, in the case that held that an individual's credit was not of public concern, the justices wrote that "content, form, and context" mattered in deciding issues of public concern and that the "essential dignity and worth of every human being" was important too, given its place "at the root of any decent system of ordered liberty." In the *Bartnicki* case, the Court suggested that matters of public concern might well not include "domestic gossip or other information of purely private concern," and in *Florida Star* it wrote that a balance was critically important because there was "sensitivity and significance of the interests presented in clashes between First Amendment and privacy rights." Its protection for data privacy is just as rich.

As evidence of a growing sensibility that something must be done, that same sort of balancing test suggested by the Supreme Court over time guides Facebook's charge to its Oversight Board, a multicultural group of human rights leaders, journalists, and professors from around the world created to help decide "some of the most difficult questions around freedom of expression online: what to take down, what to leave up, and why." This is the group that voted in 2021 to uphold Facebook's ban on Donald Trump, at least for a while, and its charter statement suggests that a balancing of rights is necessary in privacy cases too, that freedom of expression will not always win, because "there are times when speech can be at odds with . . . privacy, and dignity."

Such a balancing act could well lead to some relatively easy norms on Facebook and other places. One U.S. appellate court found certain privacy interests seemingly universal, a "desire for privacy" in nude photographs, information about sexual activity, and material in medical records that "is a mysterious but deep fact about human personality" and deserving of legal protection. Other cultures might well see things differently, but Facebook's Oversight Board with its global reach could ultimately unite the world as one.

And those categories—nudity, sexual details, medical information—are precisely the ones that constituted the core privacy interests in the United States, at least, when Sam Warren and Louis Brandeis put pen to paper and even before; they are, to paraphrase the Supreme Court, examples of *illegitimate* news interest in most cases, subjects of very little value and concern to the public. There are surely other categories deserving of such protection too, areas of private life that modern courts have danced around and protected at times, including certain criminal histories, death images, and information about sexual orientation or gender identity that could well lead to personal injury, the sorts of things that mainstream journalism would hesitate to report unless it found the information important for the public to know.

So, yes, privacy interests as they conflict with freedom of the press, freedom of speech, and freedom of expression remain in a bit of a mash. But what's most important here is that privacy has had a firm foundation for centuries in the United States, even though it's often taken a backseat in headlines and history classes to press and speech freedoms. And even though proof of privacy's importance often stems from the common law, the law that's built up over time in courts, it's pretty clear in American jurisprudence that "a common law right rises to the level of a constitutional right if it is 'deeply rooted in this Nation's history and tradition, and implicit in the concept of ordered liberty.'"

In short, an individual's dignity and her own liberty interests, however we come to define those terms, *will* at times prevail against First Amendment freedoms to publish or speak because they nearly *always* have. And that's okay. So strong are these interests that even strident First Amendment proponents say that it's certain that one day the Supreme Court will institutionalize this sort of privacy as a part of constitutional law. It's just that it hasn't happened yet.

But all that doesn't make figuring out appropriate answers in privacy cases any easier.

Arthur Ashe was a tennis champion from Virginia. He'd learned the game in the 1950s, in the segregated South, and even though he couldn't practice on the municipal courts of his home state, he'd persevered to become a collegiate tennis star and, later, the first Black man ever to win Wimbledon, the U.S. Open, and the Australian Open. He ranked as the best player in the world in both 1968 and 1975.

Throughout his tennis career and long after, Ashe also worked to end racial inequalities in the United States and beyond. He lobbied for a boycott of tennis tournaments in South Africa; he got arrested at antiapartheid rallies; he started a tennis program for inner-city children; he worked with colleges to develop tutoring programs for minority athletes. His tennis-star status had given him what Congress called "a platform to pursue social justice during a turbulent time in the civil rights era," and in the 1980s, Princeton honored Ashe with an honorary doctorate that linked his performances both "in the arena of social policy" and "on center court."

In other words, Ashe was both a superstar athlete and a passionate advocate for societal change. He was a man, they said, whose mission statement would be "for the public good."

At some point during that decade, the 1980s, Ashe needed a blood transfusion. It was there, he said, that he contracted the HIV that later developed into AIDS. Back then such a diagnosis was effectively a death sentence. By the early 1990s, he had toxoplasmosis, an AIDS complication. Even so, he didn't tell anyone other than his wife and a few others. His father's heart was failing, and his daughter was too young to fully understand. He worried that family and friends would be in distress if they knew the truth; he thought his dying was his own business.

Then, on April 8, 1992, everything changed. He suddenly called reporters to a news conference. "I have AIDS," he told them.

It's not that Ashe had wanted to reveal his diagnosis that day. It's that the day before, *USA Today* reporters had asked him if he had AIDS; they'd told him they'd gotten a tip that he did, they'd noticed he'd lost weight, and they'd started to make calls to confirm the rumor.

"I am sorry that I have been forced to make this revelation now, at this time," Ashe said that day, becoming so emotional at one point that he had to ask his wife to read his prepared statement, but he wanted to reveal his illness on his own terms. He died ten months later from AIDS complications. He was forty-nine.

"For any news organization, when any public figure becomes ill . . . there's no question that it's news," *USA Today* editors argued in defense of their reporting. "We were treating AIDS as any other illness," like cancer, for example, they explained, and Ashe was deserving of such investigation as "a public figure far beyond the world of tennis." At some point, an individual's privacy must give way to the public's interest about his life, they said. This was one of those times when, given the celebrity and his work, the public, in effect, had a right to know or, at the very least, a legitimate interest in knowing.

Those reporters who agreed with *USA Today*'s news judgment went a bit further in support of such coverage. The "redeeming purpose" for the story about Ashe's diagnosis was to "put a human face" on HIV and AIDS and to promote greater public understanding. In a perfect world, it all would lead editors across the nation and maybe even globally to publish news about the "pervasiveness of the disease," they said, and give those editors the sense that they should assign more reporters to cover the topic, creating additional public knowledge, putting pressure on government, and maybe, one day, finding a cure. Put simply, they argued, the story about Arthur Ashe's diagnosis had been that spark that could well end HIV and AIDS forever.

But that feeling was far from universal, and journalists themselves reported that they seemed split about fifty-fifty. Those opposed found it "tragic" that Ashe had, in effect, been outed in such a way, and suggested that what reporters really found newsworthy was the story's more "titillating aspects." It was not real news, that side said, because it had no redeeming value outside linking a public figure with a dread disease, and any argument otherwise was "tantamount to sacrificing virgins to save the tribe."

So conversations among journalists at a privacy conference a few months later went this way: "Where does [journalistic] interest . . . stop and [Ashe's] right to privacy begin?" one asked another. "That is the point" was the answer. "People may want to know it," a third suggested, "but is that enough reason to invade someone's privacy?" And round and round with no conclusion whatsoever.

It was Arthur Ashe himself who brought the law into it. "Are you going to be coldhearted, crass purveyors of the facts as the defenders of the First Amendment, or are you going to show some sensitivity?" Ashe asked reporters about a month after his first news conference. "Remember to temper your definition of the public's right to know with sensitivity" because "it's better to police yourself than have someone do that for you, and there soon may be a need for that."

He was right; there's now a need. But there has always been a need, and the correct answer has never been clear. If we decide to punish the revelation of medical information about Arthur Ashe, for example, and decide that First Amendment interests do not protect that particular publication of truth, would we do the same when the person is a president? What about a senator? A city council member? An elementary school teacher? If we decide that such publication is appropriate, would we do the same when the person at issue is what the law would consider a private person who has next-door neighbors who might be interested in such a diagnosis? Or is that latter person's privacy deserving of greater protection and, if so, why? Where *does* public interest stop and the right to privacy begin? What type of information do we all have the right to know?

There's a series of books published up through the 1990s that uses biographies to teach children different values. *The Value of Believing in Yourself* is taught by the story of Louis Pasteur, for example, and *The Value of Determination* is the story of Helen Keller. *The Value of Courage* is Jackie Robinson, and *The Value of Humility* is Mother Teresa. The idea behind the series is that elementary school kids will learn important principles of character by reading about another's life and be inspired to incorporate them into their own lives forever.

The Story of Arthur Ashe, supplemented by sweet cartoon drawings, teaches the value of dignity. It chronicles Arthur's early life in segregated, racist Virginia, where his family members held on to a sense of "self-worth and dignity" that they instilled in Arthur too, teaching him to "treat others as he wanted to be treated" with "respect for their dignity as human beings." Arthur becomes a tennis player, then a champion, then an advocate against apartheid and for those less fortunate. Through it all, the book explains, Ashe believed that "dignity was never out of style."

Then the story takes a somber turn. "In 1992, Arthur learned that a newspaper was about to publish the story that he had AIDS," the text reads. But as angry as Arthur was about that threatened revelation by the press, he "did not let his emotions drown his dignity." He didn't believe that the press had the right to report such a thing, so he instead stood up to newspaper reporters, took history into his own hands, and made his own heartbreaking announcement about his illness. In doing so, Ashe was, the book says, "a true American hero" and a great example to us all for "his goodness, his decency, and his unwavering dignity."

As Louis Brandeis might say, the back-fires had started to spark.

ACKNOWLEDGMENTS

I have many people to thank for their help on this book.

Thanks first to my colleagues at Tulane Law School who supported this project throughout. They include Kathy Eaton, Amberly Page, Meredith Schiro, and Tulane Law librarians who found a wide range of even obscure materials quickly, especially Carla Pritchett, Kim Glorioso, Roy Sturgeon, and James Duggan. Thanks too to Patrick Dunn and others in the mailroom who retrieved and cheerfully delivered many, many boxes of books for months. Special thanks to Todd Stamps for early insightful comments that helped to shape this book in important ways.

I also owe great thanks to those colleagues who read the book proposal, early parts (or even full drafts) of the manuscript, or otherwise discussed their thoughts on this topic with me: Erin Carroll, Erwin Chemerinsky, Jörg Fedtke, Marc Franklin, Bob Giles, Walter Isaacson, RonNell Andersen Jones, Ron Krotoszynski, Lyrissa Lidsky, Ann Lipton, Jerry Lopez, Jean McDonald, David Meyer, John Nerone, Len Niehoff, Lewis Paper, Robert Post, Neil Richards, Steve Solomon, Russ Weaver, Sonja West, and those at conferences and faculty talks where I discussed this work. I also owe thanks to Troy Miceli of NextGen Investigation Services, Cristin Morneau, and the people who very kindly responded to my out-of-the-blue request for information about their families as I attempted to investigate the mystery of Kate Nash.

A number of librarians and archivists outside Tulane University helped with this project, a process that became especially challenging during the COVID-19 pandemic. Thank you to everyone at the New York Public Library and its special collections; the Harvard Law School and Harvard University Archives; Scott Campbell, who oversees the Brandeis papers at the University of Louisville Law Library; Chloe Gerson and Anne Woodrum at Brandeis University's Robert D. Farber University Archives and Special Collections; archivists at the Massachusetts Historical Society; Lewis Wyman at the Library of Congress; Brian Harkins at the Social Law Library; Elizabeth Bouvier at the Massachusetts Supreme Judicial Court; and Adam Baler at the Superior Court in Plymouth, Massachusetts.

I also owe much to the research assistants at Tulane Law School and elsewhere who helped support this book. Special thanks goes to Ellie George, who expertly cite checked sixteen of the chapters. Thanks also to the research assistants Gianluca Cocito-Monoc, Jamie Davidian, Sarah Hunt-Blackwell, Deanna Krokos, Gabby Leonovicz, Matthew Meyer, Michael Meyer, Eden Moalem, Erin Morrissey, Molly Nelson, Denver Nicks, Suzi Roberts, P. J. Rogers, Shelby Rose, Lexi Rummel, Darcy Samuelson, Brandon Sprague, Sydney Tonic, Loretta Trezza, and Dorothea von Gablenz. Thanks to other students in my privacy, torts, media law, and journalism classes both at Tulane University and at the University of Illinois who helped shape this book in class discussions, especially my Fall 2020 Legal Writing for a Lay Audience seminar students and my Spring 2021 Media Law students at Tulane University Law School.

I very much appreciate the careful read of the manuscript and the copyediting work done by Ingrid Sterner; my thanks also to production editor Sharon Gonzalez and designers Daniel Lagin and Nayon Cho.

Thanks too to my agent, Carolyn Savarese, who encouraged this book in wonderful ways. Thanks to Terezia Cicel for helping to guide the project with professionalism and thoughtfulness.

And, finally, a huge thank-you to my editor at Viking, Wendy Wolf, who offered unfailing support and creative, incisive, and inspiring edits. It's been an honor and a joy.

NOTES

INTRODUCTION

ix **"a somewhat notorious case"**: Samuel D. Warren and Louis D. Brandeis, "The Right to Privacy," 4 *Harvard Law Review* 193 (1890).

ix **gray silk tights**: "Taken in Her Gray Tights," *New York Sun*, June 15, 1890; "Miss Manola in Distress: Will Resign Rather Than Be Photographed in Her Tights," *Boston Globe*, June 13, 1890 (Manola explains that wearing tights is a part of her profession because of the characters she plays).

ix **"a perfect abyss of weariness"**: Alan Dale, "De Wolf Hopper," *New York Evening World*, May 6, 1890.

ix **"an apparent failure"**: "Theatrical Gossip," *New York Times*, May 27, 1890.

ix **trim and attractive figure**: "The Drama in America," *Era* (London), May 17, 1890.

ix **kept audiences coming**: "Theatrical Gossip," *New York Times*, May 27, 1890 (noting that success had been plucked from the apparent failure of the show).

ix **"She is my chief soprano"**: "She Won't Be Taken in Tights: Pretty Marion Manola Rebels Against 'Castles in the Air' Orders," *New York Evening World*, June 13, 1890.

ix **WILL NOT BE PHOTOGRAPHED IN TIGHTS**: "Will Not Be Photographed in Tights: Miss Manola Will Wear Them, but There She Draws the Line," *Chicago Tribune*, June 13, 1890.

x **Broadway Theatre's balcony**: "Taken in Her Gray Tights."

x **snap camera in an upper box**: "Sensitive Actress," *Pittsburgh Dispatch*, June 15, 1890.

x **"not too slender, not too plump"**: "Taken in Her Gray Tights."

x **"The New Yorkers have nothing in view"**: "Miss Manola's Tights," *Atlanta Constitution*, June 21, 1890.

x **"entire sympathy of all of her sex"**: "Marion Manola's Whim: She Was Photographed in Tights Once Before," *New York World*, June 16, 1890.

x **Some men, on the other hand**: "Marion Manola's Whim" (quoting the manager of *Castles in the Air*: "I look at it in this light: what difference is there between Miss Manola appearing in tights before a public audience and before a photographer").

x **risqué *Boccaccio***: "Miss Manola in Distress."

x **tantalizing fringe**: Cabinet card of Marion Manola, *Newsboy* (on file with author).

x **never, ever develop the photo**: "Marion Manola Victorious: Permanent Injunction Against the Flash-Light Photographers," *New York Evening World*, June 20, 1890.

xi **it could record . . . unsuspecting victim**: Gilbert, *Photographic Advertising from A-to-Z*, 138–39 (reproducing an 1886 ad for the Peerless Detective Camera).

xi **cameras were shaped like purses**: "Haunted by Amateurs," *Waterloo (Iowa) Courier*, Feb. 15, 1888.

xi **looked so much like handguns**: Gilbert, *Photographic Advertising from A-to-Z*, 141 (reproducing an 1886 ad for the Photo Revolver).

xi **frenzied around the French actress:** "The Autograph Hunter," *Boston Globe*, May 3, 1887 (noting that Sarah Bernhardt had been "besieged" since her arrival in the United States).

xiii **"We do not hold":** *Florida Star v. B.J.F.*, 491 U.S. 524 (1989).

xiii **had poetically protected the "privacies of life":** *Riley v. California*, 573 U.S. 373 (2014) (quoting *Boyd v. United States*, 116 U.S. 616 (1886)) (internal quotation marks omitted).

xiii **same phrase:** *Olmstead v. United States*, 277 U.S. 438 (1928), *overruled in part by Berger v. State of N.Y.*, 388 U.S. 41 (1967), and *overruled in part by Katz v. United States*, 389 U.S. 347 (1967).

xiii **Supreme Court had originally written:** *Boyd v. United States*, 116 U.S. 616 (1886).

xiii **"used to lie with [his] Son's Wife":** *Publick Occurrences Both Foreign and Domestick* (Boston), Sept. 25, 1690.

xiii **shutdown of its presses for distastefulness:** Samuel Sewall, *The Diary of Chief Justice Samuel Sewall*, Sept. 25, 1690, 1:332, in Lyman Horace Weeks, "Early Massachusetts Newspapers," 3 *American Historical Magazine* 111 (1908) ("A printed sheet entitled publick Occurrences came out, which gives much distaste because not Licensed, and because of the passage referring to the French King," quoting Chief Justice Samuel Sewall's diary) (internal quotation marks omitted); *see also* David A. Copeland, "Publick Occurrences," in Sterling, *Encyclopedia of Journalism*, 1147 ("Despite the fact that England and France were at war, references to royalty and sexual indiscretions were too much for the Puritan council members."); "How Boston's First Newspaper Was Quickly Put Out of Business," *Boston Globe*, May 16, 1922.

xiii **"nothing of any possible value":** *Winters v. New York*, 333 U.S. 507 (1948).

xiii **morphine addiction:** "People of the Stage," *San Francisco Chronicle*, Sept. 2, 1894 ("It has been said in Boston for some weeks that Marion Manola was insane, and the cause was popularly attributed to the use of morphine and opium.").

xiii **died young:** "Marion Manola Dead," *Boston Globe*, Oct. 8, 1914 (stating that Manola was born only forty-nine years earlier).

xiii **didn't want her daughter to see:** "Miss Manola in Distress."

CHAPTER ONE: BRANDEIS'S SECRET

3 **oral argument:** *See* Docket of Cases for Argument, Massachusetts Supreme Judicial Court, Oct. Term, 1884 (Plymouth Superior Court case files). Present were Justices Morton, Field, Devens, W. Allen, and Holmes. Absent were C. Allen and Colburn. *See also* "Cape Cod Folks: The Famous Libel Suit Re-argued at Plymouth," *Boston Daily Advertiser*, Oct. 22, 1884 (stating that Louis Brandeis appeared for the defendants); "Plymouth County Court: The 'Cape Cod Folks' Libel Suit Argued," *Boston Post*, Oct. 22, 1884 (stating that Louis Brandeis appeared for the defendants).

3 **marble busts:** The description is taken from a photograph that is part of an online history of the court, "The Massachusetts Supreme Judicial Court in the 1880s and 1890s," Social Law Library, www.socialaw.com.

3 **Holmes had joined the Massachusetts high court:** *See* William T. Davis, *History of the Judiciary of Massachusetts: Including the Plymouth and Massachusetts Colonies, the Province of the Massachusetts Bay, and the Commonwealth* (1900), 184–85 (discussing Justice Holmes's journey to the bench and stating that he was appointed as associate justice of the Supreme Judicial Court in 1882); *see also* John Lathrop, *Massachusetts Reports: Cases Argued and Determined in the Supreme Judicial Court of Massachusetts* (1883), 134:iii (noting that Justice Holmes was appointed to the bench on December 15, 1882, and heard cases in January 1883).

3 **against Louis Brandeis:** "The 'Cape Cod Folks': A Verdict for the Plaintiff at Plymouth," *Boston Daily Advertiser*, Feb. 15, 1884 ("People generally are disposed to condemn the author of the book.").

4 **that it was Sally Pratt McLean:** "News and Notes," *Literary World*, Aug. 27, 1881 ("The authorship of *Cape Cod Folks* is ascribed, with authority, to Miss Sarah P. McLean, a daughter of Justice McLean, a well-to-do farmer of Simsbury, Conn."); "The Author of 'Cape Cod Folks,'" *Literary News*, Sept. 1881 ("The best part of the secret is that the entertaining novelist is a Hartford County lady, her home being at Simsbury, a few miles out on the Connecticut Western road. The young lady's name is Sarah McLean.").

4 **remarkably realistic prose:** Advertisement, "A Delightful Summer Book: *Cape Cod Folks*," *Literary World*, July 30, 1881 ("A remarkable realistic piece of prose fiction, combining humor and pathos with a mastery of Cape Cod dialect and Cape Cod ways; in fact, an idyl worthy of a place in every home and fireside.").

4 **"keen eye for the ridiculous"**: "Weekly Record of New Publications: Cape Cod Folks," *Publishers' Weekly*, July 23, 1881 ("She seems to have had a keen eye for the ridiculous").

4 **"quaint and homely"**: "New Publications: Cape Cod Folks," *Boston Post*, July 27, 1881 (describing the "quaint and homely people with whom [the main character] is brought in contact.").

4 **offered genuine amusement**: "Cape Cod Folks," *Literary World*, July 30, 1881 ("But one may turn the pages of many books of the present hour before he will find more genuine amusement than is afforded by these glimpses of 'Cape Cod Folks.'").

4 **"a poor little apology for a village"**: "Cape Cod Folks," *Literary News*, Aug. 1881.

4 **"one of the most desolate and forlorn places"**: "Cape Cod Folks," *Literary News*, Aug. 1881.

4 **McLean "d[id] not spare"**: "Cape Cod Folks," *Literary News*, Aug. 1881.

4 **"It's the sin and the shame"**: Zetta seems to be one of the few created names in the book. Two young women joined the lawsuit against the publisher without being named explicitly, however, so it appears likely that the story of Zetta is based upon one of them. *See* McLean, *Cape Cod Folks*, 222–25.

4 **"I should like to kiss you"**: McLean, *Cape Cod Folks*, 153.

4 **single page in the U.S. census**: Massachusetts State Census (1865).

4 **it was "too true"**: "Cape Cod Folks," *Union County Journal* (Marysville, Ohio), Nov. 17, 1881 ("The trouble with the book is that it is too true.").

4 **sorry-not-sorry apology**: "Literary and Trade Notes," *Publishers' Weekly*, Aug. 27, 1881.

5 **Adelaide had died**: "Mental Excitement: Death of Mrs. Consider Fisher, One of the Characters in 'Cape Cod Folks,'" *Boston Daily Globe*, June 23, 1882.

5 **"the unpleasant notoriety forced upon her"**: "Literary Review," *Boston Congregationalist*, Aug. 9, 1882.

5 **left behind her mariner husband**: Massachusetts State Census (1880).

5 **libel and ridicule**: *See* Docket of Cases for Argument, S.J. Court, Oct. Term 1884 (on file with author) (noting that the two causes of action involved are "libel" and "ridicule"); "Boston Notes," *American Bookseller*, Feb. 15, 1882 ("The libel suits brought against A. Williams & Co., by Adelaide A. Fisher, Luretta Nightingale, Stanton C. Fisher, and Cynthia Cahoon, residents of Cedarville, on Cape Cod, and the parties alluded to in the original edition of 'Cape Cod Folks,' are to be entered at the Superior Court at Plymouth, Mass., next week.").

5 **crushed their dignity**: "Cape Cod Folks," *Boston Daily Advertiser*, Feb. 15, 1884.

5 **proved to be a "viper"**: "A Unique Verdict: 'Cape Cod Folks' Adjudged a Libellous Work," *Boston Daily Globe*, Feb. 15, 1884.

5 **agreed to cash settlements**: *See* "City and Suburbs: About Town," *Boston Daily Advertiser*, Sept. 18, 1882.

5 **about $30,000 today**: The amount of $1,095 in 1884 was worth $29,595 in 2021. *See* CPI Inflation Calculator, www.in2013dollars.com.

5 **"on the proprieties of private life"**: "Cape Cod Folks," *Boston Daily Advertiser*, Feb. 15, 1884.

6 **question of how far**: *See* "The 'Cape Cod' Case as a Precedent," *Boston Daily Advertiser*, Feb. 18, 1884.

6 **same sort of restraint**: "The verdict in the Cape Cod Folks case has gone against the publishers, who have $1095 to pay," *Boston Congregationalist*, Feb. 21, 1884.

6 **purchased *The World***: "Greeting of the 'New World,'" *Boston Globe*, May 11, 1883.

6 **attorney who was facing disbarment**: *Cowley v. Pulsifer*, 137 Mass. 392 (Mass. 1884).

6 **"a free press [is] one"**: *Cincinnati Gazette Co. v. Timberlake*, 10 Ohio St. 548 (Ohio 1860).

7 **A LEGAL LIMIT TO "ENTERPRISE"**: "A Legal Limit to 'Enterprise,'" *Boston Daily Advertiser*, June 28, 1884.

7 **Holmes kept that newspaper clipping**: Newspaper clipping of Oliver Wendell Holmes Jr., Oliver Wendell Holmes Jr. Digital Suite, Harvard Law School Library, Addenda, 1818–1978, Biographical Materials re: OWH: box 3, folder 1, Newspaper clippings re OWH, miscellaneous, 1882–1935, seq. 3.

7 **"I don't know whether"**: Holmes to Harold J. Laski, July 21, 1921, Harvard Law School Library, Historical & Special Collections, John G. Palfrey Collection, box 7, folder 7.

7 **Holmes bench book**: Bench book of Oliver Wendell Holmes Jr., Associate Justice, Supreme Judicial Court of Massachusetts (1884–85 term), Palfrey Collection, Paige box 1. Oral argument was in October. Holmes likely was to write the original opinion because he wrote the six other opinions listed on that particular page of the bench book. It appears that after an initial reading of the Holmes decision, Justice Field took over the drafting of the opinion instead: "Nightingale v. Williams 'Cape Cod Folk' Dec. 4–7 written. Jan. 7 read. Field takes it. Settled by

parties before decision" is what Holmes wrote. Holmes had suggested in a talk to the Boston bar that he kept a "book in which I keep a docket of the decisions of the full court which fall to me to write." Felix Frankfurter, *Mr. Justice Holmes and the Constitution: A Review of His Twenty-five Years on the Supreme Court* (1927), 9n27.

7 **a case involving a truthful article:** *Lothrop v. Adams*, 133 Mass. 471 (Mass. 1881).

8 **"right of quiet occupancy":** *Newell v. Whitcher*, 53 Vt. 589 (Vt. 1880).

8 **on the "privacy of domestic life":** *Smith v. McGuire*, 67 Ala. 34 (Ala. 1880).

8 **"sacred privacy of domestic life":** *Johnson v. State*, 63 Miss. 313 (Miss. 1885).

8 **"illicit intercourse of parties":** *Felger v. Etzell*, 75 Ind. 417 (Ind. 1881).

8 **"destruction of the happiness":** *Ex parte Brown*, 72 Mo. 83 (Mo. 1880).

8 **"Of what occurs in the privacy":** *Beals v. Neddo*, 2 F. 41 (D. Kan. 1880).

8 **"lifting the veil":** *Boykin v. Boykin*, 70 N.C. 262 (N.C. 1874).

8 **A California judge had written:** *Ex parte Kearny*, 55 Cal. 212 (Cal. 1880).

8 **a catchy phrase:** Cooley, *Treatise on the Law of Torts*, 2nd ed. (1888), 29.

8 **"has no concern whatever":** *Tryon v. Evening News Association*, 39 Mich. 636 (Mich. 1878).

8 **"right to know":** *People v. Bradley*, 60 Ill. 390 (Ill. 1871) (the people have a "right to know" "why the liberty of any citizen is restrained . . . and for what reason he is confined").

9 **ridicule "laughs *down*":** "Cape Cod Folks: The Famous Libel Suit Re-argued at Plymouth."

9 **"invasion of the plaintiff's domestic privacy":** The language is from the brief filed in *Nightingale v. Williams* by Brandeis and two colleagues. Brandeis University Archives, Brandeis Collection, series 2, box 2, number 8.

9 **within a few weeks:** For example, the Holmes bench book shows that every case argued at approximately the same time as *Nightingale v. Williams* had been handed down by early January. *See* Bench book of Oliver Wendell Holmes Jr. (1884–85 term), Palfrey Collection, Paige box 1.

9 **intricate opinion:** *See, e.g., Commonwealth v. Kneeland*, 37 Mass. (1 Pick.) 206 (Mass. 1838) ("This cause was argued some time since, and partly on account of the intrinsic difficulty attending some of the questions raised in the case," Massachusetts's highest court wrote in this libel case, "and a difference of opinion among the judges on some of those questions, it has stood over for consideration and advisement, to the present time.").

9 **seventeen revised editions:** "News and Notes," *Literary World*, June 16, 1883 (noting that the new paper-covered edition was the seventeenth edition of the book).

9 **revenue from those:** As it happened, new editions kept coming for decades, and *Cape Cod Folks* eventually became a movie. *See* "Majestic," *Hartford Courant*, June 6, 1924 ("Motion pictures showing any phase of real American life are always interesting but there is an especial appeal in 'Women Who Give,' Metro's picturization of Mrs. Sarah P. McLean Greene's 'Cape Cod Folks' which heads the bill at the Majestic Theater this week.").

9 **intriguing details about the man:** *See* "Missing from Home: Unsuccessful Search for Dr. Richard C. Brandeis," *New York Times*, Dec. 26, 1884; *see also* "A Young Throat Specialist Missing," *Boston Globe*, Dec. 26, 1884 ("It is feared that he may have become temporarily deranged.").

10 **settled Lorenzo Nightingale's claim:** "The 'Cape Cod Folks' Libel Suit," *New York Times*, April 3, 1885 (suggesting that the settlement was "a percentage" of the original jury award and noting that it was "odd" that the publishers would be so certain of a win but settle).

10 **Nobody knows for sure:** Phone call and email communication with Elizabeth Bouvier, head of archives, Massachusetts Supreme Judicial Court.

10 **memento for his daughters:** Edward F. McClennen to Susan Brandeis, July 15, 1923, Brandeis University Archives, Collection of Frank Gilbert, series 11, box 2.

10 **embraced and supported the ideal:** "A 'Novel' Libel Suit," *Literary World*, Nov. 5, 1881.

10 **notorious Star Chamber:** Kent, *Commentaries on American Law*, ed. O. W. Holmes Jr., 12th ed. (1873), 2:23 ("It became the established principle of the English law, as declared in the Court of Star Chamber . . . that the truth of the libel could not be shown by way of justification, because, whether true or false, it was equally dangerous to the public peace.").

10 **ears be cut off:** *See, e.g., Faretta v. California*, 422 U.S. 806 (1975); *Brandreth v. Lance*, 8 Paige Ch. 24 (N.Y. Ch. 1839).

CHAPTER TWO: HAMILTON, JEFFERSON, AND THE GREATEST EVIL

12 **fake news:** *See, e.g., State v. Norris*, 2 N.C. (1 Hayw.) 429, 429 (N.C. 1796) ("The people in this country do not take for truth every thing that is published in a newspaper.").

12 **excited coverage of duels:** Anti-Duellist, "On the Increasing Prevalence of Duelling. No. III," *Balance and Columbian Repository (Hudson)*, Jan. 4, 1803.

12 **women's romantic inclinations:** *See* "Character and Effects of Modern Novels," *Philadelphia General Advertiser*, Nov. 9, 1792.

12 **about thirty-three thousand:** "1790 Fast Facts," U.S. Census Bureau, www.census.gov.

12 **growing citification:** "For the Connecticut Courant. The Companion. No. 3," *Hartford Courant*, Nov. 17, 1794.

12 **corrupting morals:** P., "For the Galaxy: The Rural Moralist—No. 35," *Federal Galaxy* (Brattle-boro, Vt.), Jan. 9, 1798.

12 **"One of the greatest blessings":** *United States v. Fries*, 9 F. Cas. 826 (C.C.D. Pa. 1799).

13 **concealed a voluptuary, a man:** Catullus, "For the Gazette of the United States," *Gazette of the United States* (Philadelphia), Sept. 29, 1792. Just a couple of weeks before, Jefferson had written to Washington that even though the anti-Jefferson author who was spelling Jefferson's "character at full length to the public" used a nom du plume, "neither the stile, matter, nor venom of the pieces alluded to can leave a doubt of their author." It was Hamilton. Jefferson to Washington, Sept. 9, 1792, founders.archives.gov.

13 **"For god's sake, my dear Sir":** Jefferson to Madison, July 7, 1793, founders.archives.gov.

13 **whispers in Charlottesville:** *See, e.g.,* J. T. Callender, "The President Again," *Richmond Recorder*, Sept. 1, 1802, in Thomas Jefferson Memorial Foundation, *Report of the Research Committee on Thomas Jefferson and Sally Hemings* (2000), app. E.

13 **news would be breaking:** Chernow, *Alexander Hamilton*, 407 ("Hamilton was pointing to some deeper knowledge of Jefferson's private life, perhaps his knowledge of Jefferson's liaison with Sally Hemings, based on [insider] reports.").

13 **Thomas Jefferson and his secret life:** *See, e.g.,* Phocion, "For the Gazette of the United States. No. I," *Gazette of the United States & Philadelphia Daily Advertiser*, Oct. 14, 1796.

13 **"imbibed" the subject of racial integration:** Phocion, "For the Gazette of the United States. No. III," *Gazette of the United States & Philadelphia Daily Advertiser*, Oct. 17, 1796.

13 **where Jefferson had first come to know:** *See* Betts and Bear, *Family Letters of Thomas Jefferson*, 6.

13 **must have seen all around him:** Phocion, "For the Gazette of the United States. No. II," *Gazette of the United States & Philadelphia Daily Advertiser*, Oct. 15, 1796. Many of these essays are published collectively in a sixty-two-page pamphlet, *The Pretensions of Thomas Jefferson to the Presidency Examined; and the Charges Against John Adams Refuted. Addressed to the Citizens of America in General and Particularly to the Electors of the President* (1796).

13 **sensualistic aristocratic epicurean philosopher president:** *See* Phocion, "For the Gazette of the United States. No. II."

13 **he paid Callender:** *See* Jefferson, Memorandum Book, June 20, 1797, Dec. 12, 1797, Dec. 14, 1797, Dec. 17, 1797, and Dec. 23, 1797, in *Jefferson's Memorandum Books*, 2:963, 975, 976.

13 **served as an anonymous source:** Jefferson to Callender, Oct. 6, 1799, in *New England Historical and Genealogical Register* (Boston: New England Historic Genealogical Society, 1896), 50:447.

14 **illicit correspondence with another man's wife:** Callender, *History of the United States for 1796*, 205.

14 **locked in a torrid affair:** Chernow, *Alexander Hamilton*, 364.

14 **might want some cash:** Chernow, *Alexander Hamilton*, 368–69.

14 **"Included are fifty dollars":** Callender, *History of the United States for 1796*, 220.

14 **Hamilton had once spoken publicly:** Callender, *History of the United States for 1796*, 207.

14 **ought to have concealed the imperfections:** Callender, *History of the United States for 1796*, 208.

14 **made it a crime to open another's letter:** Flaherty, *Privacy in Colonial New England*, 120.

14 **mail carriers not leave them around:** Flaherty, *Privacy in Colonial New England*, 121 (describing how Franklin ordered mail carriers to promise not to open mail and not to leave envelopes out for others to see).

14 **"Pd. Callender for Hist. of US":** Jefferson, Memorandum Book, June 20, 1797, in *Jefferson's Memorandum Books*, 2:963.

14 **He found "mortifying disappointment":** Alexander Hamilton, *Observations on Certain Documents Contained in No. V & VI of "The History of the United States for the Year 1796"* (Philadelphia: John Bioren, 1797), 4, 5, 9.

14 **"any little foible or folly":** Hamilton, *Observations on Certain Documents Contained in No. V & VI of "The History of the United States for the Year 1796,"* 4. Hamilton also published in this

document two letters by Jefferson that seemed to suggest, in Hamilton's mind at least, that Jefferson wanted Hamilton investigated. *See* apps. 44–45.

15 **one that had been highly influential:** Bird, *Revolution in Freedoms of Press and Speech*, 33.

15 **"improper, mischievous, or illegal":** *United States v. Fries*, 9 F. Cas. 826 (C.C.D. Pa. 1799) (quoting Blackstone, *Commentaries*, 4:152).

15 **exposed the husband publicly:** *See Cropp v. Tilney* (1698) 90 Eng. Rep. 1132; 3 Salk. 225 (describing an action brought by the husband for "riding Skimmington" as sufficient enough to support a libel claim); Blackstone, *Commentaries*, 3:125.

15 **"This is an age":** "Memoirs, &c. &c.," *Pennsylvania Packet, & Philadelphia Daily Advertiser*, March 6, 1789.

15 **teaching of dancing:** "Dancing," *Daily Advertiser*, Jan. 12, 1793.

15 **treatment of seminal weakness:** "Venereal Complaints," 1 *Porcupine's Gazette*, 633, 634 (1797).

15 **curing of venereal complaints:** "Venereal Complaints," 634.

15 **veil such puerilities:** "Memoirs, &c. &c."

15 **persuaded a jury to find him not guilty:** Levy, *Freedom of the Press from Zenger to Jefferson*, 61.

16 **meant to impede the work:** *See* Hamilton to Jonathan Dayton, Oct.–Nov. 1799, founders.archives.gov ("Renegade Aliens conduct more than one of the most incendiary presses in the UStates—and yet in open contempt and defiance of the laws they are permitted to continue their destructive labours.").

16 **truths not fit to be told:** Letter to the editor, *New York Weekly Journal*, Feb. 25, 1733.

16 **not yet to the states:** Rabban, *Free Speech in Its Forgotten Years*, 130 (noting that that happened in an official sense in 1925).

17 **instances of "male conduct":** Cushing to Adams, Feb. 18, 1789, founders.archives.gov. "Male conduct" back then meant immorality. *See* Theophilus Parsons, *Memoir of Theophilus Parsons, Chief Justice of the Supreme Judicial Court of Massachusetts* (Boston: Ticknor & Fields, 1859), 387–88 ("The Senate with the Governor are the court to remove these officers for misbehaviour. Those officers, in general, who are guilty of male-conduct in the execution of their office, were improper men to be appointed. Sufficient care was not taken in ascertaining their political military or moral qualifications.").

17 **plaintiff would prevail:** Adams to Cushing, March 7, 1789, founders.archives.gov.

17 **Adams put his words into action:** Act of July 14, 1798, ch. 74, § 2, 1 Stat. 596, 596–97.

17 **"every Person has little Secrets":** *See* "The Busy Body No. 4," *American Weekly Mercury*, Feb. 25, 1729.

17 **"refus'd to print":** Ben Franklin, "Apology for Printers," *Pennsylvania Gazette* (Philadelphia), June 10, 1731.

17 **libeling and personal abuse:** William Temple Franklin, *The Autobiography of Benjamin Franklin*, ed. Jared Sparks (1850), 88–89.

17 **He noted the difference:** *See* B. Franklin, "Postscript. To the Printer of the London Chronicle," *London Chronicle*, Dec. 25, 1773 (emphasis omitted).

18 **"private character to flitters":** *See* "For the Federal Gazette. An Account of the Supremest Court of Judicature of the State of Pennsylvania, viz. The Court of the Press," *Federal Gazette & Philadelphia Evening Post*, Sept. 12, 1789.

18 **"restraining and punishing incendiary":** Hamilton to Jonathan Dayton, Oct.–Nov. 1799, founders.archives.gov.

18 **"not unaware of the difficulty":** Memorandum, James Madison, Report on the Resolutions, Feb. 7, 1799, in *The Writings of James Madison*, ed. Gaillard Hunt (1906), 6:341, 387 (emphasis added).

18 **"infamous Papers":** Washington to Edmund Pendleton, Sept. 23, 1793, founders.archives.gov.

18 **"outrages on common decency":** Washington to Henry Lee, July 21, 1793, founders.archives.gov.

18 **wrote ciphered letters:** *E.g.*, Jefferson to William Carmichael, Dec. 15, 1787, founders.archives .gov ("I am very sorry you have not been able to make out the cypher of my letter of Sep. 25. because it contained things which I wished you to know at that time.").

18 **destroyed by burning:** Jefferson to Elbridge Gerry, Jan. 26, 1799, founders.archives.gov.

18 **"to avoid attracting notice":** Jefferson to Francis Hopkinson, March 13, 1789, founders .archives.gov.

18 **"to keep out of view":** Jefferson to Nicholas Lewis, Feb. 9, 1791, founders.archives.gov.

18 **"the publication of what ha[d] not been intended":** Jefferson to John Novell, June 14, 1807, founders.archives.gov.

18 "And do you not think": Jefferson to Dr. George Logan, May 19, 1816, founders.archives.gov.

18 "liberty depends on the freedom of the press": Jefferson to James Currie, Jan. 28, 1786, founders.archives.gov.

18 Jefferson shared a confidence: Jefferson to Thomas McKean, Feb. 19, 1803, founders.archives.gov.

19 "how far the licentiousness": Jefferson to Madison, Nov. 17, 1798, founders.archives.gov.

19 had a falling-out: J. T. Callender, "The President Again," *Richmond Recorder; or, Lady's & Gentleman's Miscellany*, Sept. 1, 1802, 2, reprinted in J. T. Callender, "From the Recorder. The President Again," *Baltimore Republican; or, Anti-Democrat*, Sept. 6, 1802.

19 financial help from Jefferson: *See* Callender to Jefferson, Sept. 26, 1799 ("I inclose 16 pages of the new matter, as a specimen of the Prospect."), in *New England Historical and Genealogical Register*, 50:447.

19 "tempest of malignant passions": *United States v. Callender*, 25 F. Cas. 239 (C.C.D. Va. 1800) (quoting Callender, *Prospect Before Us*, 1:30–31).

19 "hoary headed incendiary": Callender, *Prospect Before Us*, 1:143.

19 "could not have committed": Callender, *Prospect Before Us*, 1:12.

19 find him guilty and sentence him: *United States v. Callender*, 25 F. Cas. 239.

19 There was a difference between liberty: *Virginia Gazette*, "News Article," *New York Spectator*, June 14, 1800.

20 the stink: Callender to Jefferson, Aug. 14, 1800, founders.archives.gov.

20 the shrieking insane: Callender to Jefferson, Oct. 27, 1800, founders.archives.gov.

20 publish parts of a new edition: *See, e.g.*, Callender to Jefferson, Oct. 11, 1800, founders.archives.gov (suggesting that Callender had "regularly" sent sheets of the second volume as they were printed). This letter is marked "Richmond."

20 "This letter will inclose a few pages": Callender to Jefferson, Aug. 14, 1800, founders.archives.gov.

20 maybe even a postmaster job: Callender to Madison, April 27, 1801, founders.archives.gov (stating, "I have just heard that Mr. David of Richmond has got notice that he is to quit his Situation in the Post office; that this in [*sic*] one of the few situations which I would think myself qualified to fill; and that it would just about afford a genteel living for an œconomical family," especially given the "desperate lengths" Callender had gone through "to serve the party").

20 Jefferson told Callender no: Jefferson to James Monroe, July 15, 1802, founders.archives.gov (noting that Callender "took it in mortal offense" when not named postmaster).

20 he knew secrets: Jefferson to James Monroe, May 29, 1801, founders.archives.gov.

20 Callender knew nothing: Jefferson to Monroe, May 29, 1801.

20 "It is well known": Callender, "President Again" (emphasis omitted).

20 There was more: Jas. T. Callender, letter to the editor, *New York Herald*, Sept. 8, 1802.

20 published a sixty-four-page pamphlet: Junius Philaenus, *A Letter to Thomas Jefferson, President of the United States* (New York: P. R. Johnson, 1802). A notice published in the *New-York Evening Post* on November 9, 1803, showed that the book was copyrighted on November 5, 1802.

20 "A certain black strumpet": Philaenus, *Letter to Thomas Jefferson*, 46.

21 "bribed [Callender] to become a villain": Philaenus, *Letter to Thomas Jefferson*, 40.

21 "in the habits of open and shameless prostitution": Philaenus, *Letter to Thomas Jefferson*, 64.

21 coward philosopher: *See* Philaenus, *Letter to Thomas Jefferson*, 48–49, 64.

21 the responsive pamphlet: Tom Callender, *Letters to Alexander Hamilton, King of the Feds* (New York: Richard Reynolds, 1802).

21 the mark of the beast on its forehead: Callender, *Letters to Alexander Hamilton*, A2–4.

21 "made more use of that Instrumentality": Callender, *Letters to Alexander Hamilton*, A2 (emphasis omitted).

21 charity money: *See, e.g.*, "From the Washington Federalist," *North-Carolina Journal* (Halifax), Oct. 4, 1802.

21 strive to displease, vex, and torment: Editor's Note, *Hudson Wasp*, July 7, 1802.

21 "If there, perchance, should come a Bee": Myself, "From the Editor," *Hudson Wasp*, July 7, 1802.

22 "Mr. Jefferson paid one hundred dollars": R. Rusticoat, "From the Editor," *Hudson Wasp*, Sept. 9, 1802.

22 the indictment read: *People v. Croswell*, 3 Johns. Cas. 337 (N.Y. Sup. Ct. 1804).

22 most grossly slandered the private character: "Liberty of the Press. Harry Croswell's Trial," 2 *Balance & Columbian Repository* (Hudson) 258 (1803) (reproducing the language of the full indictment).

22 **libelous behavior remained against the law:** "Liberty of the Press. Harry Croswell's Trial," 258.

22 **a direct attack upon the freedom:** *See* "An Accurate Statement of Facts, Concerning Mr. Attorney General Spencer's Late Attack on the Liberty of the Press, in This Country," 2 *Balance & Columbian Repository* (Hudson) 26 (1803).

22 **writing that public men should submit to slander:** "Mr. Jefferson's Consistency," 2 *Balance & Columbian Repository* (Hudson) 259 (1803).

22 **two letters from Jefferson:** *The Speeches at Full Length of Mr. Van Ness, Mr. Caines, the Attorney-General, Mr. Harrison, and General Hamilton, in the Great Cause of the People, Against Harry Croswell, on an Indictment for a Libel on Thomas Jefferson, President of the United States* (New York: G. & R. Waite, 1804), 3–4.

23 **Callender turned up dead:** "American Citizen," *American Citizen* (New York), July 19, 1803 ("The cause was tried on Friday last at Hudson."); "From the Recorder," *Lancaster Journal*, July 30, 1803.

23 **water that was about three feet deep:** "From the Recorder," *Lancaster Journal*, July 30, 1803.

23 **buried the same day:** *Virginia Gazette*, "J. T. Callender," *Federal Gazette & Baltimore Daily Advertiser*, July 23, 1803.

23 **called the drowning accidental:** Examiner, "Mortuary Notice," *American Citizen* (New York), July 26, 1803 (reproducing the verdict after the inquest).

23 **called it a suicide:** "From the Richmond Examiner. Callender's Death," *Salem Register*, Aug. 8, 1803.

23 **plunged in by an enemy:** Adams to Benjamin Rush, June 23, 1807, in *Old Family Letters*, ed. Alexander Biddle (Philadelphia: J. B. Lippincott, 1892), 144, 149.

23 **"The grave cannot always arrest the pursuit":** "Spirit of Democracy," *Albany Centinel*, Aug. 12, 1803.

23 **But it took until the year 2000:** Thomas Jefferson Memorial Foundation, *Report of the Research Committee on Thomas Jefferson and Sally Hemings*, app. E, 10.

23 **merely scandalous tittle-tattle:** Goebel, *Law Practice of Alexander Hamilton*, 1:778.

23 **remained a part of the common law:** *See* A Tory So Called, "From the New-York Evening Post," *Washington Federalist* (Georgetown), July 6, 1803.

23 **"Mr. Jefferson's tools have resorted":** A Tory So Called, "From the New-York Evening Post" (emphasis omitted). The first "truth" here was spelled "thruth" in the original.

23 **Had the victory for newspapers:** *See* A Tory So Called, "From the New-York Evening Post."

24 **the patriot who'd wept with anxiety:** "From the Balance. The Reign of Terror," *New York Evening Post*, July 29, 1803.

24 **"The liberty of the press":** "Communication," *Hudson Bee*, July 19, 1803.

24 **the defense had little to say:** *See* "Liberty of the Press. A Correct History of Harry Croswell's Trial," *Balance & Columbian Repository* (Hudson), Sept. 6, 1803; "Liberty of the Press. A Correct History of Harry Croswell's Trial," *Balance & Columbian Repository* (Hudson), Sept. 13, 1803.

24 **He spoke for six hours:** "From the Evening Post. Review of the Croswell Case," 3 *Balance & Columbian Repository* (Hudson) 193, 196 (1804).

24 **Hamilton was "like a torrent":** Untitled news article, *New York Evening Post*, Feb. 23, 1804.

24 **Hamilton's oration was so good:** "The Patriot," *Utica Patriot*, March 12, 1804.

24 **"bold stand in favour":** "From the Balance," *New York Evening Post*, Feb. 24, 1804.

25 **"pest of society":** *Speeches at Full Length of Mr. Van Ness, Mr. Caines, the Attorney-General, Mr. Harrison, and General Hamilton*, 64.

25 **"terrible liberty":** *People v. Croswell*, 3 Johns. Cas. 337 (N.Y. Sup. Ct. 1804).

25 **"The Liberty of the Press":** *Speeches at Full Length of Mr. Van Ness, Mr. Caines, the Attorney-General, Mr. Harrison, and General Hamilton*, 63 (emphasis added).

25 **"a man's personal defects or deformity":** *People v. Croswell*, 3 Johns. Cas. 337.

25 **"uses the weapon of truth wantonly":** *Speeches at Full Length of Mr. Van Ness, Mr. Caines, the Attorney-General, Mr. Harrison, and General Hamilton*, 70.

25 **Hamilton explained in a right-to-know sort of way:** *People v. Croswell*, 3 Johns. Cas. 337.

26 **"corrupts the morals of the community":** *People v. Croswell*, 3 Johns. Cas. 337.

26 **justices split on whether Croswell:** *People v. Croswell*, 3 Johns. Cas. 337.

26 **something amiss with his "private character":** *See Particulars of the Late Duel Fought at Hoboken, July 11, Between Aaron Burr and Alexander Hamilton, Esqrs., in Which the Latter Unfortunately Fell* (New York: A. Forman, 1804), 4, 9–10.

26 **Hamilton died at the home:** Allan McLane Hamilton, *Intimate Life of Alexander Hamilton*, 273–74.

26 **"An Act to Suppress Duelling"**: Revised Code of the Laws of Virginia: Act of Jan. 26, 1810, C. 157, § 8.

26 **"an obvious bodily or mental imperfection"**: *Moseley v. Moss*, 47 Va. 534 (Va. 1850).

27 **restrictive ideals and language lived on**: *See* Marc A. Franklin, "The Origins and Constitutionality of Limitations on Truth as a Defense in Tort Law," 16 *Stanford Law Review* 789 (1964).

27 **"to make an example of"**: Jefferson to Thomas McKean, Feb. 19, 1803, founders.archives.gov.

27 **Jefferson's relationship with "Black Sall"**: *The Papers of Thomas Jefferson, 13 November 1802–3 March 1803*, ed. Barbara B. Oberg (2012), 39:552–55.

27 **was indicted for what was effectively**: *See Dennie*, 4 Yeates 267 (Pa. 1805).

27 **quoting Alexander Hamilton**: *Dennie*, 4 Yeates 267 (quoting *Speeches* at 70).

27 **"The liberty of the press consists"**: *Dennie*, 4 Yeates 267 (emphasis omitted) (quoting *Speeches* at 63–64).

27 **found the publisher not guilty**: *Dennie*, 4 Yeates 267.

27 **"If every man who does not enjoy"**: *Foot v. Tracy*, 1 Johns. 46 (N.Y. 1806).

28 **"have no interest in the matter"**: *Cowley v. Pulsifer*, 213 Mass. 392 (1884).

28 **"No state of society would be more deplorable"**: *Commonwealth v. Blanding*, 20 Mass. (3 Pick.) 304 (1825).

28 **died of alcohol poisoning**: R——, "Communication," *Providence Gazette*, Feb. 20, 1828.

28 **that sort of thing didn't belong in a newspaper**: *Blanding*, 20 Mass. (3 Pick.) 304.

28 **"Private vices," the court wrote**: *Blanding*, 20 Mass. (3 Pick.) 304.

CHAPTER THREE: LOVE AND PICTURES

29 **Judge Martin was angry**: *Denis v. Leclerc*, 1 Mart. (o.s.) 297 (La. 1811).

30 **a few public laughs at their expense**: *See* H. P. Nugent, *H. P. Nugent's Reply to the Calumnies of the Honorable F. X. Martin, One of the Judges of the Superior Court of the Territory of Orleans* (1811), 40–41 (discussing the "tender sympathies" owed to Judge Martin amid a libel suit).

30 **humans are sympathetic creatures**: *White v. Nicholls*, 44 U.S. (1 How.) 266 (1845).

31 **man had the itch and smelled of brimstone**: *White*, 44 U.S. (1 How.) 266, citing *Villers v. Monsley* (1769), 95 Eng. Rep. 886 ("Old Villers, so strong of brimstone you smell, As if not long since you had got out of hell; But this damnable smell I no longer can bear, Therefore I desire you would come no more here" and more).

31 **The happiness of individuals**: *White*, 44 U.S. (1 How.) 266.

31 **"the wounded feelings of an honorable man"**: *Brooks v. Calloway*, 39 Va. 466 (Va. 1841).

31 **"It imports nothing"**: *Brooks*, 39 Va. 466.

31 **embarrassing information was truly important news**: *White*, 44 U.S. (1 How.) 266 (quoting *Commonwealth v. Clap*, 4 Mass. (1 Tyng) 163 (Mass. 1808)).

31 **ridiculed those maidens**: *Smart v. Blanchard*, 42 N.H. 137 (N.H. 1860).

31 **dare disturb the sanctuary of domesticity**: "Slavery," *Liberator*, Sept. 6, 1834 (criticizing that such was true for white people only).

31 **the ones who feared exposure**: *District of Massachusetts' Clerk's Office, Municipal Court for the City of Boston, Trial: Commonwealth v. J. T. Buckingham, on an Indictment for a Libel* (1822), 22 (statement of defendant).

31 **press had its evil eye in every house**: Dickens, *American Notes for General Circulation*, 172.

32 **continue his secret affair**: Palko Karasz, "Dickens Tried to Send Wife to Asylum, Letters Show," *New York Times*, Feb. 24, 2019.

32 **"Alfred Moore, of North Carolina"**: *Universal Gazette* (Philadelphia), Jan. 16, 1800.

32 **"remark and approbation with every spectator"**: "Supreme Court of the U.S.," *Boston Argus*, Feb. 24, 1792.

32 **arrived the cheaper daily press**: Parton, *Life of Horace Greeley, Editor of the "New York Tribune,"* 137, 138.

32 **etiquette books advised that proper people**: Stanhope, *American Chesterfield*, 183.

32 **penny papers had started up**: "The Prospectus of the Times," *New York Times* (Jubilee Supp.), Sept. 18, 1901 ("[The Times] will canvass freely the character and pretensions of public men, the merits and demerits of all administrations of Government, National, State, and municipal, and the worth of all institutions, principles, habits, and professions.") (reprinting a *New-York Daily Times* article edited by Henry J. Raymond from August 30, 1851).

32 **great levelers, elevators:** Parton, *Life of Horace Greeley, Editor of the "New York Tribune,"* 138.

32 **wasn't very smart:** *See* "The Vacant Judgeship," *New York Herald*, Jan. 3, 1844 ("Were Mr. Webster to be only attorney of the United States' Court, behind the bar, the Chief Justice of that bench, Mr. Taney, would still be under the magic power of that magnificent intellect which Mr. Webster enjoys.").

32 **matted wad of hair:** "A Glimpse at the Supreme Judges," *Salem Register*, Feb. 10, 1845.

32 **"concealed from even his personal friends":** "Illness of Judge Bacon," *Albany Evening Journal*, April 19, 1856.

32 **"would form a rampart from behind":** *Van Ness v. Hamilton*, 19 Johns. 349 (N.Y. 1822).

32 **right to keep secret vices:** *King & Verplanck v. Root*, 4 Wend. 113 (N.Y. 1829) (quoting the jury charge).

33 **Embarrassing truthful revelations:** *Fisher v. Patterson*, 14 Ohio 418 (Ohio 1846).

33 **"a person notorious for his libidinous amours":** Nugent, *H. P. Nugent's Reply to the Calumnies of the Honorable F. X. Martin*, 7.

33 **pangs of secret love:** Nugent, *H. P. Nugent's Reply to the Calumnies of the Honorable F. X. Martin*, 40 ("Until MIRTAN [*sic*] came into power, lovers could no where find consolation for the frowns of their mistresses; but MIRTAN [*sic*], who is as well acquainted [with] the *pangs of despised love*, as with *the laws delay*, commiserates their distresses.").

33 **newspaper published a story:** H. P. Nugent, *An Account of the Proceedings Had in the Superior Court of the Territory of Orleans, Against Thierry & Nugent for Libels and Contempt of Court; with an Account of Nugent's Trial on an Indictment for a Libel* (1810), 25, 22, 26, 6–7.

33 **"extraordinary pretension":** *Denis v. Leclerc*, 1 Mart. (o.s.) 297 (La. 1811).

33 **"subject to legal control":** *State v. Buzzard*, 4 Ark. 18 (Ark. 1842).

33 **"there can be no right in printers":** *Dexter v. Spear*, 7 F. Cas. 624 (D.R.I. 1825).

33 **"discourag[ed] that licentious abuse":** *Child v. Homer*, 30 Mass. 503 (Mass. 1833).

33 **"To claim that a man may write":** *Fisher v. Patterson*, 14 Ohio 418 (Ohio 1846).

33 **"gratifying a perverted public taste":** *Hoyt v. Mackenzie*, 3 Barb. Ch. 320 (N.Y. Ch. 1848).

33 **"There are in private life":** "Proceedings of the Convention: To Form a Constitution," *Democratic Free Press* (Detroit), July 29, 1835.

34 **"published with good motives":** "Proceedings of the Convention: To Form a Constitution."

34 **"responsible for the abuse":** Mich. Const. art. 1.

34 **judge dare tell a printer:** *See* Nugent, *H. P. Nugent's Reply to the Calumnies of the Honorable F. X. Martin*, 39–40 (discussing "the absurdity of judge Martin's decision").

34 **power to decide what was news:** Parton, *Life of Horace Greeley, Editor of the "New York Tribune."*

34 **didn't include the power to publish:** *Child v. Homer*, 30 Mass. (1 Pick.) 503 (Mass. 1833).

34 **"the right of every private citizen":** "The Lawyer and His Clients," *Boston Daily Advertiser*, Jan. 30, 1871.

34 **drawings of flora and fauna:** *See, e.g.*, "The Hoopoe," *Penny Magazine of the Society for the Diffusion of Useful Knowledge* (London), Jan. 30, 1836 (providing a drawing of the Hoopoe, a "handsome bird").

34 **circus that featured two sleek racing horses:** Advertisement, "Mr. J. W. Stocking's Circus," *Newburyport (Mass.) Daily Herald*, April 27, 1840.

35 **"The Emperor Napoleon in His Coffin":** *New World* (New York), March 5, 1841.

35 **Napoleon's corpse was in excellent condition:** M. Janisch, *The Exhumation of the Remains of Napoleon Bonaparte* (1840), 16.

35 **The Reverend Dr. Hardy:** "Reverend Doctor Hardy's Case: False Impressions Corrected," *Vox Populi* (Lowell, Mass.), March 31, 1848.

35 **illustrated its sadly spelled:** *Boston Weekly Mail*, March 28, 1846.

35 **"much curiosity always exists":** "Trial of Albert J. Tirrell, for the Murder of Maria Ann Bickford, in Boston: First Day," *New York Daily Herald*, March 26, 1846.

35 **battlefield carnage:** *See, e.g.*, "The Death of Guerrilla Burroughs," *Harper's Weekly*, Feb. 20, 1864 (showing a soldier killing an enemy escaping through a window).

35 ***Harper's Weekly:*** *See, e.g.*, "A Battle as Seen by the Reserve," *Harper's Weekly*, Dec. 27, 1862 (depicting the aftermath of a battle, bodies strewn about, some being carried on stretchers, with smoke settling in the background).

35 **dead bodies added:** Alexander Gardner, *The Sharpshooter*, July 1863, in "Icons: The Ten Greatest Images of Photojournalism," *Time*, Oct. 25, 1989 (showing a photograph taken by Alexander

Gardner of a dead Civil War soldier and published as a woodcut in *Harper's Weekly* with multiple dead bodies added).

36 **moment the bullet struck President Lincoln:** "Assassination of Abraham Lincoln, President of the United States," *National Police Gazette*, April 22, 1865.

36 **Mark Twain turned an especially critical eye:** Mark Twain, *The Complete Works of Mark Twain: Mark Twain's Speeches*, 48, 52 (Mark Twain, in an 1873 speech before the Monday Evening Club of Hartford, references what he calls Police Gazettes).

36 **Newsmongers who sold the *National Police Gazette*:** *Montross v. State*, 72 Ga. 261 (Ga. 1884).

36 **hampered the enjoyment of private life:** *Thompson v. State*, 17 Tex. Ct. App. 253 (Tex. App. 1884).

36 **police raid at a brothel:** "Astounding Depravity at Alliance, Ohio," *Illustrated Police News*, Feb. 1, 1879 (showing both the unfortunate officer and his incriminating sock).

36 **readers would find multiple illustrations:** "Horrible Atrocities Practised upon Two Boys, in Monroe County, Ark." (depicting two boys being hanged by "men-devils"); "Self-Murder as an Escape from Arrest" (depicting a man shooting a gun toward his chest); "Frightful Death of Joseph Kennedy, at Lagro, Ind., Jan. 11" (depicting a boy, belly down, foot caught in his horse's stirrup, being dragged by the horse); "Murder Most Foul" (depicting two toddlers crawling over their freshly slain parents); "Buried in a Snow House" (depicting a dead man buried under a pile of snow and a spectator looking on in shock), all from *Illustrated Police News*, Feb. 1, 1879.

36 **invasive literary trash:** "Our Periodical Literature," *New York Herald*, Nov. 21, 1870.

36 **king's affair with his son's wife:** *Publick Occurrences Both Foreign and Domestick* (Boston), Sept. 25, 1690.

36 **shutdown of its presses:** David A. Copeland, "Publick Occurrences," in Sterling, *Encyclopedia of Journalism*, 1147 (shutting down the publication four days after its first circulation).

37 **"follow the example of most":** "Our Exchanges," *Magenta* (Cambridge, Mass.), March 27, 1874.

37 **Samuel D. Warren Company produced the paper:** *See* Advertisement for S. D. Warren Company, Boston (1877) (on file with author) ("S. D. Warren & Co., 220 Devonshire St., Boston, Mass., Manufacturers of all grades BOOK PAPER, TINTED AND WHITE, Sized & Super Calendered Colored Mediums, and all grades RAG NEWSPAPER.").

CHAPTER FOUR: THE WARRENS MAKE THE PAPER

38 **Warrens had started out as rag brokers:** Letter to Grant, S. D. Warren Company, Warren Family Papers, Massachusetts Historical Society.

38 **Houghton Mifflin:** Receipt in "favor" of $2,000 to S. D. Warren from Hurd & Houghton, Dec. 17, 1866, Warren Family Papers; Green, *Mount Vernon Street Warrens*, 27–29.

38 **Scribner & Co.:** Roswell Smith to S. D. Warren, Nov. 29, 1876, Warren Family Papers (expressing thanks to Warren for helping pay a student's tuition to Amherst College; Smith was one of the founders of the company).

38 **The Atlantic:** Green, *Mount Vernon Street Warrens*, 28 ("Warren [senior] supplied $20,000 to buy the *Atlantic Monthly* in 1873.").

38 **Warrens had made the paper:** Burdett and Goddard, *Biography of a Connoisseur*, 15; Sox, *Bachelors of Art*, 4. *See also* "A Just Employer," *Century Magazine*, Sept. 1888 (Samuel D. Warren Sr., death announcement, noting that he made the paper for *Century* and *St. Nicholas* magazines).

38 **a part of Scott Paper:** Seth Faison, "Scott Paper Unit Draws $1.6 Billion," *New York Times*, Oct. 11, 1994.

38 **Sam was born in 1852:** Record of Massachusetts Births, 1852. Sam's birthday is listed as January 25, and he was born Samuel Howard Warren but changed his name to Samuel Dennis Warren to honor his father when he was in his teens.

38 **boarding schools:** Class Book (1875), Harvard University Archives (including Samuel Warren's handwritten autobiography, one of many from the class of 1875).

38 **so many bedrooms:** Burdett and Goddard, *Biography of a Connoisseur*, 16 ("There were a few sunny bedrooms upstairs. . . . I was quartered in cold Northern or shadowed Eastern rooms.").

38 **two mansions would be joined as one:** Louis D. Brandeis to Frederika D. Brandeis, July 20, 1879, in Urofsky and Levy, *Family Letters of Louis D. Brandeis*, 20 (explaining that the house on Pinkney used to be a separate house, some rooms in that second house were vacant, and suggesting that Sam had suggested that Louis move into the second mansion to take one of those vacant rooms).

38 **seven servants:** U.S. Census Bureau, U.S. Federal Census (1870) (showing one housekeeper and six domestic servants).

38 **two-year-old Josiah had died:** Boston Death Registry for the Year 1853; "Deaths," *Boston Daily Atlas*, Feb. 8, 1853.

38 **lifetime of pain and disfigurement:** Burdett and Goddard, *Biography of a Connoisseur*, 437; Sox, *Bachelors of Art*, 7.

38 **skittish humans and horses:** "Table Gossip," *Boston Globe*, June 11, 1893.

39 **letters throughout Ned's life:** Cornelia Warren to Henry Warren, Sept. 3, 1892, Warren Family Papers ("Ned is certainly very fortunate in his friend, Mr. Marshall. They suit each other very well."); Cornelia Warren to Susan Warren, Aug. 1896, Warren Family Papers ("Ned and Mr. Marshall are most kind to me"). Ned also wrote to Cornelia that he wanted to be certain that his partner would be taken care of financially, independent of what might happen within the Warren family to Ned's own income. Ned Warren to Cornelia Warren, Oct. 14, 1908, Warren Family Papers. *See also* Ned Warren to Cornelia Warren, Feb. 15, 1910, Warren Family Papers ("I wanted to be as permanent [living in the United States] as my relation to Johnny would allow. Where your home is, there will your heart be also."); Ned Warren to Cornelia Warren, July 30, 1911, Warren Family Papers (lamenting that his "longed-for summer with Johnny," who by this time had married a female Warren cousin but was still keeping company with Ned, had to be cut short).

39 **"a fine, strong, and tender man":** Burdett and Goddard, *Biography of a Connoisseur*, 207.

39 **three thousand newspapers in the United States:** Mott, *American Journalism*, 216.

39 **"As he went up":** "Death for Murder," *New-York Daily Times*, May 8, 1854.

39 **coverage of the Sickles tragedy:** "The Tragedy in Washington," *Public Ledger*, March 1, 1859.

40 **strikingly handsome Philip Key:** "The Assassination at Washington," *Boston Evening Transcript*, March 1, 1859.

40 **sparked his own scandal:** "The New Minister to Spain," *Richmond Whig*, May 25, 1869 (recounting the scandals in the life of the now ambassador Sickles).

40 **"snapp[ing] his pistol at the head":** "The Sickles Tragedy," *Philadelphia Inquirer*, March 1, 1859.

40 **"A scandal in high life":** "Tragedy in Washington."

40 **THE BEECHER-TILTON SCANDAL-CASE:** *Woodhull & Claflin's Weekly*, Nov. 2, 1872.

40 **"to betray the secrets":** Holmes, *Life Thoughts*, 218–20.

41 **magnificent hussies were in attendance:** "The Philosophy of Modern Hypocrisy—Mr. L. C. Challis the Illustration," *Woodhull & Claflin's Weekly*, Nov. 2, 1872.

41 **"wickedest women in New York":** "Vic. and Tennie: The Wickedest Women in New York," *Cincinnati Daily Enquirer*, Nov. 3, 1872.

41 **sending obscene literature through the mails:** "The Woodhull-Claflin Arrest," *Commercial Advertiser*, Nov. 2, 1872. The arrest for lewd mailings came because Congress in 1873 had passed "An Act for the Suppression of Trade in, and Circulation of, Obscene Literature and Articles of Immoral Use," mandating arrest for those who would mail any "obscene, lewd, or lascivious book, pamphlet, picture, paper, print, or other publication of an indecent character." Act of March 3, 1873, ch. 258, 17 Stat. 598.

41 **a jury eventually vindicated the two:** "Court of General Sessions," *Commercial Advertiser*, March 14, 1874.

41 *Tilton v. Beecher* **lawsuit:** *Tilton v. Beecher*, 59 N.Y. 176 (1874).

41 **Reverend Beecher with Mrs. Tilton atop his knee:** *Pictorial History of the Beecher-Tilton Scandal*, 2nd ed. (1875) (containing fifty engravings "from accurate sketches").

41 **"animated with a generous anxiety":** Kent, *Commentaries on American Law*, 23.

41 **sanctity of the home and other privacies of life:** "Itch for Scandal," *Buffalo* (N.Y.) *Advocate*, Dec. 31, 1857.

41 **Publishers had burst into the sacred realm:** "Newspaper Ghouls in Our Midst," *New York Times*, April 25, 1859.

41 **unfailing mark of societal refinement:** "The Public Policy of Privacy," *Brooklyn Union*, March 20, 1868.

41 **"Flee from a woman who loves scandal":** Haines and Yaggy, *Royal Path of Life*, 80.

42 **"towering influence on all thought":** Tuchman, *Proud Tower*, 138 (attributing the quotation to the philosopher William James).

42 **a strictly private affair, a personal tidbit:** E. L. Godkin, "Editorial Perspective," *Nation*, Jan. 27, 1870.

42 **very first press association:** Stephen A. Banning, "The Professionalism of Journalism: A Nineteenth-Century Beginning," *Journalism History* 24, no. 4 (Winter 1998–99) (suggesting that the Missouri Press Association first began in 1867 and shifted toward professionalism in 1869, with a stronger shift toward it all in the early 1870s).

42 **"shape a policy of their own":** "The Colored Men," *Inter Ocean* (Chicago), Aug. 6, 1875.

42 **"everything appropriate to a student's side-board":** Ad for Alfred Wood, Grocer, *Magenta*, Jan. 24, 1873.

42 **"perfect fitting pantaloons":** Ad for Edward W. Collins & Co., *Magenta*, Jan. 16, 1874.

42 **gossamer hats:** Ad for Bent & Bush, *Magenta*, Jan. 24, 1873.

42 **"cravats, gloves, collars":** Ad for John G. Calrow, Tailor, *Magenta*, Jan. 24, 1873.

42 **teach the little tattletale:** Editorial, *Magenta*, Nov. 21, 1873.

42 **The Magenta, soon renamed The Harvard Crimson:** Secretary's Report, Harvard College Class of 1875 (1875) (noting that *The Magenta* was renamed *The Crimson* in May 1875).

42 **"I won't philosophize":** *Magenta*, Jan. 24, 1873.

43 **subscription rate of $1.50:** *Magenta*, Jan. 24, 1873.

43 **"We are perhaps too merciful":** Editorial, *Magenta*, Nov. 21, 1873.

43 **"In an editorial of our last number":** Editorial, *Magenta*, Dec. 5, 1873.

44 **"secrets of importance only to those":** Sam Warren himself was not only a member of those secret societies; he covered them for *The Magenta* and was an editor from the near start, so he surely played a role in the unsigned editorializing and privacy-minded reprimanding that followed. It fits. As a reporter, he lauded Harvard's clubs and gatherings and did little to question their exclusivity and respectability. In a story about the Institute of 1770, an invitation-only organization to which he belonged, he lamented that many neglected to honor such a venerable group, one in the foremost rank of literary societies. In a news story headlined CLASS SUPPER, a short piece about a banquet honoring Harvard's sophomore class, the arrangements were perfect, and nothing could be more brilliant or suggestive of good cheer than the welcome that the sophomores received that night. His article titled "Art in the Modern Athens" credited the Boston Art Club as one that "serv[ed] the very important purpose of bringing into more personal relations a class of men who [can] be of the greatest benefit to each other."

44 **Bowdoin newspaper shockingly flimsy:** "Our Exchanges," *Magenta*, Feb. 27, 1874.

44 **"marked improvement in general tone":** "Our Exchanges," *Magenta*, March 13, 1874.

44 **The Atlantic's variety and style:** "Our Exchanges," *Magenta*, Feb. 27, 1874.

44 **parents had been thrown from a wagon:** "State News," *Bangor Daily Whig & Courier*, April 22, 1874.

44 **golden wedding anniversary:** "City and Suburbs," *Boston Daily Globe*, May 22, 1874.

44 **scrapbook titled News Cuttings:** Scrapbook, *News Cuttings*, presented to Samuel D. Warren Jr., "by his very affectionate Grandfather and Grandmother, Jan. 25, 1875," Sam's birthday. Warren Family Papers.

44 **mementos from Harvard's exclusive clubs:** This information is both in the scrapbook and in the Harvard Yearbook for 1874, showing Samuel D. Warren Jr. as a member of Hasty Pudding, the Institute of 1770, the O.K. Society, the Cercle Français, the Glee Club, various theatrical productions on campus, and *The Magenta*.

44 **"for which I have been much interested":** Samuel Warren, Class Book (1875), Harvard University Archives (Warren's handwritten autobiography).

44 **beauty of the French language:** *See, e.g.,* "French Club," *Magenta*, Oct. 10, 1873 (without the study of French, "we lose … the pleasure of social converse in the tongue pre-eminently fitted to convey the niceties of conversation").

44 **suffering from liquor seizures:** Untitled, *Boston Globe*, Aug. 22, 1874. There was apparently another Samuel Warren who lived in Boston at the time. "Local Lines," *Boston Globe*, Oct. 16, 1888 ("Samuel Warren was this morning arrested … on the charge of stealing an overcoat.").

45 **When Dane Hall burned:** "The Passing of Dane Hall," *Harvard Crimson*, March 20, 1918.

45 **Sam and Louis part of the class of 1877:** Manual of the Harvard Law School, 1876–77 (1876), 5–6.

46 **when Louis's eyes tired:** Lief, *Brandeis: The Personal History of an American Ideal*, 22.

46 **fast friends by graduation:** Mason, *Brandeis: A Free Man's Life*, 46–47. The Mason biography was authorized; Mason was given access to a trove of materials from family and friends.

46 **Blackstone's *Commentaries*:** Manual of the Harvard Law School, 1876–77, 11.

46 **"improper, mischievous, or illegal":** Blackstone, *Commentaries on the Laws of England* 4:152.

46 **Brandeis had also prepared by reading:** *Harvard Law School Class of 1877 Sexennial Report* (1883) (Brandeis's entry explains that he "read Kent's Commentaries for two months at a law office in Louisville").

46 **a Warren family friend:** List of Members of the Thursday Club (1875), Warren Family Papers.

46 **"personal defects, or misfortunes, or vices":** James Kent, *Commentaries on American Law*, rev. ed. (1889), 26.

46 **Sam and Louis took the same sorts of classes:** Manual of the Harvard Law School, 1876–77, 10.

46 **Brandeis's notes on Torts:** Brandeis Class Notes for Ames on Torts (1875), Brandeis University Archives, Collection of Frank Gilbert, series 11, box 1.

47 **three years of study the very next year:** "President Eliot's Annual Report," *Harvard Register*, Jan. 15, 1880.

47 **It all cost students around $750:** Manual of the Harvard Law School, 1876–77, 12.

47 **trusts and property ownership:** Professor Ames to Mr. Warren (presumably Samuel junior), Feb. 5, 1876, Warren Family Papers.

47 **Brandeis had to take out a family loan:** Partial transcription of autobiographical sketch by Louis D. Brandeis (n.d.), Brandeis University Archives, Brandeis Collection, box 69 ("I went to the Harvard Law School on money lent me by my brother"). *See also* Peter Scott Campbell, "Notes for a Lost Memoir of Louis D. Brandeis," 43 *Journal of Supreme Court History* 27, 31 (2018).

47 **drawn by letter after letter from Sam:** *See, e.g.,* Warren to Brandeis, June 18, 1879, Louis D. Brandeis Collection, University of Louisville School of Law.

47 **bulldog perseverance and connections:** Brandeis to Charles Nagel, July 12, 1879, in Urofsky and Levy, *Family Letters of Louis D. Brandeis*, 16. *See also* Louis D. Brandeis to Frederika D. Brandeis, July 20, 1879, in Urofsky and Levy, *Family Letters of Louis D. Brandeis*, 20 (noting Warren's connections "from which something may come").

47 **"The former is well known to Boston":** "Personal," *Boston Post*, Aug. 16, 1879.

47 **former governor of Rhode Island:** *See, e.g.,* "Lord Roscoe and Sprague," *Cleveland Plain Dealer*, Aug. 12, 1879.

47 **The press was wrong for printing:** "Editorial," *Inter Ocean* (Chicago), Aug. 19, 1879.

47 **hit-or-miss payment:** Louis D. Brandeis to Frederika D. Brandeis, July 20, 1879, in Urofsky and Levy, *Family Letters of Louis D. Brandeis*, 20.

47 **working as a law clerk:** Partial transcription of autobiographical sketch by Brandeis ("I had offered to me a secretaryship to Chief Justice Gray . . . sitting with him five hours a day . . . [while he was] writing his opinions.").

47 **That decision involving the minister:** *Lothrop v. Adams*, 133 Mass. 471 (1882) was argued in November 1879. It appears that Justice Gray might not have been assigned to the case, however.

47 **It wasn't all work:** Louis D. Brandeis to Frederika D. Brandeis, July 20, 1879, in Urofsky and Levy, *Family Letters of Louis D. Brandeis*, 20.

48 **"the most unBostonian manner":** Louis D. Brandeis to Amy Brandeis Wehle, Nov. 25, 1880, in Urofsky and Levy, *Letters of Louis D. Brandeis*, vol. 1, *1870–1907, Urban Reformer*, 58.

48 **all the vacant rooms in the back mansion:** Louis D. Brandeis to Frederika D. Brandeis, July 20, 1879, in Urofsky and Levy, *Family Letters of Louis D. Brandeis*, 20.

48 **Louis moved in with the family:** Boston City Directory 1882. Alfred Lief put Brandeis's move to the back mansion as early as 1879. Lief, *Brandeis: The Personal History of an American Ideal*, 23.

48 **the two would hang with Oliver Wendell Holmes:** Letter from Oliver Wendell Holmes, Feb. 9, 1916, Oliver Wendell Holmes Jr. Digital Suite, Harvard University Law School (suggesting that Holmes had known Brandeis ever since Sam had imported him to Boston).

48 **talking of the highest good:** Louis D. Brandeis to Alfred Brandeis, July 31, 1879, in Urofsky and Levy, *Family Letters of Louis D. Brandeis*, 22.

48 **alcohol-enriched larks to the zoo:** Holmes to Mrs. Gray, March 25, 1922, Holmes Digital Suite (spring reminds him of larks taken with Sam in New York to the zoo, adding "alas the exquisite ravished this Country with the 18th Amendment").

48 **shared tickets to cultural events:** Holmes to Brandeis, April 13, 1881, Holmes Digital Suite (thanking Brandeis for tickets to a German play).

48 **visits to the Holmes family beach house:** Mason, *Brandeis: A Free Man's Life*, 63–64 (Brandeis "was invited to spend a week-end with Holmes and his wife at Mattapoisett").

48 **frequent meetings at a local tavern:** Mason, *Brandeis: A Free Man's Life*, 64. This is significant in that the Mason biography of Brandeis was authorized and Justice Brandeis had given Mason free access to his "memoranda, diaries, notebooks, and personal correspondence."

48 **Holmes read through Brandeis's work:** Mason, *Brandeis: A Free Man's Life*, 64. The author attributes this information to an interview he had with Justice Brandeis.

48 **Holmes's dinner parties:** Warren to Holmes, July 27, 1883, Holmes Digital Suite ("Mrs. Warren and I shall be glad to come to you for Sunday"); Holmes to Brandeis, March 9, 1881, Holmes Digital Suite (suggesting that he and Mrs. Holmes were always glad to see Brandeis).

48 **ground zero for any discussion:** Brandeis to Amy Brandeis Wehle, Dec. 4, 1879, in Urofsky and Levy, *Letters of Louis D. Brandeis*, vol. 1, *1870–1907, Urban Reformer*, 49; Warren to Holmes, July 27, 1883, Holmes Digital Suite ("Mrs. Warren and I shall be glad to come to you for Sunday the 12th August"). *See also* Lief, *Brandeis: The Personal History of an American Ideal*, 52 ("Brandeis dined at his Beacon Street home and they reviewed the judge's decisions in intimate discussion.").

48 **musings on torts:** Lief, *Brandeis: The Personal History of an American Ideal*, 25 ("Can you spare me the time and the self-sacrifice to give me this evening or a part of it and let me read over such notes as I have made for an article on Torts? It still consists of disjecta membra but I want some assistance in making up my mind whether my ideas are ripe for publication," among other missives).

48 **famous lectures on the common law:** Novick, *Honorable Justice*, 147, 158.

48 **"life of the law has not been logic":** Holmes, *Common Law*, 1, 94.

48 **Holmes's young inner circle:** Novick, *Honorable Justice*, 147, 158.

48 **by the time Holmes got appointed:** Partial transcription of autobiographical sketch by Brandeis ("As a matter of fact, I had been instrumental in getting the money for the very professorship which put Mr. Holmes there," persuading a former classmate to donate an inheritance, knowing "of the desire to get Holmes out there"); Mason, *Brandeis: A Free Man's Life*, 65 (describing Brandeis's interest in placing Holmes on the Harvard Law School faculty).

48 **"As one of the bar I rejoice":** Brandeis to Holmes, Dec. 9, 1882, Holmes Digital Suite.

48 **Holmes thanked Brandeis:** Holmes to Brandeis (dated 1902), Holmes Digital Suite.

48 **the fledgling *Harvard Law Review*:** Partial transcription of autobiographical sketch by Brandeis.

48 **Brandeis had been one of seven:** This information and the related description come from the *Harvard Law Review* original prospectus. *Harvard Law Review* archival materials, Harvard Law School Library, Historical & Special Collections.

49 **he helped to drum up potential authors:** Partial transcription of autobiographical sketch by Brandeis.

49 **was also started by Brandeis:** In a 1918 Harvard Law School publication, Brandeis is described as taking "a leading part in the formation of the Harvard Law School Association." Harvard Law School, *The Centennial History of the Harvard Law School, 1817–1917* (Harvard Law School Association, 1918), 200.

49 **Their law firm became successful too:** Partial transcription of autobiographical sketch by Brandeis (noting that by 1890 the "business had developed very much" and was beginning to be known nationally).

49 **turn away clients like Mark Twain:** Memorandum Detailing Conversation with LDB at a Dinner at the Hotel Bellevue, June 2, 1932, Felix Frankfurter Papers, Library of Congress (Brandeis "said that Mark Twain was one of his early clients, having come to him about whether to bring a libel action. His own advice was against bringing the action."). There is a reported case, *The Mark Twain Case*, 14 F. 728 (N.D. Ill. 1883), in which Mark Twain/Samuel Clemens brings a cause of action for the use of the name Mark Twain and loses. It's unclear if this is the case to which Brandeis refers.

49 **skeptical of both the claim and the man:** Brandeis to Mrs. Glendower Evans, Nov. 27, 1900, in Urofsky and Levy, *Letters of Louis D. Brandeis*, vol. 1, *1870–1907, Urban Reformer*, 150. "Do not approve of Twain. You must select someone of political, professional, or business standing," Brandeis wrote to Evans, though it is not clear what selection he was referring to. Brandeis had previously told friends that when Twain came to see him about the potential libel action, Twain was "constantly striding up and down the office as he talked, being dressed quite shabbily in clothes which at that period were not well dyed, and in an overcoat buttoned up to his neck." Memorandum Detailing Conversation with LDB at a Dinner at the Hotel Bellevue, June 2, 1932, Frankfurter Papers.

49 **nervous indigestion for the first few years:** Partial transcription of autobiographical sketch by Brandeis ("Then I got nervous indigestion, which took hold of me for about seven years. So that I had to be careful for about seven years,—until about 1886.").

49 **worried about whether the next client would show:** Louis D. Brandeis to Alfred Brandeis, July 30, 1881, in Urofsky and Levy, *Letters of Louis D. Brandeis*, vol. 1, *1870–1907, Urban Reformer*, 63 ("The outlook for next year is not good.").

49 **business quickly boomed:** The firm still exists and is known as Nutter McClennen & Fish.

49 **his seamless entry into elite Boston society:** Partial transcription of autobiographical sketch by Brandeis.

49 **because of Sam's connections:** There has been some suggestion that Sam's wife, Mabel, did not like Brandeis, but there is at least some indication that the couples enjoyed each other's company. Mabel Warren to Henry Warren (n.d.), Warren Family Papers ("Will you dine with us on Thursday at seven o'clock or 6:30 (I have asked your mother, Cornelia, & the Brandeises to come at seven)").

49 **Brandeis credited himself too:** Partial transcription of autobiographical sketch by Brandeis ("One of the reasons why I was taken up as I was in Boston society was because of the culture which I had, [I] knew more about art and about music than most of the people did. Boston did give this to me: I was then a very serious minded individual, with terribly [missing] views of life and Puritan ideals. Boston came nearer my ideal than anything") (edited for clarity).

49 **a dignity that no other city could match:** *Nutter, McClennen & Fish: The First Century*, 2.

50 **occasional mention of their philanthropic work:** *See, e.g.,* "The National Centennial," *Boston Post*, Aug. 14, 1875 (Mrs. Samuel D. Warren is mentioned as participating in a call for financial assistance for the upcoming centennial of the United States.).

50 **innocuous social events:** *See, e.g.,* "The College Regatta," *Boston Globe*, Jan. 14, 1875 (Samuel D. Warren Jr. is named as a participant in the meeting of the Rowing Association of American Colleges); "Ex-governor Claflin," *Boston Globe*, Feb. 15, 1875.

50 **a story about the paper mills:** "Kindness to Employees," *Boston Globe*, Oct. 18, 1883.

50 **booklet put out by a New York publisher:** *An Album of Portraits of Celebrities* (New York: F. M. Lupton, 1882).

50 **engagement of Mabel Bayard:** "News Observations," *News and Observer*, Oct. 21, 1882.

50 **Ditto in *The Washington Post*:** "Approaching Weddings," *Washington Post*, Oct. 23, 1882.

50 ***The Cincinnati Enquirer*:** *Cincinnati Enquirer*, Oct. 15, 1882.

50 **"The Gossip of Washington":** "The Gossip of Washington," *New York Times*, Jan. 18, 1883.

50 **"Table Gossip" column:** "Table Gossip," *Boston Globe*, Oct. 22, 1882.

50 **New York *World*:** *Boston Globe*, Oct. 23, 1882.

50 **would announce when he'd come to town:** "Personal," *Washington Post*, Dec. 26, 1882 ("Samuel D. Warren, jr., of Boston, is at Wormley's.").

50 **many other newspapers covered the wedding:** *See, e.g.,* "Gossip About People," *Milwaukee Daily Journal*, Jan. 26, 1883; "Matrimonial," *Chicago Daily Tribune*, Jan. 27, 1883.

50 **"long expected event":** "A Brilliant Bridal," *Washington Post*, Jan. 26, 1883.

50 **ten ushers, eight bridesmaids:** "The Washington Society World: Marriage of Senator Bayard's Daughter," *New York Times*, Jan. 26, 1883.

50 **"There was a bridegroom":** "Brilliant Bridal."

50 **Boston millionaire:** *New Orleans Times-Democrat*, Jan. 25, 1883.

51 **Tiffany & Co. scroll:** The scroll is kept at the Massachusetts Historical Society as part of the Warren Family Papers. It's true that Sam's brother Fiske signed the scroll and that Louis Brandeis and Ned Warren didn't, but because hundreds, newspapers said, had been invited to the wedding, it's likely that not all attendees signed. Back then, a wedding invitation was treated nearly as a royal summons, and only an emergency would be an acceptable reason to decline, so maybe both were there.

51 **"it was . . . a specific suggestion":** Brandeis to Warren, April 8, 1905, Warren Family Papers.

51 **"This, like so many of my public":** Mason, *Brandeis: A Free Man's Life*, 70.

51 **changed his middle name to Dembitz:** Lief, *Brandeis: The Personal History of an American Ideal*, 26.

51 **longtime journalist at *The Nation*:** W. M. Griswold, *A Directory of the Writers for the Literary Press*, 3rd ed. (1890), 15 (naming Lewis Dembitz as a contributor to *The Nation*). An index to *The*

Nation from the years 1881–1906 shows that Dembitz contributed more than forty articles. Daniel C. Haskell, ed., *"The Nation": Indexes of Titles and Contributors* (1951).

51 **"longing to discover truths":** Louis D. Brandeis to Stella and Emily Dembitz, April 22, 1926, in Urofsky and Levy, *Family Letters of Louis D. Brandeis*, 422.

CHAPTER FIVE: WHO WAS KATE NASH?

52 **make him happy when he died:** Nevins, *Grover Cleveland: A Study in Courage*, 2:762.

52 **"I must stop with the assertions":** Cleveland to Nash, Dec. 18, 1894, Lee Kohns Collection, New York Public Library.

52 **"I will not give you up":** Cleveland to Nash, June 26, 1895, Kohns Collection.

52 **unsigned introductory note:** Memorandum from the Kohns Collection on Manuscripts Relating to an Episode in the Life of Grover Cleveland, Kohns Collection.

53 **Kate Nash is not mentioned:** The only mention of the letters in the folder is in Joshua Kendall's 2016 book titled *First Dads*, in which he explains in the bibliography that he came upon them at the New York Public Library ("I stumbled upon four love letters of Cleveland to Kate Nash, written between 1892 and 1896, in the Lee Kohns Collection at the New York Public Library.").

53 **girls have been sending him birthday presents:** *See* Cleveland to "Little Girl," March 18, 1886, in Nevins, *Letters of Grover Cleveland*, 103; *see also* Cleveland to Nash, March 18, 1896, Kohns Collection (stating that Cleveland and Kate had "celebrated one or two of these occasions together").

53 **"I do not forget you":** Cleveland to Nash, March 18, 1896, Kohns Collection.

53 **he died in a buggy accident:** "Fatal Accident," *Fall River (Mass.) Daily Evening News*, July 24, 1875; *see also* "First Lady Biography: Frances Cleveland," National First Ladies' Library, first ladies.org (stating Frances Folsom Cleveland's birthday as July 21, 1864).

53 **he'd bought her her baby carriage:** Frances Folsom Cleveland, White House, www.whitehouse .gov.

53 **she'd called him Uncle Cleve:** "The President's Sweetheart," *New York Times*, April 27, 1886.

53 **he'd had the warmest of feelings:** Nevins, *Grover Cleveland: A Study in Courage*, 1:302–3.

54 **Cleveland became her guardian:** "Will Be a Wedding: President Cleveland and Miss Frankie Folsom Will Be Married in June," *Cleveland Plain Dealer*, May 2, 1886.

54 **she became his ward:** "Sensations of a Day: Confirmation of the Rumor That Mr. Cleveland Will Wed His Ward," *St. Louis Globe-Democrat*, April 16, 1886.

54 **became of striking appearance:** "The Hostess of the White House," *Frank Leslie's Illustrated Newspaper*, March 14, 1885.

54 **still a mere schoolgirl:** "Our Bachelor President," *New York Times*, April 18, 1886.

54 **Cleveland started dating her:** *See* Nevins, *Grover Cleveland: A Study in Courage*, 1:302–3 (suggesting that Cleveland began dating Frances just after he was elected governor, which was in 1883 when Frances was eighteen); *see also* McElroy, *Grover Cleveland: The Man and the Statesman*, 185 (suggesting that Cleveland and Frances started dating when she first entered college).

54 **the mismatch:** *See* "Our Bachelor President."

54 **wasn't a pretty man:** "The *Sunday Times* Offers to Sell 'Electrotypes of the Hon. Grover Cleveland,'" *Buffalo Morning Express*, Aug. 21, 1882 ("He can't be called a pretty man, but he wouldn't sour milk on sight.").

54 **and was portly:** "Grover Cleveland as Governor: A Sketch of His Habits and Work," *Springfield (Mass.) Republican*, June 25, 1884.

54 **leaked letter:** "President Cleveland's Engagement," *San Francisco Daily Evening Bulletin*, April 27, 1886 (the engagement "was made public by a breach of confidence on the part of friends in Buffalo").

54 **Cleveland had been her foster father:** "Don't Say a Word," *Champaign (Ill.) Daily Gazette*, April 19, 1886; "Miss Folsom's Dearest Foe," *Macon (Ga.) Telegraph*, May 10, 1886.

54 **familial love had turned to something different:** "Don't Say a Word," *Streator (Ill.) Daily Free Press*, April 19, 1886.

54 **White House chambermaids:** "The President's Photographs," *Kansas City (Mo.) Times*, June 3, 1886 (republishing an excerpt from the *Detroit Tribune*).

54 **"an outrage upon all the privacies":** "The President Righteously Indignant," *San Francisco Daily Evening Bulletin*, May 3, 1886 (internal quotation marks omitted). President Cleveland also told them that "a man, though a President, has some rights to his private affairs.").

54 **he burned his personal letters:** "President's Photographs."

54 **there'd been rumblings:** "A Terrible Tale," *Buffalo Evening Telegraph*, July 21, 1884 (suggesting that the *Rochester Union and Advertiser* had published hints that Cleveland had hidden children away).

54 **"sensational and disgusting enough":** "Cleveland Must Explain," *Jackson (Mich.) Daily Citizen*, July 23, 1884.

54 CLEVELAND'S PRIVATE LIFE: "Cleveland's Private Life: Ruining a Woman, Stealing Her Child, and Slandering a Friend," *Pittsburgh Commercial Gazette*, July 21, 1884.

54 **tricking the mother, Maria Halpin:** *See* "Cleveland's Private Life."

54 **boy christened Oscar Folsom:** "Cleveland's Private Life." *See also* "Maria Halpin Speaks," *Salt Lake Weekly Tribune*, Aug. 21, 1884 (quoting Maria Halpin that Cleveland is the father of her son, Oscar Folsom Cleveland).

55 **hide his law partner's shame:** "The Charges Disproved: How the 'Reverend' Ball Lied About Grover Cleveland," *Harrisburg (Pa.) Daily Patriot*, Aug. 9, 1884.

55 **"had the right to put in matter":** Henry Ward Beecher, "Address to the New York State Editorial Reunion at Poughkeepsie," in Wingate, *Views and Interviews on Journalism*, 233.

55 **unchaste man or an influence peddler:** E. L. Godkin, "The President as an Example," 39 *Nation* 216 (1884).

55 **decent privacy during their honeymoon:** "In the Alleghenies," *Philadelphia Inquirer*, June 5, 1886.

55 **thanks in part to police:** "The Honeymoon: Mr. and Mrs. Cleveland in Their Pretty Summer Retreat," *New York Herald*, June 4, 1886.

55 **some reporters were said to have hidden:** Joseph B. Bishop, "Newspaper Espionage," 1 *Forum* 529 (1886).

55 **only positive clippings:** "Persons and Things," *New Haven Evening Register*, July 8, 1886.

55 **company of older men:** "Persons and Things," *New Haven Evening Register*, July 23, 1886.

55 **darned her own stockings:** "Properly Domestic: The Bride Has Settled Down to Needlework," *Kansas City (Mo.) Times*, Oct. 7, 1886.

55 **his wife's millinery bill:** "Tea Table Talk," *St. Albans (Vt.) Weekly Messenger*, July 15, 1886.

55 **up to three hundred pounds:** "Presidential Possibilities," *Daily Inter Ocean* (Chicago), July 17, 1886 (republishing an excerpt from *The Boston Herald*).

55 **America had a "morbid craving":** "Lines of Propriety," *Washington Critic*, Oct. 4, 1886.

55 **"life of the *family*":** "What Has Been an Open Secret," *Montpelier (Vt.) Argus and Patriot*, Nov. 3, 1886 (emphasis added).

56 **glories of Harvard:** "The Banquet; President Cleveland's Speech," *Springfield (Mass.) Republican*, Nov. 9, 1888.

56 **tears of wrath and indignation:** Nevins, *Grover Cleveland: A Study in Courage*, 1:310.

56 **tired of the gossip:** "Banquet; President Cleveland's Speech."

56 **Cue "The Star-Spangled Banner":** "Banquet; President Cleveland's Speech."

56 **everybody who was anybody:** "President Eliot: Graduates of the University Addressed by Its Executive Head," *Boston Globe*, Nov. 9, 1886. Sam Warren's brother Fiske signed the guest book, and Sam had a stronger connection to the group by marriage than Fiske did.

56 **"All who were listening to him":** E. L. Godkin, "The President and the Newspapers," 43 *Nation* 406 (1886).

56 **"social exactions":** "Death's Sad Summons: Miss Katie Bayard Stricken by Heart Disease," *Washington Post*, Jan. 17, 1886; *see also* "Dust to Dust: The Funeral Services of Miss Bayard at Wilmington," *Philadelphia Inquirer*, Jan. 20, 1886 (reporting Miss Bayard's birth date as August 13, 1857, and death date as January 16, 1886).

57 **lying prostrate on a sofa:** "Death's Sad Summons."

57 **"There seems no doubt":** "Social Exactions at Washington," *Philadelphia Times*, Jan. 19, 1886.

57 **Newspapers reported that Sam:** "Laid in Old Swedes," *Wilmington (Del.) Morning News*, Jan. 19, 1886.

57 **Meanwhile, Mrs. Bayard, they said:** "Dust to Dust."

57 **as well as the cemetery:** "Miss Bayard's Funeral," *Washington Post*, Jan. 20, 1886.

57 **"congestion of the brain":** "Death of Mrs. Bayard: A Double Affliction Falls upon the Secretary of State," *Washington Post*, Feb. 1, 1886 (also noting that Mrs. Bayard was born on July 4, 1834, and died on January 31, 1886).

57 **"caused by grief at the loss":** "A Bereaved Family," *Hagerstown Herald and Torch Light*, Feb. 4, 1886.

57 **"hopeless invalid":** "Mr. Bayard's Wife Dead: The Secretary of State Again Bereaved," *New York Times*, Feb. 1, 1886.

57 **had mainly relied on Katie:** "Death of Mrs. Bayard."

57 **Survival looked unlikely:** "Mr. Bayard's Wife Dead."

57 **They reported great detail:** "The Late Mrs. Bayard," *Washington Post*, Feb. 2, 1886.

57 **E. L. Godkin had already written:** E. L. Godkin, "Libel and Its Legal Remedy," *Atlantic Monthly*, Dec. 1880.

58 **where the family would be vacationing:** "Table Gossip," *Boston Globe*, March 2, 1884 (the Warrens would occupy a place in Beverly for the summer).

58 **who would be vacationing with them:** "Table Gossip," *Boston Globe*, Aug. 3, 1884.

58 **Warrens visited overseas:** "Table Gossip," *Boston Globe*, Oct. 3, 1886.

58 **seaside home at Mattapoisett:** "Table Gossip," *Boston Globe*, Sept. 21, 1884.

58 **Mrs. Warren entertained:** "Table Gossip," *Boston Globe*, Jan. 15, 1888.

58 **gave a luncheon:** "Table Gossip," *Boston Globe*, Feb. 12, 1888.

58 **costly art purchases:** "Table Gossip," *Boston Globe*, April 20, 1884 ("Mrs. Samuel D. Warren has bought George Fuller's painting of 'A Quadroon,' for $3500.").

58 **building a wharf:** "Mattapoisett Matters," *Boston Globe*, July 15, 1888.

58 **and then a stable:** "Quiet Mattapoisett," *Boston Globe*, July 29, 1888.

58 **and then a boat:** "New Yacht at Mattapoisett," *Boston Globe*, May 8, 1889.

58 **India Wharf Rats:** "Boston's Blue Blooded Rats," *New York Herald*, Dec. 25, 1889; "Very Swell Boston Cooks," *Worcester (Mass.) Daily Spy*, Dec. 26, 1889; "Tony Boston Rats: The Hub Shocked at the Escapades of a Rodents' Club, with Noted Members," *Pittsburgh Dispatch*, Dec. 25, 1889 (noting that the India Wharf Rats had banded together "to have a good time in a manner that would not be allowed in the tony Somerset street Botolphian and Puritan clubs, of which the gentlemen were members").

58 **Warrens had attended White House events:** *See* "Royalty at the White House: Queen Kapiolani Calls upon President and Mrs. Cleveland," *New York Times*, May 5, 1887.

58 **dinners in honor of the First Couple:** *See* "A Gorgeous Spread," *Indianapolis Journal*, Aug. 5, 1887.

58 **Mrs. Cleveland began to visit Mrs. Warren:** "Mrs. Cleveland's Movements," *Washington Post*, Aug. 7, 1887. She returned to Mattapoisett several days later. "Mrs. Cleveland: She Takes a Morning Drive and Attends Another Entertainment at Mrs. Gilder's," *Boston Daily Advertiser*, Aug. 10, 1887.

58 **more intimate dinners together:** "Lovely in White: Reception and Dinner to Mrs. Cleveland," *Boston Globe*, Aug. 13, 1887.

58 **Breakfasts too:** "Table Gossip," *Boston Globe*, Jan. 8, 1888.

58 **had become close friends:** "People and Events," *Daily Inter Ocean* (Chicago), May 30, 1889.

58 **sort of intermediary:** *See* "Visited the President," *Raleigh (N.C.) News and Observer*, Aug. 27, 1895.

58 **coverage of the Dedham Polo Club:** *See, e.g.,* "Polo on Ponies: Dedham Scores Four Goals While Harvard Gets Two," *Boston Globe*, Nov. 10, 1889.

58 **Brandeis was also a member:** *Not a History of the Dedham Polo Club*, 8–9.

58 **Louis's single mention:** "Table Gossip," *Boston Globe*, Jan. 24, 1886.

58 **in the paper for professional reasons:** *See, e.g.,* "Against Woman Suffrage," *Boston Globe*, March 7, 1885.

59 **railroad land taxes:** "The Court Record: Supreme Court of the United States," *Washington Post*, Nov. 8, 1889.

59 **"had been ill [for] some time":** "Death of Mrs. Charles Nagel," *Louisville (Ky.) Courier-Journal*, Dec. 18, 1889.

59 **shouldn't force her to eat:** Louis D. Brandeis to Adolph Brandeis, Dec. 16, 1889, in Urofsky and Levy, *Family Letters of Louis D. Brandeis*, 34.

59 **Pulitzer's paper routinely published:** These headlines are all from "Tragedies of a Day," *New York World*, Jan. 3, 1887.

59 **ROASTED TO DEATH:** *New York World*, April 2, 1890.

59 **"On that bleak December day":** "Last Hope Abandoned," *New York World*, July 19, 1891.

59 **"Tell them how they spend their money":** "Confessions of a Yellow Journalist: The Birth of the Modern Newspaper," 38 *Public Opinion* 269 (1905).

59 **"Wall Street 'Nobility'":** Valerian Gribayédoff, "Pictorial Journalism," 11 *Cosmopolitan* 471 (1891); *see also World*, Feb. 3, 1884.

60 **"proved the starting point":** Gribayédoff, "Pictorial Journalism."

60 **"The protest was grounded":** Gribayédoff, "Pictorial Journalism."

60 **"Lovers of well-printed wood-engravings":** "Obituary: Samuel D. Warren," 23 *American Bookseller* 248 (1888).

60 **closed part of the White House grounds:** "The President Wants Privacy," *New-York Tribune*, Nov. 22, 1886.

60 **gather information:** "White House Environment: The Social Restrictions on the 'First Lady of the Land,'" *Indianapolis News*, Sept. 14, 1888.

61 **she jumped from her hammock:** "The Candidates' Wives," *Chicago Tribune*, Sept. 16, 1888.

61 **poor girl couldn't even lounge:** "Candidates' Wives."

61 **Eliza Jane Cochran:** It appears that Nellie Bly's birth name was Eliza Jane Cochran. Baptismal records from 1864 show her name as Eliza Jane, as do the 1870 and 1880 U.S. censuses, though Eliza could be Elizabeth shortened.

61 **by feigning mental illness:** "'Nellie Brown's' Story," *New York World*, Oct. 10, 1887.

61 **resulting story led to powerful change:** *See* "One Good Result," *Camden (N.J.) Daily Courier*, Nov. 3, 1887.

61 **"Should women propose?":** Nellie Bly, "Should Women Propose?," *New York World*, Nov. 11, 1888.

61 **fortune told by a witch:** "The Veiled Prophetess," *New York Evening World*, Jan. 19, 1889.

61 **"dragged from a hotel":** "Nellie Bly Arrested," *New York World*, Feb. 23, 1889.

61 **snuck into an opium den:** "A Luxurious Opium Joint," *Weekly Clarion* (Cherryvale, Kans.), March 28, 1889.

61 **had her horoscope read:** Advertisement, *New York World*, Sept. 21, 1889 (featuring Bly's upcoming story).

61 **day in a diet kitchen:** "A Day in a Diet Kitchen," *New York World*, Dec. 22, 1888.

61 **jumped into pool instruction:** "Nellie Bly in a Swimming School: How They Educate a Person Who Is Afraid of the Water," *New York World*, Aug. 16, 1889.

61 **"Frolics at the French Ball":** This is language from an ad for Nellie Bly, "Jolly at the French Ball," *New York World*, Feb. 10, 1889.

62 **"Nellie Bly at the Summer Resorts":** This is language from an ad for Nellie Bly, "Nellie Bly at Newport," *New York World*, Sept. 1, 1889.

62 **daily readership of *The World*:** *The World*'s masthead on September 21, 1889, puts the precise number at 345,875.

62 **threw himself overboard from a New York ferry:** "Leaped into the Bay," *New York World*, Feb. 19, 1890.

62 **GIRLS WHO BATHE:** "Girls Who Bathe," *New York World*, July 27, 1890.

62 **reporter hid in plain sight:** "Heard at the Telephone," *New York World*, July 1, 1890.

62 **Another hid in a sofa:** "Clinched!," *New York World*, July 6, 1890.

62 **And somebody at *The World*:** "Mrs. Burnett's Oddities," *Inter Ocean* (Chicago), Jan. 13, 1889 (republishing a story that had originally appeared in *The World*).

63 **a regular person or a reporter:** "The Decrease of Privacy," *Aberdeen Daily News*, May 8, 1887.

63 **how dare these journalists:** "The Law of Gossip," *Daily Inter Ocean* (Chicago), Nov. 30, 1888.

63 **law could and would step in to help:** "Some of the Newspaper Penny-A-Liners," *Wilmington (S.C.) Morning Star*, Feb. 13, 1889 (republishing an excerpt from a *New York Times* editorial).

63 **the "Right to Privacy":** "The Right to Privacy," *Critic*, April 27, 1889, republishing article from *The New York Times*.

63 **"Were you ever caught by the tide":** Nellie Bly, "Nellie Bly Says," *New York Evening World*, Dec. 10, 1894.

63 **"The periodical press [has] increased":** Beard, *American Nervousness*, 133.

64 **another letter in the collection:** Bissell to Nash, March 17, 1888, Kohns Collection.

64 **law partner, campaign manager:** "Wilson S. Bissell: Grover Cleveland's Friend," Western New York History, www.wnyhistory.com.

64 **attend to some "financial arrangements":** Cleveland to Bissell, Dec. 5, 1884, in Nevins, *Letters of Grover Cleveland*, 49.

64 **different-from-Frances "former ward":** *See* A. B. Farquhar, "Intimate Recollections of Grover Cleveland," *Harper's Weekly*, Aug. 1, 1908.

64 **C is likely Cleveland:** *See* Memorandum from the Kohns Collection on Manuscripts Relating to an Episode in the Life of Grover Cleveland.

64 **"I feel sure that he will misinterpret it":** Bissell to Nash, March 17, 1888, Kohns Collection.

64 **recent graduate from Wesleyan College:** "Wesleyan College: Commencement Exercises at St. Paul's Church," *Cincinnati Daily Star*, June 18, 1879.

64 **Kate Nash who lived in Cazenovia:** *See* U.S. Census for the Village of Cazenovia (1860) (listing "Catherine" Nash's age as five).

65 **This Kate Nash never married:** *See* U.S. Census for Cazenovia Township (1920).

65 **had a sister named Ellen:** *See* U.S. Census for the Village of Cazenovia (1880).

65 **"several Cleveland scrapbooks":** Library of Congress, Index to the Grover Cleveland Papers (1965), vi.

65 **A third Kate Nash:** New York State Census for the City of Rochester (1892) (listing "Miss Nash" as a clerk); *see also* New York State Census for the City of Buffalo (1892) (showing a "Miss Nash" who worked as a clerk and was twenty-six years old).

65 **she appears to have worked as a dressmaker:** U.S. Census for the City of Buffalo (1880).

65 **as a store clerk:** Buffalo Directory (1897) (identifying a "Nash Kathryne C. clk. 387 Main, h. 293 Eagle").

65 **She might have had five children:** U.S. Census for the City of Buffalo (1910).

65 **Nellie was her younger half sister:** "Nash Family Tree," Ancestry, www.ancestry.com.

65 **equated him with Thomas Jefferson:** Curtis, *True Thomas Jefferson*, 310.

65 **"I understand arrangements have been made":** Cleveland to Daniel S. Lamont, Aug. 20, 1883, in Nevins, *Letters of Grover Cleveland*, 24.

66 **Beecher was innocent "beyond question":** "The Law of It," *Buffalo Express*, Aug. 20, 1874.

66 **child would be born:** "Maria Halpin Speaks," *Salt Lake Weekly Tribune*, Aug. 21, 1884 (detailing Oscar Folsom Cleveland's birthdate as September 14, 1874).

CHAPTER SIX: "THE RIGHT TO PRIVACY"

67 **"upbraided her, called her wicked names":** "White House Felicity," *Charleston News & Courier*, Dec. 11, 1888.

67 **he later denied it:** "Denials All Around: Who Started the Gossip About the Clevelands?," *Washington Daily Critic*, Dec. 8, 1888.

67 **"as a private individual":** "Denials All Around."

67 **minister told a reporter:** "Political Villainy: The Latest and Most Vicious Campaign Lie," *Pittsburgh Daily Post*, June 9, 1888.

67 **whispers of domestic abuse:** Nevins, *Grover Cleveland: A Study in Courage*, 308.

67 **intriguing pieces of paper:** "Luck Still with Him," *Critic*, June 4, 1888.

68 **attack on Cleveland's private life:** "Cleveland Scandals," *Emporia Weekly News* (Topeka, Kans.), June 7, 1888.

68 **"I tell you this in strict confidence":** Cleveland to Bayard, Sept. 11, 1893, in Nevins, *Letters of Grover Cleveland*, 333.

68 **Cleveland was fighting cancer:** Cleveland to Bayard, Sept. 11, 1893, in Nevins, *Letters of Grover Cleveland*, 333.

68 **allegations of debauchery:** "Democratic Depravity," *St. Louis Globe-Democrat*, June 4, 1888.

68 **previous political attacks against him:** "Another Record of Failure," *Aberdeen Daily News*, May 19, 1888; "Will Mr. Bayard Retire," *New-York Tribune*, April 18, 1888; "Cabinet Characteristics: The Peculiarities of Mr. Cleveland's Colleagues," *Kansas City (Mo.) Times*, Feb. 6, 1887.

68 **would face libel charges:** "Democratic Depravity."

68 **never be welcomed back in Buffalo:** "Democratic Depravity."

68 **didn't even show for his mother-in-law's wedding:** "Why Mr. Cleveland Didn't Go," *Charleston News & Courier*, May 23, 1889.

68 **Buffalo had become the place:** Cleveland to William F. Vilas, May 20, 1889, in Nevins, *Letters of Grover Cleveland*, 207.

68 **"how I fairly yearn to be let alone":** Cleveland to Dr. S. B. Ward, June 21, 1886, in Nevins, *Letters of Grover Cleveland*, 114.

69 **larger-sized paperback book:** The July 1890 *Scribner's Magazine* is approximately seven inches wide and ten inches tall.

69 **such contraptions were pocket-sized:** "Notes & News," *Photographic Times* (New York), May 20, 1892.

69 **"of any persons or thing":** "Making a Photograph," *Herald* (Lake Geneva, Wis.), July 20, 1888.

69 **"racy" sketches:** "Tin Types," *Scribner's Magazine*, July 1890.

69 **there were only drawings inside:** Quigg, *Tin-Types Taken in the Streets of New York.*

69 **an art that Jacob Riis was already practicing:** The photographer Jacob Riis had given a lecture in 1888 incorporating eighty-five tenement photographs. Yochelson, *Jacob A. Riis: Revealing New York's Other Half,* 12.

69 **Sketches drawn from Riis photographs:** Jacob A. Riis, "How the Other Half Lives: Studies Among the Tenements," *Scribner's Magazine*, Dec. 1889.

70 **etching of a busty woman:** "Illustration of a Society Young Lady," *New York Illustrated News*, Sept. 20, 1890. "The Most Exciting and Thrilling Events of the Week Graphically Illustrated," the tabloid newspaper promised.

70 **"portraits, sketches, and news":** *New York Illustrated News*, Sept. 20, 1890. Such a call began decades before. *See New York Illustrated News*, January 21, 1860 ("Artists, Daguerreotypists, or any party capable of wielding the pencil, though roughly, throughout the country, are invited to send Sketches of any event or Scene of interest; if the same are used, they will be liberally paid for").

70 **one of Brandeis's favorite magazines:** Louis D. Brandeis to Amy Brandeis Wehle, Jan. 2, 1881, in Urofsky and Levy, *Family Letters of Louis D. Brandeis*, 24 (suggesting that the magazine published material in line with his thinking).

70 **Its caption read:** Cover drawing in *Puck*, June 11, 1890. Even babies, it seemed, could not escape such journalistic interest and the camera's lens. An 1890 issue of Boston's *Wide Awake* magazine featured an infant whose blurry but still recognizable photograph appeared just after an article titled "Confessions of an Amateur Photographer." This is relevant because a Brandeis biographer suggested that by 1890 Warren had become especially "outraged when photographers invaded his babies' privacy and snapped perambulator pictures." That seems doubtful— he wasn't *that* famous—but gossip columns did occasionally mention the Warren children, and those snap cameras shaped like other things were becoming a real worry for high-profile people.

70 **Louis had helped draw up those plans:** Partial transcription of autobiographical sketch by Louis D. Brandeis (n.d.), Brandeis University Archives, Brandeis Collection, box 69.

70 **rented a beach house just five miles:** Cleveland to Daniel S. Lamont, Sept. 13, 1890, in Nevins, *Letters of Grover Cleveland*, 231.

70 **attempted to change the *Boston Post*:** Partial transcription of autobiographical sketch by Brandeis.

70 **becoming the editor of the *Post*:** Partial transcription of autobiographical sketch by Brandeis. This occurred, Brandeis said, in 1907.

70 **He'd also fallen in love:** *See, e.g.,* Brandeis to Alice Goldmark, Sept. 6, 1890, in Urofsky and Levy, *Family Letters of Louis D. Brandeis*, 36.

70 **"bad terms" with his photographic portraits:** Brandeis to Goldmark, Sept. 9, 1890, in Urofsky and Levy, *Family Letters of Louis D. Brandeis*, 38. Writing about photographs that fail to satisfy his friends and family, Brandeis suggests that he is "on bad terms with pictorial art."

70 **ever since he was a law student:** Brandeis to Walter Bond Douglas, Nov. 13, 1877, in Urofsky and Levy, *Letters of Louis D. Brandeis*, vol. 1, *1870–1907, Urban Reformer*, 18. Brandeis suggested that his photograph was "a miserable one" and that the photographer did not treat him as well as the rest of the class.

70 **taken care to destroy them all:** Brandeis to Goldmark, Oct. 10, 1890, in Urofsky and Levy, *Family Letters of Louis D. Brandeis*, 45.

71 **got a mention in the fourth paragraph:** E. L. Godkin, "The Rights of the Citizen: To His Own Reputation," *Scribner's Magazine*, July 1890.

71 **a new American digest:** 1 *Harvard Law Review* 53 (1887).

71 **article on interstate commerce:** William R. Howland, "The Police Power and Inter-State Commerce," 4 *Harvard Law Review* 221 (1890).

71 **squib about a case:** 4 *Harvard Law Review* 241 (1890).

72 **court decision that awarded a meteorite:** 4 *Harvard Law Review* 234 (1890). The case would eventually be decided by the Iowa Supreme Court the same way. *Goddard v. Winchell*, 52 N.W. 1124 (Iowa 1892) is a relatively famous property law case.

72 **"rapidly outgrowing the experimental stage":** 4 *Harvard Law Review* 35 (1890).

72 **"a horrible octopus":** "Lo! The Poor Newspaper," *New York Times*, May 13, 1890.

73 **free-for-all use of Mrs. Cleveland's image:** *See, e.g.*, Grover Cleveland to Joseph Clarke, March 15, 1890, in Nevins, *Letters of Grover Cleveland*, 220, 302, 321, complaining that a newspaper had named Mrs. Cleveland the most popular woman in New York. There are a few letters from Cleveland that parallel these concerns: Aug. 12, 1892 (complaining of *The World*'s use of her pictures); April 15, 1893 (calling the use of Mrs. Cleveland's image in an ad "indecent"). Cleveland was surely irritated at the unauthorized use of his own image too, including in an ad for "McLane's Vermifuge," a dewormer.

73 **still routinely condemned:** Edward Thomkins, "Personality in Fiction," *Author*, June 15, 1890.

74 **Brandeis knew some French too:** Lief, *Brandeis: The Personal History of an American Ideal*, 19.

74 **by writing in a foreign language:** Samuel D. Warren and Louis D. Brandeis, "The Right to Privacy," 4 *Harvard Law Review* 193 (1890) ("En prohibant l'envahissement de la vie privée, sans qu'il soit nécessaire d'établir l'intention criminelle, la loi a entendue interdire toute discussion de la part de la défense sur la vérité des faits. Le remède été pire que le mal, si un débat avait pu s'engager sur ce terrain" is translated this way: "By prohibiting the invasion of privacy, without the need to establish criminal intent, the law intended to prohibit any argument by the defense on the facts. Had the defense debated on those grounds, the remedy would have been worse than the disease.").

74 **several quotations from British cases:** Brandeis "had a natural archival bent," a biographer would explain, "and enjoyed filing significant materials." Mason, *Brandeis: A Free Man's Life*, vii.

74 **"The right of privacy," one Missouri judge:** *Ex parte E. H. Brown*, 7 Mo. App. 484 (Mo. App. 1879), Lewis, J., dissenting.

74 **"It would be a barbarous doctrine":** *State v. Bienvenu*, 36 La. Ann. 378 (La. 1884).

74 **"Most of the world":** Brandeis to Goldmark, Dec. 28, 1890, in Urofsky and Levy, *Letters of Louis D. Brandeis*, vol. 1, *1870–1907, Urban Reformer*, 97.

76 **"Our hope," Brandeis told Alice:** Brandeis to Goldmark, Dec. 28, 1890, in Urofsky and Levy, *Letters of Louis D. Brandeis*, vol. 1, *1870–1907, Urban Reformer*, 97.

76 **"attracted a good deal of attention":** Partial transcription of autobiographical sketch by Brandeis.

76 **"the semblance of lively public interest":** Lief, *Brandeis: The Personal History of an American Ideal*, 26 (when they wanted Harvard trustees to shift a large donation toward the law school, "Brandeis sent a few lines to the *Post* and Warren to the *Transcript*, and thus the semblance of lively public interest was manifested").

76 **a certain "formula":** Lief, *Brandeis: The Personal History of an American Ideal*, 100.

76 **he kept among his files:** Reel 12, Nutter, McClennen & Fish, 1904–1916, Louis D. Brandeis Collection, University of Louisville School of Law (titled "Right to Privacy—General Correspondence").

76 **it lauded "The Right to Privacy":** "The Right to Privacy," *Boston Post*, Dec. 19, 1890; "An Abandonment of Privacy," *Boston Post*, March 11, 1891.

77 **"I have been making public opinion":** Louis D. Brandeis to Alfred Brandeis, March 20, 1889, in Urofsky and Levy, *Letters of Louis D. Brandeis*, vol. 1, *1870–1907, Urban Reformer*, 74.

77 **"The subject seems to me":** Warren to R. W. Gilder, Dec. 1, 1890, Century Company Records, New York Public Library.

77 **"a learned and interesting article":** "The Right to Be Let Alone," *Atlantic Monthly*, March 1891.

77 **a "strong" argument:** "The Right to Privacy," *Nation*, Dec. 1890 (but ultimately doubting the viability of the right given public interest in "scandal and gossip").

77 **"remarkable" work:** "The Right to Privacy," *To-Day*, Dec. 25, 1890.

77 **"very timely and very interesting":** "The Editors' Table," *New England Magazine*, May 1891.

77 **"shocking wrongs" in publishing:** "Common Law Right to Privacy," *Galveston Daily News*, Jan. 14, 1891 (citing *Life* magazine).

77 **"The Right to Privacy" even got a mention:** "Privacy Is a Sacred Privilege," *New York World*, Sept. 26, 1891. The newspaper quoted a court decision that had mentioned the *Harvard Law Review* article.

77 **"coming to be one of the most important rights":** "The Right of Privacy," *Boston Post*, Aug. 5, 1900.

77 **Brandeis remained an active trustee:** Partial transcription of autobiographical sketch by Brandeis.

77 **"an able summary":** "Recent Cases," 5 *Harvard Law Review* 146 (1891). This is followed by an update that mentioned an earlier law review article by Warren and Brandeis.

77 **"only scientific discussion":** "Recent Cases," 7 *Harvard Law Review* 183 (1893).

78 **"pleasant" to note:** "Right to Privacy Again," 7 *Harvard Law Review* 425 (1894).

78 **privacy remained a lively subject:** Brandeis to Edward H. Letchworth (editor in chief, *Harvard Law Review*), April 20, 1905, Brandeis Collection, University of Louisville School of Law. Letchworth responded to Brandeis that while he was sure that the right to privacy would begin to prevail, only the month before the editors had come across a case that had denied the existence of the right to privacy. Letchworth to Brandeis, April 21, 1905, Brandeis Collection, University of Louisville School of Law.

78 **"we shall use this one":** Edward H. Letchworth (editor in chief, *Harvard Law Review*) to Brandeis, April 21, 1905, Brandeis Collection, University of Louisville School of Law.

78 **seven hundred or so members:** "Notes," *Nation*, June 19, 1890.

78 **organization for alumni:** Partial transcription of autobiographical sketch by Brandeis.

78 **Sam enclosed a note:** Warren to Holmes, Dec. 27, 1891, Oliver Wendell Holmes Jr. Digital Suite, Harvard Law School Library.

78 **"It is satisfactory to know":** Brandeis to Walter S. Heilborn, Feb. 5, 1906, in Urofsky and Levy, *Letters of Louis D. Brandeis*, vol. 1, *1870–1907, Urban Reformer*, 404.

78 **"privacy has been defined":** John Rawle and Francis Bouvier, *Bouvier's Law Dictionary* (Boston: Boston Book Co., 1897). It would take until 1933 for a similar entry to find its way into *Black's Law Dictionary*, the third edition of the popular work.

78 **Supreme Court had mentioned the right to privacy:** *Union P. R. Co. v. Botsford*, 141 U.S. 250 (1891).

78 **Sam always thought:** Warren to Brandeis, April 10, 1905, Brandeis Collection, University of Louisville School of Law.

79 **"A study of the cases":** "What Invasions of Privacy Are Unlawful," *Case and Comment*, April 1910.

CHAPTER SEVEN: THE RIGHT TO KNOW

80 **"fearless editor":** Mott, *American Journalism*, 794.

80 **reputation as a fraud-attacking bulldog:** Gore, *Negro Journalism*, 13 (self-published pamphlet) ("Chase is especially noted for his bull-dog tenacity in exposing and attacking fraud.").

80 **"never fail[ing] to expose":** Penn, *Afro-American Press and Its Editors*, 288.

80 **"We will tackle all skunks":** "Editor Chase of the Washington Bee," *Washington Bee*, Oct. 11, 1890.

80 **"strong penchant to attack":** Hal Chase, "William C. Chase and the Washington Bee," *Negro History Bulletin* 172 (Dec. 1973).

81 **"an influential source":** David Howard-Pitney, "Calvin Chase's Washington Bee and Black Middle-Class Ideology, 1882–1900," *Journalism and Mass Communication Quarterly* 63, no. 1 (1986).

81 **"the organ of the colored people":** "A Darkey's Rebuff," *Atchison Daily Globe*, April 15, 1885.

81 **interesting, stalwart, newsy, and creditable:** "Honey for the Bee," *Washington Bee*, June 10, 1882 (collecting reviews from other newspapers).

81 **the Bee endorsed James Blaine:** "Blaine and Logan," *Washington Bee*, June 14, 1884 ("Blaine and Logan are the nominees of the Republican party, and it is the duty of every loyal republican to support the ticket. We shall support, and appeal to every true American citizen to do likewise."); *see also* "Chase Wants Revenge: Threatens to Bring President Cleveland into Court," *Washington Times*, June 7, 1895 (describing when Chase and President Cleveland first met, the president told Chase that he had a copy of *The Washington Bee* denouncing him).

81 **Chase had later worried:** William J. Simmons, *Men of Mark: Eminent, Progressive, and Rising* (1887), 129.

81 **Cleveland held up a copy of *The Washington Bee*:** Simmons, *Men of Mark*, 129–30.

81 **"I hope the colored citizens":** "Darkey's Rebuff."

81 **Then he fired Chase:** "Colored Editor Case Dismissed," *New York Times*, April 26, 1885.

81 "**It is an unwritten law of this land**": "Secret Committee Sessions," *Philadelphia Times*, Jan. 31, 1885.

82 the *Marbury v. Madison* **dispute**: *Marbury v. Madison*, 5 U.S. (1 Cranch) 137 (1803) ("anything" was spelled "any thing" in the notes written by the official reporter for the Court).

82 **the Illinois Supreme Court picked up that phrase**: *People v. Bradley*, 60 Ill. 390 (Ill. 1871).

82 **validity of election outcomes**: *State ex rel. Crawford v. Smith*, 22 A. 1020 (R.I. 1891).

82 **contracts agreed to by the government**: *State ex rel. Kinder v. Eagle Ins. Co. of Cincinnati*, 33 N.E. 1056 (Ohio 1893).

83 **contents of reports created by the government**: *Howland v. Flood*, 36 N.E. 482 (Mass. 1894).

83 **information about public offices**: *Chittenden v. Wurster*, 46 N.E. 857 (N.Y. 1897).

83 **what was going on in legislatures**: *Isley v. Sentinel*, 113 N.W. 425 (Wis. 1907).

83 **and in the courts**: *State v. Hensley*, 79 N.E. 462 (Ohio 1906).

83 **its fifty thousand readers might like to know**: "At the Very Head: What a Fresno Journal Says of Our Great Paper," *San Jose Daily Mercury*, Jan. 8, 1892 (discussing the paper's circulation of no fewer than fifty thousand copies).

83 **ordered that the courtroom be emptied**: "The Price Case: An Aged Couple Fighting for Separation in Court," *San Jose Daily Mercury*, Jan. 11, 1893.

84 "**some poor, unfortunate girl**": *In re Shortridge*, 34 P. 227 (Cal. 1893) (questioning generally how public morals can be promoted by broadcasting testimony in low and filthy divorce cases).

84 "**sensational**" **stories**: "Mrs. Hervey Answers: She Sweepingly Denies the Charge of Her Husband," *San Jose Daily Mercury*, Oct. 8, 1892.

84 "**spicy details**": "The Hervey Divorce: Further Testimony Taken in the Case," *San Jose Daily Mercury*, Jan. 10, 1893.

84 "**choice morsels**": "Muddy Waters: They Are Vigorously Stirred in the Hervey Case," *San Jose Daily Mercury*, Jan. 11, 1893.

84 *two* **pairs of shoes dropping to the floor**: "Muddy Waters."

84 "**any issue of fact**": *In re Shortridge*, 34 P. 227.

84 "**younger and livelier female companions**": "Price Case: An Aged Couple Fighting for Separation in Court."

85 **mother of thirteen**: "Tribute to the Late Mrs. Barbara Price," *San Jose Daily Mercury*, Feb. 18, 1911 (stating that Mr. and Mrs. Price had thirteen children together).

85 **inflicted with a loathsome disease**: "Price Case: An Aged Couple Fighting for Separation in Court" (stating that Mrs. Price found herself afflicted with a loathsome disease).

85 A **WIFE'S WOES**: "A Wife's Woes," *San Jose Daily Mercury*, Jan. 13, 1893.

85 "**Liberty of the press**": "Judge Lorigan's Opinion," *San Jose Daily Mercury*, Jan. 21, 1893.

85 **venereal troubles got wrapped up in the Constitution**: "All Concur: Judges Are Judges, Not Censors of Morals," *San Jose Daily Mercury*, Jan. 23, 1893 (republishing an editorial from the *Salinas Journal* titled "High-Handed Proceedings"; the *Salinas Journal* noted that "no court should have the right to prohibit [these facts]. The press, the conservator of the people's rights, will not stand any such high-handed proceedings.").

85 **courtroom to the infamous Star Chamber**: "Judges, Not Censors: Not the Court's Province to Supervise Public Morals," *San Jose Daily Mercury*, Jan. 23, 1893 (republishing an editorial from *The Antioch Ledger*).

85 **one in a place like Russia**: "Out of Latitude," *San Jose Daily Mercury*, Jan. 26, 1893 (republishing an editorial from the *Reno Gazette*).

85 "**If newspaper men are to be debarred**": "'Self Constituted Czars': If Facts Can Not Be Published What Can Be?," *San Jose Daily Mercury*, Jan. 23, 1893 (republishing an editorial from the Redlands *Citrograph*).

85 **Publicity, not secrecy, in divorce cases**: *See* "'A Cover for Crime': What Secrecy in Divorce Cases Really Amounts To," *San Jose Daily Mercury*, Jan. 17, 1893 (republishing an editorial from the *San Jose Herald* detailing that secrecy in divorce matters is "usually a cover for crime").

85 **headlines attached to stories**: "All Concur: Judges Are Judges, Not Censors of Morals," *San Jose Daily Mercury*, Jan. 23, 1893; "All Against It: No Judge Shall Dictate to the Press," *San Jose Daily Mercury*, Jan. 17, 1893; "Of One Mind: The Press of the Country Is with Us," *San Jose Daily Mercury*, Jan. 26, 1893.

85 **free speech was on trial**: "Free Speech on Trial: A Los Angeles Editor Who Says the 'Mercury' Will Win," *San Jose Daily Mercury*, Jan. 26, 1893 (republishing an editorial from the *Los Angeles Times* in a sub-headed part of the "Of One Mind" article).

85 **"unbounded liberty":** "A Chicago Comment: The 'Inter Ocean' Speaks of the Novel Judicial Proceeding," *San Jose Daily Mercury*, Jan. 26, 1893 (republishing an editorial from the *Chicago Inter Ocean* in a subheaded part of the "Of One Mind" article).

85 **"against the abridgment of the liberty":** "A Greater Contempt: Allowing Secret Trials to Parties with Misdeeds to Hide," *San Jose Daily Mercury*, Jan. 26, 1893 (republishing an editorial from the *Nevada City Transcript* in a subheaded part of the "Of One Mind" article) (quoting the *San Francisco Chronicle*).

86 **"any news which its enterprise":** "Out of Latitude" (republishing an editorial from the *Reno Gazette* in a subheaded part of the "Of One Mind" article).

86 **In the *Price v. Price* divorce case:** "Price vs. Price: Termination of the Celebrated Divorce Case," *San Jose Daily Mercury*, May 13, 1893.

86 **the court focused on the language of the statute:** *In re Shortridge*, 34 P. 227 (Cal. 1893).

86 **"Freedom of the Press Cannot Be Curtailed":** "It Was Not Contempt: The Highest Tribunal in the State Sustains the Position Taken by the 'Mercury,'" *San Jose Daily Mercury*, Sept. 12, 1893.

87 **similarly headlined their stories:** "Voice of the Press: What the Papers Say of the Decision," *San Jose Daily Mercury*, Sept. 16, 1893 (republishing other editorials from across the state).

87 **"liberty of the press must not be confounded":** *In re Shortridge*, 34 P. 227 (Cal. 1893).

87 **what the attorney for the *Daily Mercury* told:** "No Contempt: An Able Argument Before the Supreme Court," *San Jose Daily Mercury*, March 9, 1893.

87 **But headlines like THE LIBERTY OF THE PRESS:** "A Just Decision: Action of the Supreme Court Commended," *San Jose Daily Mercury*, Sept. 13, 1893 (subheaded "The Liberty of the Press Can Never Be Successfully Assailed in California").

87 **ordered journalists not to report:** "His Power," *Boston Globe*, Sept. 27, 1893. The sub-headlines read "Keeping News from Papers" and "No Boston Editor Is Allowed to Comment."

88 **Civil Service Commission found Taylor guilty:** *See* "Found Him Guilty: Recorder of Deeds Taylor and the Civil Service Law," *Washington Evening Star*, Aug. 23, 1894.

88 **"been in hot water":** "As to Mr. Heraclitus Constantine," *Washington Evening Star*, Jan. 21, 1895.

88 **commission urged President Cleveland to remove Taylor:** "Urging Taylor's Removal," *Ellsworth (Kans.) Reporter*, Aug. 30, 1894.

88 **"one of President Cleveland's discoveries":** "Both Venal and Amorous: Shocking Charges Against a Colored Washington Official," *New York Evening World*, March 1, 1895.

88 **his *Washington Bee* exploded:** "Our Defense," *Washington Bee*, Jan. 5, 1895.

89 **invasion of Taylor's privacy:** *See* "Chase Was Convicted: Jury Decided in Fifteen Minutes That He Had Libeled Taylor," *Washington Times*, March 7, 1895 ("William Calvin Chase was convicted of libel yesterday on the indictment against him for the publications regarding the private and public life of Recorder C. H. J. Taylor.").

89 **Chase's several-day trial:** "Accused of Libel: Calvin Chase on Trial on a Criminal Charge," *Washington Evening Star*, Feb. 27, 1895.

89 **troubling details about Recorder of Deeds Taylor:** "Defense Opened," *Washington Evening Star*, Feb. 27, 1895.

89 **Several women testified:** "Government Office Scandal: Recorder of Deeds Charged with Immorality," *Salt Lake Tribune*, March 1, 1895.

89 **illegal abortion and a woman's death:** "Nearing the End: Closing Up the Testimony in the Chase-Taylor Case," *Washington Evening Star*, March 4, 1895.

89 **one of the duties of the press:** "For the Defense," *Washington Evening Star*, March 6, 1895.

89 **for the public good and in the public interest:** "Defense Opened," *Washington Evening Star*, Feb. 27, 1895.

89 **exposed Taylor's "private character":** "Mr. Chase Goes to Jail: Judge Cole Imposes a Sentence of Ninety Days," *Washington Times*, March 24, 1895.

89 **good motives and justifiable ends:** "Taylor's Triumph," *Washington Evening Star*, March 7, 1895.

89 **jury would need to consider:** "Chase Was Convicted: Jury Decided in Fifteen Minutes That He Had Libeled Taylor," *Washington Times*, March 7, 1895.

89 **"If the only object of the defendant":** "Taylor's Triumph."

90 **"unusually prompt" fifteen minutes to convict:** *"Chase Was Convicted"* (stating that the jury had decided the matter in fifteen minutes); "Taylor's Triumph" (stating that Chase's conviction was the result of an "unusually prompt verdict").

90 **"to send him to prison":** "The Chase Sentence: Judge Cole Imposes Penalty in Taylor Libel Suit," *Washington Evening Star*, March 23, 1895.

90 **didn't mention race much:** Most newspaper coverage did not address the racial aspect of the case, and the Black press appeared split. "Now that a verdict has been rendered," *The Colored American* wrote, "we feel at liberty to say that the whole affair was a disgusting exhibition of washing dirty linen in public." It too worried about the implication: "It does the race no good, but thank God the race is not responsible for the doing of these two individuals." "A Bystander's Opinion," *Indianapolis Freeman*, March 16, 1895 (quoting *The Colored American*).

90 **"W. Calvin Chase . . . was to-day":** "Ninety Days for an Editor," *San Francisco Call*, March 24, 1895.

90 **president might offer him mercy:** *See* "Behind the Bars," *Washington Bee*, April 6, 1895.

90 **"This American government was founded upon":** "Our Incarceration," *Washington Bee*, April 6, 1895.

90 **The Washington press joined in:** "Chase Sentence."

90 **hoped he'd soon be free:** "Our Thanks," *Washington Bee*, April 6, 1895.

90 **"this convict maliciously published":** "Executive Clemency Denied: President Cleveland Refuses to Pardon a Man Held for Criminal Libel," *New York Times*, May 9, 1895.

90 **he'd threatened to sue:** "Chase Wants Revenge," *Washington Times*, June 9, 1895.

91 **Taylor kept his position:** "Old Alphabet Bounced," *Washington Bee*, May 22, 1897 (republishing an editorial from the *Wide Awake Bulletin* saying that Taylor was asked to hand in his title to the government, but making no mention of his past wrongdoing).

CODA PART I: THE DEATH OF SAM WARREN

92 **"I am deeply indebted to you":** Warren to Holmes, Feb. 21, 1902, Oliver Wendell Holmes Jr. Digital Suite, Harvard Law School Library.

92 **"As the years go by":** Warren to Brandeis, March 17, 1904, Warren Family Papers, Massachusetts Historical Society.

92 **helped to ease his mind:** Warren to Brandeis, Jan. 5, 1907, Warren Family Papers.

92 **"I wish I saw you oftener":** Warren to Brandeis, Aug. 31, 1904, Brandeis University Archives, Brandeis Collection, box 5, I.I.a.5.202.

92 **millionaire with three servants:** U.S. Census for Dedham, Massachusetts (1900) (listing Sarah Nickerson, Annie Plunkett, and Mary Gatety as servants for the Brandeis family; two of the women were born in Ireland, and the other came from Canada).

92 **pop in on Justice Holmes:** *See* Louis D. Brandeis to Alice Brandeis, Jan. 14, 1908, in Urofsky and Levy, *Family Letters of Louis D. Brandeis*, 115.

92 **"he had temporarily exchanged places with Atlas":** Louis D. Brandeis to Alice Brandeis, July 29, 1902, Brandeis University Archives, Brandeis Collection, box 6, I.I.b.1.63.

93 **the gossip columns:** *See, e.g.,* "Table Gossip," *Boston Daily Globe*, Sept. 1, 1901 (describing Warren's involvement in a polo game).

93 **"the well-known paper manufacturer":** "Henry C. Warren of Cambridge Dead," *Boston Globe*, Jan. 3, 1899.

93 **he had nine servants:** U.S. Census for Suffolk, Massachusetts (1900) (listing H. F. Rankin, M. G. O'Brien, Betty Nelson, J. L. Moreland, Hannah Matthews, Riera Swanson, Mary Blum, Emily Munn, and Patrick O'Brien as servants).

93 **Much of that strife sprang:** *See* "Action Called Extraordinary," *Boston Globe*, Dec. 21, 1909 (describing the complicated organization of the business and trust and noting that the trust had been drawn up in 1889).

93 **"I cannot think of the family":** Warren to Brandeis, Sept. 7, 1901, in Mason, *Brandeis: A Free Man's Life*, 389.

93 **"a very present help":** Warren to Brandeis, Sept. 7, 1901, in Mason, *Brandeis: A Free Man's Life*, 389 (internal quotation marks omitted).

93 **Sam as trustee who'd reported back:** Sam Warren to Cornelia Warren, Oct. 25, 1897, Warren Family Papers.

93 **was not always well:** *See* Sam Warren to Henry Warren, Feb. 15, 1898, Warren Family Papers.

93 **If you'd asked Sam's brother Ned:** *See* Susan Warren to Henry Warren, July 23, 1895, Warren Family Papers.

93 **"Whenever difficulties of this kind arise":** Ned Warren to Henry Warren, Dec. 10, 1896, Warren Family Papers.

93 **family agreed to lend Ned:** Sam Warren to Ned Warren, July 24, 1897, Warren Family Papers.

93 **asked for proof from Ned's doctor:** *See* Dr. Julius Althaus to Dr. A. Cabot, July 26, 1897, Warren Family Papers ("I have much pleasure in acceding to your request that I should give you a report on the case of Mr. E. P. Warren, for the information of his family").

93 **male-only commune:** Ned reported in a Harvard class update that he dwells in Lewes "with four other young Oxford men, his colleagues and assistants in his chosen profession of Classical Archeology." Harvard College Class of 1883 Fourth Report (1890–1900). *See also* Burdett and Goddard, *Biography of a Connoisseur,* 277 ("Lewes House was a monkish establishment, where women were not welcomed.").

93 **Oscar Wilde's friends would eventually find refuge:** Green, *Mount Vernon Street Warrens,* 115–16.

93 **Ned would lecture on Uranian love:** Sox, *Bachelors of Art,* 206.

93 **keen ability to spot treasures:** *See, e.g.,* Margaret Burke, *Bowdoin Collect Handbook of the Collections* (1981), 1 ("Warren's influence on taste in classical art can be seen today in museums in this country and throughout Europe by the collections he formed either as purchasing agent or through outright personal donations.").

93 **commissioned an anatomically correct version:** Sox, *Bachelors of Art,* 94.

93 **"L'organe génital de l'homme":** Burdett and Goddard, *Biography of a Connoisseur,* 279.

94 **bizarre sexual curiosities:** Glen Bowersock, "Open House for the Ancients," *New York Times,* April 18, 1999.

94 **where Sam was a trustee:** "Gen. C. G. Loring Resigns," *Boston Globe,* March 11, 1902.

94 **MFA refused to show them:** Ned's collection has "long languished in storerooms." Christine Temin, "Lifting the Curtain," *Boston Globe,* Feb. 4, 2001. The newspaper has also called the collection, pictures of which are available online on the MFA website, "smutty" (Christine Temin, "To Portland and Beyond," *Boston Globe,* Aug. 29, 1999) and "very sexually explicit" (Sebastian Smee, "More to Aphrodite Than Meets the Eye," *Boston Globe,* Oct. 30, 2011).

94 **that's called the Warren Cup:** "All Screwed Up About Sex and Art," *Observer* (London), May 9, 1999 ("The Warren Cup—as the goblet is known—was bought at the beginning of the century by the homosexual collector Edward Perry Warren.").

94 **"The collection," he'd later explain:** Boston Museum of Fine Arts, "The Secret History of the Boston Green Head," May 26, 2015, www.mfa.org.

94 **"truly a paederastic evangel":** Edward Perry Warren, *Defence of Uranian Love,* ix. This is book that suggested that its ultimate purpose was a focus on "the love of boys."

94 **liked to keep family matters within the family:** *See* Sam Warren to Cornelia Warren, March 14, 1898, Warren Family Papers.

94 **family dignity was what mattered most:** Sox, *Bachelors of Art,* 71.

94 **"Ned hates me as the author":** Sam Warren to Cornelia Warren, July 28, 1902, Warren Family Papers.

94 **Ned first hired a lawyer:** Sox, *Bachelors of Art,* 70.

94 **What about the money and the business:** Sam Warren to Cornelia Warren, July 25, 1907, Warren Family Papers.

94 **What about the treatment of workers:** Osbert Burdett and E. H. Goddard, "Edward Perry Warren: The Biography of a Connoisseur," in Kaylor, Burdett, and Goddard, *Collected Works and Commissioned Biography of Edward Perry Warren,* 1:257; Sox, *Bachelors of Art,* 76.

94 **at the business in Boston and at the mills in Maine:** Ned Warren to Cornelia Warren, Oct. 14, 1908, Warren Family Papers.

94 **Why shouldn't Ned be named a trustee:** Sox, *Bachelors of Art,* 70, 77.

94 **Ned's lawyer would uncover methods:** Burdett and Goddard, "Edward Perry Warren," 257; Sox, *Bachelors of Art,* 77.

94 **Ned threatened to sell off his share:** Ned Warren to Cornelia Warren, Oct. 14, 1908, Warren Family Papers.

94 **Ned filed a lawsuit:** Ned Warren to Cornelia Warren, Feb. 15, 1910, Warren Family Papers.

94 **"The litigants are members":** "Millions Involved in Suit," *Boston Post,* Dec. 16, 1909.

94 **WARREN BROTHERS SUED:** *Boston Daily Globe,* Dec. 16, 1909.

95 **Sam had diverted nearly $1.5 million:** "Millions Involved in Suit."

95 **the one to draw up the trust papers:** "Action Called Extraordinary," *Boston Daily Globe*, Dec. 21, 1909.

95 **"well calculated to effectuate their wishes":** "Millions Involved in Suit."

95 **drawings from the courtroom:** "Injunction Dissolved in Warren's Court Fight," *Boston Post*, Dec. 22, 1909.

95 **story had focused on Mabel Warren:** "Mrs. Warren's Dinners," *Boston Post*, Jan. 24, 1904.

95 **Sam's older son seemed in conquest:** "The Dowager's Views," *Boston Post*, June 21, 1908.

95 **proportions were Junoesque:** "Margaret Thomas Will Be the Fairest of Debutantes," *Boston Post*, Sept. 5, 1908.

95 **"a trifle too large":** "The Dowager's Views," *Boston Post*, Jan. 26, 1908.

95 **"an affair to be watched":** "The Dowager's Views," *Boston Post*, Jan. 26, 1908.

95 **called to assist a major publisher:** Urofsky and Levy, *Family Letters of Louis D. Brandeis*, 135n9.

95 **asked the partner to represent Sam's interests:** *See* Louis D. Brandeis to Alice Brandeis, Feb. 17, 1910, in Urofsky and Levy, *Family Letters of Louis D. Brandeis*, 206–7 (describing work in Washington).

95 **"dragging painfully":** Louis D. Brandeis to Alice Brandeis, Aug. 11, 1909, Brandeis University Archives, Brandeis Collection, box 8, I.I.b.3.28.

96 **"I don't suppose you know how near":** Warren to Brandeis, Dec. 27, 1884, Warren Family Papers.

96 **European honeymoon:** *See* "Table Gossip," *Boston Globe*, Feb. 6, 1910.

96 **Sam took the train to Karlstein:** Green, *Mount Vernon Street Warrens*, 197.

96 **spent some time walking the property:** "Death Halts Legal Fight over Millions," *Boston Post*, Feb. 21, 1910.

96 **chopped some wood:** Green, *Mount Vernon Street Warrens*, 197.

96 **and then shot himself:** Gal, *Brandeis of Boston*, 122, 246n53 (attributing information about the suicide from an interview with Samuel D. Warren III, Samuel Warren's grandson); Green, *Mount Vernon Street Warrens*, 197 (Warren "turned his gun against himself"). *See also* Mason, *Brandeis: A Free Man's Life*, 386 (The book is, in effect, the 1946 family-authorized biography of Brandeis given that family members gave Mason access to personal letters and other material. It suggests that Ned's lawyer had claimed that Sam's sudden understanding of Brandeis's "betrayal" with regard to the trust "had driven him to commit suicide.").

96 **"There is no doubt":** "Fight for Millions Suddenly Ended by Death of S. D. Warren," *Boston American*, Feb. 21, 1910.

96 **Samuel Warren had died of apoplexy:** *See, e.g.,* "Death Comes to Samuel D. Warren," *Boston Daily Globe*, Feb. 21, 1910; "Samuel D. Warren Dead," *New York Times*, Feb. 21, 1910.

96 **"in the hope of gaining rest":** "Death Halts Legal Fight over Millions."

96 **caused by exhaustion:** "Fight for Millions Suddenly Ended by Death of S. D. Warren."

96 **death certificate:** Death certificate of Samuel D. Warren (on file with author) (showing his date of death February 19, 1910).

96 **Brandeis was that spokesman:** "Fight for Millions Suddenly Ended by Death of S. D. Warren."

96 **"had been noticeably depressed":** "Death Halts Legal Fight over Millions."

96 **shrouded in a great deal of mystery:** "Fight for Millions Suddenly Ended by Death of S. D. Warren."

97 **Brandeis was an usher:** "S. D. Warren's Funeral: Distinguished Men at Services Today," *Boston Globe*, Feb. 23, 1910 (noting that Brandeis was an usher and failing to name Holmes when listing people in "the general attendance").

97 **"Mr. Russell":** "S. D. Warren's Funeral" (suggesting that a number of people from the "public and philanthropic bodies with which Mr. Russell had been associated" had attended the funeral).

97 **"the Warren tragedy":** Louis D. Brandeis to Alice Brandeis, Jan. 10, 1913, in Urofsky and Levy, *Family Letters of Louis D. Brandeis*, 206–7.

97 **he'd keep a photograph of Sam:** Mason, *Brandeis: A Free Man's Life*, 582 (describing that in 1940 Brandeis's study in his Cape Cod home featured "a picture of Sam Warren at the helm of an old sloop" thumbtacked to the wall).

97 **"Boston failed to appreciate":** Brandeis to Henry Warren, Sept. 27, 1935, Warren Family Papers.

97   **key to the firm's success:** Warren to Brandeis, March 6, 1884, Warren Family Papers.
97   **Louis received word from** *Hampton's Magazine*: Art director, *Hampton's Magazine*, to Brandeis, March 25, 1910 (on file with author).
97   **"somewhat broken":** Brandeis's secretary to art director, *Hampton's Magazine*, March 30, 1910 (on file with author).
97   **The short biography told readers:** "Personalities," *Hampton's Magazine*, June 1910.
97   **shot the mayor of New York:** "Gaynor Shot: X Ray Shows Bullet Split," *New York Times*, Aug. 10, 1910.
97   **blamed Hearst newspapers:** "Confessions of a Yellow Journalist," *Public Opinion*, March 4, 1905; "Yellow Journalism," *Wall Street Journal*, March 18, 1905.
97   **Hearst's sensationalistic criticism:** "Assassin Inflamed by Yellow Press: Mayor Gaynor Tells of Repeated Attacks on Him," *Washington Herald*, Sept. 20, 1910.
97   **mayor also blasted the photographers:** "Assassin Inflamed by Yellow Press."
97   **"How many more of the people's representatives":** "Mayor Gaynor's Appeal Against the Yellow Press," *Century Magazine*, Dec. 1910.
97   **"the nature and extent":** Van Vechten Veeder, "Freedom of Public Discussion," 23 *Harvard Law Review* 413 (1910).
98   **mostly withered into obscurity:** There is a mention of the article in *New York Times v. Sullivan* in a footnote, however. 376 U.S. 254 (1964).
98   **"The terms of the settlement are private":** "In Suit for Accounting," *Boston Globe*, Nov. 25, 1910.

CHAPTER EIGHT: A DIFFERENT KIND OF FIRE

101   **explosion rocked Helicon Hall:** "Sinclair Colony Routed by Early Morning Blaze," *Philadelphia Inquirer*, March 17, 1907.
101   **cause of the blast:** "Helicon Hall Destroyed," *Frederick (Md.) Daily News*, March 16, 1907.
101   **"gross and reckless assaults":** President Theodore Roosevelt, Address at the Corner Stone of the Office Building of the House of Representatives, April 14, 1906 (transcript available in the Washington Government Printing Office pamphlet).
102   **he'd tricked nearly every single newspaper:** "Upton Sinclair, Novelist Is a Native of Baltimore," *Baltimore American*, June 10, 1906 ("All but one of the metropolitan newspapers regarded the story as a real biography.").
102   **"STIRLING.—By suicide in the Hudson":** "Arthur Stirling," *New York Times*, Jan. 31, 1903 (republishing the obituary from June 9, 1902).
102   **"The reporters took it up":** *Autobiography of Upton Sinclair*, 88.
102   **dumbbell and a strong rope:** "Who Was Arthur Stirling?," *New York Times*, Jan. 24, 1903.
102   **"The reality of this":** "News and Views of Books and Their Makers: The Tragedy of a Soul Is Found in the Story of Arthur Stirling, an Author Unknown to Fame, but Who Courted It and Failed in His Quest," *Boston Journal*, Feb. 8, 1903.
102   **"to raise a sensation":** "A Hoax Which Failed to Hoax Any One," *Chicago Tribune*, May 16, 1903.
102   **who'd been tricked were aghast:** *Autobiography of Upton Sinclair*, 88 (some called it "a high crime against literature").
102   **"This matter of a faked biography":** "Books, Authors, and Arts: 'Journal of Arthur Stirling,'" *Springfield (Mass.) Republican*, Feb. 8, 1903.
102   **"came denunciation on the part":** "Upton Sinclair, Novelist Is a Native of Baltimore."
102   **a mediocre writer and a megalomaniac:** "A Literary Imposter Unmasks," *Springfield (Mass.) Republican*, May 12, 1903 ("Mediocrity and megalomania—that sums up Upton Sinclair.").
103   **After Sinclair investigated and wrote about:** "Is Chicago Meat Clean?," *Biloxi Daily Herald*, April 25, 1905.
103   **many in his profession doubted:** "Upton Sinclair, Novelist Is a Native of Baltimore."
103   **"Upton Sinclair, not being a journalist":** Seldes, *Freedom of the Press*, 173.
103   **was building a "home colony":** "A Home Colony as Planned by Upton Sinclair," *Belleville (Ill.) News-Democrat*, June 23, 1906.
103   **"there have been months":** "Sinclair's Book, 'The Jungle,'" *New York Worker*, Dec. 2, 1905.
103   **thinking big thoughts and doing big things:** *See* "Home Colony as Planned by Upton Sinclair."
103   **White people only:** "Tentative Plans Ready for Sinclair Colony," *New York Times*, Aug. 10, 1906 (reporting that the colony had decided to open its membership "to any white person of good

moral character" despite strong suggestions from the audience at an organizational meeting that it be open to all races).

103 **Sinclair regretted the need to share:** *See* "Home Colony as Planned by Upton Sinclair."

103 **the local post office reported:** "There's 'Jungle' in Every Family, He Says," *San Jose Daily Mercury*, July 17, 1906.

103 **libraries started banning *The Jungle*:** *See, e.g.*, "Muck Rake Books Burned: Topeka Public Library Declares 'The Jungle' Unfit for Its Shelves," *Morning Oregonian* (Portland, Ore.), June 30, 1906 (reporting that the Topeka, Kansas, library had found the book "unfit to be read" for its "general repulsiveness").

103 **started receiving death threats:** "Upton Sinclair Warned: Exposer of Beef Scandal Threatened with Death," *Philadelphia Inquirer*, May 31, 1906.

103 **Sinclair's Helicon Hall:** "Writers Flee from Flames: Upton Sinclair's Socialist Helicon Hall Burned This Morning," *Kansas City (Mo.) Star*, March 16, 1907.

103 **Outsiders were intrigued because rumors:** *See Autobiography of Upton Sinclair*, 130, 135.

103 **"predatory journalists":** "The Helicon Hall Invasion," *New York Times*, Feb. 20, 1907.

103 **"gutter press":** *Autobiography of Upton Sinclair*, 131.

103 **"in various disguises":** "Helicon Hall Invasion."

103 **"They wrote us up":** *Autobiography of Upton Sinclair*, 130.

104 **"All that we wish":** "Helicon Hall Invasion."

104 **turned out to be a gas leak:** "Helicon Is Gone," *Grand Rapids Evening Press*, March 16, 1907.

104 **Officials later reprimanded Sinclair:** "Helicon Hall Managers Are Indicted by Jury," *Wilkes-Barre (Pa.) Times*, March 22, 1907.

104 **"hidden secrets" of communal life:** "Helicon Hall Managers Are Indicted by Jury."

104 **somebody on the inside:** "Nobody Fired Helicon Hall," *New York Sun*, March 18, 1907.

104 **imminent financial ruin:** "Sinclair Had Been Deposed," *Kansas City (Mo.) Star*, March 21, 1907.

104 **"hopelessly in debt":** "New Site for Heliconites: Upton Sinclair's Colony Said to Have Been in Debt," *Columbus (Ga.) Daily Enquirer-Sun*, March 28, 1907.

104 **$1,000 lawsuit:** "To Investigate Helicon Fire," *New York Times*, March 18, 1907.

104 **$26,000 mortgage:** *Autobiography of Upton Sinclair*, 129.

104 **$40,000 insurance policy:** "Firebug May Have Burned Helicon Hall," *Wilkes-Barre (Pa.) Times*, March 18, 1907.

104 **"the front pages of the yellow newspapers":** *Autobiography of Upton Sinclair*, 135.

104 **what Upton usually had for breakfast:** "Upton Sinclair on Diet," *Montgomery Advertiser*, June 16, 1907.

104 **whether he'd gone undercover:** "Sinclair's Wife in Sanitarium: Victim of Nervous Collapse Due to Burning of Helicon Hall," *Pawtucket (R.I.) Evening Times*, Oct. 18, 1907.

104 **post-fire nervous breakdown:** "Sinclair's Wife in Sanitarium."

104 **"I have this to say":** "Sinclairs Are Happy: Author Denies Reports of Trouble in His Family," *Grand Rapids Evening Press*, Nov. 6, 1907.

104 **"tramp poet" from Kansas:** "The Upton Sinclairs, Who Are Going into the Divorce Court," *Wilkes-Barre (Pa.) Times-Leader*, Aug. 26, 1911.

105 **Kemp wasn't the first:** "Sinclair Sues, Names Kemp," *Kansas City (Mo.) Star*, Aug. 28, 1911 (she had "pursued several friendships with other men as if [she] w[ere] not married").

105 **sinful search for the perfect mate:** "Wife Seeks Real Mate: Mrs. Sinclair Tires of 'Essential Monogamist,'" *Bellingham (Wash.) Herald*, Aug. 29, 1911.

105 **wanted a divorce:** "Upton Sinclair to Divorce Wife," *Chicago Daily Tribune*, Aug. 24, 1911.

105 **the couple and the poet met with reporters:** "Tells Wife of Divorce Suit in Loving Terms," *Duluth News Tribune*, Aug. 29, 1911.

105 SINCLAIR FREAKY: *Morning Oregonian* (Portland, Ore.), Sept. 11, 1911.

105 SINCLAIR FIGHT ON: *Morning Oregonian* (Portland, Ore.), Oct. 10, 1911 (internal quotation marks omitted).

105 SINCLAIR TOLD ME TO TAKE HIS WIFE: *Cleveland Plain Dealer*, Dec. 25, 1911.

105 KEMP DRIFTED INTO LOVE: *Kansas City (Mo.) Star*, Dec. 27, 1911 (quoting Harry Kemp) (internal quotation marks omitted).

105 **there hadn't been any agreement:** "A Divorce for Sinclair," *Emporia (Kans.) Gazette*, Dec. 1, 1911.

105 **Meta Sinclair had not spent:** "Erroneous Impression About Mrs. Sinclair," *Gulfport (Miss.) Daily Herald*, Sept. 1, 1911; "Upton Sinclair Has Taken Another Wife," *Grand Rapids Evening Press*, April 22, 1913.

105 **"settle her affairs with Mr. Sinclair":** "Eager for a Divorce: Mrs. Upton Sinclair Surprised That Counsel Should Cause Delay," *Baltimore American*, Dec. 8, 1911.

105 **divorce case sealed:** *See* "Declares Sinclair Spurned His Wife," *Trenton Evening Times*, Dec. 30, 1911.

105 **Meta begged for reporters to drop the story:** "Mrs. Sinclair and Affinity Parted," *Morning Oregonian* (Portland, Ore.), Feb. 13, 1912.

105 **Sinclair left the United States for the Netherlands:** Sinclair, *Brass Check*, 112.

106 **"his matrimonial troubles":** "Upton Sinclair to Quit Arden Colony," *Trenton Sunday Times-Advertiser*, March 22, 1914.

106 **The "journalistic jackals":** Upton Sinclair, *The Profits of Religion: An Essay in Economic Interpretation* (1918), 227 (self-published pamphlet).

106 **the muckraker Ida Tarbell:** Lyon, *Success Story*, 266–77.

106 **"The Shame of S. S. McClure":** Lyon, *Success Story*, 277.

106 **revelations of McClure's extramarital intimacies:** Lyon, *Success Story*, 261, 267.

106 **autobiographical series for *McClure's*:** Tarbell to Frances Cleveland Preston, Sept. 14, 1938, Allegheny College Archives.

107 **"The project requires me":** Cleveland to Tarbell, June 26, 1904, Allegheny College Archives.

107 **one adventure in New York City:** Frances Cleveland to Tarbell, May 24, 1902, Allegheny College Archives; Tarbell to Frances Cleveland Preston, Sept. 14, 1938, Allegheny College Archives.

107 **"cosy time":** Frances Cleveland to Tarbell, April 28, 1903, Allegheny College Archives.

107 **"Somehow I have an idea":** Cleveland to Tarbell, March 26, 1906, Allegheny College Archives.

107 **"Have I your permission":** Tarbell to Frances Cleveland Preston, Sept. 14, 1938, Allegheny College Archives.

107 **"I always think of you":** Frances Cleveland Preston to Tarbell, Sept. 16, 1938, Allegheny College Archives.

107 **"keep them posted":** Goodwin, *Bully Pulpit*, 281 (citing David S. Barry, *Forty Years in Washington* 268 (1924)).

108 **gentleman's agreement:** David S. Barry, *Forty Years in Washington* (1924), 269.

108 **Roosevelt had Pulitzer indicted:** "Indict Five Editors for Panama Libel," *New York Times*, Feb. 18, 1909.

108 **sued a journalist for suggesting:** "Defendant Retracts in the Roosevelt Libel Case—Six Cent Verdict for Colonel," *Rochester (N.Y.) Democrat and Chronicle*, June 1, 1913. The final verdict was only six cents, however.

108 **coverage of that was incomplete:** "For whatever reason, the reading public was not well informed about Wilson's health" other than some coverage in *The New York Times*. Rutland, *Newsmongers*, 305.

108 **scandalous rumor about President Wilson:** "Notes and Gleanings," *St. Louis Fortnightly Review*, Oct. 1, 1916.

108 **"That Parkinson Affair":** Sophie Kerr, "That Parkinson Affair," *McClure's*, Sept. 1916.

108 **Mary Allen Hulbert:** Frances W. Saunders, "Love and Guilt: Woodrow Wilson and Mary Hulbert, *American Heritage*, April/May 1979.

108 **information repressed back then:** *See* Sinclair, *Brass Check*, 335–36 (suggesting that newspapers in the United States published only "dark hints" of the rumor).

108 **someone destroyed the real-life letters:** Saunders, "Love and Guilt."

108 **"resented invasions of family privacy":** Mott, *American Journalism*, 721.

109 **"There is more than one kind of parasite":** Sinclair, *Brass Check*, 13–16.

109 **"a characteristically American procedure":** *See* Sinclair, *Brass Check*, 75–76, 113, 180–81.

109 **"pernicious intrusion into private affairs":** Sinclair, *Brass Check*, 335–36.

109 **Predatory journalism had made a monkey:** Sinclair, *Brass Check*, 89.

109 **driven others to ruin and suicide:** Sinclair, *Brass Check*, 94.

109 **sparked by tipsters:** Sinclair, *Brass Check*, 105.

109 **part of the economics of reporting:** Sinclair, *Brass Check*, 93.

109 **"ethical code":** Sinclair, *Brass Check*, 417.

109 **"Cutting the Tiger's Claws":** Sinclair, *Brass Check*, 405–7.

110 **"considered disgraceful":** Upton Sinclair, "The Price I Paid," *Pearson's Magazine*, April 1917, in Sinclair, *Upton Sinclair: Biographical and Critical Opinions*.

110 **Only a few newspapers published reviews:** "The Brass Check," *Truth* (Erie, Pa.), July 17, 1920 ("only a few scattered reviews").

110 **those that did did so mostly mockingly:** *See, e.g.*, "Mr. Mencken's Dislikes," *Montgomery Advertiser*, March 19, 1920.

110 **refused to run an ad:** "The Brass Check," *Truth* (Erie, Pa.), July 17, 1920.

110 **Dr. James Melvin Lee:** "Dr. Lee Attacks 'The Brass Check,'" *New York Times*, Feb. 28, 1921.

110 *History of American Journalism:* The book was originally published in 1917 and again in 1923, but Sinclair is not mentioned in either edition.

110 **Lee first suggested:** "Dr. Lee Attacks 'The Brass Check.'"

110 *The Crimes of the "Times":* Upton Sinclair, *The Crimes of the "Times": A Test of Newspaper Decency* (1921), 3 (self-published pamphlet).

110 **not to be like Upton Sinclair:** "Defends Journalism," *New York Times*, May 22, 1921 (the director of the Columbia University School of Journalism advised the students, "Do not be deluded into the adoption of the Sinclair method of bias, of exaggeration, of sensationalism.").

110 **"I know that we still have many":** *Autobiography of Upton Sinclair*, 327.

110 **"influenced a generation of reporters":** George Seldes, "The New Gadflys," *New York Times*, Sept. 18, 1974.

110 **published a small book:** Lippmann, *Liberty and the News*, v (introductory note).

110 **"The present crisis of western democracy":** Lippmann, *Liberty and the News*, 5.

111 **"snooping at keyholes":** Lippmann, *Liberty and the News*, 74–75.

111 **"bring the publishing business":** Lippmann, *Liberty and the News*, 75.

111 **"Court of Honor":** Lippmann, *Liberty and the News*, 75.

111 **"higher law":** Lippmann, *Liberty and the News*, 3.

111 **"grace like fairness":** Lippmann, *Liberty and the News*, 8.

111 **Boston Museum of Fine Arts:** *Mrs. Fiske Warren (Gretchen Osgood) and Her Daughter Rachel*, Boston Museum of Fine Arts, www.collections.mfa.org.

111 **"the story of a Southern girl":** *Autobiography of Upton Sinclair*, 196.

112 **"very human and convincing story":** "Sylvia's Marriage," *Springfield (Mass.) Union*, Sept. 6, 1914.

112 **"Men!" an ad for Dr. Howell's practice:** Advertisement for J. S. Howell, M.D., *Cincinnati Enquirer*, March 15, 1914.

112 **Douglas van Tuiver:** *Autobiography of Upton Sinclair*, 196–97.

112 **"terrified of the gossip":** Sinclair, *Sylvia's Marriage*, 281.

112 **habit of reading society columns:** Sinclair, *Sylvia's Marriage*, 26.

112 **"I would have been embarrassed":** *Autobiography of Upton Sinclair*, 196.

113 **friendly with Fiske:** *Autobiography of Upton Sinclair*, 196–97.

113 **"old friend":** Mary C. K. Sinclair, *Southern Belle*, 258.

113 **agreed to supply Samuel D. Warren Company paper:** Sinclair, *Southern Belle*, 258–59. While it is not clear if the book was ever in fact printed on Warren paper, Fiske "had promised to let [Sinclair] have a carload of book paper" for $5,000, Mary C. K. Sinclair's autobiography, *Southern Belle*, reads, and Upton Sinclair eventually "paid his last dollar for half a carload of kraft paper" on which *The Brass Check* would be published.

CHAPTER NINE: THE LAW WON

115 **"a clappy d[amne]d son of a bitch":** *Watson v. McCarthy*, 2 Ga. 57 (Ga. 1847).

115 **"The disease imputed to the plaintiff":** *Watson*, 2 Ga. 57 (emphasis omitted).

115 **"render their judgments":** Revised Style Manual, Restatements (American Law Institute, 2015).

115 **presumed with no proof necessary:** Restatement of Torts § 572 (American Law Institute, 1938).

115 **"social and relative duties":** *Bell v. State*, 31 Tenn. (1 Swan) 42 (Tenn. 1851).

115 **unmentionable "private vices":** *Commonwealth v. Blanding*, 20 Mass. (1 Pick.) 304 (1825).

115 **"To say that a married woman has the pox":** James Kent, *Commentaries on American Law*, ed. Oliver Wendell Holmes, 12th ed. (1873), 2:20n1.

116 **"colored to suit a gross":** Samuel D. Warren and Louis D. Brandeis, "The Right to Privacy," 4 *Harvard Law Review* 193 (1890).

116 **"A person who unreasonably":** Restatement of Torts § 867 (American Law Institute, 1939).

116 **manufacturing cardboard containers:** "Rochester," *American Stationer* (New York), March 14, 1895.

116 **make local tobacco seem more exotic:** "Cigarette Boxes for Japan," *Paper Box Maker* (New York), Aug. 1898.

117 **ad for Minkota Milling Company:** Advertisement for Minkota Milling Co., *Weekly Northwestern Miller* (Minneapolis), Jan. 4, 1899.

117 **ad designed for Franklin Mills Flour:** "The 'Right of Privacy,'" *Profitable Advertising* (Boston), Aug. 1902 (reproducing the lithograph).

117 **she was seventeen:** "Famous Picture Case Was Argued," *Rochester (N.Y.) Democrat and Chronicle*, April 2, 1901 (describing Miss Abigail Roberson as "a 17-year-old girl of remarkable beauty").

117 **meant for her boyfriend's eyes alone:** Dave Concannon, "It Was a Day to Remember," *Rochester (N.Y.) Democrat and Chronicle*, Jan. 15, 1967 (stating that Abbie Roberson "had some pictures made" for her boyfriend).

117 **"Little did I realize":** Concannon, "It Was a Day to Remember."

117 **had seen herself in the window:** Concannon, "It Was a Day to Remember" (stating that Abbie Roberson was "shocked" to see herself on a poster in a grocery store).

117 **twenty-five thousand such posters:** William Ringle, "Miss Roberson Fought for Right to Privacy," *Rochester (N.Y.) Democrat and Chronicle*, Jan. 15, 1967.

117 **found their way into warehouses:** *Roberson v. Rochester Folding Box Co.*, 32 Misc. 344 (N.Y. Sup. Ct. 1900).

118 **Abbie was "made sick":** Ringle, "Miss Roberson Fought for Right to Privacy."

118 **one of the founders of Rochester Folding Box:** Association of the Bar of the City of New York, "Memorial of Elbridge Laphan [*sic*] Adams," in *Yearbook for 1934* (1934), 293. He is also mentioned as president of the Rochester Folding Box Company in a brief biography, "Adams, Elbridge Lapham," a short biography published in *Cyclopaedia of American Biography*, ed. J. E. Homans (1924), 10:271.

118 **third-largest box manufacturer:** "Merger Ties Box Factory, Paper Firm," *Rochester (N.Y.) Democrat and Chronicle*, March 27, 1938.

118 **judges were powerless to protect Abbie:** *Roberson*, 32 Misc. 344.

118 **"the acts complained of":** *Mackenzie v. Soden Mineral Springs Co.*, 244 Abb. N. Cas. 402 (N.Y. Sup. Ct. 1891) (the court granted an injunction).

118 **"Every woman has a right":** *Roberson*, 32 Misc. 344.

118 **"The unauthorized circulation of the portraits":** "The Right of Privacy," *Fourth Estate: A Newspaper for the Makers of Newspapers* (New York), Aug. 11, 1900.

118 **those judges cited Judge Cooley's right:** *Roberson v. Rochester Folding Box Co.*, 71 N.Y.S. 876 (N.Y. App. Div. 1901).

119 **"This decision is interesting":** "Notes," *Photo-Miniature: A Magazine of Photographic Information* (New York), July 1901.

119 **"bordering upon the absurd":** *Roberson*, 64 N.E. 442.

119 **"Others would have appreciated the compliment":** *Roberson.*, 64 N.E. 442.

119 **swindling the Earl of Rosslyn:** "Fights Record as Rogue," *New York Times*, Jan. 3, 1903.

119 **police remove his photo:** "Picture Must Stay in Gallery," *New York Evening World*, March 28, 1903.

119 **"to escape the sleepless surveillance":** "The Right of Privacy," *Rochester (N.Y.) Democrat and Chronicle*, July 26, 1904.

119 **"Curses and chickens":** "Right of Privacy," *Rochester (N.Y.) Democrat and Chronicle*, July 26, 1904.

120 **ditty about a fictional girl:** "Maud Muller and Judge Parker," *Rochester (N.Y.) Democrat and Chronicle*, July 31, 1904.

120 **New York legislature passed a law:** 1903 N.Y. Laws 308 (describing chapter 132 as "An Act to Prevent the Unauthorized Use of the Name or Picture of Any Person for the Purposes of Trade").

121 **"Needless to say, as illustrated":** *Foster v. Svenson*, 7 N.Y.S.3d 96 (N.Y. App. Div. 2015).

121 **"The right of privacy, or the right of the individual":** *Pavesich v. New England Life Ins. Co.*, 50 S.E. 68 (Ga. 1905).

121 **"the invasion of privacy by reporters":** Roscoe Pound, "Interests of Personality," 28 *Harvard Law Review* 445 (1915).

122 **Elbridge Adams, a distant relative:** "Adams, Elbridge Lapham," in *Cyclopaedia of American Biography*, 10:270.

122 **suddenly began arguing in support:** Elbridge L. Adams, "The Law of Privacy," *Current Literature* 33 (Oct. 1902).

122 **"began to stagger, and sank":** "Down in a Moment," *Boston Daily Globe*, Oct. 8, 1890.

122 **extramarital sexual behaviors:** "E. L. Adams, Lawyer, Is Sued for Divorce," *New York Times*, Sept. 15, 1929.

122 **Everyone in the world:** Elbridge L. Adams, "The Right of Privacy and Its Relation to the Law of Libel," *Journal of Social Science* 41 (Aug. 1903) (noting that the *Roberson* decision "excited much discussion all over the world").

122 **"meet a condition of modern society":** Adams, "Law of Privacy," *Current Literature* 33 (Oct.1902).

122 **Courts should simply extend:** *See* Elbridge L. Adams, "The Law of Privacy," *North American Review* 175, no. 550 (1902) (discussing the "growing disregard for the rights of privacy").

123 **failed to identify himself:** Adams, "Right of Privacy and Its Relation to the Law of Libel," *Journal of Social Science* 41 (Aug. 1903) (a "demurrer was interposed to this complaint").

123 **"The Right of Privacy, and Its Relation to the Law of Libel":** Elbridge L. Adams, "The Right of Privacy, and Its Relation to the Law of Libel," 39 *American Law Review* 37 (1905).

123 **to students at the *Harvard Law Review*:** Brandeis to Edward H. Letchworth, April 20, 1905, Louis D. Brandeis Collection, University of Louisville School of Law (directing the editor in chief of the *Harvard Law Review*, Edward H. Letchworth, to review the "January–February, 1905, number of the American Law Review which contains a summary of the law of privacy up to that date," which is the Elbridge L. Adams law review article).

123 **"a vital force":** Brandeis to Warren, April 8, 1905, Brandeis Collection, University of Louisville School of Law; *see also* Elbridge L. Adams, "The Right of Privacy, and Its Relation to the Law of Libel," 39 *American Law Review* 37 (1905) (referred to in Brandeis's letter to Warren, dated April 8, 1905).

123 **was finding judicial recognition:** Brandeis to James Bettner Ludlow, April 20, 1905, in Urofsky and Levy, *Letters of Louis D. Brandeis*, vol. 1, *1870–1907, Urban Reformer*, 306 (stating that "the right to Privacy is at last finding judicial recognition").

123 **"a very live one":** Brandeis to Edward H. Letchworth, April 20, 1905, Brandeis Collection, University of Louisville School of Law.

123 **giving a paper titled:** Louis D. Brandeis, "The Incorporation of Trades-Unions," *Journal of Social Science* 41 (Aug. 1903) (an abstract of the address given to the American Social Science Association on May 14, 1903).

123 **"one of the most brilliant excursions":** Adams, "Right of Privacy and Its Relation to the Law of Libel," *Journal of Social Science* 41 (Aug. 1903).

124 **his notorious role:** *Plessy v. Ferguson*, 163 U.S. 537 (1896), *overruled by Brown v. Bd. of Ed. of Topeka, Shawnee Cty., Kan.*, 347 U.S. 483 (1954).

124 **"exceedingly doubtful":** Henry Billings Brown, "The Liberty of the Press," 3 *Brief of Phi Delta Phi* 214 (1900) (emphasis added).

124 **"No right is held more sacred":** *Union Pac. Ry. Co. v. Botsford*, 141 U.S. 250 (1891).

124 **tight rein on journalists:** *See* "God Save the Honorable Court," *Chicago Tribune*, Jan. 4, 1891 (the paper explains, "Woe be to you if you violate any of the rules."); *see also* "The Dignity of the Court," *Atlanta Constitution*, March 4, 1887 ("Note books are also prohibited, and the attorney or spectator who attempts to make an abstract of the proceedings is quickly notified to desist.").

124 **shocking leaks to the media:** *See, e.g.*, "The Income Tax Opinion," *Philadelphia Inquirer*, April 8, 1895 ("It is an undeniable fact that opinions of the court, some of them affecting the stock market, have been known to interested persons in advance of their official announcement.").

124 **liquor to loosen justices' lips:** "Supreme Court Leaks: Instances of Decisions Becoming Known in Advance of Their Announcement," *Baltimore Sun*, March 27, 1888, suggesting that the justices would at times enjoy "fine brands of liquors" and that information would thereafter be relayed to outsiders.

124 **justices' salaries:** "The Supreme Bench," *Trenton Evening Times*, May 22, 1895 (stating that the chief justice's salary is "but $10,500 a year, while associates get only $10,000").

124 **gambling problems:** "A Mysterious Scandal," *Cleveland Plain Dealer*, Dec. 20, 1882.

124 **apparent senility:** "United States Supreme Court," *St. Albans (Vt.) Daily Messenger*, March 17, 1881 (stating that Justice Clifford "has passed into a state of senile disability and lost even the power to write his resignation").

125 **"I only want to live long enough":** "Gossip from the Capital," *Omaha World-Herald*, Dec. 31, 1899.

125 **choosing just one to marry:** "Justice Gray's Engagement," *Philadelphia Inquirer*, March 22, 1889.

125 **Annie Van Vechten:** *See, e.g.*, "Miss Cleveland at Atlantic City," *New York Times*, April 3, 1886 (suggesting that Annie Van Vechten was with Rose Cleveland); Lachman, *Secret Life*, 321.

125 **It was for Justice Gray's fiancée:** "Justice Gray's Engagement."
125 **wife's apparent alcoholism:** "A Supreme Court Scandal," *Kansas City (Mo.) Star*, Jan. 22, 1887.
125 **"Adonis lover":** "The Moral of the Sprague-Conkling Affair," *Chicago Daily Tribune*, Aug. 22, 1879.
125 **curing waters:** "Away for the Summer," *Washington Post*, Aug. 11, 1889.
125 **husband's liquor habit:** "Mrs. Aubrey Sues for Divorce," *New York Times*, March 12, 1895.
125 **he'd shot a burglar:** "A Daring Burglary," *Detroit Free Press*, June 12, 1885.
126 **"A reporter for *The Free Press*":** "The Other One Identified," *Detroit Free Press*, Oct. 17, 1885.
126 **journalists had erroneously reported:** "Our High Court," *Los Angeles Times*, Oct. 8, 1893 (in a section with the subhead "Judges with Histories").
126 **eyesight was fading:** "Justice Brown's Eyesight Impaired," *Baltimore Sun*, Dec. 17, 1897.
126 **could not have children:** *See* "Wives of the Justices of the Supreme Court," *Washington Post*, March 5, 1899.
126 **become an invalid:** Augusta Prescott, "Our Modern Daniels," *Washington Post*, May 6, 1894.
126 **"I feel like the man who was told":** "Sons of Yale Dine," *Washington Post*, Jan. 17, 1894.
126 **meeting of the New York State Bar Association:** The talk was later published in article form: Henry Billings Brown, "The Liberty of the Press," 2 *Brief of Phi Delta Phi* 128 (1900), and Henry Billings Brown, "The Liberty of the Press," 3 *Brief of Phi Delta Phi* 214 (1900).
126 **Adams in attendance:** A few years later, Adams would change his privacy sensibilities a bit after he purchased the personal letters sent between the playwright George Bernard Shaw and the actress Ellen Terry; Adams suggested that he had needed to woo Shaw into publication because Shaw's wife didn't want them published. The letters eventually made their way into a book, *Ellen Terry and Bernard Shaw: A Correspondence.*
126 **"The media often seeks":** *Flowers v. Mississippi*, 139 S. Ct. 2228 (2019) (Thomas, J., dissenting).
127 **"assaults upon private character":** Brown, "Liberty of the Press," 2 *Brief of Phi Delta Phi* 128, 134 (1900).
127 **"violently in love":** Charles A. Kent, *Memoir of Henry Billings Brown: Late Justice of the Supreme Court of the United States* (1915), 53, 69.
127 **very fond of young ladies:** Kent, *Memoir of Henry Billings Brown*, 34 ("He was very fond of society, especially that of young ladies.").
127 **invade "one's right to privacy":** Brown, "Liberty of the Press," 2 *Brief of Phi Delta Phi* 128, 135 (1900).
127 **"The freedom of speech and of the press":** *Robertson v. Baldwin*, 165 U.S. 275 (1897).
127 **"the intimacies of the marriage relation":** *Cannon v. United States*, 116 U.S. 55 (1885).
127 **"the privacies of life":** *Boyd v. United States*, 116 U.S. 616 (1886).
128 **"The most tender affections":** *Douglas v. Stokes*, 149 S.W. 849 (Ky. 1912).
128 **"the license which the press assumes":** *Young v. Fox*, 49 N.Y.S. 634 (N.Y. App. Div. 1898) (a libel case decided before *Roberson*) (internal quotation marks omitted).
128 **sneaking into a jury room:** *People ex rel. Choate v. Barrett*, 9 N.Y.S. 321 (N.Y. Gen. Term. 1890).
128 **letters of "extreme affection":** *Baker v. Libbie*, 97 N.E. 109 (Mass. 1912).
128 **"a person who enters upon a public office":** *Post Publ'g Co. v. Hallam*, 59 F. 530 (6th Cir. 1893).
128 **Sensationalism was neither good nor justifiable:** *Dorr v. United States*, 195 U.S. 138 (1904).
128 **"if there is one department":** *People ex rel. Attorney Gen. v. News-Times Publ'g Co.*, 84 P. 912 (Colo. 1906).
129 **punishment for overstepping:** *Patterson v. Colorado*, 205 U.S. 454 (1907).
129 **"No state of society":** *Commonwealth v. Blanding*, 20 Mass. (1 Pick.) 304 (Mass. 1925).
129 **"Mutual Weekly" newsreels:** *Mut. Film Corp. v. Indus. Comm'n of Ohio*, 236 U.S. 230 (1915), *overruled in part by Joseph Burstyn Inc. v. Wilson*, 343 U.S. 495 (1952).
129 **"Do not become a tool":** Bowen, *This Fabulous Century*, vol. 2, *1910–1920*, 234.
129 **newspaper could be held liable:** *Toledo Newspaper Co. v. United States*, 247 U.S. 402 (1918), *overruled in part by Nye v. United States*, 313 U.S. 33 (1941).

CHAPTER TEN: HOLMES AND BRANDEIS
AND THE (REGULATED) MARKETPLACE OF IDEAS

131 **marketplace of ideas:** *Abrams v. United States*, 250 U.S. 616 (1919) (Holmes, J., dissenting) ("But when men have realized that time has upset many fighting faiths, they may come to believe

even more than they believe the very foundations of their own conduct that the ultimate good desired is better reached by free trade in ideas—that the best test of truth is the power of the thought to get itself accepted in the competition of the market, and that truth is the only ground upon which their wishes safely can be carried out. That at any rate is the theory of our Constitution.").

131 **credited the power of the press:** *Near v. Minnesota*, 283 U.S. 697 (1931) ("In determining the extent of the constitutional protection, it has been generally, if not universally, considered that it is the chief purpose of the guaranty to prevent previous restraints upon publication.").

131 **keep his letters private:** *See, e.g.*, Holmes to Felix Frankfurter, Jan. 10, 1925, Oliver Wendell Holmes Jr. Digital Suite, Harvard Law School Library (letter is marked "Private" in the top-left-hand corner, with a note indicating "My letter is private . . ." as a postscript).

131 **colleagues' strong disapproval:** Holmes to Clara Sherwood Stevens, Oct. 26, 1907, Holmes Digital Suite ("Some of my brethren have intimated an opinion that it is improper to write a private letter on this paper.").

131 **He had "many longings":** Holmes to Clara Sherwood Stevens, Oct. 26, 1907, Holmes Digital Suite (also stating that if she complained again about him not wanting to see her, he would slap her and drop her).

132 **"lusty":** Ernst, *The Best Is Yet . . .*, 121.

132 **"the feeling of family privacy":** Holmes to Harold J. Laski, Feb. 22, 1929, in Howe, *Holmes-Laski Letters*, 2:1133.

132 **"anything that had the least touch of privacy":** Holmes to Lewis Einstein, Sept. 5, 1930, Holmes Digital Suite.

132 **"I am much obliged to you":** Holmes to Richard W. Gilder, Nov. 4, 1894, Century Company Records, New York Public Library.

132 **"She hates to have people talk":** Holmes to Nina Gray, April 26, 1929, Holmes Digital Suite.

132 **"were all rascals":** Holmes to Edward A. Ross, March 15, 1912, Holmes Digital Suite.

132 **"real information" regarding "important matters":** Holmes to Edward A. Ross, March 15, 1912, Holmes Digital Suite.

132 **"a casual unknown dame":** Holmes to Nina Gray, March 25, 1922, Holmes Digital Suite.

132 **"deep sense of privacy":** *See, e.g.*, Budiansky, *Oliver Wendell Holmes: A Life in War, Law, and Ideas*; Bowen, *Yankee from Olympus*, 347 ("always hated publicity"); Mark DeWolfe Howe to Charles P. Curtis, Aug. 4, 1942, Holmes Digital Suite (Holmes had a "sensitive instinct for privacy").

132 **"plaintiff's private papers were stolen":** *Burdeau v. McDowell*, 256 U.S. 465 (1921) (Brandeis, J., dissenting).

132 **"By the by I never have asked":** Holmes to Laski, July 21, 1921, Holmes Digital Suite.

133 **two-volume set of books:** *See generally*, Howe, *Holmes-Laski Letters*.

133 **replaced with an ellipsis:** Holmes to Laski, July 21, 1921, in Howe, *Holmes-Laski Letters*, 1:351.

133 **"private facts":** Norman Hapgood, "Journalism" (address delivered in the Page Lecture Series before the Sheffield Scientific School, Yale University, 1909), in *Every-Day Ethics* (1910), 4.

133 **lest journalism foul its own nest:** Hapgood, "Journalism," 12–13 ("A newspaper might expose anything it liked, so long as it did not expose another paper. Such criticism was called fouling one's own nest, with the obvious implication that it would be better to foul the nest of some one else.").

133 **"What Publicity Can Do":** Louis D. Brandeis, "What Publicity Can Do," *Harper's Weekly*, Dec. 20, 1913 ("Require a full disclosure to the investor of the amount of commissions and profits paid; and not only will investors be put on their guard, but bankers' compensation will tend to adjust itself automatically to what is fair and reasonable.").

133 **He taught family members:** *See, e.g.*, Louis D. Brandeis to Susan Brandeis Gilbert, Jan. 6, 1927, in Urofsky and Levy, *Family Letters of Louis D. Brandeis*, 20 ("If by any chance such speed has been made in framing that this has already been done, please hang the letters in the privacy of your bedroom where no one else will see them.").

133 **destroyed most of the correspondence:** Brandeis to Leila E. Colburn, Aug. 22, 1934, in Urofsky and Levy, *Letters of Louis D. Brandeis*, vol. 5, *1921–1941, Elder Statesman*, 545.

133 **his wife's depression:** Urofsky, *Louis D. Brandeis: A Life*, 122–25.

133 **"Privacy was one of the things":** *See, e.g.*, Urofsky, *Louis D. Brandeis and the Progressive Tradition*, 11.

133 **Holmes wrote a famous dissent:** *Lochner v. New York*, 198 U.S. 45 (1905) (Holmes, J., dissenting), *overruled in part by Day-Brite Lighting Inc. v. Missouri*, 342 U.S. 421 (1952), and *overruled in part by Ferguson v. Skrupa*, 372 U.S. 726 (1963), and *abrogated by W. Coast Hotel Co. v. Parrish*, 300 U.S. 379 (1937).

134 **Brandeis had designed a plan:** Charles S. Groves, "William S. Youngman of Boston Testifies on Brandeis," *Boston Evening Globe*, Feb. 28, 1916.

134 **"probably claimed as much of the attention":** Urofsky and Levy, *Letters of Louis D. Brandeis*, vol. 4, *1916–1921, Mr. Justice Brandeis*, 69. n. 7. Urofsky and Levy wrote this assessment as a footnote to Brandeis's quick mention of the Warren matter in a February 17, 1916, letter to Edward Francis McClennen.

134 **banner headlines:** Charles S. Groves, "Brandeis Attacked Own Acts," *Boston Evening Globe*, Feb. 15, 1916.

134 **"have preferred to be let alone":** Louis D. Brandeis to Alfred Brandeis, Feb. 12, 1916, in Urofsky and Levy, *Letters of Louis D. Brandeis*, vol. 4, *1916–1921, Mr. Justice Brandeis*, 54.

135 **"should . . . make clear beyond peradventure":** Brandeis to Cornelia Lyman Warren, Feb. 17, 1916, in Urofsky and Levy, *Letters of Louis D. Brandeis*, vol. 4, *1916–1921, Mr. Justice Brandeis*, 71–72.

135 **"would not protect a man in falsely shouting fire in a theatre":** *Schenck v. United States*, 249 U.S. 47 (1919) (Justice Holmes writing for the unanimous Court).

135 **"the First Amendment . . . cannot have been":** *Frohwork v. United States*, 249 U.S. 204 (1919) (Justice Holmes writing for the unanimous Court).

135 **"'Whatever a man publishes'":** *Wash. Post v. Chaloner*, 250 U.S. 290 (1919).

135 **wartime case involving the publication:** *Abrams v. United States*, 250 U.S. 616 (1919).

135 **Holmes had recently reread:** Holmes to Laski, Feb. 28, 1919, in Howe, *Holmes-Laski Letters*, 1:186.

136 **Holmes also read H. G. Wells:** Holmes to Patrick A. Sheehan, July 17, 1909, in Burton, *Holmes-Sheehan Correspondence*, 40 (writing, "I find among the books waiting for me one by H. G. Wells"); Holmes to Laski, April 20, 1917, in Howe, *Holmes-Laski Letters*, 1:79 (writing, "Wells is best employed on stories").

136 **"When Joan left Highmorton":** H. G. Wells, *Joan and Peter: The Story of an Education* (1918), 330.

136 **"faults, foibles, deformities":** *Commonwealth v. Blanding*, 20 Mass. 304 (Mass. 1825).

136 **"general American trouble is that we make public":** Brandeis to Frankfurter, Feb. 17, 1920, in Urofsky and Levy, *Letters of Louis D. Brandeis*, vol. 4, *1916–1921, Mr. Justice Brandeis*, 449.

137 **"within the permissible *curtailment* of free speech":** *Schaefer v. United States*, 251 U.S. 466 (1920) (Brandeis, J., dissenting) (emphasis added).

137 **"men feared witches and burnt women":** *Whitney v. California*, 274 U.S. 357 (1927) (Brandeis, J., concurring), *overruled in part by Brandenburg v. Ohio*, 395 U.S. 444 (1969).

137 **"men's affairs":** *Federal Trade Commission v. American Tobacco Co.*, 264 U.S. 298 (1924).

137 **First Amendment absolutism:** *Pennekamp v. Florida*, 328 U.S. 331 (1946) (Frankfurter, J., concurring).

137 **"become encysted in phrases":** *Pennekamp*, 328 U.S. 331 (Frankfurter, J., concurring) (citing *Hyde v. United States*, 225 U.S. 347 (1912) (Holmes, J., dissenting)).

137 **"is not a freedom from responsibility":** *Pennekamp*, 328 U.S. 331 (Frankfurter, J., concurring).

137 **Olmstead v. United States:** *Olmstead v. United States*, 277 U.S. 438 (1928), *overruled in part by Berger v. New York*, 388 U.S. 41 (1967), and *overruled in part by Katz v. United States*, 389 U.S. 347 (1967).

138 **Brandeis had played a behind-the-scenes role:** Ruth Finney, "Seeks Probe of Espionage," *El Paso Evening Post*, Dec. 16, 1927.

138 **One editor had finally taken the bait:** Ruth Finney, "He Snoops to Conquer," *Pittsburgh Press*, May 3, 1927.

138 **grant certiorari and hear the case:** Brandeis to Frankfurter, May 21, 1927, in Urofsky and Levy, *Letters of Louis D. Brandeis*, vol. 5, *1921–1941, Elder Statesman*, 285; Strum, *Louis D. Brandeis: Justice for the People*, 326, 464–65.

139 **He'd been just as worried:** *Olmstead v. United States* File, Louis D. Brandeis Papers, Historical & Special Collections, Harvard Law School Library.

139 **very obviously impossible:** Paper, *Brandeis: An Intimate Biography of One of America's Truly Great Supreme Court Justices*, 312.

139   **"privacies of life":** *Olmstead v. United States*, 277 U.S. 438 (Brandeis, J., dissenting) (quoting *Boyd v. United States*, 116 U.S. 616 (1886).

139   **quoting that Supreme Court case from 1886:** *Boyd v. United States*, 116 U.S. 616 (1886).

139   **"I fear that your early stated zeal":** Note from Holmes to Brandeis, Feb. 23, 1928, Brandeis Papers, Historical & Special Collections, Harvard Law School Library.

139   **"given this case so exhaustive an examination":** *Olmstead v. United States*, 277 U.S. 438 (Holmes, J., dissenting).

139   **"It has always been recognized":** *Sinclair v. United States*, 279 U.S. 263 (1929), *overruled by United States v. Gaudin*, 515 U.S. 506 (1995).

139   **"The State has, of course, power to afford protection":** *Senn v. Tile Layers Protective Union*, 301 U.S. 468 (1937).

139   **including entire chapters:** Arthur and Crosman, *Law of Newspapers*, 212 (chapter titled "Right of Privacy"); Loomis, *Newspaper Law*, 159 (chapter titled "Privacy").

140   **saved freedom of the press:** *See generally*, Fred W. Friendly, *Minnesota Rag*.

140   **very first edition of *The Saturday Press*:** H. A. Guilford and J. M. Near, "Following a Custom," *Saturday Press* (Minneapolis), Sept. 24, 1927.

140   **paying a ransom of sorts:** This practice had started early and extended beyond Minnesota. *See Iowa v. Lewis*, 65 N.W. 295 (Iowa 1895) (the object "was to extort money from prominent citizens, by means of threats and covert insinuations of the purpose to expose their crimes and shortcomings in said newspaper").

141   **threatened to arrest anyone:** J. M. Near, "If So, Why?," *Saturday Press* (Minneapolis), Oct. 1, 1927.

141   **Minnesota's nuisance law:** *State ex rel. Olson v. Guilford*, 219 N.W. 770 (Minn. 1928) (quoting 1925 Minn. Laws 358–60).

141   **Guilford was shot:** J. M. Near, "The Shooting of Howard A. Guilford and Some Twin City Reporter History," *Saturday Press* (Minneapolis), Oct. 1, 1927, 2–3, 7. Sadly, the prediction would come true: Guilford was shot to death three years after the Supreme Court decided *Near v. Minnesota*, and police never arrested anyone for the crime. James Eli Shiffer, "Murder of a Minneapolis Muckraker," *Star Tribune*, March 5, 2010.

141   **"a selection of scandalous and defamatory articles":** *State ex rel. Olson v. Guilford*, 219 N.W. 770 (Minn. 1928).

141   **"in harmony with the public welfare":** *State ex rel. Olson v. Guilford*, 228 N.W. 326 (Minn. 1929).

141   **published *Washington Merry-Go-Round*:** *See generally* Pearson and Allen, *Washington Merry-Go-Round*.

142   **unconstitutional prior restraint:** *Near v. Minnesota ex rel. Olson*, 283 U.S. 697 (1931) ("There is nothing new in the fact that charges of reprehensible conduct may create resentment and the disposition to resort to violent means of redress, but this well-understood tendency did not alter the determination to protect the press against censorship and restraint upon publication.").

142   ***The Kansas City Star* reported:** *Kansas City (Mo.) Star*, June 6, 1931.

142   ***The Miami Herald* read:** *Miami Herald*, June 2, 1931.

142   **Hundreds of other newspapers:** "Court Approves Press Freedom," *Elmwood (Ind.) Call Leader*, June 2, 1931; "U.S. Supreme Court Upholds the Freedom of the Press," *Santa Cruz Evening News*, June 3, 1931; William S. Neal, "Press Gag Law Held Unconstitutional: Supreme Court Guarantees Freedom of the Press," *Tyrone (Pa.) Daily Herald*, June 2, 1931.

142   **injunctions would be appropriate:** *Near*, 238 U.S. 697 (citing Roscoe Pound, "Equitable Relief Against Defamation and Injuries to Personality," 20 *Harvard Law Review* 640 (1916)).

143   **"You are dealing here not with a sort":** "Brandeis Criticizes Minnesota Gag Law," *New York Times*, Jan. 31, 1931.

143   **had become editor of *The World*:** "Lippmann Sees End of 'Yellow' Press," *New York Times*, Jan. 13, 1931.

CHAPTER ELEVEN: BE DECENT

144   **press-sponsored tournament:** Carter Field, "Harding, Fussed by Crowd, Loses Press Golf Honor by a Stroke," *New-York Tribune*, May 27, 1922.

144   **Harding's ethics advice:** "President Aggrieved at Attacks upon Administration Officials," *Baltimore Sun*, June 3, 1922; "Declares Harding Would Muzzle Press," *New York Times*, June 4, 1922.

145 **Harding's Creed:** Chester T. Crowell, "As Man to Man," *Independent* (London), Aug. 28, 1920; "Harding's Newspaper Rules," *Oregon Exchanges*, Nov. 1920.

145 **make journalism more respectable:** "Harding's Creed," *Pratt (Kans.) Republican*, July 20, 1920.

145 **"If he had been discussing":** "President Aggrieved at Attacks upon Administration Officials."

145 **"The President speaks in such matters":** "Washington's Passing Show," *Christian Science Monitor*, June 3, 1922.

145 **"President Harding has some fairly fixed ideas":** "Attacks on Officials Incense Harding; Nettled by Space the Press Gives Them," *New York Times*, June 3, 1922.

145 **Harding's meeting with reporters:** *See* "Sinclair Consolidated in Big Oil Deal with U.S.," *Wall Street Journal*, April 14, 1922.

145 **Harding had had longtime affairs:** *See, e.g.,* Britton, *President's Daughter*.

145 **burn them when he died:** Britton, *President's Daughter*, 71.

146 **"shape a policy of their own":** "The Colored Men," *Inter Ocean* (Chicago), Aug. 6, 1875.

146 **Colored Press Association:** "The Colored Press Convention in Washington," *Independent*, Aug. 10, 1882.

146 **"Journalism and Journalism Ethics":** "National Colored Press Convention," *Washington Bee*, July 2, 1887.

146 **had become a leader of the organization:** "To the Colored Press," *Washington Bee*, Aug. 19, 1893.

146 **refused their invitation to speak:** "Governor O'Ferrall Writes a Letter," *Alexandria Gazette*, Sept. 13, 1894.

146 **telegram petitioning members:** American Society of Newspaper Editors, *Problems of Journalism: Proceedings of the First Annual Meeting* (1923), 118.

146 **"pay their respects":** "Society of Editors," *Wausau Daily Herald*, April 27, 1923.

146 **they'd named a special member:** "Ethics of Press Topic of Editors," *Washington Evening Star*, April 27, 1923.

146 **input on their ethics plan:** "President Talks Shop with Editors," *Brooklyn Daily Eagle*, April 29, 1923.

147 **Cornell University taught journalism:** Andrew D. White to Charles F. Wingate, May 29, 1875, in Wingate, *Views and Interviews on Journalism*, 359–60.

147 **the program lagged:** *See* Sutton, *Education for Journalism in the United States*, 129–37 (Cornell is not listed as having a program in journalism).

147 **"any prescribed course of study":** J. J. White (acting president, Washington and Lee University) to Charles F. Wingate, May 25, 1875, in Wingate, *Views and Interviews on Journalism*, 360.

147 **"practical printing and journalism":** Sutton, *Education for Journalism in the United States*, 7.

147 **University of Missouri students were starting:** Sutton, *Education for Journalism in the United States*, 10.

147 **Courses in Journalism program:** Sutton, *Education for Journalism in the United States*, 11.

147 ***Reporting for the Newspapers*:** Hemstreet, *Reporting for the Newspapers*, 7.

147 **used newsreel films to teach students:** "Movies Teach Columbia Students How to Be Newspaper Reporters," *Morning Oregonian*, June 21, 1914.

147 **Fisk University had included:** Gore, *Negro Journalism*, 21.

147 **"agitating for a set of rules of conduct":** "The Journalistic Code of Ethics," *Ohio State University Bulletin*, Feb. 18, 1922, 3.

147 **local and regional ethics codes:** The code provisions outlined in this paragraph are taken from "The Journalist's Creed," *University of Missouri Bulletin: Journalism Series*, Sept. 1915, 6.

148 **"the most distinguished journalist":** American Society of Newspaper Editors, *Problems of Journalism: Proceedings of the First Annual Meeting*, 160.

148 **Harding had titled his talk "Journalism":** "Editors Aroused over Lack of Seasoned Newspapermen," *Washington Evening Star*, April 28, 1923.

148 **there was never a time:** "Harding Denies Bankers Bring Plan for Court," *Chicago Tribune*, April 29, 1923.

148 **he was appalled at the lack:** "President Talks Shop and Visits Baseball Game," *Sacramento Bee*, April 24, 1923, quoting Harding, who begged for greater accuracy in reporting: "I have been crucified as a destroyer of sticks, eight in number in five weeks."

148 **Comforting truth was better than scandal:** "Harding Denies Bankers Bring Plan for Court."

148 **"everything of a vicious character":** American Society of Newspaper Editors, *Problems of Journalism: Proceedings of the First Annual Meeting*, 164.

148 **"the excessive publication of sensational vice":** "Harding Denies Bankers Bring Plan for Court."

149 **keep his misdeeds out of the paper:** American Society of Newspaper Editors, *Problems of Journalism: Proceedings of the First Annual Meeting*, 164–65.

149 **repay their debt to America:** "Harding Denies Bankers Bring Plan for Court."

149 **by drafting an ethics code:** American Society of Newspaper Editors, *Problems of Journalism: Proceedings of the First Annual Meeting*, 165.

149 **"often times when the news":** "1923 Record Year in Journalism," *Editor & Publisher*, Jan. 26, 1924.

149 **seven separate sections:** "Canons of Journalism Adopted," *Chicago Tribune*, April 29, 1923.

149 **"details of crime and vice":** "Canons of Journalism Adopted."

149 **"a right to violate with pen":** American Society of Newspaper Editors, *Problems of Journalism: Proceedings of the First Annual Meeting*, 81.

149 **called privacy a "right":** American Society of Newspaper Editors, *Problems of Journalism: Proceedings of the First Annual Meeting*, 51.

149 **"the Bible of the American journalist":** Walker, *City Editor*, 169.

149 **Upton Sinclair was the first to report:** Nasaw, *Chief*, 509.

149 **Harding praised the new ASNE code:** "Harding Denies Bankers Bring Plan for Court."

149 **especially the privacy-protecting part:** American Society of Newspaper Editors, *Problems of Journalism: Proceedings of the First Annual Meeting*, 164.

149 **one of Harding's mistresses published:** Britton, *President's Daughter*, 5.

150 **"true account of the relations":** "Harding Smirched in Britton Book," *Brooklyn Daily Eagle*, July 8, 1927.

150 **she was thirteen:** Britton, *President's Daughter*, 9.

150 **Their first kiss would come:** Britton, *President's Daughter*, 29.

150 **he'd register her at hotels as his niece:** Britton, *President's Daughter*, 37.

150 **"obscene, lewd and indecent":** "Sumner and Vice Leaguers Sued by Mother over Book," *New York Daily News*, July 9, 1927.

150 **"a real Harding":** Britton, *President's Daughter*, 177.

150 **jury convicted Secretary Fall:** "Fall Found Guilty in Bribery Trial," *Washington Evening Star*, Oct. 25, 1929.

150 **the Library of Congress released:** Library of Congress, "President Warren Harding's Love Letters Open to the Public," press release, July 29, 2014, www.loc.gov.

150 **journalism scholars began to study:** Kingsbury and Hart, *Newspapers and the News*, 6, 103.

150 **Even the notorious *Police Gazette*:** *See, e.g.*, *National Police Gazette*, Nov. 22, 1930. The *Gazette* "of three-quarters of a century and more ago . . . little is now known" is a description from 1930. Van Every, *Sins of New York as "Exposed" by the "Police Gazette,"* 9.

150 **"the model of decent and dignified journalism":** *See* Advertisement, "The Model of Decent and Dignified Journalism," *New York Times*, 1896 (on file with author).

151 **"the beginning of the end":** Mott, *American Journalism*, 671.

151 **growing newspaper responsibility:** *See* Mott, *American Journalism*, 689–711.

151 **Mickey's policy at *The Daily War-Drum*:** Disney, *Mickey Mouse Runs His Own Newspaper*, 30, 34, 410.

152 **celebrity journalism had been a thing:** "Greenroom Jottings," *Motion Picture Story Magazine*, July 1912, 130–31; "Answers to Inquiries," *Motion Picture Story Magazine*, July 1912, 146.

152 **"armed with the new flashlight contrivance":** Charles Shepard Washburne, "'Tricks' of the Newspaper Photographer," *Technical World Magazine*, May 1913.

152 **Harris's autobiographical series:** Harris, *My Life and Loves* (privately printed in multiple volumes throughout the 1920s).

152 **Guy de Maupassant:** Harris, *My Life and Loves* (1925), 2:237–38, 240.

152 **Aubrey Beardsley:** Harris, *My Life and Loves* (1922), vol. 1.

152 **Walt Whitman:** Harris, *My Life and Loves* (1922), 1:239.

152 **real-life, noncelebrity conquests:** *See, e.g.*, Harris, *My Life and Loves* (1927), 3:159–73 (chapter 10: Grace).

152 **most amatory experience:** *See* Harris, *My Life and Loves* (1927), 4:154–71 (chapter 8: San Remo).

152 **agreed to a bizarre remedy:** Harris, *My Life and Loves* (1922), 1:221–24.

152 **Holy Spirit of Truth:** Harris, *My Life and Loves* (1922), 3:54.

152 **"I am resolved to dare speak":** Harris, *My Life and Loves* (1925), 2:11.

152 **First Amendment soldier:** Frank Harris, introduction to Eugene V. Debs, *Pastels of Men* (1919).

152 **he found few comrades:** *See* Harris, *My Life and Loves* (1925), 2:9.

153 **vile, inexcusable, and poisonous:** Tobin and Gertz, *Frank Harris*, 314.

153 **"a serious blow to the cause of freedom":** Harold E. Stearns, "French Moral Issues Are Partly Political," *Baltimore Sun*, May 1, 1923.

153 **privacy required a wronged plaintiff:** A book titled *Lies and Libels of Frank Harris* was eventually published in the United States, but it does not appear that anyone ever sued Harris on privacy or other grounds. Smith, Smith, and Stephens, *Lies and Libels of Frank Harris*.

153 **"pernicious animals, or *an obscene book*":** *Livingston v. Van Ingen*, 9 Johns. 507 (N.Y. 1811).

153 **"slight social value as a step":** *R. A. V. v. St. Paul*, 505 U.S. 377 (1992), citing *Chaplinsky v. New Hampshire*, 315 U.S. 568 (1942).

153 **judges in the 1940s sent bookshop owners:** "5 Days in Jail Is Penalty for Sale of Harris' Book," *Detroit Free Press*, Aug. 1, 1945.

153 **up to $150 on the black market:** "Have You a Question," *Dallas Morning News*, Aug. 30, 1959 (putting the "banned book" at $100 to $150).

153 **edited-for-certain-content version:** Richard L. Brown, "Books of the Day," *Kansas City (Mo.) Star*, Oct. 13, 1963.

153 **"I had hardly any sex-thrill":** Frank Harris, "My Life and Loves," *Eros* (Winter 1962): 41.

153 **finding all "the requisite elements":** *United States v. Ginzburg*, 224 F. Supp. 129 (E.D. Pa. 1963).

153 **affirmed the *Eros* obscenity conviction:** *Ginzburg v. United States*, 383 U.S. 463 (1966).

154 **"to secure 'the widest possible'":** *New York Times v. Sullivan*, 376 U.S. 254 (1964) (citing *Associated Press v. United States Trib. Co.*, 326 U.S. 1 (1945)).

154 **more than $1,000:** Sale Listing, "My Life and Loves—Five Volumes in One," Abebooks, accessed March 30, 2021.

154 **"a landmark in erotic literature":** Sale Listing, "My Life and Loves (Literary Classics) Paperback—November 1, 1999," Amazon, accessed March 24, 2021.

154 **"things that the public has no right to know":** Harris, *My Life and Loves* (1922), 2:253.

154 **"heroic adventure":** *Smith v. Suratt*, 7 Alaska 416 (D. Alaska Territory 1926).

154 **"Certainly, this Court should proceed":** *Berg v. Minneapolis Star & Trib. Co.*, 79 F. Supp. 957 (D. Minn. 1948).

154 **they can lose their jobs:** *See, e.g.,* Howard Kurtz, "Ethics Pressure Squeezes a Few out the Door," *Washington Post*, May 2, 2005.

155 **"Minimize Harm" section:** Society of Professional Journalists, "SPJ Code of Ethics" (2014), www.spj.org.

CHAPTER TWELVE: PANDORA'S BOX, THE SOURCE OF EVERY EVIL

157 ***Croswell* case:** *People v. Croswell*, 3 Johns. Cas. 337 (N.Y. Sup. Ct. 1804) (emphasis omitted).

157 **"Four-Dimensional Bodies":** "11-Year-Old Lecturer," *New York Sun*, Jan. 6, 1910.

157 **"gazed in wonder":** "Boy Explains 4th Dimension," *Chicago Daily Tribune*, Jan. 6, 1910 ("Distinguished mathematical professors gazed in wonder as the boy placed on the blackboard row after row of figures to prove his difficult and profound theories. Many of them again and again called on him to explain anew some theory.").

157 **compared him with Jesus at the Temple:** "Harvard's Quartet of Mental Prodigies: Unique Problem for Psychologists in Education of Young Sidis and His Three Companions," *New York Times*, Jan. 16, 1910.

157 **the Greek mathematician Euclid reincarnated:** *See* "Euclid in Sidis: Theosophists Believe Harvard Prodigy Is the Mathematician Reborn," *Gulfport (Miss.) Daily Herald*, April 20, 1910.

157 ***The Baltimore Sun* headlined its story:** *Baltimore Sun*, Jan. 16, 1910.

157 **"the grip" and "overstudy":** "Boy Prodigy Ill: W. J. Sidis Confined to Home by Grip," *New-York Tribune*, Jan. 26, 1910.

157 **he was "breaking down":** "Harvard Prodigy Seriously Ill," *Fall River (Mass.) Daily Evening News*, Jan. 26, 1910.

158 **"from the wearisome exclamations":** "The Prodigy's Collapse: May Be Due to Pestering More Than Overburdened Mind," *Washington Post*, Jan. 31, 1910.

158 **BOY WIZARD IS NOW A GRADUATE:** *Marion (Ohio) Daily Star*, June 19, 1914.

158 **personal vow of celibacy:** "Oh Lis-ten! Women Mean Naught to Youthful Prodigy," *Syracuse Herald*, April 18, 1915.

158 **newspapers called him a freak:** "Musings of a Tenderfoot," *Riverside (Calif.) Enterprise*, April 19, 1915 (describing Sidis as an "educated freak and Harvard mathematical prodigy").

158 **dream was to become a lawyer:** William Aronoff, letter to the editor, *Christian Science Monitor*, July 31, 1944.

158 **entered Harvard Law School:** Wallace, *Prodigy*, 125 (stating that Sidis enrolled in Harvard Law School in September 1916).

158 **injunctions were appropriate in privacy cases:** Roscoe Pound, "Equitable Relief Against Defamation and Injuries to Personality," 29 *Harvard Law Review* 640 (1916).

158 **dropped out in his third year:** Wallace, *Prodigy*, 135.

158 **"curious tragedy":** "Boy Prodigy Is Now 26 and Is Paid $23 Weekly," *Sayre (Pa.) Evening Times*, Jan. 10, 1924.

158 **"a remarkable instance of the rise and fall":** "Prodigy as Baby, Sidis at 26 Clerks for $23 a Week," *New York Daily News*, Jan. 10, 1924.

158 **ALL HEAD AND NO HEART:** "Over Education Does Not Pay," *Brainerd (Minn.) Daily Dispatch*, Jan. 10, 1924.

158 **"asks merely that he be let alone":** "Prodigy as Baby, Sidis at 26 Clerks for $23 a Week."

159 **photograph featuring a deceased child:** *Bazemore v. Savannah Hosp.*, 155 S.E. 194 (Ga. 1930), finding that the parents had stated a claim for relief.

159 **abdominal X-ray:** *Banks v. King Features Syndicate*, 30 F. Supp. 352 (S.D.N.Y. 1939).

159 **woman lying outside, overcome by gas fumes:** *Peed v. Wash. Times Co.*, 54 Wash. L. Rep. 182 (D.C. 1927).

159 **photographs of a criminal defendant:** *Ex parte Strum*, 136 A. 312 (Md. 1927).

159 **former prostitute had a right to privacy:** *Melvin v. Reid*, 297 P. 91 (Cal. Ct. App. 1931).

159 **"Interference with Privacy":** Restatement of Torts § 867 (American Law Institute, 1939).

160 **by following a person around for a week:** Restatement of Torts § 867, illus. 1.

160 **by publishing a film of an abdominal operation:** Restatement of Torts § 867, illus. 3.

160 **by secretly capturing a photograph:** Restatement of Torts § 867, illus. 6.

160 **those public people:** Restatement of Torts § 867, cmt. c.

160 **"without a scratch on freedom of speech":** "Text of President's Message to Nation," *New Orleans States*, Jan. 4. 1939.

160 **Depression-era National Recovery Act:** *See, e.g.*, "Newspapers and the New Deal," *Brooklyn Daily Eagle*, Nov. 19, 1933 (the "status of newspapers" as part of the "National Recovery Act" had been "agitating newspaper publishers for quite some time").

161 **picture of a man as part of criminal coverage:** *Reed v. Real Detective Publ'g Co.*, 162 P.2d 133 (Ariz. 1945).

161 **"starving glutton":** *Barber v. Time Inc.*, 159 S.W.2d 291 (Mo. 1942).

161 **"vivid and intimate character sketch":** *Cason v. Baskin*, 20 So. 2d 243 (Fla. 1944).

161 **"whether the occasion or incident":** *Barber*, 159 S.W.2d 291.

161 **"the unwarranted appropriation of one's personality":** *Right of Privacy*, 138 American Law Reports 22 (1942).

162 **"International Bill of Rights":** William Draper Lewis to the Advisers of the American Law Institute on the International Bill of Rights Project, June 7, 1943.

162 **"everyone shall have the right":** Draft Report of the International Bill of Rights from the Advisers of the American Law Institute on the International Bill of Rights Project, Personal Rights Subcommittee, June 7, 1943.

162 **he'd read numerous documents:** The story is told in Michael Traynor, "The President's Letter: The Statement of Essential Human Rights—a Groundbreaking Venture (Part II)," *ALI Reporter* 29, no. 3 (2007) (statement of John Humphrey, the director of the United Nations Human Rights Division, who prepared a first draft of what was to become the Universal Declaration of Human Rights).

162 **Universal Declaration of Human Rights:** Convention for the Protection of Human Rights and Fundamental Freedoms, Nov. 4, 1950, 213 U.N.T.S. 221 (*entered into force* Sept. 3, 1953).

162 **protection of people:** For a more complete view of privacy around the world, see Ronald J. Krotoszynski Jr., *Privacy Revisited: A Global Perspective on the Right to Be Left Alone* (2016).

162 **the highest court in the United Kingdom:** *PJS v. News Group Newspapers Ltd.* [2016] UKSC 26.

163 **mysterious PJS:** "Elton John Betrayed by Cheating Husband!," *National Enquirer*, April 6, 2016.

163 **"by a decent respect":** Code of Ethics, American Newspaper Guild (1934); "Code of Ethics, Adopted by the American Newspaper Guild (TNG), at Its Second Annual Convention in 1934," Accountable Journalism, www.accountablejournalism.org.

164 **"Unless newspapermen in the aggregate":** "Talk of the Town," *New Yorker*, July 10, 1937.

164 **Thurber was assigned "The Talk of the Town":** Jon Michaud, "Eighty-five from the Archive: James Thurber," *New Yorker*, June 2, 2010.

164 **he continued his contributions:** *The New Yorker* website credits Thurber with authoring "The Talk of the Town" for the November 13, 1937, issue. *See* "Contributors: James Thurber," *New Yorker*, Nov. 13, 1937.

164 **discrediting ethics for reporters:** *See, e.g.,* James Thurber, "The Greatest Man in the World," in *Writings and Drawings of James Thurber* (1996), 291.

164 **class on American Indians:** Stephen Bates, "The Prodigy and the Press: William James Sidis, Anti-intellectualism, and Standards of Success," *Journalism and Mass Communication Quarterly* 88, no. 2 (2011).

164 **"Where Are They Now?":** James Thurber and Jared L. Manley, "Where Are They Now? April Fool!," *New Yorker*, Aug. 14, 1937. Thurber used the pen name Jared L. Manley but is credited on *The New Yorker* website as authoring the piece. *See* "Contributors: James Thurber," *New Yorker*, Aug. 14, 1937 (showing that Thurber coauthored the issue's "Where Are They Now? April Fool!" with Jared L. Manley).

164 **show parents how not to raise their children:** *See* Thurber, *Years with Ross*, 212 ("My sincere feeling [was] that the piece would help to curb the great American thrusting of talented children into the glare of fame or notoriety, a procedure in so many cases disastrous to the later career and happiness of the exploited youngsters.").

164 **"The Secret Life of Walter Mitty":** James Thurber, "The Secret Life of Walter Mitty," *New Yorker*, March 18, 1939.

165 **"'It's strange,' said William James Sidis:** Thurber and Manley, "Where Are They Now? April Fool!"

165 **"may recall a recent account":** Jared L. Manley, "Where Are They Now? Prodigy," *New Yorker*, Dec. 25, 1937.

165 **"began, in an American way":** James Q. Whitman, "The Two Western Cultures of Privacy: Dignity Versus Liberty," 113 *Yale Law Journal* 1151 (2003).

165 **It started at the trial level:** *Sidis v. F-R Publ'g Corp.*, 34 F. Supp. 19 (S.D.N.Y. 1938).

165 **On appeal, the three-judge panel:** *Sidis v. F-R Publ'g Corp.*, 113 F.2d 806 (2d Cir. 1940).

166 **The Supreme Court voted not to hear:** *Sidis v. F-R Publ'g Corp.*, 311 U.S. 711 (1940).

166 **Brandeis had retired from the Court:** "Brandeis Quits; Roosevelt Will Pick 4th Jurist," *Chicago Tribune*, Feb. 14, 1939 (stating that on February 13, 1939, Justice Brandeis announced his retirement, effective immediately).

166 **"A free press stands":** *Grosjean v. Am. Press Co. Inc.*, 297 U.S. 233 (1936).

166 **Newspapers enthusiastically covered the pro-press court:** *See, e.g.,* "W. J. Sidis Loses in $150,000 Suit," *Portsmouth (N.H.) Herald*, July 23, 1940 (recounting the appellate court decision); "No Privacy for Prodigy: High Court Refuses to Grant Seclusion Thirty Years After," *New York Times*, Dec. 17, 1940.

166 **"Life again made a mockery":** "Former Child Prodigy Fails in Effort to Guard Privacy," *Boston Daily Globe*, Dec. 17, 1940.

166 **"without justifiable motives or good ends":** Wallace, *Prodigy*, 265.

166 **In 1944, he won that case, in effect:** Wallace, *Prodigy*, 269 (while there appears to be no record of the amount, some put the figure at $600); *see also* Bates, "The Prodigy and the Press" (putting the amount at $3,000).

166 **"I feel that it was at last":** Sidis to "Friend," April 10, 1944, www.sidis.net.

167 **Newspaper headlines announcing his death:** "Mental Genius Who Gave Up Thinking Dies," *Chicago Daily Tribune*, July 18, 1944; "Intellectual Genius Dies, Obscure, Broke," *Burlington (Vt.) Free Press*, July 18, 1944; "W. J. Sidis, Former Child Prodigy, Dies Destitute at 46," *Boston Daily Globe*, July 17, 1944.

167 **focused on Sidis's "career":** "W. J. Sidis, Former Child Prodigy, Dies Destitute at 46."

167 **"William Sidis had one great cause":** Shirley S. Smith, letter to the editor, *Boston Daily Globe*, July 22, 1944.

167 **newspapers that had dogged him:** William Aronoff, letter to the editor, *Christian Science Monitor*, July 31, 1944.

167 **"once a public figure":** Thurber, *Years with Ross*, 211.

167 **"forever celebrated":** Thurber, *Years with Ross*, 210.

167 **"vital legal right":** Ernst and Schwartz, *Privacy*, xiii.

167 **"declin[ing] to report events":** Ernst, *So Far So Good*, 51.

168 **Ernst would say that he loved Brandeis:** Morris L. Ernst, letter to the editor, *Commentary*, Jan. 1949.

168 **whenever he touched a lamp:** Ernst, *Best Is Yet . . .* , 25–26.

CHAPTER THIRTEEN: BODIES AND BREATHING SPACE

169 **leather-masked murderess:** *New York Daily News*, Jan. 13, 1928. Even back then, ethics suggested that publications publish such imagery only if the pictures served some instructive purpose, such as a spur to face reality or find a cure for a modern plague. Vitray, Mills, and Ellard, *Pictorial Journalism*, 388.

169 **violation of journalism ethics:** *See, e.g.,* Joe Hight and Frank Smyth, *Tragedies and Journalists* (2003), 5 (suggesting that journalists ask themselves "whether the images are pertinent or will do unnecessary harm" to individuals within the community).

170 **"Though we can see nothing":** *Winters v. New York*, 333 U.S. 507 (1948).

170 **Hutchins Commission:** Commission on Freedom of the Press, *A Free and Responsible Press* (1947), 80.

170 **speech that embarrasses doesn't lose protection:** *NAACP v. Claiborne Hardware Co.*, 458 U.S. 886 (1982).

170 **speech that offends can't be suppressed:** *FCC v. Pacifica Found.*, 438 U.S. 726 (1978).

170 **First Amendment requires adequate breathing space:** *Hustler Magazine v. Falwell*, 485 U.S. 46 (1988).

170 **press responsibility can't be legislated:** *Miami Herald Publ'g v. Tornillo*, 418 U.S. 241 (1974).

171 **a whopping 72 percent of Americans:** Megan Brenan, "Americans' Trust in Mass Media Edges Down to 41%," Gallup, Sept. 26, 2019 (explaining that in 1976, 72 percent of Americans said that they trusted the media).

171 *Cox Broadcasting v. Cohn*: *Cox Broadcasting v. Cohn*, 420 U.S. 469 (1975).

171 **"Members of the press":** *Oklahoma Publi'g Co. v. District Court*, 430 U.S. 308 (1977).

172 **"If the information is lawfully obtained":** *Smith v. Daily Mail Publi'g Co.*, 443 U.S. 97 (1979).

172 *Florida Star v. B.J.F.:* *Florida Star v. B.J.F.*, 491 U.S. 524 (1989).

173 **"full agency disclosure":** S. Rep. No. 813, 89th Cong., 1st Sess., 3 (1965).

173 **presumed open to the public:** *See, e.g.,* Illinois freedom-of-information statutory language, 5 Ill. Comp. Stat. Ann. 140/1 and 140/1.2 ("the people of this State have a right to full disclosure of information relating to the decisions, policies, procedures, rules, standards, and other aspects of government activity that affect the conduct of government and the lives of any or all of the people" and "all records in the custody or possession of a public body are presumed to be open to inspection or copying").

173 **33 percent of the public was worried:** Charles Piller, "Privacy in Peril," *MacWorld*, July 1993. It put the rate in the 1970s at "about a third of those polled."

173 **might be shared and published:** *See, e.g.,* Mayer, *Rights of Privacy*, xiii–xiv, linking privacy worries with the Supreme Court decision in the Pentagon Papers case and public awareness that their personal data was in the hands of the government and might therefore be published without liability.

174 **Ken Starr . . . suggested with worry:** Ken Starr, "Thursday Luncheon Session," *A.L.I. Proceedings*, May 18, 1989.

174 **"on one occasion, the President inserted a cigar":** Kenneth Starr, *The Starr Report: The Official Report of the Independent Counsel's Investigation of the President* (1998), 18.

174 **One book about Supreme Court decisions:** Hachten, *Supreme Court on Freedom of the Press*, viii–ix.

174 **the press had but two limitations:** Chenery, *Freedom of the Press*, 65 (suggesting specifically that "subject to the laws of libel, citizens may write or say what they please").

174 **"the right of privacy is not a major impediment":** Pember, *Mass Media Law*, 211.

174 **privacy was dead:** "Is Privacy Dead?," *Newsweek*, July 27, 1970.

175 **sexual privacy was dying:** Frank Trippett, "What's Happening to Sexual Privacy," *Look*, Oct. 20, 1970.

175 **"clear that the news media":** "Jousts Without Winners," *Time*, July 6, 1987.

175 **"right to be let alone had disappeared":** Joshua Quittner, "Invasion of Privacy," *Time*, Aug. 25, 1997.

175 **solidified the shift against privacy:** *Bartnicki v. Vopper*, 532 U.S. 514 (2001).

175 **"Our Bill of Rights assures the press freedom" . . . is the way:** American Society of Newspaper Editors, *Problems of Journalism: Proceedings of the 1964 Convention*, 53.

176 **privacy-promoting language:** This is especially interesting in light of a recent empirical study showing that modern Supreme Court justices have more often written about the press in a negative light. RonNell Andersen Jones and Sonja R. West, "The U.S. Supreme Court's Characterizations of the Press: An Empirical Study," 100 *North Carolina Law Review* ___ (2022).

176 *Beauharnais v. Illinois*: *Beauharnais v. Illinois*, 343 U.S. 250 (1952).

176 *Sweezy v. New Hampshire*: *Sweezy v. New Hampshire*, 354 U.S. 234 (1957).

176 *Watkins v. United States*: *Watkins v. United States*, 354 U.S. 178 (1957).

176 *NAACP v. Alabama*: *NAACP v. Alabama ex rel. Patterson*, 357 U.S. 349 (1958).

176 *Mapp v. Ohio*: *Mapp v. Ohio*, 367 U.S. 643 (1961).

176 *New York Times v. Sullivan*: *New York Times v. Sullivan*, 376 U.S. 254 (1964).

177 *Garrison v. Louisiana*: *Garrison v. Louisiana*, 379 U.S. 64, 72 (1964).

177 *Griswold v. Connecticut*: *Griswold v. Connecticut*, 381 U.S. 479 (1965).

177 **"respect for the inviolability":** *Tehan v. United States*, 382 U.S. 406 (1966) (internal quotation marks omitted; the quotation is from a footnote in the majority opinion).

177 **Sam Sheppard case:** *Sheppard v. Maxwell*, 384 U.S. 333 (1966).

177 *Time v. Hill*: *Time v. Hill*, 385 U.S. 374 (1967).

177 **"Fuck the Draft" jacket:** *Cohen v. California*, 403 U.S. 15 (1971).

177 *Rosenbloom v. Metromedia*: *Rosenbloom v. Metromedia*, 403 U.S. 29 (1971).

178 **Pentagon Papers case:** *New York Times v. United States*, 403 U.S. 713 (1971).

178 *Branzburg v. Hayes*: *Branzburg v. Hayes*, 408 U.S. 665 (1972).

178 *Doe v. McMillan*: *Doe v. McMillan*, 412 U.S. 306 (1973).

178 *Roe v. Wade*: *Roe v. Wade*, 410 U.S. 113 (1973).

179 **for private reading:** *Stanley v. Georgia*, 394 U.S. 557 (1969).

179 **"in the penumbras of the Bill of Rights":** Jill Lepore points out that women, not mentioned in the Constitution, had to write themselves into it by way of analogy and that Roe's attorney "was willing to use any kind of argument the court would accept," including privacy. Lepore, *These Truths*.

179 *United States v. Nixon*: *United States v. Nixon*, 418 U.S. 683 (1974).

179 *Nixon v. Administrator of General Services*: *Nixon v. Adm'r of Gen. Servs.*, 433 U.S. 425 (1977).

179 *Nixon v. Warner Communications*: *Nixon v. Warner Commc'ns*, 435 U.S. 589 (1978).

180 **released all portions of the tapes:** Christopher Goffard and Paloma Esquivel, "Nixon's Final Tapes," *Los Angeles Times*, Aug. 22, 2013.

180 *Time v. Firestone*: *Time v. Firestone*, 424 U.S. 448 (1976).

180 *Paul v. Davis*: *Paul v. Davis*, 424 U.S. 693 (1976).

180 *Air Force v. Rose*: *Dep't of Air Force v. Rose*, 425 U.S. 352 (1976).

180 *Nebraska Press Association v. Stuart*: *Neb. Press Ass'n v. Stuart*, 427 U.S. 539 (1976).

180 **human cannonball act:** *Zacchini v. Scripps-Howard Broad. Co.*, 433 U.S. 562 (1977).

180 *Whalen v. Roe*: *Whalen v. Roe*, 429 U.S. 589 (1977).

181 **"not like animals in a zoo":** *Houchins v. KQED*, 438 U.S. 1 (1978).

181 **access to ordinary criminal trials:** *Richmond Newspapers v. Virginia*, 448 U.S. 555 (1980).

181 **privacy interests of victims:** The Court suggested that a trial judge weigh the victim's age, the nature of the crime, the victim's psychological state, and more. *Globe Newspaper v. Superior Court for the County of Norfolk*, 457 U.S. 596 (1982).

181 **or potential jurors:** *Press-Enterprise Co. v. Superior Court of Cal.*, 464 U.S. 501 (1984).

181 *Landmark Communications v. Virginia*: *Landmark Commc'ns v. Virginia*, 435 U.S. 829 (1978).

181 **"Filthy Words":** *FCC v. Pacifica Found.*, 438 U.S. 726 (1978).

181 *Herbert v. Lando*: *Herbert v. Lando*, 441 U.S. 153 (1979).

181 **68 percent of Americans expressed concern:** Piller, "Privacy in Peril."

181 **Kissinger had privacy:** *Kissinger v. Reporters Comm. for Freedom of the Press*, 445 U.S. 136 (1980).

181 *Seattle Times v. Rhinehart*: *Seattle Times v. Rhinehart*, 467 U.S. 20 (1984).

181 **"no public issue":** *Dun & Bradstreet v. Greenmoss Builders*, 472 U.S. 749 (1985).

181 *Hazelwood v. Kuhlmeier*: Hazelwood School Dist. v. Kuhlmeier, 484 U.S. 260 (1988).

182 *Hustler Magazine v. Falwell*: Hustler Magazine v. Falwell, 485 U.S. 46 (1988).

182 **"a special benefit of the privacy":** *Frisby v. Schultz*, 487 U.S. 474 (1988).

182 **trash bags:** *California v. Greenwood*, 486 U.S. 35 (1988).

182 **so-called rap sheets:** *U.S. Dep't of Justice v. Reporters Comm. for Freedom of the Press*, 489 U.S. 749 (1989).

182 **confidentiality to a source:** *Cohen v. Cowles Media*, 501 U.S. 663 (1991).

182 **so-called ride alongs:** *Wilson v. Layne*, 526 U.S. 603 (1999).

182 *Lawrence v. Texas*: Lawrence v. Texas, 539 U.S. 588 (2003).

183 **Vince Foster autopsy photos:** *Nat'l Archives and Records Admin. v. Favish*, 541 U.S. 157 (2004).

183 *Snyder v. Phelps*: Snyder v. Phelps, 562 U.S. 443 (2011).

183 *NASA v. Nelson*: NASA v. Nelson, 562 U.S. 134 (2011).

183 **tracking through cell phone towers:** *Carpenter v. United States*, 138 S. Ct. 2206 (2018).

183 **privacies found on cell phones:** *Riley v. California*, 573 U.S. 373 (2014).

184 **"There *is* a zone of privacy":** *Cox Broadcasting v. Cohn*, 420 U.S. 469 (1975) (emphasis added).

184 **"we do not hold that truthful publication":** *Florida Star v. B.J.F.*, 491 U.S. 524 (1989).

185 **popular newspaper database:** Search done on newspapers.com, a database of "20,700+ newspapers from the 1700s–2000s," showing privacy mentioned 468,000 times.

185 **the facts danced:** "Making Facts Dance" is a chapter in Kerrane and Yagoda, *Art of Fact*.

185 **stone-block bastille:** "A New Look at Bridgewater," *Boston Globe*, Sept. 30, 1967.

186 **"material needs":** Richard A. Powers, "Inmates Stage Follies," *Boston Globe*, Oct. 3, 1965.

186 **"stir up community interest":** Sara Davidson, "N.Y. Justice Denies Bridgewater Film Ban," *Boston Globe*, Sept. 29, 1967.

186 **at election time:** "New Look at Bridgewater."

186 **Wiseman didn't film the inmate Albert DeSalvo:** Ray Richard, "Producer Denies Film Editing Pact," *Boston Globe*, Oct. 10, 1967.

186 **releases from about a hundred of the competent:** David B. Wilson, "Producer of 'Titicut' Denies Doublecross," *Boston Globe*, Oct. 25, 1967.

186 **hottest ticket:** Sara Davidson, "'Titicut Follies' Switches Moods," *Boston Globe*, Sept. 29, 1967 (noting that several hundred people waited in line in the rain even after all tickets had been distributed).

187 **"public institutions in a democracy":** "Ask Fred," *Independent Lens*, accessed Jan. 24, 2006.

187 **The day of its premiere:** "State Trying to Halt N.Y. Showing of Film of Bridgewater Inmates," *Boston Globe*, Sept. 28, 1967.

187 **"extremely intimate and confidential situations":** "And Some Cross-Purposes," *Boston Globe*, Sept. 30, 1967.

187 **hired the Morris Ernst law firm:** Davidson, "N.Y. Justice Denies Bridgewater Film Ban."

187 **he won a temporary restraining order:** "Court Retains Ban on Movie on Bridgewater," *Boston Globe*, Sept. 26, 1967.

187 **"Where the hell are the liberals":** Ray Richard, "House Asks U.S. to Ban Titicut Follies," *Boston Globe*, Oct. 18, 1967.

187 **American Civil Liberties Union had represented:** Wilson, "Producer of 'Titicut' Denies Doublecross."

187 **"civil liberties on both sides":** "Civil Liberties Union Postpones Stand on 'Follies,'" *Boston Globe*, Oct. 29, 1967.

187 **revenge porn:** *See, e.g.*, Anne Flaherty, "'Revenge Porn' Victims Press for New Laws," *Danville (Ky.) Advocate-Messenger*, Nov. 17, 2013 (suggesting that the ACLU had successfully fought and watered down a revenge porn bill in California and quoting an ACLU attorney who argued that if a woman shared her image willingly with another, constitutional issues would be raised upon the other's later publication of the photo).

187 **"the control individuals have":** The language was taken from the national ACLU website in 2020.

188 **"nightmare of ghoulish obscenities":** Joseph M. Harvey and Ray Richard, "Court Upholds 'Titicut' Ban," *Boston Globe*, Jan. 5, 1968.

188 **mostly endorsed that ban:** *Commonwealth v. Wiseman*, 249 N.E.2d 610 (Mass. 1969).

188 **And some people argued:** Joseph Harvey, "Rights to Privacy in Kennedy Case," *Boston Globe*, Oct. 9, 1969.

189 **justices voted not to hear:** *Wiseman v. Massachusetts*, 398 U.S. 960 (1970), dissent from denial of certiorari by Justices Harlan, Douglas, and Brennan.

189 **"No amount of 'free debate'":** *Commonwealth v. Wiseman*, Reply Brief for Petitioners, 1969 WL 120223 (1969).

189 **only if Wiseman blurred out the faces:** Irene Sege, "Court Eases 22-Year Ban on 'Titicut Follies,'" *Boston Globe*, Sept. 29, 1989.

189 **"not a film about faceless people":** Sege, "Court Eases 22-Year Ban on 'Titicut Follies.'"

189 **So Wiseman refused:** Dana Kennedy, "Film Maker to Appeal Blurred Decision on 'Titicut Follies,'" *Berkshire (Mass.) Eagle*, Sept. 30, 1989.

189 **could be seen by the general public:** "Long-Banned 'Titicut Follies' Can Now Be Shown, Judge Rules," *Berkshire (Mass.) Eagle*, Aug. 2, 1991.

190 **"I don't flatly reject":** David Mills, "Restrictions Lifted on 'Titicut Follies,'" *Philadelphia Inquirer*, Aug. 3, 1991.

190 **Warren and Brandeis privacy tort was dead:** Diane L. Zimmerman, "Requiem for a Heavyweight: A Farewell to Warren and Brandeis's Privacy Tort," 68 *Cornell Law Review* 291 (1983).

190 **Constitution was a "nearly insurmountable" barrier:** Bezanson, Cranberg, and Soloski, *Libel Law and the Press*, 115.

190 **"The American press has never been more free":** Abrams is quoted in Wagman, *First Amendment Book*, xiii.

190 **Some ads featured a single prominent image:** *Titicut Follies* ad, *Los Angeles Weekly*, Oct. 17, 1991.

CHAPTER FOURTEEN: REAL CHUTZPAH, REAL HOUSEWIVES

191 *An American Family*: "Family Documentary Appears Thursday," *Hutchinson (Kans.) News*, Jan. 5, 1973.

191 **Camera-enhanced** *Cops*: Tracie Cone, "Fox Turns Traffic Stop into Network Event," *Miami Herald*, Feb. 15, 1989.

191 **most cringe-worthy snippets:** "'Candid Camera' Back on CBS in One-Hour Special," *Elmira (N.Y.) Star-Gazette*, Jan. 3, 1990.

191 *Unsolved Mysteries*: "Prime Time: Wednesday, January 3, 1990," *Elmira (N.Y.) Star-Gazette*, Jan. 3, 1990.

191 **mushroomed into a new genre:** Linda Shrieves, "'Firefighters' Is Latest Entry in the Reality-TV Craze," *Odessa (Tex.) American*, Feb. 7, 1993 (internal quotation marks omitted).

191 **entangled in the wreckage:** *Shulman v. Grp. W Prods.*, 59 Cal. Rptr. 2d 434 (Cal. Ct. App. 1996).

191 **she thought she was dreaming:** *Shulman v. Grp. W Prods.*, 955 P.2d 469 (Cal. 1998).

192 *On Scene: Emergency Response*: Susan King, "Daytime Play: NBC Retells the Truth, KCAL Holds a Trump Card," *Los Angeles Times*, Sept. 9. 1990.

192 **"sensational, sometimes fatal car wrecks":** Zan Dubin, "'On Scene': Life, Death, and Roving Minicams," *Los Angeles Times*, Dec. 14, 1990.

192 **"delirious head-injury patient":** The California Supreme Court opinion suggests that the syndicated episode featuring the Shulman accident aired on September 29, 1990. That week, the description in the *San Bernardino County Sun* television listings describes one of the stories in the episode as "an auto accident," but the *Miami Herald* describes one of the stories as "delirious head-injury patient resists treatment." *See* "Saturday TV Highlights," *San Bernardino County Sun*, Sept. 29, 1990; "Daily Listings," *Miami Herald*, Sept. 30, 1990.

192 **"I was not at my best":** *Shulman*, 955 P.2d 469.

192 **public did in fact want to watch:** Shrieves, "'Firefighters' Is Latest Entry in the Reality-TV Craze."

192 **"All media that uses a camera":** Dubin, "'On Scene': Life, Death, and Roving Minicams."

192 **"There is no social value":** Maura Dolan, "Justices Hear Case Involving Media and Privacy Issues," *Los Angeles Times*, March 4, 1998 (internal quotation marks omitted).

193 **Media lawyers argued in turn:** Maura Dolan, "The Right to Know vs. the Right to Privacy," *Los Angeles Times*, Aug. 1, 1997.

193 **"any injury [they] suffered":** This is language from the release for the hidden-camera program *Betty White's Off Their Rockers* (on file with author).

193 **The California Supreme Court began its decision:** *Shulman v. Grp. W Prods.*, 955 P.2d 469 (Cal. 1998) (quoting Samuel D. Warren and Louis D. Brandeis, "The Right to Privacy," 4 *Harvard Law Review* 193 (1890)).

194 **in such cases was "well-settled":** Defendants' Petition for Review, *Shulman v. Grp. W Prods.*, 1997 WL 33630698 (1997).

194 **"upheld many of the long-established principles"**: Manny Fernandez, "Tabloid TV Dealt Blow in Ruling on Privacy," *San Francisco Chronicle*, June 2, 1998.

194 **"The law is literally unfolding"**: Dolan, "The Right to Know vs. the Right to Privacy."

194 **pants unwittingly unzipped:** *Neff v. Time Inc.*, 406 F. Supp. 858 (W.D. Pa. 1976).

194 **wearing only a dish towel:** *Cape Publ'ns Inc. v. Bridges*, 423 So. 2d 426 (Fla. Dist. Ct. App. 1982).

195 **involuntary sterilization:** *Howard v. Des Moines Reg. & Trib. Co.*, 283 N.W.2d 289 (Iowa 1979).

195 **psychiatric history:** *Gilbert v. Med. Econ. Co.*, 665 F.2d 305 (10th Cir. 1981).

195 **secret adoption:** See *Hall v. Post*, 372 S.E.2d 711 (N.C. 1988).

195 **incestuous birth:** *Anonsen v. Donahue*, 857 S.W.2d 700 (Tex. Ct. App. 1993).

195 **victim of a rape:** *Ross v. Midwest Commc'ns Inc.*, 870 F.2d 271 (5th Cir. 1989).

195 **called it all privileged conduct:** *Howell v. N.Y. Post Co. Inc.*, 612 N.E.2d 699 (N.Y. 1993).

195 **basketball players' lousy grades:** *Bilney v. Evening Star Newspaper Co.*, 406 A.2d 652 (Md. Ct. Spec. App. 1979).

195 **"dispel the false public opinion"**: *Sipple v. Chron. Publ'g Co.*, 201 Cal. Rptr. 665 (Cal. Ct. App. 1984).

195 **Sipple had argued in broken:** Daryl Lembke, "Ford to Thank S.F. Man Who Deflected Gun," *Los Angeles Times*, Sept. 26, 1975.

195 **rape had been videotaped by her attacker:** *Anderson v. Blake*, 2006 WL 314447 (W.D. Okla. Feb. 9, 2006), *aff'd sub nom. Anderson v. Suiters*, 499 F.3d 1228 (10th Cir. 2007).

195 **"By airing the videotape"**: *Anderson*, 499 F.3d 1228 (citing *Gilbert v. Med. Econ. Co.*, 665 F.2d 305 (10th Cir. 1981)).

196 **"Courts do not have license"**: *Howard v. Des Moines Reg. & Trib. Co.*, 283 N.W.2d 289 (Iowa 1979).

196 **"a newspaper's privilege to publish news"**: *Cape Publ'ns Inc. v. Bridges*, 423 So. 2d 426 (Fla. Dist. Ct. App. 1982).

196 **"engage in after-the-fact judicial 'blue-penciling'"**: *Anderson v. Blake*, 2006 WL 314447 (W.D. Okla. Feb. 9, 2006), *aff'd sub nom. Anderson v. Suiters*, 499 F.3d 1228 (10th Cir. 2007).

196 **protections given publishers:** See, e.g., Teeter, Le Duc, and Loving, *Law of Mass Communications*.

196 **"when a person becomes involved"**: Goldstein, *Associated Press Stylebook and Libel Manual*, 292.

196 **Outsiders who questioned the media's right:** Burl Osborne, foreword to Wagman, *First Amendment Book*, ix. The book is dedicated to Justice Brennan, who "worked tirelessly in the defense of freedom of expression and protecting the rights of individuals under the First Amendment."

196 **right to sell T-shirts:** *Peckham v. New England Newspapers Inc.*, 865 F. Supp. 2d 127 (D. Mass. 2012).

196 **anonymous commenters:** *In re Indiana Newspapers Inc.*, 963 N.E.2d 534 (Ind. Ct. App. 2012).

196 **state university undergraduate applications:** *Chi. Trib. Co. v. Univ. of Ill. Bd. of Trs.*, 781 F. Supp. 2d 672 (N.D. Ill. 2011) (the trial court agreed with the *Tribune*, but the request was never renewed by the newspaper).

196 **collecting from police the mug shots:** The *Chicago Tribune*'s "Mugshots in the News" for December 18, 2018, for example, featured people arrested for theft and burglary. The *Tribune* has since stopped publishing this feature.

197 **"See the Mug Shot, Guess the Crime"**: Jessica Roy, "Quiz: See the Mug Shot, Guess the Crime," *New York: Intelligencer*, Dec. 5, 2014.

197 **DOOMED, the *Post* cover read:** *New York Post*, Dec. 4, 2012 (captioned "Ki Suk Han of Queens, hurled to the tracks, tries to climb to safety yesterday as a train bears down on him in Midtown. He was fatally struck seconds later.").

197 **survivors forever "haunted" by that image:** Laura Collins and Meghan Keneally, "'He Wouldn't Leave Me Alone So I Pushed Him': Chilling Confession of Suspect Who Pushed Man onto Subway Tracks Comes as His Widow Tells How She and Daughter Are Haunted by Photos of Her Husband's Final Seconds," *Daily Mail*, Dec. 5, 2012.

197 **"passion for peeping"**: James Poniewozik, "Television: We Like to Watch," *Time*, June 26, 2000.

197 **"a scandal press corps"**: Gardner, Csikszentmihalyi, and Damon, *Good Work*, 135 (quoting the *Washington Post* reporter Bob Woodward).

197 **"the weird, the stupid, the coarse"**: Dave Ranney, "Watergate Journalist Says Media Losing Public Trust," *Lawrence (Kans.) Journal-World*, April 16, 2005 (quoting the *Washington Post* reporter Carl Bernstein) (internal quotation marks omitted).

197 **"The First Amendment's guarantees"**: Lewis, *Freedom for the Thought That We Hate*, 80.

198 **"it is beyond doubt"**: *Lemerond v. Twentieth Century Fox Film Corp.*, 2008 WL 918579 (S.D.N.Y. March 31, 2008).

198 **trust in it had fallen:** Gallup, "Americans' Trust in Mass Media Sinks to New Low," gallup.com, Sept. 14, 2016 (finding that only "32% say they have 'a great deal' or 'a fair amount' of trust" in media).

198 **privacy interests had risen:** An Equifax poll in 1990 showed that 79 percent of people believed that privacy belonged in the Constitution as a fundamental right. Equifax, "Consumers in the Information Age," Roper Center for Public Opinion Research, Jan. 11, 1990–Feb. 11, 1990 (survey by Louis Harris & Associates and Cornell University).

198 **Mentions of the right to privacy in court decisions:** This, of course, would include mentions of the right to privacy in situations outside the tort context as well, including Fourth Amendment search-and-seizure criminal matters, but the numbers are interesting nevertheless.

198 **"not only relevant, but essential to the narrative":** *Shulman v. Grp. W Prods.*, 955 P.2d 469 (Cal. 1998).

199 **"a major defeat for media corporations":** "Court Allows Lawsuit over Newsgathering," *Sheboygan (Wis.) Press*, June 2, 1998 (quoting Shulman's attorney Antony Stuart) (internal quotation marks omitted).

199 **"For the legitimate news media":** Fernandez, "Tabloid TV Dealt Blow in Ruling on Privacy" (quoting the media attorney Neil Shapiro) (internal quotation marks omitted).

199 *The World's Nastiest Neighbors:* Brian Lowry, "Hidden Cameras Move In," *Los Angeles Times*, Oct. 17, 1998; *see also* Jim Rutenberg, "TV Notes: More Reality," *New York Times*, May 24, 2000 (stating that UPN picked up *The World's Nastiest Neighbors* after it was refused by Fox).

200 **"may be offensive to some":** Rutenberg, "TV Notes: More Reality."

CODA PART II: IT DOES NOT FOLLOW

201 **"I should tremble":** Wingate, *Views and Interviews on Journalism*, 353–54. The quotation is from an interview with David G. Croly, author of *Miscegenation: The Theory of the Blending of the Races, Applied to the American White Man and Negro* (1864).

201 **CYBERPORN cover:** *Time*, July 3, 1995.

201 **"there is in this vast world":** 141 Cong. Rec. 8469 (1995) (statement of Rep. Christopher Cox).

201 **"deter online porn merchants":** J. W. Huttig, "Putting Porn in Its Place?," *PC Novice*, July 1995.

201 **"ban indecent":** "Plan Would Let Parents Control Internet Access," *Los Angeles Times*, June 22, 1995.

202 **"No provider or user":** 141 Cong. Rec. 8447 (1995).

202 **"We want to make sure that everyone":** 141 Cong. Rec. 8469 (1995) (statement of Rep. Christopher Cox).

202 **Others in Congress agreed:** 141 Cong. Rec. 8471 (1995) (statement of Rep. Bob Goodlatte).

203 **"both the private sector and the public interest":** Presidential statement on signing the Telecommunications Act of 1996, 32 Weekly Comp. Pres. Doc. 218 (Feb. 8, 1996).

203 **oddly unplugged time:** For a history of Section 230, see Kosseff, *Twenty-Six Words That Created the Internet.*

203 **20 percent of households:** Kathleen Yanity, "Learning to Live on the World Wide Web," *Providence Journal*, March 10, 1996.

203 **less than 10 percent of Americans:** Doug Abrahms, "Exon Move on Internet Porn Grabs Lawmakers," *Washington Times*, July 19, 1995.

203 **"like a gigantic electronic filing cabinet":** Dana Tofig, "Fire Department's Home Page to Debut on World Wide Web," *Hartford Courant*, Feb. 9, 1996.

203 **"lets people access information":** L. A. Lorek, "Web Sites Offer Who, What, When, Wares—Hundreds of Businesses from Solo Entrepreneurs to Corporations in S. Florida Are Using the Internet to Strut and Sell Their Stuff," *South Florida Sun-Sentinel* (Fort Lauderdale), Jan. 1, 1996.

203 **Even Congressman Cox had suggested:** 141 Cong. Rec. 8469 (1995) (statement of Rep. Christopher Cox).

203 **"sites with sounds":** Kate McKee, "Sites with Sounds Are Proliferating on the Internet," *Tulsa World*, Feb. 9, 1996.

203 **"gradually catching the attention":** Yanity, "Learning to Live on the World Wide Web."

203 **most important invention since Velcro:** Robert Grede, "For Getting Message Out, Web Site Is Cutting Edge," *Milwaukee Journal-Sentinel*, Feb. 12, 1996.

204 **"One reason the Web is so great":** Evan Ramstad, "Big Internet News of '95: World Wide Web Got Wider; Part of Web's Popularity Stems from Its Flexibility and Lack of Rules," *Austin American-Statesman*, Jan. 1, 1996.

204 **NO ONE INVITED HER:** "No One Invited Her," thedirty.com, Jan. 20, 2011.

205 **"In a word—NO":** "Legal FAQs," thedirty.com, thedirty.com/legal-faqs/.

205 **$10,000 a month:** Kashmir Hill, "The Dirty Business: How Gossipmonger Nik Richie of TheDirty.com Stays Afloat," *Forbes*, Nov. 11, 2010, suggesting that The Dirty's creator was "cagey" about his income from the site, but that he had purchased his fiancée a $130,000 engagement ring.

205 **slept with every Cincinnati Bengals football player:** *Jones v. Dirty World Ent. Recordings LLC*, 755 F.3d 398 (6th Cir. 2014).

205 **"You dug your own grave":** *Jones*, 755 F.3d 398.

206 **"grounded in core First Amendment standards":** Brief for Amicus Curiae Online Service Providers, *Jones v. Dirty World Ent. Recordings LLC*, 2013 WL 6221286 (2013) (filing on behalf of Advance Publications, Amazon, Avvo, *BuzzFeed*, CNN, and *Gawker*, among others).

206 **"threaten[ed] the broad diversity":** Motion for Leave to File Amicus Brief, *Jones v. Dirty World Ent. Recordings LLC*, 2013 WL 11105898 (2013) (filing by the ACLU of Kentucky, among others, in support of defendants-appellants).

206 **Facebook, Google, Microsoft:** Brief for Amici Curiae, *Jones v. Dirty World Ent. Recordings LLC*, 2013 WL 6409350 (2013) (filing in support of defendants-appellants AOL Inc., eBay Inc., Facebook Inc., Google Inc., LinkedIn Corp., Microsoft Corp., Tumblr Inc., Twitter Inc., and Zynga Inc.).

206 **"Congress enacted [Section 230] to preserve":** *Jones*, 755 F.3d 398.

206 **"home wrecking whore":** thedirty.com, Sept. 24, 2014 (deleted post on file with author). The title of this post identifies the subject by her full name.

206 **other websites that trafficked:** dirtyphonebook.com, March 25, 2010 (original post on file with author); juicycampus.com, Feb. 7, 2008 (original post on file with author); collegeacb.com, May 31, 2009 (original post on file with author); blipdar.com, April 25, 2009, and Oct. 18, 2011 (original posts on file with author); "Oh, Crap!," peopleofwalmart.com, Jan. 29, 2011. People of Walmart has remained an active website.

207 **earnings at $20,000 a month:** "'Revenge Porn' Website Founder Launching New 'Scary as S**t Venture,'" *Daily Mail*, Dec. 2. 2012.

207 **"Anyone have K——D——?":** This material is from the "College Bitches" link on a website that calls itself Anon, anonme.tv/cb, one that appears to be located outside the United States, even though "College Bitches" is United States focused. The women's full names appear in the requests for photographs.

207 **granted the website backpage.com immunity:** *Jane Doe No. 1 v. Backpage.com LLC*, 817 F.3d 12 (1st Cir. 2016).

207 **rising suicide rates, depression, and anxiety:** Howard K. Koh et al., "Confronting the Rise and Fall of U.S. Life Expectancy," 322 *Journal of the American Medical Association* 1963 (2019).

208 **Facebook's own damning internal assessment:** Georgia Wells, Jeff Horwitz, and Deepa Seetharaman, "Facebook Knows Instagram Is Toxic for Teen Girls, Company Documents Show," *Wall Street Journal*, Sept. 14, 2021.

208 **they would feel "kinda bad":** Mia, Comment to "No One Invited Her," thedirty.com, Jan. 20, 2011.

208 **"Let's be real for a second":** Camille Dodero, "Hunter Moore Makes a Living Screwing You," *Village Voice*, April 4, 2012.

208 **"encourages the unfettered and unregulated development":** *Batzel v. Smith*, 333 F.3d 1018 (9th Cir. 2003) *superseded by statute on other grounds.*

208 **"preserve [its] vibrant and competitive free market":** 47 U.S.C.A. § 230(b)(1)-(2) (2018).

208 **"offer a forum for a true diversity":** 47 U.S.C.A. § 230(a)(3) (2018) (emphasis added).

208 **"*educational* and *informational* resources":** 47 U.S.C.A. § 230(a)(1) (2018) (emphasis added).

208 **"harassment by means of computer":** 47 U.S.C.A. § 230(b)(5) (2018).

208 **"an American hero who saved the internet":** "Sarah Jones vs. Dirty World," thedirty.com, June 16, 2014.

CHAPTER FIFTEEN: MISS VERMONT, JUDGE MIKVA, AND THE WRESTLER

213 **"an inexperienced girl reacting":** The description is from a post titled "The Miss Vermont Story," accessed from tuckermax.com in September 2003. "The Miss Vermont Story," *Tucker Max*, www.tuckermax.com (PDF of post on file with author).

213 **"outside the bounds of all social norms"**: Bill Douthat, "Lurid Details Fuel Internet Privacy Duel," *Palm Beach (Fla.) Post*, June 16, 2003 (reporting that Max stated that he operates "outside the bounds of all social norms").

213 **"of people putting their lives"**: Douthat, "Lurid Details Fuel Internet Privacy Duel."

213 **"autobiographical account of their relationship"**: "Judge Orders Chicago Man to Take Beauty Queen's Name Off Web," *Pensacola News Journal*, June 3, 2003.

214 **"the time I had sex with a midget"**: Tucker Max, "The Midget Story: The Time I Had Sex with a Midget," *Tucker Max*, Aug. 28, 2019, www.tuckermax.com.

214 **"Tucker Tries Buttsex"**: Tucker Max, "Tucker Tries Buttsex; Hilarity Does Not Ensue," *Tucker Max*, Aug. 28, 2019, www.tuckermax.com.

214 *We're All Journalists Now*: Gant, *We're All Journalists Now.*

214 **deserved public accountability:** Notice of Removal, *Johnson v. Max*, No. 03-Civ-80515-Hurley/Lynch (S.D. Fla. June 6, 2003).

214 **one impassioned newspaper editorial:** Editorial, "Don't Chip Away at 1st Amendment," *Victoria (Tex.) Advocate*, June 15, 2003.

214 **another was headlined:** Howard Goodman, "Judge's Ruling Harms Our Freedom to Print Views," *South Florida Sun-Sentinel* (Fort Lauderdale), June 17, 2003.

214 **"the same principle generally applies":** Editorial, "Don't Chip Away at 1st Amendment."

214 **"even the disreputable":** Sam Hemingway, "Column: Sam Hemingway," *Burlington (Vt.) Free Press*, June 8, 2003.

215 **"cyberphobia":** Editorial, "Cyberphobia Gossip Dents First Amendment," *News-Journal* (Daytona Beach, Fla.), June 9, 2003.

215 **some blamed Miss Vermont:** Joe Bob Briggs, "Joe Bob's Week in Review," United Press International, May 9, 2003 ("Of course, NOBODY will read it now. Just say no, Katy").

215 **"but we hold the First Amendment":** Editorial, "Don't Chip Away at 1st Amendment."

215 **"It's not good manners":** Goodman, "Judge's Ruling Harms Our Freedom to Print Views."

215 **"I am proud that I was able":** "Delray Woman Drops Suit over Alleged Lies on Web," *South Florida Sun-Sentinel* (Fort Lauderdale), July 22, 2003.

215 **"If you read the briefs":** Tucker Max, "Case Dismissed," *Tucker Max*, www.tuckermax.com (PDF of post on file with author).

215 **"true free marketplace of ideas":** Brief for Amicus Curiae ACLU, *Johnson v. Max*, Case No. 03-80515-CIV-HURLEY (filed June 17, 2003).

215 **"Watch out!" he wrote:** Abner J. Mikva, "In My Opinion, Those Are Not Facts," 11 *Georgia State University Law Review* 291 (1995).

216 **"romantic" view of First Amendment rights:** Anna Stolley Persky, "50 Years After New York Times v. Sullivan, Do Courts Still Value Journalists' Watchdog Role?," *ABA Journal*, March 2014.

216 *Sports Illustrated* **was one:** *M.G. v. Time Warner Inc.*, 107 Cal. Rptr. 2d 504 (Cal. Ct. App. 2001).

216 **"A jury could find that a reasonable member":** *Green v. Chi. Tribune*, 675 N.E.2d 249 (Ill. App. Ct. 1996).

217 **"I love you, Calvin":** William Recktenwald and Colin McMahon, "Deadly End to a Deadly Year," *Chicago Tribune*, Jan. 1, 1992.

217 **"unlikely that an unmarried, professional woman":** *Benz v. Wash. Newspaper Grp.*, 2006 WL 2844896 (D.D.C. Sept. 29, 2006).

218 **Conradt told the tween:** Luke Dittrich, "Tonight on Dateline This Man Will Die," *Esquire*, Sept. 2007.

218 **"When these people came after him":** "The Shame Game," *Columbia Journalism Review*, Jan./Feb. 2007.

218 **judge ruled that Conradt's sister:** *Conradt v. NBC Universal Inc.*, 536 F. Supp. 2d 380 (S.D.N.Y. 2008).

219 **prove the actual malice necessary:** *Palin v. N.Y. Times Co.*, 940 F.3d 804 (2d Cir. 2019).

219 *Sullivan* **should be overturned:** Justice Thomas wrote this concurring in the denial of certiorari in *McKee v. Cosby*, 139 S. Ct. 675 (2019). No other justice joined him in the concurrence. Other justices have criticized *Sullivan*, however, including Justice Neil Gorsuch, who wrote a dissenting opinion in *Berisha v. Lawson*, 141 S. Ct. 2424 (2021) ("What started in 1964 with a decision to tolerate the occasional falsehood to ensure robust reporting by a comparative handful of print and broadcast outlets has evolved into an ironclad subsidy for the publication of falsehoods by means and on a scale previously unimaginable").

219 **"I do think," he wrote:** Denny Chin, "Privacy, Newsworthiness, and a View from the Bench," 93 *Tulane Law Review* 1079 (2019).

220 **"no 'legitimate purpose of disseminating news'":** *Toffoloni v. LFP Publ'g Grp.*, 572 F.3d 1201 (11th Cir. 2009).

220 **Gawker headlined its news story:** A. J. Daulerio, "Even for a Minute, Watching Hulk Hogan Have Sex in a Canopy Bed Is Not Safe for Work but Watch It Anyway," *Gawker*, Oct. 4, 2012 (article on file with author).

220 **flouting journalism's ethics codes:** Jeff Bercovici, "A Candid Conversation with Gawker's Nick Denton," *Playboy*, March 2014. This would include, Denton suggested, images of people engaging in sexual activity because such images would be beneficial for society.

221 **worldwide attention to a North Carolina teen:** *Araya v. Deep Dive Media*, 966 F. Supp. 2d 582 (W.D.N.C. 2013).

221 **"The Constitution does unambiguously accord":** John Cook, "A Judge Told Us to Take Down Our Hulk Hogan Sex Tape Post. We Won't," *Gawker*, April 25, 2013, www.gawker.com.

221 **Many commentators agreed:** *See, e.g.*, Alison Frankel, "Why Does Hulk Hogan Even Have a Case Against Gawker?," Reuters, March 14, 2016, www.blogs.reuters.com.

221 **A child under the age of four:** Charles Harder, "Hulk Hogan's Lead Lawyer Explains How His Team Beat 'Arrogant,' 'Defiant' Gawker," *Hollywood Reporter*, April 5, 2016.

221 **Shock-wave-inspired headlines:** Editorial, "First Amendment Trashed," *New York Daily News*, Aug. 19, 2016; Ken White, "Even the Loathsome Have Rights," *Los Angeles Times*, June 14, 2016.

221 **chilled the press:** *See* Fabio Bertoni, "The Stakes in Hulk Hogan's Gawker Lawsuit," *New Yorker*, March 23, 2016.

221 **"America has incomparable free-speech protections":** Margaret Sullivan, "Free Speech Is Precious. What's Happening with Gawker and Facebook Threaten It," *Washington Post*, May 29, 2016.

222 **a man who'd been outed by Gawker:** Alyssa Rosenberg, "A Sex Tape and an Empty Victory," *Tampa Bay Times*, March 11, 2018.

222 **case ultimately settled for $31 million:** Sydney Ember, "Gawker and Hulk Hogan Reach $31 Million Settlement," *New York Times*, Nov. 2, 2016.

222 **"Hulk Hogan Syndrome":** Paul Farhi, "Rolling Stone Verdict May Reflect Hostility Toward Media," *Washington Post*, Nov. 6, 2016.

222 **"First Amendment could no longer be invoked":** O'Neil, *First Amendment and Civil Liability*, x–xi.

222 **"As the ability to do harm":** *Welling v. Weinfeld*, 866 N.E.2d 1051 (Ohio 2007).

222 **National Football League player's medical chart:** *Pierre-Paul v. ESPN Inc.*, 2016 WL 4530884 (S.D. Fla. Aug. 29, 2016).

222 **Illinois driver's license database:** *Dalstrom v. Sun-Times Media LLC*, 777 F.3d 937 (7th Cir. 2015).

223 **Title IX complaints:** *Doe v. HarperCollins Publishers LLC*, 2018 WL 1174394 (N.D. Ill. March 6, 2018) (quoting *Haynes v. Alfred A. Knopf Inc.*, 8 F.3d 1222 (7th Cir. 1993)) (internal quotation marks omitted).

223 **The First 48:** *Smart v. City of Miami*, 740 Fed. App'x 952 (11th Cir. 2018).

223 **video from a fatal accident scene:** *Gonzalez v. Am. News & Info. Serv.*, 2018 WL 3383123 (Conn. Super. Ct. June 22, 2018) (quoting *Gleason v. Smolinski*, 125 A.3d 920 (Conn. 2015)) (internal quotation marks omitted).

223 **"falls outside the protection":** *Jackson v. Mayweather*, 217 Cal. Rptr. 3d 234 (Cal. Ct. App. 2017).

223 **"This is a unique crime":** *People v. Austin*, 155 N.E.3d 439 (Ill. 2019) (quoting *State v. VanBuren*, 214 A.3d 791 (Vt. 2019)) (internal quotations omitted).

224 **80 percent of people:** "Americans and Privacy: Concerned, Confused, and Feeling Lack of Control over Their Personal Information," Pew Research Center, Nov. 15, 2019.

CHAPTER SIXTEEN: GIRLS GONE WILD (PRIVACY IN PUBLIC)

225 **tens of millions of doorbells:** Drew Harwell, "Home-Security Cameras Have Become a Fruitful Resource for Law Enforcement—and a Fatal Risk," *Washington Post*, March 2, 2021 (estimating the number at somewhere in the millions). In 2020, some put the number at more than twenty million.

225 **"Millions of unsuspecting people":** Harwell, "Home-Security Cameras Have Become a Fruitful Resource for Law Enforcement."

226 **cameras look like weeds and sticks:** Eggers, *Circle*, 63.

226 **"If you've ever peed"**: Chelsea Brasted, "If You've Ever Peed Outside This New Orleans Bar, You May Have Been Caught on Camera," nola.com, June 3, 2019.

226 **"A is drunk on the public street"**: Restatement (Second) of Torts § 652B, cmt. b, cmt. c, illus. 6 (American Law Institute, 1977).

226 **"Fundamental respect for human dignity"**: *Shulman v. Grp. W Prods.*, 955 P.2d 469 (Cal. 1998).

226 **"It has now been affirmed"**: Maura Dolan, "News Media Ruled Liable for Undue Intrusion," *Los Angeles Times*, June 2, 1998 (quoting Antony Stuart, Shulman's lawyer) (internal quotation marks omitted).

226 **"the privacy that we enjoy"**: *Project Veritas Action Fund v. Rollins*, 982 F.3d 813 (1st Cir. 2020).

227 **"Even if photographs are accurate"**: *Roe v. McClellan*, 2009 WL 94014 (Cal. Ct. App. Jan. 15, 2009).

227 **"a variety of young women"**: *Padilla v. MRA Holding LLC*, 2004 WL 2988172 (Cal. App. Dec. 28, 2004).

227 **A rowdy Mardi Gras party**: *Capdeboscq v. Francis*, 2004 WL 463316 (E.D. La. March 10, 2004).

227 **waters on a public lake**: *Padilla*, 2004 WL 2988172.

227 **detaining a citizen-photographer**: *Frasier v. Evans*, 992 F.3d 1003 (10th Cir. 2021).

227 **"the objections of individuals"**: *Paff v. Ocean Cty. Prosecutor's Off.*, 192 A.2d 975 (N.J. 2018).

228 **"sheer morbidity and gossip"**: *Catsouras v. Dep't of Cal. Hwy. Patrol*, 104 Cal. Rptr. 3d 352 (Cal. App. 2010).

228 **"is wide of the mark"**: *Safari Club Int'l v. Rudolph*, 862 F.3d 1113 (9th Cir. 2017).

228 **"as the law now stands"**: William Safire, "The Great Unwatched," *New York Times*, Feb. 18, 2002.

228 **44 percent of people**: ABC News/Washington Post Poll, "Future Terrorist Attacks/Catholic Church/Watergate, Question USABCWP.061002.R09," Roper Center for Public Opinion Research, June 7–June 9, 2002.

229 **"Put the pen in your pocket"**: "16 Hour Voice Activated Recorder Pen," SpyGuy, www.spyguy.com.

229 **rock-shaped hidden cameras**: Xtreme Life RockCam Outdoor Hidden Camera and DVR with Remote Control, Amazon, accessed Feb. 18, 2021.

229 **facial recognition technology**: Kim Hart, "Facial Recognition Surges in Retail Stores," *Axios*, July 19, 2021.

229 **"smart contact lenses"**: Ina Fried, "How the Wearable Hardware Battle Is Shaping Up," *Axios*, July 2, 2021.

229 **"legal and etiquette issues"**: Mike Allen, "Debut Ina Fried Column: Your Smartphone Is Breaking Up," *Axios AM*, July 2, 2021.

229 **commercially available geolocation tracking data**: "Pillar Investigates: USCCB Gen Sec Burrill Resigns After Sexual Misconduct Allegations," pillarcatholic.com, July 20, 2021.

229 **"a structural failure"**: Shira Ovide, "The Nightmare of Our Snooping Phones," *New York Times*, July 21, 2021.

229 **front porch could indeed be a "private space"**: *King v. Paxton*, 576 S.W.3d 881 (Tex. App. 2019).

229 **In Europe, for example, a homeowner's camera**: Case C-212/13 *Ryneš v. Úřad pro ochranu osobních údajů*, ECLI:EU:C:2014:2428 (Dec. 11, 2014) ("The image of a person recorded by a camera constitutes personal data.").

229 **Prince William and Kate Middleton**: A court in France awarded them approximately $130,000 after *Closer* magazine published the photographs. Kim Willsher, "Court Awards Duchess of Cambridge Damages over Topless Photos," *Guardian*, Sept. 5, 2017.

230 **"fear or suspicion"**: *Bartnicki v. Vopper*, 532 U.S. 514 (2001), citing President's Commission on Law Enforcement and Administration of Justice, *The Challenge of Crime in a Free Society* (1967), 202.

230 **"a growth industry"**: Aspen Institute, "Justice Elena Kagan on Privacy," youtube.com, June 30, 2013.

230 **marshals would confiscate recording devices**: *See* Bob Herbert, "A Justice's Sense of Privilege," *New York Times*, April 12, 2004.

230 **"First Amendment right not to speak"**: "Understanding Justice Scalia," rcfp.org, Spring 2004.

230 **"profoundly disconcerting"**: Sotomayor, *My Beloved World*, ix–x.

230 **"veil of privacy"**: Sonia Sotomayor, "The Arthur Miller Freedom to Write Lecture," PEN America, May 5, 2013, www.pen.org (transcribed by Micah Zeno, on file with author); *see also* "Arthur Miller Freedom to Write Lecture: Sonia Sotomayor," youtube.com, May 13, 2013.

230 **"talk like girlfriends"**: Sotomayor, "Arthur Miller Freedom to Write Lecture."

230 **"the spear of an individual's individual freedom"**: Sotomayor, "Arthur Miller Freedom to Write Lecture."

CHAPTER SEVENTEEN: KATE NASH REDUX (PRIVACY IN DATA)

231 **"There are companies"**: "Federal Judge Speaks Out for First Time After Son's Murder," NBC 4 New York, Aug. 3, 2020, www.nbcnewyork.com.

231 **"home addresses, cellphone numbers"**: Sarah Lyall and Mark Landler, "Tabloid Hired Gun Tells of Shady Hunt for Meghan Markle Scoops," *New York Times*, March 18, 2021.

232 **that sort of information wasn't protected**: *See, e.g., Busse v. Motorola Inc.*, 813 N.E.2d 1013 (Ill. App. Ct. 2004).

233 **"In a single search"**: "TLOxp Social Media Basic Search and Comprehensive Report," TransUnion, www.tlo.com/social-media.

233 **available on the internet**: MyLife, www.mylife.com.

234 **California Consumer Privacy Act**: Cal. Civ. Code § 1798.100.

234 **"a global leader"**: This information is from Experian's website, www.experian.com.

235 **certain journalism websites do track and share**: Erin C. Carroll, "News as Surveillance," 59 *Washburn Law Journal* 431 (2020) ("Although journalists have admirably revealed and explained the ways in which government and businesses surveil us online, they have been mostly mum on a key fact: the press is spying on us as well").

236 **new state laws restricting police access**: Virginia Hughes, "Two New Laws Restrict Police Use of DNA Search Method," *New York Times*, May 31, 2021.

236 **93 percent of Americans**: Kyle Daly, "Exclusive: Poll Reveals Americans' Data Privacy Frustrations," *Axios*, Aug. 13, 2020.

236 **"ruthless exposure of private lives"**: *Watkins v. United States*, 354 U.S. 178 (1957).

236 **"embarrassingly intimate picture"**: Westin, *Privacy and Freedom*, 299.

236 **"Even as you read this"**: Brenton, *Privacy Invaders*. This quotation is sourced from the cover.

236 **"Here's how snoop devices"**: Packard, *Naked Society*. This quotation is sourced from the cover of the Pocket Cardinal edition.

236 **Congress was holding hearings**: *The Computer and Invasion of Privacy: Hearings Before the S. Comm. on Invasion of Privacy of the Comm. on Gov't Operations*, 89th Cong. 2 (1966).

236 **"Is Privacy Dead?"**: *Newsweek*, July 27, 1970.

237 **public school data compiled**: *Doe v. McMillan*, 412 U.S. 306 (1973).

237 **"the 'sacred precincts'"**: *See, e.g.*, 120 Cong. Rec. 36969 (daily ed. Nov. 21, 1974) (statement of Rep. Drinan). Representative Robert Drinan was also a priest and a law professor at Georgetown University Law Center.

237 **passed the Privacy Act**: *U.S. Dep't of Justice v. Reporters Comm. for Freedom of the Press*, 489 U.S. 749 (1989) (citing H.R. Rep. No. 93-1416, at 7 (1974)).

237 **"the threat to privacy implicit"**: *Whalen v. Roe*, 429 U.S. 589 (1977).

237 **"the implications of computerized data banks"**: *U.S. Dep't of Justice v. Reporters Comm. for Freedom of the Press*, 489 U.S. 749 (1989).

237 *New Media* **magazine**: Curtis Lang, "Privacy in the Digital Age," *New Media*, April 1994.

237 *MacWorld* **magazine**: Charles Piller, "Privacy in Peril," *MacWorld*, July 1993.

237 **68 percent of Americans had already expressed**: Piller, "Privacy in Peril."

237 **"You already have zero privacy"**: Robert Scheer, "Nowhere to Hide," Yahoo Internet Life, Oct. 2000 (quoting Scott McNealy).

237 **they didn't**: *See, e.g.*, Zuboff, *Age of Surveillance Capitalism*.

237 **98 percent by some measures**: The Data Privacy Feedback Loop 2020, the poll cited in Daly, "Exclusive: Poll Reveals Americans' Data Privacy Frustrations." As *Axios* explained, "The company behind the survey is Transcend, which builds data privacy dashboards."

237 **Now we have doxing**: *Vangheluwe v. Got News LLC*, 365 F. Supp. 3d 850 (E.D. Mich. 2019).

237 *Facebook, Social Media Privacy*: *Facebook, Social Media Privacy, and the Use and Abuse of Data: Hearing Before the S. Comm. on Commerce, Science, and Transp. and the Comm. on the Judiciary*, 115th Cong. 1 (2018).

238 **Cambridge Analytica's use of Facebook data**: *In re Facebook Inc.*, 402 F. Supp. 3d 767 (N.D. Cal. 2019).

238 **restricted from scanning faces**: *See Patel v. Facebook Inc.*, 932 F.3d 1264 (9th Cir. 2019).

238 **Birth dates have been protected**: *True the Vote v. Hosemann*, 43 F. Supp. 3d 693 (S.D. Miss. 2014).

238 **as have cell phone numbers**: *Rocky Mountain Wild v. U.S. Bureau of Land Mgmt.*, 445 F. Supp. 3d 1345 (D. Colo. 2020).

238 **Social Security numbers:** *Mandelbaum v. Arseneault*, 2017 WL 4287837 (N.J. Super. Ct. App. Div. Sept. 28, 2017).

238 **internet browsing histories:** *In re Facebook Internet Tracking Litig.*, 956 F.3d 589 (9th Cir. 2020).

238 **"personal reading information":** *Lin v. Crain Commc'n*, 2020 WL 248445 (E.D. Mich. Jan. 16, 2020).

238 **Federal judges in 2021 similarly allowed:** *Brooks v. Thomson Reuters Corp.*, 2021 WL 3621837 (N.D. Cal. Aug. 16, 2021) (dossiers); *Lopez v. Apple, Inc.*, 2021 U.S. Dist. LEXIS 171307 (N.D. Cal. Sep. 2, 2021) (personal assistants).

238 *redacted* **abortion records:** *Northwestern Mem'l Hosp. v. Ashcroft*, 362 F.3d 923 (7th Cir. 2004).

238 **Illinois Biometric Information Privacy Act:** 740 ILCS 14/5.

239 **"a landmark result":** *In re Facebook Biometric Info. Privacy Litig.*, 2021 U.S. Dist. LEXIS 36801 (N.D. Cal. Feb. 26, 2021).

239 **company's conduct is fully protected:** Johana Bhuitan, "Suit Targets Firm's Scraping Photos to ID People," *Los Angeles Times*, March 10, 2021.

239 **"become wildly popular among strangers":** Drew Harwell, "This Facial Recognition Website Can Turn Anyone into a Cop—or a Stalker," *Washington Post*, May 14, 2021.

239 **"who put those pictures on the Internet":** Harwell, "This Facial Recognition Website Can Turn Anyone into a Cop—Or a Stalker."

240 **deepfakes:** Geoffrey A. Fowler, "Anyone with an iPhone Can Now Make Deepfakes," *Washington Post*, March 25, 2021.

240 **"When someone takes a photo of you":** Katie Campione, "Khloé Kardashian Speaks Out After Unauthorized Photo's Release: 'How I Choose to Look Is My Choice,'" people.com, April 7, 2021.

240 **Some insurance companies now use:** Bryan Walsh, "Bringing Life Insurance into the Age of Big Data," *Axios*, April 24, 2021.

240 **that an applicant is said to be either:** These categories are from my Experian data report.

240 **New Jersey passed a law:** 2020 N.J. ALS 125, 2020 N.J. Laws 125, 2020 N.J. Ch. 125, 2020 N.J. A.N. 1649.

240 **forces publishers to take down:** "Governor Murphy Signs 'Daniel's Law,'" 2020 Legis. Bill Hist. NJ A.B. 1649.

241 **"privacy concerns":** *Americans for Prosperity Foundation v. Bonta*, 141 S. Ct. 2373 (U.S. 2021).

241 **Similar worries have led Google Maps:** Google Maps suggested in 2021 as a part of Google Maps Help in a post titled "Blur or Remove 360 Photos with the Street View App" that "if Google is the owner of the photo, you can request blurring or report the photo, as long as it contains: Your face, home, or other identifying information."

241 **"shows your home or apartment":** Ben Smith, "Is an Activist's Pricey House News? Facebook Alone Decides," *New York Times*, April 25, 2021.

241 **"data protection is sacrosanct":** Felix Steiner, "Merkel Entitled to Privacy over Health Concerns," Deutsche Welle, July 13, 2019.

CHAPTER EIGHTEEN: THE RIGHT TO BE FORGOTTEN (PRIVACY IN THE PAST)

242 **"Beating and then taking a bribe":** Eric D. Lawrence, "4 Police Officers Face Bribery, Drug Charges," *Detroit Free Press*, Jan. 26, 2013.

242 **Those arrestees, the marshals said:** Detroit Free Press Inc.'s Supplemental Brief on Rehearing En Banc, *Detroit Free Press Inc. v. U.S. Dep't of Justice*, 2016 WL 368467 (2016).

243 **"significant public interest in the disclosure":** *Detroit Free Press Inc. v. U.S. Dep't of Justice*, 73 F.3d 93 (6th Cir. 1996), *overruled by Detroit Free Press Inc. v. U.S. Dep't of Justice*, 829 F.3d 478 (6th Cir. 2016).

243 **public have access to mug shots:** *See* Brief of Amici Curiae the Reporters Committee for Freedom of the Press and 36 Media Organizations in Support of Appellee Seeking Affirmation, *Detroit Free Press Inc. v. U.S. Dep't of Justice*, 2015 WL 301755 (2015) (additionally, amici explained, "A thorough survey of state laws undertaken by amici demonstrates that, in the vast majority of states, there is no privacy interest in mugshots that would allow them to be withheld from the public. To the contrary, booking photographs are available or presumptively available to the public under the open records laws of at least 40 states.").

243 **"booking photos appeared on television":** *Detroit Free Press Inc. v. U.S. Dep't of Justice*, 829 F.3d 478 (6th Cir. 2016).

243 **"A mug shot preserves":** *Times Picayune Publ'g Co. v. U.S. Dep't of Justice*, 37 F. Supp. 2d 472 (E.D. La. 1999).

244 **"the details about his past":** *Hartzell v. Cummings*, 2015 WL 7301962 (2015) (C.P. Phila. Cty. Nov. 4, 2015).

244 **decades-old incarceration information:** *Taha v. Bucks Cty. Pennsylvania*, 408 F. Supp. 3d 628 (E.D. Pa. 2019).

244 **European Court of Justice ordered:** Case C-131/12, *Google Spain SL. v. Agencia Española de Protección de Datos*, ECLI:EU:C:2014:317 (May 13, 2014).

244 **"an individual's right to privacy":** Mark Scott, "French Official Campaigns to Make 'Right to Be Forgotten' Global," *Bits, New York Times*, Dec. 3, 2014, www.nytimes.com.

244 **any European right will surely not cross the Atlantic:** John Timpane, "Can the Internet Learn to Forget?," *Philadelphia Inquirer*, June 28, 2014.

244 **credit reports are not matters of public concern:** *Dun & Bradstreet v. Greenmoss Builders*, 472 U.S. 749 (1985).

245 **"unambiguously male":** *Grimes v. Cty. of Cook*, 455 F. Supp. 3d 630 (N.D. Ill. 2020).

245 **gender-affirming surgery:** *Diaz v. Oakland Tribune*, 188 Cal. Rptr. 762 (Cal. Ct. App. 1983).

245 **"incompetence and insubordination":** *Bloomgarden v. Nat'l Archives and Records Admin.*, 798 F. App'x 674 (D.C. Cir. 2020), *cert. denied*, 141 S. Ct. 556 (2020) (quoting *Bloomgarden v. U.S. Dep't of Justice*, 874 F.3d 757 (D.C. Cir. 2017)) (internal quotation marks omitted).

245 **"greatly diminished" over time:** *Bloomgarden v. U.S. Dep't of Justice*, 2016 WL 471251 (D.D.C. Feb. 5, 2016).

245 ***timeliness boundaries* limited the amount:** *Toffoloni v. LFP Publ'g Grp.*, 572 F.3d 1201 (11th Cir. 2009) (emphasis added).

245 **nearly 90 percent of people:** Brooke Auxier, "Most Americans Support Right to Have Some Personal Info Removed from Online Searches," Pew Research Center, Jan. 27, 2020, www .pewresearch.org ("Nearly nine-in-ten Americans (87%) agree with this idea when it comes to potentially embarrassing photos and videos. Majorities also think Americans should have a right to have personal financial data collected by a tax preparer (79%) and personal medical data collected by a health care provider (69%) deleted by the organization or person who holds the information. Far fewer (36%) think personal data collected by law enforcement—like criminal records or mugshots—should be able to be deleted, which tracks with the findings around the removal of such data from public online search results.").

245 **minors the right to erase the past:** Cal. Bus. & Prof. Code § 22581.

245 **it would be "barbarous" to allow:** *Louisiana v. Bienvenu*, 36 La. Ann. 378 (La. 1884) (emphasis added).

245 **"to wreck honorable old age":** *Riley v. Lee*, 11 S.W. 713 (Ky. 1889).

246 **"she would have been justified":** This was likely a deflection given that the parents had sued the doctor for invasion of privacy. The May 1898 issue of *The St. Louis Medical and Surgical Journal* suggested that the family was out only for money and that maybe it was the parents who were ultimately responsible by allowing the doctor to take such a photograph in the first place.

246 **"unsavory incidents" in her past:** *Melvin v. Reid*, 297 P. 91 (Cal. Dist. Ct. App. 1931).

246 ***World* had refused to touch:** "Discrediting Journalism," *New York World*, Feb. 10, 1888.

246 **"Jean Valjean, an ex-convict":** Restatement (Second) of Torts § 652D, cmt. k, illus. 26 (American Law Institute, 1977).

246 **interviewee changes his mind:** *See Virgil v. Time Inc.*, 527 F.2d 1122 (9th Cir. 1975).

247 **"offensive facts that occurred 25 years ago":** *Sheaffer v. Shippensburg Chron.*, 2 Pa. D & C 3d 662 (C.P. Cumberland Cty. 1977).

247 **"some of [a man's] past history":** Restatement (Second) of Torts § 652D, cmt. b.

247 **Modern courts continue to cite:** *See, e.g., Robinson v. Wichita State Univ.*, 2017 WL 2378332 (D. Kan. May 31, 2017).

247 **"pose[d] serious threats" to publishers:** Charles D. Tobin and Christine N. Walz, "*Right to Be Forgotten, Expungement Laws Raise New Challenges on the 40th Anniversary of Cox Broadcasting v. Cohn*," *Communications Lawyer* (Fall 2015).

247 **"a man's forgotten misconduct":** *Garrison v. State of Louisiana*, 379 U.S. 64 (1964) (quoting 69 Hansard, Parliamentary Debates Hist. Eng. 1230 (3d series) (H.L. June 1, 1843) (Report of Lord Campbell)) (internal quotation marks omitted).

247 **protected student data:** *Doe v. McMillan*, 412 U.S. 306 (1973).

247 **"outgrown youthful indiscretions":** *McMillan*, 412 U.S. 306 (Douglas, J., concurring).

247 **once-famous woman into a private figure:** *Time Inc. v. Firestone*, 424 U.S. 448 (1976).

247 **Air Force Academy cadets:** *Dep't of the Air Force v. Rose*, 425 U.S. 352 (1976).

247 **Freedom of Information Act decision:** *U.S. Dep't of Justice v. Reporters Comm. for Freedom of the Press*, 489 U.S. 749 (1989) (emphasis added).

248 **"In the era of the Internet":** "Gazette Article Removal Request," *Cedar Rapids (Iowa) Gazette*, www.thegazette.com.

248 **certain states prohibited their release:** *See, e.g.*, 5 Ill. Comp. Stat. 140/2.15 (West 2019) (the Illinois statute restricts police from releasing certain mug shots, including some of people charged with certain misdemeanor crimes).

248 **"live forever" on the internet:** Keri Blakinger, "Newsrooms Rethink a Crime Reporting Staple: The Mugshot," Marshall Project, www.themarshallproject.org.

249 **In 2021, the *Tribune* announced:** Colin McMahon, "How the Chicago Tribune Handles Police Booking Photos," *Chicago Tribune*, Feb. 10, 2021.

249 **"it was gone":** Aaron Krolik and Kashmir Hill, "The Slander Industry," *New York Times*, April 24, 2021.

249 **"THE RIGHT TO BE FORGOTTEN":** Lisa Selin Davis, "'The Right to Be Forgotten': Should Teens' Social Media Posts Disappear as They Age?," *Washington Post*, June 14, 2021.

249 **"The 30-Year Secret":** Nigel Jaquiss, "The 30-Year Secret," *Willamette Week*, May 11, 2004, www.wweek.com.

CHAPTER NINETEEN: A PRESIDENT AND HIS TAX RETURNS (PRIVACY IN POLITICS)

251 **professional photographers grabbed their cameras:** Andrea Salcedo, "To Capture Trump Golfing as Biden Won, Photographers Clicked Away Across the Potomac," *Washington Post*, Nov. 10, 2020.

252 **"relentlessly positive":** Peter Baker and Maggie Haberman, "Trump's Symptoms Described as 'Very Concerning' Even as Doctors Offer Rosier Picture," *New York Times*, Oct. 3, 2020.

252 **Trump claimed a right to privacy in his health:** Ricardo Alonso-Zaldivar, "Trump's Doctor Leans on Health Privacy Law to Duck Questions," Associated Press, Oct. 5, 2020.

252 **journalists interested in it sick and dangerous:** John Bowden, "Trump Asked for Nondisclosure Agreements Last Year from Walter Reed Physicians," *Hill*, Oct. 8, 2020.

252 **nondisclosure agreements:** Carol E. Lee and Courtney Kube, "Trump Asked Walter Reed Doctors to Sign Nondisclosure Agreements in 2019," nbcnews.com, Oct. 8, 2020.

252 **NDA was unusual:** Lee and Kube, "Trump Asked Walter Reed Doctors to Sign Nondisclosure Agreements in 2019."

252 **"undisclosed health issue":** Bowden, "Trump Asked for Nondisclosure Agreements Last Year from Walter Reed Physicians."

252 **"extremely depressed oxygen levels":** Noah Weiland et al., "Trump Was Sicker Than Acknowledged with Covid-19," *New York Times*, Feb. 11, 2021.

253 **"will protect the president":** Marcy Gordon, "Mnuchin Says He'll Protect Trump Privacy if Taxes Requested," Associated Press, March 14, 2019.

253 **the Biden administration:** Maegan Vazquez and David Goldman, "Biden Administration Investigates 'Illegal' Leak of Jeff Bezos, Elon Musk and Warren Buffett's Tax Information," cnn.com, June 9, 2021.

253 **"perhaps there is very little":** William Prosser, "Privacy," 48 *California Law Review* 383 (1960).

253 **most recent Restatement:** Restatement (Second) of Torts § 652D, cmt. h (American Law Institute, 1977).

253 **aside from a few reporters:** *The New York Times*, in a news story about its decision to publish information from the tax returns but not the tax returns themselves, suggested that this was to protect the confidentiality of its sources. Dean Baquet, "An Editor's Note on the Trump Tax Investigation," *New York Times*, Sept. 27, 2020, www.nytimes.com.

254 **giant white box truck:** Tom Kludt, "Truck Blocks Cameras from Filming Trump on Golf Course," cnn.com, Dec. 27, 2017.

254 **it ordered that *Closer* pay the equivalent:** Reuters, "Actress Julie Gayet Gets $20,000 Judgment Against Tabloid Linking Her to President François Hollande," *New York Daily News*, March 27, 2014.

254 **health was a private matter:** Nico Fried, "Angela Merkel: Das Zittern der Kanzlerin," *Süddeutsche Zeitung*, June 28, 2019.

254 **"entitled to a privilege":** Felix Steiner, "Merkel Entitled to Privacy over Health Concerns," *Deutsche Welle*, July 13, 2019.

255 **"The public *needs* to know":** Margaret Mead, "The Right to Privacy vs. the Public Right to Be Informed," *Redbook*, April 1967.

255 **the most impenetrable ever:** Denver Nicks, "Study: Obama Administration More Secretive Than Ever," *Time*, March 17, 2014.

255 **"had been used to prevent the release":** Jeffrey Scott Shapiro, "Lawsuit Accuses Obama White House of Thwarting Release of Public Data Under FOIA," *Washington Times*, Aug. 19, 2014.

255 **"real dangerous in this country":** Gwen Ifill, "Clinton Defends His Privacy and Says the Press Intruded," *New York Times*, Jan. 27, 1992.

256 **"Even presidents have private lives":** Peter Baker and John F. Harris, "Clinton Admits to Lewinsky Relationship, Challenges Starr to End Personal 'Prying,'" *Washington Post*, Aug. 17, 1998.

256 **was once a journalist:** *See* Talese, *The Kingdom and the Power*, 124–25.

256 **"I do not know whether you silenced":** John F. Kennedy, "The Religious Issue in Politics" (address at the American Society of Newspapers Convention), in American Society of Newspaper Editors, *Problems of Journalism: Proceedings of the 1960 Convention*, 58, 63.

256 **"discuss some things intelligently":** Lester Markel, "The Flow of the News to Marilyn Monroe" (address at the American Society of Newspapers Convention), in American Society of Newspaper Editors, *Problems of Journalism: Proceedings of the 1960 Convention*, 73–74.

256 **she was good friends:** Monroe to Markel, March 29, 1960, Julien's Auctions: Lot 74, Marilyn Monroe Correspondence with Lester Markel, Property from the Collection of David Gainsborough-Roberts, the Estate of Lee Strasberg, and Déjà Vu, Julien's Auctions, www.julienslive.com.

257 **"if private behavior didn't interfere":** Holzer, *The Presidents vs. the Press*, 214 (quoting Ben Bradlee, Kennedy's friend) (internal quotation marks omitted).

257 **woman whom Kennedy had "seduced":** Kathy Ehrich Dowd, "How President Kennedy Seduced a White House Intern—Inside the Bedroom He Shared with Jackie," people.com, Sept. 20, 2017.

257 **"far too close to the men":** James Reston, "The Embattled Press" (address at the American Society of Newspapers Convention), in American Society of Newspaper Editors, *Problems of Journalism: Proceedings of the 1972 Convention*, 213.

257 **"gentlemen's agreement":** Davis, *Scandal*, 141.

257 **Helen Thomas was an anomaly:** David Stout, "50 Years of Tough Questions and 'Thank You, Mr. President,'" *New York Times*, July 20, 2013.

257 **"not be informed of the President's whereabouts":** Eugene S. Pulliam Jr. to Pierre Salinger, Feb. 15, 1961, in American Society of Newspaper Editors, *Problems of Journalism: Proceedings of the 1961 Convention*, 177 (internal quotation marks omitted).

257 **"he has little, if any, claim to privacy":** Salinger to Eugene S. Pulliam Jr., April 18, 1961, in American Society of Newspaper Editors, *Problems of Journalism: Proceedings of the 1961 Convention*, 178.

257 **Nelson Rockefeller's divorce:** *See* Newbold Noyes Jr. et al., "If I Were Editor: A Round-Table Discussion by Four Reporters (address at the American Society of Newspapers Convention), in American Society of Newspaper Editors, *Problems of Journalism: Proceedings of the 1962 Convention*, 85–93.

258 **"biggest political story":** Noyes et al., "If I Were Editor," 85.

258 **"had nothing whatever to do":** Noyes et al., "If I Were Editor," 91.

258 **"professional self-discipline":** "Dallas Revisited: A Panel on the Role of the Press in the Events of November 22, 1963," panel discussion at the American Society of Newspapers Convention, in American Society of Newspaper Editors, *Problems of Journalism: Proceedings of the 1964 Convention*, 25 (quoting Joseph Costa).

258 **"Freedom and Responsibility of the Press":** Arthur J. Goldberg, "Freedom and Responsibility of the Press" (address at the American Society of Newspapers Convention, in American Society of Newspaper Editors, *Problems of Journalism: Proceedings of the 1964 Convention*, 53, 55.

258 **protect President Kennedy even in death:** *See, e.g., Maritote v. Desilu Prods. Inc.*, 230 F. Supp. 721 (N.D. Ill. 1964).

258 **keep paparazzi from invading their privacy:** *Galella v. Onassis*, 353 F. Supp. 196 (S.D.N.Y. 1972), *aff'd in part, rev'd in part*, 487 F.2d 986 (2d Cir. 1973).

258 **Kennedy's autopsy records would be protected:** *Katz v. Nat'l Archives and Records Admin.*, 68 F.3d 1438 (D.C. Cir. 1995).

258 **written during a dustup:** Richard Dougherty, "Foes of Mrs. Kennedy Routed in Book Fight," *Los Angeles Times*, Dec. 25, 1966.

258 **"personal communications":** *Nixon v. Adm'r of Gen. Servs.*, 433 U.S. 425 (1977).

259 **"the American public stands to gain little":** *Cook v. Nat'l Archives and Records Admin.*, 921 F. Supp. 2d 148 (S.D.N.Y. 2013).

259 **Obama's FBI background check:** *Archibald v. U.S. Dep't of Justice*, 950 F. Supp. 2d 80 (D.D.C. 2013).

259 **publishing income tax records:** *U.S. v. Dickey*, 268 U.S. 378 (1925).

259 **"an upsurge of opposition":** Charles W. Maynes, "Disclosing Tax Information," *Progressive*, Oct. 1974.

259 **Taxpayer Bill of Rights:** This document was available at www.irs.gov in May 2021.

259 **"no officer or employee":** 26 U.S.C. § 6103.

259 **Restatement agrees that income tax returns:** Restatement (Second) of Torts § 652D, cmt. b (American Law Institute, 1977).

259 **"is not public and there is an invasion":** *U.S. Dep't of Just. v. Reporters Comm. for Freedom of the Press*, 489 U.S. 749, 763 (1989).

260 **"Some will raise questions":** Baquet, "Editor's Note on the Trump Tax Investigation."

260 **"rigorously confined the policy":** Arthur Schlesinger Jr., "Of Privacy and the Press," *Wall Street Journal*, Oct. 24, 1978.

260 **"the wholesale investigations":** Samuel D. Warren and Louis D. Brandeis, "The Right to Privacy," 4 *Harvard Law Review* 193 (1890) (emphasis added).

261 **unless he's involved with a lobbyist:** *See, e.g.*, Editorial Board, "Advice to Lawmakers: If You're Going to Have an Affair, Don't Have It with a Lobbyist," *South Florida Sun-Sentinel* (Fort Lauderdale), Sept. 13, 2019; "Inside the Beltway," *Washington Times*, June 28, 2000 ("I didn't believe and still don't believe that the private life of a public figure is necessarily the public's business," including extramarital love affairs, but explaining that, here, the reported affair was with a lobbyist).

261 **voting against gay rights:** Kelly McBride, "Thresholds of Coverage: When to Say He's Gay," poynter.org, Aug. 29, 2007.

261 **senator Larry Craig:** "Senator Pleaded Guilty, Reportedly After Bathroom Stall Incident," cnn .com, Aug. 27, 2007.

261 **once had relationships with teenagers:** Brian Lyman, "'Absolutely Not': Shelby Won't Vote for Roy Moore," *Montgomery (Ala.) Advertiser*, Nov. 16, 2017.

261 **"breathing space":** Joint Status Report, *Moore v. Cohen*, 1:19-cv-4977-ALC, filed July 15, 2020.

261 **federal judge initially refused to dismiss:** Ashley Cullins, "Sacha Baron Cohen Points to 'Borat' Wins in Defamation Suit over 'Who Is America?,'" *Hollywood Reporter*, Feb. 9, 2021. The trial court judge eventually dismissed the lawsuit in July 2021.

262 **"protect[ed] the personal integrity":** Hon. Stephen G. Breyer, "Reflections of a Junior Justice," 54 *Drake Law Review* 7 (2005).

EPILOGUE: DIGNITY AND LIBERTY

263 **"about an incident in the 1980s":** *Richard v. British Broad. Corp.* [2018] EWHC 1837 (Ch).

263 **"It was an extraordinary thing":** *Piers Morgan's Life Stories*, ITV 1 (London) television broadcast, Nov. 1, 2020.

264 **his dignity had been forever damaged:** Katie Hodge, "'BBC Ruined My Life': Sir Cliff Richard's 'Reputation and Private Life Were Shattered' After the BBC Filmed a Police Raid of His House, His Lawyer Claims," *Sun* (London), April 12, 2018.

264 **"Sir Cliff had privacy rights":** *Richard v. British Broad. Corp.* [2018] EWHC 1837 (Ch).

264 **approximately $3 million:** Converter X, www.currencyconverterx.com.

264 **"the anonymity in America":** Jemma Carr, "Sir Cliff Richard Abandons Britain and Moves to New York After Legal Battle over False Child Sex Abuse Allegations," *Daily Mail*, May 25, 2019, www.dailymail.com.

265 **"safeguards for freedom":** *New York Times v. Sullivan*, 376 U.S. 254 (1964).

265 **"It is only the more *flagrant* breaches"**: Samuel D. Warren and Louis D. Brandeis, "The Right to Privacy," 4 *Harvard Law Review* 193 (1890).

265 **United States does not value that liberty exclusively**: *See, e.g.*, Solove, *Understanding Privacy*.

265 **privacy protected the woman who'd refused**: *Union P. R. Co. v. Botsford*, 141 U.S. 250 (1891) (suggesting that "to compel any one, and especially a woman, to lay bare the body, or to submit it to the touch of a stranger, without lawful authority, is an indignity").

265 **"a matter of human dignity"**: *Hawley v. Prof'l Credit Bureau*, 76 N.W.2d 835 (Mich. 1956) (Smith, J., dissenting).

266 **"a different rule"**: *Galella v. Onassis*, 487 F.2d 986 (2d Cir. 1973) ("Privacy essential to individual dignity and personal liberty underlies the fundamental rights guaranteed in the Bill of Rights.").

266 **"fundamental respect for human dignity"**: *Shulman v. Grp. W Prods. Inc.*, 955 P.2d 469 (1998).

266 **"publicly humiliate[d] a public servant"**: *Conradt v. NBC Universal Inc.*, 536 F. Supp. 2d 380 (S.D.N.Y. 2008).

266 **"dignity . . . of the individual"**: Warren and Brandeis, "Right to Privacy."

266 **stand the chance to go viral**: Hannah Knowles, "A Zoom Hearing for Her Domestic Violence Case Went Viral," *Washington Post*, March 12, 2021 (the parties appeared to be Zooming in from the same location).

266 **"the privacies of life"**: *Boyd v. United States*, 116 U.S. 616 (1886).

267 **"are entitled to respect for their private lives"**: *Lawrence v. Texas*, 539 U.S. 558 (2003).

267 **"a document guaranteeing people"**: Strum, *Privacy*, 203 (quoting Breyer during his Supreme Court confirmation hearings in 1994) (internal quotation marks omitted).

267 **data protections often stem**: *See* Richards, *Intellectual Privacy*, 73.

267 **"We are beginning to learn"**: Jeffrey Rosen, "Why Internet Privacy Matters," *New York Times Magazine*, April 30, 2000.

267 **"The man who is compelled"**: Edward J. Bloustein, "Privacy as an Aspect of Human Dignity: An Answer to Dean Prosser," 39 *New York University Law Review* 962 (1964).

267 **"essential to peace and happiness"**: *In re Application of the Pacific Railway Commission*, 32 F. 241 (N.D. Cal. Cir. 1887) (Justice Stephen Field sat as a federal appellate court judge for this case and wrote the opinion).

267 **"pursuit of happiness"**: James Q. Whitman, "The Two Western Cultures of Privacy: Dignity Versus Liberty," 113 *Yale Law Journal* 1151 (2003).

267 **99 percent of people in the United States**: In a 2017 poll, 87 percent called "the right to privacy" "essential to their own sense of freedom." Pew Research Center for the People and the Press, "America's Complex Relationship with Guns," June 22, 2017, www.pewsocialtrends.org. Another 12 percent suggested that it was "important but not essential."

268 **"an elasticity which shall take account"**: Warren and Brandeis, "The Right to Privacy."

268 **"there has to be some balancing"**: Denny Chin, "Privacy, Newsworthiness, and a View from the Bench," 93 *Tulane Law Review* 1079 (2019).

268 **"best men"**: Rosenberg, *Protecting the Best Men*, 10–11.

268 **"moulded out of faults"**: William Shakespeare, *Measure for Measure*, act 5, scene 1.

268 **"raising the curtain"**: *State v. Rhodes*, 61 N.C. (Phil.) 453, 459 (N.C. 1868).

269 **"roll[s] back dignity"**: "Rolling Back Dignity" is the subtitle of the *People of Walmart Adult Coloring Book*, published in 2016, a compilation of colorable drawings from photographs of Walmart shoppers sent in by readers to the website, drawings that, the introductory note reads, may cause a reader "the sudden urge to vomit" due to the individuals' "ass-cracks, side-boob[s]," and other oddities.

269 **"the deck seems stacked"**: *Berisha v. Lawson*, 141 S. Ct. 2424 (2021) (Gorsuch, J., dissenting).

269 **Section 230 protects free expression**: Tony Room and Elizabeth Dwoskin, "Trump Signs Order That Could Punish Social Media Companies for How They Police Content, Drawing Criticism and Doubts of Legality," *Washington Post*, May 28, 2020.

270 **those who rioted and broke into the Capitol**: Mike Allen, "Capitol Defendants Use Journalism as Defense," *Axios*, April 18, 2021.

270 **"is a subject of *legitimate* news interest"**: *Snyder v. Phelps*, 562 U.S. 443 (2011) (emphasis added).

270 **"content, form, and context"**: *Dun & Bradstreet v. Greenmoss Builders*, 472 U.S. 749 (1985).

270 **"domestic gossip"**: *Bartnicki v. Vopper*, 532 U.S. 514 (2001).

270 **"sensitivity and significance"**: *Florida Star v. B.J.F.*, 491 U.S. 524 (1989).

271 **Facebook's ban on Donald Trump:** "Oversight Board Upholds Former President Trump's Suspension, Finds Facebook Failed to Impose Proper Penalty," www.oversightboard.com, May 2021.

271 **"there are times when speech can be at odds":** This language is from the Oversight Board's Charter, available at www.oversightboard.com in May 2021.

271 **a "desire for privacy":** *Haynes v. Alfred A. Knopf, Inc.*, 8 F.3d 1222 (7th Cir. 1993).

272 **"a common law right rises":** *Marsh v. County of San Diego*, 680 F.3d 1148 (9th Cir. 2012), citing *Washington v. Glucksberg*, 521 U.S. 702 (1997).

272 **First Amendment proponents say:** Bollinger, *Images of a Free Press*, 46.

272 **Arthur Ashe:** Resolution in honor of Arthur Ashe, H.R. Res. 1054, 115th Cong. (2018) (enacted).

272 **"a platform to pursue social justice":** Resolution in honor of Arthur Ashe.

272 **honorary doctorate:** James Barron, "Volcker Is Honored as 1,024 Graduate at Princeton," *New York Times*, June 8, 1982.

273 **"for the public good":** American Press Institute, "Arthur Ashe: Did We Really Need to Know?," in *The Public, Privacy, and the Press: Have the Media Gone Too Far? J. Montgomery Curtis Memorial Seminar, September 13, 14, 15, 1992* (Reston, Va.: American Press Institute, 1992).

273 **blood transfusion:** Hal Bock, "Tennis Great Arthur Ashe: 'I Have AIDS,'" Associated Press, April 8, 1992; Hal Bock, "Ex–Tennis Star Ashe Has AIDS," *Chicago Sun-Times*, April 8, 1992.

273 **on his own terms:** Bock, "Ex–Tennis Star Ashe Has AIDS."

273 **"For any news organization":** Bock, "Tennis Great Arthur Ashe: 'I Have AIDS'" (quoting *USA Today*'s managing editor for sports) (internal quotation marks omitted).

274 **"tantamount to sacrificing virgins":** American Press Institute, "Arthur Ashe: Did We Really Need to Know?"

274 **conversations among journalists:** American Press Institute, "Arthur Ashe: Did We Really Need to Know?"

274 **"Remember to temper":** Stephen Power, "Ashe Urges Media to Show 'Sensitivity,'" *Boston Globe*, May 27, 1992.

275 ***The Story of Arthur Ashe:*** Johnson, *Value of Dignity*, 7, 9, 45, 58, 61, 62.

BIBLIOGRAPHY

Abramson, Albert. *The History of Television, 1880 to 1941.* Jefferson, N.C.: McFarland, 1987.

Acton, Patricia Nassif. *Invasion of Privacy: The Cross Creek Trial of Marjorie Kinnan Rawlings.* Gainesville: University of Florida Press, 1988.

Adams, Katherine. *Owning Up: Privacy, Property, and Belonging in U.S. Women's Life Writing.* New York: Oxford University Press, 2009.

Adams, Katherine H., Michael L. Keene, and Jennifer C. Koella. *Seeing the American Woman, 1880–1920: The Social Impact of the Visual Media Explosion.* Jefferson, N.C.: McFarland, 1954.

Agee, James, and Walker Evans. *Let Us Now Praise Famous Men.* Boston: Houghton Mifflin, 2001.

Alderman, Ellen, and Caroline Kennedy. *The Right to Privacy.* New York: Vintage Books, 1997.

Alexander, Ruth M. *The "Girl Problem": Female Sexual Delinquency in New York, 1900–1930.* Ithaca, N.Y.: Cornell University Press, 1995.

Algeo, Matthew. *The President Is a Sick Man: Wherein the Supposedly Virtuous Grover Cleveland Survives a Secret Surgery at Sea and Vilifies the Courageous Newspaperman Who Dared Expose the Truth.* Chicago: Chicago Review Press, 2011.

Alger, Horatio, Jr. *Dan, the Newsboy: The Story of a Boy's Life in the Streets of New York.* New York: A. L. Burt, 1893.

Amar, Akhil Reed. *America's Constitution: A Biography.* New York: Random House, 2005.

The American Domestic Cyclopedia: A Volume of Universal Ready Reference for American Women in American Homes. New York: F. M. Lupton, 1890.

American Law Institute. *Principles of the Law: Data Privacy.* Tentative Draft for Consideration at the Ninety-sixth Annual Meeting on May 20, 21, and 22, 2019. (Submitted April 15, 2019.)

Angwin, Julia. *Dragnet Nation: A Quest for Privacy, Security, and Freedom in a World of Relentless Surveillance.* New York: Times Books, 2014.

Arthur, Timothy Shay. *Ten Nights in a Bar-Room, and What I Saw There!* Philadelphia: L. Johnson, 1858.

Arthur, William R., and Ralph L. Crosman. *The Law of Newspapers: A Text and Case Book for Use in Schools of Journalism and a Desk-Book for Newspaper Workers.* New York: McGraw-Hill, 1928.

Aspinall, Arthur. *Politics and the Press, 1780–1850.* London: Home & Van Thal, 1949.

The Associated Press Stylebook and Briefing on Media Law 2018. New York: Basic Books, 2018.

Attwood, F. G. *Manners and Customs of Ye Harvard Studente.* Boston: J. R. Osgood, 1877.

Baker, Alfred. *Reporting Hints and Practice, Designed for the Student-Reporters and Others Qualifying for Newspaper Work.* London: Isaac Pitman & Sons, 1889.

Baker, Liva. *The Justice from Beacon Hill: The Life and Times of Oliver Wendell Holmes.* New York: HarperCollins, 1991.

Baker, Nicholson, and Margaret Brentano. *The World on Sunday: Graphic Art in Joseph Pulitzer's Newspaper (1898–1911).* New York: Bulfinch Press, 2005.

Baldasty, Gerald J. *The Commercialization of News in the Nineteenth Century.* Madison: University of Wisconsin Press, 1992.

Balk, Alfred, and James Boylan, eds. *Our Troubled Press: Ten Years of the "Columbia Journalism Review."* Boston: Little, Brown, 1971.

Barbas, Samantha. *Laws of Image: Privacy and Publicity in America.* Stanford, Calif.: Stanford University Press, 2015.

———. *Newsworthy: The Supreme Court Battle over Privacy and Press Freedom.* Stanford, Calif.: Stanford University Press, 2017.

Barrow, Andrew. *Gossip: A History of High Society from 1920 to 1970.* New York: Coward, McCann & Geoghegan, 1979.

Bartee, Alice Fleetwood. *Privacy Rights: Cases Lost and Causes Won Before the Supreme Court.* Lanham, Md.: Rowman & Littlefield, 2006.

Bartow, Edith Merwin. *News and These United States.* New York: Funk & Wagnalls, 1952.

Bausum, Ann. *Muckrakers: How Ida Tarbell, Upton Sinclair, and Lincoln Steffens Helped Expose Scandal, Inspire Reform, and Invent Investigative Journalism.* Washington, D.C.: National Geographic, 2007.

Bazzell, Michael. *Extreme Privacy: What It Takes to Disappear.* 2nd ed. Edited by Y. Varallo, Ashley Martin, and M. S. Williams. 2020.

Beard, George M. *American Nervousness: Its Causes and Consequences: A Supplement to Nervous Exhaustion (Neurasthenia).* New York: Putnam, 1881.

Beatty, Jack. *Age of Betrayal: The Triumph of Money in America, 1865–1900.* New York: Vintage Books, 2007.

Behrnd-Klodt, Menzi L., and Peter J. Wosh, eds. *Privacy and Confidentiality Perspectives: Archivist and Archival Records.* Chicago: Society of American Archivists, 2005.

Bell, Emily, and Taylor Owen, eds. *Journalism after Snowden: The Future of the Free Press in the Surveillance State.* New York: Columbia University Press, 2017.

Bender, David L., ed. "How Should the Right to Privacy Be Defined?" In *Civil Liberties: Opposing Viewpoints,* 16–68. San Diego: Greenhaven Press, 1994.

Benson, Ivan. *Fundamentals of Journalism.* New York: Prentice-Hall, 1937.

Berger, Meyer. *The Story of "The New York Times," 1851–1951.* New York: Simon & Schuster, 1951.

Bernstein, Carl, and Bob Woodward. *All the President's Men.* New York: Simon & Schuster, 1974.

Betts, Edwin Morris, and James Adam Bear, eds. *The Family Letters of Thomas Jefferson.* Columbia: University of Missouri Press, 1966.

Bezanson, Randall P. *How Free Can the Press Be?* Urbana: University of Illinois Press, 2003.

Bezanson, Randall P., Gilbert Cranberg, and John Soloski. *Libel Law and the Press: Myth and Reality.* New York: Free Press, 1987.

Bickel, Alexander M. *The Unpublished Opinions of Mr. Justice Brandeis.* Cambridge, Mass.: Belknap Press of Harvard University Press, 1957.

Bickel, Karl A. *New Empires: The Newspaper and the Radio.* Philadelphia: J. B. Lippincott, 1930.

Biddle, Francis. *Mr. Justice Holmes.* New York: Charles Scribner's Sons, 1943.

Bird, Wendell. *The Revolution in Freedoms of Press and Speech: From Blackstone to the First Amendment and Fox's Libel Act.* New York: Oxford University Press, 2020.

Black, Jay, Bob Steele, and Ralph Barney. *Doing Ethics in Journalism: A Handbook with Case Studies.* 3rd ed. Boston: Allyn and Bacon, 1999.

Blackstone, William. *Commentaries on the Laws of England.* 4 vols. Edited by William Carey Jones. Reprint, Baton Rouge, La.: Claitor's, 1976.

Bleyer, Willard Grosvenor. *Main Currents in the History of American Journalism.* Cambridge, Mass.: Riverside Press, 1927.

Boling, Patricia. *Privacy and the Politics of Intimate Life.* Ithaca, N.Y.: Cornell University Press, 1996.

Bollinger, Lee C. *Images of a Free Press.* Chicago: University of Chicago Press, 1991.

Bowen, Catherine Drinker. *Yankee from Olympus: Justice Holmes and His Family.* Boston: Little, Brown, 1944.

Bowen, Ezra, ed. *This Fabulous Century.* Vol. 1, *1900–1910.* New York: Time-Life Books, 1969.

———. *This Fabulous Century.* Vol. 2, *1910–1920.* New York: Time-Life Books, 1969.

Boylan, James. *The World and the 20's: The Golden Years of New York's Legendary Newspaper.* New York: Dial Press, 1973.

Bradley, Mabel Warren. *Samuel Dennis Warren.* Published by the author, 1956.

Bradley, Patricia. *Making American Culture: A Social History, 1900–1920.* New York: Palgrave Macmillan, 2009.

Brady, Kathleen. *Ida Tarbell: Portrait of a Muckraker.* Pittsburgh: University of Pittsburgh Press, 1984.

Brands, H. W. *American Colossus: The Triumph of Capitalism, 1865–1900*. New York: Anchor Books, 2010.

——. *Heirs of the Founders: The Epic Rivalry of Henry Clay, John Calhoun, and Daniel Webster, the Second Generation of American Giants*. New York: Doubleday, 2018.

Breckenridge, Adam Carlyle. *The Right to Privacy*. Lincoln: University of Nebraska Press, 1970.

Brenton, Myron. *The Privacy Invaders*. New York: Crest Books, 1964.

Bridgham, Percy A. *One Thousand Legal Questions Answered by the "People's Lawyer" of the "Boston Daily Globe."* Boston: Lyman B. Brooks, 1891.

Brin, David. *The Transparent Society: Will Technology Force Us to Choose Between Privacy and Freedom?* Reading, Mass.: Addison-Wesley, 1998.

Britton, Nan. *The President's Daughter*. New York: Elizabeth Ann Guild, 1927.

Brockway, Beman. *Fifty Years in Journalism: Embracing Recollections and Personal Experiences with an Autobiography*. Watertown, N.Y.: Daily Times Printing and Publishing House, 1891.

Brookhiser, Richard. *James Madison*. New York: Basic Books, 2011.

Broun, Heywood. *It Seems to Me, 1925–1935*. New York: Harcourt, Brace, 1935.

Bruce, John. *Gaudy Century, 1848–1948: San Francisco's One Hundred Years of Robust Journalism*. New York: Random House, 1948.

Budiansky, Stephen. *Oliver Wendell Holmes: A Life in War, Law, and Ideas*. New York: W. W. Norton, 2019.

Bulla, David W. *Lincoln's Censor: Milo Hascall and the Freedom of the Press in Civil War Indiana*. West Lafayette, Ind.: Purdue University Press, 2008.

Bunting, Henry S. *The Elementary Laws of Advertising and How to Use Them*. Chicago: Novelty News Press, 1913.

Burdett, Osbert, and E. H. Goddard. *Edward Perry Warren: The Biography of a Connoisseur*. London: Christophers, 1941.

Burgh, James. *The Dignity of Human Nature; or, A Brief Account of the Certain and Established Means for Attaining the True End of Our Existence*. 2nd ed. Hartford: John Babcock, printer, 1802.

Burns, Eric. *Infamous Scribblers: The Founding Fathers and the Rowdy Beginnings of American Journalism*. New York: PublicAffairs, 2006.

Burton, David H., ed. *Holmes-Sheehan Correspondence: Letters of Justice Oliver Wendell Holmes Jr. and Canon Patrick Augustine Sheehan*. Rev. ed. New York: Fordham University Press, 1993.

Byrne, Julia Clara Bush. *Gossip of the Century: Personal and Traditional Memories—Social Literary Artistic &c*. Vol. 1. London: Ward and Downey, 1892.

Callender, James Thomson. *The History of the United States for 1796; Including a Variety of Interesting Particulars Relative to the Federal Government Previous to That Period*. Philadelphia: Snowden & McCorkle, 1797.

——. *The Prospect Before Us*. Richmond: M. Jones, S. Pleasants Jr., and J. Lyon, 1800.

Campbell, W. Joseph. *The Year That Defined American Journalism*. New York: Routledge, 2006.

——. *Yellow Journalism: Puncturing the Myths, Defining the Legacies*. Westport, Conn.: Praeger, 2001.

Campbell-Copeland, T. *The Ladder of Journalism: How to Climb It*. New York: Allan Forman, 1889.

Cappello, Lawrence. *None of Your Damn Business: Privacy in the United States from the Gilded Age to the Digital Age*. Chicago: University of Chicago Press, 2019.

A Century of Journalism: An Anthology of Outstanding Feature Articles from the "New York Post," New York's Oldest Newspaper, Founded in 1801. Vol. 2, *In Peace and War*. New York: New York Post, 1943.

A Century of Journalism: An Anthology of Outstanding Feature Articles from the "New York Post," New York's Oldest Newspaper, Founded in 1801. Vol. 3, *Panorama*. New York: New York Post, 1943.

Chapin, E. N. *American Court Gossip; or, Life at the National Capitol*. Marshalltown, Iowa: Chapin & Hartell Bros., 1887.

Charle, Christophe. *Birth of the Intellectuals, 1880–1900*. Translated by David Fernbach and G. M. Goshgarian. Malden, Mass.: Polity, 2015.

Chauncey, George. *Gay New York: Gender, Urban Culture, and the Making of the Gay Male World, 1890–1940*. New York: Basic Books, 1994.

Chenery, William L. *Freedom of the Press*. New York: Harcourt, Brace, 1955.

Cheney, Lynne. *James Madison: A Life Reconsidered*. New York: Viking, 2014.

Chermayeff, Serge, and Christopher Alexander. *Community and Privacy: Toward a New Architecture of Humanism*. Garden City, N.Y.: Anchor Books, 1963.

Chernow, Ron. *Alexander Hamilton*. New York: Penguin Press, 2004.

Citron, Danielle Keats. *Hate Crimes in Cyberspace*. Cambridge, Mass.: Harvard University Press, 2014.

Claitor, Diana. *100 Years Ago: The Glorious 1890s*. New York: Gallery Books, 1990.

Clayton, Charles C. *Fifty Years for Freedom: The Story of Sigma Delta Chi's Service to American Journalism, 1909–1959*. Carbondale: Southern Illinois University Press, 1959.

Clayton, Richard, and Hugh Tomlinson. *Privacy and Freedom of Expression*. Reprinted from *The Law of Human Rights*. Oxford: Oxford University Press, 2001.

Cleland, John. *Memoirs of Fanny Hill: A New and Genuine Edition from the Original Text (London, 1749)*. Lexington, Ky.: Filiquarian, 2010.

Cleveland, Rose E. *The Social Mirror: A Complete Treatise on the Laws, Rules, and Usages That Govern Our Most Refined Homes and Social Circles*. St. Louis: J. L. Herbert, 1888.

Cloud, Stanley, and Lynne Olson. *The Murrow Boys: Pioneers on the Front Lines of Broadcast Journalism*. Boston: Houghton Mifflin, 1996.

Cobb, Irvin S. *Stickfuls: Compositions of a Newspaper Minion*. New York: George H. Doran, 1923.

Cobbett, William. *The Republican Judge; or, The American Liberty of the Press, as Exhibited, Explained, and Exposed in the Base and Partial Prosecution of William Cobbett, for a Pretended Libel Against the King of Spain and His Embassador, Before the Supreme Court of Pennsylvania: With an Address to the People of England*. London: printed for J. Wright, 1798. Reprinted by Ecco Print Editions.

Cohen, Daniel. *Yellow Journalism: Scandal, Sensationalism, and Gossip in the Media*. Brookfield, Conn.: Twenty-First Century Books, 2000.

Cohen, Patricia Cline, Timothy J. Gilfoyle, and Helen Lefkowitz Horowitz. *The Flash Press: Sporting Male Weeklies in 1840s New York*. Chicago: University of Chicago Press, 2008.

Colclough, Stephen. *Consuming Texts: Readers and Reading Communities, 1695–1870*. New York: Palgrave Macmillan, 2007.

Commission on Freedom of the Press. *A Free and Responsible Press: A General Report on Mass Communication: Newspapers, Radio, Motion Pictures, Magazines, and Books*. Edited by Robert D. Leigh. Chicago: University of Chicago Press, 1947.

Conboy, Martin. *Journalism: A Critical History*. London: Sage, 2004.

Cook, David A. *A History of Narrative Film*. New York: W. W. Norton, 1981.

Cook, Elizabeth Christine. *Literary Influences in Colonial Newspapers, 1704–1750*. Port Washington, N.Y.: Kennikat Press, 1966.

Cooley, Thomas M. *A Treatise on the Law of Torts; or, The Wrongs Which Arise Independent of Contract*. Chicago: Callaghan, 1879.

Copeland, David A. *Colonial American Newspapers: Character and Content*. Newark: University of Delaware Press, 1997.

Coquillette, Daniel R., and Bruce A. Kimball. *On the Battlefield of Merit: Harvard Law School, the First Century*. Cambridge, Mass.: Harvard University Press, 2015.

Couser, G. Thomas. *Vulnerable Subjects: Ethics and Life Writing*. Ithaca, N.Y.: Cornell University Press, 2004.

Coyle, Erin K. *The Press and Rights to Privacy: First Amendment Freedoms vs. Invasion of Privacy Claims*. El Paso, Tex.: LFB, 2012.

Crane, Stephen. *Maggie: A Girl of the Streets and Other Writings About New York*. New York: Barnes & Noble Classics, 2005.

Cronkite, Walter. *A Reporter's Life*. New York: Alfred A. Knopf, 1996.

Cumberland Mills. *Samuel Dennis Warren, September 13, 1817–May 11, 1888: A Tribute from the People of Cumberland Mills*. Cambridge, Mass.: Riverside Press, 1888.

Curtis, William Eleroy. *The True Thomas Jefferson*. Philadelphia: J. B. Lippincott, 1901.

Czitrom, Daniel J. *Media and the American Mind: From Morse to McLuhan*. Chapel Hill: University of North Carolina Press, 1982.

Dabney, Virginius. *The Jefferson Scandals: A Rebuttal*. Lanham, Md.: Madison Books, 1981.

Daly, Christopher B. *Covering America: A Narrative History of a Nation's Journalism*. Amherst: University of Massachusetts Press, 2012.

Dann, Martin E. *The Black Press, 1827–1890: The Quest for National Identity*. New York: G. P. Putnam's Sons, 1971.

Davies, Marion. *The Times We Had: Life with William Randolph Hearst*. New York: Ballantine Books, 1975.

Davis, Lanny. *Scandal: How "Gotcha" Politics Is Destroying America*. New York: Palgrave, Macmillan, 2006.

Davis, Noah K. *Elements of Ethics*. Boston: Silver, Burdett, 1900.

Davis, Richard. *Justices and Journalists: The U.S. Supreme Court and the Media*. New York: Cambridge University Press, 2011.

DeCew, Judith Wagner. *In Pursuit of Privacy: Law, Ethics, and the Rise of Technology*. Ithaca, N.Y.: Cornell University Press, 1997.

Dennis, Donna. *Licentious Gotham: Erotic Publishing and Its Prosecution in Nineteenth-Century New York*. Cambridge, Mass.: Harvard University Press, 2009.

Derry, T. K., and Trevor I. Williams. *A Short History of Technology: From the Earliest Times to A.D. 1900*. New York: Oxford University Press, 1961.

Dicken-Garcia, Hazel. *Journalistic Standards in Nineteenth-Century America*. Madison: University of Wisconsin Press, 1989.

Dickens, Charles. *American Notes for General Circulation*. London: Chapman and Hall, 1850.

Dickerson, Donna Lee. *The Course of Tolerance: Freedom of the Press in Nineteenth-Century America*. New York: Greenwood Press, 1948.

Disney, Walt. *Mickey Mouse Runs His Own Newspaper*. Racine, Wis.: Whitman, 1937.

Dotson, Carrol Baker. *The N.I.A. Handbook for Writers: The Texts and Reference Manual of a Training Course in Modern Writing, Applying Metropolitan Journalistic Practices, and Employing the Copy Desk Method*. New York: Newspaper Institute of America, 1945.

Downie, Leonard, Jr., and Robert G. Kaiser. *The News About the News: American Journalism in Peril*. New York: Vintage Books, 2003.

Duniway, Clyde Augustus. *The Development of Freedom of the Press in Massachusetts*. New York: Burt Franklin, 1906.

Dyar, Ralph E. *News for an Empire: The Story of the "Spokesman-Review" of Spokane, Washington, and of the Field It Serves*. Caldwell, Idaho: Caxton Printers, 1952.

Eastman, Max. *Journalism versus Art*. New York: Alfred A. Knopf, 1916.

Editorials from the Hearst Newspapers. New York: Albertson, 1906.

Eggers, Dave. *The Circle*. New York: Vintage Books, 2014.

Elliot, Edward. *Biographical Story of the Constitution: A Study of the Growth of the American Union*. New York: G. P. Putnam's Sons, 1910.

Ellis, Joseph J. *American Sphinx: The Character of Thomas Jefferson*. New York: Alfred A. Knopf, 2005.

Emerson, Edwin. *A History of the Nineteenth Century, Year by Year*. 3 vols. New York: Collier and Son, 1902.

Emery, Edwin. *The Press and America: An Interpretative History of the Mass Media*. 3rd ed. Englewood Cliffs, N.J.: Prentice-Hall, 1972.

———, ed. *The Story of America as Reported by Its Newspapers, 1690–1965*. New York: Simon & Schuster, 1965.

Epps, Garrett, ed. *The First Amendment, Freedom of the Press: Its Constitutional History and the Contemporary Debate*. Amherst, N.Y.: Prometheus Books, 2008.

Ernst, Morris L. *The Best Is Yet . . .* New York: Harper, 1945.

———. *So Far So Good*. New York: Harper Brothers, 1948.

Ernst, Morris L., and Alan U. Schwartz. *Privacy: The Right to Be Let Alone*. New York: Macmillan, 1962.

File, Patrick C. *Bad News Travels Fast: The Telegraph, Libel, and Press Freedom in the Progressive Era*. Amherst: University of Massachusetts Press, 2019.

Filler, Louis. *Crusaders for American Liberalism: The Story of the Muckrakers*. New York: Collier Books, 1961.

Fisher, Joseph R., and James Andrew Strahan. *The Law of the Press: A Digest of the Law Specially Affecting Newspapers; with a Chapter on Foreign Press Codes; and an Appendix Containing the Text of All the Leading Statutes*. London: W. Clowes, 1891.

Flaherty, David H. *Privacy in Colonial New England*. Charlottesville: University Press of Virginia, 1967.

Flanagan, Maureen A. *America Reformed: Progressives and Progressivisms, 1890s–1920s*. New York: Oxford University Press, 2007.

Foley, Elizabeth Price. *Liberty for All: Reclaiming Individual Privacy in a New Era of Public Morality*. New Haven, Conn.: Yale University Press, 2006.

Forman, Allan, ed. *The Journalist: A Pictorial Souvenir, 1884–1887*. New York: Wynkoop, Hallenbeck, 1887.

Foster, G. J. *Women and Temperance*. London: National Temperance Publication Depot, 1888.

Fowler, O. S. *Creative and Sexual Science; or, Manhood, Womanhood, and Their Mutual Inter-relations: Love, Its Laws, Power, Etc.* Toronto, Calif.: C. R. Parish, 1870.

Foy, Jessica H., and Thomas J. Schlereth, eds. *American Home Life, 1880–1930: A Social History of Spaces and Services.* Knoxville: University of Tennessee Press, 1992.

Fraleigh, Douglas M., and Joseph S. Tuman. *Freedom of Speech: In the Marketplace of Ideas.* New York: St. Martin's Press, 1997.

Frank, Elizabeth. *True Stories; or, Interesting Anecdotes of Young Persons: Designed Through the Medium of Example, to Inculcate Principles of Virtue and Piety.* Philadelphia: Benjamin & Thomas Kite, 1811.

Franklin, Marc A., David A. Anderson, Lyrissa Barnett Lidsky, and Amy Gajda. *Media Law: Cases and Materials.* 9th ed. St. Paul: Foundation Press, 2016.

Friedman, David M. *Wilde in America: Oscar Wilde and the Invention of Modern Celebrity.* New York: W. W. Norton, 2014.

Friedman, Lawrence M. *Guarding Life's Dark Secrets: Legal and Social Controls over Reputation, Propriety, and Privacy.* Stanford, Calif.: Stanford University Press, 2007.

Friendly, Fred W. *Minnesota Rag: Corruption, Yellow Journalism, and the Case That Saved Freedom of the Press.* Minneapolis: University of Minnesota Press, 2003.

The Future of the Common Law. Cambridge, Mass.: Harvard University Press, 1937.

Gabler, Neal. *Winchell: Gossip, Power, and the Culture of Celebrity.* New York: Vintage Books, 1994.

Gal, Allon. *Brandeis of Boston.* Cambridge, Mass.: Harvard University Press, 1980.

——. "Brandeis, Progressivism, and Zionism: A Study in the Interaction of Ideas and Social Background." PhD diss., Brandeis University, 1976.

Gans, Herbert J. *Deciding What's News: A Study of "CBS Evening News," "NBC Nightly News," "Newsweek," and "Time."* Evanston, Ill.: Northwestern University Press, 2004.

Gant, Scott. *We're All Journalists Now: The Transformation of the Press and Reshaping of the Law in the Internet Age.* New York: Free Press, 2007.

Gardner, Howard, Mihaly Csikszentmihalyi, and William Damon. *Good Work: When Excellence and Ethics Meet.* New York: Basic Books, 2007.

Garfinkel, Simson. *Database Nation: The Death of Privacy in the 21st Century.* Sebastopol, Calif.: O'Reilly & Associates, 2000.

Garrow, David J. *Liberty and Sexuality: The Right to Privacy and the Making of Roe v. Wade.* New York: Macmillan, 1994.

Gibbs, Philip. *Adventures in Journalism.* London: William Heinemann, 1923.

Gilbert, George. *Photographic Advertising from A-to-Z: From the Kodak to the Leica.* Cedartown, Iowa: Portertown Products, 1970.

Gilbert, Martin. *A History of the Twentieth Century.* Vol. 1, *1900–1933.* New York: Avon Books, 1997.

——. *A History of the Twentieth Century.* Vol. 2, *1933–1951.* New York: Avon Books, 1999.

Giles, Robert. *When Truth Mattered: The Kent State Shootings 50 Years Later.* Traverse City, Mich.: Mission Point Press, 2020.

Given, John L. *Making a Newspaper.* New York: Henry Holt, 1907.

Gleason, Timothy W. *The Watchdog Concept: The Press and the Courts in Nineteenth-Century America.* Ames: Iowa State University Press, 1990.

Goddard, Morrill. *What Interests People and Why.* New York: American Weekly, 1935.

Goebel, Julius, Jr. *The Law Practice of Alexander Hamilton: Documents and Commentary.* Vol. 1. New York: Columbia University Press, 1964.

Goffman, Erving. *Stigma: Notes on the Management of Spoiled Identity.* New York: Simon & Schuster, 1963.

Goldstein, Norm, ed. *The Associated Press Stylebook and Libel Manual.* Reading, Mass.: Perseus Books, 1998.

Goodman, Robert F., and Aaron Ben-Ze'ev, eds. *Good Gossip.* Lawrence: University Press of Kansas, 1994.

Goodwin, Doris Kearns. *The Bully Pulpit: Theodore Roosevelt, William Howard Taft, and the Golden Age of Journalism.* New York: Simon & Schuster, 2013.

Gordon, Matthew. *News Is a Weapon.* New York: Alfred A. Knopf, 1942.

Gore, George W. *Negro Journalism: An Essay on the History and Present Conditions of the Negro Press.* Greencastle, Ind.: self-published, 1891.

Gosse, Edmund. *Gossip in a Library.* New York: John W. Lovell, 1891.

Grannan, Joseph. *Grannan's Warning Against Fraud, and Valuable Information: A Treatise upon Subjects Relating to Crime and Business, and Also Embracing Many Practical Suggestions for Everyday Life.* Cincinnati: Grannan Detective Bureau, 1889.

Grant, James. *The Newspaper Press: Its Origin—Progress—and Present Position*. Vol. 1. London: Tinsley Brothers, 1871.

Green, Martin. *The Mount Vernon Street Warrens: A Boston Story, 1860–1910*. New York: Charles Scribner's Sons, 1989.

——. *The Problem of Boston: Some Readings in Cultural History*. New York: W. W. Norton, 1966.

Griffin, Brett. *Yellow Journalism, Sensationalism, and Circulation Wars*. New York: Cavendish Square Publishing, 2019.

Gross, Gerald, ed. *The Responsibility of the Press*. New York: Fleet, 1966.

Hachten, William A. *The Supreme Court on Freedom of the Press: Decisions and Dissents*. Ames: Iowa State University Press, 1968.

——. *The Troubles of Journalism: A Critical Look at What's Right and Wrong with the Press*. Mahwah, N.J.: Lawrence Erlbaum Associates, 1998.

Hadlock, Edwin Harvey. *Press Correspondence and Journalism*. San Francisco: United Press Syndicate, 1910.

——. *Profitable Authorship: How to Write and Where to Sell Short Stories and Other Manuscripts*. San Francisco: United Press Syndicate, 1910.

Haines, T. L., and L. W. Yaggy. *The Royal Path of Life; or, Aims and Aids to Success and Happiness*. Chicago: Western, 1881.

Halaas, David Fridtjof. *Boom Town Newspapers: Journalism on the Rocky Mountain Mining Frontier, 1859–1881*. Albuquerque: University of New Mexico Press, 1981.

Hale, William G., and Ivan Benson. *The Law of the Press: Text, Statutes, and Cases*. 2nd ed. St. Paul: West, 1933.

Hale, William Harlan. *Horace Greeley: Voice of the People*. New York: Harper & Brothers, 1950.

Hall, William T. *The Turnover Club: Tales Told at the Meeting of the Turnover Club, About Actors and Actresses*. Chicago: Rand, McNally, 1890.

Halsey, Francis W. *Our Literary Deluge and Some of Its Deeper Waters*. New York: Doubleday, Page, 1902.

Hamilton, Alexander, James Madison, and John Jay. *The Federalist Papers*. Edited by Clinton Rossiter. New York: Mentor Books, 1961.

Hamilton, Allan McLane. *The Intimate Life of Alexander Hamilton: Based Chiefly upon Family Letters and Other Documents, Many of Which Have Never Been Published*. New York: C. Scribner's Sons, 1910.

Hannigan, William. *New York Noir: Crime Photos from the "Daily News" Archive*. New York: Rizzoli, 1999.

Harder, Charles. *Gawker Slayer: The Professional and Personal Adventures of Famed Attorney*. Coppell, Tex., 2021.

Harland, Marion. *Eve's Daughters; or, Common Sense for Maid, Wife, and Mother*. New York: John R. Anderson & Henry S. Allen, 1882.

Harris, Frank. *My Life and Loves*. 4 vols. Paris: Obelisk Press, 1931.

The Harvard Law School, 1817–1917. Published for Distribution to the Graduates of the Law School by the Harvard Law School Association, 1917.

Haskell, Barbara. *The American Century: Art and Culture, 1900–1950*. New York: W. W. Norton, 1999.

Hawthorne, Nathaniel. *The Scarlet Letter: A Romance*. 2nd ed. Boston: Ticknor, Reed and Fields, 1850.

Hayter, Thomas. *An Essay on the Liberty of the Press, Chiefly as It Respects Personal Slander*. Dublin: printed for M. Williamson, 1755. Reproduction printed by Ecco Print Editions.

Healy, Thomas. *The Great Dissent: How Oliver Wendell Holmes Changed His Mind—and Changed the History of Free Speech in America*. New York: Metropolitan Books, 2013.

Heller, Steven, and Louise Fili. *Cover Story: The Art of American Magazine Covers, 1900–1950*. San Francisco: Chronicle Books, 1996.

Hemstreet, Charles. *Reporting for the Newspapers*. New York: A. Wessels, 1901.

Hesse, George W. *Camera Journalism with the Miniature Camera*. Canton, Ohio: Fomo, 1936.

Heyman, Steven J. *Free Speech and Human Dignity*. New Haven, Conn.: Yale University Press, 2008.

Hicks, Donna. *Dignity: Its Essential Role in Resolving Conflict*. New Haven, Conn.: Yale University Press, 2011.

Hill, Edwin C. *The Human Side of the News*. New York: Walter J. Black, 1934.

Hocking, William Ernest. *Freedom of the Press: A Framework of Principle: A Report from the Commission on Freedom of the Press*. Chicago: University of Chicago Press, 1947.

Hofstadter, Samuel H. *The Development of the Right of Privacy in New York*. Edited by George Horowitz. New York: Grosby Press, 1954.

Holmes, Alfred I. *Life Thoughts from Pulpits and from Poets*. Brooklyn: A. I. Holmes, 1871.

Holmes, Oliver Wendell, Jr. *The Common Law*. Boston: Little, Brown, 1881.

———. *Speeches*. Boston: Little, Brown, 1891.

Holsinger, Ralph L. *Media Law*. Edited by Peter Sandman. New York: Random House, 1987.

Holt, Hamilton. *Commercialism and Journalism*. Boston: Houghton Mifflin, 1909.

Holzer, Harold. *Lincoln and the Power of the Press: The War for Public Opinion*. New York: Simon & Schuster, 2014.

———. *The Presidents vs. the Press: The Endless Battle Between the White House and the Media*. New York: Dutton, 2020.

———, ed. *Lincoln as I Knew Him: Gossip, Tributes, and Revelations from His Best Friends and Worst Enemies*. Chapel Hill, N.C.: Algonquin Books, 2009.

Hooker, Richard. *The Story of an Independent Newspaper: One Hundred Years of the "Springfield Republican," 1824–1924*. New York: Macmillan, 1924.

Horwitz, Morton J. *The Transformation of American Law, 1870–1960: The Crisis of Legal Orthodoxy*. New York: Oxford University Press, 1992.

Howe, Mark deWolfe, ed. *Holmes-Laski Letters: The Correspondence of Mr. Justice Holmes and Harold J. Laski, 1916–1935*. 2 vols. Cambridge, Mass.: Harvard University Press, 1953.

Hudson, Frederic. *Journalism in the United States, from 1690 to 1872*. New York: Harper & Brothers, 1873.

Ickes, Harold L., ed. *Freedom of the Press Today: A Clinical Examination by 28 Specialists*. New York: Vanguard Press, 1941.

Igo, Sarah E. *The Known Citizen: A History of Privacy in Modern America*. Cambridge, Mass.: Harvard University Press, 2018.

Jefferson, Thomas. *Jefferson's Memorandum Books*. Vol. 2, Accounts, with Legal Records and Miscellany, 1767–1826. Edited by James A. Bear and Lucia C. Stanton. Princeton, N.J.: Princeton University Press, 1997.

Jewett, Paul K. *Who We Are: Our Dignity as Human: A Neo-evangelical Theology*. Edited by Marguerite Shuster. Grand Rapids: William B. Eerdmans, 1996.

Johnson, Ann Donegan. *The Value of Dignity: The Story of Arthur Ashe*. Los Angeles: Value Tales, 1994.

Johnson, Gerald W. *What Is News? A Tentative Outline*. New York: Alfred A. Knopf, 1926.

Jones, Robert W. *The Law of Journalism: Including Matters Relating to the Freedom of the Press, Libel, Contempt of Court, Property Rights in News, and Regulation of Advertising*. Washington, D.C.: Washington Law Book Co., 1940.

"The Journalist," a Pictorial Souvenir: Issued on the Completion of Its Third Year of Continuous Publication. New York: Wynkoop, Hallenbeck, 1887.

Kalb, Marvin. *One Scandalous Story: Clinton, Lewinsky, and 13 Days That Tarnished American Journalism*. New York: Free Press, 2001.

Kaylor, Michael Matthew, Osbert Burdett, and E. H. Goddard, eds. *The Collected Works and Commissioned Biography of Edward Perry Warren*. Vol. 1. Brno, Czech Republic: Masaryk University, 2013.

Keizer, Garret. *Privacy*. New York: Picador, 2012.

Kendall, Joshua. *First Dads: Parenting and Politics from George Washington to Barack Obama*. New York: Grand Central Publishing, 2016.

Kenny, Herbert A. *Newspaper Row: Journalism in the Pre-television Era*. Chester, Conn.: Globe Pequot Press, 1987.

Kent, James. *Commentaries on American Law*. Vol. 2. 2nd ed. New York: O. Halstead, 1832.

Kenyon, Andrew T., ed. *Comparative Defamation and Privacy Law*. Cambridge, U.K.: Cambridge University Press, 2016.

Kerrane, Kevin, and Ben Yagoda, eds. *The Art of Fact: A Historical Anthology of Literary Journalism*. New York: Touchstone, 1998.

King, Martin Luther, Jr. *All Labor Has Dignity*. Edited by Michael K. Honey. Boston: Beacon Press, 2011.

Kingsbury, Susan M., and Hornell Norris Hart. *Newspapers and the News: An Objective Measurement of Ethical and Unethical Behavior by Representative Newspapers*. New York: G. P. Putnam's Sons, 1937.

Kipple, Andrew, Adam Kipple, and Luke Wherry. *People of Walmart.com Adult Coloring Book: Rolling Back Dignity*. Lexington, Ky.: Day Drankin' Press, 2016.

Knowlton, Steven R., and Patrick R. Parsons, eds. *The Journalist's Moral Compass: Basic Principles*. Westport, Conn.: Praeger, 1995.

Knudson, Jerry W. *Jefferson and the Press: Crucible of Liberty*. Columbia: University of South Carolina Press, 2006.

Kobre, Sidney. *The Yellow Press and Gilded Age Journalism*. Tallahassee: Florida State University, 1964.

Koltay, András, ed. *Comparative Perspectives on the Fundamental Freedom of Expression*. Budapest: Wolters Kluwer, 2015.

Kosseff, Jeff. *The Twenty-Six Words That Created the Internet*. Ithaca, N.Y.: Cornell University Press, 2019.

Kovach, Bill, and Tom Rosenstiel. *The Elements of Journalism: What Newspeople Should Know and the Public Should Expect*. 1st rev. ed. New York: Three Rivers Press, 2001.

Kroeger, Brooke. *Nellie Bly: Daredevil, Reporter, Feminist*. New York: Times Books, 1994.

Labunski, Richard. *James Madison and the Struggle for the Bill of Rights*. New York: Oxford University Press, 2006.

Lachman, Charles. *A Secret Life: The Lies and Scandals of President Grover Cleveland*. New York: Skyhorse, 2012.

LaFeber, Walter, Richard Polenberg, and Nancy Woloch. *American Century: A History of the United States Since the 1890s*. 2nd ed. Armonk, N.Y.: M. E. Sharpe, 2008.

Lahey, Thomas A. *The Morals of Newspaper Making*. Notre Dame, Ind.: Notre Dame University Press, 1924.

LaMay, Craig L., ed. *Journalism and the Debate over Privacy*. Mahwah, N.J.: Lawrence Erlbaum Associates, 2003.

Lane, Frederick S. *American Privacy: The 400-Year History of Our Most Contested Right*. Boston: Beacon Press, 2009.

Lawrence, D. H. *Pornography and Obscenity*. New York: Alfred A. Knopf, 1930.

Lebovic, Sam. *Free Speech and Unfree News: The Paradox of Press Freedom in America*. Cambridge, Mass.: Harvard University Press, 2016.

Lee, James Melvin. *History of American Journalism*. 1917; Garden City, N.Y.: Garden City Publishing, 1923.

Lee, Kai-Fu. *AI Super-Powers: China, Silicon Valley, and the New World Order*. Boston: Houghton Mifflin Harcourt, 2018.

Leff, Laurel. *Buried by the "Times": The Holocaust and America's Most Important Newspaper*. New York: Cambridge University Press, 2005.

Lepore, Jill. *The Mansion of Happiness: A History of Life and Death*. New York: Vintage Books, 2012.

———. *These Truths: A History of the United States*. New York: W. W. Norton, 2018.

———. *This America: The Case for the Nation*. New York: Liveright, 2019.

Lesy, Michael. *Wisconsin Death Trip*. Albuquerque: University of New Mexico Press, 1973.

Levmore, Saul, and Martha C. Nussbaum, eds. *The Offensive Internet: Speech, Privacy, and Reputation*. Cambridge, Mass.: Harvard University Press, 2010.

Levy, Leonard W. *Emergence of a Free Press*. New York: Oxford University Press, 1985.

———. *Freedom of the Press from Zenger to Jefferson*. Durham, N.C.: Carolina Academic Press, 1996.

———. *Jefferson and Civil Liberties—the Darker Side*. Cambridge, Mass.: Harvard University Press, 1963.

Lewis, Anthony. *Freedom for the Thought That We Hate: A Biography of the First Amendment*. New York: Basic Books, 2007.

Lief, Alfred. *Brandeis: The Personal History of an American Ideal*. Harrisburg, Pa.: Telegraph Press, 1936.

———, ed. *The Brandeis Guide to the Modern World*. Boston: Little, Brown, 1941.

Linkof, Ryan. *Public Images: Celebrity, Photojournalism, and the Making of the Tabloid Press*. London: Bloomsbury, 2018.

Lippmann, Walter. *Liberty and the News*. New York: Harcourt, Brace and Howe, 1920.

———. *A Preface to Politics*. 1914. Ann Arbor: University of Michigan Press, 1962.

———. *Public Opinion: A Classic in Political and Social Thought*. 1922. Jersey City: Start Publishing, 2015.

Long, Edward V. *The Intruders: The Invasion of Privacy by Government and Industry*. New York: Frederick A. Praeger, 1967.

Loomis, William Warner. *Newspaper Law: A Digest of Court Decisions on Commercial and Legal Advertising, Subscriptions, Contracts, Official Papers, Libel, Lotteries, Contempt, and Copyright, Classified and Indexed for Quick Reference*. LaGrange, Ill.: Citizen, 1921.

Lord, Chester S. *The Young Man and Journalism*. New York: Macmillan, 1922.

Lord, Walter. *The Good Years: From 1900 to the First World War*. New York: Harper & Brothers, 1960.

Lyon, Peter. *Success Story: The Life and Times of S. S. McClure*. New York: Scribner, 1963.

MacCarthy, James Philip. *The Newspaper Worker: A Manual for All Who Write*. New York: Frank-Maurice, 1925.

Machlin, Milt. *The Gossip Wars: An Exposé of the Scandal Era*. Cammeray, N.S.W.: Horwitz, 1981.

MacPherson, Myra. *The Scarlet Sisters: Sex, Suffrage, and Scandal in the Gilded Age*. New York: Twelve, 2014.

Madison, James. *The Mind of the Founder: Sources of the Political Thought of James Madison*. Edited by Marvin Meyers. Hanover, N.H.: University Press of New England, 1981.

Mainardi, Patricia. *Another World: Nineteenth-Century Illustrated Print Culture*. New Haven, Conn.: Yale University Press, 2017.

Mallinson, Rufus H. *Free-Lance Journalism with a Camera*. London: British Periodicals Limited, 1926.

Margolis, Stacey. *The Public Life of Privacy in Nineteenth-Century American Literature*. Durham, N.C.: Duke University Press, 2005.

Marx, Karl. *On Freedom of the Press and Censorship*. Vol. 4 of *The Karl Marx Library*. Translated by Saul K. Padover. New York: McGraw-Hill, 1974.

Marzio, Peter C. *The Men and Machines of American Journalism: A Pictorial Essay from the Henry R. Luce Hall of News Reporting*. Washington, D.C.: National Museum of History and Technology, Smithsonian Institution, 1973.

Mason, Alpheus Thomas. *Brandeis: A Free Man's Life*. New York: Viking Press, 1946.

Mathews, Nancy Mowll. *Moving Pictures: American Art and Early Film, 1880–1910*. With Charles Musser. Manchester, Vt.: Hudson Hills Press, 2005.

Maverick, Augustus. *Henry J. Raymond and the New York Press, for Thirty Years*. Hartford: A. S. Hale, 1870.

Mayer, Michael F. *Rights of Privacy*. New York: Law-Arts, 1972.

McArthur, Benjamin. *Actors and American Culture, 1880–1920*. Philadelphia: Temple University Press, 1984.

McChesney, Robert W., and Victor Pickard, eds. *Will the Last Reporter Please Turn Out the Lights: The Collapse of Journalism and What Can Be Done to Fix It*. New York: New Press, 2011.

McClellan, Grant S., ed. *The Right to Privacy*. New York: H. W. Wilson, 1976.

McCormick, Robert R. *The Freedom of the Press: A History and an Argument Compiled from Speeches on This Subject Delivered over a Period of Fifteen Years*. New York: D. Appleton–Century, 1936.

McElroy, Robert. *Grover Cleveland: The Man and the Statesman*. New York: Harper & Brothers, 1923.

McKinney, Megan. *The Magnificent Medills: America's Royal Family of Journalism During a Century of Turbulent Splendor*. New York: HarperCollins, 2011.

McLaren, Angus. *The Trials of Masculinity: Policing Sexual Boundaries, 1870–1930*. Chicago: University of Chicago Press, 1997.

McLean, Sarah Pratt. *Cape Cod Folks*. Boston: A. Williams, 1881.

McNair, Brian. *News and Journalism in the UK*. 4th ed. London: Routledge, 1994.

McRae, Milton A. *Forty Years in Newspaperdom: The Autobiography of a Newspaper Man*. New York: Brentano's, 1924.

Melanson, Philip H. *Secrecy Wars: National Security, Privacy, and the Public's Right to Know*. Washington, D.C.: Brassey's, 2001.

Mencken, H. L. *Newspaper Days, 1899–1906*. New York: Alfred A. Knopf, 1941.

Merrill, Samuel. *Newspaper Libel: A Handbook for the Press*. Boston: Ticknor, 1888.

Meyer, Michael J., and W. A. Parent, eds. *The Constitution of Rights: Human Dignity and American Values*. Ithaca, N.Y.: Cornell University Press, 1992.

Miller, Arthur R. *The Assault on Privacy: Computers, Data Banks, and Dossiers*. New York: Mentor Books, 1971.

Miller, William Lee. *The Business of May Next: James Madison and the Founding*. Charlottesville: University Press of Virginia, 1992.

Mills, Jon L. *Privacy: The Lost Right*. New York: Oxford University Press, 2008.

———. *Privacy in the New Media Age*. Gainesville: University Press of Florida, 2015.

Milton, John. *Areopagitica*. Oxford: Clarendon Press, 1894.

Milton, Joyce. *The Yellow Kids: Foreign Correspondents in the Heyday of Yellow Journalism*. New York: Harper & Row, 1989.

Mindich, David T. Z. *Just the Facts: How "Objectivity" Came to Define American Journalism*. New York: New York University Press, 1998.

Mitchell, Dwight Emerson. *Journalism and Life: A Textbook for Secondary Schools*. Boston: Little, Brown, 1939.

Moore, Barrington, Jr. *Privacy: Studies in Social and Cultural History*. New York: M. E. Sharpe, 1984.

Morris, James McGrath. *Pulitzer: A Life in Politics, Print, and Power*. New York: Harper Perennial, 2010.

Mott, Frank Luther. *American Journalism: A History, 1690–1960*. 3rd ed. New York: Macmillan, 1962.

———. *Jefferson and the Press*. Baton Rouge: Louisiana State University Press, 1943.

———, ed. *Interpretations of Journalism: A Book of Readings*. New York: F. S. Crofts, 1937.

Nasaw, David. *The Chief: The Life of William Randolph Hearst*. New York: Mariner Books, 2001.

Nash, W. G. *A Century of Gossip; or, The Real and the Seeming*. Chicago: W. B. Keen, Cooke, 1876.

National Press Photographers Association and the University of Missouri School of Journalism. *The Best of Photojournalism: The Year in Pictures*. Vol. 17. Durham, N.C.: National Press Photographers Association, 1991.

———. *The Best of Photojournalism: The Year in Pictures*. Vol. 18. Durham, N.C.: National Press Photographers Association, 1992.

———. *The Best of Photojournalism: The Year in Pictures*. Vol. 19. Durham, N.C.: National Press Photographers Association, 1993.

Nelson, Deborah. *Pursuing Privacy in Cold War America*. New York: Columbia University Press, 2002.

Nelson, Harold Lewis. *Freedom of the Press from Hamilton to the Warren Court*. Indianapolis: Bobbs-Merrill, 1976.

Nelson, William, ed. *Documents Relating to the Colonial History of the State of New Jersey*. Vol. 25, *Extracts from American Newspapers, Relating to New Jersey*. Vol. 6, *1766–1767*. Paterson, N.J.: Call Printing and Publishing, 1903.

Nevins, Allan. *Grover Cleveland: A Study in Courage*. 2 vols. Norwalk, Conn.: Easton Press, 1932.

———, ed. *Letters of Grover Cleveland, 1850–1908*. Boston: Houghton Mifflin, 1933.

Newell, Martin L. *The Law of Defamation, Libel, and Slander in Civil and Criminal Cases as Administered in the Courts of the United States of America*. Chicago: Callaghan, 1890.

Nicholson, Virginia. *Among the Bohemians: Experiments in Living, 1900–1939*. New York: William Morrow, 2002.

Nock, Albert Jay. *Jefferson*. New York: Harcourt, Brace, 1926.

Not a History of the Dedham Polo Club: Containing Misstatements Concerning the Club from 1893 to 1907: Author Escaped. Walton Advertising and Printing Company, 1907.

Novick, Sheldon M. *Honorable Justice: The Life of Oliver Wendell Holmes*. Boston: Little, Brown, 1989.

Nutter, McClennen & Fish: The First Century, 1879–1979. Privately printed, 1979.

O'Brien, Frank M. *The Story of "The Sun": New York, 1833–1918*. New York: George H. Doran, 1918.

O'Connor, Richard. *Haywood Broun: A Biography*. New York: G. P. Putnam's Sons, 1975.

Oliver, James A. *The Pamphleteers: The Birth of Journalism, Emergence of the Press, and the Fourth Estate*. London: Information Architects, 2010.

O'Malley, Charles J. *It Was News to Me*. Boston: Bruce Humphries, 1939.

O'Neil, Robert M. *The First Amendment and Civil Liability*. Bloomington: Indiana University Press, 2001.

Onuf, Peter S. *Jeffersonian Legacies*. Charlottesville: University Press of Virginia, 1993.

Orvell, Miles. *The Real Thing: Imitation and Authenticity in American Culture, 1880–1940*. Chapel Hill: University of North Carolina Press, 1989.

Packard, Vance. *The Naked Society*. New York: David McKay, 1965.

Paneth, Donald. *The Encyclopedia of American Journalism*. New York: Facts on File, 1983.

Paper, Lewis J. *Brandeis: An Intimate Biography of One of America's Truly Great Supreme Court Justices*. Englewood Cliffs, N.J.: Prentice-Hall, 1983.

Parker, Alison M. *Purifying America: Women, Cultural Reform, and Pro-censorship Activism, 1873–1933*. Urbana: University of Illinois Press, 1997.

Parker, George F., ed. *The Writings and Speeches of Grover Cleveland*. New York: Cassell, 1892.

Parr, Leslie, Andrea Hicks, and Marie Stareck, eds. *Sears, Roebuck and Co.: The Best of 1905–1910 Collectibles*. New York: Skyhorse, 2011.

Parton, J. *The Life of Horace Greeley, Editor of the "New York Tribune."* New York: Mason Brothers, 1855.

Pasternack, Susan A. *Justice Louis Dembitz Brandeis: Guided by the Light of Reason*. Waltham, Mass.: Brandeis University, 2007.

Paterson, James. *The Liberty of the Press, Speech, and Public Worship: Being Commentaries on the Liberty of the Subject and the Laws of England*. London: Macmillan, 1880.

Patterson, Philip, and Lee Wilkins. *Media Ethics: Issues and Cases.* 6th ed. Boston: McGraw-Hill, 2008.

Payton, Theresa M., and Theodore Claypoole. *Privacy in the Age of Big Data: Recognizing Threats, Defending Your Rights, and Protecting Your Family.* Lanham, Md.: Rowman & Littlefield, 2014.

Pearson, Drew, and Robert S. Allen. *Washington Merry-Go-Round.* New York: Horace Liveright, 1931.

Pember, Don R. *Mass Media Law.* 4th ed. Dubuque, Iowa: Wm. C. Brown, 1987.

——. *Privacy and the Press: The Law, the Mass Media, and the First Amendment.* Seattle: University of Washington Press, 1972.

Penn, Irvine Garland. *The Afro-American Press and Its Editors.* Springfield, Mass.: Willey, 1891.

Perry, Eugene H. *A Socrates for All Seasons: Alexander Meiklejohn and Deliberative Democracy.* Bloomington, Ind.: iUniverse, 2011.

Personal Privacy in an Information Society: The Report of the Privacy Protection Study Commission. Washington, D.C.: Superintendent of Documents, U.S. Government Printing Office, 1977.

Phillips, Cabell, Duncan Aikman, William C. Bourne, Homer Joseph Dodge, and William A. Kinney, eds. *Dateline: Washington: The Story of National Affairs Journalism.* Garden City, N.Y.: Doubleday, 1949.

Pickett, Calder M. *Voices of the Past: Key Documents in the History of American Journalism.* Columbus, Ohio: Grid, 1977.

Pictured Encyclopedia of the World's Greatest Newspaper: A Handbook of the Newspaper as Exemplified by the "Chicago Tribune"—Issued to Commemorate Its Eightieth Birthday. Chicago: Tribune Company, 1928.

Pitcairn, Frederick Wilson, and Elizabeth J. Williard. *Woman's Guide to Health, Beauty, and Happiness.* Philadelphia: National Publishing Company, 1906.

Plain Words on Important Topics: Recent Articles in the "Century" Magazine on Strike Violence, General Lawlessness, Yellow Journalism, and Bad Manners. New York: Century, 1910.

Planel, Philippe. *Locks and Lavatories: The Architecture of Privacy.* London: English Heritage, 2000.

Pollard, James E. *The Newspaper as Defined by Law.* Columbus: Ohio State University Press, 1940.

Ponder, Stephen. *Managing the Press: Origins of the Media Presidency, 1897–1933.* New York: Palgrave, 1998.

Powe, Lucas A., Jr. *The Fourth Estate and the Constitution: Freedom of the Press in America.* Berkeley: University of California Press, 1991.

The Privacy Act of 1974: An Assessment: Appendix 4 to the Report of the Privacy Protection Study Commission. Washington, D.C.: Superintendent of Documents, U.S. Government Printing Office, 1977.

Problems of Journalism: Proceedings of the 1940, 1960–70, and 1972–75 Conventions, American Society of Newspaper Editors. New York: American Society of Newspaper Editors, multiple years.

Quigg, Lemuel Ely. *Tin-Types Taken in the Streets of New York.* New York: Cassell, 1890.

Quinn, Susan. *Eleanor and Hick: The Love Affair That Shaped a First Lady.* New York: Penguin Press, 2016.

Rabban, David M. *Free Speech in Its Forgotten Years.* Cambridge, U.K.: Cambridge University Press, 1997.

Rayne, M. L. *What Can a Woman Do; or, Her Position in the Business and Literary World.* Petersburgh, N.Y.: Eagle, 1893.

Record Linkage and Privacy: Issues in Creating New Federal and Statistical Information. Washington, D.C.: U.S. General Accounting Office, 2001.

Reel, Guy. *The "National Police Gazette" and the Making of the Modern American Man, 1879–1906.* New York: Palgrave Macmillan, 2006.

Reeves, Richard. *What the People Know: Freedom of the Press.* Cambridge, Mass.: Harvard University Press, 1998.

Remini, Robert V. *The Election of Andrew Jackson.* Philadelphia: J. B. Lippincott, 1963.

Richards, Neil. *Intellectual Privacy: Rethinking Civil Liberties in the Digital Age.* New York: Oxford University Press, 2015.

Richardson, Megan. *The Right to Privacy: Origins and Influence of a Nineteenth-Century Idea.* Cambridge, U.K.: Cambridge University Press, 2017.

Rodgers, Ronald R. *The Struggle for the Soul of Journalism: The Pulpit Versus the Press, 1833–1923.* Columbia: University of Missouri Press, 2018.

Rosen, Jeffrey. *Louis D. Brandeis: American Prophet.* New Haven, Conn.: Yale University Press, 2016.

——. *The Unwanted Gaze: The Destruction of Privacy in America.* New York: Vintage Books, 2000.

Rosen, Michael. *Dignity: Its History and Meaning.* Cambridge, Mass.: Harvard University Press, 2012.

Rosenberg, Norman L. *Protecting the Best Men: An Interpretive History of the Law of Libel.* Chapel Hill: University of North Carolina Press, 1986.

Ross, Charles G. *The Writing of News: A Handbook.* New York: Henry Holt, 1911.

Ross, Ishbel. *Ladies of the Press: The Story of Women in Journalism by an Insider.* New York: Harper & Brothers, 1936.

Rotenberg, Marc, Julia Horwitz, and Jeramie Scott. *Privacy in the Modern Age: The Search for Solutions.* New York: New Press, 2015.

Rothman, Jennifer E. *The Right of Publicity: Privacy Reimagined for a Public World.* Cambridge, Mass.: Harvard University Press, 2018.

Rozenberg, Joshua. *Privacy and the Press.* Oxford: Oxford University Press, 2004.

Rule, James, Douglas McAdam, Linda Stearns, and David Uglow. *The Politics of Privacy.* New York: Mentor Books, 1980.

Rules Governing Newspaper Style. Prepared by Staff of the Department of Journalism. Austin: University of Texas, 1934.

Rutland, Robert Allen. *James Madison: The Founding Father.* New York: Macmillan, 1987.

——. *The Newsmongers: Journalism in the Life of the Nation.* New York: Dial Press, 1973.

S. D. Warren Company. *Paper Permanence: Preserving the Written Word.* Boston: S. D. Warren Company, 1983.

Sachsman, David B., ed. *After the War: The Press in a Changing America, 1865–1900.* London: Routledge, 2017.

Sachsman, David B., and David W. Bulla, eds. *Sensationalism: Murder, Mayhem, Mudslinging, Scandals, and Disasters in 19th Century Reporting.* New Brunswick, N.J.: Transaction, 2013.

Sacks, Jonathan. *The Dignity of Difference: How to Avoid the Clash of Civilizations.* New York: Continuum, 2002.

St. John, Christopher, ed. *Ellen Terry and Bernard Shaw: A Correspondence.* New York: Knickerbocker Press, 1931.

Sanford, Bruce W. *Don't Shoot the Messenger: How Our Growing Hatred of the Media Threatens Free Speech for All of Us.* New York: Free Press, 1999.

Sappenfield, James A. *A Sweet Instruction: Franklin's Journalism as a Literary Apprenticeship.* Carbondale: Southern Illinois University Press, 1973.

Schaelchlin, Patricia A. *The Newspaper Barons: A Biography of the Scripps Family.* San Diego: San Diego Historical Society in association with Kale Press, 2003.

Schiller, Dan. *Objectivity and the News: The Public and the Rise of Commercial Journalism.* Philadelphia: University of Pennsylvania Press, 1981.

Schneider, Carl D. *Shame, Exposure, and Privacy.* New York: W. W. Norton, 1992.

Schoeman, Ferdinand D., ed. *Philosophical Dimensions of Privacy: An Anthology.* London: Cambridge University Press, 1984.

Schroeder, Joseph J., ed. *Sears, Roebuck and Co.: Consumers Guide, Fall 1900.* Catalog No. 110. Reprint, Northfield, Ill.: DBI Books, 1970.

Schroeder, Theodore. *"Obscene" Literature and Constitutional Law: A Forensic Defense of Freedom of the Press.* New York: privately printed, 1911.

Schudson, Michael. *Discovering the News: A Social History of American Newspapers.* New York: Basic Books, 1978.

——. *The Power of News.* Cambridge, Mass.: Harvard University Press, 1995.

Schwartz, Bernard. *A Commentary on the Constitution of the United States: Rights of the Person.* Vol. 1, *Sanctity, Privacy, and Expression.* New York: Macmillan, 1968.

——. *A Commentary on the Constitution of the United States: Rights of the Person.* Vol. 2, *Equality, Belief, and Dignity.* New York: Macmillan, 1968.

Sears, Roebuck and Co. Catalogue No. 114. Reprint, New York: Skyhorse, 2012.

Sedgwick, Ellery. *The Happy Profession.* Boston: Little, Brown, 1946.

Seldes, George. *Even the Gods Can't Change History: The Facts Speak for Themselves.* Secaucus, N.J.: Lyle Stuart, 1976.

——. *Freedom of the Press.* Cleveland: World, 1935.

——. *You Can't Print That! The Truth Behind the News, 1918–1928.* New York: Payson & Clarke, 1929.

Shamir, Milette. *Inexpressible Privacy: The Interior Life of Antebellum American Literature.* Philadelphia: University of Pennsylvania Press, 2006.

Shapiro, Bruce. *Shaking the Foundations: 200 Years of Investigative Journalism in America*. New York: Thunder's Mouth Press, 2003.

Shaw, David. *Journalism Today: A Changing Press for a Changing America*. New York: Harper's College Press, 1976.

Shermer, Michael. *The Science of Good and Evil: Why People Cheat, Gossip, Care, Share, and Follow the Golden Rule*. New York: Henry Holt, 2004.

Sherover, Max. *Fakes in American Journalism*. Buffalo, N.Y.: Buffalo Publishing Company, 1914.

Shields-West, Eileen. *The World Almanac of Presidential Campaigns: All the Facts, Anecdotes, Scandals, and Mudslinging in the History of the Race for the White House*. New York: World Almanac, 1992.

Shuman, E. L. *Practical Journalism: A Complete Manual of the Best Newspaper Methods*. New York: D. Appleton, 1914.

Simonis, H. *The Street of Ink: An Intimate History of Journalism*. London: Cassell, 1917.

Sinclair, Upton. *The Autobiography of Upton Sinclair*. New York: Harcourt, Brace & World, 1962.

——. *The Brass Check: A Study of American Journalism*. Pasadena, Calif.: published by the author, 1919.

——. *Sylvia's Marriage: A Novel*. Long Beach, Calif.: published by the author, 1914.

——. *Upton Sinclair: Biographical and Critical Opinions*. Pasadena, Calif.: published by the author, 1923.

Skinner, B. F. *Beyond Freedom and Dignity*. New York: Alfred A. Knopf, 1972.

Skinner-Thompson, Scott. *Privacy at the Margins*. Cambridge, U.K.: Cambridge University Press, 2021.

Skog, Jason. *Yellow Journalism*. Minneapolis: Compass Point Books, 2007.

Smith, Gene, and Jayne Barry Smith, eds. *The Police Gazette*. New York: Simon & Schuster, 1972.

Smith, Gerrit, and Mary Caldwell Smith, eds. *Lies and Libels of Frank Harris*. With Arguments by Kate Stephens. New York: Antigone Press, 1929.

Smith, Jeffery Alan. *Printers and Press Freedom: The Ideology of Early American Journalism*. New York: Oxford University Press, 1988.

Smith, Richard Norton. *The Colonel: The Life and Legend of Robert R. McCormick*. New York: Houghton Mifflin, 1997.

Smith, Robert Ellis. *Ben Franklin's Web Site: Privacy and Curiosity from Plymouth Rock to the Internet*. Providence: Privacy Journal, 2004.

——. *Privacy: How to Protect What's Left of It*. Garden City, N.Y.: Anchor Press, 1979.

Snowden, Edward. *Permanent Record*. New York: Picador, 2019.

Soderlund, Gretchen. *Sex Trafficking, Scandal, and the Transformation of Journalism, 1885–1917*. Chicago: University of Chicago Press, 2013.

Solomon, Stephen D. *Revolutionary Dissent: How the Founding Generation Created the Freedom of Speech*. New York: St. Martin's Press, 2016.

Solove, Daniel J. *The Future of Reputation: Gossip, Rumor, and Privacy on the Internet*. New Haven, Conn.: Yale University Press, 2007.

——. *Understanding Privacy*. Cambridge, Mass.: Harvard University Press, 2008.

Solove, Daniel J., and Paul M. Schwartz. *Privacy and the Media*. 2nd ed. New York: Wolters Kluwer, 2015.

Somervill, Barbara A. *Ida Tarbell: Pioneer Investigative Reporter*. Greensboro, N.C.: Morgan Reynolds, 2002.

Sotomayor, Sonia. *My Beloved World*. New York: Alfred A. Knopf, 2013.

Sox, David. *Bachelors of Art: Edward Perry Warren and the Lewes House Brotherhood*. London: Fourth Estate, 1991.

Spencer, David R. *The Yellow Journalism: The Press and America's Emergence as a World Power*. Evanston, Ill.: Northwestern University Press, 2007.

Stackpole, E. J. *Behind the Scenes with a Newspaper Man*. Philadelphia: J. B. Lippincott, 1927.

Stanhope, Philip Dormer. *The American Chesterfield; or, Way to Wealth, Honour, and Distinction; Being Selections from the Letters of Lord Chesterfield to His Son; and Extracts from Other Eminent Authors, on the Subject of Politeness: With Alterations and Additions, Suited to the Youth of the United States*. Philadelphia: Lippincott, Grambo, 1828.

Starr, Paul. *The Creation of the Media: Political Origins of Modern Communications*. New York: Basic Books, 2004.

Stasz, Clarice. *The Rockefeller Women: Dynasty of Piety, Privacy, and Service.* New York: St. Martin's Press, 1995.

Steigleman, Walter A. *The Newspaperman and the Law.* Dubuque, Iowa: W. C. Brown, 1950.

Stein, M. L. *Freedom of the Press: A Continuing Struggle.* New York: Julian Messner, 1966.

Steinberg, Cobbett S. *TV Facts.* New York: Facts on File, 1980.

Steinberg, Stacey. *Growing Up Shared.* Naperville, Ill.: Sourcebooks, 2020.

Stephens, Mitchell. *Beyond News: The Future of Journalism.* New York: Columbia University Press, 2014.

Sterling, Christopher H., ed. *Encyclopedia of Journalism.* Los Angeles: Sage, 2009.

Stern, Philip Van Doren, and Herbert Asbury, eds. *The Breathless Moment: The World's Most Sensational News Photos.* New York: Alfred A. Knopf, 1935.

Stevens, John D. *Sensationalism and the New York Press.* New York: Columbia University Press, 1991.

Stoddard, Henry Luther. *Horace Greeley: Printer, Editor, Crusader.* New York: G. P. Putnam's Sons, 1946.

Strum, Philippa. *Louis D. Brandeis: Justice for the People.* New York: Schocken Books, 1984.

———. *Privacy: The Debate in the United States Since 1945.* Fort Worth, Tex.: Harcourt Brace College Publishers, 1998.

Sullivan, Harold W. *Contempts by Publication: The Law of Trial by Newspaper.* 3rd ed. Privately printed, 1941.

Sutton, Albert Alton. *Education for Journalism in the United States from Its Beginning to 1940.* Evanston, Ill.: Northwestern University, 1945.

Swanberg, W. A. *Citizen Hearst: A Monumental and Controversial Biography of One of the Most Fabulous Characters in American History.* New York: Galahad Books, 1961.

Swindler, William F. *A Bibliography of Law on Journalism.* New York: Columbia University Press, 1947.

———. *Problems of Law in Journalism.* New York: Macmillan, 1955.

Talese, Gay. *The Kingdom and the Power: Behind the Scenes at "The New York Times": The Institution That Influences the World.* New York: World, 1977.

Tarbell, Ida M. *The History of the Standard Oil Company.* Edited by David M. Chalmers. New York: W. W. Norton, 1966.

Tebbel, John. *The Compact History of the American Newspaper.* New York: Hawthorn Books, 1963.

Teeter, Dwight L., Don R. Le Duc, and Bill Loving. *Law of Mass Communications: Freedom and Control of Print and Broadcast Media.* 9th ed. New York: Foundation Press, 1998.

Terry, Ellen, and Bernard Shaw. *Ellen Terry and Bernard Shaw: A Correspondence.* Edited by Christopher St. John. New York: Knickerbocker Press, 1931.

Thayer, Frank. *Legal Control of the Press: Concerning Libel, Privacy, Contempt, Copyright, Regulation of Advertising and Postal Laws.* 4th ed. Brooklyn: Foundation Press, 1962.

Things I Shouldn't Tell. Philadelphia: J. B. Lippincott, 1925.

Thomas, Isaiah. *The History of Printing in America: With a Biography of Printers in Two Volumes.* New York: Burt Franklin, 1874.

Thurber, James. *The Years with Ross.* New York: Little, Brown, 1957.

Tiffin, Walter F. *Gossip About Portraits, Including Engraved Portraits.* London: John Russell Smith, 1867.

Time-Life Books. *Prelude to the Century, 1870–1900.* New York: Bishop Books, 1999.

———. *This Fabulous Century.* Vol. 3, *1920–1930.* New York: Time-Life Books, 1969.

———. *This Fabulous Century.* Vol. 4, *1930–1940.* New York: Time-Life Books, 1969.

Tobin, A. I., and Elmer Gertz. *Frank Harris: A Study in Black and White.* Chicago: Madelaine Mendelsohn, 1931.

Todd, A. L. *Justice on Trial: The Case of Louis D. Brandeis.* Chicago: University of Chicago Press, 1964.

Townshend, John. *A Treatise on the Wrongs Called Slander and Libel, and on the Remedy by Civil Action for Those Wrongs, to Which Is Added in This Edition a Chapter on Malicious Prosecution.* 3rd ed. New York: Baker, Voorhis, 1877.

Trager, Robert, Joseph Russomanno, and Susan Dente Ross. *The Law of Journalism and Mass Communication.* New York: McGraw-Hill, 2007.

Tuchman, Barbara W. *The Proud Tower: A Portrait of the World Before the War, 1890–1914.* New York: Macmillan, 1966.

Twain, Mark. *The Complete Works of Mark Twain: Mark Twain's Speeches.* New York: Harper & Bros., 1923.

———. *Journalism in Tennessee and Other Humorous Sketches*. Girard, Kans.: Haldeman-Julius, 1924.

Tweed, Paul. *Privacy and Libel Law: The Clash with Press Freedom*. Haywards Heath, U.K.: Bloomsbury Professional, 2012.

Underwood, Agness. *Newspaperwoman*. New York: Harper & Brothers, 1949.

Urofsky, Melvin I. *Louis D. Brandeis: A Life*. New York: Schocken Books, 2009.

———. *Louis D. Brandeis and the Progressive Tradition*. Edited by Oscar Handlin. Boston: Little, Brown, 1981.

———. *A Mind of One Piece: Brandeis and American Reform*. New York: Charles Scribner's Sons, 1971.

Urofsky, Melvin I., and David W. Levy, eds. *The Family Letters of Louis D. Brandeis*. Norman: University of Oklahoma Press, 2002.

———. *Letters of Louis D. Brandeis*. Vol. 1, *1870–1907, Urban Reformer*. Albany: State University of New York Press, 1971.

———. *Letters of Louis D. Brandeis*. Vol. 2, *1907–1912, People's Attorney*. Albany: State University of New York Press, 1972.

———. *Letters of Louis D. Brandeis*. Vol. 3, *1913–1915, Progressive and Zionist*. Albany: State University of New York Press, 1973.

———. *Letters of Louis D. Brandeis*. Vol. 4, *1916–1921, Mr. Justice Brandeis*. Albany: State University of New York Press, 1975.

———. *Letters of Louis D. Brandeis*. Vol. 5, *1921–1941, Elder Statesman*. Albany: State University of New York Press, 1978.

Van Every, Edward. *Sins of New York as "Exposed" by the "Police Gazette."* New York: F. A. Stokes, 1930.

Villard, Oswald Garrison. *The Disappearing Daily: Some Chapters in American Newspaper Evolution*. New York: Alfred A. Knopf, 1944.

Vincent, David. *Privacy: A Short History*. Malden, Mass.: Polity, 2016.

Vitray, Laura, John Mills Jr., and Roscoe Ellard. *Pictorial Journalism*. New York: McGraw-Hill, 1939.

Wacks, Raymond. *Privacy and Media Freedom*. Oxford: Oxford University Press, 2013.

Wagman, Robert J. *The First Amendment Book*. New York: Pharos Books, 1991.

Walker, James Herbert. *The Johnstown Horror!!! or, Valley of Death, Being a Complete and Thrilling Account of the Awful Floods and Their Appalling Ruin*. Philadelphia: John C. Winston, 1889.

Walker, Stanley. *City Editor*. New York: Blue Ribbon Books, 1934.

Wallace, Amy. *The Prodigy: A Biography of William James Sidis*. New York: E. P. Dutton, 1986.

Walls, Jeannette. *Dish: How Gossip Became the News and the News Became Just Another Show*. New York: Avon Books, 2000.

Ward, Stephen J. A. *The Invention of Journalism Ethics: The Path to Objectivity and Beyond*. Montreal: McGill-Queen's University Press, 2004.

Warren, Cornelia. *A Memorial of My Mother*. Boston: Merrymount Press, 1908.

———. *Miss Wilton*. Boston: Houghton, Mifflin, 1892.

Warren, Edward Perry. *A Defence of Uranian Love*. Edited by Michael Matthew Kaylor. Translated by Mark Robert Miner. Kansas City: Valancourt Books, 2009.

———. *The Prince Who Did Not Exist*. Forest Park, Ill.: Acorn Press, 1958.

Warren, Henry Clarke. *Buddhism in Translations: Passages Selected from the Original Pali into English*. Cambridge, Mass.: Harvard University Press, 1922.

Warren, J. A. *A History of S. D. Warren Company, 1854–1954*. Portland, Ore.: Anthoensen Press, 1954.

Warren, Samuel D., and Louis D. Brandeis. *The Right to Privacy*. 1890. New Orleans: Quid Pro Law Books, 2010.

Watson, Elmo Scott. *A History of Newspaper Syndicates in the United States, 1865–1935*. Chicago, 1935.

Weinberg, Steve. *Taking on the Trust: The Epic Battle of Ida Tarbell and John D. Rockefeller*. New York: W. W. Norton, 2008.

Weingarten, Marc. *The Gang That Wouldn't Write Straight: Wolfe, Thompson, Didion, and the New Journalism Revolution*. New York: Crown, 2006.

Wells, Richard A. *Manners, Culture, and Dress of the Best American Society*. Springfield, Mass.: King, Richardson, 1891.

Westin, Alan F. *Privacy and Freedom*. New York: Atheneum, 1968.

White, Llewellyn. *The American Radio: A Report on the Broadcasting Industry in the United States from the Commission on Freedom of the Press*. Chicago: University of Chicago Press, 1947.

Whiting, Lilian. *Kate Field: A Record*. Boston: Little, Brown, 1900.

Whitman, Walt. *Leaves of Grass*. 1855. New York: Oxford University Press, 2005.

Whitney, A. D. T. *A Golden Gossip: Neighborhood Story Number Two*. Boston: Houghton, Mifflin, 1892.

Wickwar, William Hardy. *The Struggle for the Freedom of the Press, 1819–1832*. London: George Allen & Unwin, 1928.

Wilde, Oscar. *The Trial of Oscar Wilde: From the Shorthand Reports*. London: Forgotten Books, 2017.

Willard, Roger. *Missing Persons USA: How to Hunt Down and Find Anyone, Anywhere*. Boulder, Colo.: Paladin Press, 1994.

Williams, Sara Lockwood. *Twenty Years of Education for Journalism: A History of the School of Journalism of the University of Missouri, Columbia, Missouri, U.S.A.* Columbia, Mo.: E. W. Stephens, 1929.

Williams, Talcott. *The Newspaper Man*. New York: Charles Scribner's Sons, 1922.

Wilson, Jean Moorcroft. *Siegfried Sassoon: The Journey from the Trenches: A Biography, 1918–1967*. New York: Routledge, 1999.

———. *Siegfried Sassoon: The Making of a War Poet: A Biography, 1886–1918*. New York: Routledge, 2003.

Winfield, Betty Houchin. *FDR and the News Media*. Urbana: University of Illinois Press, 1990.

———, ed. *Journalism 1908: Birth of a Profession*. Columbia: University of Missouri Press, 2008.

Wingate, Charles F., ed. *Views and Interviews on Journalism*. New York: F. B. Patterson, 1875.

Wolfe, Tom. *The New Journalism*. New York: Harper & Row, 1973.

Woman: Her Dignity and Sphere. New York: American Tract Society, 1870.

Wood, J. G. *The Uncivilized Races of Men in All Countries of the World: Being a Comprehensive Account of Their Manners and Customs, and of Their Physical, Social, Mental, Moral, and Religious Characteristics, in Two Volumes*. Vol. 2. Hartford: J. B. Burr, 1870.

Woody, Robert Henley. *Psychological Information: Protecting the Right to Privacy: A Guidebook for Mental Health Practitioners and Their Clients*. Madison, Conn.: Psychosocial Press, 2001.

The World War in Photographs, Uncensored. New York: International Newspaper Syndicate, 1934.

Wright, William. *Harvard's Secret Court: The Savage 1920 Purge of Campus Homosexuals*. New York: St. Martin's Press, 2005.

Wyatt, Wendy N., ed. *The Ethics of Journalism: Individual, Institutional, and Cultural Influences*. New York: Palgrave Macmillan, 2014.

Yochelson, Bonnie. *Jacob A. Riis: Revealing New York's Other Half: A Complete Catalogue of His Photographs*. New Haven, Conn.: Yale University Press, 2015.

Young, John H. *Our Deportment; or, The Manners, Conduct, and Dress of the Most Refined Society*. Detroit: F. B. Dickerson, 1881.

Young, John P. *Journalism in California: Pacific Coast and Exposition Biographies*. San Francisco: Chronicle, 1915.

Zelermyer, William. *Invasion of Privacy*. New York: Syracuse University Press, 1959.

Zelezny, John D. *Communications Law: Liberties, Restraints, and the Modern Media*. 4th ed. Belmont, Calif.: Wadsworth, 2004.

Ziff, Larzer. *The American 1890s: Life and Times of a Lost Generation*. New York: Viking Press, 1966.

Zittrain, Jonathan. *The Future of the Internet and How to Stop It*. New Haven, Conn.: Yale University Press, 2008.

Zuboff, Shoshana. *The Age of Surveillance Capitalism: The Fight for a Human Future at the New Frontier of Power*. New York: Hachette, 2019.

INDEX

abortion choice, privacy in, xvi, 178–79, 223, 238
Abrams, Floyd, 190, 239
Abrams v. United States, 131, 135
academic freedom, 176
Adams, Elbridge, 118, 119, 122–24, 126
Adams, John
  on abuses of the press, 17
  and Alien and Sedition Acts (1798), 17, 19
  and Callender's death, 23
  Callender's pamphlet criticizing, 19, 20, 26
  on right to publish embarrassing truth, 264–65
  and truthful libel, 17
adoptions, secret, 195
adultery, 83–87
advertising, using a woman's likeness in, 116–19
AIDS, 273
Air Force Academy, 180, 247
Air Force v. Rose, 180
An Album of Portraits of Celebrities, 50
Alien and Sedition Acts (1798), 16, 17, 19, 23–24
Amazon, 233–34
The American Bookseller, 60
American Civil Liberties Union (ACLU)
  and Miss Vermont's suit against Max, 215
  and revenge porn, 187, 223
  and Section 230 of the Communications Decency Act, 206, 208
  and Wiseman's *Titicut Follies*, 187
An American Family, 191
American Journalism (Mott), 80, 151
American Law Institute
  "International Bill of Rights" project of, 161–62, 163

"Principles of the Law: Data Privacy" project of, 237
  reformulation of privacy section in the Restatement, 173
  "right to privacy" phrase embraced by, 159
  on time's impact on privacy, 246
  See also Restatement of the Law of Torts
American Nervousness, 63, 208
American Social Science Association, 123
American Society of Newspaper Editors (ASNE), 146–47, 148–50, 256, 257
America's Funniest Home Videos, 191
anxiety, 207
Aquarian Foundation, 181
arrest records, 237, 247
art works, 120–21
artificial intelligence, 239, 240
artistic rights, 73
Ashe, Arthur, 272–75
Assault on Privacy: Computers, Data Banks, and Dossiers (Miller), 236
Associated Press, 110
associates included in background checks, 232–33
athletes
  medical records of, 222, 253
  poor grades of, 195
Atlanta Constitution, x
The Atlantic, 44
Atlantic Monthly, 77
authority, positions of, 88–91

background checks, 232–33
backpage.com, 207
Baltimore Sun, 145, 157
bank account activity, 233
bankruptcies, 233, 244

Baquet, Dean, 260
Bartnicki v. Vopper, 175, 184, 270
Bayard, Miss Katie, 56–57
Bayard, Mrs., 56–57
Bayard, Thomas, 50, 56, 68
Bayard, William, 26
Bayard family tragedies, 56–59
BBC, 263–64, 266
Beauharnais v. Illinois, 176
The Bee, 21, 24
Beecher, Henry Ward, 40, 55, 65–66
Benoit, Nancy, 220, 245
Bernhardt, Sarah, xi
Bernstein, Carl, 197
Bickford, M. A., 35
Biden, Joe, 251, 253
Big Brother, 197
Bill of Rights
    and guarantee of personal privacy, 179
    limited applicability of, in early American
        society, 16
    and Miss Vermont's suit against Max, 215
    predated by privacy, 177
    and press freedom balanced with
        privacy, 258
binding precedents, xviii
biometrics, 238–39
birth control, restrictions on, 177
birth date, public availability of, 232, 233
Bissell, Wilson, 64, 65
Black, Hugo, 171, 178
Black American press, 42
Black community, 81, 90, 146
Black Lives Matter, xii, 268
blackmailers, potential, 236
Blackstone's *Commentaries on the Laws of
    England*, 15, 46, 142
Blaine, James, 81
Blipdar website, 206
bloggers, 156
bloodshed, news about, 170
Bly, Nellie, xiii, 60–62, 63, 101
Boccaccio (Broadway play), x, xiii
Borat films, 198, 261
Boston, Massachusetts, 36, 94
Boston American, 96
Boston Daily Advertiser, 5–6, 7
Boston Daily Globe, 94–95
Boston Globe
    on Brandeis, 58
    on Sidis, 166, 167
    on Titicut Follies case, 187
    on Warren family matters, 50, 96, 98
    on Warren's death, 97
Boston Herald, 6, 55
Boston Journal, 102
Boston Museum of Fine Arts, 94, 111–13
Boston Post, 47, 70, 76, 94, 95, 96

Brandeis, Louis
    and Adams, Elbridge, 123
    and *Cape Cod Folks* (*Nightingale* case), 3–6,
        7, 8–10, 11, 47, 58, 73, 74, 87
    correspondence of, 133
    death of sister, 59
    early law career of, 47–48, 49
    and Ernst, 168
    as First Amendment legend, 131
    on First Amendment's limitations, 137
    and *Harvard Law Review*, 48–49, 77–78
    at Harvard Law School, 45–47
    and Holmes, 48
    impact of, on privacy, 121
    and Manola's tights, ix
    and marketplace-of-ideas language, 135,
        136–37
    and *Near* case, 143
    and Ned Warren, 39, 134
    newspaper publishing experience of, 70
    and Nixon's radio address on privacy, 260
    Olmstead dissent of, 138–39, 179, 267
    personal motives for privacy aims, xii
    and police wiretaps, 138–39
    premium placed on privacy, 131, 133
    press coverage of, 58–59
    on publication of tax records, 259
    success of, 92
    on Supreme Court, xiv, 98, 129–30, 166
    Supreme Court confirmation hearings,
        134–35
    on Toledo's newspaper editorials, 129–30
    and Warren family trust, 70, 93, 95–96, 98
    and Warren's death, 96–97
    Warren's friendship with, 45–46, 92
    See also "The Right to Privacy"
Brandeis, Richard, 9–10, 59
Branzburg v. Hayes, 178
*The Brass Check: A Study of American
    Journalism* (Sinclair), 106, 109–10,
        113, 143
Brennan, William, 178, 189
Breyer, Stephen, 261–62, 267
Bridgewater State Hospital, 185–90
broadcasters and power of FCC, xvii
Brother XII, 181
Brown, Henry Billings, 123–27
Browning, Robert, 154
Burnett, Frances Hodgson, 62–63
Burr, Aaron, 26
Bush, George W., 259

California
    and biometrics privacy, 239
    right to be forgotten in, 245, 246
    state constitution's provision on right to
        privacy, xvi
California Consumer Privacy Act, 234

California Supreme Court, 85–87, 193, 266
California v. Greenwood, 182
Callender, James, 13–14, 16, 19–21, 22–23, 24, 26
Cambridge Analytica's use of personal data, 238
cameras
    as addressed in "The Right to Privacy," 72
    in *To Catch a Predator*, 217
    court rulings with implications for photographers, 119
    doorbells with video cameras, 225–26
    hidden cameras, 199–200, 228, 229
    marketed for purpose of invading privacy, x–xi
    and paparazzi, 229–30
    and photo of Manola's tights, x
    portable, 69
    used to record police use of force, 227
Candid Camera, 191
Cape Cod Folks (McLean)
    and Brandeis work on "The Right to Privacy," 74
    lawsuit prompted by, 5
    and loss of dignity, 5, 265
    and *Nightingale* case, 5–6, 7, 8–10, 11, 47, 58, 73, 87
    subject matter of, 3–5
Capitol riots, January 6, 2021, 270
Carlin, George, 181
Carpenter v. United States, 183
cars
    black boxes, 235
    public availability of ownership records, 232
Carter, Jimmy, 215
Case and Comment magazine, 79
Castles in the Air (Broadway play), ix–x
Catherine, Duchess of Cambridge, 229–30
Catholic priest's use of hookup app, 229
Cedarville, Massachusetts, 3–6
cell phone towers, tracking through, 183
Century Magazine, 77, 97, 132
Cercle Français, 74
charities, donors to, 241
Chase, W. Calvin, 80–81, 88–91, 146
cheatersandbastards.com, 206
Chicago Sun-Times, 222
Chicago Tribune, 216–17, 249
children, publication of personal information about, 178
Chin, Denny, 219, 266, 268, 269–70
Christian Science Monitor, 145, 151
Cincinnati Enquirer, 50
The Circle, 226
civil rights, xi, 171
civil-law systems, xviii
Claflin, Tennie, 40

Clementi, Tyler, 207
Cleveland, Frances Clara, xi
Cleveland, Frances Folsom
    Bly's story on, 60–61
    and husband's relationship with Nash, 53
    husband's role in youth of, 53–54
    image used in advertising, 73, 116
    marriage of, 52, 54
    public interest in, 55–56, 58
    rumors about private life of, 67, 68
    and Tarbell, 107
    and the Warrens, 58, 70
Cleveland, Grover
    and Chase, 80–81, 88–91
    compared with Jefferson, 65
    demands for privacy, 54, 56, 268
    as guardian of Frances, 53–54
    and Kate Nash, 52–53, 63–66
    law partner of, 53–54
    marriage of, 52, 54
    personal motives for privacy aims, xii
    public interest in, 55–56
    reelection campaign, 67–68
    and "The Right to Privacy," 75
    and rumors of domestic abuse, 67
    secrets of, 54–55, 91, 256
    and Tarbell, 106–7
    on Tilton-Beecher adultery case, 65–66
    and the Warrens, 58, 70
Clinton, Bill
    and Chin's judicial appointment, 219
    and Communications Decency Act, 203
    pleas for privacy, 255–56
    sexual indiscretions of, 255–56
    and Starr's report, 174
Clinton, Hillary, 255
Closer magazine, 254
cloud-based storage, 138
CNN, 206, 208
Cohen, Sacha Baron, 198, 261
College ACB website, 206
college sports, reporting on, 195
Colorado Supreme Court, 128–29
Colored Press Association, 146
Columbia University, 147
Commentaries on the Laws of England (Blackstone), 15, 46, 142
common law (court-created law)
    about, xv, xvii–xviii
    and citations to other court decisions, xix
    countries that apply, xviii
    and evolving needs of society, xxii
    firming up of right to privacy in, 121
    and history of right to privacy, 223, 272
    and statutory law, xx
Commonwealth v. Blanding, 28, 129, 136, 142

confessions from defendants in criminal cases, 180
Congress, U.S.
  and biometrics privacy, 239
  and cyberporn, 201
  on data collection concerns, 236
  passage of legislation, xx
  and Privacy Act, 237
  and Section 230 of the Communications Decency Act, 202, 205, 207
Conradt, Bill, 217–19
Constitution of the United States
  blessings of liberties ensured by, 266–67
  and *Lochner* dissent of Holmes, 134
  and *Price v. Price* divorce case, 85–87
  and stare decisis, xv
  as supreme law of the land, xx
constitutional law, xv–xvi
Cooley, Thomas, 8, 85, 87, 118, 121, 124
Cops, 191
copyright protections, 269
Cornell University, 147
correspondence, personal
  of Brandeis, 133
  European Convention on Human Rights on, 162
  and freedom of the press, 33, 34
  of Harding, 145, 150
  of Holmes, 131–33
  legislation protecting, 14
  lower courts on privacy of, 128
  Martin's ruling on newspapers printing, 29–30
  protection of, 33, 121
  Restatement on privacy of, 247
courts
  and dicta regarding right to privacy, xix–xx
  official status of right to privacy in, 160
  "right to privacy" phrase used by, 146, 151, 159
  See also Supreme Court, U.S.; *specific cases and justices*
COVID-19, 251–52, 253
Cowley v. Pulsifer, 6–7
Cox, Christopher, 201, 202, 203
Cox, James M., 145
Cox Broadcasting v. Cohn, 171
Craig, Larry, 261
creativity, 267
credit card activity, 233
credit reports, privacy of, 181, 244
crimes and criminal cases
  and arrest records, 182, 237, 247
  and criminal histories, 182
  criminal law, xvi
  and exclusion of media from trials, 181
  included in background checks, 233
  media publicity for murder trials, 177

and mug shots, 180, 196–97, 242–43, 248–49
  photographs of murder scenes, 169
  press coverage of, 249
  and privacy protections, 159, 271
  and publication of confessions, 180
  and right to be forgotten, 242–44
  stories or photographs of crime scenes, 169–70
  and warrantless tracking through cell phone towers, 183
The Crimes of the "Times" pamphlet (Sinclair), 110
Cross Creek (Rawlings), 161
Croswell, Harry, 22–24, 80
Croswell case
  cited by Pound, 158
  Hamilton's argument in, 24–26, 27, 28, 87, 121, 268
  on motives for publishing the truth, 268
  and "Pandora's box" comment, 157, 168
  as precedent, 30
  ruling in, 24
Cushing, William, 17, 264–65
cyberporn, 201–2

Dana, Charles, 39
data, personal
  Americans' interest in privacy of, 181, 236, 237
  available for purchase, 233
  and background checks, 232–33
  and biometrics, 238–39
  Cambridge Analytica's use of, 238
  in dossiers, 231–33, 238, 241
  justices' concerns about, 178
  laws protecting, 235, 240–41, 267
  maintained by data collection companies, 234–35
  and Salas's family tragedy, 231, 236, 240
Dateline, 217–19
Davies, Marion, 149
death of privacy, claims of, 174, 175, 190, 236
deaths
  executions, 39, 169
  and *Hustler*'s misappropriation of Benoit images, 220
  invasive coverage of, 56–59, 183, 197
  and privacy protections, 271
  publication of photographs of, 169–70
  and statement of a grieving mother, 216–17
  video of fatal accident scene, 223
Debs, Eugene, 152
debt proceedings, 244
Declaration of Independence, 267
deepfakes, 240
defamation, 114–15, 170, 180, 181
Delaware, 239

Dembitz, Lewis, 51, 77
democracy, 265
Democratic National Convention (1888), 67–68
Denis, Henry, 29–30, 33, 265
Dennie, Joseph, 27
depression, 207
Dershowitz, Alan, 189
DeSalvo, Albert, 186
Detroit Free Press, 242, 243
Detroit News, 148
Deutsche Welle, 254
Dickens, Charles, 31–32
dicta regarding right to privacy, xix–xx
dignity
    of Ashe, 275
    and BBC's invasion of Richard's privacy, 264
    as counterbalance to press freedoms, 266
    in culture of transparency, 267
    and First Amendment freedoms, 272
    "The Right to Privacy" on, 266
    value placed on, 264, 265–66
The Dirty, 204–6, 208–9
dirtyphonebook.com, 206
dish towel, woman escaping abduction wearing, 194, 196, 198
disinformation, 208
divorces
    discussed in school newspaper article, 181–82
    Price v. Price divorce case, 83–87
    of Rockefeller, 257–58
    Supreme Court on release of details from, 180
DNA test results, 235–36
Doe v. McMillan, 178
domestic violence, 266, 268
doorbells with video cameras, 225–26, 229
dossiers, personal, 231–33, 238, 241
Douglas, William O., 178, 189
doxing, 237
driver's licenses, 222, 232
Driver's Privacy Protection Act, 235
driving record, public availability of, 232
drug testing, xi

Eggers, Dave, 226
elites/prominent individuals
    as best arbiters of privacy standards, 73
    Boston newspapers' criticisms of, 95
    Chase's penchant for attacking, 80
    as target of penny press, 40
    targeted by Pulitzer's *The World*, 59–60
email, 203
embarrassing truths, 15, 30–33, 106, 269
emotional harm
    and *Closer* ruling, 254
    and *Conradt* case, 218

considered in court decisions, 30–31
Gawker sued for, 221
websites trafficking in, 206–9, 269
employment history, data on, 233
England
    privacy laws in, 74
    Star Chamber of, 10–11, 85, 268
Ernst, Morris, 167–68
Eros magazine, 153–54
ESPN, 222
ethnicity, public availability of, 233
etiquette advice on scandals, 32
Europe
    European Court of Justice, 244
    freedom of expression in, 244, 254
    General Data Protection Regulation, 234
    privacy expectations in, 229–30, 253, 254
European Convention on Human Rights, 162, 254
The Evening World, 88
excessive privacy, xii
executions, 39, 169
Experian, 234–35, 240
exposé reporting, 60–63

Facebook
    ban of Trump, 271
    and Cambridge Analytica, 238
    liability of users on, 156
    Oversight Board of, 271
    privacy protection measures of, 241
    and Section 230 of the Communications Decency Act, 206, 208
    and "Tag Suggestions" program, 239
Faces of Death, 197
facial recognition technology, 229, 238, 239
Fair Credit Reporting Act, 235
Fall, Albert, 145
false light, xviii, 173, 177
Falwell, Jerry, 182
family matters, privacy in, 8, 162, 179, 183, 254
family members included in background checks, 232–33
family trees in public databases, 66
Favish case, 183
Federal Communications Commission (FCC), xvii, 181
Field, Walbridge, 7
Fifth Amendment, 179
"Filthy Words" (Carlin), 181
fingerprints, 238–39
The First 48, 223
First Amendment
    backlash against doctrine, 215–17
    Brandeis on limitations of, 137
    Brown on limitations of, 127
    and courts on publishers' violations of secrets, 33

First Amendment (*cont.*)
  and cultural/legal shift to right to
    know, 174
  in early American society, 16, 17
  and early freedom of the press cases, 6–7, 26
  Holmes and Brandeis as defenders of, 131
  in Internet age, 156
  and journalists' rights, 196
  judiciary's refocus on, 41
  and marketplace-of-ideas language, 136
  and Miss Vermont's suit against Max,
    214–15
  newsworthy information protected by, 196,
    223, 260
  and *Sidis* case, 165–68, 185
  Supreme Court on limitations of, 135
  and value placed on liberty, 264
  See also freedom of expression; freedom of
    speech; freedom of the press
Fisher, Adelaide, 5
Fisk University, 147
fitness trackers, 235
Florida Star v. B.J.F.
  and later rulings, 182
  on liberty/privacy balance, 270–71
  and privacy-promoting language, 184
  ruling in, 172, 174, 265
Folsom, Oscar, 53–54
Ford, Gerald, 195
Foster, Vince, 183
Founding Fathers
  and Brandeis's *Olmstead* dissent, 139
  and *People v. Croswell* case, 11
  privacy prioritized by, 17–19
  public interest in personal lives of, xiii
Fourteenth Amendment, 179, 266
Fourth Amendment, 179
France, privacy laws in, 74, 254
Frank Leslie's Illustrated Newspaper, 35
Frankfurter, Felix, 136, 137, 138, 170
Franklin, Ben, 14, 17–18
Franklin Mills Flour Company, 117–19
Free Press, 126
freedom of expression
  as American value, 264–65
  balanced with right to be let alone, 268
  and BBC's invasion of Richard's privacy, 264
  in Europe, 162, 244, 254
  as First Amendment right, xv
  and First Amendment work of Holmes and
    Brandeis, 131
  in Internet age, 156, 269
  and liberty/privacy balance, 271
  and *New York Times v. Sullivan*, 154
  and Section 230 of the Communications
    Decency Act, 269
freedom of information, xi, xxi
Freedom of Information Act (1966), 172–73, 183

"Freedom of Public Discussion" (*Harvard Law
  Review*), 97–98
freedom of speech
  Brandeis on, 137
  in early American society, 16
  as First Amendment right, xv
  and *Headquarters Detective* case, 170
  Lewis on need for balance, 197
  limitations of, 85, 127, 137, 143
  and Miss Vermont's suit against Max, 213
  and *New York Times v. Sullivan*, 265
  Roosevelt on, 160
  shifts from right to privacy to, 177
  and state constitutions, 33–34
  Supreme Court decisions on, 135–37
  and websites trafficking in emotional/
    reputational harm, 207
freedom of the press
  as American value, 264–65
  and BBC's invasion of Richard's privacy, 264
  and Blackstone's *Commentaries*, 46
  Brandeis on restraints of, 130
  compared to Pandora's box, 157, 168
  courts/rulings privileging privacy over,
    33, 159
  and *Croswell* case, 22, 24–26, 27, 28
  cultural/legal shift away from right to
    privacy to, 177
  database search for term, 185
  democracy's dependence on, 265
  dignity as counterbalance to, 266
  in early American society, 6–7, 16
  and early concepts of right to privacy, xi
  as First Amendment right, xv
  and Founding Fathers, 17–19
  Frankfurter on limitations of, 137
  Goldberg on, 258
  and government corruption, 140–43
  and Jefferson's criticisms of the press,
    18–19
  Lewis on need for balance, 197
  and Martin on newspapers printing private
    correspondence, 30
  and Miss Vermont's suit against Max,
    214–15
  and *Near v. Minnesota*, 140–43
  and *Price v. Price* divorce case, 83–87
  and right to be forgotten, 244
  right to privacy as counterbalance to, xii
  "The Right to Privacy" on, 265
  and right to publish embarrassing truths,
    264–65
  and *Sidis* case, 165–68, 185
  and sources of journalists, 178, 182
  and state constitutions, 33–34
  Supreme Court on, 125–29, 140–43, 170–75,
    178, 180–81
  and value placed on liberty, 264

and Zenger, 15–16
See also journalism and the press
freedom-of-information laws, 82
Freemark Communications, 203
frequent shopper cards of grocery stores, 235
Friend of the Laws newspaper, 29–30
Friendly, Fred, 140, 141
"Fuck the Draft" jacket, 177
funeral picketing case, 183
Furnish, David, 163

Garrison v. Louisiana, 177
Gawker
    and Hogan sex tape, 116, 184–85,
        220–22, 223
    and Section 230 of the Communications
        Decency Act, 206
    and teen's lawsuit for emotional harm, 221
    and Thiel, 222
Gayet, Julie, 254
Gaynor, William, 97
Gazette of the United States, 12–13
gender identity, 245, 271
General Data Protection Regulation, 234
Georgia, right to privacy in, 121
Germany, 254
Girls Gone Wild, 227
Godkin, E. L.
    on Cleveland's presidential campaign, 55
    on Cleveland's speech, 56
    influence of, 106
    on reporting on family tragedies, 57
    "The Rights of the Citizen: To His Own
        Reputation," 71
    and Sinclair's criticism of media, 101
    on standards in publishing, 41–42
    on threats to dignity, 71, 265
Goldberg, Arthur, 175, 258
Goldmark, Alice, 70
Goldschmidt, Neil, 249–50
Google, 206, 208, 249
Google Maps, 241
Gorsuch, Neil, 269
gossip, 72, 73, 264, 270
government
    and Alien and Sedition Acts (1798),
        16, 17
    arrests of critical journalists, 16
    and Chase-Cleveland clash, 88–91
    criticisms of, 15–16
    data collected by, 237
    exposure of corruption in, 140–43
    and limitations of freedom of the press, 142
    and *Olmstead* dissents of Brandeis and
        Holmes, 139
    and Pentagon Papers case, 171, 178
    and police wiretaps, 138–39
    and right to know, 82–83

Supreme Court on media's responsibility to
    report on, 171
    and *Titicut Follies* documentary, 185–90
Gray, Horace, 78, 125, 179
Griswold v. Connecticut, 177
Guilford, Howard, 140–43

hacking, 138
Halpin, Maria, 54, 55, 66
Hamilton, Alexander
    affair of, revealed, 13–14, 25
    cited by judges, 32–33
    and *Croswell* case, 24–26, 28, 87, 121, 268
    death of, 26
    and *Nightingale* case, 10
    personal motives for privacy aims, xii
    and Philaenus pseudonym, 21
    privacy prioritized by, 18
    pseudonymous attacks on Jefferson,
        12–13
    quoted in latter cases, 27
    and state constitutions' protections,
        33–34
    and Washington's personal
        correspondence, 14
Hampton's Magazine, 97
Han, Ki Suk, 197
hand scans, 238, 239
Hansen, Chris, 217–19
Hapgood, Norman, 133
happiness, necessity of privacy for, 73
Harding, Warren G.
    on ethical standards in journalism, 144–45,
        146–47, 148–49, 270
    personal correspondence of, 145, 150
    secret child of, 149–50, 256
    self-interested use of privacy by, 268
    sexual indiscretions of, 145, 268
    and Teapot Dome scandal, 145, 146
Harding's Creed, 145, 147
Hardy, Dr., 35
Harlan, John Marshall (1877–1911), 124–25
Harlan, John Marshall, II (1899–1971), 189
Harper's Weekly, 35
Harris, Frank, 152–55
Harrison, Benjamin, 70, 88
Harry, Prince, Duke of Sussex, 231–32
Harvard College
    class song of 1875, 44–45
    The Magenta (later *The Harvard Crimson*),
        36–37, 42–44
    Warren at, 36–37, 42, 44–45
Harvard Law Review
    "Freedom of Public Discussion," 97–98
    "The Right to Privacy" promoted in, 77–78
    "The Right to Privacy" published in, xx,
        71–72
    Warren and Brandeis's roles in, 48–49

Harvard Law School, 45–47
Harvard Law School Association, 49, 78
hate speech, 176
Hazelwood v. Kuhlmeier, 181–82
Headquarters Detective: True Cases from the Police Blotter magazine, 169–70
Health Insurance Portability and Accountability Act, 235
Hearst, William Randolph, 149
Hearst newspapers, 97
Hemings, Sally, 13, 20–21, 23, 27, 28
Herbert v. Lando, 181
High Court of Justice in London, 264
high courts, xvii–xviii
"highly offensive" revelations, xvii–xviii
history of right to privacy, xi, 265, 271–72
The History of the United States for 1796 (Callender), 13–14, 20
"History of U.S. Decision-Making Process on Viet Nam Policy," 178
HIV and AIDS, 273
Hogan, Hulk, 116, 184–85, 220–22, 223
Hollande, François, 254
Holmes, Fanny, 132
Holmes, Oliver Wendell
    and Brandeis, 47, 48
    correspondence of, 7, 131–33
    and court decision restricting truthful article, 6, 27–28
    and *Cowley v. Pulsifer*, 6–7
    as First Amendment legend, 131
    and Kent's *Commentaries on American Law*, 46
    and *Lochner* dissent, 133–34
    and marketplace-of-ideas language, 135–36, 137
    on newspaper libel, 128, 129
    on newspapers' standards, 132
    and *Nightingale* case, 3–6, 10
    Olmstead dissent of, 139
    premium placed on privacy, 131–33
    on publication of tax records, 259
    and "The Right to Privacy," 78
    and sensationalism in newspapers, 6
    Supreme Court appointment of, 48, 128
    on Toledo's newspaper editorials, 130
    and Warren, 48, 92, 97
    and wiretaps of police, 138
Holmes-Laski Letters (Howe), 133
home, privacy of, 8, 182
home address, public availability of, 232, 233, 240–41
homosexuality, 183
House Un-American Activities Committee, 176
Hulbert, Mary Allen, 108
human cannonball act, news broadcast of, 180
human rights documents, 162

human trafficking, 207
humiliating secrets/truths, 3, 28, 136, 242, 266
Hustler
    Hustler Magazine v. Falwell, 182
    misappropriation of Benoit images, 219–20, 245
Hutchins Commission on Freedom of the Press, 170
hypothetical cases, xix–xx

identity, use of another's, xviii. *See also* misappropriation
Illinois, xx, 222
Illinois Biometric Information Privacy Act, 238–39
Illinois Supreme Court, 82, 223
Illustrated Police News, 36
illustrations in newspapers
    drawn from photographs, 69–70
    emergence of, 34–36
    impact on circulation numbers, 60
    in *Scribner's*, 69
    of Tilton on Beecher's knee, 41, 55
    of women, 60
    in *The World*, 59–60
incestuous births, media coverage of, 195
Ingalls, John, 67
injustices, privacy's facilitation of, xii
inmates, right to interview, 181
insurance information, 233
intellectual property rights, 73
"Interference with Privacy" provision in the Restatement, 159–61
Internal Revenue Service's Taxpayer Bill of Rights, 259
"International Bill of Rights" project of American Law Institute, 161–62
international movement toward right to privacy, 161–62
internet
    and bloggers, 156
    and *To Catch a Predator*, 217
    and copyright/trademark protections, 269
    and cyberporn, 201–2
    and dignity considerations, 266
    and doxing, 237
    and facial recognition technology, 238, 239
    and freedom of expression, 156, 269
    and identities of online commentators, 196
    images of death posted on, 183
    and liability of service providers, 202
    as marketplace of ideas, 204, 215
    parents' sharing of child's information on, 245–46
    pictures on, 239
    privacy scenarios originating in, xix
    regulation of (*see* Section 230 of the Communications Decency Act)

and revenge porn, 187, 207, 208, 223,
    266, 269
and Richie's The Dirty, 204–6
sites trafficking in emotional/reputational
    harm, 206–9, 269
video of accident scene posted on, 223
intrusion into seclusion, xviii, 173, 198,
    199, 226
invasion of privacy
    defamation compared to, 115
    legal standards of, 115–16
investigatory companies, 233
Iredell, James, 32
iris scans, 238, 239
Is Anyone Up? 208

Jaquiss, Nigel, 249–50
Jefferson, Thomas
    Callender's criticisms of, 20, 22–23, 24
    Callender's publications sponsored by, 14,
        19–20, 21, 22, 23, 26
    Cleveland compared to, 65
    criticisms of the press, 18–19, 268
    Croswell's criticisms of, 21–22, 23–26
    Hamilton's attacks on, 12–13
    on need for libel charges against
        publishers, 27
    personal motives for privacy aims, xii,
        18–19
    Philaenus's pamphlet criticizing, 20–21
    secret relationship with Hemings, 13, 20–21,
        22, 23, 27, 28
John, Elton, 163
Jones, Sarah, 205–6
Jones v. Dirty World, 205–6, 208
The Journal of Arthur Stirling (Sinclair), 102, 109
Journal of the American Medical Association,
    207–8
journalism and the press
    Adams's criticisms of, 122
    as addressed in "The Right to Privacy,"
        72, 75
    Brown's criticisms of, 123–27
    and Capitol riots, January 6, 2021, 270
    courts' deference to judgement of, 154, 168,
        194, 196, 216, 219
    and cultural/legal shift toward right to
        know, 174
    education/training programs for, 147
    emotional harm caused by, 30–31
    ethical standards in, 41–42, 146–51, 154–56,
        218–19, 258, 261, 269–70
    excluded from trial proceedings, 181
    First Amendment claims of, 196
    and Founding Fathers, 17–19
    and Harding, 144–45, 146–47, 148–49, 270
    and interviewees' rights, 246
    Jefferson's criticisms of, 18–19, 268

and Kennedy assasination, 258
liability for invading privacy, 160
and Miss Vermont's suit against Max,
    214–15
and motives for publishing the truth, 268
muckraking, 101–2
and mug shots, 248–49
newsworthiness standard of, 178, 184, 188,
    196, 198, 260
and Nightingale case, 3–6, 7, 9–10
paparazzi, 229–30, 258, 265–66
politicians' relationships with journalists,
    107–8, 256–58, 261
Pound's criticisms of oversteps, 121–22
press-protective judicial language, 170–72,
    265 (see also New York Times v. Sullivan)
professionalism of, 151
publication of tax records, 259
reporters ordered out of courtrooms,
    84–85
Restatement examples of media liability,
    160, 161, 177, 183
and Richie's The Dirty, 206
and ride-alongs with police, 182
and right to be forgotten, 248
right to privacy as norm in, 143, 154–56
and school newspapers, 181–82
and self-censorship concerns, 181
and Sidis case, 165–68, 185, 194
and Sinclair's The Brass Check, 106, 109–10,
    113, 143
and sources, 178, 182
and Star Chamber of England, 268
trust in, 198
truth as defense in, 19, 22, 23, 30, 184
and truthful libel, 17–19
Woodward and Bernstein's criticisms
    of, 197
and Zenger, 15–16
and zone of privacy surrounding
    individuals, 184
See also freedom of the press; media;
    newspapers
judgments, public availability of, 233
Juicy Campus website, 206
The Jungle (Sinclair), 101, 102, 103
Juno, 203
juvenile defendants, identities of, 171–72,
    173, 184

Kagan, Elena, 230
Kansas, 148
Kansas City Star, 142
Kardashian, Khloé, 240
Kemp, Harry, 105
Kennedy, Caroline, 258
Kennedy, Jackie, 258, 265–66
Kennedy, John F., 256–57, 258

Kennedy, Ted, 188–89
Kent's *Commentaries on American Law*, 46, 115
Key, Philip, 40
Kimbrough, Mary Craig, 105
Kissinger, Henry, 181
Kopechne, Mary Jo, 188–89

Landmark Communications v. Virginia, 181
Laski, Harold, 7, 132–33
law review articles, xx–xxi
Lawrence v. Texas, 182–83
Lee, James Melvin, 110
Lee, Robert E., 147
legal publications, xx–xxi
legislation on privacy
    in New York, 120
    Privacy Act (1974), 172, 237
    Warren on need for, 78–79
Les Misérables (Hugo), 246, 250
Let Us Now Praise Famous Men (Agee and
    Evans), 269
Letter to Thomas Jefferson (Junius Philaenus),
    20–21
*Letters to Alexander Hamilton, King of the
    Feds*, 21
Levine, Lee, 194
Lewis, Anthony, 197
libel
    as inadequate to address privacy
        breeches, 73
    seditious libel, 10, 15–16
    See also truthful libel; *specific cases*
liberty
    balanced with privacy rights, 268
    constitutional promises of, 266–67
    and First Amendment freedoms, 272
    privacy as protective of, 268
    "The Right to Privacy" on, 267
    value placed on, 264, 265
Liberty and the News (Lippmann), 110
liens, public availability of, 233
life insurance policies, 240
Life magazine, 77, 177
likeness of another, use of, 116–19
Lincoln, Abraham, 36
Lippmann, Walter, 110–11, 112, 143, 150
The Literary World, 10
Little League team photograph, 216
Lochner v. New York, 133–34
Lockup, 197
Look magazine, 174–75, 257–58
Lorigan, William, 83–84, 85, 86
Los Angeles Times, 194
lower courts, xv–xvi, xix
lynchings of Black men, 146

Mackenzie, Sir Morell, 118
MacWorld magazine, 237

Madison, James, 13, 18, 171
The Magenta (later *The Harvard Crimson*),
    42–44
Manley, Jared L. [pseudonym of Thurber], 164
Manola, Marion, ix–x, xii, xiii, 69, 73,
    116, 117
Mapp v. Ohio, 176
Marbury v. Madison, 82
Marion Star, 148, 158
Markel, Lester, 256–57
marketplace of ideas
    and *Abrams* case, 135
    Brandeis and Holmes's role in, 131, 135–37
    internet as, 204, 215
    language of, 135–36
    regulation of, 135–37
    and *Titicut Follies* documentary, 189
Markle, Meghan, 231–32
marriage, privacy of relations in, 127
Marshall, Thurgood, 178
Martin, François Xavier, 29–30, 33, 265
Massachusetts
    criminal libel in, 75–76
    Massachusetts Supreme Judicial Court, 7–8,
        47, 188–89
    and *Titicut Follies* documentary, 185–90
Maupassant, Guy de, 152
Max, Tucker, 213–15, 223
Mayweather, Floyd, 223
McCarthyism, 176, 266–67
McClure, S. S., 106
McClure's, 106–7, 108, 169
McLean, Sally Pratt, 4–5
Mead, Margaret, 255, 258
media
    brash, invasive reporting of, xiii
    and cases emphasizing right to know,
        194–95
    Gawker's publication of Hogan sex tape,
        220–22
    and identities of online commenters, 196
    newsworthiness standard of, 198, 199, 223,
        244, 248
    and "privileged conduct," 195
    pushback against, in favor of privacy,
        215–22
    and Richie's The Dirty, 206
    and right to be forgotten, 247
    and *Shulman* case, 191–94, 198–99, 209
    and *Titicut Follies* documentary,
        185–90
    trust in, 198
    See also journalism and the press
medical/health information, personal
    Ashe's AIDS diagnosis, 273–74
    availability of data for purchase, 233
    and HIPAA, 252
    and Kennedy assasination, 258

laws protecting, 235
and liability for invading privacy, 159, 160, 161
of Merkel, 254
of professional athletes, 222, 253
Restatement on privacy of, 247
of Trump, 251–52
as universal privacy concern, 271
Meghan, Duchess of Sussex, 231–32
Merkel, Angela, 254
#MeToo movement, xii, 89, 268
Miami Herald, 142
Michigan, 33–34
microphones, 192, 199
Microsoft, 206
Middleton, Kate, 229–30
Mikva, Abner, 215–16, 219
Mill, John Stuart, 135
Miller, Arthur, 236
Milton, John, 135
Minnesota, 140–43
Minnesota Supreme Court, 141–42
misappropriation, xviii, 116–19, 173
Miss Vermont, 213–15, 223
Mnuchin, Steven, 253
Monroe, James, 20
Monroe, Marilyn, 256–57
Moore, Alfred, 32
Moore, Roy, 261
mortgage information, public availability of, 232
Mott, Frank Luther, 80, 151
Mrs. Fiske Warren (Gretchen Osgood) and Her Daughter Rachel (Sargent), 111
muckraking journalism, 101–2
mug shots, 180, 196–97, 242–43, 248–49
murders, 169, 177
"Mutual Weekly" newsreels, 129
My Life and Loves (Harris), 152–55
myex.com, 207

NAACP v. Alabama, 176
NASA v. Nelson, 183
Nash, Kate, 52–53, 63–66
The Nation, 41–42, 55, 77
National Archives and Records Administration v. Favish, 183
National Enquirer, 163
National Football League (NFL), 222, 253
National Police Gazette, 35–36, 128, 150
National Public Radio, 155
National Recovery Act, 160
Near, Jay, 140–43
Near v. Minnesota, 131, 140–43, 187, 214
Nebraska Press Association v. Stuart, 180
necessity of privacy, 73
The Neighbors art series, 120–21
net worth, public availability of, 233

New England Magazine, 77
New Jersey, 240
New York City, 120–21
New York *Daily News*, 158, 169
New York Illustrated, 69–70
New York Illustrated News, 73
New York Post, 197
New York state
    and biometrics privacy, 239
    population of, 12
    privacy legislation in, xvii, 120
    and *Roberson* case, 119
New York State Bar Association, 126
New York *Sun*, 39, 108
New York Times
    ethical standards of, 150–51, 155
    on exposé journalism, 63
    on Google's removal of content, 249
    and Harding on ethical standards in journalism, 145
    on hidden-camera programs, 200
    on Sidis, 157
    and Sinclair, 102, 104, 109–10
    on Trump's medical condition, 252, 253
    on Trump's tax returns, 259–60
    Warren's critique of, 44
    and Warren's wedding, 50
New York Times v. Sullivan
    and *Eros* obscenity conviction, 153–54
    and *Gawker* case, 221
    and Goldberg on journalistic standards, 258
    press-protective language of, 154, 170, 176, 265
    role of, in exposing truths, 265
    Thomas's call to overturn, 219
New York *World*, 146
The New Yorker, 163–67
news consumption patterns, 235
Newspaper Guild, 163
newspapers
    and Bayard family tragedies, 56–59
    and death coverage, invasive, 56–59
    Hamilton's attacks on Jefferson in, 12–13
    and Holmes, 6, 132
    illustrations in, 34–36, 41, 55, 59–60, 69–70
    and liability for invading privacy, 160, 161
    penny press, 32, 39–42, 49
    printing personal correspondence, 29–30
    and pro-press decisions in *Sidis* case, 166
    rise of, 3
    use of "right to know" phrase, 81
    Victorians' perspectives on, 41
    See also journalism and the press
newsreels, 129
Newsweek magazine, 174, 236
New-York Daily Times, 39

New-York Tribune, 69
Nightingale, Lorenzo, 5–6, 8–9, 10
Nightingale case, 5–6, 7, 8–10, 11, 47, 58
911 calls, 197
Nixon, Richard
    radio address on privacy, 260
    tape recordings made by, 179–80, 258–59
    tax records of, 259
    and Watergate scandal, 171, 172, 174, 179,
        255, 261
Nixon v. Administrator of General Services, 179
Nixon v. Warner Communications, 179–80
nondisclosure agreements (NDA), 252
nudity, 121, 271

Obama, Barack, 219, 255, 259
obscenity, 153
O'Ferrall, Charles, 146
"offensive" revelations, xvii–xviii
Ohio Supreme Court, 222
Oklahoma Publishing Co. v. District Court,
    171–72
Olmstead v. United States, 137–39, 179, 267
On Scene: Emergency Response television
    program, 191–94, 198–99
opinion, freedom of, 162
Oregon, 148
out-of-state decisions, xix

Palin, Sarah, 219
palm recognition technology, 239
Pandora's box, freedom of the press compared
    to opening, 157, 168
paparazzi, 229–30, 258, 265–66
Parker, Alton, 119–20
Paul v. Davis, 180
Pennsylvania, 246–47
penny press, 32, 39–42, 49
Pentagon Papers case, 171, 178
People of Walmart, 206, 269
People v. Croswell. See *Croswell* case
personal assistants, voice-activated, 238
personal information, accumulation of, 180
personal liberty, Fourteenth Amendment's
    concept of, 179
Philaenus, Junius, 20–21
phone numbers, public availability of, 232
photographers and photographs
    as addressed in "The Right to Privacy," 72, 75
    court rulings with implications for, 119
    of crime scenes, 169
    of Hollande and Gayet, 254
    illustrations drawn from, 69–70
    internet scans for, 239, 240
    and liability for invading privacy, 128, 160
    in *The Neighbors* art series, 120–21
    and nudity, 271
    and privacy in public spaces, 227

"PJS," 162–63
police
    AI and biometrics used by, 239
    and bodycam videos, 227–28
    and DNA test results, 236
    and media ride alongs, 182
    mug shots of, 242–43
    privacy interests used to protect,
        242–43, 268
    and reality shows recording arrests, 223
    and recordings of use of force, 227
    right to search trash, 182
    and warrantless tracking through cell
        phone towers, 183
politicians
    claims to privacy, 250, 261
    in Europe, 254
    journalists' relationships with, 107–8,
        256–58, 261
    and matters of public concern, 75
    private character of, 83
    See also specific individuals
pornography
    cyberporn, 201–2
    revenge porn, 187, 207, 208, 223, 266, 269
Pound, Roscoe, 121–22, 142, 158
precedents, legal, xix
prescription information, 233
presidents
    personal communications of, 258–59
    presidential election of 2016, 238
    and presidential privilege, xi
    privacy afforded to, 179, 253, 260
    public's concern with, 255, 256
    secrets of, kept by press, 256–58
    tax returns of, 252–53, 259–60
    and Washington press corps, 108,
        144, 257
    See also specific presidents
The President's Daughter (Britton), 149–50
Price v. Price divorce case, 83–87
"Principles of the Law: Data Privacy"
    (American Law Institute), 237
privacy, definition of, xi–xii
Privacy Act (1974), 172, 237
privacy interests of Americans
    after terrorist attacks of 9/11, 228
    increasing levels of, 198, 224
    regarding personal data, 181, 236, 237
    and sense of freedom/liberty, 267
Privacy: The Right to Be Let Alone (Ernst),
    167–68
Prodigy web service company, 202
proper and justifiable truth, 74
The Prosect Before Us (Callender), 19, 20, 22
Prosser, William, 253
pseudonyms, use of, 114
psychiatric history, media coverage of, 195

psychiatric hospitals, photographers
    trespassing on grounds of, 195
public databases, 66
public figures and public officials
    Ashe's AIDS diagnosis, 272–74
    and BBC's invasion of Richard's privacy,
        263–64, 266
    To Catch a Predator's pursuit of Conradt,
        217–19, 266
    and celebrity sex tapes, 116, 184–85,
        220–22
    personal data of public servants, 240
    pleas for privacy, 240
    Restatement on privacy standards
        for, 160
    right to privacy of, 128
    right to publish embarrassing truths about,
        264–65
    self-interested pursuit of privacy by,
        xii–xiii, 268
    sex lives of, 217
    Sidis case, 163–67
public interest/concern
    in Arctic expedition, 154
    and Ashe's AIDS diagnosis, 272–74
    balancing right to privacy with, 268
    and BBC's invasion of Richard's
        privacy, 264
    Brandeis on, 143
    and courts' deference to journalists, 196
    and credit reports, 181, 244
    as defense against privacy claims, 214
    and *Hustler*'s misappropriation of Benoit
        images, 220
    and limits on privacy claims, 75
    and medical records of athletes, 222
    in mug shots, 243
    in presidents' personal information,
        253, 255
    "The Right to Privacy" on matters of, 75, 175,
        260, 265
    and sex lives of public figures, 217
    and *Shulman* case, 192, 193
    and *Sidis* case, 165–66
    Supreme Court on standards for legitimate,
        270–71
    and teacher/student texts, 223
    and Westboro Baptist Church
        picketing, 183
public places, privacy in, 225–30
public schools' data on students, 237
public servants, personal data of, 240
publicity given to private life, 173
Publick Occurences, 36
Puck, 70
Pulitzer, Joseph
    and Columbia's journalism school, 147
    and illustrations of women, 60

purchase of *The World*, 6, 49
    and Roosevelt's libel lawsuit, 108
    sensational coverage cultivated by, 59
Punk'd, 198

radio
    ethical standards in radio journalism, 155
    station's broadcast of cell phone
        conversation, 175, 184
    stations' broadcasts of Carlin's "Filthy
        Words," 181
Radio Television Digital News Association, 155
railroad passenger's right to be let alone, 78,
    124, 179, 265
rap sheets (criminal histories), 182, 247
rape and sexual assault victims, identities of
    and cases emphasizing journalism's rights,
        171, 172, 173, 185, 195
    and privacy-promoting language of
        courts, 184
    and videotaped rape case, 195, 196
Rawlings, Marjorie Kinnan, 161
reading habits, information on, 238
The Real Housewives, 197
The Real World, 197
reality television
    arrests recorded for, 223
    emergence of, 197–98
    and media releases, 193
    and *Shulman* case, 191–94
The Recorder, 20
regulations, xv, xvii
relatives included in background checks,
    232–33
releases, media, 193
religion, public availability of, 233
religious groups, members and donors
    of, 181
Reporters Committee for Freedom of the
    Press, 206, 208
Reporting for the Newspapers, 147
reputational harm
    and BBC's invasion of Richard's privacy, 264
    and sexually transmitted diseases, 115
    Supreme Court on newspapers
        inflicting, 135
    websites trafficking in, 206–9
respect, 267
Restatement of the Law of Torts
    about, xxi, 115
    definition of privacy, 116
    and examples of liability of media, 160, 161,
        177, 183
    on income tax records, 259
    "Interference with Privacy" provision in,
        159–61
    on invasion of privacy, 226
    on peering in on another, 199

Restatement of the Law of Torts (*cont.*)
  on presidents' lack of privacy, 253
  on privacy in public spaces, 226
  on privacy relative to time/place, 249
  on right to know, 260
  on sexual relations, 247
  on sexually transmitted diseases, 115
  on time's impact on privacy, 246, 250
  update of privacy section, 173–74
Reston, James, 185, 257
retina scans, 238, 239
revenge porn, 187, 207, 208, 223, 266, 269
Reynolds, Maria, 14, 25
Richard, Sir Cliff, 263–64, 266
Richardson, Elliot, 187
Richie, Nik, 204–6, 208–9
right to be forgotten, 242–50
  Americans' support for, 245
  in Europe, 244
  and freedom of the press, 244
  historical cases supporting, 245–46
  and mug shots, 242–43, 248–49
  and past crimes, 244
right to be let alone
  after terrorist attacks of 9/11, 228
  balanced with liberty of expression, 268
  and Brandeis's *Olmstead* dissent, 267
  Cooley's treatise on, 8, 118, 121
  cultural/legal shift away from, 174, 175
  and human dignity, 265
  as meaning of privacy, xii
  and railroad passenger's case, 78, 124,
    179, 265
  and Warren and Brandeis vision of privacy,
    76, 174
right to know and truthful revelations
  and Ashe's AIDS diagnosis, 273–74
  as balanced with right to privacy, xii, 82
  and Chase-Cleveland clash, 80–81, 88–91
  courts' decisions protecting, 154, 171
  and Croswell's criticisms of Jefferson, 24–26
  cultural/legal shift away from right to
    privacy to, 174, 177, 194
  dignity as counterbalance to, 266
  emergence of concept, 8
  and Freedom of Information Act (1966),
    172–73
  government behavior linked to, 82–83
  growing prioritization of, 172
  media cases emphasizing, 194–95
  and mug shots, 242–43
  and newspapers' right to publish truth, 7
  newspapers' use of phrase, 81
  and *Price v. Price* divorce case, 83–87
  Restatement on, 260
  and right to be forgotten, 244
  and right to publish embarrassing
    truths, 265

and *Shulman* case, 191–94
tension with right to privacy, xiii
time's impact on, 245, 246
and *Titicut Follies* documentary, 189
and Watergate scandal, 171, 172, 174
right to privacy (phrase), 146, 151, 159
"The Right to Privacy" (Warren and Brandeis)
  and *Bartnicki v. Vopper*, 175
  on circumstantial nature of cases, 268
  cited by courts and scholars, xx–xxi, 75, 178,
    193, 224, 248
  and Cleveland's secrets, 65–66
  on dignity, 266
  five main points of, 72–74
  as foundation for privacy law, 71
  on freedom of the press, 265
  goal of, 74
  influence of, xi, 127, 190
  language of, 75, 76
  on liberty, 267
  on matters of public interest/concern, 75,
    175, 260, 265
  and modern Supreme Court language, xiii
  on new technologies/devices, 72–73, 75, 138,
    193, 199, 226
  and *Olmstead* dissent of Brandeis, 138
  origins of, 51
  and Parker's ruling in *Roberson* case, 119
  praised by E. Adams, 123
  and Privacy Act (1974), 237
  promotion of, 76–78
  on publication of women's images, 73, 116
  published in *Harvard Law Review*, xx,
    71–72
  Schlesinger's interpretation of, 260
  and Sinclair's *Sylvia's Marriage*, 112
  statutory language included in, 75–76
"The Rights of the Citizen: To His Own
  Reputation" (Godkin), 71
Riis, Jacob, 69
Riley v. California, 183–84
Roberson, Abbie, 117–19, 122, 123
Roberson case, 121, 122, 123, 173
Rochester Folding Box Company, 116–19, 123
Rockefeller, Nelson, 257
Roe v. Wade, xxi–xxii, 178–79
Rollins, Clara Sherwood, 131–32
Roosevelt, Franklin Delano, 160
Roosevelt, Theodore, 101–2, 107–8
Rosenbloom v. Metromedia, 177–78

Sad Sam's Tavern in Waukesha, Wisconsin, xix
Safire, William, 228, 229
salary information, data on, 233
Salas, Esther, 231, 236, 240
Salinger, Pierre, 257
Samuel D. Warren Company, 37, 38, 60, 69, 70,
  93–94

San Francisco 49ers National Football League
team, 243
San Jose Daily Mercury, 83–87, 90
Sargent, John Singer, 111
The Saturday Press, 140–43
Scalia, Antonin, 230
scandals/scandalous truths
Adams on, 17
etiquette advice on, 32
government related, 17, 19
and the penny presses, 39–42
public interest in, 3
Scare Tactics, 198
Schlesinger, Arthur, 260
school newspapers, 181–82
Scribner's Magazine, 69, 71
Scripps-Howard newspapers, 138
Seattle Times v. Rhinehart, 181
Section 230 of the Communications Decency
Act, 202–8
amending, 269
copyright/trademark protections in, 269
and data privacy concerns, 237, 240
harm caused by, 269
impact of, 202–3
and Miss Vermont's suit against Max, 213
passage of, 200, 202
and websites trafficking in emotional/
reputational harm, 204–8
seditious libel, 10, 15–16
Seldes, George, 103, 110
self-incrimination, 229
September 11, 2001, terrorist attacks, 228
sexual harrassment, 88–89
sexual information, personal
as addressed in "The Right to Privacy," 72
Catholic priest's use of hookup app, 229
celebrity sex tapes, 116, 184–85, 221
and cultural/legal shift away from right to
privacy, 175
and early privacy cases, 8
in France, 254
and gossip column about news producer's
sex life, 217
and Harris's *My Life and Loves*,
152–55
lower courts on privacy of, 128
and Miss Vermont's suit against Max,
213–15, 223
of presidents/politicians, 255–57, 260
Restatement on privacy of, 247
revenge porn, 187, 207, 208, 223, 266, 269
and right to be forgotten, 249–50
sexual abuse, 216
sexual orientation, xvii, 195, 271
sexually transmitted diseases, 111–12,
114–15, 152
Supreme Court on, 127, 183

and teen's lawsuit of *Gawker*, 221
as universal privacy concern, 271
Shakespeare, William, 268
Sheppard, Sam, 177
Shulman, Ruth, 191–94, 198–99, 253
Shulman case
and human dignity, 226, 266
intrusion into seclusion aspect of,
198–99, 226
and media releases, 193
Supreme Court ruling on, 193–94
Sickles tragedy, press coverage of, 39–40
Sidis, William, 157–58, 164–67, 215
Sidis case
current caution exercised with, 168
influence of, 174, 194
and loss of dignity, 166
pro-press court decisions in, 165–68, 185
as Restatement example, 173–74
Sinclair, Meta, 104–5
Sinclair, Upton
*The Brass Check: A Study of American
Journalism*, 106, 109–10, 113, 143
The Crimes of the "Times" pamphlet, 110
and Fiske Sinclair, 111–13
and Harris's *My Life and Loves*, 152–53
on Hearst's mistress, 149
Helicon Hall colony of, 101, 103, 104, 106
The Jungle, 101, 102, 103
marital troubles and divorce of, 104–6
media coverage of, 103–6
and Stirling hoax, 102, 109, 110
Sylvia's Marriage, 111–13, 114
Sipple, Oliver, 195
smartphones, xiii, 229
Smith v. Daily Mail Publishing Co., 172
Snyder v. Phelps, 183, 270
social media
and facial recognition technology, 238
included in background checks, 233
negative psychological impacts of, 207–8
and right to be forgotten, 249
See also internet
Social Security number, public availability of,
232, 238
Society of Professional Journalists, 155,
218–19
Soden Mineral Springs Company, 118
Sotomayor, Sonia, 230, 267–68
sources of journalists, 178, 182
Sports Illustrated, 216
Springfield Republican, Massachusetts, 102
Standard Oil, 106
Star Chamber, 10–11, 85, 268
stare decisis, xv, xvii–xviii, xix
Starr, Ken, 174, 256
state constitutions, xvi, 33–34
state legislatures, xx

state universities, college applications
    to, 196
statutory law
    about, xv, xvi–xvii
    common law trumped by, xx
    and history of right to privacy, 223
sterilization, involuntary, 195, 196
The Story of Arthur Ashe (Johnson), 275
street photography, 69
students
    privacy of records of, 247
    public schools' data on, 237
    publication of personal information
        about, 178
    and teacher/student texts, 223
subscription information, 238
Süddeutsche Zeitung, 254
suicides
    of Conradt in sting operation, 218–19
    and interviews of county inmates, 181
    and websites trafficking in emotional/
        reputational harm, 207–8
suing for privacy invasions, xviii
Sun Microsystems, 237
Supreme Court, U.S.
    cases in the 1950s, 175–76
    cases in the 1960s, 176–77
    cases in the 1970s, 177–81
    cases in the 1980s, 181–82
    cases in the 1990s and onward, 182–84
    and data privacy, 236, 241
    deferential First Amendment decisions
        of, 216
    dicta regarding right to privacy, xx
    first mention of right to privacy, 78
    on freedom of the press, 125–29, 140–43,
        170–75, 178, 180–81
    and government-related cases,
        xxi–xxii
    on income tax records, 259
    journalists covering, 124–25
    on liberty as "sacred right," 266
    on liberty/privacy balance, xv–xvi, xx,
        270–71
    on line between right to privacy and right
        to know, xiii
    on obscenity, 153–54
    press-protective language of, 170–72,
        175–76
    on "privacies of life," xiii, 127, 139, 176,
        183–84, 266
    and privacy in public spaces, 230
    and privacy of justices, 124–25, 230
    privacy-promoting language of, 176–84
    on public-interest standards, 270–71
    Restatement cited by, xxi
    and right to be forgotten, 247
    on sensationalism in media, 177

shifts from right to know to right to privacy,
    181, 182
shifts from right to privacy to right to
    know, 175, 177
and *Sidis* case, 166
and *Titicut Follies* documentary, 189
and truthful information, 170
*See also individual cases and justices,
    including* Holmes, Oliver Wendell
Sweezy v. New Hampshire, 176
Sylvia's Marriage (Sinclair), 111–13, 114

tape recordings of Nixon, 179–80
Tarbell, Ida, 101, 106–7, 108
tax information
    of presidents, 252–53, 259–60
    publication of, 259
    right to privacy in, 252–53
Taylor, C. H. J., 88–91
Teapot Dome scandal, 145, 146
technology
    biometrics, 238–39
    and challenges of modern privacy, 262
    as considered in "The Right to Privacy,"
        72–73, 75, 138, 193, 199, 226
    and data collection/sharing (*see* data,
        personal)
    deepfakes, 240
    doorbells with video cameras, 225–26, 229
    for facial recognition, 229, 238, 239
    geolocation tracking, 229
    and *The Neighbors* art series, 120–21
    and new media, xiii
    and *Olmstead* dissent of Brandeis, 138–39
    and privacy in public spaces, 229–30
    secret recording devices, 199–200, 228, 229
    and self-incrimination, 229
    of Victorian age, 69
teen pregnancy, 181–82
telegrams, privacy of, 8
telephone conversations, 181
telephone numbers, 240
terrorist attacks of September 11, 2001, 228
Texas, 229, 239
Thiel, Peter, 222
"The 30-Year Secret" (Jaquiss), 249–50
Thomas, Clarence, 126, 219
Thomas, Helen, 257
Thomas Jefferson Foundation, 23
Thurber, James, 164–67, 180
Tilton-Beecher adultery case, 41, 55, 65–66
Time magazine, 175, 197, 201
Time v. Firestone, 180
Time v. Hill, 170–71, 177
The Times of Philadelphia, 81
Tin-Types Taken in the Streets of New York
    (Quigg), 69
Tirrell, Albert J., 35

Titicut Follies documentary, 185–90
To Catch a Predator, 217–19, 266
To-Day, 77
tort law, xviii, xxi, 48
Totally Hidden Video, 191
trademark protections, 269
tragedies, press coverage of, 56–59
transparency, culture of, 267
trash, right of police to search, 182
true-crime periodicals, 169
Trump, Donald
    and Capitol riots, January 6, 2021, 270
    coronavirus diagnosis of, 251–52, 253
    Facebook's ban of, 271
    premium placed on privacy, xii, 252, 253, 255
    pussy-grabbing boast of, 254
    targeted by photographers, 251, 254
    tax returns of, 252–53, 259–60
truth
    and Blackstone's *Commentaries*, 15
    as defense against privacy claims, 19, 22, 23,
        30, 115, 173, 184, 214
    embarrassing truths, 15, 30–33, 106, 269
    emotional harm caused by, 31
    growing prioritization of, 172
    humiliating secrets/truths, 3, 28, 136,
        242, 266
    as insufficient for constitutional
        protection, 184
    motives of press in publishing, 268
    newspapers' right to publish, 7
    and Nixon presidency, 179
    proper and justifiable truth, 74
    publication of, as invasion of privacy, 115
    right to privacy as counterbalance to, xii
    shifts from right to privacy to, 177
    and Star Chamber of England, 10–11
    Supreme Court case prioritizing, 170
truthful libel
    Adams on, 123
    and Blackstone's *Commentaries*, 15
    as common law concept, 16
    Dennie arrested for, 27
    emergence of idea in early privacy cases, 10
    Godkin on, 57, 73
    "the greater the truth. . . ." mantra of, 15,
        23, 71
    and Hamilton, 14
    and *Sidis* case, 166
Twain, Mark, 36, 49
typewriters, 69

United Kingdom, 162–63, 263–64
United Nations, 162
United Press International, 257
United States v. Nixon, 179
Universal Declaration of Human Rights, 162
University of Missouri, 147

University of Pennsylvania, 147
Unsolved Mysteries, 191
unzipped pants, picture of man with, 194, 198
*U.S. Department of Justice v. Reporters
    Committee for Freedom of the Press*, 247
USA Today, 273

Vietnam, reporting on war in, 171
The Village Voice, 208
Virginia, 26
voice, biometrics based on, 238, 239
voter registration records, 232
Vox Populi, 35, 36

Wall Street Journal, 145
Walt Disney, 151
Walter Reed Medical Center, 251, 252
Walton, Lester, 146
Warren, Cornelia, 134–35
Warren, Edward Perry (Ned), 39, 93–95, 98, 111,
    134–35
Warren, Fiske, 70, 111–13
Warren, Gretchen Osgood, 111–13
Warren, Mabel Bayard
    Boston newspapers' criticisms of, 95
    and the Clevelands, 58, 70
    marriage of, 58
    public interest in, 50, 58
Warren, Samuel D.
    abhorrence of invasions of social privacy, 51
    background of, 38
    and Bayard family tragedies, 56–57
    and Boston Museum of Fine Arts, 111
    Brandeis's friendship with, 45–46, 92
    and the Clevelands, 58, 70
    and Cleveland's speech on privacy, 56
    critiques of publications in *The Magenta*,
        36–37, 44
    death of, xiv, 96–97
    dignity as personal value of, 94, 266
    and family paper business, 70, 93–94
    and family privacy/dignity, 50–51, 94, 98
    and family strife, 93–96
    and family trust, 70, 93–96, 98
    handwriting of, 92
    at Harvard College, 36–37, 42, 44–45
    and *Harvard Law Review*, 48–49
    at Harvard Law School, 45–47
    and Holmes, 48, 92
    impact of, on privacy, 121
    law career of, 49, 97
    and Manola's tights, ix, x
    marriage of, 49–51, 58
    media coverage of, 50–51, 58, 94–97
    on need for privacy legislation, 78–79
    personal motives for privacy aims, xii
    scrapbook of, 44–45
    See also "The Right to Privacy"

Warren family, 38, 48, 93, 111, 112
Washington, George
    Callender's pamphlet criticizing, 19, 20, 26
    and Hamilton's attacks on Jefferson, 13
    Hamilton's remarks on letters from, 14
    privacy prioritized by, 18
Washington Bee, 80–81, 88–91, 146
Washington Examiner, 217
Washington Federalist, 23
Washington Merry-Go-Round (Anonymous),
    141–42
Washington Post
    on doorbells with video cameras, 225
    on impact of Hogan jury verdict, 222
    on pictures posted on internet, 239
    on right to be forgotten, 249
    on Sidis, 157–58
    and Warren's wedding, 50
Washington press corps, 108, 144, 257
Washington state, 239
The Wasp, 21–22, 24, 34
Watergate scandal, 171, 172, 174, 179, 255, 261
Watkins v. United States, 176
Watterson, Henry, 67
Weegee (Ascher Fellig), 169
Weekly Mail, 35, 36
Wells, H. G., 136
Wells, Ida B., 146
Westboro Baptist Church, 183
Whalen v. Roe, 180
"What Publicity Can Do" (Hapgood), 133
Wherry, Edith, 106
White, Byron, 178
Whitman, Walt, 152
Whitney v. California, 137
Willamette Week (Oregon), 249–50
William, Prince, Duke of Cambridge, 229–30
Wilson, Woodrow, 108, 136–37
Wilson v. Layne, 182

Winchell, Walter, 151
Winters v. New York, 170
wiretapping phones, 138–39
Wisconsin, xix
Wiseman, Frederick, 186–90
women
    and accusations of sexually transmitted
        diseases, 115
    and journalistic ethics standards, 148
    likeness reproduced in newspapers, 60, 73,
        116–19
    and Section 230 of the Communications
        Decency Act, 269
    technology enabling stalking of, 239
    and websites trafficking in emotional/
        reputational harm, 207
Woodhull, Victoria, 40
Woodhull & Claflin's Weekly, 40–41
Woodward, Bob, 197
The World newspaper
    and Bly's reporting, 60–62, 63
    circulation of, 62
    coverage of tragedies, 59
    ethical standards exercised by, 246
    exposé reporting in, 60–63
    and Hearst newspapers, 97
    illustrations in, 59–60
    Pulitzer's purchase of, 6, 49
    on "The Right to Privacy," 77
    and Roosevelt's libel lawsuit, 108
    sensational coverage cultivated at, 59–60
World War II, 161–62
World's Nastiest Neighbors, 199–200
Wyden, Ron, 202

Yahoo, 203

Zenger, John Peter, 15–16, 27, 80
zone of privacy surrounding individuals, 184